ch. 20 in Stats book
p. 911

marketing research

wiley series in marketing   David A. Aaker, Editor

Third Edition

marketing research

David A. Aaker
University of California, Berkeley

George S. Day
University of Toronto

John Wiley & Sons

NEW YORK   CHICHESTER   BRISBANE   TORONTO   SINGAPORE

Cover Design by Carolyn Joseph
Cover Photo by Comstock, Inc./Tom Grill

Library of Congress Cataloging-in-Publication Data

Aaker, David A.
  Marketing research.

  Includes bibliographical references and indexes.
  1. Marketing research. I. Day, George S.
II. Title.
HF5415.2.A14 1986   658.8′3   85-32301
ISBN 0-471-83875-6

Printed in the United States of America

10 9 8 7 6 5 4 3 2

PREFACE

There are perhaps three changes in the third edition that will be most visible to those familiar with prior editions. First, a major chapter on advertising research has been added that provides a comprehensive look at one of the most interesting and important marketing research application areas. Second, advances in marketing research methodology caused by the computer and related technologies have dramatically changed the field. Thus, new material has been added on topics such as computer retrievable data bases, scanner-based data bases, scanner-based new product and advertising testing, computer-driven interviewing, and marketing decision support systems. Third, ten new cases have been added. The data from two cases, Pacific Gas and Electric (B) and New Food are available on floppy disks.

For those new to the book, it may be helpful to review our overall objectives:

1 To write for the user of marketing research as well as the student interested in a research career. The user needs to known when marketing research can and should be used, what research alternatives exist, how to recognize effective and ineffective research, and how to interpret and apply the result.

2 To emphasize the "front end" of marketing research, the development of a research purpose linked to decision making and research objectives that truly guide the research. We believe that this material (to which two full chapters are devoted) is the key to effective research.

3 To use examples, applications, and illustrations throughout to provide interest and understanding. In particular, there are four chapters that provide an in-depth discussion of the application areas of advertising, market analysis, forecasting, and new product research, and 43 cases of varying levels of complexity.

4 To provide a clear and comprehensive treatment of modern data analysis topics. Each chapter includes simple numerical examples to help students get a hands-on feel for the material.

5 To provide thorough coverage of the most advanced and current marketing research methodologies, pointing out limitations as well as their potential for enhancing research results.

ACKNOWLEDGMENTS

Many debts have been accumulated during the eleven years in which the three editions of this book took shape. We are especially grateful to our students, who gave us feedback from the consumer's perspective and whose field research projects provided many of the illustrations and problems; to our colleagues, who stimulated us and brought new ideas and approaches to our attention; and to our clients, who gave us many opportunities to put the ideas in this book into practice and thus broadened our understanding of marketing research as it is currently practiced. It has been a continuing pleasure to associate with a class publisher, John Wiley & Sons, and a competent, helpful editor and friend, Rich Esposito.

A host of helpful and insightful reviews on the first two editions were received from Scott Armstrong, Ronald Beall, Andrew Brogowicz, Melvin Crask, William R. Dillon, Chris T. Ford, Gary T. Ford, Chris Lovelock, Barry Mason, Douglas L. MacLachlan, Shelby McIntyre, Thomas Pilon, Peter Riesz, Eli Seggev, Subrata Sen, Terence A. Shimp, Allan Shocker, Judy Wilkinson, and Noel Zabriskie. This third edition benefited from the help of Don Bruzzone, Michael Hagerty, and Gary Russell. We owe a special debt of gratitude for the support and patience of our wives, Kay and Marilyn. This book is dedicated to them as a small recognition of this debt.

David A. Aaker
George S. Day

CONTENTS

8 ATTITUDE MEASUREMENT   205

section C CAUSAL RESEARCH   239

9 EXPERIMENTATION   241

13   HYPOTHESIS TESTING   373

14   INTRODUCING A THIRD VARIABLE   405

15   PRESENTING THE RESULTS   423

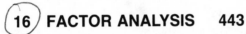

GLOSSARY   639

APPENDIX: TABLES   649

INDEX   657

marketing research

part 1

THE MARKETING RESEARCH PROCESS

1

A DECISION-MAKING PERSPECTIVE ON MARKETING RESEARCH

The purpose of marketing research is to support marketing decision making. The scope of marketing research activities is therefore determined by the nature of these decisions. At the same time, each decision situation has unique requirements for information, as we see from the following examples:

Coca Cola. For years Coke endured television commercials in which Pepsi won taste tests hands down. One result was continued erosion in the Coke share of supermarket cola sales. In late summer 1984 a new formula was developed to replace the original secret formula introduced in 1886. Would consumers taste the difference? Would they prefer the new Coke to the old formula and Pepsi? Should the formula be changed without telling anyone?

San Francisco Museum of Modern Art. The director of the museum was convinced of the need for self-guiding educational materials for visitors. However, numerous questions arose. What types of people visit the museum? Do they need a basic introduction to modern art, a historical background on the painters, or interpretations of individual works? Would they prefer a pamphlet or some kind of cassette recording? How much, if anything, would they be willing to pay?

Ameritech. In October 1983 Ameritech offered the first cellular mobile radio service in Chicago providing phone service in vehicles. A strong challenge was mounted by the Cellular One company which entered in January 1985 with lower prices, a television blitz and inducements to customers who switched over from Ameritech. Before they responded, Ameritech management needed to know how many subscribers they would likely lose. What would be the effect of increased awareness of cellular radio and rapidly sinking prices on the total market size?

3

Budget Rent-A-Car Corporation. In seeking growth opportunities in the car rental market against three dominant competitors, Budget uncovered a ''professional care'' segment who felt ''that nobody cares about me anymore.'' The next question was: What kind of programs would be appealing to this segment?

These examples could be multiplied by thousands, for virtually every private- and public-sector organization encounters the same pressures for more and better information about its markets. Whether the organization serves customers in competitive market environments or clients in a public-sector enterprise, there is a need to understand and satisfy the changing needs of diverse groups of people. This task is greatly complicated within the private sector by the nature of competitive action, which is relatively unpredictable and seldom in the best interests of the firm. Competition also exists in many parts of the public sector. For example, private delivery services are effectively supplementing the faltering postal services in many cities, and publicly operated clinics compete with privately financed and operated health maintenance organizations.

Overall, the similarities outweigh the differences between the private and the public sector so far as the functions of marketing research in the organization are concerned. This is reflected in the following definition, which serves equally well in both decision-making situations:

> Marketing research links the organization with its market environment. It involves the *specification, gathering, analyzing,* and *interpretation* of information to help management understand the environment, identify problems and opportunities, and develop and evaluate courses of marketing action.

This definition highlights the role of marketing research as an aid to decision making. An important feature is the inclusion of the specification and interpretation of needed information. Too often marketing research is considered narrowly as the gathering and analyzing of data for someone else to use. Finally, marketing research is defined as an informational input to decisions, not simply the evaluation of decisions that have been made.

The purpose of this chapter is to illustrate and discuss the role that marketing research does—or should—play in the organization: When should marketing research be used? What are some examples of useful marketing research? Why is it used? For what kinds of decisions? What do the users expect? This chapter begins with a discussion of the role of marketing research in analyzing markets and developing and controlling marketing strategies and programs. The concept of a coordinating marketing planning and information system will then be introduced. Next, the factors that contribute to successful marketing research are reviewed. The chapter then concludes with an overview of the research industry to clarify the relationships among various information providers and the ultimate users they serve.

MARKETING RESEARCH AND MARKETING MANAGEMENT

To understand the various contexts in which marketing research is used, an overview of the marketing management process is useful. The information requirements of marketing management and its many associated decisions are what generate the need for marketing research. Figure 1–1 structures the marketing management process as involving three very different phases. The first is market analysis; the other two phases involve the development and control of the marketing program. We next elaborate this process and describe the types of information needs associated with each step.

Market Analysis

Effective marketing programs are built upon an in-depth understanding of the market. Table 1–1 provides a partial list of the information needs of a consumer goods manufacturer. Information is needed about the market characteristics, such as customer perceptions and problems, competitor strategies, and changes in the distribution channel. Further, a market analysis would be incomplete without information about the market environment. Technological, social, political, and cultural developments and trends can affect the demand for present and prospective products.

One objective of market analysis is to identify problems and opportunities that will require the development or major modification of a marketing program. A problem could be caused by the emergence of a new distribution channel. The job of marketing research

---

Step 1 Market Analysis
       Understanding the market
       Identifying opportunities and problems
       Understanding opportunities and problems

Step 2 Developing the Marketing Problem
       Segmentation decisions
       Product decisions
       Distribution decisions
       Advertising and promotion decisions
       Personal selling decisions
       Price decisions

Step 3 Controlling the Marketing Program
       Performance monitoring and evaluation
       Refining the marketing program

FIGURE 1–1   The marketing management process

TABLE 1–1
Scope of Market Analysis for a Consumer Goods Manufacturer

1. CONSUMER BEHAVIOR
   a. *What they buy*
      A product or service? A convenience, shopping, or specialty good? A satisfaction . . .
   b. *Who buys*
      Everybody? Women only? Teenagers? (i.e., demographic, geographic, psychographic classification)
   c. *Where they buy*
      Will they shop around or not? Outlet types
   d. *Why they buy*
      Motivations, perceptions of product and needs, influences of peers, prestige, influence of advertising, media
   e. *How they buy*
      On impulse, by shopping (i.e., the process they go through in purchasing)
   f. *When they buy*
      Once a week? Every day? Seasonal changes?
   g. *How much they buy at a time*
   h. *Anticipated change*
      Incidence of new products, shifts in consumers' preferences, needs
2. MARKET CHARACTERISTICS
   a. *Size*
      Potential market, actual market, selected segments of market
   b. *Location*
   c. *Competition*
      Who is competition, what are their characteristics, what is their likely behavior in marketing activities (promotion, pricing, new products, etc.)?
   d. *Competitive products*
      Their nature and number
   e. *Economic conditions*
3. MARKET ENVIRONMENT
   a. *Technology*
      What new technologies will emerge?
   b. *Culture*
      What is becoming fashionable?
   c. *Economic trends*

SOURCE: Adopted from Murray A. Cayley, "Marketing Research Planning and Evaluation," *Business Quarterly*, Spring 1975, pp. 30–36.

is to insure that such a development is detected and then, if necessary, to learn enough about it so that decisions can be made as to what marketing program would be most responsive. An opportunity might be represented by dissatisfaction that customers have with existing products. Marketing research could be called on to detect the dissatisfaction and perhaps determine how many people are dissatisfied and the level and nature of that dissatisfaction.

A variety of research approaches is used to analyze the market. Perhaps the simplest is to organize information already obtained from prior studies, from magazine articles that have been filed, and from comments made by customers to a firm's sales representatives. Another approach is to have small groups of customers discuss their use of a product. Such a technique, called a focus group, can provide many ideas for new marketing programs.

Especially when a problem or opportunity has been identified and it is necessary to understand it in more depth, a survey is often employed. For example, to understand the competitive position of Québec in the tourism market, a survey was conducted to determine the benefits sought by visitors and nonvisitors as well as the risks they perceived. The results identified a large group who felt highly insecure in new and/or foreign environments and were not attracted by the appeals of uniqueness in culture, traditions, and architecture used by Québec to differentiate its product.

Taylor California Cellars used extensive survey research to identify opportunities in the premium generic wine business.[1] By following the implications they were able to build a 100 million dollar business between 1980 and 1985. When planning began in 1977 the competitors, such as Almaden and Inglenook, were basing their strategies on research showing that wine drinkers knew little about wine and drank it mainly during social, romantic or celebratory occasions. This research said little about frequent wine drinkers. While they were only 4 percent of all wine drinkers they accounted for 53 percent of consumption. Taylor management wanted to learn much more about this group. Further research found that the frequent drinkers were much more interested in taste-related attributes such as crispness, bouquet and dryness, than in the symbolic role of wine. At the time of this research no other brand was addressing these benefits. One finding—that 58 percent of the target market had recently attended a wine tasting—became the basis for the advertising campaign "The Great California Wine Tasting." This theme was an ideal way to impart a message of superior taste.

Developing the Marketing Program

The emphasis now shifts to the development of the marketing program that will exploit the opportunity or solve the problem. Marketing program development involves a host of decisions, each of which often will benefit by the information provided by marketing research. Table 1–2 provides a sample list of some of those decisions.

[1]Charles Overholser, "Digging Beyond Research Yields Vintage Success for Winemaker," *Marketing News* (April 26, 1985), 7.

TABLE 1–2
Developing the Marketing Program—Representative Decisions
That Draw upon Marketing Research

---

1. Segmentation Decisions
   Which segment should be the target?
   What benefits are most important to each segment?
   Which geographic area should be entered?
2. Product decisions
   What product features should be included?
   How should the product be positioned?
   What type of package is preferred by the customers?
3. Distribution decisions
   Which type of retailer should be used?
   What should be the markup policy?
   Should a few outlets be employed or many?
4. Advertising and promotion decisions
   What appeals should be used in the advertising?
   In which vehicles should the advertising be placed?
   What should the budget be?
   What sales promotions should be used, and when should they be scheduled?
5. Personal selling decisions
   What customer types have the most potential?
   How many salespeople are needed?
6. Price decisions
   What price level should be charged?
   What sales should be offered during the year?
   What response should be made to a competitor's price change?

To illustrate some of the possible research approaches that are employed we will focus on the series of market research studies that were conducted to help Johnson Wax Company successfully introduce Agree Cream Rinse in 1977 and Agree Shampoo in 1978. The story begins with a major market analysis survey of hair-care practices conducted in the early seventies. The study showed that there was a trend away from hair sprays but a trend toward shampooing more frequently and a growing concern about oily hair. This led to a strategic decision to enter the shampoo and creme rinse market with products targeted toward the "oiliness" problem. This decision was supported by other studies on competitive activities in the market and on the willingness of the retailers to stock new shampoos.[2]

A total of 50 marketing research studies conducted between 1975 and 1979 supported

[2]"Key Role of Research in Agree's Success is Told," *Marketing News* (January 12, 1979) 14–15.

the development of these two products. A series of focus group discussions was held to understand the oiliness problem and people's perceptions of existing shampoo products. The firm was particularly interested in learning about teenagers, since most of its products were sold to homemakers. One goal of these focus groups was to get ideas for a copy theme. Subsequently, more focus groups were held to get reaction to the selected advertising theme, "Helps Stop the Greasies." Several tests of advertising were employed in which customers were exposed to advertisements and their reactions were obtained. In fact, over 17 television commercials were created and tested.

More than 20 of the studies helped to test and refine the product. Several blind comparison tests were conducted in which 400 women were asked to use the new product for two weeks and compare it to an existing product. (In a "blind" test, the products are packaged in unlabeled containers and the customers do not know which contains the new product.)

Several tests of the final marketing program were conducted. One was in a simulated supermarket where customers were asked to shop after they had been exposed to the advertising. The new product, of course, was on the shelf. Another test involved placing the product in a real supermarket and exposing customers to the advertising. Finally, the product was introduced using the complete marketing plan in a limited test area involving a few selected communities including Fresno, California and South Bend, Indiana. During the process, the product, the advertising, and the rest of the marketing program were being revised continually. The effort paid handsome dividends: The Agree Creme Rinse took a 20 percent share of the market for its category and was number one in unit volume, while the Agree Shampoo also was introduced successfully.

Controlling the Marketing Program

The beginning of the phase is signaled by a decision to proceed with a new program or strategy and the related commitments to objectives, budgets, and timetables. At this point the focus of marketing research shifts to such questions as:

Did the elements of the marketing program achieve their objectives?

　How did sales compare with objectives?

　In what areas were sales disappointing? Why?

　Were the advertising objectives met?

　Did the product achieve its distribution objectives?

　Are any supermarkets discontinuing the product?

Should the marketing program be continued, discontinued, revised, or expanded?

　Are customers satisfied with the product?

　Should the product be changed? More features added?

　Should the advertising budget be changed?

　Is the price appropriate?

For research to be effective at this stage, it is important that specific measurable objectives be set for all elements of the marketing program. Thus, there should be sales goals by geographic area; distribution goals, perhaps in terms of number of stores carrying the product; and advertising goals, such as achieving certain levels of awareness. The role of marketing research is to provide measures against these objectives and to provide more focused studies to determine why results disappointed or surpassed expectations.

Often underlying this phase of marketing management is uncertainty about the critical judgments and assumptions that preceded the decision. For example, in 1982, Xerox, Canon, and IBM each launched new products into the office copier market. Prior to this, some companies had emphasized very large copiers, while others had ignored this end of the market. One reason for these differences in strategic emphasis was a fundamental assumption as to whether customers tended to centralize or decentralize their processing of copies. In response to this uncertainty, the companies undertook research studies with the dual purpose of measuring the acceptability of the new product entries and of monitoring the copy processing policies of the target customers.

There is overlap among all three phases of the marketing process. In particular, the third phase, by identifying problems with the marketing program, and perhaps opportunities as well, really blends into the market analysis phase of some other follow-up marketing program.

THE MARKETING PLANNING AND INFORMATION SYSTEM

In most organizations there will be many marketing programs under way or being developed at any one time. There also can be many marketing research projects either completed or under way. How is all this activity and information directed and coordinated? The answer for many organizations is an integrated marketing planning and information system or MPIS. As will be shown in Chapter 2 and elsewhere in the book, a marketing planning and information system can help marketing research be more effective by precipitating and scheduling marketing research projects and by providing a "home" for their resulting reports. The MPIS consists of a strategic or long-range planning system, a tactical or short-range planning system, and an information system.

Strategic Plans

The strategic plan usually has a horizon of more than one year. It focuses upon strategic decisions, which are major questions of resource allocation with long-run performance implications, such as:

- Which segments should the organization serve?
- Within these segments, which wants and needs should be highlighted?

- What products or services will be offered?
- Which product markets should the organization move into or withdraw from?
- Which distribution channels should be developed?

The strategic planning activity draws heavily upon market analysis activities. The size and characteristics of product markets in the future, technological developments, and changes in the market environment all need to be explored. The identification of problems and opportunities in the market also is important for strategic planning. Directions will be suggested toward which the organization can move in terms of new markets, new products, or both.

Tactical Plans

These usually cover a one-year period or less. They specify in detail the decisions that need to be made and the actions that must be taken to develop and implement current marketing programs. For example, the tactical plan may include plans for the launching of a new product. Such a plan could include a sales forecast by region and district, a pricing strategy, a complete advertising and promotional program, a plan to ship and store inventory, and a dealer-incentive program. It also will include a timetable for the various activities. If candidate brand names must be selected by June, then a market research study to evaluate the alternative names must be conducted by March so the name can be selected by June. Marketing research to help select an advertising theme must be completed by July so first advertisements will be ready by September and can be tested in October.

The Information System

An information system supports the planning system by (1) *anticipating* the types of information that are likely to be required by decision makers and (2) *organizing* information that has been collected to insure it will be readily accessible when needed. Whereas marketing research is concerned with the actual content of the information and how it is collected, the information system focuses on managing the flow of relevant information to decision makers. The actual system for organization, storing, and retrieving may be as simple as a set of filing cabinets or as complex as a computer-based system with on-line access capabilities. The latter is becoming more feasible for almost all organizations, as the rapid developments in systems software are reducing their costs and simplifying their operation.

Marketing information systems contain three types of information. The first is the recurring market and accounting data that flow into the organization as a result of market analysis research and accounting activities. For example, automobile firms use government sources for monthly data on new-car sales by brand and geographic area. In addition, surveys are conducted yearly to determine the age and type of automobiles currently driven, the lifestyles of the drivers (their activity and interest patterns), and their media habits, and intentions to replace their car. The accounting department will submit sales and inventory data for each of its dealers on a continuing basis, to update and supplement the information system.

A second type of information system content is intelligence information about influences relevant to the future strategy of the business. Automobile firms, for example, will collect reports and information about new ways to use steam or electricity to power automobiles. This information could come from scientific meetings, trade magazines, or perhaps from government reports. It also could include information from salesmen or dealers about new-product tests being conducted by competitive firms. Marketing intelligence is difficult to develop, because it usually involves diverse and changing sets of topic and information sources and is rarely collected in a systematic manner.

A third input to the information system is the marketing research studies that are not of a recurring nature. The potential usefulness of a marketing research study can be multiplied manyfold if it can be placed in an information system instead of being filed and forgotten. When it resides in an information system, the potential exists that others may use the study, although perhaps in a manner that was not originally intended.

SUCCESSFUL MARKETING RESEARCH: SOME GUIDELINES

All marketing decisions involve uncertainty, both in the information on which they are based and the forecasts of the consequences. We have emphasized—and will emphasize throughout this book—that successful marketing research is decision oriented. This means, first, that marketing research should be undertaken only when the results will reduce uncertainty and influence decisions. Indeed, there is no point in doing research if the decision maker isn't in a position to alter anything. More specifically, marketing research will make a contribution when it is **relevant** to current or anticipated decisions, **timely, efficient,** and **accurate.**

Relevant Research

Research should not be conducted to satisfy curiosity or confirm the wisdom of previous decisions. Relevance comes through support of strategic and tactical planning activities, that is, by anticipating the kinds of information that will be required. This information is the backbone of the ongoing information system. As new circumstances arise and decision alternatives become more specific, research projects may be undertaken. Throughout the planning of these projects the focus must be constantly toward decisions.

Timely Research

Research decisions are constrained by the march of events. Often these decisions are fixed in time and must be taken according to a specified schedule, using whatever information is available. If a new product is to be launched in the spring, all the research-based decisions on price, product formulation, name, copy appeals, and other components must be conducted far in advance. One role of the planning system is to schedule needed market research so that it can be conducted in time to influence decisions. The formulation of responses to competitive actions puts the greatest time pressure on researchers, for the results are always wanted "yesterday." There are, of course, many situations where the timing of decisions is contingent upon the research results. Even so, there is still time pressure stemming from the recognition that failure to take corrective action or pursue an opportunity as quickly as possible will result in opportunity costs.

Efficient Research

There are two senses in which marketing research must be efficient. The first asks: What is the maximum quality of information the researcher can provide with the minimum expenditure of time and money? Most often this question is phrased in terms of the consequences of a reduced expenditure on research. The second asks: Is the research study appropriate to the decision context? The study should be expensive and elaborate only if the decision is important and the research information will be helpful and timely. Sometimes the conclusion is that the research is not justifiable, although it clearly can contribute to the decision. In such a case, the costs of a minimally acceptable study exceed the foreseeable benefits of increased revenue and profits, improved client satisfaction, or other performance criteria. The dictates of efficiency also influence the kind of research that is done. One well-known policy researcher advocates ". . . research designs and research procedures that give good results with high probability, rather than more sophisticated approaches that give excellent results if they are correct, but may be very inaccurate if some of their assumptions are not met."[3]

Accurate Research

Relevance, timing, and efficiency requirements should not compromise the accuracy of the results. Throughout this book we will discuss a variety of methods and procedures that will help ensure accuracy. Despite careful research design it is inevitable that biases will arise due to question wording or interpretation, the sampling plan, and other elements of the research design. One way to reduce bias is to use more than one approach to address a research problem. If several approaches with different kinds of biases yield similar conclusions, the accuracy will be enhanced.

[3]James S. Coleman, *Policy Research in the Social Sciences* (Morristown, N.J.: General Learning Press, 1972), p. 24.

IMPLEMENTING MARKETING RESEARCH

Marketing research is unquestionably a growth industry. Between 1975 and 1985 real expenditures on marketing research (that is, after adjusting for inflation) more than doubled! This is largely a consequence of economic and social changes that have made better marketing an imperative.

> *"With marketing the new priority, marketing research is the rallying cry. Companies are trying frantically to get their hands on information that identifies and explains the needs of powerful new consumer segments now being formed. Kroger Co., for example, holds more than 250,000 consumer interviews a year to define consumer wants more precisely. Some companies are pinning their futures to product innovations, others are rejuvenating timeworn but proven brands, and still others are doing both."*[4]

Not only are those companies that always did marketing research doing a great deal more, but the breadth of research activities also continues to expand:

- Senior management is looking for more support for their strategic decisions; so researchers are doing more acquisition and competitor studies, segmentation and market structure analyses, and basic strategic position assessments.

- Other functions, such as the legal department, now routinely use marketing research evidence. Corporate Affairs wants to know shareholders', bankers', analysts', and employees' attitudes toward the company. The service department continuously audits service delivery capability and customer satisfaction.

- Entire industries that used to be protected from the vagaries of competition and changing customer needs by regulatory statutes are learning to cope with a deregulated environment. Airlines, banks, and financial services groups are looking for ways to overcome product proliferation, advertising clutter, and high marketing costs brought on by more sophisticated customers and aggressive competitors.

Information Suppliers

The growing needs for marketing research information are satisfied by two types of suppliers shown in Figure 1–2, in-company and outside-company. Both can feed information directly to their clients who are users with decision-making needs. More often the outside suppliers will get their direction, and provide information to an inside research group. These inside suppliers translate the problems of their clients into specific information requirements, decide how the information will be collected and by whom, and then interpret the findings.

[4]"Marketing: The New Priority," *Business Week* (November 21, 1983), 96.

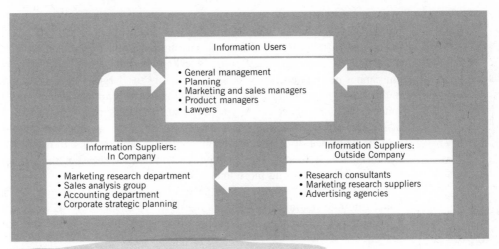

FIGURE 1–2 Participants in marketing research activities

In-Company Suppliers. The importance and influence of the marketing research function can be assessed in part by the position of the marketing research department within the organization. One approach is to have it report to the highest levels of general management and thus have its responsibilities merge with those of the strategic planning group. For example, Coca-Cola has a senior vice-president in charge of market research. Another approach is to have the department report to the top marketing officer, either directly or indirectly through a marketing services group. A third possibility is to have marketing research activities dispersed throughout the organization; however, there is then the risk that the marketing research activities will be fragmented and lack credibility and visibility. Further, if the research group is associated with sales or advertising, its mission naturally will be narrowed by the interests of that group.

The Marketing Research Industry. The information suppliers outside the company, as described in Figure 1–2, comprise the marketing research industry. There is no satisfactory measure of the size of this industry, although it is known that the top 40 U.S.-controlled research firms had revenues of $1450 million in 1984. This is an international industry; 24 percent of this revenue came from outside the United States.[5]

The total industry revenue was estimated to be at least $1.9 billion in 1984, after taking account of research revenues by another 350 for-profit research organizations, as well as research conducted in house by such large manufacturers as General Foods and by advertising agencies. There are two distinct tiers within the industry. The top four firms are known as data-bank or syndicated-services companies and account for more than 50 percent of all research revenues. In Chapter 4 we will analyze the syndicated services of A. C. Nielsen, IMS International, SAMI, and Arbitron to see why their

[5]Jack V. Honomichl, "Top Research Companies Revenues Rise 13.7%," *Advertising Age* (May 23, 1985), 16–17.

revenues are as large as the rest of the companies combined. Within the second tier are predominantly specialists in customized individual research projects, such as Burke International, Market Facts, Chilton Research, and Louis Harris and Associates.

The U.S. Bureau of the Census is technically outside the industry as defined earlier, but cannot be ignored, for it is unquestionably the largest survey research organization in the world. Revenue in 1984 was approximately $98 million, which was almost entirely funded by federal agencies. A typical Census Bureau study conducted for the Department of Health, Education and Welfare, was designed to redefine the measure of poverty, provide incidence of disability, school enrollment figures, health insurance coverage and the incidence of food stamp recipiency. This was a one-shot survey, spread out over several years and costing more than $10 million.

Most organizations rely on some facet of the market research industry to at least collect the information they need. In the next two chapters we will take the viewpoint of the researcher within the organization and see how the decision to use outside suppliers is made.

SUMMARY

Marketing research links the organization with its market environment. It involves the specification, gathering, analyzing, and interpretation of the information to help management understand that market environment, identify its problems and opportunities, and develop and evaluate courses of marketing action. The marketing management process involves market analysis, marketing program development, and marketing program control. Each of these areas includes a host of decisions that need to be supported by marketing research information. The marketing planning and information system (MPIS) helps to plan and coordinate these decisions and the information flow associated with them. Marketing research, to be effective, should be relevant, timely, efficient, and accurate. Among the participants in marketing research activities are information users; external information suppliers, such as the marketing research firms; and the information suppliers within the organization.

QUESTIONS AND PROBLEMS

1 How might the following use marketing research? Be specific.
   a A resident ballet company
   b A small sporting goods store
   c AMTRAK
   d Washington State University
   e Toronto Blue Jays Baseball Team

f Sears Roebuck

g Apple Computers

2 Consider the first illustrative decision in each of the six decision areas listed in Table 1–2. How might marketing research be used to support that decision? For example, how might marketing research help select a target segment? Assume that you are a marketing manager for the Bank of America.

3 Design a marketing information system for the Beta Electronics Company, makers of display equipment such as oscilloscopes. The primary interest is to support the long-range planning effort by learning about the technological trends and developments in about five technical areas and of trends and developments in the area of competitor products and customer applications. Specify the nature of the information to be included and the sources of that information.

4 Is there a parallel between an accounting system that provides information on costs of products and a marketing information system that provides information on product demand?

5 In some companies strategic planning and marketing research functions both report to the same executive and may be more or less integrated. What are the advantages to locating the research function in this part of the organization? What arguments could be made in opposition to this arrangement?

2

THE RESEARCH PROCESS

How is the market research project conceived, planned, and executed? The answer, in part, is through a research process, consisting of stages or steps that guide the project from conception through the final analysis, recommendation, and ultimate action. The research process provides a systematic, planned approach to the research project and helps ensure that the research project involves stages and elements that are consistent with each other. In particular, it is important that the research design and implementation be consistent with the research purpose and objective. The research process should help provide that consistency.

In this and the following chapter the research process is described. This chapter provides an overview of the research process, a discussion of the research purpose and research objectives, and a consideration of the value of research information. Chapter 3 contains an overview of the research design and its implementation. Together these two chapters provide a foundation and structure for the balance of the book.

OVERVIEW OF THE RESEARCH PROCESS

There are several steps in the process of designing and implementing a research study. They are:

1 Obtaining agreement on the purpose of the research. This involves determining the decisions that are to be supported, the problems or opportunities that are to be studied, or the market analysis task that exists.

2 Translating the research purpose into specific research objectives.

3 Estimating the value of the research information.

4 Designing the research study. Research design usually involves both the selection of a research approach (i.e., a survey *vs.* an experiment *vs.* using secondary data) and

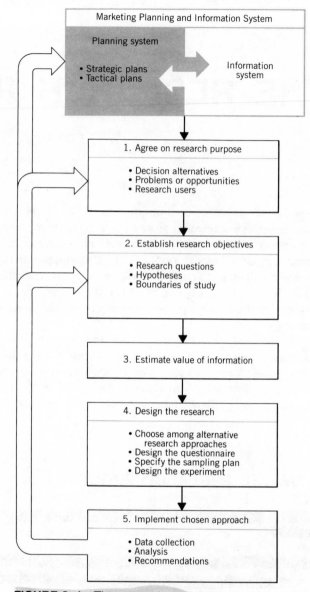

FIGURE 2–1 The research process

the specification of aspects of the study, such as the questionnaire and the sampling plan.

5 Implementing the design—collecting and analyzing the data, and preparing a report.

These steps are linked in a sequential order in Figure 2–1. Also shown in Figure 2–1 is the MPIS, the Marketing Planning and Information System, introduced in the previous chapter. The concept of MPIS plays a useful role in showing how the need for research is created and how the results ultimately are used.

The development of a research purpose that links the research to decision making and the creation of research objectives that serve to guide the research are unquestionably the most important elements of good research. If they are right, then the research will have an excellent chance of being useful and appropriate. If they are bypassed or are not correct, the research almost surely will be wasteful and irrelevant. These aspects of research, too often neglected by researchers, will be discussed in detail in this chapter.

Also discussed in this chapter is the concept of the value of the research information. It makes no sense to conduct research when the cost will outweigh any value. Thus, it is important early in the research design process to attempt to justify the research economically.

The research design and the implementation stages are presented in Chapter 3. They involve selecting the research approach, designing experiments, creating questionnaires, developing sampling plans, planning and conducting field work, analyzing the results, and presenting the conclusions.

THE ROLES OF THE MPIS

The MPIS, the Marketing Planning and Information System, has several important roles to play in the marketing research process, as the flow chart in Figure 2–2 suggests. These roles serve to link the MPIS with marketing research. Such links can enhance greatly the effectiveness of marketing research by avoiding the all-too-common situation where marketing research is a series of isolated, *ad hoc* projects that are conceived occasionally when there is a particular and immediate need for information.

As Figure 2–2 indicates, one role of the MPIS is to receive the outputs of the marketing research study. Virtually all research studies should be aimed at influencing a decision that is imbedded in a planning system; thus, the research output will flow into the planning system, which provides a context for the decision and identifies the relevant decision makers. In addition, the research output also may flow into the information system. The information system, which can be a sophisticated interactive computer system or a simple filing system, draws heavily upon marketing research. Market analysis studies can contribute current information on competitor actions or in-depth information on customer profiles. Program development studies can provide comparison benchmarks—such as what level of recall previous advertisements have achieved. Performance monitoring research

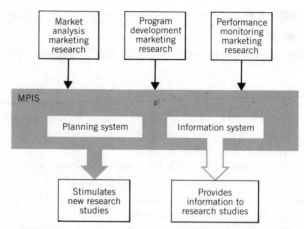

FIGURE 2–2 The roles of the MPIS

allows the tracking of relevant performance measures, such as sales over time. If the information system can make prior research studies visible and accessible, their data can contribute to research questions that might be quite different from those motivating the original study.

Another role of the information system component of the MPIS is to provide information that can be used to answer research questions directly. As will be discussed in Chapter 3, one research approach is to access the information system. It is foolish to conduct a survey or experiment if the information system has the needed information.

The third and perhaps the most important role of the MPIS is to precipitate new research. For research to be conducted, someone initially must perceive a need for information that a market research project can satisfy. Many potentially valuable research studies are simply never conducted because the perceived need never became visible at the appropriate time. The MPIS can reduce this all-too-frequent occurrence by systematically identifying information needs.

The planning system can anticipate the need for research information. The development of the strategic plan requires information that will signal changes in the market that may indicate the existence of new problems or opportunities. The implementation of a strategic plan often will suggest more specific information needs. For example, the strategic plan for a retail chain could include expansion into new cities in the coming years. Thus, information that could help the organization select the best cities would be helpful. The need to develop a product line to serve a new product market would be another example. In such a case, people's opinions of existing products might provide useful information.

The short-run could generate many anticipated needs for information. For example, a sales promotion might be planned for the fall. Thus, in the spring, marketing research could be called upon to test three alternative promotions. Further, marketing research might be needed after the promotion to conduct evaluation research. If a public health agency is opening two new offices, marketing research might be required to determine the mix of demands that is expected to be placed upon each office so that they can be adequately staffed and equipped.

No organization can develop a set of plans that can anticipate all information needs. There always will be unanticipated needs as problems, changes, and new circumstances arise during the implementation of a plan. These emergent needs for information frequently will be identified by components of an information system. For example:

- Performance (sales, market share, contributions, patronage) may be unsatisfactory relative to objectives. Perhaps the condition can be traced to a specific geographic area, but the underlying reasons still must be sought before action can be taken.

- A competitor may launch a new product or employ a new advertising appeal, with unknown consequences for the firm's competitive position.

- An unavoidable increase in costs puts pressures on profitability (or, in the case of a transit system, increases the subsidy requirements to an unacceptable level). Various possible increases in fares or prices must be evaluated.

- An upsurge in interest in health and nutrition may suggest to a snack company a new product line directed toward responding to this interest. Concept testing might be a first step in exploring this opportunity.

Given the sometimes chaotic and usually uncertain nature of most market environments, a large number of problems and some opportunities can emerge. Very few of these will ever be given formal consideration: there may be no further need for clarification, the implications may not appear serious, or the response may appear evident in the judgment of the decision maker. Our interest is in those problems or opportunities that need to be clarified, whose consequences are uncertain, or which involve the development of new programs, products, or services.

The MPIS serves to emphasize that marketing research should not exist in isolation as a single effort to obtain information. Rather, it should be part of a more systematic and continuous effort by the organization to improve the decision-making process.

RESEARCH PURPOSE

One of the most important contributions of an effective marketing researcher is to help the manager understand the purpose of the research. It is safe to say that most managers will not know fully what they want and they may have defined incorrectly the problems they have recognized or the decision alternatives to be evaluated. It is also essential for the researcher to have a clear picture of the purpose of the research, for this will guide the rest of the research process. For these reasons the research purpose is possibly the most crucial step in the research process.

The research purpose comprises a shared understanding between the manager and the researcher of the following:

1 Decision alternatives to be evaluated
   • What are the alternatives being studied?
   • What are the criteria for choosing among the alternatives?
   • What is the timing or importance of the decision?
2 Problems or opportunities to be studied
   • Which problems or opportunities are anticipated?
   • What is the scope of the problems and the possible reasons?
3 Users of the research results
   • Who are the decision makers?
   • Are there any covert purposes?

Decision Alternatives

If research is to be effective, it should be associated with a decision. Marketing research is committed to the principle of utility. In general, if research is not going to have an effect on decisions, it is an exercise in futility. The researcher should always be sensitive to the possibility that either there are no decision alternatives—and therefore no decision—or that the research findings will not affect the decision—usually because of resource or organizational constraints. In such circumstances, the research will have no practical value and probably should not be conducted.

When a decision does exist, it is important to identify it explicitly, because the research then can be designed to have maximum effectiveness. For example, researchers frequently are asked to assess the potential of a market that is unfamiliar to the company. But what are the decisions facing the manager? Is he thinking of acquiring a company serving that market? Has the lab produced a new product which might be sold as a component to the industry serving that market? The answers will have a significant influence on the design of the research.

A most useful way to clarify the decision motivating the research is to ask: (1) What alternative actions are being considered? (2) What actions would be taken, given the various feasible outcomes of the research? This line of questioning can be very enlightening for the decision maker, as well as for the researcher, in terms of clarifying exactly what is to be accomplished by the research. The story in the following box illustrates how both can learn from a focus on decisions.

> **POLITICAL
> CAMPAIGN RESEARCH**
>
> The meeting between Hugh Godfrey and two project directors from Pollsters Anonymous, a well-known survey research company, had taken a surprising turn. Here were two researchers suggesting that no research be undertaken.
>
> Godfrey was campaign manager for John Crombie, a university professor and erstwhile Democratic challenger of the Republican incumbent for the local House of Representatives seat. He and his candidate were anxious to undertake a program of research. They thought it would be a good idea to have surveys in May and September (five months and six weeks prior to the election) of voter awareness of the candidate, attitudes toward him, issue salience and intentions to vote. The results would be helpful in clarifying the candidate's position and deciding on media expenditures. Positive results would be useful in soliciting campaign contributions, which loomed as a big problem.
>
> During the meeting the researchers had asked what Godfrey expected to find. He was sure that the initial survey would reveal low awareness, and would confirm other information he had that there was a low level of voter registration among Democrats in the area. The next question was whether any foreseeable results would persuade him not to spend all his available resources on a voter registration drive. He had to admit also that the preliminary estimate of $6000 for a May survey was a large chunk of his available funds. In fact, he was thinking, "With the money for the survey I could hire enough canvassers to get at least 1500 to 2000 registrations."

Sometimes the decision involved is highly specific. A copy test is used to select a copy alternative. A concept test is employed to determine if a concept should be developed further. Sometimes the decision can be very general. What markets should be the primary targets of our organization? Should our marketing program be changed? It is desirable to be as specific as possible because the research purpose then will be more effective in guiding the development of the research design. However, even if the decision is necessarily general, it needs to be clearly stated.

Criteria for Choosing Among Alternatives.   It is essential for the researcher to know how the decision maker will choose among the available alternatives. Suppose a product manager is considering three possible package redesigns for a health-care product with declining sales. This would seem to be a straightforward research undertaking, as the decision alternatives are completely specified. Yet the product manager could use some or all of the following criteria to choose the best of the three alternative packages:

1   Long-run sales
2   Trial purchases by users of competing brands

3 Amount of shelf space assigned to the brand

4 Differentiation from competitive packages

5 Brand-name recognition

The researcher and decision maker need to discuss all possible criteria in advance and choose those which are appropriate. If the criteria for comparison is to be long-run sales results, the research approach will be much more elaborate than if the choice were based simply on brand-name recognition.

Timing and Importance.   These are always pivotal questions in the research process. How crucial is the decision? If the wrong decision is made, what will the consequences be? Obviously, the decision to go national with a new government program represents a much larger commitment than the decision to pursue a new program idea a bit further. Other questions are concerned with the timing of the decision. What is the time pressure on the decision? Is information needed quickly or is there time to develop an optimal research design?

Problem or Opportunity Analysis

Recall in Chapter 1 that three phases of marketing program development were identified.

1 Market analysis

2 Developing the marketing program

3 Controlling the marketing program

When the second or third phases are involved, the research purpose usually involves fairly well-defined decision alternatives. However, in the market analysis phase, the decision motivating the research may be rather vague. In such cases, it is useful to specify the involved problem or opportunity, as well as the possible decisions.

Research is often motivated by a problem or opportunity. The fact that sales are below expectations in the East might be a problem requiring research. The fact that people are consuming fewer sweets could be a problem or potential opportunity for a candy company. Increased leisure time might be viewed as an opportunity by a recreation-oriented organization. In such cases the research purpose should specify the problem or opportunity to be explored.

The manager needs to make certain that the *real* problem is being addressed. Sometimes the recognized problem is only a symptom or perhaps merely a part of a larger problem. A sobering illustration of this is the plight of Compton Corp.,[1] a manufacturer of capital equipment costing between $10,000 and $25,000. The company was dominant in its market, with a share as large as the next two biggest competitors. All the companies

[1]Adapted from Irving D. Canton, ''Do You Know Who Your Customer Is?'' *Journal of Marketing* (April 1976) 83.

sold their equipment through a network of independent distributors, each of which sold the products of at least two competitors. For several years this market leader had been losing share. In an attempt to reverse the trend they changed advertising agencies. When the new agency funded a study of end-users, they found to their surprise that the previous agency had done a superb job in creating awareness and favorable attitudes. However, many of the equipment purchasers who favored Compton were actually buying from the competitor. This problem had little to do with the performance of the advertising agency. A new study, oriented toward the distributors, found that Compton's distributor relations program was very weak relative to competitors. One competitor emphasized sales contests, another offered cash bonuses to salespeople, and a third was particularly effective with technical sales assistance directed to difficult accounts. Not surprisingly, these factors influenced the distributors when they were asked for advice, or when the prospective purchaser didn't have a firm commitment to Compton equipment.

In this case, the real problem was ultimately isolated, but only after much time and energy had been directed toward the wrong problem. It is important, when defining the problem, to think broadly about the possible causes—or influential variables. This may justify a separate exploratory research study.

The Research Users

The Decision Makers.   When the research results will be used to guide internal problem solving, the researcher must be sure that he knows the objectives and expectations of the actual decision makers. The bigger the problem, the more difficult this becomes, for not only are a large number of people likely to be involved, but the contact person may simply be acting as a liaison whose interpretation of the problem and the need for research may be secondhand. The major benefit from making an effort to reach all the decision makers is that the research purpose is likely to be specified more adequately. These contacts also will tell the researcher (especially an outside supplier who is called in to undertake the work) a good deal about the resources that are available to deal with the problem. This is very helpful in developing a realistic proposal.

Increasingly, marketing research is entering the public domain, which introduces a new set of users who frequently have very different criteria for evaluating research results. For example:

- A public utility presents a research study to a regulatory body in support of a request for a rate change or introduction of a change in service level.

- An industry trade association conducts research designed to influence proposed legislation or trade regulations. Thus the Direct Mail Marketing Association has sponsored a study of mail-order buyers in response to a proposed Federal Trade Commission order that would require sellers to offer a refund if they could not ship the ordered goods within a month.

- A regional transit agency wants to build public support for the continuation of an experimental program involving "dedicated" bus lanes (part of a road or highway on which no automobile traffic is permitted). The research demonstrating the effectiveness of the program is to be presented to various public bodies and citizen groups.
- Increasingly the Federal Trade Commission is using research to support their prosecution of deceptive advertising. Often this research is obtained by subpoenaing company files during the investigation.

In most cases, the research in the above examples is used to support a decision alternative. However, the examination of the results is often conducted in an adversary setting, which means more criticism of shortcomings and necessitates a higher quality of research.

Overt and Covert Purposes.   It would be naive to presume that research is always conducted to facilitate rational problem-solving activity or that the decision maker will always be willing or able to share his reasons for initiating the research.

Most researchers have encountered situations where the main purpose for their efforts was to serve someone's *organizational goals*. Thus, research can be used to postpone an awkward decision or to lend respectability to a decision that has been made already. A related purpose is to avoid responsibility. When there are competing factions, the manager making a difficult choice looks to research for the decision. This has the further advantage that, if the decision is later proved to be wrong, the manager can find someone else to blame.

In addition, research has a public relations value. A manager, believing he has a successful program, hopes that a research study will make his efforts more visible.[2] Usually the researcher has to guess at these covert purposes, for the decision maker will be understandably unwilling to reveal them. Worse, he may not disclose all the overt purposes. In highly sensitive situations the decision maker may want to minimize the number of people with full knowledge. This problem is confronted often by outside research suppliers. Another reason may be a lack of confidence in the abilities of the researcher—in such cases the researcher's scope is limited to the mechanical aspects. Finally, the manager simply may not want the researcher to acquire any additional power that might come from greater familiarity with the decision-making process.[3]

It is to be hoped that the researcher now understands the manager's purposes. The decision and the decision maker have been identified. The agreed-upon statement of purpose should not be static. Rather, it should be the basis of a continuing dialogue as the research process enters the design stage. In particular, there should be a continuing

---

[2]Edward A. Suchman, "Action for What? A Critique of Evaluative Research," in *The Organization, Management and Tactics of Social Research*, Richard O'Toole, ed. (Cambridge, Mass.: Schenkman Publishing Co., 1970).

[3]Stewart A. Smith, "Research and Pseudo-Research in Marketing," *Harvard Business Review, 56*, (March–April 1974), 73–76.

effort to make the purpose as specific as possible. The next step is to determine the research objective.

RESEARCH OBJECTIVE

The research objective is a statement, in as precise terminology as possible, of what information is needed. The research objective should be generated so that obtaining the information will improve the decision described in the research purpose. Thus, the research purpose will motivate the development of research objectives.

Research objectives have three components. The first is the research question. It specifies the information needed by the decision maker. The second and third elements help the researcher make the research question as specific and precise as possible. The second element is the development of hypotheses that are basically alternative answers to the research question. The research determines which of these alternative answers is correct. It is not always possible to develop hypotheses, but the effort should be made. The third is the scope or boundaries of the research. Is the interest in only current customers or in all potential customers, for example?

Research Question

The research question asks what specific information is required to achieve the research purpose. If the research question is answered by the research, then the information should aid the decision maker.

An illustration comes from a company in the toiletries and cosmetics business which was interested in acquiring a smaller firm with an apparently complementary product line. One anticipated benefit of the acquisition was the opportunity to eliminate one of the sales forces. The *purpose* of the research was to assess whether the company could use its existing sales force to distribute the products of the acquired company. The corresponding research *objective* was to determine how much the retail distribution patterns of the two companies overlapped. There was some preliminary evidence that suggested (that is, hypothesized) that distribution coverages would differ by geographic area and store type. The resulting study found that there was very little overlap, for the acquiring company emphasized major metropolitan areas, while the other company was largely represented in smaller cities and suburbs.

It is possible to have several research questions for a given research purpose. Thus, if the purpose is to determine if a specific advertisement should be run, the following research questions could be posted:

- Will the advertisement be noticed?
- Will it be interpreted accurately?
- Will it influence attitudes?

These questions correspond to the criteria used to evaluate the advertising alternatives. Similarly, if the purpose is to determine how to improve the services of a bank, possible research questions might be:

- What aspects of the current service are customers most pleased with and which are they most dissatisfied with?
- What types of customers use the various services?
- What benefits do people seek from banks?

Each of these questions should pass the test of being relevant to the purpose. For example, if customer types are identified that use a service like traveler's checks, it may be possible to modify that service to make it more convenient or attractive to them.

Sometimes the researcher can select a major objective and some supporting objectives. An example is a study conducted for the Department of Defense to address the problem of declining strength of the National Guard and the reserve components such as the Army Reserve.[4] The research purpose was to determine what job characteristics (product dimensions) would increase the enlistment levels and the reenlistment levels of various demographic types. Job characteristics such as salary, fringe benefits, education opportunity, travel, job image, and hair regulations were among the possible policy variables that could be adjusted. The overall objective of the study, to examine motivation factors in enlistment and reenlistment, lead to several supporting objectives. The first of these was to measure young men's propensity to serve (or reenlist). The second was to determine current perceptions of the reserve in terms of 12 key attributes. The third was to determine the relative importance of the 12 key job attributes that could provide the basis for influencing young men to join and remain in the service.

The researcher will always try to make the research question as specific as possible. Suppose the research question as to which customer types use the various bank services could be replaced by the research question: What are the lifestyle and attitude profiles of the users of credit cards, automatic overdraft protection, and traveler's checks? This increase in specificity will aid the researcher in the development of the research design by suggesting who to survey and what questions to include. The role of the research objective is to provide guidance to the research design. The more specific the research question is, the more practical guidance will be provided.

When a research question is set forth, it is sometimes difficult to realize that the question can and should be made more specific. The remaining two elements of the research objective—hypothesis development and the research boundaries—provide exercises to help the researcher make the research question more specific.

---

[4]"Conjoint Analysis of Values of Reserve Component Attitudes," a report prepared for the Department of Defense by Market Facts, Chicago, Illinois: November 1977.

Hypothesis Development

A hypothesis is a possible answer to the research question. The researcher should always make the time and effort to speculate as to possible research-question answers that will emerge from the research. In doing so, the fact that everyone already knows the answer sometimes becomes apparent. More often, the effort will add a considerable degree of specificity to the research question.

A hypothesis could speculate that sales are down in the Northeast because the level of competition has been abnormally high there during the past two months. Such a hypothesis provides considerable detail to a research question that asks what the problem is in the Northeast. It guides the research by ensuring that competitive promotions are included in the research design. One important role of a hypothesis is to suggest variables to be included in the research design—in this case, competitive promotion.

A research problem might be to estimate the demand for a new product. The hypothesis that the product will do well in the North but not in the South adds the concept of geographic location to the problem. It suggests that the sampling plan should include people from both regions. If the hypothesis suggests that the product will not do well in the South because it is not compatible with the southern lifestyle, it becomes evident that the research should measure not only purchase intentions, but also how the product would be used.

Normally there will be several competing hypotheses, either specified or implied. If all the hypotheses were known in advance to be true, there would be little reason to conduct the research. Thus, one objective of research is to choose among the possible hypotheses. A good illustration of the role of competing hypotheses is the problem recently faced by a major Canadian cable television company. A cable TV company picks up TV and radio signals with a large, sophisticated antenna and "pipes" the high-quality signals through cable into subscribers' homes. In 1978 this company provided service to 75 percent of the households within the total service area. The problem facing the company was that there were several areas where the penetration rate was far below average. The population in these areas represented about 15 percent of the total service area. Bringing these areas closer to the average would significantly improve profitability. Before remedial action could be taken it was necessary to establish the reasons for the low penetration. A variety of reasons were suggested by management, including:

1 Good television reception is available without cable.
2 Residents are illegally connecting their sets to the cable network.
3 There is a very transient population.
4 Residents have had poor previous experience with cable service.
5 The price is too high, given the incomes in the area.
6 The salesforce coverage has been inadequate.
7 A large percentage of the residents of the area are in age or social class groups that watch little television.

The challenge for the researcher is to devise a research approach which will provide information that can test each of these hypotheses.

Hypotheses are not appropriate for all situations. As the upcoming discussions on exploratory research in Chapter 3 will make clear, there are times when there simply is insufficient information on which to develop a hypothesis.

There are also times when the most reasonable hypothesis statement is simply a trivial restatement of the research question. For example:

Research

Question: Will the advertisement attract attention?

Hypothesis: It will attract attention.

In such cases the hypothesis will not add anything to the research and should simply be omitted. Hypothesis development should not be viewed as an item on a checklist to be quickly satisfied but rather as an opportunity to communicate information and to make the research question more specific.

How does the researcher generate hypotheses? The answer is that whatever information is available is used to speculate on which answers to the research questions are possible and which are likely.

There are three main sources of information the researcher can use to develop hypotheses, as Figure 2–3 illustrates. First, the researcher can draw upon previous research efforts; in fact, it is not uncommon to conduct exploratory research to generate hypotheses for future large-scale research efforts. The research purpose might be whether to conduct the large-scale studies.

A second source of hypotheses is theory from such disciplines as psychology, sociology, marketing, or economics. Thus, economic theory might suggest the importance of price in explaining the loss of retail sales. Marketing theory could indicate that distribution was important in predicting new-product acceptance. The use of attitude might be suggested by psychological theory as a measure of advertising impact.

A third and perhaps the most important source of hypotheses is the manager's experience with related problems, coupled with a knowledge of the problem situation and

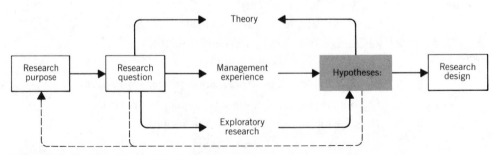

FIGURE 2–3 Hypothesis development

the use of judgment. This source is illustrated by the manufacturer who has discovered an unusual increase in selling costs.[5] Past experience with similar problems, plus a preliminary investigation into the reasons for the problem, point to an increase in the proportion and number of small orders received. The tentative hypothesis is: Small orders (suitably defined) have increased in both number and proportion, and this increase, coupled with a higher cost of processing these orders, has raised selling costs. The research would then be directed at the questions of (a) the extent of increase in small orders (and the reasons for the increase), and (b) the additional unit costs involved in processing orders of different sizes.

Research Boundaries

Hypothesis development helps make the research question more precise. Another approach is to indicate the scope of the research or the boundaries of the study. Is the interest in the total population, is it restricted to men only, or only to those on the West Coast? Is the research question concerned with the overall attitude toward the proposed new automobile, or is it necessary to learn customer attitudes about trunk space, handling, gas economy, styling, and interior appearance?

Actually, often much of the communication between the researcher and the decision maker will be directed at clarifying the boundaries of the study. For example, a manager may wish a study of the *effects* of government price controls on *conditions* in his *industry*. During the process of hypothesis development the possible effects may be isolated. This still leaves a number of areas of ambiguity. What is meant by "condition"—profitability, competitive position in world markets, labor relations, or what? How is the "industry" to be defined? What geographic areas are to be considered? What time period is to be appraised?

A final question of research scope regards the desired precision or accuracy of the results. This will, of course, depend on the research purpose. If a multimillion-dollar plant is to be constructed on the basis of the research results, a high degree of accuracy will be required. If, however, the decision involves the investment of a small sum in research and development on a new product idea, then a crude judgment as to the potential of the product would be acceptable.

ESTIMATING THE VALUE OF INFORMATION

Before the research approach can be selected, it is necessary to have some estimate of the value of the information, that is, the value of obtaining answers to the research questions. Such an estimate will help determine how much, if anything, should be spent on the research.

[5]Robert Ferber, Sidney Cohen, and David J. Luck, *The Design of Research Investigations* (Chicago: American Marketing Association, 1958).

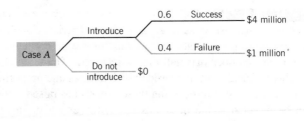

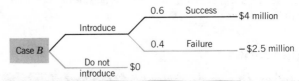

FIGURE 2–4   Illustrative decision models

The value will depend upon the importance of the decision as noted in the research purpose, the uncertainty that surrounds it, and the influence of the research information on the decision. If the decision is highly significant in terms of investment required or in terms of its impact upon the long-run success of the organization, then information may have a high value. However, uncertainty that is meaningful to the decision also must exist for the information to have value. If the outcomes are already known with certainty or if the decision will not be affected by the research information, the information will have no value.

To illustrate and expand these concepts, consider the simplified examples in Figure 2–4. In Case A the decision to introduce a new product is shown as a decision tree. The first two branches represent the decision alternatives—to introduce the product or to decide not to introduce it. The second branch represents the uncertainty. Our descriptive model indicates that if the product is successful, a profit of $4 million will result. The indication is that there is a probability of 0.6 that the product will be successful. However, if the product is not successful, the profit would be only $1 million, an event that will occur with probability 0.4. How much should we be willing to pay for perfect information in this case? If someone came to us with the claim that she could tell us, in advance, and with certainty, whether the product would be successful or not, how much would we pay her? The correct answer is nothing! The fact is that regardless of the information our decision would be the same. We would introduce the product, for even if the product were not well accepted, we would still make $1 million. In this case, not only is the decision insignificant to the organization, it is nonexistent. There is only one viable alternative. Without alternatives there is no decision contest, even if uncertainty exists; therefore, there is no need for additional information.

In the second case, the estimate is that, if the product is not successful, a loss of $2.5 million will occur. Since the expectation of the new product's eventual performance is still, on balance, positive, the product would be introduced.[6] However, in this case,

---

[6]The expected value of introducing the product would be 0.6(4M) + 0.4(−2.5M) = 1.4M.

perfect information now would have value. If we knew in advance that the product definitely would not be accepted, we would decide against introducing it and save $2.5 million. Since our best estimate of the probability of the product's not being accepted is 0.4, the value of the information would be 0.4 times $2.5 million, or $1 million. Thus, if this decision contest could be repeated many times, perfect information would save us $2.5 million about 40 percent of the time and would save us nothing (since it would not alter our decision) about 60 percent of the time. On average, it would save us $1 million. By spending money on research, we might improve knowledge as to how the product will be accepted. But market research is unlikely to be as good as perfect information, and therefore its value will be less than $1 million. Obviously, if the cost associated with an unsuccessful product were lower, or if the probability of an unsuccessful product were smaller, the value of information would be less. (The Appendix to this chapter extends this example to include the possibility of using a concept test to predict whether or not the product will succeed. A method is developed to determine the value of the concept test to the decision maker.)

PLANNING A NEW HMO

To see how a research purpose and a set of research objectives are developed, we join a meeting that took place at the Fraser General Hospital in September 1983.

The five doctors had a dilemma. They had spent a useful morning confirming that their hospital had the resources to operate a Health Maintenance Operation (the concept of an HMO is described in the boxed insert). These resources were substantial, as would be expected in a 1000-bed teaching and research hospital with a strong regional reputation.

**WHAT
IS AN HMO?**

There are two basic kinds of health coverage. The Health Maintenance Organization (HMO) is the best example of the *prepaid group practice* type. This involves fixed monthly payments directly to a group of doctors or clinic who are then responsible for all the health needs covered by the plan. The other is the *insurance* type which involves a company which collects premiums from subscribers who can go to any clinic or doctor they choose. The insurance company pays for the services covered by the policy. In both cases there may be limits to the coverage of such items as hospitalization, drugs and office visits.

The big drawback of the HMO is restriction of the choice of physicians and hospitals to those affiliated with the HMO. Generally, the total annual cost of an HMO to the consumer is lower than for group insurance plans. One reason is that the flat-free formula discourages doctors from hospitalizing patients longer than necessary. Also the emphasis on preventative care produces fewer seriously sick patients.

The September 10, 1983 meeting was one in a long series of informal talks, investigations, and efforts to build support for the idea within the hospital. These efforts had brought them to a critical point; their problem was how to determine whether there was enough market demand in the region to support another HMO. While each member of the planning group was convinced of the prospective benefits to the community, the hospital teaching program, and the bed utilization rate, they knew they needed persuasive evidence before the hospital trustees would provide start-up funds. After all, the trustees were even reluctant to approve funds for initial planning. What would it take before they would approve an initial investment in excess of $400,000?

The trustees weren't the only hurdle. Each of the doctors in the HMO planning group knew at least one colleague who was openly skeptical due to the presence of competitive health care programs. There was a well-established HMO about eight miles away, plus several clinics operating on a fee-for-service basis. Many of the clinic doctors had privileges at the Fraser General Hospital.

At lunch the planning group was joined by Herb Ellis, a partner of a local research and consulting firm. He had been invited by one of the doctors who knew him socially. During lunch the doctors enthusiastically described the HMO concept, what it meant for subscribers—especially those on low incomes, and some of the innovations such as consumer inputs to operations and procedures.

After lunch, John Akitt, a surgeon and the originator of the HMO proposal, reviewed some of the tentative decisions that would influence the market analysis. First, they intended to offer fairly comprehensive services from the beginning, including internal medicine, pediatrics, surgery, orthopedics, obstetrics, and gynecology. However, they weren't sure whether they should also offer dentistry and optometry at an additional fee. Such an array of services was felt to be competitively necessary, but when combined with a high doctor–enrollee ratio to ensure a high service level, the result was very high fixed costs.

All the doctors agreed that one way to keep initial costs down was to concentrate on larger employer groups. This meant a two-stage marketing effort would be required; first to get the employer to agree to offer the HMO plan as a subsidized benefit and then to persuade the employees to switch from their present health care plan. The largest employer in the vicinity was the state university, two miles away, with over 13,000 faculty, staff, and married students who could join a health plan. The vice-president of finance of the university appeared committed to offering the HMO plan. There were three other large employers nearby, representing an additional 20,000 possible enrollees. However, they had been much less enthusiastic about offering the Fraser Hospital HMO as a benefit, and implied that they wouldn't consider it until it had been successfully operating for a few months. This was upsetting to the doctors, for a sizable enrollment base had to be generated quickly if the HMO was to achieve its objectives. Still, if significant adoption of the HMO within the university occurred they felt they could get close to the break-even target in the short run.

As the discussion progressed, Ellis realized that the extent and rate of acceptance of the HMO would depend on the marketing effort and the fee level. Marketing was a real problem since solicitation of patients was, strictly speaking, unethical. This probably did not prevent personal selling and other communications efforts to explain the differences between fee-for-service and HMO plans. Pricing seemed to be a big factor; the prepaid feature of the HMO meant the prospective enrollee would see a bigger monthly salary bite, although over the long run total health costs would be lower. Since a large proportion of costs were fixed, a high enrollment target could help to lower fees. Otherwise, to lower fees it would be necessary to reduce services, which would make the HMO less attractive. Without knowledge of the price sensitivity of the market it would be hard to establish a fee structure. But who was the target market? Here the doctors had many conflicting opinions and the meeting became quite heated. Was the HMO concept most attractive to young families, older families with or without children or enrollees in the competitive HMO? No one was sure just how big an area an HMO could serve. While some existing HMOs attracted only people within a 10-mile radius of the hospital, there was a feeling that convenience and driving time were more important than distance.

At this point Herb Ellis felt he had some understanding of the doctors' marketing problems. Rather than discuss research approaches he asked for another meeting at which specific research purposes and objectives could be discussed. These would be the basis for a research proposal. He already knew that a big constraint on his planning would be the available budget. There was no way that more than $10,000 could be found to finance marketing research, no matter what the economic value of the research information to the hospital.

Prior to a second meeting with the planning committee Herb Ellis had done some background reading on the HMO concept, talked to several doctors in private practice, and informally interviewed four members of the competitive HMO. With this background he was ready to discuss preliminary research purposes and objectives which could be used to guide the design of the study.

During the second meeting with the hospital planning committee, quick agreement was reached that the primary purpose of the study was to address the decision as to whether the proposal for an HMO should be pursued to the point of making major investments in its implementation. The accompanying research objective consists of the research question and a statement of the study scope.

Research

Question: What is the demand for the new HMO?

Scope: Limited to students, staff, and faculty of the University.

The study was limited to University students, staff, and faculty because of several reasons. First, the University administration was disposed toward the plan, giving it the best chance of success in that environment. If support from that group was not in evidence, then the prospects would be dim in other organizations. Second, the budget limitation made it unlikely that any worthwhile research could be conducted with more than one organization. No geographical limits were placed on the study, as it was thought that distance from the home to the HMO would have only a weak influence on individual interest in the proposed HMO.

Much more time was spent on developing the supporting purposes and objectives, with Ellis constantly challenging the usefulness of each proposed purpose and objective. Because of the tight budget constraint he was fearful that overly ambitious objectives would be difficult to achieve with the alternative research designs he had in mind. Finally, the following set of supporting purposes and objectives was developed:

Purpose: What target market segments should the HMO emphasize?

Objective: Identify the market segments most interested in the proposed HMO. Estimate their probable rate of utilization of medical services from their past medical experience.

Purpose: What services should be provided at what price level?

Objective: Identify the attributes or characteristics of health plans that would have the greatest influence on an individual's choice among alternatives.

During the meeting a number of hypotheses were advanced as to who was the most likely to be interested in the plan. Of course, they would have to express strong interest in the plan as described to them. In addition, good prospects would be those who were dissatisfied with the coverage or quality of their present plan, didn't have a long-standing relationship with a family doctor, had favorable attitudes toward the Fraser General Hospital, and weren't enrolled in other plans through their spouses. At the end of the meeting the chairman indicated he wanted a proposal in time for the trustees' meeting on October 3. If the proposal were approved they would need the results of the study no later than the first week in February.

In the next chapter we will complete our overview of the steps in the research process. Most of the attention will be given to the major research design alternatives; however, each step is important in the development of a proposal.

SUMMARY

The research process consists of a series of stages or steps that serve to guide the research project from its conception through to the final recommendations. An overview of the process and a detailed discussion of the research purpose and research objective were presented in this chapter. The following chapter will provide a discussion of the research design and implementation stages. Together, the two chapters will provide a structure for the rest of the book.

The MPIS serves to stimulate research. The planning system allows managers to anticipate decisions and therefore the need for research systems. The information systems contain various environmental surveillance projects that can detect problems and opportunities that merit research efforts. The MPIS also serves as a vehicle for using the research. The research feeds into the planning system to influence not only the decision motivating the research but, perhaps, others. The information system can help the research findings build a cumulative understanding.

The specification of the research purpose involves first the identification of the decision involved, its alternatives, and the timing and importance of it. Sometimes the decision is as general as "should our marketing program be changed?" In such cases it is also useful to specify the problem or opportunity that is motivating the research or the environmental surveillance objective. The purpose statement also should consider who the research users are. There are times in which the identification of the research users and the subsequent understanding of their decisions and motives can improve significantly the effectiveness of the research.

The research objective involves the identification of the research questions. The answer to an appropriate research question should be relevant to the research purpose. The research question should be as specific as possible. In particular, hypotheses should be developed whenever possible. The research boundaries specification is also part of the research objective statement.

Even at the early stages of research conceptualization it is useful to consider what value the resulting information is likely to have. This exercise can lead to a decision to forego the research or at least make a judgment about the scale of research project that would be appropriate to consider.

QUESTIONS AND PROBLEMS

1 Jim Mitchell, a speaker of the California State Assembly, is considering running for the Democratic nomination for governor against the incumbent, Governor Brown. Mitchell and his backers do not want to enter the race unless there is a reasonable chance of winning. What are some research questions and hypotheses that, if answered, could help him make the decision?

2 At the beginning of Chapter 1 there are three examples of management information needs: Coca Cola, San Francisco Museum of Modern Art, Ameritech and Budget Rent-a-Car. Review each of these situations and develop an appropriate set of research purposes and objectives.

3 In the United Kingdom, cars are polished more frequently when the owners do not have garages. Is the lack of a garage a good variable for predicting sales of car polish? Are there other hypotheses that might explain this finding?

4 Can you think of additional research objectives for the HMO study?

5 The president of a small chain of women's clothing stores was concerned about a four-year trend of decreasing profits. The stores have been characterized as being rather conservative over the years in respect to their product line, store decor, and

advertising. They have consistently avoided trendy clothes, for example. Their market is now becoming extremely competitive because several aggressive fashion stores are expanding and are aiming at the young fashion-conscious buyer. As a result of this competition and the disappointing profit trend, the president is considering making the product line appear less conservative and more oriented to the young buyer. Before making such a risky change, the president felt it prudent to conduct some marketing research to learn the exact status of his chain. What should be the research purpose? Compose a set of research questions that would be helpful.

6 Explain the roles of the MPIS in the marketing research process. Illustrate your explanation using the Agree Cream Rinse example discussed in Chapter 1.

7 Consider the example in Figure 2–5 in the Appendix. What would be the expected value of perfect information if the loss would be $1 million instead of $2.5 million? How about if the loss would be $10 million instead of $2.5 million? What would it be if the probability of failure would be .2 instead of .4? Explain in words what is meant by the expected value of perfect information and what its implication is.

8 Consider the example explained in Figure 2–5 in the Appendix. Determine the value of research information under the following situations:

a Pr(Neg|F) = .9 and Pr(Pos|F) = .1 and all else remains the same

b Pr(Pos|S) = .7 and Pr(neg|S) = .3 and all else remains the same

c Pr(Pos|S) = .9, Pr(Neg|S) = .1, Pr(Neg|F) = .9, Pr(pos|F) = .1

APPENDIX
THE VALUE OF RESEARCH INFORMATION
USING BAYESIAN DECISION THEORY

In the discussion surrounding Figure 2–4, the value of perfect research information for Case B was determined to be $1 million. Perfect research information would indicate with certainty that the product would be a success or a failure. In this appendix, the more realistic question as to the value of imperfect research information will be addressed.

The Case B example of Figure 2–4 is shown at the top of Figure 2–5. A decision to introduce a new product has two possible outcomes. A "success" is given a prior probability of 0.6 and will result in a profit of $4 million. A "failure" is given a prior probability of 0.4 and will result in a profit of $-2.5 million. Symbolically,

$$\text{Product Success} = S = \$4 \text{ million}$$
$$\text{Product Failure} = F = -\$2.5 \text{ million}$$
$$\text{Probability of Success} = \Pr(S) = 0.6$$
$$\text{Probability of Failure} = \Pr(F) = 0.4$$

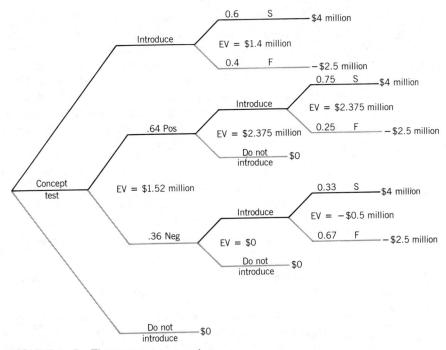

FIGURE 2–5 The concept test option

The expected value of introducing the product is then the sum of the two possible payoffs, each weighted by its probability of occurring:[7]

$$EV = \text{Expected Value} = S \times Pr(S) + F \times Pr(F)$$
$$= (\$4 \text{ million}) \times 0.6 + (-\$2.5 \text{ million}) \times 0.4 = \$1.4 \text{ million}$$

This expected value is shown in Figure 2–4 between the two outcomes, success and failure. The alternative of not introducing will result in a profit of zero. Thus, the product will be introduced. If it were possible to obtain perfect information about the outcome of the product introduction then the potential would be created to avoid the result of losing $2.5 million. The maximum amount that would be paid for perfect information would be $2.5 million times .4, the probability that a failure will result, which amounts to $1 million. Only when a failure results will the decision be affected; therefore, the firm will save some money.

---

[7]To understand expected value consider the following game. Ten balls numbered from one to 10 are placed in a bowl. One ball is selected at random. If the number is 1, 2, 3, 4, 5 or 6, you receive $4 million. If it is 7, 8, 9, or 10, you must pay $2.5 million. If you played this game thousands of times you would earn $1.4 million, on the average, each time the game was played.

Figure 2–5 has added the alternative of evaluating the new product with a concept test, such as a focus-group interview in which a group of eight to ten people are asked to discuss the concept. Let us assume that the concept test will either be positive (Pos) or negative (Neg). Now assume that the concept test is not a perfect indicator of the ultimate result. In particular, those who have worked with this concept test several times before believe that for successful products the concept test is positive 80 percent of the time (and thus negative 20 percent of the time). For the failed products, the concept test is believed to be negative 60 percent of the time (and thus positive 40 percent of the time). In terms of conditional probabilities,

Probability of a Pos concept test given a successful product
$$= Pr(Pos|S) = .8$$

Probability of a Neg concept test given a successful product
$$= Pr(Neg|S) = .2$$

Probability of a Neg concept test given a failed product
$$= Pr(Neg|F) = .6$$

Probability of a Pos concept test given a failed product
$$= Pr(Pos|F) = .4$$

The expected value of the "introduce the product immediately" option is $1.4 million. We need to determine the expected value of the concept test alternative in order to determine how much value, if any, there will be in conducting the test. To proceed we first need to determine

Pr(Pos)   = The probability of a positive concept test
Pr(Neg)   = The probability of a negative concept test
Pr(S|Pos) = The probability that the product will be successful given a positive concept test
Pr(F|Pos) = The probability that the product will be a failure given a positive concept test
Pr(S|Neg) = The probability that the product will be successful given a negative concept test.
Pr(F|Neg) = The probability that the product will be successful given a negative concept test

The first two terms are obtained from the following formula.[8]

$$Pr(Pos) = Pr(Pos|S)Pr(S) + Pr(Pos|F)Pr(F)$$
$$= .8 \times .6 + .4 \times .4 = .64$$
$$Pr(Neg) = Pr(Neg|S)Pr(S) + Pr(Neg|F)Pr(F)$$
$$= .2 \times .6 + .6 \times .4 = .36$$

[8]The formulas are easily expanded if there are more than two outcomes to the decision. For example, suppose that there were three outcomes, Success (S), Failure (F) and Indeterminant (I). The formula would then be:

$$Pr(Pos) = Pr(Pos|S) \times Pr(S) + Pr(Pos|I) \times Pr(I) + Pr(Pos|F) \times Pr(F)$$

To obtain the balance of the expressions we apply a formula known as Bayes Theorem, which is the basis of Bayesian Decision Theory:

$$\text{Pr}(S|\text{Pos}) = \frac{\text{Pr}(\text{Pos}|S) \times \text{Pr}(S)}{\text{Pr}(\text{Pos})} = \frac{.8 \times .6}{.64} = .75$$

$$\text{Pr}(F|\text{Pos}) = \frac{\text{Pr}(\text{Pos}|F) \times \text{Pr}(F)}{\text{Pr}(\text{Pos})} = \frac{.4 \times .4}{.64} = .25$$

$$\text{Pr}(S|\text{Neg}) = \frac{\text{Pr}(\text{Neg}|S) \times \text{Pr}(S)}{\text{Pr}(\text{Neg})} = \frac{.2 \times .6}{.36} = .33$$

$$\text{Pr}(F|\text{Neg}) = \frac{\text{Pr}(\text{Neg}|F) \times \text{Pr}(F)}{\text{Pr}(\text{Neg})} = \frac{.6 \times .4}{.36} = .67$$

The information is now at hand to evaluate the concept test alternative. We first consider what happens if there is a positive concept test and the product is introduced. The probability of obtaining a successful product, which would earn $4 million, is $\text{Pr}(S|\text{Pos})$ or .75. The failure probability is of course $\text{Pr}(F|\text{Pos})$ or .25. The expected value, the sum of the two outcomes each weighted by its probability, is then

$$S \times \text{Pr}(S|\text{Pos}) + F \times \text{Pr}(F|\text{Pos})$$
$$= (\$4 \text{ million}) \times .75 + (-\$2.5 \text{ million}) \times .25 = \$2.375 \text{ million}$$

Since $2.375 million is more than the value of the "do not introduce" alternative, the product would be introduced after a positive concept test, and an expected value of $2.375 million would result, as shown in Figure 2–4.

A similar analysis reveals that the expected value of introducing the product after a negative concept test would be

$$(\$4 \text{ million}) \times .33 + (-\$2.5 \text{ million}) \times .67 = -\$.5 \text{ million}$$

Thus, given a negative concept test, the preferred alternative would be "do not introduce," which would yield zero.

Therefore an expected value of $2.375 million (associated with a positive concept test) will occur with a probability of .64 [recall that $\text{Pr}(\text{Pos}) = .64$]. Further, an expected value of zero (associated with a negative concept test) will occur with probability .36. The expected value of a concept test alternative is thus

$$(\$2.75 \text{ million}) \times .64 + (\$0) \times .36 = \$1.52 \text{ million}$$

Note that

Expected Value of "Concept Test" Alternative	= $1,520,000
Expected Value of "Introduce" Alternative Difference	= $1,400,000
	= $120,000

Thus the value of a concept test is $120,000, considerably less than value of perfect information ($1 million), but still substantial. A researcher should be willing to pay up to $120,000 for a concept test. Of course, if another concept test could be found that would predict success or failure more accurately, then its value would be higher, as the reader could demonstrate.

CASE 2–1

San Francisco Museum of Modern Art (A)[9]

In 1976 the San Francisco Museum of Modern Art reopened its permanent collections after one year in storage. Although a catalog describing individual works existed, it was out of date, unavailable for purchase, and was written more for a knowledgeable audience of art historians than for the average museum visitor. Hence, there was no way for the visitor to learn about the collection or about modern art, other than through taking courses at universities or colleges in the area or leafing through art history texts. For these reasons, Linda Robinson, the education director, argued that the development of a self-guide to the collection was one of the museum's major priorities for 1978.

THE MUSEUM

The San Francisco Museum of Modern Art (SFMMA) is the West's oldest museum featuring modern art. In 1890 the San Francisco Art Association, a coalition of Bay Area artists, was given the Mark Hopkins Mansion to convert into galleries for exhibitions. After being forced to close due to the mansion being destroyed in the 1906 earthquake and fire, the museum relocated several times before occupying its current residence on the fourth floor of the Veterans Building in the Civic Center War Memorial Complex.

Under its first director, Dr. Grace McCann Morky, the museum brought understanding and acceptance of new forms of twentieth-century art and encouraged the work of San Francisco artists. The museum shared major travelling exhibitions with leading contemporary art institutions and originated many shows. Since 1970, the museum had expanded to the third floor of the Veterans Building, renovated the fourth-floor galleries, and added a bookshop and cafe and a painting conservation laboratory.

The education department sponsored many regular programs and special events. Studio and classroom

[9]Prepared by Linnea Bohn and David A. Aaker for use as the basis of a class discussion.

courses were scheduled throughout the year, and concerts, dance programs, and poetry readings were regular events. Films covering every form of cinema art were presented weekly. Tours were provided two or three times a week by volunteers (docents) from the community.

The museum was supported entirely by the members, through contributions and endowments. The director of the museum oversaw a staff of 44, including curators, conservators, education specialists, researchers, and technicians.

THE SELF-GUIDE DECISION

The museum had explored a number of alternatives meeting the objectives of the permanent collection; namely, educating the visitor with respect to modern art. Various forms of guides were considered, but there was no obvious best choice for this particular collection. Among the many questions raised were: Would the visitor be more likely to pick up a pamphlet that could be used in the museum and then taken home, or would a recorded tour be more appealing? What about a catalogue that could be used while in the museum but could not be taken home? Perhaps guides could be placed on the wall near the art works? The content and level of writing also might affect use of the guide. Would adult visitors be insulted by simple explanations aimed more at the younger visitor? Would a more complex, esoteric style turn off the novice visitor? Because of the limited resources available for the development and production of a self-guide, there was no room for error in deciding format or content. Money committed to an unusable guide would mean the museum could meet neither its educational objectives nor its larger purpose of serving the public. Further, a successful guide would demonstrate the museum's responsiveness to meeting the needs of its public and, in turn, encouraged increased memberships and funding through donations and grants.

In order to improve the museum's decision-making

process with respect to evaluating alternate approaches to the self-guide design, the education director decided that market research could provide helpful information. About six months was available to conduct research and to test preliminary guides.

It is important to note that the museum, because of the nature of the organization and because of tradition, had operated historically in a different way from most business organizations. Museums do not have a consumer outlook, despite a commitment to public service. They allow people who cannot afford to purchase paintings and sculptures to enjoy art for education and entertainment. Rather than following the marketing concept of providing for the consumers' needs, museums rely on the judgments of administrators as to what is good for the public to decide on the services to be offered. However, the contraction of government support was forcing these administrators to step off their pedestals and become more responsive to their visitors.

At the same time, art organizations were skeptical as to how business practices could help their situation. Businesses are fueled by profits, museums by civic duty. Marketing research also was seen as an intrusion of an individual's privacy. This study was therefore being viewed in part as an experiment for the museum. Linda Robinson and the other administrators wanted to see whether marketing research could be a valuable tool for improving their decisions.

QUESTIONS FOR DISCUSSION

1 Develop a research purpose and set of research questions and hypotheses. Justify the research questions by linking them to the research purpose.

2 What research approaches would you recommend? Provide as much specific detail as possible about the research you recommend, especially any exploratory research.

CASE 2–2
National Chemical Corporation[10]

TIGER-TREAD

On January 20, 1980, Charley Omsrud, marketing director, and Matt Perspex, technical director, of the New Products Division of National Chemical Corporation, met to respond to the division general manager's request to advance the introduction of Tiger-Tread, a spray compound designed to free cars stuck in ice or snow. The two men were jointly responsible for presenting a marketing plan, a manufacturing plan, and a preliminary budget to the general manager by the end of the month.

Tiger-Tread consisted of resins dissolved in methanol. The user sprayed Tiger-Tread on the exposed portion of a stuck tire, then slowly rotated the wheels. As

[10]Reproduced with permission of HBS Case Services and Professor Richard Cardozo, University of Minnesota.

the treated portion of the tire contacted the water, the resins formed a sticky layer, providing traction so the user could drive away. Tiger-Tread was a "spin-off" product from a basic technology whose patent would expire in 1984.

Both men knew that Dow had withdrawn Liquid Tire Chain, a similar product, in the early 1970s, because of product difficulties that the National Chemical product appeared to have overcome. "I don't know why Dow didn't take it back into the lab to iron out the problems," Charley pondered; "from what I heard, one in five households in their test market tried it, and four of five of those bought a second can."

"I don't know whether these results are relevant for Tiger-Tread or not," Charley continued, "because we're looking for an industrial market." National Chemical had recently experienced difficulty in penetrating consumer markets other than those its Household

Products Division served through the grocery trade. As a result, National Chemical senior management had charged the New Products Division to seek opportunities for developing and introducing new products intended for industrial markets. Because existing products appeared unlikely to provide the sales growth to which corporate management was committed, there was pressure on the New Products Division to accelerate its activities.

Charley Omsrud defined the industrial market for Tiger-Tread as fleets of 10 or more passenger cars. Such fleets accounted for more than seven million vehicles in 1979. The following table shows approximate fleet size by type of operator.

Almost 75 percent of all the cars in business fleets were used for sales calls; nearly all the remainder, for service calls.

Fleets in which 25 or more cars were used in a particular area generally operated their own garages and purchased supplies centrally. Operators of large, dispersed fleets ordinarily negotiated blanket service contracts, which might include supplies, with automobile dealers who sold the brands of cars represented in the fleet. Small fleets might arrange a service agreement with a local garage or service station, or simply reimburse vehicle users for maintenance expenses.

Fleet owners who operated garages bought supplies either directly from manufacturers or through automotive parts wholesalers, who purchased from manufacturers. Garages and service stations typically acquired supplies from wholesalers.

A manufacturer's average receipts per unit varied with the margins obtained by wholesalers and garages, the discount available to direct purchasers and the proportion of sales made direct and through wholesalers. One industry source estimated that an item like Tiger-Tread would, on average, yield the manufacturer about 45 cents on every dollar that garages or service stations charged vehicle users for the product.

National Chemical customarily priced its specialty chemicals at three times factory cost. The industry average prices for specialty chemical products were about two times factory cost.

Matt Perspex noted that costs depended on the size of the spray can used and the volume of cans expected to be filled. "At volume production, a 10-ounce can cost about 25 percent more than a 5-ounce can. We should be able to produce Tiger-Tread at about 75 to 80 cents for a 5-ounce can if we can make 100,000 or more a month. At 50,000 cans a month we'd add another 5 to 10 cents a can. Below that, our costs could easily run up to $1.25. Cost aside, we have to know what capacity to commit and schedule it at least 10 weeks in advance. Our planning horizon's really longer than that, because we'll have to order cans, labels, boxes, and any other materials three to six months ahead."

As a basis for forecasting sales, Charley reviewed

Table 1

Operator	Average Fleet Size	Number of Fleets	Percent of Total Fleet Vehicles
Business (25+ cars)	200	12,000	35
Business (10–24 cars)	20	35,000	10
Rental	1,050	450	7
Federal Government Agencies	850	400	5
State & Local Governments & Agencies	300	3,000	13
Police	500	580	4
Taxi	30	6,680	3
All other	n.a.	n.a.	23

a study about winter driving habits which showed that 18 percent of the cars in snowbelt states were stuck at least once in a typical winter, and that the average driver got stuck 1.6 times a winter. Because that study was more than 10 years old, Charley thought that smaller, lighter cars had increased the incidence of trouble.

Charley then reported on informal conversations he had held with National Chemical executives. The dozen or so executives to whom Charley and Matt had given samples of Tiger-Tread were impressed with its potential:

1 Jerry (another division executive) and I flew in late and couldn't get out of the airport parking lot—it was like a skating rink. We were literally spinning our wheels till I remembered that can. Jerry was so sure it wouldn't work he went to find a cab. It took me just about a minute to "spray and rotate, then be patient," just like the label said to, and then I drove out—picked up Jerry at the cab stand. He's a lot less skeptical now. Anybody who drives a lot—and most sales, marketing and general management people do—shouldn't be without it.

2 My last trip to Pittsburgh made me a believer. I had a really tight schedule, and when the rain turned to snow, I got stuck in curbside parking spaces. Even though I was on an incline both times, Tiger-Tread got me out. Can you get me another can?

3 I told Newhouse (operations vice-president of a large customer) about Tiger-Tread over a drink after our meeting. He was excited about the possibility of developing a longer lasting compound that he could spray on their lift-truck tires. They have a problem with moisture on the plant floor, and he says they've had several near-accidents. I asked Matt to send someone to visit with him.

Some executives found family uses for their samples. One said, "I gave the can to my kid, who goes out in all kinds of weather. He used it twice, and says he got out when he otherwise would've called me for help. I figure that can's bought me at least four hours

of sleep." Another executive, who had placed the can in his wife's car, said, "She's never used it, but I feel better knowing it's there."

Charley had also visited with fleet operators, who found the concept of Tiger-Tread interesting. One commented that, ". . . it would be a lot cheaper to use Tiger-Tread than to send a tow truck." An official of a car rental company thought Tiger-Tread might help his firm's image: "When people get stuck, they blame the car—not themselves. Sometimes they'll just walk away, and we'll get the keys in the mail with a nasty letter."

Matt was enthusiastic about the product:

We distributed 200 samples (4-ounce aerosol cans) to our personnel in the Toledo lab. More than 150 people used it, and half of them reported that it worked "like a miracle" for them. Most of the other half evidently didn't know how to use it properly, from what they told us afterwards.

Tiger-Tread is much more powerful than Dow's original product, and we have a far more effective applicator. We've spent almost 30 months getting it right. It'll work, and we can make it. Now, Charley, it's up to your guys to figure out how to sell it.

National Chemical's sales force did not presently call on automotive parts distributors or fleet operators, but could do so if the New Products Division were willing to "buy" some of its time. (The National Chemical sales force covered a variety of industrial accounts, and "sold" its time to the company's product divisions.) Sales force time was available at a cost of 15 percent of sales volume, with a minimum charge of $150,000 per division. An alternative route to distributors and users was through independent manufacturers' representatives, who would charge from 5 to 15 percent of sales.

Many suppliers who served the fleet industry advertised in *Automotive Fleet,* whose circulation exceeded 17,000. A full-page ad in *Automotive Fleet* costs about $2500.

3

RESEARCH DESIGN AND IMPLEMENTATION

A *research design* is the detailed blueprint used to guide the implementation of a research study toward the realization of its objectives.

The process of designing a research study involves many interrelated decisions. The most significant decision is the choice of **research approach**, for this determines how the information will be obtained. Typical questions at this stage are: Should we rely on secondary sources such as the census? What is more appropriate, an exploratory approach with group discussions or a survey? Is a mail, telephone, or personal interview survey better for this problem?

Tactical research decisions are made once the research approach has been chosen. Here the focus is on the specific measurements to be made or questions to be asked, the structure and length of the questionnaire, and the procedure for choosing a sample to be interviewed. These tactical decisions also are constrained by time and budget availability. So, before a study can be implemented, the estimated costs must be compared to the anticipated value.

To design something also means to ensure that the pieces fit together. The achievement of this fit between objectives, research approach, and research tactics is inherently an iterative process in which earlier decisions are constantly reconsidered in light of subsequent decisions. This may mean a revision of the research objectives as new insights are gained into the complexities of the population to be sampled, or a reassessment of the research approach in light of realistic cost estimates. Consequently, few researchers find they have designed their research studies in the neat and linear fashion that is implied by Figure 3–1; however, this figure is a useful overview of major research design topics to be introduced in this chapter. Also in this chapter we will discuss the research proposal as a vehicle for summarizing significant decisions made during the research design process.

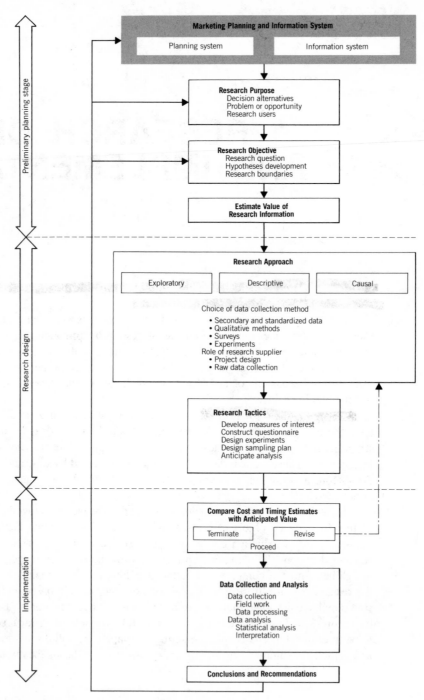

FIGURE 3–1 The research process

RESEARCH APPROACH

Types of Research

All research approaches can be classified into one of three general categories of research: exploratory, descriptive, and causal. These categories differ significantly in terms of research purpose, research questions, precision of the hypotheses that are formed, and the data collection methods that are used.

Exploratory Research.   Exploratory research is used when one is seeking insights into the general nature of a problem, the possible decision alternatives, and relevant variables that need to be considered. There is typically little prior knowledge upon which to build. The research methods are highly flexible, unstructured, and qualitative, for the researcher begins without firm preconceptions as to what will be found. The absence of structure permits a thorough pursuit of interesting ideas and clues about the problem situation.

Exploratory research hypotheses are either vague and ill-defined or do not exist at all. Table 3–1 illustrates this point with three examples. In the first example, the research question asks what alternative ways there are to provide lunches for school children. It was precipitated by information suggesting problems with existing school lunch programs. In this case, there simply is no information that would suggest the most tentative of hypotheses. In the second, the research question is to determine what benefits people seek from the product. Since no previous research considered consumer benefits, it is difficult to even provide a list of them. In the third, the hypothesis is advanced that a root cause of customer dissatisfaction is an image of impersonalization. However, this hypothesis is extremely tentative and provides at best only a partial answer to the research question.

Exploratory research is also useful for establishing priorities among research questions and for learning about the practical problems of carrying out the research. What kinds of questions will respondents be able to answer? What are the barriers to contacting the appropriate respondents? When should the study be conducted?

A variety of productive exploratory approaches will be discussed in Chapters 4 and 5, including literature reviews, individual and group unstructured interviews, and case studies.

Descriptive Research.   Descriptive research embraces a large proportion of marketing research. The purpose is to provide an accurate snapshot of some aspect of the market environment, such as

• The proportion of the adult population that supports the United Fund
• Consumer evaluation of the attributes of our product versus competing products

TABLE 3–1

Three Research Approaches

Research Purpose	Research Question	Hypothesis
Exploratory research		
1. What new product should be developed?	What alternative ways are there to provide lunches for school children?	———
2. What product appeal will be effective in advertising?	What benefits do people seek from the product?	Constructs unknown.
3. How can our service be improved?	What is the nature of any customer dissatisfaction?	Suspect that an image of impersonalization is a problem.
Descriptive research		
4. How should a new product be distributed?	Where do people now buy similar products?	Upper-class buyers use specialty stores and middle-class buyers use department stores.
5. What should be the target segment?	What kinds of people now buy the product, and who buys our brand?	Older people buy our brand, whereas the young marrieds are heavy users of competitors'.
6. How should our product be changed?	What is our current image?	We are regarded as being conservatives and behind the times.
Causal research		
7. Will an increase in the service staff be profitable?	What is the relationship of size of service staff and revenue?	For small organizations an increase of 50% or less will generate marginal revenue in excess of marginal costs.
8. Which advertising program for public transit should be run?	What would get people out of cars and into public transit?	Advertising program A generates more new riders than program B.
9. Should a new budget or "no frills" class of airfare be introduced?	Will the "no frills" airfare generate sufficient new passengers to offset the loss of revenue from existing passengers switching from economy class?	The new airfare will attract sufficient revenue from new passengers.

- The socioeconomic and demographic characteristics of the audience of a magazine
- The proportion of all possible outlets that are carrying, displaying, or merchandising our products

In descriptive research, hypotheses often will exist but they may be tentative and speculative. In general, the relationships studied will not be causal in nature. However, they may still have utility in predicting.

In the fourth example in Table 3–1, the research question is concerned with where people buy a particular type of product. One hypothesis is that upper-class families buy this type of product in specialty stores and middle-class families use department stores. There is no explicit cause–effect relationship. The question is simply to describe where people buy. With this hypothesis it is clear that if data are gathered, it will be important to include indicators of social class and to be prepared to analyze the data with respect to stores classified as specialty and department stores. Thus, the development of the hypothesis provides guidance to the researcher by introducing more detail to the research question. Similarly, in the sixth example, the hypothesis suggests that when image is being measured it is necessary to include measures of innovativeness.

Causal Research. When it is necessary to show that one variable causes or determines the values of other variables, a causal research approach must be used. Descriptive research is not sufficient, for all it can show is that two variables are related or associated. Of course, evidence of a relationship or an association is useful, for otherwise we would have no basis for even inferring that causality might be present. To go beyond this inference we must have reasonable proof that one variable preceded the other and that there were no other causal factors that could have accounted for the relationship.

Suppose we had evidence that territories with extensive sales coverage, as measured by the number of accounts per salesperson, had higher per capita sales. Is this sufficient grounds for a decision to increase the sales coverage in areas where sales are currently weak? The answer would depend first on whether past increases in sales coverage had led to increases to sales. Perhaps the allocation of the sales force annual budget was based on the previous year's sales. Then we might conclude that past sales increases led to an increase in sales coverage—a conclusion with dramatically different implications. Secondly, we would have to be sure that there were not other reasons for differences in sales between territories. Perhaps the weak sales territories had special requirements due to climate differences and our product was at a disadvantage, or perhaps the weak territories were served by competitors with local advantages. In either case, adding more salespeople to weak sales territories would not improve sales, for the basic problems still would be present.

Because the requirements for proof of causality are so demanding, the research questions and relevant hypotheses are very specific. The examples in Table 3–1 show the level of detail that is desirable.

The Detective Funnel

The three types of research—exploratory, descriptive, and causal—each have a distinct and complementary role to play in many research studies. This is most evident in studies that are initiated with this question: Why are our sales (share, patronage, contributions) below our objectives or below last year's performance? The first step is to use exploratory techniques to generate all possible reasons for the problem (see insert). Thereafter, a combination of descriptive and causal approaches is used to narrow the possible causes. Hence, the research is used in exactly the same way that a detective proceeds to eliminate unlikely suspects. Descriptive research evidence is often sufficient to filter out many of the possible causes.

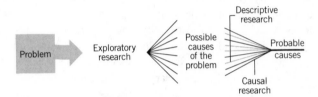

For example, a municipal transit company, seeking to understand why ridership has declined suddenly, can dispose quickly of weather-related factors by examining weather records to see whether the recent weather pattern has been unusual. Similarly, evidence from customer records can be used to determine whether or not telephone complaints about the quality of service have increased. Also, their surveys of customers will reveal that service frequency and fares are the two most important factors in evaluating transit service, whereas riders are indifferent to the amount and type of advertising inside buses. If fares haven't risen (or the costs of competitive transportation modes such as car parking or operating costs haven't declined), then attention can be focused on service frequency. Whether this is the causal factor depends on whether there was a reduction in frequency that preceded the decline in ridership.

Data Collection Methods

The research designer has a wide variety of methods to consider, either singly or in combination. They can be grouped first according to whether they use secondary or primary sources of data. **Secondary data** are already available, because they were collected for some purpose other than the present problem. Included here are (1) the existing company information system; (2) data banks of other organizations, including government sources such as the Census Bureau or trade association studies and reports; and (3) syndicated data sources, such as consumer purchase panels, where one organization collects reasonably standardized data for use by client companies. These secondary sources are discussed

TABLE 3–2
Methods for Collecting Primary Data

1. *Qualitative research:* Unstructured interviews with small samples, usually intended to generate ideas and hypotheses
   A. *Expert opinion:* Discussions with people who have specialized insights into the nature of markets
   B. *Depth interviews:* The emphasis is on the depth and richness of information from a few respondents
   C. *Focus-group interviews:* Groups of six to ten people engage in a lengthy discussion of subjects related to the research question
2. *Survey research:* Structured collection of data directly from representative samples of respondents:
   A. *Mail interviews*
   B. *Telephone interviews*
   C. *Personal interview:* These can be done either in the respondent's home or work place or at a central location such as a shopping mall
3. *Experimental research:* The intent is to determine the effect of a change in one variable on another variable. This requires the researcher to introduce the change into the environment and then measure the resulting effect
   A. *Laboratory experiments:* Variables are manipulated in an artificial setting
   B. *Field experiments:* Variables are manipulated in a natural setting

in Chapter 4. **Primary data** is collected especially to address a specific research objective. A variety of methods—ranging from qualitative research to surveys to experiments—can be employed. These methods are described in more detail in Table 3–2.

Some methods are better suited to one category of research than another. The breakdown is as follows:

Data Collection Method	Category of Research		
	Exploratory	Descriptive	Causal
Secondary sources			
information system	**	*	
data banks of other organizations	**	*	
syndicated services	**	*	*
Primary sources			
qualitative research	**	*	
surveys	*	**	*
experiments		*	**

**Very appropriate method.
*Somewhat appropriate method.

Because different methods serve different purposes, a researcher often will use several in sequence so the results from one method can be used by another. For example, in investigating the potential for a new frozen dessert product, a researcher may begin by consulting secondary sources, such as Census statistics or industry trade association statistics, or by studying the performance of similar products that have been launched into the same market. Then qualitative research would be used to gain insights into the benefits sought by customers and into sources of dissatisfaction with the existing products. These tentative insights could be confirmed with telephone survey interviews of a representative sample of potential buyers. Finally, a controlled store experiment might be used to test the appeal of different packages.

Choosing a Research Approach for the HMO Study

Seldom is a data collection method perfectly suited to a research objective. A successful choice is one that has the greatest number of strengths and the fewest weaknesses, relative to the alternatives. Often this is achieved by combining several methods to take advantage of their best features and minimize their limitations. This was what Herb Ellis had to do to get the amount of information required by the research objectives and still remain within the budget limit.

From the beginning it was clear that the overall research approach would involve preliminary qualitative research followed by a survey to expose the concept of a health maintenance organization to a large representative sample and test the specific hypotheses. Ellis proposed to conduct two focus groups to establish the vocabulary used by the target respondents and the attributes they used to evaluate a health plan, as well as explore their knowledge and expectations of health plans and their reasons for past or prospective changes. The problem was deciding the kind of survey to conduct.

The principal survey options were mail questionnaires and personal or telephone interviews. Each, however, had a serious drawback. Personal interviews using trained interviewers were simply too costly and would have been feasible only with a sample that was too small to identify adequately the differences among the three segments. Telephone interviews would have been difficult to conduct, both because of the length of the questionnaire and the evident need for multiple category questions, which are awkward to communicate verbally. The questionnaire could have been administered by mail, but experience suggested that the response rates would be low unless substantial incentives and followups were used.

The solution was a self-administered questionnaire, with door-to-door delivery and pick-up by untrained survey assistants. The advantage of the telephone in economically reaching large samples was utilized both to establish contact and then get agreement to participate. During the initial phone call, arrangements were made to deliver and pick up the questionnaire. Before the pick-up, a reminder phone call was made to ensure the questionnaire was completed. In some instances the respondent was given a stamped, addressed envelope so the questionnaire could be returned by mail.

The research approach was successful in achieving a high response rate at a low cost per completed interview. The key to success was the matching of the approach to the objectives of the study and the characteristics of the population, notably, the presence of an up-to-date listing, the limited geographic area to be covered, and their inherent interest in the subject of the survey. In Chapter 6 we will return to discuss this process of matching in more detail.

Choice of Research Supplier

Virtually all research users will at some time use the services of outside research specialists. Their role may be limited to raw-data collection, according to the research approach, questionnaire, and sampling method provided by the client. At the other extreme, the client may assign the entire problem to an outside consultant who is responsible for every step to the completed report and action recommendations. Other possibilities are to bring in outside specialists for special problems (such as a sampling expert to draw a complex sample), or to employ services that have special facilities or data.

Many related considerations will influence the decision to go outside:[1]

1 Internal personnel may not have the skills or experience. Few but the largest companies have specialists in all areas, from psychologists able to conduct focus-group interviewing, to electronics engineers with MBAs who have studied the telecommunications equipment market.

2 Outside help may be called in to boost internal capacity in response to an urgent deadline.

3 Often it is cheaper to go outside. Specialists who have encountered similar problems with other clients are probably more efficient in dealing with the problem, and because they are not on the staff there is no risk of underutilization of their time.

Shared cost and multiclient studies coordinated by an outside supplier offer considerable savings possibilities. Multiclient studies are feasible when several organizations have related needs for information about a major topic, such as the future of Electronic Funds Transfer Systems. Each client will pay an agreed share of the total cost. The ultimate in shared cost studies are the large standardized data collection services, such as store audits of product sales activity or omnibus surveys which combine questions from several clients.

4 Often outside suppliers have special facilities or competencies (an established national interviewing field force, conference rooms with one-way mirrors, banks of telephone lines, or test kitchens) which would be costly to duplicate for a single study.

[1]Lee Adler and Charles S. Mayer, *Managing the Marketing Research Function* (Chicago: American Marketing Association, 1977).

5 Political considerations may dictate the use of an outside research specialist whose credentials are acceptable to all parties to an internal policy dispute. Research people within the organization may be well advised to avoid being on one side or the other of a sensitive issue.

6 Marketing research is increasingly used in litigation or in proceedings before regulatory or legislative bodies. The credibility of the findings generally will be enhanced if the study is conducted by a respected outsider. Also, this kind of research often is subjected to critical questioning or cross-examination and is likely to stand up only if designed to high standards, which may exceed those used within the organization for routine decision-making purposes.

Once the decision has been made to go outside there still remains the question of which consultant or supplier to retain. A crucial factor in the choice is the judgment as to whether the supplier or consultant actually can deliver the promised data, advice, or conclusions. This judgment should be made only after the following steps have been followed:

1 A thorough search for names of people and companies who have acknowledged expertise in the area of the study.[2]

2 The selection of a small number of bidders on the basis of recommendations of colleagues or others who have had similar needs.

3 Personal interviews with the person who would be responsible for the project, asking for examples of work on similar problems, their procedures for working with clients, and names of previous clients who could provide references.

4 A check of the references of each potential supplier, with special attention to comments on their depth of competence and expertise, their creativity in dealing with problems, and the quality and adequacy of resources available.

5 Selection on the basis of how well the problem and objectives have been understood,[3] the comments by the references, and whether the quoted price or fee is a good value in light of the research approach that is proposed. Seldom is the lower quotation going to be the best value. To minimize the problem of comparability, have all bidders respond to the same study specifications.[4]

---

[2]Useful sources are *Greenbook: International Directory of Marketing Research Houses and Services* (New York: American Marketing Association, Annual); *Consultants and Consulting Organizations Directory* (Detroit: Gale Research Co., Triennial with annual supplements); *Bradfords Directory of Marketing Research Agencies in the U.S. and Around the World* (Fairfax, VA: Bradford Publishing Co., 1984.)

[3]Warren J. Wittreich, "How to Buy/Sell Professional Services," *Harvard Business Review, 44* (March–April 1966), 127–136.

[4]Raymond D. Speer, "Follow These Six Steps to Get Most Benefits from Marketing Research Consultant Project," *Marketing News* (September 18, 1981) 12, 13.

RESEARCH TACTICS AND IMPLEMENTATION

Once the research approach has been chosen, the specifics of the measurements, the plan for choosing the sample, and the methods of analysis must be developed.

Measurements

The first step is to translate the research objective into information requirements and then into questions that can be answered by anticipated respondents.

For example, one of the objectives in the HMO study is to estimate probable demand for the proposed HMO. This means that information will be needed on (1) the respondents' overall evaluation of the proposed HMO, (2) their preference for the proposed HMO relative to their present health plan, and (3) their likelihood of adopting the new plan if it becomes available. As we will see in Chapters 7 and 8, there are many ways to ask questions to obtain this kind of attitudinal information.

Once the individual questions have been decided, the measuring instrument has to be developed. Usually this instrument is a questionnaire, but it also may be a plan for observing behavior or recording data. The researcher designing an effective questionnaire must be concerned with how sensitive questions on topics such as income can be asked, what the order of the questions should be, and how misinterpretations can be avoided.

The Sampling Plan

Most marketing research studies will be limited to a sample or subgroup of the total population relevant to the research question, rather than a census of the entire group. The sampling plan describes how the subgroup is to be selected. One approach is to use probability sampling, in which all population members have a known probability of being in the sample. This choice is indicated whenever it is important to be able to show how representative the sample is of the population. Other critical decisions at this stage are the size of the sample, as this has direct implications for the project budget, and the means of minimizing the effect on results of sample members who cannot be reached or refuse to cooperate.

Anticipating the Analysis

When one is bogged down in the details of tactical research problems it is easy to lose sight of the research objectives. Before actual data collection begins the researcher must be alert to the possibility that the data will not be adequate for testing the hypotheses, or will be interesting but incapable of supporting action recommendations. Once the data have been collected it is too late to lament, "Why didn't we collect data on that variable?" or "Why didn't we foresee there wouldn't be enough respondents to test that hypothesis?"

With these concerns in mind the researcher should plan how each of the data items is to be analyzed. One useful device is to generate fictional (dummy) data from the questions in the measurement instrument. These dummy data can be analyzed for the study, to ensure the results of the analysis address the objectives. For example, a great deal of preliminary data analysis consists of cross-tabulating one question by a second question. Each of the anticipated tables should be reviewed in terms of its relevance to the research question. Any shortcomings identified here will help guide the changes to the questionnaire before it is sent into the field.

Analysis of Value versus Cost and Time Involved

At this stage of the design most of the cost has yet to be expended. Yet the research is now completely specified and a reliable cost estimate should be available. Thus, a more detailed cost–benefit analysis should be possible to determine if the research should be conducted as designed or if it should be conducted at all.

One component of cost to be considered is the time involved. A research study can take six months or more. It may be that such a time period will delay a decision, thus creating the risk that a set of attractive conditions will be missed. For example, if the research designed to test a new product takes too long, a competitor may preempt the market with its own version of the product.

The analysis can conclude that either the research design is cost effective and should proceed or that it is not and should be terminated. Usually, instead of termination, consideration will be given to a revised research design that will be less costly. Perhaps a smaller sample could be used or a laboratory experiment substituted for a field experiment. Throughout the whole research process new information is uncovered that makes it useful to alter the purpose, the research question, the research approach, or some aspect of tactics. Indeed, it is much more accurate to think of the research process as a series of iterations and reconsiderations, rather than an ordered sequence of well-defined steps.

THE RESEARCH PROPOSAL

A proposal describes a plan for conducting and controlling a research project. While it has an important function as a summary of the major decisions in the research process, it is useful for a number of other reasons. Administratively it is the basis for a written agreement or contract between the manager and researcher, as well as a record of what was agreed. As such it provides a vehicle for reviewing important decisions. This helps ensure that all parties are still in agreement on the scope and purpose of the research, and it reduces later misunderstandings. Frequently proposals are used to make a choice among competing suppliers and to influence positively the decision to fund the proposed study. For these latter purposes, a proposal should be viewed as a persuasive device that demonstrates the researcher's grasp of the problem and ability to conduct the research and also highlights the benefits of the study.

Like other communications the structure and coverage of a proposal must be tailored to the situation. However, the following content outline has been used widely, as it ensures that likely questions will be anticipated.

Basic Contents of a Proposal

1	Executive summary	A brief overview of the contents of the proposal. It may be the only part read by some people, so it should be sufficient to give them a basic understanding of the proposal.
2	Purpose and Scope	A description of the management problem, the possible reasons for the problem, and the decision alternatives being studied.
3	Objectives	Defines the information to be obtained in terms of research questions to be answered. This information must be related explicitly to the management problem.
4	Research approach	Presents the important features of the research methods to be used, with justification of the strengths and limitations of the chosen method relative to the alternatives. All aspects of the research that might be elements of a contract should be discussed, such as sample size, quality control procedure, and data collection method. Details of questionnaire format, sample selection procedures, and so forth should be confined to an appendix.
5	Time and cost estimates	This encompasses all negotiated aspects, including total fees, payments, provisions, treatment of contingencies such as the clients' decision to expand or cancel the study, and the schedule for submission of interim, draft, and final reports.
6	Appendices	Any technical matters of interest to a small minority of readers should be put at the back end of the proposal.

SUMMARY

In this chapter the focus has shifted from the manager's problems and information needs—as expressed in the research purpose and objectives—to the strategic and tactical decisions that will achieve the objectives of the research approach. The various research approaches included qualitative research, surveys, observation, and experimentation. Tactical research design decisions include the choice of a research supplier, the questionnaire development, the design of the experiment, the sampling plan, and the anticipation of data analysis. Implementation involves a final cost-benefit check plus data collection, data analysis, and the development of conclusions and recommendations.

An important distinction can be made between exploratory, descriptive, and causal research. Exploratory research, which tends to involve qualitative approaches such as group interviews, is usually characterized by ill-defined or nonexistent hypotheses. Descriptive research, which tends to use survey data, is characterized by tentative hypotheses that fall short of specifying causal relationships. Causal research, which tends to rely upon experimentation, involves more specific hypotheses involving causal relationships.

The major decisions during the research process are summarized in the research proposal. This step is essential to ensuring that the manager's problems have been translated into a research study that will yield relevant, timely, and accurate information—and not cost more than the information is worth.

QUESTIONS AND PROBLEMS

1 Is a research design always necessary before a research study can be conducted?

2 In what ways do exploratory, descriptive, and causal research designs differ? How will these differences influence the relative importance of each research approach at each phase of the marketing program development process described in Chapter 1?

3 What alternative research approaches should Herb Ellis consider for the HMO study? What are the strengths and weaknesses of the possible approaches?

4 A manufacturer of hand tools uses industrial supply houses to reach its major markets. The company is considering a new automatic inventory control procedure. How would you proceed with an exploratory study in advance of a larger study of the dealers' reactions to this new procedure?

5 What problems can you foresee in a test of the hypothesis that federal food stamps issued to low-income individuals are being used to supplement food budgets rather than replace former spending on food?

6 The problem of a large Canadian cable TV company was described in Chapter 2. A number of hypotheses were offered by management to account for the poor penetration in several areas comprising 15 percent of the population of the total service area. If you were the researcher assigned to study this problem, how would you proceed? Specifically, is the statement of purpose of the research adequate? What alternative research designs should be considered? Will one design be adequate to test all the hypotheses?

CASE 3–1
Maple Leaf Insurance Company

In late January of 1979, Jim King, a market research assistant at Maple Leaf Life, faced a difficult problem. Two weeks earlier, he had been asked by Paul Till, vice president of marketing, to put together a proposal for a market research study that would clarify the reasons for the growing numbers of terminated individual life insurance policies. Mr. Till had told King that he wasn't sure whether increased marketing effort was desirable or whether it should be in the direction of advertising, personal selling, or price discounts for renewals. Since then, Jim King had consulted with the sales manager, the assistant sales manager, and one of the company's most successful salespeople. In addition, King had surveyed the information available through the company's own internal reporting system and had researched the topic at the company library. He now was sorting through all of this information in order to prepare his market research proposal for Till.

Maple Leaf Life Insurance Company, headquartered in Toronto, was one of Canada's largest insurance companies. In addition, Maple Leaf had extensive foreign operations in the United States, the United Kingdom, and throughout the Caribbean. Besides individual life insurance policies, the company sold a large number of other insurance lines, such as health, pension, and group life policies.

THE TERMINATION PROBLEM

In 1977, approximately 15,000 of Maple Leaf's Canadian individual life policies were terminated. These policies accounted for five percent of the company's total policies in force (300,000) and 80 percent of the 19,000 new life insurance policies sold in 1977. With 80 percent of the new policies sold just to maintain current company policy levels, only 20 percent of new sales went to expanding the policyholder base.

Since the new policies written in 1978 had higher dollar face values than those being terminated, because of the effect of inflation, the annual premium income

from the terminated policies was only 54 percent of the premium income of the new policies. Nontheless it was clear that a major source of growth was available to the company if it could decrease the number of terminations.

Relatively little information was available within the company as to the reasons for terminations. There was a weekly report from each branch, which was filled out by the branch secretary. According to summaries of these reports, the major reasons for termination were:

1 The policy was paid up (no more premiums were due). 9%

2 The policy was cashed in before being paid up so the policyholder could get the cash surrender value. 48%

3 The policy matured. 7%

4 The policyholder died. 12%

5 The policy lapsed because the policyholder stopped paying premiums before the policy was paid up. 24%

100%

The data from the branch reporting system were problematic because the categories used to describe the reason for the termination were too general and the agents were relied on for the necessary information. (The agents were not always unbiased, and, in any event, a lapsed policyholder was generally uncooperative in telling the agent the real reason for the lapse.) The summary reports, however, did indicate the magnitude of the problem and the degree of variability in termination experience between branches (*see* Exhibit 3–1).

AVAILABLE SECONDARY INFORMATION

In the company library, King found several studies published by various life insurance associations. The Contemporary Research Centre for the Canadian Life In-

EXHIBIT 3–1

Maple Leaf Life Insurance Company Quarterly New Policies Terminations Report

Branch	Annual Premiums Written July–September, 1978 (1)	Annual Premiums For Terminated Policies July–September 1978 (2)	Percent- age (1:2)
Vancouver	$ 123,951	$ 85,029	69%
Victoria	11,938	5,637	47
Alberta	38,256	63,832	167
Saskatchewan	89,510	41,758	47
Manitoba	125,313	26,718	21
Thunder Bay	1,104	10,031	908
Western Canada	390,072	233,005	60
Central Toronto	143,574	52,492	36
North Toronto	51,265	25,647	50
South Toronto	65,545	34,081	52
East Toronto	22,295	40,104	179
West Toronto	69,039	55,567	80
Toronto	350,718	207,891	60
Hamilton	27,010	20,514	75
London	71,766	28,359	39
Windsor	44,367	11,736	26
Ottawa	80,511	12,219	15
Belleville	97,400	43,753	45
Sudbury	29,250	19,788	67
Niagara	18,609	10,276	55
Ontario (excluding Toronto)	369,063	146,645	40
New Brunswick	32,954	36,489	110
Nova Scotia	42,222	6,029	14
Newfoundland	69,068	22,861	33
Sherbrooke	65,953	35,110	53
Quebec City	72,564	25,366	35
Three Rivers	29,126	17,517	60
Eastern Canada	144,244	65,379	45
Central Montreal	101,550	95,005	93
North Montreal	97,270	47,247	48
South Montreal	59,424	37,318	62
East Montreal	76,056	28,584	37
West Montreal	38,863	27,298	70
Montreal	373,163	235,452	63
Canada Total	$1,794,903	$996,365	54%

surance Association (CLIA) had published two national attitude surveys, *Life Insurance in 1974* and *Life Insurance in 1976*. Both surveys measured respondents' attitudes toward such things as life insurance costs, agents, policy features, sources of cost comparison information, and reasons for buying insurance. No specific questions were asked about termination in these surveys. A similar study by Daniel Yankelovitch and his associates, *Monitoring Attitudes of the Public*, carried out in the United States for the Institute of Life Insurance also was available. There was no indication in these studies that there were shifts in preferences for term versus whole-life insurance or that inflation was having an adverse effect on the perceived need for insurance.

VIEWS OF THE SALES STAFF

The first person King contacted in the sales department was Dick Elliot, sales manager (individual life policies). When King explained that he was preparing a research proposal for studying the lapse problem, Elliott told King:

Well, I think you're wasting your time. The problem is simple. First, in the 10 years I've had this job, I've never seen salesmen who take it so easy, especially the younger ones. Maybe the salaries are too high. And, that new sales commission scheme we introduced last year didn't exactly help either. It cut the commissions on renewals and boosted them on new policies. Second, the customers themselves are changing too. They just aren't as loyal to the same company anymore. They just go from one company to another. I guess there's little we can do about that though.

Elliot went on to say that perhaps it would be a good idea to study how often the salespeople visited their clients. In addition, he thought that a check on the reasons for branch differences in the number of terminations would be interesting. King then talked the

matter over with the assistant sales manager, Peter Kirkley, a recent M.B.A. graduate. Kirkley told King:

. . . that's a great idea. You know I've been pushing for a study since I arrived here last year. We should be finding out what kinds of policies are needed by our customers. Our present policies were designed in the fifties. Plus, our overall company image is, well, a pretty old-fashioned one.

Kirkley went on to say that he thought the cheapest approach to the study of the problems of policy design and image was through in-depth interviews. He suggested that a dozen customers and a dozen former customers be interviewed in this manner. In addition, Kirkley thought that some general company awareness data would be good to have.

Finally, King visited the company's best individual life policy salesman, Frank Bellweather. Bellweather told King:

I think the main cause of the terminations due to cash surrender value (C.S.V.) is the current situation of tight money. People are simply cashing in their policies in order to meet the rising cost of living. Also, I don't know how you could do it, but I think some information concerning our competitors' prices would be useful. I've heard that they offer a substantial discount for customers who renew their policies. Actually, everyone's policies are so different I guess they would be difficult to compare.

King, as we leave him here, now begins the task of preparing a research proposal based on his findings.

QUESTIONS FOR DISCUSSION

1 Why are policyholders terminating their life insurance policies?

2 What are the possible purposes for research in this situation?

3 What purpose would you recommend?

4 What research objectives and data collection methods are consistent with this purpose?

CASES FOR PART I

THE MARKETING RESEARCH PROCESS

CASE I–1 CLOVER VALLEY DAIRY COMPANY

In the fall of 1978, Vince Roth, General Manager of the Clover Valley Dairy Company, was considering whether a newly developed multipack carrier for yogurt was ready for market testing and, if so, how it should be tested.

Since 1930, the Clover Valley Dairy Company had sold, under the trade name Valleyview, milk, ice cream, and other milk byproducts—such as yogurt, cottage cheese, butter, skim milk, buttermilk, and cream—in Camden, New Jersey. The raw milk was obtained from independent farmers in the vicinity of Camden and was processed and packaged at the Clover Valley Dairy.

Clover Valley's sales had grown steadily from 1930 until 1973 to an annual level of $3.75 million. However, between 1973 and 1977, a series of milk price wars cut the company's sales to $3.6 million by 1977. During this time, a number of other independent dairies were forced to close. At the height of the price wars, milk prices fell to 75¢ per half gallon. In the spring of 1977, an investigation of the milk market in Camden was conducted by the Federal Trade Commission and by Congress. Since then, prices had risen so that Clover Valley had a profit for the year to date.

Clover Valley served approximately 130 grocery store accounts, which were primarily members of a cooperative buying group or belonged to a 10-store chain that operated in the immediate area. Clover Valley no longer had any major chain accounts, although in the past they had sold to several. Because all three of the major chains operating in the area had developed exclusive supply arrangements with national or regional dairies, Clover Valley was limited to a 30 percent share of the Camden area dairy product market.

Although Clover Valley had a permit to sell its products in Philadelphia, a market six times the size of Camden, management decided not to enter that market and instead concentrated on strengthening their dealer relationships. In addition, it was felt that, if a price war were to ensue, it might extend from Philadelphia into the Camden area.

With the healthier market and profit situation in early 1978, Clover Valley began to look for ways to increase sales volume. One area that was attractive because of apparent rapid growth was yogurt. During the previous three years management had felt that this product could help to reverse Clover Valley's downward sales trend, if given the correct marketing effort. However, the financial problems caused by the loss of the national grocery chains and the price war limited the firm's efforts. As a result, Mr. Roth felt that Clover Valley had suffered a loss of share of yogurt sales in the stores they served.

Since 1975, Mr. Roth had been experimenting with Clover Valley's yogurt packaging with the hope that a new package would boost sales quickly. All dairies in Clover Valley's area packaged yogurt in either 8-oz or 1-lb tubs made of waxed heavy paper. Clover's 8-oz tub was about 5 inches high and $2\frac{1}{2}$ in. in top diameter, tapering to $1\frac{3}{4}$ in. at base.

The first design change to be considered was the use of either aluminum or plastic lids on the traditional yogurt tubs. However, these were rejected because the increased costs did not seem to be justified by such a modest change. Changing just the lid would not make their tubs appear different from their competitors' tubs, it was felt.

By 1976, Mr. Roth had introduced a completely different package for Clover Valley's yogurt. The 8-oz tubs were replaced by 6-oz cups, designed for individual servings. In addition, the new cups were made of plastic and had aluminum foil lids. The 1-lb tubs were unchanged. No special promotional effort was undertaken by Clover Valley, but unit sales of the new 6-oz cups were more than triple the unit sales of the old 8-oz tubs (see Exhibit I–1). While the increased sales volume was welcomed, the new plastic cups increased unit packaging costs from 7.2¢ to 12.0¢. This more than offset the saving of 4¢ because of the reduction in the amount of yogurt per container. Retail prices were reduced from 41¢ to 34¢ for the new 6-oz cup, while the price for the 1-lb tub remained at 75¢. The increased sales then increased the total dollar contribution to fixed costs from yogurt by only 5 percent. (All dairies priced their yogurt to give retailers a 10-percent margin on the retail selling price. Competitors' retail prices for their 8-oz tubs remained at 41¢.)

Mr. Roth felt that both the change to plastic and the convenience of the smaller size were responsible for the increased sales. However, he was disappointed with the high packaging costs and began to look at ways of reducing them, without changing the package much further. He felt another package change would be too confusing to consumers. Because of the economies of scale needed to produce plastic containers, costs could be reduced if more units were produced and sold. Mr. Roth felt that packaging a number of cups together would make the 6-oz cups easier to carry home, which might increase sales, and would certainly reduce packaging costs.

By 1978, work had begun on developing a multipack holder to hold six cups together. A single strip of aluminized plastic would serve both as holder and as the top for two rows of three yogurt cups. A single cup could be readily separated from the others in the pack. Dairy personnel constructed wooden models of several different cups for use with the holder and with plastic-molding experts, choosing one that would mold easily and cheaply. Eventually, some of these carriers were made to order for testing in the plant and among Clover Valley employee families.

Several problems soon became apparent. The holder did not always fasten securely to all six cups in the multipack. While the holder strip was being put on, the side walls of the cups were slightly compressed, causing some cups to crack at the edges. When consumers tried to remove one of the cups, they sometimes pulled the top from an adjacent

EXHIBIT I–1

Clover Valley Dairy Company: Sales Results

	1974	1975	1976	1977	1978
Unit Sales of Yogurt—8-Ounce Tubs (6-Ounce After June 1977)					
January		1,203	3,531	7,899	18,594
February		996	3,651	7,629	20,187
March		960	3,258	6,677	20,676
April		853	3,888	6,081	20,199
May		861	4,425	5,814	18,420
June		915	4,044	12,726*	14,424
July		978	3,546	13,422	16,716
August		1,254	3,696	15,105	16,716
September		1,212	3,561	23,601	18,657
October	1,740	1,485	4,731	23,214	
November	1,437	2,928	4,499	22,146	
December	1,347	3,528	6,177	17,916	
Unit Sales of Yogurt—1-Pound Tubs					
January	3,882	3,715	3,937	3,725	2,971
February	4,015	3,596	3,833	3,510	3,232
March	4,061	3,670	3,285	3,344	2,866
April	3,573	3,405	3,333	3,503	3,392
May	3,310	3,482	3,609	3,101	2,390
June	3,252	3,376	3,366	3,537	2,094
July	3,383	3,366	2,837	2,827	2,589
August	3,721	3,307	2,616	3,103	2,384
September	3,415	3,275	2,729	2,871	2,895
October	3,276	3,450	2,816	3,028	
November	3,865	4,650	3,375	2,796	
December	4,110	3,908	3,386	3,086	

*6-ounce tubs

cup. The problem was the strength of the aluminized plastic, which made it difficult to tear even when perforated.

The multipack was redesigned and again tested in the plant and by employee families. It appeared that the new package was performing satisfactorily. Negotiations with Clover Valley's carton supplier resulted in an estimated price of 8.5¢ for the first 100,000 units. Thereafter unit costs would drop to 7.5¢ per 6-oz cup.

Mr. Roth decided that the best multipack carrier presently possible had been designed. His attention then turned to methods of testing the new packs for consumer acceptance.

Mr. Krieger, his father-in-law and president of Clover Valley, sent him the following letter concerning market testing:

Dear Vince,

Concerning the market test of the new cups and carriers, I have a few suggestions that may be helpful, although the final decision is yours. I think we should look for a few outlets where we are not competing with the other dairies, perhaps the Naval Base or Bill's Market. Actually, if we use Bill's, then the test could be conducted as follows:

1. Give Bill a special deal on the multipacks for this weekend.
2. In the next two weeks, we'll only deliver the multipacks and no single cups at all.
3. In the third week we'll deliver both the packs and the single cups.
4. During the third weekend we'll have someone make a survey at the store to determine its acceptance.
5. Here is how it could be conducted:
    a. Station someone at the dairy case.
    b. After the shoppers have chosen either single cups or the multipacks, question them.
    c. If they chose the multipacks, ask them why.
    d. If they chose the single cups ask them why they didn't buy the packs.
    e. Thank them for their help and time.

Yours,

CHARLES KRIEGER
(signed)

Questions for Discussion

1 Should the new multipack carrier be tested?

2 If a test is judged necessary, what should be the criteria for success or failure?

3 How useful is the proposed test in addressing the management problem? What changes, if any, would you recommend?

CASE I-2   INFO–MED[1]

Tim Findlay was troubled as he studied the PMR proposal on his desk. He had expected a much more detailed outline of the market research task that Precision Market Research would do and had found the proposal provided few details. Furthermore, he had just received a phone call from the author of the PMR proposal, asking that they meet next week to begin planning the project. The researcher added that he hoped Findlay would give further thought to the objectives of the study, as well as provide reactions to the proposed design. Findlay now decided to go back over the pilot research study in order to see whether a second study was really needed and, if needed, what kind of study it should be.

Background

The PMR research was to guide the formation of a new business, called INFO-MED. The concept of the new business came from Dr. Arthur Lam, who envisioned a new method of supplying physicians with up-to-date medical information: a computerized medical abstract retrieval system. The doctor would have a computer CRT terminal in his office that would allow him to search a carefully selected data base of the abstracts of articles dealing with problems faced by the practicing doctor. An on-line, "natural language" keyword search technique would allow the doctor, quickly and simply, to find and read the abstracts dealing with new developments in the treatment of the case in hand.

The Need for INFO-MED

Dr. Lam felt such a service should be aimed at the practicing "primary" physician—those doctors practicing general medicine who were the first line of medical care (general and family practitioners and internists). Most cases were treated by the primary physician, but it was often necessary to know when and where to send patients when they required the attention of a specialist.

Because medical knowledge had a half-life of about five years, a doctor who had been out of medical school for five years and had not attempted to keep up-to-date would find 50 percent of his knowledge to be obsolete. With the many pressures of running a private practice, few physicians had time to read medical journals. Furthermore, journal articles were reports of problems and solutions as they occurred and were therefore difficult to access when needed by the doctor.

Lam found that, while some doctors kept large literature indices on their bookshelves, these indices often were outdated and required a trip to the library to read the actual article. More often, a physician relied on colleagues or on literature from drug companies to keep informed about recent developments. This was especially true in rural areas. Because of the these factors, Lam felt that INFO-MED could satisfy a significant need.

[1]This case was provided through the courtesy of Dr. Robert V. Illa of the Medical Abstract Retrieval Service.

INFO-MED: The Service

Because Dr. Lam knew little about computers, he interested a systems analyst, Fred Junkin, in assisting him to develop the idea. The heart of INFO-MED was to be the data base, containing abstracts of articles appearing in selected medical journals. The articles would be selected for their problem-solving relevance, by a board of prestigious doctors. The data base would be updated continuously.

By operating the computer terminal, the doctor could access all abstracts containing the key words chosen. Generally, the abstract alone would be sufficient to solve most problems. The terminals would be connected by phone lines to the INFO-MED computer, so that the service would be available throughout the country. While conventional computer services usually charged by hour of terminal time (e.g., $100 per hour), Junkin felt that this would make most doctors nervous. A better alternative seemed to be a modest monthly charge of $60 per month to cover the terminal rental and a charge of $8.00 per completed search.

Market and Financial Analysis

Since neither Lam nor Junkin had any business experience, they turned to Tim Findlay, a local accountant, for help in establishing the new venture. Findlay thought the idea was a good one and contacted a few companies that he thought might be interested. These contacts pointed out that past attempts to market computer services often had been disastrous and that the mix of computers and doctors was even worse. Findlay felt that it was too early in the development of this idea to be able to make a persuasive case that this service would be any different.

With the help of Lam and Junkin, Findlay was able to develop estimates of break-even volume. In addition to start-up costs of $650,000, primarily to prepare the data base and absorb initial losses, there would be fixed operating costs of $135,000 per month. It was estimated that the contribution[2] from 1260 terminals would cover this fixed cost. This was encouraging inasmuch as the available data from the American Medical Association indicated a very large market, as follows:

Segment I: *Group practices:* There were 12,200 groups in either general practice or multiple specialties; each group had an average of five doctors

Segment II: *Small hospitals with inadequate medical library facilities:* There were 8000 hospitals with less than 150 beds

Segment III: *Solo physicians:* There were 81,200 doctors in general practice or internal medicine not associated with a group

---

[2]The contribution was estimated on the assumption that each terminal would be used for 30 searches per month and 10 abstracts would be accessed during each search.

EXHIBIT I–2

Arthur Lam, M.D.
Harrison Road
Oakbrook, Illinois
April 5, 1979

Dear Sir:

I am interested in your opinion of the possible utility of the system described in the following abstract:

"On-Line Continuing Education for the Primary Physician by Lam, A. and Junkin, F.

Participation in programs of continuing education by the busy practitioner has been impeded by a number of factors, such as time, geographic location, financial considerations and, in some instances, course content, which he may judge to be irrelevant. We propose as a partial solution to this problem the installation in the physician's office of a computerized literature retrieval system which would allow quick, convenient and relevant access to that portion of the medical literature for which he would have the greatest need. We discuss the feasibility of such a system, and suggest advantages over traditional methods of access."

Within this system, a physician in his office operates a keyboard-video display terminal, whereby groups of keywords can be combined to carefully select abstracts from the computer files of articles from selected medical journals in the data base. The physician is continually advised of the number of abstracts stored that correspond to his current request. For example, by combining the key words "**DIGOXIN**" and "**ARRYTHMIA**," the physician might find that there are ten relevant abstracts. At that point, he can then request a display of the abstracts of interest.

In addition to abstracts of articles from the current medical literature, the data base would include abstracts of reviews, and other important past articles. The service would provide advantages over current **MEDLINE** searches, in terms of ready accessibility, ease of use, specificity and quality of information provided.

Please note your response on the enclosed postcard.

Thank you for your cooperation.

Yours truly,

ARTHUR LAM, M.D.

Enclosure

Preliminary Market Study

It was clear to Findlay that a direct assessment of the doctors' interest in this service was necessary before any company would invest any money into developing this idea. Consequently, a pilot assessment of market acceptance was conducted by sending 200 doctors in the Chicago area a letter and return postcard, asking them for their opinions (Exhibits I–2 and I–3). Their names were taken from lists of doctors affiliated with three large medical centers in the area.

The overall response rate was 52 percent, yielding 104 usable responses. There were 63 respondents who said they were interested; among this group 13 indicated they ''would probably use such a system'' and a further 11 respondents indicated they would ''probably use such a system if the cost were below $300 per month.''

Research Proposal

At this point, it seemed that too much weight was being placed on the pilot market survey, so Findlay decided to investigate the possibility of having a market research firm conduct a full-scale study. Findlay felt a private market research firm would be a relatively objective source with the credibility necessary to convince potential investors that there was a reasonable chance of success for the business.

Consequently, Lam, Junkin, and Findlay decided to invest up to $10,000 in a market survey. Findlay contacted Precision Market Research (PMR) and asked that a research proposal be developed for the introduction of INFO-MED. PMR said a survey of about 40 doctors could be done in three geographic clusters in Illinois and Ohio for a little over $10,300 and submitted this proposal to Lam, Junkin, and Findlay for approval (Exhibit I–4).

The PMR study was given initial approval by Findlay and the others. PMR was anxious to get started and requested a planning session where the objectives and methods of the project could be decided. So far, it was agreed that the best way to conduct the

EXHIBIT I–3
Questionnaire Return Card

_____ I am interested in the idea.
_____ I would probably use such a system in my office.
_____ I would probably use such a system in my office if the cost were below $300 per month.
_____ Please send me a copy of the paper.
_____ I would have no use for such a system.
   Other comments:

EXHIBIT I–4

Precision Market Research, Incorporated

Proposal No. RPP79-257

September 12, 1979

Mr. Tim Findlay, F.C.A.
966 Franklin Ave., Suite 501
Chicago, Illinois 21402

Dear Mr. Findlay:

The following is a proposal to perform research for a new venture, INFO-MED. The proposal is divided into three sections: Our Approach to the Problem, Estimated Time, and Estimated Costs.

Our Approach to the Problem

PMR has conducted several studies in the past that appear to parallel this form of new venture in the medical industry. Based on our knowledge of the existing market and the potential in the future (1985), we view this assignment as having three major phases.

The first phase will be to interview on a personal basis key decision-makers in hospitals and group and solo practices in Illinois and Ohio. The purpose of these interviews is to assess the likely reaction to such a service among potential purchasers in terms of current needs and pricing.

The second phase is an analysis of the perceived present and future competition. This step involves interviews with executive sources at firms and associations, i.e., nonprofit groups, who currently operate, or have the potential to develop, a service competitive with that contemplated by INFO-MED.

At the conclusion of the first two phases, PMR will prepare and deliver a brief (10-page) written report of the findings, conclusions, and recommendations.

The third phase of the assignment will involve limited ongoing assistance and consultation in marketing and financial areas until the final decision is made in late December.

Estimated Time

Given our present workload and experience with projects of a similar nature, we are prepared to perform this work according to the following schedule:

Phase	Description	Timing	Estimated Days of Professional and Research Assistant Work
1.	Perform field interviews and evaluate response	10/7/79 to 10/25/79	15
2.	Assess competitive environment	10/21/79 to 10/30/79	5
	Prepare, deliver, and discuss report	11/4/79	5
3.	Provide ongoing consultation	11/5/79 to 12/31/79	5

This schedule allows a minimum of two weeks for field interviews of key decision-makers. During these interviews, an INFO-MED employee will assist the PMR staff in the demonstration of a CRT device using a product algorithm similar to that which is currently contemplated.

The project will be conducted under the direction of Bill Skelly. The project leader will be Sam Kellner. Brief descriptions of their professional backgrounds and related experience are attached.

Estimated Cost

The charge for the proposed project is $10,300 including personnel, travel, and related charges. To provide the working capital required for this project, the initial payment due on acceptance of the proposal is $5300 to be followed by two monthly payments of $2500 each.

This proposal will remain in effect until October 1, 1979; we will be pleased to consider an extension if requested.

We feel that our qualifications will meet with your approval. We look forward to this most interesting and challenging assignment and await your authorization to proceed.

Respectfully yours,
SAM KELLNER

Approved:
PAT PEPALL, General Manager

Accepted: _____ Date: _____

survey would be to have Junkin demonstrate the service in the doctor's office during the interview with a portable CRT terminal. This demonstration approach was thought necessary because a working prototype would help greatly to communicate the concept.

Aside from the demonstration idea during a personal interview, however, little else had been decided. Even so, Findlay was not completely convinced that personal interviews were the most cost-effective method. He still had no idea as to how to structure the interview questionnaire, what segments to contact, and how to interpret the results. As he thought about the upcoming planning session with PMR the following week, he kept wondering whether this was the best way to spend $10,300 of their capital. He knew that further funding for research was very unlikely.

Questions for Discussion

1   What are the most serious gaps in market knowledge?

2   How should the purpose of the research be specified?

3   What specific research objectives need to be addressed?

4   Should the PMR proposal be accepted? If not, how can the information needs be satisfied?

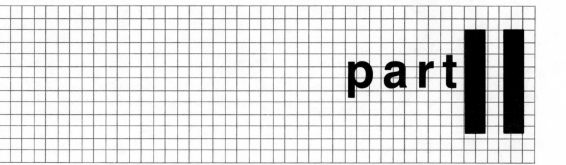

part II

DATA COLLECTION

---

section A
Exploratory and
Secondary Research

4

SOURCES OF MARKETING DATA

Many data sources were identified in the previous chapters, yet they are only suggestive of the vast array of possibilities that can literally submerge the manager and researcher in numbers. The real problem with this ''data explosion'' is not the quantity but the variability of the sources with respect to quality, availability, cost, timeliness, and relevance to the needs of the decision maker. In this chapter, we begin the task of bridging the gap between **data** (which are unassimilated facts about the market) and **information** (which answers the specific questions of the decision maker).

One of the hallmarks of a competent marketing researcher is familiarity with the basic sources pertaining to the market being studied, coupled with sensitivity to their respective strengths and weaknesses. This means that time is not lost in an aimless search for nonexistent data, but neither is time and money wasted on a premature decision to go into the field to obtain the data.

Most search procedures follow a distinctive pattern, which begins with the most available and least costly sources. Figure 4–1 summarizes the principal sources available to a researcher who is responding to a research question or considering what data to collect in order to anticipate future information needs. The ordering from top to bottom roughly corresponds to the order in which the alternative sources should be considered. It may also correspond to the likelihood of the type of data being incorporated into the marketing information system. That is, almost all information systems are initially based on routinely collected internal data and expand through the inclusion of data from secondary and standardized sources.

The emphasis in the remainder of this chapter will be on externally available *secondary* sources—where the specification, collection, and recording of the data are done by some agency other than the user. Subsequent chapters will deal with the many problems of collecting primary or original data when the immediate and special needs of the decision maker cannot be satisfied with data collected for other purposes.

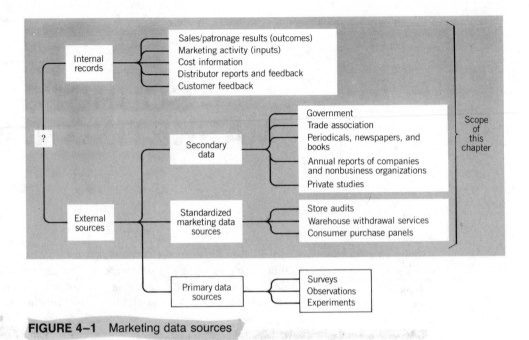

FIGURE 4–1   Marketing data sources

INTERNAL RECORDS

The internal accounting and control systems provide the most basic data on marketing *inputs* and the resulting *outcomes*. The principal virtues of this data are ready availability, reasonable accessibility on a continuing basis, and relevance to the organization's situation.

Data on *inputs*—marketing effort expended—can range from budgets and schedules of expenditures to salespeople's call reports that describe the number of calls per day, who was visited, problems and applications discussed, and the results of the visit.

Extensive data on *outcomes* can be obtained from the order-shipping-billing records maintained in the accounting system. In many industries the resulting sales reports are the single most important piece of data used by marketing managers because they can be related (via exception reporting methods) to plans and budgets to determine whether performance is meeting expectations. Also, they may be compared with costs in order to assess profitability.[1]

---

[1]Thomas C. Kelley, Jr., "The Marketing-Accounting Partnership in Business," *Journal of Marketing*, 3 (July 1966), 9–11.

Using Internal Data Effectively

Many diagnostic studies can potentially be undertaken with various combinations of internal and external data, to address such questions[2] as

- What is the effect of marketing inputs (number of sales calls or types of distribution channels) on outcomes such as profitability and unit sales within regions or sales territories?
- Is our sales performance within key market segments or types of retailers improving or deteriorating?
- Are current sales and marketing expenditures above or below the levels set in the annual budget and sales plan?

Such insightful analyses, however, often are thwarted because of limitations in the accounting system and distortions in the data.

The first problem is that accounting systems are designed to satisfy many different information needs. As a result, the reporting formats frequently are rigid and inappropriate for marketing decisions.[3] Often the accounting data is too highly aggregated into summary results and is not available for key managerial units, such as geographic areas, customer types, or product types. Efforts to break down sales and profitability data by different units may involve special, time-consuming studies. It also is possible that production, sales, and profit figures are each measured in slightly different time frames, which are all at variance with external data such as bimonthly store-audit data.

A second problem is the quality of the data found in the internal records. On the input side, the reports of salespeople's call activity may be exaggerated if they are being evaluated on this basis. Indeed the well-known optimism of salespeople may unconsciously pervade all the data from this source. Accounting data are not exempt from such problems. The usual interpretation of a sales invoice is compromised if liberal return privileges are permitted or if the product is purchased at one location but delivered or used in another place. In general, whenever there is a long distribution channel, with several places where inventories can be accumulated, the data on orders received or invoices billed may not correspond to actual sales activity.[4]

Nonbusiness organizations are highly variable in their maintenance of decent records. Procedures are often in place to collect comprehensive information about those who were served or who participated or contributed. For example, pupils in schools, patients in hospitals, and clients of family planning clinics supply a good deal of background information about themselves and their situations.

[2]J. M. Hulbert and N. E. Toy, "A Strategic Framework for Marketing Control," *Journal of Marketing,* (April 1977) 12–20.

[3]Thomas C. Kelley, Jr., "The Marketing-Accounting Partnership in Business, " *op cit.*

[4]Se John C. Chambers, Satinder K. Mullick, and Donald D. Smith, *An Executive's Guide to Forecasting,* New York: John Wiley, 1974.

The usefulness of this information is often compromised when it is stored in an inaccessible or indigestible state or only converted into a more usable form long after it could have contributed to the identification and resolution of problems. Evaluators of social programs often find other shortcomings to the available data:

> *Incompleteness plagues many agency systems. If the participants do not supply certain items of information or if the staff fails to enter data, nobody checks on the missing items and follows up. . . . Agencies sometimes change record-keeping procedures and . . . there is the possibility of distortion. Agency records are often based on the reporting of practitioners, and when they know that they are being "judged" by the data in the records, they may intentionally or unintentionally bias their accounts.*[5]

Customer Feedback

Increasingly, companies are augmenting their internal records with systematic compilations of product returns, service records, and customer correspondence, in a manner that permits easy retrieval. *Complaint letters* are being used as sources of data on product quality and service problems. One reason is the insight they can provide into the problems of small groups with unusual requirements, reactions, or problems. For example, a premarket skin abrasion test of a new talc-base bath powder uncovered no problems, but the complaint letters that poured in shortly after the reformulated product was introduced revealed serious problems among a small group with sensitive skin.

Yet complaint letters present an incomplete and distorted picture. People who write such letters are not typical clients or customers. They are most likely to be highly educated, articulate, and fussy, with more than average amounts of free time. A letter of complaint is actually a rather infrequently used method of resolving a dissatisfaction; instead people are more likely to switch brands, shop in a different store, or complain to their friends. Manufacturers are almost completely cut off from knowledge of customer unhappiness because most complaints are voiced to retailers and there is little systematic feedback from retailers to manufacturers.

SECONDARY DATA

Secondary data are by far the most popular source of marketing information. Not only are the data readily available, but they often are sufficient to answer the research question. For example:

- A marketing manager studying development in the wine industry will use trade association data to learn how the total consumption of wine is broken down by type of

---

[5]Weiss, *Evaluation Research* (Englewood Cliffs, N.J.: Prentice-Hall, 1974), p. 54.

customers, geographic area, type of wine, brand name, and distribution outlet. These data are available annually and sometimes quarterly, so significant trends can be isolated readily.

- A person starting a new specialty shop will use census data on family characteristics and income to support a likely location for the shop.
- Local housing planners rely on census data on the characteristics of housing and households in their locality to judge the need for new housing construction or housing rehabilitation.

Sometimes there is simply no way to get the data. The Census Bureau, for example, can require retailers to divulge sales, expense, and profit information, which would not be revealed to anyone else.

Even when it is obvious that the research project will require primary data collection, it is desirable first to consult the appropriate secondary sources. The results of the search may help answer the research question. Secondary sources also may facilitate the **research process** by

- Expanding the understanding of the problem
- Suggesting hypotheses and research design alternatives, and perhaps indicating some preliminary basis for choosing among alternative designs
- Helping to plan the sample and to provide a basis for validating the obtained sample. Whenever possible the demographic distribution of respondents in a sample should be compared with census results. This requires that the same classifications be used in the study as in the census.

The prospective user of secondary data also is confronted with the problem of matching a specific need for information with a bewildering array of secondary data sources of variable and often indeterminate quality. What is needed is, firstly, a flexible *search* procedure that will insure that no pertinent source is overlooked and, secondly, some general *criteria* for evaluating quality. These issues will be dealt with in the next two sections.

Finding Secondary Sources

The major sources are the various governments (federal, state, provincial, and local), periodicals and journals, and publicly available reports from such private groups as foundations, publishers, trade associations, unions and companies. Of all these sources the most valuable data for the marketing researcher come from the government census and various registration requirements. The latter encompass births, deaths, marriages, income tax returns, unemployment, export declarations, automobile registrations, and so on. A detailed description of the scope and nature of census data and other government publications is provided in the Appendix to this chapter.

How should someone who is unfamiliar with a market or research topic proceed? The following diagram suggests two basic rules to guide the search effort: (1) start with the general and go to the specific and (2) make use of all available expertise.[6] The four main categories are:

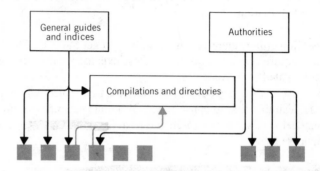

Authorities. Knowledge of pertinent sources—and of their limitations—comes from continued experience. Thus, the best starting point is someone else who has been doing research on the same subject. Trade associations and specialized trade publications are particularly useful, for they often compile government data and collect additional information from their subscribers or members.[7] If information about a specific geographic area is sought, the local chamber of commerce is a good place to begin. When the problem or topic is too large or ill-defined, there is no substitute for a well-informed reference librarian.

General Guides and Indices. Within this category there is a hierarchy of generality. At the top are the "guides to the guides," such as Constance Winchell, *Guide to Reference Books,* the *Bibliographic Index: A Cumulative Bibliography of Bibliographies,* the *Cumulative Book Index,* and Doris B. Katz *et al.,* editors, *Guide to Special Issues and Indices of Periodicals.*

At the next level of reference materials are the guides to general business information sources. Several important bibliographies are the *Encyclopedia of Business Information Sources, Encyclopedia of Geographic Information Sources,* and the *Statistical Reference*

[6]More extensive discussion of data sources and how to locate them can be found in Lorna Daniells, *Business Information Sources* (Berkeley, California: University of California Press, 1985); Lorna Daniells, *Note on Sources of External Marketing Data* in B. Shapiro, R. Dolan, J. Quelch, *Marketing Management* Vol. II, Appendix (Richard D. Irwin Inc., 1985) Barbara E. Brown, Canadian Business and Economics: *A Guide to Sources of Information* (Ottawa: Canadian Library Association, 1984).

[7]A comprehensive listing of these associations can be found in the Encyclopedia of Associations, National Gale Research Co., 1984.

Index. At a third level of generality, business periodical indices contain references to a large number of journals, periodicals and newspapers. Several of these can be referenced through computers, an increasingly prevalent way of accessing indices and abstracts of articles on specific topics. This subject is discussed further in the section on computer-retrievable data bases. Several general business indices are *Business Periodicals Index*, *Business Publications Index and Abstract*, *Management Contents*, *Public Affairs Information Service Bulletin*, *Applied Science and Technology Index*, *Index of Economic Journals*, *Psychological Abstracts*, and *Sociological Abstracts*. Specific indices for several newspapers are also available, such as the *Wall Street Journal*, *Washington Post*, and *New York Times*.

This list is suggestive of the kinds of material found in most libraries, but hardly exhausts the possibilities. Other valuable published sources include the section of the *Journal of Marketing* devoted to "Marketing Abstracts," *Predicast Forecasts* (a summary of industry forecasts), the *Marketing Information Guide* of the U.S. Department of Commerce (an annotated bibliography of materials relevant to domestic and foreign marketing), and the *Monthly Catalog of U.S. Government Publications*. The *Journal of Business* reviews recent books and lists recent doctoral dissertations by subject area.

For studies of international markets there is the *International Bibliography of Marketing and Distribution*. Each country has its own reference guides to domestic periodicals. For example, in Canada there is the (Annual) *Statistics Canada Catalogue*, the *Canadian Business Index*, and in the United Kingdom there is the *Annual Abstract of Statistics*. Most countries have reference guides to state and provincial jurisdictions. For example, *Canadiana* includes a regular listing of provincial and municipal government publications.

Information on nonprofit organizations is available in the following periodicals:

- *Current Index to Journals in Education*
- *Abstracts of Hospital Management Studies*
- *Sage Public Administration Abstracts*
- *Urban Affairs Abstracts*

Compilations. These are intermediate sources, in that they facilitate access to the original sources. This is particularly desirable with statistical information. The standard work in this area is the *Statistical Abstract of the United States*, which contains selections from the various censuses as well as data collected by other agencies. For example, data on the number of industrial robots installed world wide, by country, are compiled by the U.S. International Trade Commission. General purpose marketing statistics are published in volumes such as *Market Guide*, *Marketing Economics Guide* and the *Rand McNally Commercial Atlas and Marketing Guide*. Other valuable compilations are the *Sales and Marketing Management* annual statistical issues detailing the Survey of Buying Power which includes industrial incomes, sales of six types of retail stores, market potential indices for states, countries, and metropolitan areas, and similar statistics for Canada.

Directories. These are useful for locating people or companies that could provide information. Trade directories supply a wealth of information on individual companies, including address, names of executives, product range, and brand names. Information on parent companies and/or subsidiaries often is provided. The *Thomas Register of American Manufacturers* lists such data on manufacturers in 75,000 product classifications. The *Canadian Trade Index* lists over 13,000 firms in Canada. Some directories are narrowly focused, such as *McKitrick's Directory of Advertisers*, or the *Pulp and Paper Directory of Canada*. There are a number of directories such as the *World Who's Who in Finance and Industry* and *Standard and Poor's Register of Corporations, Directors and Executives* (that covers the United States and Canada) that provide general biographical information on individuals.

It is important to realize that only a few of the better known sources have been described or mentioned here. The researcher is always best advised to seek the assistance of a qualified reference librarian whenever a new area or topic is being studied.

Computer-Retrievable Databases

Even with the array of printed bibliographies, directories, and indices, a search can be very time consuming. Recent advances in computer technology have resulted in more efficient methods of cataloging, storing, and retrieving published data. The growth in the number of databases available electronically through computers has been dramatic. It is estimated that over 2500 "online" databases are available to researchers and analysts working in almost every area of business, science, law, education and the social sciences. Many of these databases are now accessible from personal computers, as well as terminals equipped with an appropriate telephone linkage. And increasingly, the software developed for the user's communication with the database system is designed to be "user-friendly". As a result, use of these electronic information sources has expanded rapidly to facilitate almost any search for information and is no longer limited to computer specialists.

Classifying Databases. The large number of databases can be overwhelming.[8] A useful classification is that databases provide either reference or source information.

Reference databases refer users to articles and news contained in other sources. They provide on-line indices and abstracts and are therefore referred to as bibliographic databases. This is a quick and efficient method for researching a subject before obtaining a large amount of detailed information. Reference databases provide three distinct search features:

1 They are up-to-date summaries or references to a wide assortment of articles appearing in thousands of business magazines, trade journals, government reports, and newspapers throughout the world.

[8]Martha E. Williams, *Computer-Readable Data Bases: A Directory and Data Source-book*, (1982), White Plains, N.Y.: Knowledge Industry Publications, 1982; *Directory of Online Databases* (quarterly), Santa Monica, Ca: Cuadra Associates, Inc.; *The Computer Bank Book*, New York, N.Y. Find/SVP. *Information Market Place*, New York, N.Y. R.R. Bowker Co. *Encyclopedia of Business Information Sources*, Detroit, Michigan Gale Research Co.

2 The information is accessed through the use of natural language key words, rather than by author or title. For example, the word ''steel'' will cause the computer to retrieve all abstracts which contain the word ''steel''.

3 Key words can be combined in a search for articles which cover a number of related topics.

Source databases provide either numerical data, a complete text, or a combination of both. These include the many economic and financial data bases and the textual source databases which contain the complete texts of newspaper or journal articles.

Accessing and Using Databases. Databases are accessible both from their producers and increasingly from online information services.[9] Database producers originate the information in the database. Many are older information suppliers, such as the Dow Jones Information Service or Mead Data Central's Lexis database for lawyers. The United States government is a large-scale producer of data which is accessed from commercial database services.

Online services provide a network of numerous databases from one central access point. They evolved from the data processing industry and attempt to provide users with increasingly simple and standardized methods for searching a number of databases using one online vendor. There are several large networks of databases, or online information vendors, offering the same databases as well as ''exclusive'' information services. They can be distinguished by their support services to users, the ease of information search and retrieval, and the fee for online information. Most online services have a fee for access to each database and a charge for the amount of information retrieved, and possibly supplemental charges, depending on the nature of the information or the contract arrangements. In 1985 a one-hour search for online information cost an average of $100 while a five minute search of a familiar database source cost $5.

Reference Databases. Examples of the more widely-used reference (bibliographic) databases include:

1 *PTS (Predicasts Terminal System) F & S Index.* Brief descriptive annotations of articles and publications covering U.S. and international company, product, and industry information.

2 *PTS Prompt.* (Predicasts Overview of Markets and Technology). Primary source of information on product introductions, market share, corporate directors, and ventures in every industry with detailed summaries of articles from trade and industry sources. Citations of business literature on market and strategic planning, new techniques and products, and regulation in major industries.

3 *ABI/INFORM.* A widely-used database providing extensive summaries of selected

[9]''Who's Who in the Information Business and How to Find Which One is Right for You'', *Business Marketing* (October 1983).

articles from 550 English-language business and management journals, including indices and abstracts of all articles in 300 journals.

4 *Management Contents.* Indices and abstracts of articles in over 700 English-language business/management periodicals, and proceedings.

5 *Adtrack.* Description of advertisements from 150 U.S. consumer magazines—provides competitive tracking and product announcements.

6 *FIND/SVP Reports and Studies Index.* Summaries of industry and market research reports, surveys from U.S. and international sources, market, industry and company analyses.

7 *Harfax Industry Data Sources.* Description of sources for financial and marketing data in major industries worldwide.

8 *AMI.* (Advertising and Marketing Intelligence). A new database indexing recent articles and news in marketing magazines. It abstracts articles and news appearing in over 60 marketing and trade journals as well as several newspapers.

Source Databases. Source databases provide complete text or numeric information in contrast to the indices and summaries contained in the reference database. They can be classified into: (1) Full text information sources, (2) Economic and financial statistical databases, and (3) Online data and descriptive information on companies.

Nexis is a full text database which includes the text of stories and articles in the major wire services, ten newspapers including the New York Times and Washington Post, 48 magazines and journals, and the Encyclopedia Britannica.

The economic and financial statistical databases were among the first databases to be offered online. Several of the more widely-known statistics vendors provide general economic information as well as specific industry analyses and forecasts. These include: Chase Econometrics/Interactive Data Corp, Citicorp Economic Division, Data Resources, Merrill Lynch Economics, Wharton Econometric Forecasting, Predicasts Forecasts and Predicasts Worldcasts. General economics and business statistics can also be accessed through the online information vendors. Examples are:

1 *BI/Data Time Series.* A computerized database containing 300 economic, demographic, trade and other time series for 131 countries.

2 *Donnelly Demographics.* U.S. Demographic information including 1980 census, current year estimates, and five-year projections from zip code level to the U.S. summary.

In addition to the various major databases providing financial information about companies and stocks, such as Standard and Poor's *Compustat* services and the *Value Line* Database, there are a number of online sources of non-financial information about companies. Several examples are:

1 *EIS* (Economic Information Systems) *Industrial Plants and EIS Non-manufacturing Establishments.* These provide the following information for 150,000 industrial plants

with over 20 employees, and for 350,000 nonmanufacturing establishments: address, SIC industry code, value of shipments, employment size class, share of market estimates, and headquarters address.

2 *D & B—Dun's Market Identifiers.* Directory of over 1 million public and private companies with 10 or more employees, listing address, products, sales executives, corporate organization, subsidiaries, industry information, sales prospects.

Advantages of Computer Retrieval Methods. The main advantage is the scope of the information available on databases. They now cover several thousand U.S. and worldwide information sources. A second advantage is the speed of information access and retrieval. Often, much of the information is available from a computer before it is available in published form, due to the time required for printing and mailing printed material. Thirdly, commercially available search procedures provide considerable flexibility and efficiency in cross-referenced searching. For example, by using the EIS Plants database, it is possible to locate plants that simultaneously meet several criteria, such as geographic location, industry code, and market share.

Limitations of Computer Retrieval Methods. The main limitations of the reference databases are the reliance on the accuracy of the abstract author, the dependence on the journal and article selection policy of the database producer, and the idiosyncracies of the search procedures of the different databases as well as the different database network vendors.[10]

Because the computer search is based on finding certain key words within the abstract, there is the possibility that some important information is missed if an abstract is missing a key word. On the other hand, a lot of irrelevant data may be generated if certain key words used to limit a search are not cited in an abstract. For example, a manufacturer of minicomputers may not want to retrieve the entire data base on computers if he is interested only in developments pertaining to minicomputers. However, the abstract may contain the work "computer" regardless of size, and accessing information on minicomputers would also yield general computer information.

Another limitation arises from the enormous amount of information now available online. It is often quite difficult to know which of the myriad sources has the correct information most readily accessible. Finally, the researcher using online database retrieval services must weigh the benefits of the research procedure, including timeliness, speed, and scope of information retrieval, against the costs of searching and accessing computer-retrievable data bases.

Appraising Secondary Sources

Users of secondary sources rapidly develop a healthy skepticism. Unfortunately there are many reasons why a forecast, historical statistic, or estimate may be found to be irrelevant

---

[10]An interesting compilation of reasons why a database search might not meet with success is provided in Jeff Pemberton, "Faults and Failures—25 Ways That On-line Searching Can Let you Down", *Online*, *7*, September 1983.

or too inaccurate to be useful. Before such a judgment can be made the researcher should have answers to the following questions:

1 *Who?* This question applies especially to the reputation of the collecting agency for honest and thorough work and the character of the sponsoring organization, which may influence the interpretation and reporting of the data. A related question is whether either organization has adequate resources to do a proper job. The problems do not end here, for the original data source (that provided the count, estimate, or other basis for the reported result) may have their own motives for biasing what they report. A company that is pressed by a trade association, chamber of commerce, or government agency may be unwilling to report the true state of affairs or to take the time to collect the data, which may result in a biased guess.

2 *Why?* Data which are collected to further the interests of a particular group are especially suspect. Media buyers, for example, soon learn to be wary of studies of media. It is easy to choose unconsciously those methods, questions, analysis procedures, and so forth that favor the interests of the study sponsor, and it is certainly unlikely that unfavorable results will be exposed to the public.

3 *How?* It is impossible to appraise the quality of secondary data without knowledge of the methodology used to collect the data. Therefore, one should immediately be suspicious of any source that does not describe the procedures used—including a copy of the questionnaire (if any), the nature and size of the sample, the response rate, the results of field validation efforts, and any other procedural decisions that could influence the results. The crucial question is whether any of these decisions could bias the results systematically.

The need for caution is illustrated by a study to determine the best locations for new bank branches. The researchers initially used the projections of population in different parts of the city, which were provided by the city planning commission. These ostensibly valuable data had to be discarded when it was found that the commission arrived at their projections by subdividing on maps the areas to be developed and multiplying each area by the density of families in the established areas of the city. When this methodology was discovered, a proper projection was made by canvassing every real estate developer in the area regarding his future plans. The difference between the two projections, both in extent and timing of population increases, was great.

4 *What?* Even if the available data is of acceptable quality it may prove difficult to use or inadequate to the need. One irritating and prevalent problem is the classifications that are used. Wide variations in geographic, age and income groupings across studies are common, and there is no accepted definition for the minimum number of stores in a supermarket chain, for example.

5 *When?* There is nothing less interesting than last week's newspaper. Sooner or later the pace of change in the world in general, and in markets in particular, renders all secondary data equally obsolete and uninteresting except to the historian. The rate of

obsolescence varies with the types of data, but in all cases the researcher should know when the data were collected. There may be a substantial lag between the time of collection and the publication of the results.

6 *Consistency?* With all the possible pitfalls in secondary data, and the difficulty in fully identifying them, the best defense is to find another source which can be used as a basis of comparison. Ideally, the two sources should use different methodologies to arrive at the same kind of data. In the likely event that there is some disagreement between the two sets of data the process of reconciliation should first identify the respective biases in order to narrow the differences and determine which set is the most credible.

CENSUS DATA

The demographic, economic and social statistics contained in great detail in the census are key aspects of many marketing studies. For example:

> *Company Y must decide where to locate a new shopping mall and which kinds of stores to install. These decisions will require (1) Census of Population information about the populations with access to the proposed locations. (2) Census of Retail Trade information about likely competitors and local wage levels. (3) Census of Construction Industries information about land development, contractors, and construction costs, available by state and metropolitan area.*

Understanding the Census

All countries conduct a mandatory enumeration of important facts about their population and the economic and social environment. The major national and international census data collection agencies and some of their major publications are the U.S. Bureau of the Census, Statistics Canada, Statistical Office of the European Communities (Social Statistics, Industrial Statistics), Great Britain Central Statistical Office (Annual Abstract of Statistics), Japan Bureau of Statistics (Japan Statistical Yearbook), and the United Nations (Statistical Yearbook).

The United States Bureau of the Census is illustrative of the scope of these undertakings. There are actually eight regular Economic Censuses, taken in the years ending with the numbers 2 and 7, and Censuses of Population and Housing that are taken every 10 years in the year ending with 0. The eight Economic Censuses compile detailed statistics on the structure and functioning of the major economic sectors: agriculture, construction industries, manufacturers, mineral industries, retail trade, service industries, transportation, and wholesale trade. A more detailed account of these censuses is found in the Appendix.

Although the scope and detail of the information in the Economic Censuses is large, several years will pass from the time the data is gathered until it is completely published in permanent volumes. It is therefore often necessary to consult numerous special studies and interim estimates that are described in the Bureau of Census Catalog,[11] published monthly with quarterly and annual cumulations. Other federal government agencies also publish current statistics. The Appendix provides references to these and a brief listing indicating the extent of government-originated statistics. There is also a vast quantity of tabulated but unpublished data which are available at cost—usually in microfiche or machine-readable form.

To use census data effectively one must be able to locate quickly the specific information relevant to the research topic. The *Index to Selected 1980 Census Reports* and the *Index to 1980 Census Summary Tapes* list all the titles of tables available from the 1980 census in either printed or tape form. Each table is described in terms of the variable and the level of aggregation used. For example, one table may be described as "Education by Sex" with an indication of the level of aggregation available.

An especially useful publication is the Census Bureau's *Measuring Markets: A Guide to the Use of Federal and State Statistical Data*, which is a guide to the market information available in federal statistics. In addition, it contains a bibliography of all governmental sources of data, a list of state statistical abstracts, and other marketing research information.

Census data can be obtained at many levels of aggregation (see Figure 4–2).[12] The smallest identifiable unit is the city block bounded by four streets and some other physical boundaries. City blocks then are combined arbitrarily to form block groups. The block groups then are collected together to make up census tracts, which are generally used to approximate neighborhoods. Census tracts have populations of above 4000 and are defined by local communities. In urban areas, census tracts are combined to form metropolitan statistical areas (MSAs), which are counties containing a central city with populations of at least 50,000.

The general concept of a metropolitan area is one of a large population nucleus, together with adjacent communities which are determined to have a high degree of economic and social integration with that central nucleus. In June 1983 the federal government replaced the old standard metropolitan statistical area (SMSA) designation with new definitions. Such changes in the criteria for definitions occur periodically and often require revisions of older data. To maintain comparability, data for an earlier period are revised where possible to reflect the MSA boundaries of the more recent period. In addition to the new standard MSAs, the largest defined areas are consolidated metropolitan statistical areas (CMSA), which are metropolitan complexes containing separate component areas. There are 261 MSAs and 21 CMSAs in the United States (including Puerto Rico).

Finally, the whole country is divided into four large regions (northeast, mid-west, south, and west). In addition, census data are available by civil divisions, such as states, counties, cities, and wards.

---

[11]Write to Divisions of Public Documents, Washington, D.C. 20402, or visit one of the 700 U.S. Depository Libraries.

[12]See generally, *A Student's Workbook on the 1970 Census* (Washington D.C.: U.S. Department of Commerce, Bureau of the Census, September 1976); and Solomon Butka, Lester R. Frankel, and Irving Roshwalb, *A Marketer's Guide to Effective Use of 1980 Census Data.* (New York: Audits and Surveys, Inc., 1981).

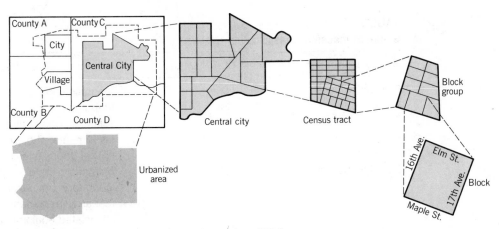

FIGURE 4-2 Geographic subdivisions of an MSA

Data for some levels of aggregation may be available only on magnetic tape. If these data are seldom needed by the market researcher, it may be more economical to obtain them from a private firm rather than purchase the tape and write the appropriate computer programs. Private firms also can provide some manipulation of census data into different formats, such as zip code statistics. In addition, both the U.S. Bureau of the Census and Statistics Canada provide specialized data to order from their tapes.

Standard Industrial Classification System

The key to obtaining census data in the industrial and services market is the Standard Industrial Classification System (SIC). This is a uniform numbering system for classifying establishments according to their economic activities. The total economy is first divided into 11 divisions, such as mining, manufacturing, retail trade, and public administration. Within each of these divisions, the major industry groups are classified by two-digit numbers. Thus, SIC 22 includes all manufacturers of textile mill products within division D, which contains all manufacturing industries. Industry subgroups are defined by a third digit, and detailed industries are defined by a fourth digit. As many as seven digits are available to classify specific products. Table 4-1 illustrates the different levels. Each plant or establishment is given the SIC number that comes closest to describing the principal activity at the location.[13]

There are many sources of SIC related data. The most detailed source is the *U.S. Census of Manufacturers,* which provides data down to the 5- and 7-digit level. As it is published at four- and five-year intervals, it is frequently out-of-date. Other Census Bureau sources are *U.S. Industrial Outlook* and *County Business Patterns.* There are also many

---

[13]These numbers are obtained from the Office of Management and Budget, *1972 Standard Industrial Classification Manual* (Washington, D.C.: U.S. Government Printing Office, 1972).

TABLE 4–1
Standard Industrial Classification System

Classification	SIC Number	Description
Division	D	Manufacturing
Major group	38	Manufacturers of professional, scientific, and controlling instruments; photographic and optical goods; watches and clocks
Industry subgroup	381	Manufacturers of engineering, laboratory, and scientific and research instruments and associated equipment
Detailed industry	3811	Manufacturers of engineering, laboratory, and scientific and research instruments and associated equipment
Manufactured products	38112	Manufacturers of all other laboratory and scientific instruments, *excluding* aircraft, nautical, and navigational instruments, and industrial instruments
Manufactured products	3811264	Manufacturers of laboratory and scientific instruments including medical laboratory instruments using diagnostic reagent chemicals

SOURCE: Robert W. Haas, "SIC System and Related Data for More Effective Marketing Research," *Industrial Marketing Management,* 6 (1977), pp. 429–35.

directories that publish information on individual companies within SIC categories. Other sources are:[14]

1 Predicasts quarterly reports on past industry trends and summaries of long-term growth forecasts, by a seven-digit SIC number.

2 Dun and Bradstreet's "Market Identifiers" service is a continuous file on approximately 3,250,000 U.S. and Canadian establishments. For each establishment such information as the name, address, telephone number, number of employees at the location, credit rating, and so forth is provided.

[14]Robert W. Haas, "SIC System and Related Data for More Effective Market Research," *Industrial Marketing Management,* 6 (1977), pp. 429–35.

3 Mailing-list companies such as Polk and National Business Lists Co. provide mailing lists and labels on SIC-classified establishments.

ZIP Market Cluster Analysis

Traditionally, the analysis of households using census data has been limited to geographic and demographic variables. Another perspective has been provided recently by describing the census data according to postal code or ZIP code areas. The resulting PRIZM system[15] (Potential Rating Index Zip Markets) is based on evidence that people with similar cultural backgrounds and circumstances will gravitate naturally toward one another. Each of the 35,600 ZIP markets was first described according to 34 key demographic factors. These ZIP markets then were clustered into 40 distinct groups, which were each very homogenous within themselves and very different from other groups.

Each of the 40 groups has been labeled according to its dominant characteristics. For example, ZIP code areas labeled as "Young Influentials" were those with many high-income families having one or two small children, who do not take extensive vacations but are among the nation's heaviest imbibers of wines. By contrast, "Bunker's Neighbors" describes areas with predominantly 50-plus blue-collar workers with high incomes. These groups travel extensively, make large purchases such as mobile homes, and are high alcoholic beverage users.

Since every market is composed of ZIP code areas, it is possible to estimate the sales potential of a market by ZIP Market Clusters. As an example, a power tool manufacturer was able to create a PRIZM profile of product warranty cards mailed by recent buyers. This told the manufacturer which ZIP code areas should be chosen as target markets and helped to allocate media spending and sales force effort.

SYNDICATED MARKETING DATA SOURCES

The more specific and topical the need for information, the smaller the likelihood that relevant secondary data will be found. The researcher then has the choice of designing a special study or taking advantage of standardized data collection and analysis procedures. The latter alternative generally exists whenever several information users have common information needs and when the cost of satisfying an individual user's need is prohibitive. These conditions are most often encountered with consumer goods sold to large, diffuse markets and repurchased at frequent intervals. A further condition—especially important for data sources such as store audits and continuous consumer panels—is that the information needs are recurrent and can be anticipated. Thus the data supplier can enter into long-term relationships with clients and be sure of covering the heavy fixed costs. The clients get continuity of data series, which is essential for monitoring and evaluation purposes.

[15]"PRIZM Adds Zip to Consumer Research", *Advertising Age* (November 10, 1980) 22.

This section describes and evaluates the major syndicated sources of marketing data—including store audits, panels, warehouse withdrawal services, consumer purchase panels and scanner-based systems. Each source has a distinctive profile of strengths and weaknesses that reflects differences in orientation, types of measures, and their location in the distribution channel. To get a full picture of the market situation of a product category or brand it is usually necessary to use several sources in combination. Unfortunately, when this is done the result is more often confusion rather than clarity of insight, because of information overload. This is such a prevalent problem that the last section of this chapter will be devoted to recently developed decision support systems that help cut the confusion.

Standardized Research Services

The largest standardized research services are those which supply consumer product companies with audit or panel data on retail sales activity and distribution coverage. To understand why, consider the problems of a manufacturer of cold remedies who has to rely on factory shipment data for information about sales. Management is especially interested in the reaction to a new convenience package that was introduced at the beginning of the cold season in December. By the end of January, the following information has been received from the accounting department:

WEEK ENDING	FACTORY SHIPMENTS
December 28	12,700 cases
January 4	19,800 cases
January 11	18,200 cases
January 18	14,100 cases
January 25	11,050 cases

All the usual problems of interpreting times series data are compounded in this example by the ambiguities in the data. The peak in factory shipments during the week ending January 4 represents a substantial amount of "pipeline filling," and an unknown amount of product sold for that reason still remains on the shelves. Also unknown is competitive performance during this period; did the new package gain sales at the expense of competition, or was there a loss of market share? Shipment data provide no diagnostic information, so these questions remain: How many retail stores used the special displays of the new product? Were competitors making similar or more effective offers? Was there a carry-over of last year's stock in the old package? Without answers to these questions the manager is in no position to either correct problems or continue the strong points; thus, there is a strong motivation to acquire data from one or more syndicated services that provide information on the flow of products (1) through retailers, as provided by store audit services; (2) through wholesalers, as provided by warehouse withdrawal services; (3) purchased by consumers, as provided by consumer purchase panels; or (4) bought in supermarkets (data from check-out scanners are becoming more readily available). The rest of this section will describe these four types of services in turn.

Retail Stores Audits[16]

Every two months a team of auditors from a research firm visits a sample of stores to count the inventory on hand and record deliveries to the store since the last visit. Sales during the two-month period, for any desired classification of the product category (including brands, sizes, package types, flavors, etc.), are arrived at by computing

Beginning Inventory + Deliveries − Ending Inventory = Sales for the Period

TABLE 4–2
Contents of a Nielsen Store Audit Report

Each of the following variables can be subdivided as follows:
- a. sales districts
- b. size of county (A, B, C, or D)
- c. type of store (e.g., chain versus large-medium-small independents)
- d. 32 largest metropolitan markets
1. *Sales* (volume, trend and share) on the basis of retail dollars and units, pounds or equivalent cases for total market, and major brands by sizes, flavors, types etc. as appropriate to the category
2. *Distribution*
    - a. percentage of all stores, and all commodity sales, carrying each brand and size
    - b. out-of-stock conditions
    - c. retail inventories
    - d. stock cover (the length of time the stocks will last, assuming current rates of sales)
    - e. source of delivery (wholesaler, rack jobbers, manufacturer, chain warehouse or inter-store transfers)
3. *Selling prices,* and volume sold at each price or deal
4. *Retailer support* in terms of shelf facings, special displays, in-store advertising and newspaper advertising
5. *Media advertising* for total market and major brands
6. *Special analyses* (illustrative)
    - a. analyses of combinations of brands stocked to determine the extent to which individual brands compete together
    - b. cumulative distribution of new products

[16]Garry Arnott, "Trade Research," in Robert M. Worcester, ed., *Consumer Market Research Handbook* (London: McGraw-Hill, 1973), pp. 120–142.

These sample results then are projected—to arrive at nationwide and regional estimates of total sales, inventories, and so forth—and reported to the client between six and eight weeks after the end of the period. During each store visit the auditor also may collect such observable information as shelf prices, display space, presence of special displays, and in-store promotion activity.

Nielsen Retail Index.   The A. C. Nielsen Co. is the biggest research company in the world (with 1982 revenues of $433 million), primarily because of their auditing services. There are four major reporting groups: (1) grocery products, (2) drugs, (3) mass merchandisers, and (4) alcoholic beverages. Within the grocery products group the auditors cover a 1300-store sample, which is weighted toward high-volume stores. One of every 39 of the large chain stores is taken in the sample, while only one of every 360 small independent stores is taken. These stores are paid for their cooperation.

The data provided by Nielsen, or other auditing companies such as Audits and Surveys, are incredibly rich. Table 4–2 summarizes the information that is provided routinely in the bimonthly report. For most companies this becomes the basis of their marketing information system. Beyond basic analyses of market position and competitive activity, the data can be used to analyze the impact of marketing activities. Since products purchased regularly are reported separately from those items sold with a promotional offer, it is possible to judge the effect of a promotion by comparing several periods of data. As an example, consider the following chart. Sales of regular or nonpromotional merchandise (the dark-shaded portions of the bars) went from an 8.5-percent share of the market to an 11.3-percent share. If nothing else changed, then this gain could be credited to the coupon promotion run during March and April.

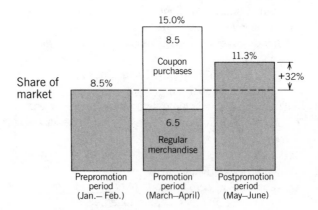

Audits and Surveys: National Total Market Audit.   This is a bimonthly audit that focuses on products, regardless of the type of retail outlet carrying the product. This is especially useful for categories such as personal care products, batteries, and candy and confectionary, which are sold through many types of outlets other than grocery stores or drugstores. The audit samples 4000 outlets to obtain brand-by-brand retail (consumer) sales, dealer purchases, retail inventory, distribution and out-of-stocks. Clients purchase only the outlet types and sample size needed to suit a particular need. Because this audit is conducted regularly, it provides continuous measures of how well a brand is doing in terms of share, distribution coverage, inventory in stock and so forth.

For infrequently purchased products, such as housewares, writing instruments, and sunglasses, where bimonthly audit data are less important than a very large sample of outlets, Audit and Surveys conducts an annual Retail Census of Product Distribution. This census entails personal store visits to 40,000 retail outlets of all types from catalog showrooms to variety stores. The detail collected from each type of store on a product such as bakeware and cookware, as shown in Figure 4–3, permits manufacturers to analyze the strengths and weaknesses of their distribution. With the census results, for example, a manufacturer of hair sprays can ask, ''Is the wholesaler getting my brand into the smaller stores in more remote areas, or merely 'skimming the cream' off the market?''

Warehouse Withdrawal Services

SAMI (Selling Areas—Marketing, Inc.) is a major competitor to Nielsen in the audit business. Their approach differs in that they carry out the auditing at the warehouse or wholesale level rather than at the retail level. Basically SAMI reports the amount of product shipped from chain warehouses, wholesalers, and health-and-beauty-aid rack jobbers to food stores in the market area served by the warehouses. Warehouse withdrawal data are available for 42 major market areas which account for 80 percent of total food sales in the United States. On average, the product shipment information gathered in a market area by SAMI represents about 75 percent of that market area's all-commodity food volume. There are over 550 warehouse operators and 110,000 stores participating in this service.

Subscribers to the SAMI service receive a report every four weeks showing product description, package size, case movement, the item's dollar share of total category sales, and the number of food operators carrying the product. A sample (disguised) subscriber report is shown in Figure 4–4. The data can be broken out for each of the 42 SAMI areas, and presented as trends by showing the results from the 13 most recent reporting periods. These trend data can be used to measure the effectiveness of promotions offered in different areas by comparing average case movement before the promotion with average case movement during the promotion.

A limitation of the basic SAMI service is that it doesn't say anything about what is happening at the point of sale; for example, which brands have distribution in which stores, what shelf location each brand occupies, the kinds of displays in effect, and so forth. To partially overcome this problem, SAMI offers a supplementary distribution report called SARDI (an acronym for SAMI Retail Distribution Index). A typical SARDI report shows retail distribution for each brand, item, and consumer deal pack within the category, as a proportion of all-commodity volume (ACV). This takes into account the great dif-

**BAKEWARE/COOKWARE *(NON-ELECTRIC)*
DINNERWARE**

I. METAL COOKWARE/BAKEWARE *(Non-Electric)*

Definitions: Cookware—used on top of range
Bakeware—used in oven

Note: Brand name can be found on bottom of each item.

CLUB (Club American)—*Cookware*
Coated *(i.e. Teflon, Silverstone)*........................☐ 31-y
Uncoated ....☐ -x
FARBERWARE—*Cookware*
Coated *(i.e. Teflon, Silverstone)*........................☐ -0
Uncoated ....☐ -1
REVERE WARE—*Cookware*
Coated *(i.e. Teflon, Silverstone)*........................☐ -2
Uncoated ....☐ -3
ANY OTHER METAL COOKWARE ....☐ -4
ANY METAL BAKEWARE.....................................☐ -5

II. GLASS COOKWARE/BAKEWARE

REFER TO ILLUSTRATIONS INCLUDED WITH MATERIALS
FOR ADDITIONAL PICTURES.
NOTE: The brand name can be found on the bottom side
of each item. If uncertain, ask person in charge.

1. NUMBER OF ITEMS: Check below for the appropriate *number
of items* for each brand carried. An item is defined as either. . .

(A)	(B)
A grouping of pieces sold together = *1 item*	A piece sold individually = *1 item*
Example: 3-piece mixing bowl set = *1 item*	*Example:* 4-Qt. covered casserole = *1 item*

Do not count the same item more than once *(i.e. if there are two
3-piece mixing bowl sets, count it only once.)*

2. SETS—A grouping of pieces sold together *(i.e. 3-piece mixing
bowl set):* Check below where indicated if any item checked in
Q.1 is a set.

	1.NUMBER OF ITEMS		2. ANY
	10 or less	11 or more	SETS
ANCHOR HOCKING			
Clear	☐ 32-y	☐ 33-y	☐ 34-y
Amber *(Brown Tint)*	☐ -x	☐ -x	☐ -x
Opal *(White Translucent— Plain and Design)*	☐ -0	☐ -0	☐ -0
DURAND BAKEWARE	☐ -1	☐ -1	■
CORNING WARE			
Cornflower	☐ -2	☐ -2	■
Wildflower	☐ -3	☐ -3	■
Spice O'Life	☐ -4	☐ -4	■
"Just White"	☐ -5	☐ -5	■
French White	☐ -6	☐ -6	■

(Continues next column)

II. GLASS COOKWARE/BAKEWARE *(cont'd)*

	1. NUMBER OF ITEMS		2. ANY SETS
	10 or less	11 or more	
PYREX			
Clear	☐ 35-y	☐ 36-y	☐ 37-y
Fireside—*Amber (Brown Tint)*	☐ -x	☐ -x	☐ -x
Opal *(White Translucent— Plain or Design)*	☐ -0	☐ -0	☐ -0

Now check each "PYREX OPAL" design found in this store.

Autumn Harvest ....☐ 38-y
Butterfly Gold ....☐ -x
Homestead ....☐ -0
Spring Blossom Green ....☐ -1
Woodland ....☐ -2
ANY OTHER GLASS COOKWARE/BAKEWARE.......☐ -3

III. DINNERWARE

Check here whether the dinnerware items
below are being sold as open stock *(a cup,
a plate, etc.)* or as a set *(a complete setting).*

Note: Brand name can be found on bottom
of each item.

	HOW SOLD	
	Open Stock	In Sets
ANCHOR HOCKING	☐ 39-y	☐ 41-y
ARCOPAL/ARCOPAL TABLE/ARCOROC	☐ -x	☐ -x
CORELLE *(REGULAR)*		
Butterfly Gold	☐ -0	☐ -0
Old Towne Blue	☐ -1	☐ -1
Spring Blossom Green	☐ -2	☐ -2
Winter Frost White	☐ -3	☐ -3
Woodland Brown	☐ -4	☐ -4
CORELLE *EXPRESSIONS*		
April	☐ -5	☐ -5
Batik	☐ -6	☐ -6
Blue Heather	☐ -7	☐ -7
Indian Summer	☐ -8	☐ -8
Meadow	☐ -9	☐ -9
Wildflower	☐ 40-y	☐ 42-y
DURAND	☐ -x	☐ -x
FRANCISCAN	☐ -0	☐ -0
JEANETTE	☐ -1	☐ -1
JEPCOR	☐ -2	☐ -2
MIKASA	☐ -3	☐ -3
ROYAL	☐ -4	☐ -4
SANGO	☐ -5	☐ -5
TAYLOR, SMITH & TAYLOR	☐ -6	☐ -6

FIGURE 4–3 Retail census of product distribution

100

SAMI

MANUFACTURER: NON-CONTRACT
CONTRACT NO.:
MARKET AREA:

CATEGORY: COFFEE, REGULAR
ISSUE NUMBER: 116

UNITS: DOLLAR VOLUME / CASE VOLUME
CURRENT 4 WK PERIOD: 07/05/75 - 08/01/75
PERIOD COVERED: 07/30/74 - 08/01/75

STANDARD DOLLAR REPORT	ITEM SIZE	PACK PER CASE	AVG. SHELF PRICE	MEASURED CASE VOLUME 4 WEEKS	MEASURED CASE VOLUME 52 WEEKS	MEASURED DOLLAR SALES 4 WEEKS	MEASURED DOLLAR SALES 52 WEEKS	DOLLAR SHARE OF BRAND 4 WEEKS	DOLLAR SHARE OF BRAND 52 WEEKS	DOLLAR SHARE OF CATEGORY 4 WEEKS	DOLLAR SHARE OF CATEGORY 52 WEEKS	# OF SHIP PNG WEEKS	NEW (N) DROP (D) ITEM IN MARKET PERIOD ENDING
YUBAN COFFEE ALL PURPOSE	2 LB	12	2.068	675	6.204	16.752	190.655	30.611%	21.999%	1.197%	.971%	*	•
YUBAN COFFEE REGULAR	2 LB	12	2.710	46	377	1.496	12.447	2.734%	1.436%	.107%	.063%	*	•
YUBAN COFFEE DRIP	2 LB	12	2.700	35	2.572	1.134	84.937	2.072%	9.801%	.081%	.432%	7	
YUBAN COFFEE ELECTRAMATIC	1 LB	24	1.374	232	3.918	7.648	130.937	13.975%	15.108%	.546%	.667%	7	
YUBAN COFFEE ELECTRAMATIC	2 LB	12	2.130	767	10.544	19.600	325.775	35.815%	37.590%	1.401%	1.658%	6	
FOLGERS				14.405	193.431	446.064	5.916.015	100.000%	100.000%	31.874%	30.116%	8	
FOLGERS COFFEE REG	8 OZ	24	.721	26	410	450	7.052	.101%	.119%	.032%	.036%	8	
FOLGERS COFFEE REG	1 LB	24	1.297	2.385	22.585	74.248	710.901	16.645%	12.017%	5.305%	3.619%	•	
FOLGERS COFFEE REG	2 LB	12	2.604	1.039	24.027	32.469	747.589	7.297%	12.637%	2.230%	3.806%	8	
FOLGERS COFFEE REG	3 LB	8	3.821	1.448	20.109	44.262	589.614	9.923%	9.966%	3.163%	3.001%	8	
FOLGERS COFFEE DRIP	1 LB	24	1.300	1.529	14.073	47.717	443.029	10.697%	7.489%	3.410%	2.255%	8	
FOLGERS COFFEE DRIP	2 LB	12	2.624	826	15.670	26.013	485.829	5.832%	8.212%	1.859%	2.473%	8	
FOLGERS COFFEE DRIP	3 LB	8	3.801	1.116	13.365	33.932	394.721	7.607%	6.672%	2.425%	2.009%	8	
FOLGERS COFFEE FINE	1 LB	24	1.287	259	2.606	7.999	82.444	1.793%	1.394%	.572%	.420%	5	
FOLGERS COFFEE FINE	2 LB	12	2.599	89	1.691	2.776	53.292	.622%	.901%	.198%	.271%	8	
FOLGERS COFFEE ELECTRIC PRK	1 LB	24	1.306	2.574	24.814	80.672	778.244	18.085%	13.155%	5.765%	3.962%	8	
FOLGERS COFFEE ELECTRIC PRK	2 LB	12	2.599	1.181	28.425	36.832	882.427	8.262%	14.916%	2.632%	4.492%	8	
FOLGERS COFFEE ELECTRIC PRK	3 LB	8	3.796	1.933	25.656	58.694	740.873	13.158%	12.523%	4.194%	3.771%	8	
HIGH POINT				874	6.487	32.051	239.690	100.000%	100.000%	2.290%	1.220%	6	
HIGH POINT COF DRIP DECAF	1 LB	24	1.535	261	2.300	9.616	85.685	30.002%	35.748%	.687%	.436%	8	0214N
HIGH POINT COF DRIP DECAF	1 LB	12	3.048	124	757	4.536	27.666	14.152%	11.542%	.324%	.141%	5	0214N
HIGH POINT COF EL PERK DECAF	1 LB	24	1.535	275	2.081	10.133	77.278	31.615%	32.241%	.724%	.393%	8	0214N
HIGH POINT COF EL PERK DECAF	2 LB	12	3.024	214	1.349	7.766	49.061	24.230%	20.469%	.555%	.250%	7	0214N
CHASE SANBORN				583	21.733	17.951	653.726	100.000%	100.000%	1.283%	3.328%	4	
CHASE SANBORN COF REG	2 LB	12	2.576	224	8.193	6.923	249.779	38.566%	38.209%	.495%	1.272%	4	
CHASE SANBORN COF DRIP	2 LB	12	2.596	98	3.288	3.053	96.177	17.007%	14.712%	.218%	.490%	4	
CHASE SANBORN COF ELC PRK	2 LB	12	2.546	261	10.252	7.975	307.770	44.426%	47.079%	.570%	1.567%	4	
FRENCH MARKET				4	18	62	280	100.000%	100.000%	.004%	.001%	•	
FRENCH MARKET COF CHIC REG	1 LB	12	1.292	4	18	62	280	100.000%	100.000%	.004%	.001%	•	0314N
OLD JUDGE				1.847	33.829	54.275	1.060.584	100.000%	100.000%	3.878%	5.399%	6	
OLD JUDGE COFFEE REG	1 LB	24	1.304	299	6.418	9.360	203.224	17.246%	19.162%	.669%	1.035%	5	
OLD JUDGE COFFEE REG	2 LB	12	2.322	474	6.389	13.205	199.850	24.330%	18.843%	.944%	1.017%	6	
OLD JUDGE COFFEE REG	3 LB	8	3.822	59	2.510	1.804	77.465	3.324%	7.304%	.129%	.394%	•	
OLD JUDGE COFFEE DRIP	1 LB	24	1.303	127	1.892	3.972	59.711	7.318%	5.630%	.284%	.304%	•	

*ASTERISK INDICATES 3 OR LESS FOOD OPERATOR SHIPPING.

FIGURE 4–4 Report form for warehouse withdrawal service

ference in the size of stores. Thus, an 80-percent ACV distribution means the brand has distribution in stores that account for the 80 percent of total sales in the product category, which is not necessarily 80 percent of the total number of stores.

SARDI reports are based on the assumption that if a retail store makes a withdrawal of a product from a central warehouse during a given time period (usually four weeks) then the store has sold the product. In 1984, a sample of 5800 stores within SAMI reporting areas reported this withdrawal information.

Consumer Purchase Panels

From store audits and warehouse withdrawal services we can learn how much product is moving through the distribution channel. As this information is one step removed from the actual purchase transaction, we still don't know who bought, how frequently they bought, or whether the seeming stability of market shares reflects stable purchasing patterns or a great deal of switching back and forth between brands and stores in response to short-term promotional efforts. To answer these questions, we need detailed records of purchasing activity by the same people over an extended period of time. Here are two methods for collecting this data:

1   The **home audit** approach in which the panel member agrees to permit an auditor to check the household stocks of certain product catergories at regular intervals. A secondary condition is that the panel member save all used cartons, wrappers, and so on for recording by the auditor.

2   In the **mail diary method** the panel member records the details of each purchase in certain categories and returns the completed diary by mail at regular intervals (biweekly or monthly). The detail that can be collected is illustrated for two of the 88 clothing, food, and personal care products recorded by members of the American Shoppers Panel (see Figure 4–5).

Both types of panels are used extensively in Europe, while in the United States and Canada the mail diary method is dominant. When comparisons have been possible, the two methods have produced equally accurate market-share and trend data.[17]

In 1981 there were at least six syndicated panels operating in the United States and Canada and another 25 of various types operating in the rest of the world.[18] Not all of these were purchase panels. Indeed, the best-known panel is the Nielsen television viewing panel, from which the Nielsen program ratings are obtained. Each panel member has a meter attached to her or his television set. The meter records on a tape the time the set is in operation and the channel to which the set is tuned. The actual audience is obtained from a viewing diary, in which the viewing times of household members (and guests) are

---

[17]John Parfitt, "Panel Research," in Robert M. Worcester, *Consumer Market Research Handbook* (London: McGraw-Hill, 1972), pp. 143–177.

[18]Seymour Sudman and Robert Ferber, *Consumer Panels* (Chicago: American Marketing Association, 1979).

NOTE: Extra space page 1. Free Gifts and Samples, inside front cover.

Date of month purchase was made	Write in **BRAND NAME** as shown on label **RAZOR BLADES** Including free blades with purchase of razor or travel and shaving kits. Write in all of the words which together describe the complete brand name.	HOW MANY of each kind did you buy?	HOW MUCH DID YOU PAY?					WHERE DID YOU PURCHASE?					CHECK (✓) ONE			CHECK (✓) ONE Type of Blade							Write in: Number of blades or cartridges per package or number of shaving edges per continuous band	CHECK (✓) ONE Kind of Blade								WRITE IN AGE, SEX OF PURCHASER		WRITE IN AS MANY AS APPLY TO THE ITEM, AGE AND SEX OF USERS											
		Write in number of packages, or other containers	TOTAL CASH PAID Don't include taxes		Was this a special price or merchandise offer?			NAME OF STORE (or company if purchased from door-to-door or home delivery salesperson)	KIND OF STORE Check (✓) or write in																									User No. 1		User No. 2		User No. 3		User No. 4		User No. 5		User No. 6	
			$	¢	IF NO, Check here ✓	If YES, describe kind, such as: • Price-Off marked on package • Store Coupon from newspaper • Other Coupon from newspaper • Coupon from magazine or received in mail • Gift on or in package • Special refund offer such as cash refund or merchandise offer • Store sales • Other deals	Total ¢ off if any		GROCERY OR FOOD	DRUGS	DISCOUNT	Other — Describe	BLADES ONLY	RAZOR INCLUDING BLADES	KIT INCLUDING BLADES	SINGLE EDGE	DOUBLE EDGE	INJECTOR	CONTINUOUS EDGE (BAND)	BONDED	TWIN (2) BLADED CARTRIDGE	OTHER		BLUE	SUPER BLUE	STAINLESS STEEL	CHROMIUM	PLATINUM	TUNGSTEN	THINS	OTHER	Age	Sex	AGE	SEX	AGE	SEX	AGE	SEX	AGE	SEX	AGE	SEX	AGE	SEX

NOTE: Extra space page 1. Free Gifts and Samples, inside front cover.

CARBONATED SOFT DRINKS DIARY TIPS: First of all, enter in the diary only those purchases which are brought home from the store. This includes items which may later be taken on a picnic or to the beach as well as items which are consumed at home. • Do **not** enter items which are consumed at the place of purchase. Usually, these include vending machine purchases, restaurants, refreshment stands, ball games, etc. • When you make a purchase entry, fill in the answers under every column all the way across the page. • Be sure to enter purchases brought home by all family members.

Date of month purchase was made	Write in **BRAND NAME** as shown on label **CARBONATED SOFT DRINKS** Write in all of the words which together describe the complete brand name.	HOW MANY of each kind did you buy?	HOW MUCH DID YOU PAY?					WHERE DID YOU PURCHASE?			WEIGHT (SIZE) SHOWN ON LABEL	Check (✓) one TYPE OF PACK							Check (✓) one TYPE OF CONTAINER				WRITE IN FLAVOR	Check (✓) one	
		Write in number of packages, or other containers	TOTAL CASH PAID Don't include taxes		Was this a special price or offer?			NAME OF STORE (or company if purchased from door-to-door or home delivery salesperson)	KIND OF STORE Check (✓) or write in		Write in the amount of weight per item or container and tell us the kind of weight such as pounds and/or ounces, pints, quarts, etc.								Glass Bottle				Such as: Orange, Chocolate, Cola, Lemon, Cherry, etc. COPY FROM LABEL		
			$	¢	IF NO, Check here ✓	IF YES, describe kind such as store sale, cents-off coupon, gift on or in package, etc. How much savings in total? DESCRIBE SPECIAL PRICE OR OFFER	Total ¢ off		GROCERY OR FOOD	Other — Describe		SINGLES	2 PACK	4 PACK	6 PACK	8 PACK	CASE	OTHER	RETURN	THROW AWAY	PLASTIC BOTTLE	CAN		REGULAR	LOW CALORIE

FIGURE 4–5 Illustrations of recording forms used in mail diary panels

recorded. From these data are estimated the total audience for each program and their composition by age, sex, and so forth.

MRCA (Market Research Corporation of America) has operated a mail-diary panel since 1941. The MRCA data on consumer purchases of items sold in food and drugstores are obtained from a panel of approximately 7500 families throughout the United States. For each purchase, the following information is recorded by the participating families:

Date and day of week

Brand name

Number of items purchased

Type of container (glass, tin, etc.)

Exact weight or quantity

Where purchased (including store name)

Normal transaction or deal

Price paid

The 7500 families used in the sample are selected on a probability basis to be representative of the total population on major characteristics such as geographic region, city size, income, presence of children, education, size of family, and age of homemaker. When a family is selected for the panel, a personal call is used to enlist their cooperation and train them in the reporting procedures. Each family receives compensation in the form of points, which are exchangeable for merchandise.

Each month MRCA delivers a report for the preceeding month showing total consumer purchases of each brand in the category, plus sales overall, which can be converted into volume and dollar market shares. Each quarter, an analysis of purchases by regions and by type of retail outlet is provided.

Advantages of Panels.   The data from a panel can be analyzed as a series of snapshots—providing information on *aggregate* sales activity, brand shares, and shifts in buyer characteristics and types of retail outlets from one month to the next. But, just as a motion picture is more revealing than a snapshot, it is the ability to measure changes in the behavior of *individuals* that is the real advantage of a panel.[19] Knowledge of the sequence of purchases makes it possible to analyze

- Heavy buyers and their associated characteristics
- Brand switching rates and the extent of loyal buying (evidence of stable purchase activity in the aggregate usually masks a great deal of individual movement)
- Cumulative market penetration and repeat purchase rates for new products (the success of new products depends jointly on the proportion who have tried them once and then purchased a second, third, or fourth time)

[19]These and other uses are described in Parfitt, *op. cit.*, and Seymour Sudman and Robert Ferber, *op. cit.*

A continuous panel is an excellent vehicle for conducting quasi-experiments. A change in price, advertising copy, or package can be implemented in one region and the results compared with other regions where no change was made. Also, because of the lengthy relationship with members of continuous panels, there is much more opportunity to collect classification and attitudinal information to help understand the observed changes in behavior.

By comparison with interview methods, although not audits, the continuous panel has an advantage of accuracy. Several studies have found that interview respondents will exaggerate their rate of purchasing (an effect that is most pronounced for infrequently purchased products) and dramatically oversimplify brand-switching behavior.[20] Apparently, survey respondents tend to equate their most recent brand buying behavior to their "normal" behavior—whether or not this is accurate.

Limitations of Consumer Panels. The limitations all relate to the vulnerability of panels to various biases. The first encountered is *selection* bias, because of the high rates of refusal and the resulting lack of representativeness. It is estimated that panel recruitment rates may vary from as low as 10 to 15 percent when the initial contact is made by mail in the United States, to 50 percent or more for personal contacts made on behalf of panels in Great Britain.[21]

A related problem is **mortality,** which may mean a dropout rate in excess of 20 percent a year. Some of this is unavoidable, due to moves and illness. To reduce both the refusal and mortality rates, all panels offer some incentive for continuing participation; these include direct money payments and stamp schemes in exchange for gifts.

There is little doubt that those who refuse or drop out differ from those who participate and remain. In particular those lacking in interest in the topic are most likely to drop out. These losses are replaced by new members with similar characteristics. This amounts to a matching procedure, and of course it is not possible to match on all important characteristics. In a subsequent chapter we will examine the problem of refusals, which afflicts all forms of survey work. As a consequence, however, all panels underrepresent the very rich, the very poor, and the transitory.

Panels are also subject to a variety of **testing effects.** There is a definite tendency for new panel members to report unusual levels of purchasing because of the novelty of the reporting responsibility. This effect is so pronounced that the first month's results are usually discarded. Surprisingly there is little evidence to suggest that there is a long-run conditioning behavior that would lead to great brand loyalty or price consciousness that would produce systematically biased data.

Finally, it should be kept in mind that it is usually the wife that does the recording of purchases. Whenever a product—such as cigarettes or toothpaste—is purchased by several members of the household, there is a good chance that some purchases will be missed. These products are also troublesome to analyze, for what appears to be brand

---

[20]Seymour Sudman, "On the Accuracy of Recording of Consumer Panels," *Journal of Marketing Research*, 1 (August 1964), 69–83.
[21]Parfitt, "Panel Research" *op. cit.,* 156.

switching simply may be the purchasing of different brands for (or by) different members of the household.

Scanner-Based Research Services

Computerized scanner checkouts are beginning to revolutionize syndicated research activities. Their promise of richer, more detailed and more comprehensive data that address many more marketing questions had to wait until sufficient scanner checkouts were in place to generate the data, and research systems could cope with this deluge of data. By 1984 these conditions were largely realized. Over 7200 supermarkets had been equipped with scanners. These represented almost half of stores with sales of more than $80,000 per week. These large stores accounted for almost 70 percent of total supermarket volume.

Within supermarkets equipped with scanner checkouts, purchases are recorded by passing them over a laser scanner, which automatically reads the bar-coded description (the Universal Product Code) printed on each package. This in turn actuates the cash register, which relates the product code to its current price—held in computer memory–and calculates the amount due. All the pertinent data on the purchase then are stored in the computer and can be accessed instantly for analysis.

Scanner-based Audit Services. The most immediate benefits of scanner data are a high degree of accuracy, time savings and the ability to study very short time periods of sales activity. To appreciate these benefits, consider the introduction of a new food product into a test market monitored by a scanner-based audit service. This service includes weekly visits to stores to measure display activity and retailer newspaper advertising.

According to the standard bimonthly reports from the store audit service, there was steady progress in building the market share. During the second bimonthly period (see Figure 4-6), share more than doubled, as retailer advertising and coupon promotions were stepped up.

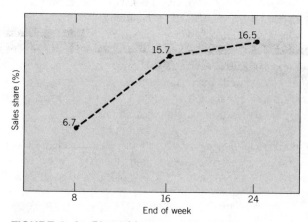

FIGURE 4–6 Bimonthly store audit results

The results from the third period normally would not be available for six to eight weeks. With scanning data, however, weekly reports on this product were available within two to three weeks of the end of the period. These weekly reports were also far more revealing, as we see from the data shown in Figure 4-7 for the same time period following the launch. The first 11 weeks followed a fairly typically new-brand cycle, with share by week 10 only half of the initial peak. Back-to-back price and coupon promotion in weeks 12 and 13 boosted shares to twice the introductory level. Shares then declined, until a further promotion in week 18. Fortunately, postpromotion shares were always higher than prepromotion shares through week 22. The sharp decline in week 23 was traced to a shortage of the most popular size of package, which was rectified during the next week.

In 1984 there were three scanner-based audit services, providing nationally–or locally–representative results within two weeks of the end of the reporting period. The largest was National Scanning Services covering 700 stores in more than 100 SMSA's; the others were TRIM and Nielsen's National Scantrack with somewhat smaller store samples. Each of these services reported full detail on each universal product code in a product category, including product description, size, price, unit movement and unit share, and dollar sales and share. These are combined with weekly checks of in-store display and shelf-space conditions and monitoring of newspaper ads. Virtually any combination of stores could be isolated, to look at sales by a particular chain or geographic area down to the level of an individual store.

Behavior Scan. This is a market testing service that fully exploits the potential for extensive and detailed electronic monitoring of sales. By 1985 this service made it possible for supermarket goods manufacturers to monitor the sales of their product through every checkstand, in one of four pairs of eight communities, on a daily basis. Each of these communities is reasonably self-contained, with its own newspaper and cable TV, and is demographically representative of the United States.

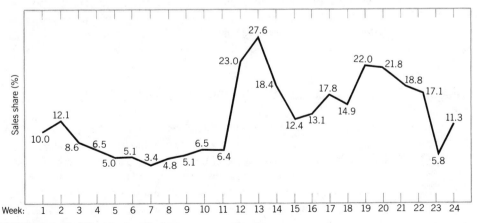

FIGURE 4–7 Weekly results from scanner service

More detailed data was available on the purchases of a panel of 2500 households in each community. Each panel member had an identification card that was presented at the scanner-equipped grocery store each time a purchase was made. This card alerted the checkout terminal to send an item-by-item record of those purchases to a computer file. Then researchers could relate the details of a household's purchase of each product to previously collected classification information about the family and any promotional stimuli to which the family was exposed.

These panel households could also be individually targeted for newspaper advertising, so a marketer could experiment with different combinations of advertising copy and/or exposure, discount coupons and in-store price discounts and promotions. The effects of these different programs could be unobtrusively monitored in the supermarket and each panel member's purchases compared with what they had purchased before the test. To control for competitive activity the service also tracked the amount of features, displays and couponing activity in each supermarket.

The most striking feature of BehaviorScan is the ability to control the advertising seen by panel members and monitor the station to which the TV is tuned. For example, it is possible to send a Duncan Hines cake mix commercial only to Betty Crocker customers, to find out if they can be induced to switch. Then television viewing of these households is electronically monitored by five-second intervals, providing detailed records of exposure to programming and specific commercials.

In a typical application of the BehaviorScan system, the research purpose was to establish the cost-effectiveness of a product sample as either an alternative or an accompaniment to TV commercials to sell a children's food product. The panel was divided into four groups and given different combinations of samples and advertising. Sales doubled in all groups receiving samples during the test period; however, the group also exposed to advertising was more loyal to the brand during subsequent weeks. The major advantages BehaviorScan had over conventional market tests, for this kind of market response question, were (1) the availability of extensive pretest sales records, (2) immediate availability of test results, and (3) the ability to compare the purchases of households receiving a specific ad during the test, with their own purchases prior to the test as well with purchases of those who had not been exposed to the new product ad.

MARKETING DECISION SUPPORT SYSTEMS

A typical marketing manager regularly receives some or all of the following data: factory shipments or orders; syndicated aggregate (industry) data services; sales reports from the field sales force; consumer panel data; scanner data; demographic data and internal cost and budget data. These data may also come in various levels of detail and aggregation. Often they use different reporting periods and incompatible computer languages. Add to this sales estimates about competing brands and advertising, promotion and pricing activity and there is a data explosion.

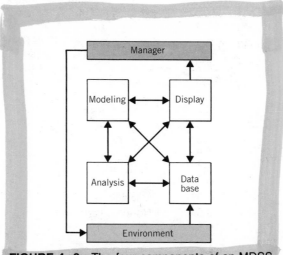

FIGURE 4–8 The four components of an MDSS

But managers don't want data. They need decision-relevant information in accessible and preferably graphic form for (1) routine comparisons of current performance against past trends on each of the key measures of effectiveness, (2) periodic exception reports to assess which sales territories or accounts have not matched their previous years purchases, and (3) special analyses to evaluate the sales impact of particular marketing programs, and to predict what would happen if changes were made. In addition different divisions would like to be linked to enable product managers, sales planners, market researchers, financial analysts and production schedulers to share information.

The purpose of a marketing decision support system (MDSS) is to combine marketing data from diverse sources into a single data base which line managers can enter interactively to quickly identify problems and obtain standard, periodic reports as well as answers to analytical questions. More specifically, an MDSS is assembled from the four components shown in Figure 4-8.[22]

The Data Base. This contains data from all the sources described in this chapter and others to come. It is stored in a sufficiently disaggregated way so that it can be analysed by product item, sales district, trade account and time period. The best systems have data bases that can be easily updated with new information and have sufficient flexibility that data can be readily analysed in new ways. Since most analyses deal with a subset of a larger data base the supporting software should permit random access to any and all data to create appropriate subsets.

Reports and Displays. The capabilities of an MDSS range from simple ad hoc tables and reports to complex plots, charts and other graphic displays. Any report or display can include calculations such as variances and running totals, or the results of statistical procedures found in the system. Typical reports produced with an MDSS include status

---

[22]The section adapted from a manual on Express EASYTRAC, published by Management Decision Systems, 1984.

Comparison Matrix
Issue 203 Ending 04.02.82

% Change in Category Sales vs Year Ago

	28.7		Memphis	9.8
	20.3		San Antonio	14.0
	13.3		Oklahoma City	10.5
	13.1		Cleveland	6.5
	12.8		Kansas City	9.3
	12.8		Detroit	4.1
	11.6		Cincinnati/Dayton	4.1
	10.9	Indianapolis 0.0		
	10.1		Houston	6.3
	9.6	Milwaukee −0.4		
	9.3	Norfolk/Richmond 0.9		
	9.3		Phoenix/Tucson	6.4
Above	9.3		Minneapolis/St. Paul	8.4
	8.5		Omaha/Des Moines	6.3
	8.5		St. Louis	12.1
	8.4	Pittsburgh −1.5		
	7.9		Buffalo	7.1
	7.8		New Orleans	7.7
	7.8	Albany/Schnectedy −4.5		
	7.8		New York	3.1
	7.1		Salt Lake City	11.1
	7.1		Boston/Providence	7.7
	7.0		Dallas/Ft. Worth	6.7
	6.6		Jacksonville/	7.8
	6.0	Syracuse 1.3		
	5.9		Charlotte	4.0
U.S. Avg	5.8			
	5.3		Portland	3.6
	4.8		Nashville/Knoxville	3.2
	4.6	Birmingham/Mobile −0.9		
	4.4		Denver	2.6
	3.9	Baltimore/Washington −3.1		
	2.9		Seattle/Tacoma	7.1
Below	2.7		Atlanta	10.1
	1.7	Miami −0.3		
	1.2	Chicago 1.3		
	0.3	Los Angeles/San Diego −0.2		
	−0.6	Philadelphia −4.7		
	−2.3	Raleigh/Greensboro −0.2		
	−5.2	San Francisco −9.6		

Below   2.0   Above

U.S. Avg

% Change in Mama Mia Sales vs Year Ago

FIGURE 4–9 Comparison of Brand Performance With Industry Trend

reports that track current trends, exception reports on troubled brands and markets, and variance reports showing budget and actuals for sales and profits. The report in Figure 4-9 answers the question: In which regions is the Mama Mia brand not keeping up with the industry trend? Figure 4–9 shows that the product category sales were up 5.8 percent whereas Mama Mia sales were up only 2.0%. On a more detailed level product category sales was up 13.1% in Cleveland and 1.7% in Miami while Mama Mia sales rose 6.5% in Cleveland and fell 0.3% in Miami.

Analysis Capabilities. These are used to relate the data to the models, as well as clarify relationships, identify exceptions, and suggest courses of action. These capabilities should include the ability to make calculations such as averages, lags and percentage changes versus a previous period, and conduct seasonal analyses and standard statistical procedures such as regression, correlation, and factor analysis. These procedures will be covered in subsequent chapters of this book.

Models. These represent assumptions about how the world works, and specifically how brand sales, shares, and profits respond to changes in elements of the marketing mix. Models are used to test alternative marketing programs, answer "what if" questions, and assist in the setting of more realistic objectives. For example, managers want help with such questions as: What is the impact on profitability of achieving wider distribution? What is the optimal call level for each sales representative for each account and prospect? What objectives should be set for coupon redemption and the profitability of promotion programs? The models used to address these questions can range from simple forecasts to complex simulations of relationships among marketing, economic and other factors.

SUMMARY

The theme of this chapter is the wealth of data available to the marketing researcher. Many problems can be resolved by recourse to internal records or such secondary records as government statistics, without undertaking the collection of original data. The key to successful usage of these sources is the development of an effective search procedure, coupled with a healthy skepticism of the accuracy and meaningfulness of what is found.

Between the generally available secondary sources (which are economic and quickly found but perhaps not relevant) and primary data (which is designed to be directly relevant but consumes considerable time and money) there are various standardized information services. These exist whenever there are economies of scale in collecting data for a number of users with similar information needs. Consumer panels and store audits were examined in detail because they are so widely used. Numerous other services exist to satisfy such common needs as media audience measurement, advertising testing (for planning the advertisements and then evaluating their effects), identifying specific industrial market opportunities, and appraising the progress and impact of new technologies.

The remainder of this book will emphasize the collection and analysis of primary data, for it is here that the greatest problems and opportunities are found. Knowledge of the methods of primary data collection is also essential to informed usage of secondary sources.

QUESTIONS AND PROBLEMS

1 You are opening a new retail store that will sell personal computers and software. What secondary data are available in your area to aid you in deciding where to locate the store? Would the same data be relevant to someone opening a convenience copying center?

2 How will the introduction of the universal product code and computerized store check-outs affect the market data available to the store manager? Will channel relationships be altered?

3 Of the three types of external sources, that is, secondary records, standardized data sources, and primary data sources, which is the most accurate? Are internal records more accurate than external sources? How can the accuracy of internal records be improved?

4 A large chain of building supply yards was aiming to grow at a rate of three new yards per year. From past experience this meant carefully reviewing as many as 20 or 30 possible locations. You have been assigned the task of making this process more systematic. The first step is to specify the types of secondary information that should be available for the market area of each location. The second step is to identify the possible sources of this information and appraise their usefulness.
From studies of the patrons of the present yards you know that 60 percent of the dollar volume is accounted for by building contractors and tradesmen. The rest of the volume is sold to farmers, householders, and hobbyists. However, the sales to do-it-yourselfers have been noticeably increasing. About 75 percent of the sales were lumber and building materials, although appliances, garden supplies, and home entertainment systems are expected to grow in importance.

5 Which of these two, a product audit (such as the Audits and Surveys National Market Audit) or a store audit (such as the Nielsen Retail Index), would be more suitable for the following products: (1) peanut butter, (2) cameras, (3) engine oil additives, (4) chewing gum? Why?

6 The manager of a supermarket in Hoboken, N.J. has two local newspapers competing for his weekly ads. The salesman for newspaper A claims that although his rates are significantly higher than paper B, he's got the best circulation in the market. Also, his readership studies show that area residents really scrutinize the paper's pages. The salesman for newspaper B concedes his publication doesn't have the widest circulation, but points to readership studies showing his ads are equally effective. "Why pay twice as much for an ad,'' he says, ''when my paper can do as strong a job for less money?'' This problem has been unresolved for some time. Recently the store has had nine scanner check-outs installed. The manager would like your advice on how to use the scanner sales data from his store to compare the effectiveness of the two newspapers.

APPENDIX
THE CENSUS AND OTHER
GOVERNMENT STATISTICS

This Appendix reviews the scope of four different classes of census conducted in the United States: Economic, Population, Housing and Government.

Economic Census

The Ecomomic Censuses are conducted every five years in years ending in 2 and 7.

Census of Agriculture. Based on the organization of the 1978 census, five volumes are published:

Volume 1: State and Country Data. Data is given on farms, farm characteristics and farm products.

Volume 2: Statistics by Subject. Reports on farms, tenure, farm expenditures, and other subjects

Volume 3: Agricultural Services

Volume 4: Irrigation

Volume 5: Special Reports

The U.S. Department of Agriculture publishes a considerable amount of data apart from the Census. In particular, its annual volume of *Agricultural Statistics* should be consulted for current sources.

Census of Construction Industries. Detailed data for each state on the operations of construction establishments. *The Industry Series* reports on 27 four-digit industries covering general contractors, land subdividers, and developers. *The Geographic Series* is arranged by state and MSA.

Census of Manufacturers. This is the principal source of data on the organization and operations of manufacturing industries in the U.S. *The Industry Series* reports information such as, the number and size of 452 SIC industries, shipments, detailed costs of production, inventories, value of fixed assets, capital expenditures, and value-added. *The Geographic Area Series* arranges similar statistics by MSAs, counties, and cities. *The Subject Series* reports on specific statistics, such as size of establishments, and concentration ratios in manufacturing.

Current information is compiled in the *Annual Survey of Manufacturers* and *Current Industrial Reports*.

Census of Mineral Industries. *The Industry Series* reports on similar statistics as the Census of Manufacturers for 42 mineral industries.

Census of Retail Trade. Four series are published:

1 *Geographic Area Series*: Statistics on 100 classifications of retail establishments, by geographic area and by subject.
2 *Industry Series*: Includes data on total sales, number of employees, payouts, number of establishments.
3 *Merchandise Line Sales Series*: Numbers of establishments handling the line, sales and other data by merchandise line.
4 *Major Retail Center Series*: Similar statistics arranged by central business district and major retail centers within each MSA.

Census of Service Industries. Statistics similar to the Census of Retail Trade, for 200 service industries including business, health, legal, educational services, museums, and recreation.

Census of Transportation. Covers data on passenger transportation, truck usage and bus carriers. Information is gathered in three surveys:

1 Truck Inventory and Use Surveys
2 1983 Commodity Transportation Survey
3 Selected Statistics for Transportation Industries

Census of Wholesale Trade. *Geographical Area Series* report on the structure and operations of wholesaling establishments. *The Industry Series* contain detailed data on sales, size of firm, legal form of organization, and other statistics.
A summary set of statistics, published as *Enterprise Statistics*, is compiled into a *General Report on Industrial Organizations* indicating the nature of structural changes in U.S. industrial organizations.

Population Census is conducted every ten years in the year ending in 0.

Reports the count of population by numerous geographical classifications: State, county, metropolitan area, urbanized area, incorporated, unincorporated places, and other civil divisions. General population, social and economic characteristics are described—sex, age, marital status, race, mobility, education, family composition, employment status, occupation, income and others. Specific subject and supplementary reports are also published.

More current, less detailed, statistics are compiled in *Current Population Reports*.

The Census of Housing is conducted every ten years in the year ending in 0. This report contains detailed housing and occupancy statistics, such as type, age, and size of structure, major appliances, sewage disposal, rent or mortgage, occupancy.
Five volumes are published:

Volume 1. Characteristics of housing units

Volume 2. Metropolitan housing characteristics

Volume 3. Subject reports

Volume 4. Components of inventory change

Volume 5. Residential finance

A joint enumeration with the Census of Population contains data by city block, census tracts, and governmental divisions. More recent statistics are published in *Current Housing Reports* and *Annual Housing Surveys*.

The Census of Governments is conducted every five years. It covers detailed data on the characteristics of state and local governments, employment by levels of government, payrolls, revenue and indebtedness of school districts and other governmental divisions.

Information in Government Statistics Many federal government agencies publish statistics monthly, quarterly, or annually. A complete index of government statistical publication is contained in the monthly *American Statistics Index*, found in large public or university libraries. A useful and more accessible reference is the *Statistical Abstract of the United States*, published annually by the U.S. Bureau of the Census. A brief list of other publications, (published M-Monthly or A-Annually) indicates the extent of current government statistics.

- *Business Conditions Digest* (**M**)
- *Bureau of Economic Analysis*
- *Economic Indication* (**M**)
- *U.S. Council of Economic Advisers*
- *Federal Reserve Bulletin* (**M**)
- *Board of Governors Federal Reserve System*
- *Handbook of Basic Economic Statistics* (*A*, with monthly supplements)

- *Economics Statistics Bureau.*
- *Monthly Labour Review* (**M**)
- *U.S. Bureau of Labour Statistics*
- *Survey of Current Business* (**M**)
- *Bureau of Economic Analysis*
- *U.S. Industrial Outlook* (A)
- *Bureau of Industrial Economics.*

CASE 4-1
Barkley Foods (A)

Joyce Stevenson, the manager of marketing research for Barkley Foods, had just left an emergency meeting with the firm's president. An opportunity to buy an established line of gourmet (high quality/high priced) frozen dinners had arisen. Because there were other interested buyers a decision had to be made within three or four weeks. This decision depended on judgments about the future prospects of the gourmet frozen dinner market and whether Barkley could achieve a competitive advantage. The marketing research group was asked to provide as much useful information as possible within a 10 day period. Although uncomfortable with the time pressure involved, Joyce was pleased that marketing had finally been asked to participate in the analysis of acquisition prospects. She had pressed for such participation and now she had to deliver.

Because of prior work on frozen fruit juices, Joyce had some knowledge of the gourmet frozen market. It was pioneered by Stouffer who introduced the "Lean Cuisine" line of entrees in 1981. Since then other firms have entered the industry with complete gourmet dinners (including Swanson's Le Menu and Armour's Dinner Classics). The distinction between entrees, dinners, and the three main types of food offered, conventional, ethnic (i.e. Benihana Restaurant Classics) or low-calorie (i.e. Weight Watchers or Light & Elegant) define relevant submarkets. Joyce hypothesized that the gourmet frozen food buyer differs from the buyer of conventional "TV dinners" in several respects. The gourmet frozen food buyers are generally young, upper

socioeconomic group people who probably have microwaves, are more health-conscious, and are likely to be working women and others who want the sophisticated cuisine, but lack the time to prepare it.

Barkley Foods was a diversified food company with sales of 2.3 billion dollars. Over 80 percent of its sales came from branded packaged food products sold nationally through grocery stores. Its largest product areas were canned tomato products, frozen orange juice, cake mixes, and yogurt. Barkley was known to have strengths in operations (product preparation), distribution (obtaining distribution and managing the shelves), and advertising. Their brands typically held a solid second place position in the supermarket. There was no effort at umbrella brand identification, so each product area was carried by its own brand.

Joyce Stevenson had previous been in strategic planning and reviewed the type of information and analysis that would be required to support a strategic decision like this one. She wrote down the following four sets of questions to guide the thinking of the research group:

1 Market Analysis
- What is the size, current growth rate, and projected growth rate, of the industry and its relevant subsets (such as ethnic dinners) for the next five and ten years?
- What are the important industry trends?
- What are the emerging production technologies?

- What are the distribution trends?
- What are current and future success factors (a competitive skill or asset needed to compete successfully)?

2 Environmental Analysis

- What demographic, cultural, economic, or governmental trends or events could create strategic threats or opportunities?
- What major environmental scenarios (plausible stories about the future) can be conceived?

3 Customer Analysis

- What are the major segments?
- What are their motivations and unmet needs?

4 Competitor Analysis

- Who are the existing and potential competitors?

- What are their current or forecasted levels of sales, market shares, and profits?
- What are their strengths and weakness?
- What strategies are they following, and how are they differentiating themselves in the market?

QUESTIONS FOR DISCUSSION

1 What secondary data sources would be useful? What types of questions might be answered by each?

2 Identify one piece of information from the library that would be helpful and relevant. How did you locate it?

3 What other mechanisms would you use to gather information?

CASE 4-2
Delisle Paper Products, Incorporated

Delisle Paper Products was a medium-sized manufacturer of branded products, principally paper towels, toilet paper, and table napkins. The vast majority of sales were through retail food outlets in major urban centers. For the past 15 years the company had subscribed to the A.C. Nielsen store audit service for detailed information on sales through retail food outlets. This policy was being questioned by a newly appointed vice-president of marketing who had come from a company with a similar product line. This company did not use the Nielsen service, but subscribed instead to a warehouse withdrawal service plus a diary panel to obtain the necessary market information. The director of marketing research for Delisle knew that during the next marketing committee meeting he would be called on to defend the suitability of the Nielsen service versus the alternatives that were more familiar to the new vice-president. As the review of the options proceeded the research director began to wonder whether the Nielsen service was superior, in view of the high costs relative to the alternatives. At the insistence of some members of the research group the review was expanded to include scanner-based audit services. After some initial

screening, it was decided to limit the consideration to the National Scanning Services audit, because they provided tracking information on more than 700 stores. The question was whether this could replace Nielsen, and if so whether it needed to be used in combination with other syndicated services.

The Delisle Paper Products company used a conventional marketing mix. Sales coverage was obtained with a full-time salesforce that called on chain-store buyers, managers of large independent supermarkets, and wholesalers. To support the direct sales effort the company spent heavily on media advertising and promotion. Included in promotional spending were coupons, in-store displays, trade deals, and cooperative advertising. Until three years ago the total communications budget had been equally divided between advertising and promotion. According to the marketing plan for the coming year promotion expenditures would be double the advertising budget. Some managers were questioning this shift in allocation, although admitting that the sales evidence seemed to favor spending more on promotion. The principal evidence on promotional effectiveness came from a series of studies on the shifts in retail sales and market shares recorded by the Nielsen audit before, during, and after a promotion.

The company's reliance on Nielsen store-audit data stemmed from (1) the richness of the information on distribution coverage; (2) the competitive information on prices, out-of-stocks, availability of special packages, and allocations of retail shelf space to individual brands; and (3) Nielsen's ability to separate the merchandise purchased regularly from that purchased during a promotion.

Store-audit data were not cheap. The annual cost of the basic A.C. Nielsen service for the major products sold by Delisle was more than $200,000 per year. This was almost 40 percent of the total marketing research budget for the company. By contrast, SAMI warehouse withdrawal data for the same products were available at a cost of $87,000 per year, the MRCA consumer panel would cost about $125,000 per year, and National Scanning Services would charge between $95,000 and $110,000 per year depending on the number of categories and store detail to be provided.

QUESTIONS FOR DISCUSSION

1 How are product movement data used in this organization?

2 Should the research director consider alternative methods for collecting product movement and market position data?

3 What would you recommend he do? What arguments should he use to the new vice-president?

CASE 4-3
Kerry Gold Products, Ltd.[23]

In late May of 1980, the research manager for Kerry Gold Products met with the product manager for margarine to review the company's first experience with Nielsen scanner data. A year-long test in a single chain organization, which began in April of 1979, had been completed recently.

The first purpose of their review was to interpret the findings. They decided to concentrate on the results

Brand	Share of Total Sales				Share of Sales in Nonpromotional Weeks	
	1st $\frac{1}{2}$ yr.		2nd $\frac{1}{2}$ yr.		1st $\frac{1}{2}$ yr.	2nd $\frac{1}{2}$ yr.
Kerry Gold	39%	(34%)[a]	13%	(7%)	18.9%	19.3%
B	17%	(8%)	42%	(35%)	30.4%	30.3%
C	29%	(13%)	28%	(18%)	33.1%	33.9%
D	15%	(11%)	17%	(12%)	17.6%	16.5%
	100%	(66%)	100%	(72%)	100%	100%

[a]Figures in parentheses are deal merchandise shares of market. In the first half of the year, 66 percent of total unit sales in the category were on deal.

[23]Source: Derek Bloom, "'The Renaissance of Retail Auditing," *Journal of Advertising Research*, 20 (June 1980), 9-17. Adopted with permission of the Advertising Research Foundation.

of the first 18 weeks of the tests, which are summarized in Figure 4-10. The size of the bars represents the weekly unit sales for Kerry Gold brand and the three competing brands also sold by the chain organization. In addition to the weekly data there were summary data on share of total sales for the first and second halves of the year. This distinction was important because Kerry Gold had

spent relatively little on promotion in the second half of the year. Since Nielsen had full records of all sales on deal, they were also able to examine their share of sales during weeks when no brands offered price-reduction promotions. These data are shown in the two right-hand columns in the preceding table.

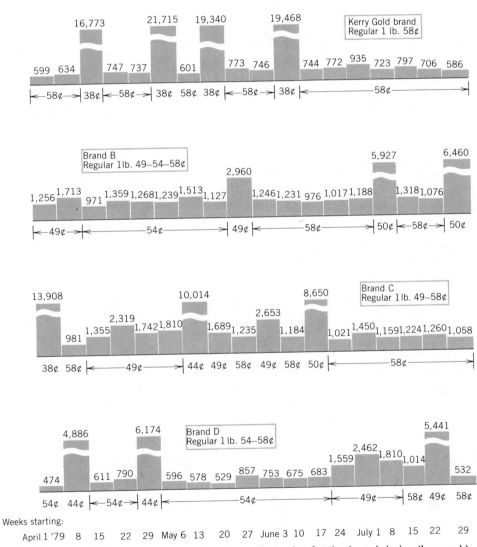

FIGURE 4–10 Unit sales per week (and prevailing price for the brand during the week)

While the research manager was reviewing these results he also was wondering whether scanner data would be useful for other grocery products sold by Kerry Gold. Many of them were as heavily promoted as margarine. Judgments on the desirability of consumer promotions for these products usually were based on a combination of store-audit data plus periodic controlled experiments.

5

INFORMATION COLLECTION: QUALITATIVE AND OBSERVATIONAL METHODS

This chapter shifts the focus from the utilization of already available secondary data to the collection of primary data for a specific purpose. Seldom, however, is enough known about a marketing problem or situation for the researcher to be able to proceed directly to the design of a structured study yielding representative and quantifiable results. Instead, the researcher needs to spend time getting *oriented* to the range and complexity of consumer activity and concerns, *clarifying* the problem, and *identifying* likely methodological problems.

A variety of qualitative methods can be used for such exploratory purposes. Specifically, we will discuss individual and group interviews and case studies. Within the category of qualitative methods are projective techniques that are used when self-reports are likely to be misleading. Although projective techniques are utilized during exploratory research, they also are used as a primary data-collection method.

Also in this chapter we will introduce observational methods. The observation of ongoing behavior is a widely used exploratory method, as well as an effective way to collect quantitative information when direct questioning is not possible.

QUALITATIVE RESEARCH METHODS

Collectively, these methods are *less structured* and *more intensive* than standardized questionnaire-based interviews. There is a longer, more flexible relationship with the respondent, so the resulting data have more depth and richness of context—which also means a greater potential for new insights and perspectives. The numbers of respondents are small and only partially representative of any target population, making them preludes to, but not substitutes for carefully structured, large-scale field studies.

There are three major categories[1] of acceptable uses of qualitative research methods:

Exploratory

—Defining problems more fully.

—Suggesting hypotheses to be tested in subsequent research.

—Generating new product or service concepts, problem solutions, lists of product features and so forth.

—Getting preliminary reactions to new product concepts.

—Pretesting structured questionnaires.

Orientation

—Learning the vantage point and vocabulary of the consumer.

—Educating the researcher to an unfamiliar environment: needs, satisfactions, usage situations and problems.

Clinical

—Gaining insights into topics that otherwise might be impossible to pursue with structured research methods.

The range of possible applications of these methods can be seen from the following examples:

- A telephone equipment supplier wanted to know what features to incorporate in an answering device located in a telephone substation (rather than in the home or office). From several group discussions came ideas for many features such as variable-length messages and accessibility from any telephone. Specific features and price expectations were tested in a subsequent survey.

- An advertising agency was asked to prepare a public information pamphlet on venereal disease, especially for teenagers. Group sessions were arranged in which teenagers discussed venereal disease in their own terms and pointed out areas of confusion. The questions and problems became the actual text for the pamphlet.[2]

- Before Beckman Instruments entered the process control equipment market it conducted four separate group interviews with instrumentation engineers. Participants came to the three-hour sessions in part because of the opportunity to talk with others in the field. Their complaints and comments about lack of readability of scales and unreliability of recording equipment were very influential in subsequent design decisions.[3]

---

[1]The implications of these differences are discussed in depth in Bobby Calder, "Focus Groups and the Nature of Qualitative Research," *Journal of Marketing Research* (August 1977) 353–364.

[2]Myril D. Axelrod, "Marketers Get an Eyeful When Focus Groups Expose Products, Ideas, Images, Ad Copy, etc. to Consumers," *Marketing News* (February 28, 1975) 6.

[3]"Beckman Gets Customers to Design Its Product," *Business Week,* August 17, 1974, 52.

- The Volvo automobile company wanted to undertake a study of the differences between buyers and those who considered but did not buy Volvos. The purpose of the research was to learn the *reasons* for buying and the *resistances* to buying a Volvo. During the exploratory work they found great differences among people in the way they considered Volvos, including talking with Volvo owners, reading articles in car magazines, paying more attention to Volvo advertisements, visiting a showroom, and negotiating over price. These actions became the basis for a series of questions in the field study.[4]

Individual In-Depth Interviews

There are two basic types of in-depth interviews.[5] They are **nondirective** and **semistructured**, and their differences lie in the amount of guidance provided by the interviewer.

Nondirective Interviews.   Here the respondent is given maximum freedom to respond, within the bounds of topics of interest to the interviewer. Success depends on: (1) the establishment of a relaxed and sympathetic relationship; (2) the ability to probe in order to clarify and elaborate interesting responses—without biasing the content of the responses; and (3) the skill of guiding the discussion back to the topic outline when digressions are unfruitful, always pursuing reasons behind the comments and answers. Such sessions are normally one to two hours long and may be tape recorded (always with the permission of the respondent) for later interpretation.

Semistructured or Focused Individual Interviews.   Here the interviewer attempts to cover a specific list of topics or subareas. The timing, exact wording, and time allocated to each question area are left to the discretion of the interviewer.

This mode of interviewing is especially effective with busy executives, technical experts, and thought leaders. Basic market intelligence, such as trends in technology, market demand, legislation, competitive activity, and similar information are amenable to such interviews. The open structure ensures that unexpected facts or attitudes can be pursued easily.

This type of interview is extremely demanding, and much depends on the skill of the interviewer. First the interviewer must be sufficiently persuasive to get through the shield of secretaries and receptionists around many executives, in order to get an appointment. The major challenge is to establish rapport and credibility in the early moments of the interview and then maintain that atmosphere. For this there is no substitute for an informed, authoritative person who can relate to respondents on their own terms. This can be achieved by asking the respondent to react to specific information provided by the interviewer. Care should be taken to avoid threatening questions. A good opener might be, ''If you

[4]Thomas D. Dupont, ''Exploratory Group Interviews in Consumer Research A Case Example,'' in Beverlee B. Anderson, ed., *Advances in Consumer Research,* vol. 3 (Chicago: Association for Consumer Research, 1976).

[5]Peter Sampson, ''Qualitative Research and Motivation Research,'' in Robert M. Worcester, *Consumer Market Research Handbook* (Maidenhead, England: McGraw-Hill, 1972), pp. 7–27.

had to pick one critical problem affecting your industry, what would it be?'' Cooperation sometimes can be improved by offering a *quid pro quo*, such as a summary of some of the study findings.

A difficult problem with these interviews is the matter of record-keeping.[6] Some executives dislike tape recorders, so it may be necessary to use a team of interviewers alternating the asking of questions and recording of responses. To keep the interview as short as possible it is usually best to leave behind a structured questionnaire for any specific data that are wanted, since this can be assigned to staff for answering. Finally, since the appropriate respondents for these studies are often difficult to identify—and may encompass many parts of an organization—it is always advisable to ask for recommendations regarding which other people it might be useful to interview.

Focus-Group Discussions

The emphasis in this method is on the results of *group interaction* when focused on a series of topics introduced by a discussion leader. Each participant in a group of five to nine or more persons is encouraged to express views on each topic and to elaborate or react to the views of the other participants. The objectives are similar to unstructured in-depth interviews, but the moderator plays a more passive role than does an interviewer.

The group discussion situation certainly offers more stimulation to the participants than an interview; presumably this makes new ideas and meaningful comments more likely.[7] Among other advantages it is claimed that discussions often provoke more spontaneity and candor than can be expected in an interview. Some proponents feel that the security of being in a crowd encourages some participants to speak out.

As a rule, three or four group sessions are usually sufficient. From the first discussion the analyst invariably learns a great deal. The second interview produces much more, but less is new. Usually by the third or fourth session much of what is said has been heard before and there is little to be gained from continuing.[8] The exceptions to this rule occur if there are distinct segments to cover, such as regional differences in tastes, the differences between wives working in the home and outside the home, or the differences between married or unmarried women.

A focus group is not an easy technique to employ. Further, a poorly conducted or analyzed focus group can yield very misleading results and waste a good deal of money. (In 1984, the recruitment costs, payments to participants, space rental, moderation, and analyst fees easily could exceed $1500 per focus group for consumer studies. The typical cost for an industrial focus group is approximately $3000.) The key success factors are

---

[6]This is a controversial question in any setting, but especially in executive interviews. For competing viewpoints, see P. H. Berent, ''The Depth Interview,'' *Journal of Advertising Research, 6* (June 1966), 32–39 and Aubrey Wilson, ''Industrial Marketing Research in Great Britian,'' *Journal of Marketing Research, 6* (February 1969), 15–27.

[7]A. E. Goldman, ''The Group Depth Interview,'' *Journal of Marketing, 26* (July 1962), 61–68.

[8]William D. Wells, ''Group Interviewing,'' in Robert Ferber, ed., *Handbook of Marketing Research* (New York: McGraw-Hill, 1974), pp. 2–138.

(1) planning the agenda, (2) recruiting participants, (3) effective moderation, and (4) analysis and interpretation of the results.[9]

Planning the Agenda.   This starts by translating the research purpose into a set of questions that will be asked of the research results. This ensures that client and moderator are in agreement on specific objectives before the study begins. From these questions the group moderator can prepare a topic outline. This serves as a checklist of the specific issues and topics to be covered; however, this list is strictly for general guidance as it is not desirable to have formal questions that are read to the group. As Wells notes, "it is far more important to listen perceptively to what participants are saying, than to emit a volley of questions."[10]

An important issue is the ordering of topics by the moderator. Usually it is desirable to proceed from a general discussion to increasingly specific questions, for if the specific issue is addressed first it will influence the general discussion. Further, it is easier for respondents to relate to a specific issue when it has been preceded by a general discussion. For example, Mother's Cookies was interested in concept testing a new fruit-filled cookie and a proposed introductory promotion involving tickets to a circus. The moderator started with a general discussion about snacks and then moved to the use of cookies as snacks and the question of buying versus making cookies. Only after this general discussion was the more specific topic addressed. As another example, Pacific Gas and Electric conducted a series of focus-group discussions to test the concept of automatically turning air conditioners on and off to conserve energy. They started with a discussion of the energy crisis, of things people had done to conserve energy, and their perceptions of government controls, before moving to the more specific topic.

The set of topics covered may change after each focus-group experience. The moderator and client may decide that a question is not generating useful, nonrepetitive information and drop it in the remaining focus groups. Or a new, interesting idea may emerge and reactions may be sought from subsequent groups.

Recruitment.   When *recruiting* participants it is necessary to provide for both similarity and contrast within a group. As a rule it is undesirable to combine participants from different social classes or stages in the life cycle, because of differences in perceptions, experiences, and verbal skills. Within an otherwise similar group some contrast in opinions can be achieved, for example, by including both users and nonusers of the product.

Moderation.   Effective *moderating* encourages all participants to discuss their feelings, anxieties, and frustrations as well as the depth of their convictions on issues relevant to

[9]This section is adapted from Wells, *op. cit.;* and Myril D. Axelrod, "Ten Essentials for Good Qualitative Research," *Marketing News,* March 14, 1975, 10–12.

[10]Wells, *op. cit.,* p. 2–140.

the topic, without being biased or pressured by the situation. The following are critical moderating skills:

- Ability to establish rapport quickly by listening carefully, demonstrating a genuine interest in the views of each participant, dressing like the participants, and avoiding the use of jargon or sophisticated terminology that may turn off the group.
- Flexibility, observed by implementing the interview agenda in a manner that the group finds comfortable. Slavish adherence to an agenda means the discussion loses spontaneity and degenerates into a question-and-answer session.
- Ability to sense when a topic has been exhausted or is becoming threatening and to know which new topic to introduce to maintain a smooth flow to the discussion.
- Ability to control group influences to avoid having a dominant individual or subgroup, which might suppress the total contribution.

Analysis and Interpretation of the Results. This is complicated by the wealth of disparate comments usually obtained, which means that any analyst can find something that agrees with their view of the problem. A useful report of a group session is one that captures the range of impressions and observations on each topic and interprets them in light of possible hypotheses for further testing. When reporting comments, it is not sufficient merely to repeat what was said without putting it into a context so the implications are more evident.

Several features of group interactions must be kept in mind during the analysis. An evaluation of a new concept by a group tends to be conservative; that is, it favors ideas that are easy to explain and therefore not very new. There are further problems with the order of presentation when several concepts, products, or advertisements are being evaluated. If group participants have been highly critical of one thing, they may compensate by being uncritical of the next.

Projective Techniques

These techniques often are used in conjunction with individual nondirective interviews. The central feature of all projective techniques is the presentation of an ambiguous, unstructured object, activity, or person that a respondent is asked to interpret and explain.[11] The more ambiguous the stimulus, the more the respondent has to project himself or herself into the task, thereby revealing hidden feelings and opinions.

Projective techniques are used when it is believed that respondents will not or cannot respond meaningfully to direct questions about (1) the *reasons* for certain behaviors or attitudes or (2) what the act of buying, owning, or using a product or service *means* to them. People may be unaware of their own feelings and opinions, unwilling to make

---

[11]Harold H. Kassarjian, ''Projective Methods,'' in Robert Ferber, ed., *Handbook of Marketing Research* (New York: McGraw-Hill, 1974), pp. 3–87.

admissions that reflect badly on their self-image (in which case they will offer rationalization or socially acceptable responses), or too polite to be critical to an interviewer.[12]

Originally, projective techniques were used in conjunction with clinical "motivation research" studies. One such study was done on Saran Wrap, a plastic food wrap, when it was first introduced. Because it was very clingy, it was effective in sealing food, but also quite difficult to handle. As a result, strong negative attitudes toward the product became evident. To clarify the reasons for this dislike a series of in-depth, nondirective clinical interviews was conducted. During the fifties, there were many homemakers who disliked and even hated their role of keeping house and cooking. At that time, prior to the resurgence of the women's movement, there was no acceptable outlet for this dislike among women. It could not be verbalized openly, and women were even inhibited from admitting it to themselves. The study concluded that many homemakers found an outlet for this dislike by transferring it upon Saran Wrap. The frustrations they had with the use of the product came to symbolize their frustrations with their role and lifestyle. As a result of the study, the product was made less clingy and nonkitchen uses were stressed.

The underlying assumption of the clinical approach is that people often cannot or will not verbalize their true motivations and attitudes. They may be embarrassed to reveal that they dislike cooking. Alternatively, they may have suppressed this dislike and may not even be conscious of it. They simply may believe that their dislike is caused by the plausible judgment that Saran Wrap is awkward to use. The difficulty with clinical research is that the true motivations are seldom clear. Indeed, two different clinical analysts working from different theoretical backgrounds may arrive at totally different interpretations. These problems eventually have brought considerable disrepute to motivation research. At present, this type of research is relegated to a distinctly secondary role; however, projective techniques for asking indirect questions, when direct questions may not provide valid answers, are used more extensively. The following categories of projective techniques will be discussed: (1) word association, (2) completion tests, (3) picture interpretation, (4) third-person techniques, and (5) role playing.

Word Association. Here the respondent is asked to give the first word or phrase that comes to mind after the researcher presents a word or phrase. The list of items used as stimuli should include a random mix of such neutral items as "chair," "sky," and "water," interspersed with the items of interest, such as "shopping downtown," "vacationing in Greece," or "Hamburger Helper." This technique has been particularly useful for obtaining reactions to potential brand names and advertising slogans. For example, Bell Telephone found that one theme for advertising, "The System Is the Solution," triggered negative, "big-brother-is-watching-you" reactions among some people.

Completion Tests. The simplest test involves giving a respondent an incomplete and ambiguous sentence, which he is asked to complete with a phrase. Again he is encouraged

---

[12]A. M. Oppenheim, *Questionnaire Design and Attitude Measurement* (London: Heinemann, 1966).

to respond with the first thought that comes to mind. Sentences are usually in the third person ("The average person considers television _____." "People drawing unemployment compensation are _____."), but may refer directly to the object or activity ("Insurance of all kinds is _____.") This test can be expanded readily to involve the completion of a story presented as an incomplete narrative or simply as a cartoon.

Picture Interpretation. This technique is based on the Thematic Apperception Test (TAT). The respondent is shown an ambiguous picture in the form of a line drawing, illustration, or photograph and asked to describe it. This is a very flexible technique, for the pictures can be adapted readily to many kinds of marketing problems.

Third-Person Techniques. By asking how friends, neighbors, or the average person would think or react in the situation, the researcher can observe, to some extent, the respondents projecting their own attitudes onto this third person, thus revealing more of their true feelings. Magazines successfully use this technique to identify the articles to feature on the cover to stimulate newsstand sales. Direct questioning as to the articles of greatest interest to the respondent tends to be confounded by socially desirable responses. For example, articles on complex issues of foreign affairs are rated highly interesting to the respondent during direct questioning, but are not thought to be of interest to the neighbors.

A variant of this technique provides a shopping list or a description of activities of a person and asks respondents to describe the person. The respondents' attitudes toward the activities or items on the list will be reflected in their descriptions of the person. Usually two lists are prepared and presented to matched sets of respondents; these could be grocery shopping lists in which all items are identical except that Nescafé instant coffee on the first list is replaced by Maxwell House (drip grind) coffee on the second list,[13] or the contents of a billfold which differ only in the inclusion of a Bank Americard in one list. Differences in the descriptions attributed to the two lists can be revealing of the underlying attitudes toward the product or activity that is being studied.

Role Playing. Here a respondent assumes the role or behavior of another person, such as a salesperson in a store. This person then can be asked to try to sell a product to consumers, who raise objections. The method of coping with objections may reveal the respondents' attitudes, if they project themselves fully into the role without feeling uncomfortable or embarrassed.

Another technique with similar expressive objectives is the "role rehearsal" procedure used as part of a focus-group discussion. The participants in a focus group are encouraged, by offering them an incentive, to alter their behavior pattern in some extreme way. Abelson

---

[13]This was the design of the classic study by Mason Haire, "Projective Techniques in Marketing Research," *Journal of Marketing, 14* (April 1950), 649–656. However, recent validation studies have found that differences in the two descriptions also are influenced by the relationship of the two test products to the items in the shopping list, so the interpretation is anything but straightforward. See also James C. Andersen, "The Validity of Haire's Shopping List Projective Technique," *Journal of Marketing, 15* (November 1978), 644–649.

describes a study in which housewives were asked to serve chicken to their families three times a week for a year, in return for $15.00 a week and an agreement to not tell the family about the arrangement.[14] The reaction of the participants to this offer, as they "rehearsed" the problems and objections they would likely encounter, gave useful insights into their attitudes toward chicken. This technique is used toward the end of the focus-group session, and respondents must be told that the offer was fictional when the exercise is finished.

Case Studies

A case study, in the research sense, is a comprehensive description and analysis of a single situation. The data for a case study is usually obtained from a series of lengthy, unstructured interviews with a number of people involved in the situation, perhaps combined with available secondary and internal data sources.

Case studies are very productive sources of research hypotheses. This approach was used by a food company to suggest the factors that might characterize successful district sales managers. A successful and an unsuccessful manager from otherwise similar territories (that is, the territories had similar market structure, potential, and competitive situations) were studied closely for two weeks. They were interviewed, observed during sales calls and trips with their salespeople, and given a series of personality tests. The differences were used to develop a series of surveys that were administered to all the managers.

There are circumstances where a case study may be the only way to understand a complex situation. For example, the decision-making processes in large organizations may be imperfectly understood by any single participant. This problem makes it difficult to understand the sequence of decisions leading to, for example, the choice of a telephone service that customers use to call for reservations or information or place purchase orders. A telecommunication manager simply may be a technical consultant on the telephone system for the using company and not know how the system is used in the business. The functional managers in marketing or operations may actually make the decision to offer the service to the customers but not know the intricacies of the switching network. To get a picture of the company's use of the service, all parties must be interviewed.

Limitations of Qualitative Methods

Most of the limitations of these methods stem from the susceptibility of the results to misuse, rather than from inherent shortcomings in the methods. There is a great temptation among many managers to accept small sample exploratory results as sufficient for their purposes because they are so compelling in their reality. Here are real consumers speaking directly about their reactions, dissatisfactions, and beliefs. The dangers in uncritical ac-

[14]Herbert Abelson, "A Role Rehearsal Technique for Exploratory Research," *Public Opinion Quarterly, 30* (1966), 302–305.

ceptance of the unstructured output from a focus group or brief series of informal interviews are twofold. First, the results are not necessarily representative of what would be found in the population and hence are not projectible. Second, there is typically a great deal of ambiguity in the results. The flexibility that is the hallmark of these methods gives the moderator or interviewer great latitude in directing the questions; similarly, an analyst with a particular point of view may interpret selectively the thoughts and comments to support that view. In view of these pitfalls, these methods should be used strictly for insights into the reality of the consumer perspective and to suggest hypotheses for further research.

OBSERVATIONAL METHODS[15]

Observation is limited to providing information on current behavior. Too often this limitation becomes an excuse for not considering observational methods, and the resulting lack of exposure of many researchers to these methods means they do not appreciate their considerable benefits. However, there are strong arguments for considering observation of ongoing behavior as an integral part of the research design. Some of these are:

- Casual observation is an important exploratory method. Managers continually monitor such variables as competitive prices and advertising activity, the length of lines of customers waiting for service, and the trade journals on executives' desks, to help to identify problems and opportunities.

- Systematic observation can be a useful *supplement* to other methods. During a personal interview the interviewer has the opportunity to note the type, conditon, and size of the residence, the race of the respondent, and the type of neighborhood with regard to mixed types and qualities of home and apartments. Seldom is this data source adequately exploited in surveys.

- Observation may be the *cheapest* and most *accurate* method of collecting purely behavioral data such as in-store traffic patterns or traffic passing a certain point on a highway system. Thus, people's adherence to pedestrian safety rules before and after a safety campaign can be measured most easily by counting the number of people who cross against the light or outside the sidewalks.

- Sometimes observation is the *only research alternative*. This is the case with physiological phenomena or with young children who cannot articulate their preferences or motives. Thus, the Fisher-Price Company operates a nursery school in a residential area as a means of field testing potential new toys.

[15]The analysis of secondary records, as discussed in the previous chapter, is an observational method. In this chapter, however, we are restricting ourselves to observation of ongoing behavior.

Direct Observation

This method is frequently used to obtain insights into search behavior and related issues, such as packaging effectiveness. One firm uses an observer, disguised as a shopper, to watch grocery store shoppers approach a product category, to measure how long they spend in the display area, and to see whether they have difficulty finding the product, whether the package is read, and if so, whether the information appeared hard to find.[16] This kind of observation can be highly *structured*—with a detailed recording form prepared in advance—or very *unstructured*. When making an unstructured observation the observer may be sent to mingle with customers in the store and look for activities that suggest service problems. This is a highly subjective task because the observer must select a few things to note and record in varying amounts of detail. This inevitably will draw subjective inferences from the observed behavior. For example, just what was meant by the frown on the face of the shopper waiting at a cash register?[17]

Regardless of how the observation is structured, it is desirable that the respondents not be aware of the observer. Once conscious of being observed, people may alter their behavior, but in very unpredictable ways. One-way mirrors, disguises, and cameras are some of the common solutions. Care should be taken, however, that there is not an invasion of privacy.

Contrived Observation

These methods can be thought of as behavioral projective tests; that is, the response of people placed in a contrived situation will reveal some aspects of their underlying beliefs, attitudes, and motives. Many direct-mail offers of new products or different kinds of books fall into this category, as do tests of variations in shelf space, product flavors, and display locations.[18] The ethics of such offers can be very dubious, as in the example where a manufacturer decides to produce a product only *after* receiving an acceptable number of orders from a direct-mail advertisement.

A variant of this method uses buying teams, disguised as customers, to find out what happens during the *normal* interaction between the customer and the retailer, bank, service department, or complaint department. This method has provided useful insights into the discriminatory treatment of minorities by retailers, and the quality of public performance by employees of government agencies, banks, and airlines. One is hard pressed to think of other ways of finding out about the knowledgeability, helpfulness in meeting customers' needs, and efficiency of the staff. Clouding this picture are some serious, unresolved questions of ethics.

[16]David A. Schwartz, "Research Can Help Solve Packaging Functional and Design Problems," *Marketing News* (January 16, 1976) 8.
[17]William D. Wells and Harry A. Lo Scuito, "Direct Observation of Purchasing Behavior," *Journal of Marketing Research* (August 1966) 227.
[18]Michael L. Ray, "Unobtrusive Marketing Research Techniques," in Gerald Zaltman and Philip D. Burger, *Marketing Research* (New York: Dryden Press, 1975).

Physical Trace Measures

This approach involves the recording of the natural "residue" of behavior. These measures are rarely used because they require a good deal of ingenuity and usually yield a very gross measure. When they work, however, they can be very useful.[19] For instance, (1) the consumption of alcohol in a town without liquor stores has been estimated from the number of empty bottles in the garbage; (2) an automobile dealer selected radio stations to carry his advertising by observing the most popular dial settings on the radios of cars brought in for servicing; (3) one magazine readership research method employs small glue spots in the gutter of each page spread of a magazine, so broken glue spots are used as evidence of exposure; and (4) a museum gauges the popularity of individual exhibits by measuring the rate of wear on the floor tiles in front of the exhibit and by the number of nose smudges on the glass of the case around the exhibit.

The home audit approach to purchase panels (described in Chapter 4) is yet another type of physical trace measure. The auditor describes the inventory in several prespecified categories. This method is not very useful if used on a one-shot basis, for it then requires a very tenuous assumption that possession is indicative of purchase and usage. However, if the inventory is made over an extended period and supplemented with a record of cartons and wrappers, an indication of rate of purchase is possible.

Behavior Recording Devices

Various devices have been developed to overcome particular deficiencies of human observers. The most obvious example is the *traffic counter*, which operates continuously without getting tired and consequently is cheaper and probably more accurate than humans. For the same reasons, as well as for unobtrusiveness, *cameras* may be used in place of human observers. Someone still has to interpret what is recorded on the film, but the option exists of sampling segments of the film, slowing the speed, or having another observer view it for an independent judgment.

There are certain situations where human observation is completely out of the question and a recording device is needed. A good example is the audimeter, described in the previous chapter, which records when radio and television are turned on and off and to which stations they are tuned. This device is placed very discreetly on the set and does not interfere with normal operation. Nonetheless, there is some doubt that families, who know they have an audimeter on their set, will follow their normal viewing and listening patterns. Departures from normal, to the extent they occur, probably will be most pronounced just after the unit is installed.

Some types of observation are beyond human capabilities. All physiological reactions fall into this category. Thus devices are available to measure changes in the rate of perspiration as a guide to emotional response to stimuli (the psychogalvanometer), and changes in the size of pupils of subjects' eyes which are presumed to indicate the degree

---

[19]For a fuller discussion see Eugene J. Webb, Donald T. Campbell, Richard D. Schwartz, and Lee Sechrest, *Unobtrusive Measures: Non-reactive Research in the Social Sciences* (Chicago: Rand-McNally, 1966).

of interest in the stimulus being viewed (the pupilometer). These devices can only be used in laboratory environments and often yield ambiguous results.

Recent experience with *eye movement* recorders has been more successful.[20] This device records the experience of viewing a picture of an advertisement, package, sign, or shelf display at a rate of 30 readings per second. The recorded eye movements show where in the picture the subject started to view, the order in which the elements of the image were examined and reexamined, and the amount of viewing time given each element. One application is to test the visual impact of alternative package designs.

Limitations of Observational Methods

The vast majority of research studies use some form of questionnaire. Observation methods, despite their many advantages, have one crucial limitation: They cannot observe motives, attitudes or intentions, which sharply reduces their diagnostic usefulness. To be sure, these cognitive factors are manifested in the observed behavior, but so are many other confounding factors. For example, the Zippo Lighter Company seemingly has a valuable measure of advertising effectiveness in the volume of their lighters sent in for repair. Despite the mention of the free repair privilege in the advertising, it is questionable whether such a measure can unambiguously test for impact.

Observation methods suffer other limitations as well. They are often more costly and time consuming and may yield biased results if there are sampling problems or significant observer subjectivity is involved. However, these biases are usually very different in character from those that affect obtrusive, questionnaire methods. This is one of the underexploited strengths of observation methods: They help to increase our confidence in questionnaire measures if they yield essentially similar results when used as a supplement.

SUMMARY

Exploratory research is an essential step in the development of a successful research study. In essence, this kind of research is insurance that major elements of the problem or important competing hypotheses will not be overlooked. It further ensures that both the manager and the researcher will see the market through the consumer's eyes. Fortunately, research design is an iterative and not a sequential process, so major initial oversights are not necessarily irreversible. In particular, the exploratory technique of semistructured interviews should be reemployed later when the structured study is pretested. Properly handled, a pretest should provide opportunities for respondents to express their frustrations with the specific questions, as well as identify deficiencies in the scope of the questions.

In this chapter we also discussed observational methods. These are useful during the

---

[20]Elliot Young, "Eye Movement Recorder Blows the Lid Off Past Tests of Print Ads, Packages and Other Marketing Materials," *Marketing News* (September 10, 1976) 3.

exploratory stage of the research design but are even more valuable as a data collection method. The advantages of observational methods will become even more apparent in the next chapter as we examine the errors that are inherent when an interviewer starts to interact with a respondent.

QUESTIONS AND PROBLEMS

1 What are the significant differences between nondirective and semistructured individual interviews? In what circumstances would a nondirective interview be more useful than a semistructured interview?

2 Motivation research is the branch of marketing research that relies heavily on projective techniques and nondirective individual interviews. What is the appropriate role of motivation research in marketing research? Is it a sufficiently powerful tool that marketers can be called "hidden persuaders" (as was done by Vance Packard in a popular book of the sixties)? What are the ethical problems with the use of motivation research techniques?

3 You have conducted two group meetings on the subject of telephone answering devices. In each group there were seven prospective users of such devices, and in the two groups there were four users of telephone answering services. (These services use an operator to intercept calls and record messages.) When the New Product Development Manager from the client heard the tapes and read the transcripts of the two meetings, his first reaction was, "I knew all along that the features I wanted to add to our existing model would be winners, and these people are just as enthusiastic. Let's not waste any more research effort on the question of which features are wanted." What do you say?

4 There have been a number of complaints in your city that minorities receive discriminatory treatment from local retailers of major appliances (with respect to prices, trade-ins, sales assistance, and credit). How would you use the techniques described in this chapter to study this question?

5 A local consumer organization is interested in the differences in food prices among major stores in the area. How should they proceed in order to obtain meaningful comparisons?

6 How could a political candidate use observational methods to determine the level of support for his or her candidacy in a forthcoming electon?

7 Toothpaste manufacturers have found consistently that if they ask for detailed information on the frequency that people brush their teeth, and then make minimal assumptions as to the quantity of toothpaste used on each occasion as well as spillage and failure to squeeze the tube empty, the result is a serious over-statement of toothpaste consumption. How would you explain this phenomena? Would it be possible to design a study to overcome these problems and obtain more accurate estimates of consumption? Describe how such a study would be conducted.

CASE 5–1

Mountain Bell Telephone Company[21]

Jim Martin, marketing research manager for Mountain Bell, studied the final research design for the hospital administrator study that had been prepared by Industrial Surveys, a marketing research firm in Denver. He realized that he needed to formulate some recommendations with respect to some very specific questions. Should individual personal interviewers be used as suggested by Industrial Surveys, or should a series of one to six focus-group interviews be used instead? Was the questionnaire satisfactory? Should individual questions be added, deleted, or modified? Should the flow be changed? Exactly who should be sampled, and what should the sample size be?

THE RESEARCH SETTING

About 20 field salespeople at Mountain Bell Telephone Company were involved in sales of communication equipment and services to the health care industry. Because of job rotations and reorganizations, few salespeople had been in their present positions for more than three years. They were expected to determine customer needs and problems and to design responsive communication systems. In addition, there was a health care industry manager, Andy Smyth, who had overall responsibility for the health care industry marketing effort at Mountain Bell, although none of the sales personnel reported directly to him. He prepared a marketing action plan and worked to see that it was implemented. The marketing action plan covered:

Sales objective by product and by segment

Sales training programs

Development of sales support materials and information

Andy Smyth was appointed only recently to his current position, although he had worked in the health care market for several years while with the Eastern Bell Telephone Company. Thus, he did have some first-hand knowledge of customer concerns. Further, there was an AT&T marketing plan for the health care industry which included an industry profile; however, it lacked the detailed information needed, especially at the local level. It also lacked current information as to competitive products and strategies.

Mountain Bell had long been a quasimonopoly, but during the past decade had seen vigorous aggressive competitors appear. Andy Smyth thought it imperative to learn exactly what competitive products were making inroads, in what applications, and the basis of their competitive appeal. He also felt the need for some objective in-depth information as to how major Mountain Bell customers in the health care industry perceived the company's product line and its salesforce. He hypothesized that the salesforce was generally weak in terms of understanding customers' communication needs and problems. He felt that such information would be particularly helpful in understanding customer concerns and in developing an effective sales training program. He hoped that the end result would be to make the salesforce more customer oriented and to increase revenues from the health care market.

While at Eastern Bell, Andy Smyth had precipitated a mail survey of hospital administrators that had been of some value. Several months before, he had approached Jim Martin with the idea of doing something similar at Mountain. Jim's reaction was that the questionnaire previously used was too general (i.e., one question was: What basic issues confront the health care area?) or too difficult to answer (How much do you budget monthly for telecommunications equipment or service? 0–$1,000; $1,000–$2,000; etc.) Further, he felt that in-depth individual interviews would be more fruitful. Thus, he contacted Industrial Surveys, which, after considerable discussion with both Jim and Andy, created the research design. They were guided by the following research objectives:

1 What are the awareness and usage levels of competitive telecommunications products by the hospital?

[21]This case was prepared by D. Aaker and J. Seydel as a basis for class discussion.

2 What is the perception of Mountain Bell's salesforce capabilities as compared to other telecommunications vendors?

3 What is the decision-making process as it pertains to the identification, selection, and purchase of telecommunications equipment?

4 What concerns/problems impact most directly upon the hospital's (department's) daily operations?

5 What are the perceived deficiencies and suggestions for improvement of work/information flow?

THE RESEARCH DESIGN

Field interviews will be conducted in seven Denver area hospitals with the hospital administrator and, where possible, with the financial officer and the telecommunications manager. A total of 14 interviews are planned. Interviews will be held by appointment, and each respondent will be probed relative to those questions that are most appropriate for his/her position and relevant to the study's overall objectives. The cost will be from $6,500 to $8,500, depending upon the time involved to complete the interviews. The questionnaire to be used follows:

A Awareness and Usage of Competitive Telecommunications Equipment

1 What departments presently use non-Bell voice communications equipment (paging, intercom, message recording, etc.)? What were the main considerations in selecting this equipment?

2 What departments use non-Bell data terminals (CRTS)? What are the major functions/activities that this equipment is used for? What were the main considerations in selecting this equipment?

3 How do you view the capabilities of Bell System voice-communications equipment to meet your operations needs?

4 How do you view the capabilities of Bell System data terminals to meet your records- and information-retrieval needs?

5 What do you feel are Mounatin Bell's main

strengths and/or weaknesses in meeting your hospital's overall telecommunications needs?

B Perceptions of the Mountain Bell Salesforce

1 What should a telecommunications specialist know about the hospital industry in order to adequately address your voice-communications and data-processing needs?

2 Have you ever worked with any Mountain Bell marketing people in terms of your communications needs? If so, how knowledgeable do you perceive the Mountain Bell salesforce to be with respect to both the health care industry and their telecommunications equipment? How do they compare to non-Bell vendors of such products?

C The Purchasing Decision

1 What is the standard procedure for selecting and authorizing a telecommunications purchase? Is this based primarily upon the dollar amount involved or type of technology?

2 Who has the greatest input on the telecommunications decision (department manager, administrator, physicians, etc.)?

3 What are the most important considerations in evaluating a potential telecommunications purchase (equipment price, cost-savings potential, available budget, etc.)?

4 What supplier information is most important in facilitating the purchasing decision? How effective has the Mountain Bell salesforce been in providing such information?

D Specification of the most important problems or concerns relating to effective hospital management.

1 What are the most important problems or concerns confronting you in managing the hospital?

2 What type of management data are required in order to deal effectively with these problems or concerns?

3 How are these data presently recorded, updated, and transmitted? How effective would you say your current Information Retrieval System is?

4 Do you have any dollar amount specifically budgeted for data or telecommunications improvements in 1979–1980? What specific information or communication functions are you most interested in upgrading?

E Achieving maximum utilization of hospital facilities.

   1 Do you experience any problems in obtaining accurate, up-to-date information on the availability of bed space, operating rooms, or lab services?

   2 Do you see _____ hospital as competing with other area hospitals or HMOs in the provision of health care services? If so, with which hospitals? Do you have a marketing plan to deal with this situation?

F Efficient Use of Labor Resources

   1 How variable is the typical daily departmental workload, and what factors most influence this variance?

   2 How do you document and forecast workload fluctuations? Is this done for each hospital department?

   3 To what extent (if any) do you use outside consulting firms to work with you in improving the delivery of hospital services?

G Reimbursement and Cash Flow

   1 Which insurer is the primary provider of funds? How is reimbursement made by the major insurers?

   2 What information do you need to verify the existence and type of insurance coverage when an individual is being processed for admission or outpatient hospital services? What, if any, problems are experienced in the verification and communication of insurance information?

CASE 5–2

U.S. Department of Energy (A)

Judy Ryerson, the head of the newly formed windmill power section of the U.S. Department of Energy, was considering what types of qualitative marketing research would be useful to address a host of research questions.

The U.S. Department of Energy was formed to deal with the national energy problem, which was considered by many to be the nation's most serious concern. One of its goals was to encourage the development of a variety of energy sources, including the use of windmill power. One difficulty was that almost nothing was known about the current use of windmill power and the public reaction to it as a power source. Before developing windmill power programs, it seemed prudent to address several research questions to obtain background information and to formulate testable hypotheses.

THE CURRENT USE OF WINDMILLS IN THE UNITED STATES

How many power generating windmills are there? Who owns them? What power generating performance is being achieved? What designs are being used? What applications are involved?

PUBLIC REACTION

What are the public attitudes to various power sources? How much premium would the public be willing to pay for windmill power sources, both in terms of money and in terms of "visual pollution"? What is the relative acceptance of six different windmill designs ranging from the "old Dutch windmill" design to an eggbeater design?

ASSIGNMENT

Design one or more qualitative research designs to address the research questions and to develop hypotheses for future testing. If focus-group interviews are considered, provide a set of questions to guide the moderator.

section B
Descriptive Research

6

INFORMATION FROM RESPONDENTS: SURVEY METHODS

The survey is the overwhelming choice of researchers for the collection of primary data. The methods already discussed—qualitative and observational research and secondary data analysis—are more likely to be used to improve or supplement the survey method than take its place.

The principal advantage of a survey is that it can collect a great deal of data about an individual respondent at one time. The data may include: (1) depth and extent of **knowledge;** (2) **attitudes,** interests, and opinions; (3) **behavior**—past, present, or intended; and (4) **classification variables,** such as demographic and socioeconomic measures of age, income, occupation, and place of residence. It is perhaps only stating the obvious to say that for most of these kinds of data the respondent is the only, or the best, source. The second advantage of this method is versatility; surveys can be employed in virtually any setting—whether among teenagers, old-age pensioners, or sailboat owners–and are adaptable to research objectives that necessitate either a descriptive or causal design.

These advantages are not easy to achieve. Effective implementation requires considerable judgment in choice of survey method, whether personal or telephone interview or mail questionnaire. There also are some distinct disadvantages to surveys, which stem from the social interaction of interviewer and respondent. Indeed, a survey cannot be developed or properly interpreted without a knowledge of the errors that may intrude into the data during this interaction. These are discussed in the next section as a prelude to the analysis of the methods of collecting survey data, the principal focus of this chapter.

SOURCES OF SURVEY INTERVIEW ERROR

The process by which respondents are questioned appears deceptively simple. The reality, however, is closer to Oppenheim's opinion that ". . . questioning people is more like

141

trying to catch a particularly elusive fish, by hopefully casting different kinds of bait at different depths, without knowing what is going on beneath the surface."[1]

The problem of getting meaningful results from the interview process stems from the need to satisfy reasonably the following conditions:

- Population has been defined correctly
- Sample is representative of the population
- Respondents selected to be interviewed are available and willing to cooperate
- Questions are understood by the respondents
- Respondents have the knowledge, opinions, attitudes, or facts required
- Respondents are willing and able to respond
- Interviewer correctly understands and records the response

These conditions often are not satisfied because of interviewer error, ambiguous interpretation of both questions and answers, and errors in formulating responses. These types of errors are shown in Figure 6–1, as filters or screens that distort both the question and response. Ambiguity is usually a consequence of poor question wording, which is covered in the next chapter. In this section, we will deal with the factors that influence prospective respondents' willingness to cooperate and provide accurate answers to whatever questions are asked.

Nonresponse Errors Due to Refusals

Refusal rates are highly variable. They can be as low as three to five percent of those contacted for a short interview on a street corner or at a bus stop, to 30 or 35 percent and higher for lengthy personal and telephone interviews or mail questionnaires, which are of little interest to most subjects. High refusal rates are a major source of error, for those who refuse to be interviewed are likely to be very different from those who cooperate.

Why Do People Cooperate? Although refusals are a growing problem, the vast majority of people remain willing to be interviewed. To understand the problem of refusals, we should start with the satisfactions and motives that can be tapped to insure a high level of participation. First and foremost, people are willing to be *helpful*, just out of friendliness, politeness, or a desire to help the interviewer do his job. Such willingness is increased substantially by an interest in the topic or a positive identification with the sponsor. Surprisingly, there is no evidence that the public's willingness to help is related to their opinions regarding the benefits of marketing research studies to the public.[2] Second, an

[1]A. N. Oppenheim, *Questionnaire Design and Attitude Measurement* (London: Heinemann, 1966).
[2]P. B. Hodgsen, "An Examination of Market Research's Public Image—Will the Public Continue to Cooperate?" *ESOMAR Proceedings,* 1972.

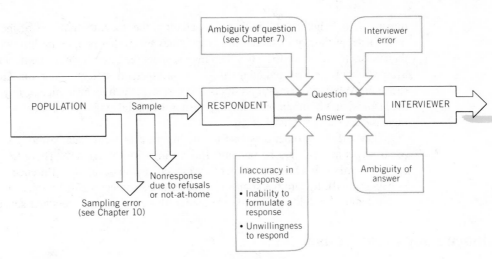

FIGURE 6–1   Sources of error in information from respondents

interview provides a chance for a *social interaction*.[3] For people who are lonely or bored it is a welcome break in the daily routine. For others it is an opportunity to share experiences with a sympathetic listener. Nor should we underestimate how flattering it is to be asked for one's opinion by an interested, attentive listener. Third, and less important, is *curiosity*. While most people have heard about polls and surveys, they may not know what is involved and will participate because it is a "novel experience." A 1980 telephone survey with 500 respondents found that 59 percent had been interviewed at some time in the past and 56 percent of those who had participated in a survey in the past year had done so more than once. This motive may be less significant in the future, and potential respondents might become antagonistic because of too-frequent impositions.[4]

Finally, some people will cooperate for a *reward* or a direct benefit. As we will see, this factor can have a big influence on mail-survey response rates. Thus far, it has not been necessary to pay people (with cash or gifts) to participate in one-time interviews. However, it is well accepted that participants in focus groups, members of diary panels, and so forth will be compensated for their effort. As surveys become more frequent—and less novel—respondents can be expected increasingly to ask, "What is in this for me?" Those who interview busy executives are already familiar with this problem.

Factors Contributing to Refusals.   The bond of trust and goodwill that is the ultimate basis for respondent cooperation is both subtle and fragile. Perhaps the greatest

---

[3]R. L. Kahn and C. F. Cannel, *The Dynamics of Interviewing* (New York: Wiley, 1967).

[4]Frank D. Walker, "Researchers Image Dips but Remains High among U.S. Consumers," *Marketing News* (June 12, 1981) 4. The proportion previously surveyed may be understated, for 41 percent of those contacted refused to participate in the survey.

threat is *fear*, whether of a potential assailant at the door, the motives of the interviewer, or the uses of the data.[5] Increasing crime rates mean that people are less willing to open their doors to any stranger. They also may suspect the interviewer of being a tax collector, a representative of a credit bureau, or a salesperson selling under the guise of doing research. Mention of certain products and services, such as insurance of any kind, books, magazines, and home improvements, during the initial stages of an interview will sharply increase the rate of refusal.

There are many other reasons for unwillingness to participate.[6] Among some segments of society a survey may be perceived as an invasion of privacy. There may be hostility either toward the interviewer (if there are evident and undesirable differences in personality or background), toward the sponsor, or toward the subject matter. Subjects such as death, sexual habits, or debts may generate anxiety because of their personal sensitivity.

Inaccuracy in Response

Respondents may be *unable* to give any response, or *unwilling* to give a complete and accurate response.

Inability to Respond. Respondents may not know the answer to a question because of ignorance, forgetting, or an inability to articulate. The last two problems are sources of error in their own right; however, all three problems create further errors when respondents contrive an answer because they don't want to admit they don't know the answer or because they want to please the interviewer.

Respondents are especially likely to be *ignorant*—in the sense of having never known the answer–when they are not qualified to answer. This may occur when a respondent is asked about the behavior or attitudes of other members of the household. Many housewives, for example, are not aware of the financial status of the family (such as insurance, investments, and benefits). In general, it is dangerous to assume that one person can speak for the rest of the household.

The likelihood of *forgetting* an episode such as a visit to a doctor, a purchase, an airplane trip, or an exposure to an advertisement depends on both the recency of occurrence and the importance of the event—as well as what else was happening at the same time.[7]

Ideally, questions should be asked only about recent behavior. This may mean as short a period as the past 24 hours in the case of something with as modest an impact as an advertising exposure.[8] If retrospective questions, going back a long period of time,

---

[5]George S. Day, ''The Threats to Marketing Research,'' *Journal of Marketing Research, 12* (November 1975), 462–467.

[6]Donald P. Warwick and Charles A. Lininger, *The Sample Survey: Theory and Practice* (New York: McGraw-Hill, 1975), and Frederick Wiseman and Mariane Schafer, ''If Respondents Won't Respond, Ask Nonrespondents Why,'' *Marketing News,* September 9, 1977, 8–9.

[7]Charles F. Cannel, Lois Oksenberg, and Jean M. Converse, ''Striving for Response Accuracy: Experiments in New Interviewing Techniques,'' *Journal of Marketing Research, 14* (August 1977), 306–315.

[8]One general interest magazine found that the recall of ads in its pages averaged 25.1 percent 24 hours after the respondent read the magazine, but this declined to 20.1 percent after 48 hours. Harper W. Boyd and Ralph L. Westfall, *Marketing Research,* New York: Richard D. Irwin, 1972.

are required, the accuracy of recall can be improved by questioning the respondent about the context in which an event occurred. If one is interested in the choice of credit source used to pay for a major appliance, it may be necessary to ask also about the choice of retail outlets and the reasons for the purchase in order to get a full picture. The caveat about limiting questions to recent behavior also implies that questions that ask respondents to generalize about their behavior over long periods of time are likely to be inaccurate. When asked to state the frequency of engaging in leisure-time activities such as golf, swimming, and tennis, it appears that people respond in terms of their most recent behavior. For this reason it is preferable to ask about specific occasions of an activity.[9]

Memories also may be sharpened by aided recall techniques. These attempt to stimulate recall with specific cues, such as copies of magazines, pictures, or lists. In a study of consumer expenditures the unaided recall question might be, "What groceries did you buy this week?" and the aided recall counterpart might be, "Did you buy any frozen corn?" While aided recall reports always uncover more activity, they are not necessarily more accurate. It is essential to keep in mind that most respondents want to be cooperative; when in doubt they prefer to give too much rather than too little information. Memory distortions compound this source of error by **telescoping** time, so that an event is remembered as occurring more recently than it actually did.[10]

Finally, respondents may be unable to respond because they cannot *formulate* an adequate answer. This is especially true of direct questions about motivations. Many choice decisions are made without conscious consideration of the reasons. So when someone is asked why they responded to a charitable appeal, bought a particular brand of analgesics, or watched a certain television program, the reasons that are given are likely to be incomplete and superficial. Worse, they may represent a respondent's guess as to a conveniently acceptable answer. There may be respondents with thoughtful and complete answers, but it is difficult to know how many respond this way. One alternative is to use indirect methods such as the projective techniques described in the previous chapter.

Unwillingness to Respond Accurately.   During the interview a number of biasing factors may come into play to subvert the positive motivations that were present when the respondent agreed to participate. Questionnaires that are lengthy and boring are especially vulnerable to these biases, a fact that too often is forgotten by researchers who succumb to the temptation to ask "just one more question" because the results may be interesting.

1   *Concern about invasion of privacy.* While most respondents don't regard a survey, as such, as an invasion of privacy, their tolerance may not extend to detailed personal questions. As many as 20 percent of the respondents in a telephone or personal interview survey may refuse to answer an income question, while others may distort their answer. In their view such a question is not appropriate from someone they don't

---

[9]Lester Frankel, "The Design of Leisure Time Activity Studies," *ESOMAR Proceedings,* 1973, 213–227.
[10]Seymour Sudman and Norman M. Bradburn, "Effects of Time and Memory Factors on Response in Surveys", *Journal of the American Statistical Association, 68* (December 1973), 805–815.

know, who could conceivably misuse the answer. To some extent assurances of confidentiality and full explanations of the need for the data will reduce this problem.

2 *Time pressure and fatigue.* As a lengthy interview proceeds the accuracy of responses is bound to decline. Those respondents who initially were reluctant to participate because they were busy become anxious about the time that seems to be required. Not surprisingly, they may decide that giving abrupt answers and avoiding requests for clarification are the best ways to terminate the interview quickly. Even those who willingly and fully respond to all questions will become fatigued eventually if the interview is too long (length, of course, is very subjective—a dull 20-minute personal interview may seem longer than an imaginative 45-minute personal interview on a topic of interest). The resulting bias is most likely random, but is sometimes in a consistent direction if the respondent decides to retaliate by grouping all answers about some point on a scale.[11]

3 *Prestige seeking and social desirability response bias.* Here we begin to see the consequences of the interview as a process of social interaction. There is mounting evidence that respondents will distort their answers in ways that (they believe) will enhance their prestige in the eyes of the interviewer and will not put them at variance with their perception of the prevailing norms of society. Consequently, questions that have implications for prestige—such as income, education, time spent reading newspapers, tastes in food, or even place of residence—may be biased subtly in ways that reflect well on the respondent. In deference to what is socially desirable, respondents may subordinate their own attitudes or be reluctant to mention inappropriate behaviors, such as abusing the health delivery system, violating sexual codes, or misusing alcoholic beverages.

4 *Courtesy bias.* There is a general tendency to limit answers to pleasantries that will cause little discomfort or embarrassment to the interviewer, or to avoid appearing uncooperative. We have seen already how this bias can inflate responses to aided recall questions. It also is encountered in concept-testing situations when a respondent gives a "courtesy endorsement" to the description of a new idea, even though he or she may have little interest in the idea.[12]

5 *Uninformed response error.* Simply asking someone a question implies that the questioner expects the respondent to have an answer. This expectation, plus a desire to appear cooperative, may induce respondents to answer a question despite a complete lack of knowledge about the topic. When a sample of the general public was asked a question about a fictitious organization, the National Bureau of Consumer Complaints, an astonishing 75 percent of those who returned the questionnaire expressed an opinion about the effectiveness of the organization in obtaining relief for consumers.[13]

[11]James Hulbert and Donald R. Lehmann, "Reducing Error in Question and Scale Design: A Conceptual Framework," *Decision Sciences, 6* (January 1975), 166–173.

[12]Bill Iuso, "Concept Testing: An Appropriate Approach," *Journal of Marketing Research, 12* (May 1975), 228–231.

[13]Del I. Hawkins and Kenneth A. Coney, "Uninformed Response Error in Survey Research," *Journal of Marketing Research, 13* (August 1981), 370–374.

6 *Response style*. Evaluative questions requiring a good–bad, positive–negative judgment are afflicted by systematic tendencies of certain respondents to select particular categories of response regardless of the content of the question. For example, there is an acquiescence response set, which is the tendency to favor affirmative over negative responses. This is different from ''yeasaying,'' which is a tendency to give exaggerated responses; that is, good becomes very good and bad becomes very bad. For example. Wells found that yeasayers consistently gave higher ratings to favorably evaluated advertisements and were more likely to exaggerate self-reports of product purchases.[14]

Interviewer Error

Interviewers vary enormously in personal characteristics, amount of previous experience, style of interviewing, and motivation to do a thorough job. There don't seem to be any

"That's the worst set of opinions I've heard in my entire life."

Drawing by Weber; © 1975. The New Yorker Magazine, Inc.

[14]William D. Wells, ''The Influence of Yeasaying Response Style,'' *Journal of Advertising Research, 1* (June 1963), 8–18.

consistently useful personality or other characteristics that can be used to identify good interviewers, other than the obvious fact that minimum levels of education, intelligence, and social skills must be present. The biggest influence on the kinds of people that are attracted is the nature of the job: it is part-time work, often in the evenings, for compensation that is close to the minimum wage; and it is usually loosely supervised. The differences among interviewers also mean a great deal of variability in the way interviews are conducted; these are a particularly serious source of error in personal interviews. These errors arise from the impression the respondent has of the interviewer, as well as the way the interviewer asks questions, follows up partial answers, and records the responses.

The Respondent's Impression of the Interviewer. For most respondents a personal interview is a sufficiently novel experience that they have little knowledge and few expectations to help guide their reaction. Therefore, the interviewer becomes a major source of clues as to appropriate behavior. Subtle signs of approval, pleasure, encouragement, or hostility become important. At the outset, the interviewer must be seen as a person who is capable of understanding the respondent's point of view, and of doing so without rejecting his opinion.[15] This kind of rapport is most likely to be established quickly when respondent and interviewer share basic characteristics such as sex, age, race, and social class.

The attitudes the interviewer reveals to the respondent during the interview can have a great effect on the level of interest and willingness to answer openly. Especially important is the sense of assurance and ease with the task. If the interviewer is apologetic about the study, fumbles with the questionnaire, overexplains the purpose of the questions, and generally seems uneasy with the task, the respondent will be disturbed and uncomfortable. Communication will be inhibited further if the interviewer appears flippant or bored or fails to express interest, constantly interrupts the person when speaking, or is too immersed in notetaking to look up.[16] Obviously, proper selection coupled with good training can reduce many of these problems.

Questioning, Probing, and Recording. The way an interviewer asks a question and follows up by probing for further details and clarification will be colored by (1) the interviewer's own feelings about the "appropriate" answer to the questions and (2) expectations about the kind of answers that "fit" the respondent. For example, when interviewing a person with limited education, the interviewer might shift unconsciously from a question worded, "Have any of your children attended college?" to "I don't imagine any of your children have gone to college, have they?" In one study it was found that, in response to a question on sources of advice on financial problems, one interviewer

---

[15]Kahn and Cannel, *op. cit.*
[16]Warwick and Lininger, *op. cit.*, pp. 198, 203.

obtained eight percent saying they solved the problem themselves, while another interviewer obtained 92 percent choosing this option.[17]

Perhaps the most common interviewer error is insufficient probing. The respondent may not be expected to have much to say about the subject or may have given an answer that the interviewer thinks is "right." One study found that this error occurred in 52 percent of the instances.[18] Furthermore, interviewer expectations will influence both what is "heard"–especially if the answer is long and rambling—and the phrases and ideas that are selected for recording.

Fraud and Deceit.   Modest interviewer compensation and the problems of monitoring the activities of personal interviewers out in the field, or telephone interviewers calling from their home, provide ample incentive for cheating. This may be as serious as outright fabrication of an entire interview or judicious filling in of certain information that was not obtained during the interview. It also may occur in the respondent selection process. Because it is such a serious potential source of error, most commercial research firms validate 10 to 15 percent of the completed interviews. This entails reinterviewing a sample of those who were reported to have been interviewed, to verify that an interview actually took place and that the questions were asked. Some indication of the extent of the problem comes from the experience of the Advertising Research Foundation (ARF), which conducts validations for member firms on request. During 1972 and 1973 the ARF found that 5.4 percent of the interviews in 33 separate studies could not be verified. An additional 7.9 percent contained at least two performance errors. The results are especially disturbing because it is generally believed that the surveys submitted for validation are among the best that are executed in the advertising field.[19]

Conclusions

The array of problems and sources of error, summarized in Table 6–1, have the greatest effect on the personal interview method. Some can be lived with and others can be compensated for during the interpretation of the results. The best solution by far is to minimize the problems by proper recruiting, selecting, training, motivation, and control of interviewers. This is a large and complex topic, which is often given only lip service by harassed project directors and field supervisors intent on meeting deadlines and living with tight budgets. Yet the potential is enormous.[20]

[17]J. Freeman and E. W. Butler, "Some Sources of Interviewer Variance in Surveys," *Public Opinion Quarterly,* Spring 1976, 84–85.

[18]Herbert Hyman, William J. Cobb, Jacob J. Feldman, Clyde W. Hart, and Charles Stembler, *Interviewing in Social Research* (Chicago: University of Chicago Press, 1954).

[19]Benjamin Lipstein, "In Defense of Small Samples," *Journal of Advertising Research, 15* (February 1975), 33–40.

[20]Good discussions of what can be found in Warwick and Lininger, *op. cit.;* Seymour Sudman, *Reducing the Cost of Surveys* (Chicago: Aldine, 1967); and Robert Ferber, ed., *Handbook of Marketing Research* (New York: McGraw-Hill, 1974), pp. 2.124–2.132, 2.147–2.159.

TABLE 6–1
Sources of Error in Interview Surveys

1. *Nonresponse errors due to refusals*
   (a) Fear of the consequences of participation
   (b) Resentment of an invasion of privacy
   (c) Anxiety about the subject
2. *Inaccuracy in responses*
   (a) Inability to give a response
       i. Ignorance of the answer
       ii. Forgetting
       iii. Problems in formulating an answer
   (b) Unwillingness to respond accurately
       i. Concern about invasion of privacy
       ii. Time pressure and fatigue
       iii. Desire to enhance prestige
       iv. Desire to appear cooperative
       v. Biased response style
3. *Errors caused by interviewers*
   (a) Provision of clues as to "appropriate" responses
   (b) Inadequate questioning and probing
   (c) Fraud and deceit

While other methods of data collection are less prone to interview error, they have offsetting problems, as we will see in the following section.

METHODS OF DATA COLLECTION

The choice of data collection method is a critical point in the research process. The decision is seldom easy, for there are many factors to be considered and many variations of the three basic methods of (1) personal interview, (2) telephone interview, and (3) mail survey. In this section, we will look at the advantages and limitations of the three basic methods, and such variants as the mail panel, the omnibus personal and mail interview, and combinations of methods. The following factors will be used to evaluate the methods:

1 Accuracy (absence of systematic interviewer error or response bias)

2 Amount of data that can be collected (how much time and effort can be reasonably expected from each respondent)

3 Flexibility (potential for employing a variety of questioning techniques)

4 Sample bias (ability to draw a representative sample and obtain cooperation)

5 Direct cost per completed interview

6 Speed (elapsed time from the start to completion of data collection in the field)

7 Administrative problems (such as recruiting, training, supervising, auditing, and controlling)

Because each research problem will have a different ranking of the importance of these factors, and no data collection method is consistently superior on all factors, few generalizations can be made. Much depends on the skill of the researcher in adapting the method to the circumstances. Overall, however, the telephone is the dominant method for conducting surveys. By 1983, it was estimated that 40 to 45 percent of all interviews were done by telephone.[21] Door-to-door personal interviews accounted for approximately ten percent; 20 to 25 percent were done at shopping centers and central location facilities; and 25 to 30 percent were mail surveys.

Personal Interviewing

Advantages. An interviewer, face to face with a respondent, can do a great deal to arouse initial interest and thereby increase the rate of participation and establish continuing rapport. To reduce the likelihood of a respondent refusing to finish the interview with an interviewer, it is also feasible to ask complex questions and enhance their meaning with pictorial and mechanical aids, clarify misunderstandings, and probe for more complete answers. For these reasons the personal interview is usually preferred when a large *amount* of information is required and the questions are complex or involve tasks such as sorting cards into ordered piles or evaluating visual cues such as pictures of product concepts or mock-ups of advertisements.

The personal interview questionnaire has a high degree of *flexibility*. Questions can be asked in a variety of sequences which might depend on the characteristics of the respondent or previous answers. For example, if the answer to "Have you ever heard of (a COMMUNITY AGENCY)?" is "yes," then ask questions A and B, but if the answer is "no" go to the next agency. Additional flexibility comes because the interviewer can observe both overtly (for example, asking to see certain records or inspect the medicine cabinet) or covertly (to note the respondent's ethnicity, quality of furnishings, neighborhood, and so forth).

Generalizations about the **accuracy** of personal interview responses are hazardous. On one hand, interviewer probes and clarifications maximize respondent understanding and yield complete answers, especially to open-ended questions. Possibly offsetting these advantages are the problems of prestige seeking, social desirability, and courtesy biases discussed earlier. In relative terms it seems that for questions about neutral topics, all three methods are equally satisfactory, while for embarrassing topics the personal interview is at a disadvantage.

[21]Frank Walker, "From the Respondent's Viewpoint: Evaluating Survey Research," in Frederick Wiseman, *Improving Data Quality in Sample Surveys* (Cambridge, MA: Marketing Science Institute, 1983).

TABLE 6–2

Comparative Indices of Direct Costs per Completed Interview (including travel and telephone charges, interviewer compensation, training, and direct supervision expenses)

Data Collection Method	Index of Cost[a]
1. Mail survey (costs depend on return rate, incentives, and follow-up procedure)	0.3–0.8
2. Telephone interviews	
(a) 7-minute interview with head of household in metropolitan area	0.5–0.8
(b) 15-minute interview with small segment of national population from a central station	1.3–1.7
3. Personal interviews	
(a) 10-minute personal interview in middle-class suburban area (2 call-backs and 10 percent validation)	1.5–1.8
(b) 40- to 60-minute interview of national probability sample (3 call-backs and 10 percent validation)	2.5–3.5
(c) Executive (VIP) interviews	4.0–15.0+

[a]In 1985, an index value of 1.0 corresponded to a cost of $14.00.

Finally, there is an advantage to having a personal interviewer when an explicit or current list of households or individuals is not available. The interviewer can be assigned to specific census tracts, blocks, or residences as defined by census data. Once a residence is chosen, the researcher can control who is interviewed and how much assistance is obtained from others in the household.

Limitations. Personal interview studies are time consuming, administratively difficult, and costly. The *time requirements* are understandable in light of the need to travel between interviews, set up appointments, and perhaps schedule return visits to complete interrupted interviews. Only 30 to 40 percent of an interviewer's time on the job is devoted to interviewing itself.[22] One can use more interviewers to reduce the elapsed time, but then problems of quality control increase. Because of the time and administrative problems the *cost per completed personal interview* tends to be higher than for mail or telephone surveys. Direct comparisons of the costs of different methods are difficult, in part because of the wide variability in the implementation of each method. However, Table 6–2 provides some approximate indices of the *direct cost* of a completed interview, to help compare data collection methods. In 1985 an index value of 1.0 corresponded to a cost of $14.00. Thus, in 1985, one could expect a 7-minute telephone interview with a head of household

[22]Sudman, *Reducing the Costs of Surveys, op. cit.*

in a metropolitan area to cost between $7.00 (0.5 × $14.00) and $11.20 (0.8 × $14.00). This cost assumes the study was conducted by a commercial research supplier. A nonprofit organization could reduce this cost substantially by using students or volunteers, getting donated use of telephones (for example, on the weekend or during evenings at the donor's office), and (in the United States) using low, nonprofit organization mailing rates.

Until recently, it was thought that the personal interview method was always the best way to reduce nonresponse bias from refusals and not-at-homes. Interviewers can track down hard-to-find respondents and minimize refusals by being physically present at the door and exerting charm, flattery, and enthusiasm. Unfortunately, the costs of the call-backs needed to achieve high response rates are becoming excessive. This is especially a problem in the inner-city areas, which interviewers are reluctant to visit and may refuse to enter at night even though they work in teams.[23]

Shopping center interviews are a popular solution when funds are limited, and the respondent must see, feel, or taste something. They often are called shopping mall *intercept* surveys, in recognition of the interviewing procedures. Interviewers, stationed at entrances or selected locations in a mall, randomly approach respondents and either question them at that location or invite them to be interviewed at a special facility in the mall. These facilities have equipment that is adaptable to virtually any demonstration requirement, including

- Interview rooms and booths
- Kitchens with food preparation areas
- Conference rooms for focus groups
- Closed-circuit television and sound systems
- Monitoring systems with one-way mirrors
- On-line video-screen interviewing terminals

Since interviewers don't travel and respondents are plentiful, survey costs are low. However, shopping center users are not representative of the general population, visit the center with different frequencies, and shop at different stores within the center.[24] These problems can be minimized with the special sampling procedures described in Chapter 10.

Omnibus surveys are regularly scheduled (weekly, monthly, or quarterly) personal interview surveys with questions provided by a number of separate clients. Within each questionnaire there could be sequences of questions on topics ranging from the market for fiber tip pens and wood paneling, attitudes toward double-knit fabrics, and the effect of a cut in federal withholding taxes upon spending and saving.

There are impressive advantages to the omnibus approach whenever only a limited

[23]Eugene Telser, "Data Exorcises Bias in Phone vs. Personal Interview Debate," *Marketing News,* Sept. 10, 1976.

[24]Seymour Sudman, "Improving the Quality of Shopping Center Sampling," *Journal of Marketing Research, 17* (November 1980), 423–431.

number of personal interview questions is needed. The total costs are minimized since the rates are based on the number of questions to be asked and tabulated. The results are available quickly because all the steps are standardized and scheduled in advance. The regularity of the interview schedule and the assurance that the independent samples are matched make this a suitable base for continuous ''tracking'' studies and before–after studies. Some omnibus operators offer split-run facilities, so that half of the sample receives one stimulus (one version of a question or concept) and the other matched half gets another version. Also, by accumulating over several waves of interviews it is possible to conduct studies of low-incidence activities such as the extent of salt-free diets and shortwave transmitter ownership.

Telephone Interviewing

The telephone gradually has become the dominant method for obtaining information from large samples, as the cost and nonresponse problems of personal interviews have become more acute. At the same time, many of the accepted limitations of telephone interviewing have been shown to be of little significance for a large class of marketing problems.

Advantages.   Telephone interviews may be conducted either from a central location, at prescribed hours under close supervision, or from the interviewer's home, unsupervised and at their own hours. The former is preferred because problems can be isolated quickly and greater uniformity is possible.[25] Supervisors can double-record interviews by listening on an extension and gradually weed out incompetent interviewers. A competent, full-time staff is also easier to retain, for the morale-sapping isolation of the interviewer in the field is not a factor.

Regardless of how the telephone interviews are conducted, the obvious advantages are the same: (1) more interviews can be conducted in a given time period, because no time is lost in traveling and locating respondents; (2) more hours of the day are productive—especially the evening hours when working women and singles are likely to be at home and apartment doors are locked; and (3) repeated call-backs at different times of the day can be made at very low cost. At one time, mileage costs were less than telephone costs. This is no longer the case in many metropolitan areas, and is definitely not so for national or regional surveys. The key to the low costs for the latter surveys is the Wide Area Telephone Service (WATS), which provides unlimited calls to a given zone in Canada or the United States for a fixed monthly charge.

Overall, the telephone method dominates the personal interview with respect to *speed, absence of administrative problems,* and *cost per completed interview.* As we saw in Table 6–1, the costs of a telephone survey seldom will exceed two-thirds of the comparable

---

[25]Joseph O. Eastlack and Henry Assael, ''Better Telephone Surveys through Centralized Interviewing,'' *Journal of Advertising Research, 6* (March 1966), 2–7.

costs for a personal interview.[26] Costs can be reduced further with omnibus surveys. In 1985 four closed-end questions could be asked of a national probability sample of 1000 adults for $2800. This cost included results tabulated by major demographic variables. The advantages are the same as for personal interview omnibus surveys.

For better or worse the telephone is an "irresistible intruder."[27] A ringing telephone literally compels us to answer. Long-distance calling brings a further dimension of urgency and importance to reaching the desired respondent. (This tends to counteract the fact that it is easier for a person to terminate midway through a telephone interview.) The telephone is a particularly effective method for gaining access to hard-to-reach people such as busy executives. The receptionist who thwarts the personal interviewer will readily connect a telephone interview request. Thus, Payne found that 94 percent of the interviews attempted with responsible persons in the 600 largest companies were successfully completed.[28] In this case the responsible person could be identified readily by title. Often this is not so easy, as when influential buyers and decision makers are being sought. Here the telephone has been used to interview as many as seven or eight people in a single company location regarding the extent of their involvement in a decision.[29]

The intrusiveness of the telephone, plus the ease of making call-backs, means there should be less *sample bias* due to nonresponse. Judging from a recent analysis of 182 telephone surveys,[30] these benefits are often not realized:

> . . . *the median noncontact rate (not-at-homes, busy signals, disconnected phones, etc.) was 39%. That is, in half the surveys more than 39% of the selected respondents or households with known phone numbers were not contacted. However, if four or more attempts were made to reach the number, the noncontact rate dropped to 23%. Surprisingly, in 36% of all surveys, only one attempt was made to contact a potential respondent. . . . the median refusal rate was 28%. When an appointment was made to call again at a more convenient time the refusal rate was 22%. When no appointment was suggested the refusal rate was 38%.*

Overall, the nonresponse performance was poor, but significant improvements were well within the capacity of the research suppliers.

For most topics there is likely to be little difference between telephone and personal interviews in the *accuracy* of responses. The Survey Research Center (University of Michigan) found similar aggregate results were obtained by the two methods in the quarterly interview of consumer intentions. However, less differentiated responses were

---

[26]Stanley L. Payne, "Data Collection Methods: Telephone Surveys," in Robert Ferber, ed., *op. cit.*, pp. 2.105–2.123.

[27]Donald W. Ball, "Toward a Sociology of Telephone and Telephoners," in Marcello Truzzi, eds., *Sociology and Everyday Life* (Englewood Cliffs, N.J.: Prentice-Hall, 1968), pp. 59–75.

[28]Payne, *op. cit.*, 2.116.

[29]John E. Morrell, "Industrial Advertising Pays Off," *Harvard Business Review*, March–April 1970, 4 *et. seq.*

[30]Frederick Wiseman and Philip McDonald, "Noncontact and Refusal Rates in Consumer Telephone Surveys," *Journal of Marketing Research, 16* (November 1979), 478–484.

obtained over the telephone.[31] Studies of health practices and perception of water resource problems also found the two methods gave similar results. In the latter study, about three percent considered that water resources constituted a major problem when either telephone or personal interview was used.[32]

During the telephone interview the respondent's only impression of the interviewer is that conveyed by the voice. The lack of rapport is offset to a degree by lessened interviewer bias and greater anonymity of the situation. However, the research on whether the respondent will reply with greater candor to personal questions (such as alcohol consumption) is quite mixed.

Limitations. Relatively few of the problems with the telephone method are completely insurmountable. The most obvious problem is the inability to *employ visual aids or complex tasks*. For example, it does not appear feasible to ask respondents to retain the names of nine department stores in their minds and then ask them to choose one store (which is "easiest to get to from here," "has the highest quality," etc.). There have been ingenious solutions to this problem—including separate delivery of the product, or asking the respondent to treat the telephone dial as a 10-point rating scale (from "1" for extreme like to the "0" for extreme dislike). A related problem with the telephone is that the interviewer must rely solely on verbal cues to judge the reaction and understanding of respondents.

There is some controversy regarding the *amount* of information that can be collected with a telephone interview—hinging largely on assumptions regarding the feasible length. Most telephone interviews are kept as short as five to ten minutes, because of the belief that a bored or hurried respondent would be likely to hang up the phone. However, 20- to 30-minute interviews are increasingly frequent and successful, but only with interesting topics and capable interviewers.

A further limitation of telephone interviewing is the potential for *sample bias,* which is a consequence of some people being without phones, having unlisted phones, and telephone directories being unable to keep up with a mobile population. A subsequent chapter on sampling will discuss some of the solutions to these sampling problems, as well as the use of call-backs to reduce the frequency of not-at-homes.

Mail Surveys

Advantages. One solution to rising costs and problems of interviewer error is to dispense with that source of cost and error. While the most likely reason for choosing a mail survey is *cost,* there are others, as illustrated by the decision of the Census Bureau to switch from a personal interview to a census by mail to gain "better results, including

---

[31]J. B. Lansing and J. N. Morgan, *Economic Survey Methods,* Ann Arbor, Michigan, University of Michigan, Institute for Social Research, 1971, 203–243.

[32]Charles A. Ibsen and John A. Balliveg, "Telephone Interviews in Social Research: Some Methodological Considerations," *Quality and Quantity, 8* (1974), 181–192.

a shortening of the period for collecting the data and more reliable answers supplied directly by respondents instead of through a more-or-less inhibiting intermediary, the enumerator.''[33] This approach worked well for the 1970 census, when forms were mailed to 60 percent of American households, of which 87 percent were completed voluntarily. More recent tests, to larger segments of the population, have not been so encouraging. Response rates in one test were as low as 50 to 55 percent.[34]

There is consistent evidence that mail surveys yield more accurate results—*among those completing the survey*. Because the mail questionnaire is answered at the respondent's discretion, the replies are likely to be more thoughtful and others can be consulted for necessary information. Mail surveys generally are superior when sensitive or potentially embarrassing topics, such as sexual behavior and finances, are covered (so long as the respondent is convinced that the answers will be taken in confidence). For example, a 1973 study of Boston residents, which compared the three basic methods of data collection, found that each of them gave equivalent results for neutral topics such as giving funds for an SST. But on sensitive topics where socially undesirable responses were possible there were large differences. On the question of legalizing abortion, 89 percent of mail survey respondents were in favor, compared to 62 and 70 percent for telephone and personal interview respondents, respectively.[35]

Limitations. The absence of an interviewer means a large number of variables are controlled inadequately, including

- The identity of the respondent (was it the addressee who answered, or an assistant or spouse?)
- Whom the respondent consults for help in answering questions
- The speed of the response (the usual time lag before receipt of a questionnaire delays the study and makes the responses vulnerable to external events taking place during the study)[36]
- The order in which the questions are exposed and answered (the respondent can look ahead to see where the questions are leading, so it is not possible to funnel questions from the general to the specific, for example)
- Respondent understanding of the questions (there is no opportunity to seek clarification of confusing questions or terms, so many respondents return their questionnaire partially completed)

[33]Quoted from Census Bureau sources by Paul L. Erdos, ''Data Collection Methods: Mail Surveys,'' in Robert Ferber, ed., *Handbook of Marketing Research, op. cit.,* pp. 2–91.

[34]''Census Bureau Ponders Ad Drive to Encourage Response to 80 Count,'' *Advertising Age* (November 29, 1976), 56.

[35]Frederick Wiseman, ''Methodological Bias in Public Opinion Surveys,'' *Public Opinion Quarterly, 36* (Spring 1972), 105–108. Results from other comparative studies have not been so clear-cut. See, for example, W. Locander, S. Sudman, and N. Bradburn, ''An Investigation of Interviewer Method, Threat and Response Distortion,'' *Journal of the American Statistical Association,* June 1976, 262–275.

[36]Michael J. Houston and Neil M. Ford, ''Broadening the Scope of Methodological Research on Mail Surveys,'' *Journal of Marketing Research, 13* (November 1976), 397–403.

One consequence of these problems is that long questionnaires with complicated questions cannot be used without destroying the response rate. As a rule of thumb, six to eight pages is the upper limit on topics of average interest to respondents.[37]

Mail surveys are limited to situations where a mailing list is available and the cost of the list is not prohibitive. There are many sources for such lists: city directories, telephone directories, business directories (such as Poors and Thomases), membership lists of associations, publication subscription lists, and lists compiled for sale by specialty firms.[38] Unfortunately, there are a number of possible flaws in all such lists: obsolescence, omissions, duplications, and so forth. This makes it difficult to find the ideal list, which consists entirely of the type of person to be contacted but also represents all of those who exist. Great care must be taken at this stage to ensure that the study objectives can be achieved without excessive compromise.

If the boon of mail surveys is cost, then the bane is *response rates*. The problem is not that acceptable response rates cannot be achieved, but rather that the rate is hard to forecast and there is substantial risk that an acceptable rate may not be achieved. Many factors combine to influence the response rate, including (1) the perceived amount of work required, which in turn depends on the length of the questionnaire and the apparent ease with which it can be completed; (2) the intrinsic interest of the topic; (3) the characteristics of the sample; (4) the credibility of the sponsoring organization; and (5) the level of induced motivation. A poorly planned mail survey on a low-interest topic may achieve only a 10- to 15-percent response rate. Under the right circumstances, 90-percent response rates are also possible.

Coping with Nonresponse to Mail Surveys.

Nonresponse is a problem because those who respond are likely to differ substantially from those who do not respond. The best way to protect against this bias is to improve the response rate. The most consistently effective methods for achieving high response rates involve some combination of monetary incentives and follow-ups or reminders.[39] The inclusion of a 25¢ coin in the mailing, which is the usual reward, has been found to improve response rates by increments of 18 to 27 percent when compared to returns when no incentive is used. Comparable improvements have been obtained from the single or multiple follow-up letter. Although each follow-up brings additional responses, the optimum number seems to be two. It is a moot point whether the inclusion of another questionnaire in the follow-up letter is worthwhile. Other techniques for improving response rates, such as providing a stamped, return envelope and a persuasive cover letter, appear to have a lesser but still worthwhile effect. Surprisingly, there is no clear evidence that personalization of the mailing, promises of anonymity, color, and methods of reproduction make much difference.

Another approach to the nonresponse problem is to determine the extent and direction of bias by studying the differences between responders and nonresponders. This sometimes

---

[37] Paul L. Erdos, *op. cit.*

[38] *1973–1974 Catalog of Mailing Lists,* New York: Fritz S. Hofheimer, Inc., 1972.

[39] Leslie Kanuk and Conrad Berenson, ''Mail Surveys and Response Rates: A Literature Review,'' *Journal of Marketing Research, 12* (November 1975), 440–453.

can be done by taking a subsample of the nonrespondents and using a variety of methods to get a high response rate from this group. Of course, when the questionnaire is anonymous or time is short, this cannot be done. In this situation it may be possible to compare the results of the survey with "known" values for the population, using such variables as age and income. Alternatively, one can use extrapolation methods, which assume that those who respond less readily are more like nonrespondents.[40] "Less readily" can be defined as either being slower-than-average in answering a simple mailing, or responding to the extra prodding of a follow-up mailing. With data from two waves of mailings a trend can be established in the pattern of answers; nonrespondents can be assumed to be like either the last respondent to the second wave or like a projected respondent at the midpoint of the nonresponse group. This is represented graphically in the following chart.

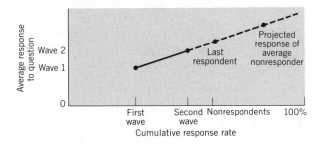

Mail Panels.   In this context a panel means a representative national sample of people who have agreed to participate in a limited number of mail surveys each year. A number of these panels are operated by firms such as Market Facts, Home Testing Institute, and National Family Opinion, Inc. The latter firm, for example, offers a number of panels which contain 130,000 people. The major advantage is the high response rate, which averages 75 to 85 percent.

A typical application of a mail panel is the Conference Board Survey of Consumer Confidence. Each quarter a large sample, drawn from the National Family Opinion Panel, is sent a questionnaire in the card format shown in Figure 6–2. This card is sent with cards from as many as 10 other studies, which spreads the costs of the survey. Since the questions and the sampling procedures are the same every quarter, the Conference Board has a standard measuring stick for tracking fluctuations in consumer attitudes and buying intentions.

Panels are recruited to match the general population with respect to geographic location, city size, age of homemaker, and family income. Inevitably, those people who agree to serve on such panels will be different from the rest of the population—perhaps because they are more interested in such research, have more time available, and so forth. Little is known about the impact of such differences on questionnaire responses.

[40]J. Scott Armstrong and Terry S. Overton, "Estimating Nonresponse Bias in Mail Surveys," *Journal of Marketing Research, 14* (August 1977), 396–402.

11044-2

ANSWER THIS SIDE FIRST

1. How would you rate the present general business conditions in your area?

☐ GOOD ☐ NORMAL ☐ BAD

a. SIX MONTHS from now do you think they will be:

☐ BETTER? ☐ SAME? ☐ WORSE?

2. What would you say about available jobs in your area right now?

☐ PLENTY ☐ NOT SO MANY ☐ HARD TO GET

a. SIX MONTHS from now do you think there will be:

☐ MORE? ☐ SAME? ☐ FEWER?

3. How would you guess your total family income to be SIX MONTHS from now?

☐ HIGHER ☐ SAME ☐ LOWER

4. Does anyone in your household plan to buy a house in the next SIX MONTHS?

☐ YES ☐ NO ☐ MAYBE

a. If YES: ☐ NEW? ☐ LIVED IN? ☐ DON'T KNOW?

5. Does anyone in your household plan to buy a car in the next SIX MONTHS?

☐ YES ☐ NO ☐ MAYBE

a. If YES: ☐ NEW? ☐ USED? ☐ DON'T KNOW?

MAKE?____________________ ☐ DON'T KNOW?

CONTINUE →

FIGURE 6–2 Conference Board mail panel survey of consumer confidence

ANSWER OTHER SIDE FIRST

6. Please check which, if any, of the items you plan to buy in the next SIX MONTHS, and which <u>brand</u> you are most likely to choose:

BRAND PREFERENCE

Refrigerator.........0 1☐ _____

Washing Machine......0 2☐ _____

Black/White TV.......0 3☐ _____

Color TV.............0 4☐ _____

Vacuum Cleaner.......0 5☐ _____

Ranges...............0 6☐ _____

Clothes Dryer........0 7☐ _____

Air Conditioner......0 8☐ _____

Dishwasher...........0 9☐ _____

Microwave Oven.......1 0☐ _____

Sewing Machine.......1 1☐ _____

Carpet (over 4' x 6')1 2☐ _____

☐ NONE OF THESE

7. Do you plan to take a vacation <u>away from home</u> between NOW and the next SIX MONTHS?

☐ YES   ☐ NO   ☐ UNDECIDED

a. Where will you spend the <u>most</u> of your time while on vacation?

☐ HOME   ☐ OTHER   ☐ FOREIGN
   STATE   STATE(S)   COUNTRY

b. How will you mainly travel?

<u>AIRPLANE</u>   <u>CAR</u>   <u>TRAIN</u>   <u>BOAT</u>   <u>BUS</u>

☐   ☐   ☐   ☐   ☐

Name of airline: _____

During the recruitment interview a large amount of classification information is obtained, including occupation of principal earner, number of years married, willingness to be telephoned (and most convenient hours), and ownership of boats, trailers, pets, cars and trucks. These make it possible to draw special samples of particular occupation groups (such as lawyers), age categories (such as teenagers), and geographic areas. Large samples can be obtained quickly in test-market areas, for example.

Combinations of Survey Methods

Since each of the basic methods of data collection has different strengths and weaknesses, it is sometimes desirable to combine them and retain the best features of each while minimizing the limitations. Some of the feasible combinations (or sequences) are illustrated below:

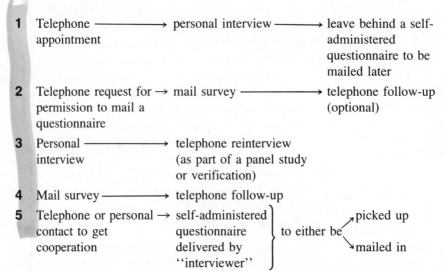

1 Telephone ⟶ personal interview ⟶ leave behind a self-appointment administered questionnaire to be mailed later

2 Telephone request for → mail survey ⟶ telephone follow-up permission to mail a (optional) questionnaire

3 Personal ⟶ telephone reinterview interview (as part of a panel study or verification)

4 Mail survey ⟶ telephone follow-up

5 Telephone or personal → self-administered contact to get questionnaire to either be ⟋ picked up cooperation delivered by ⟍ mailed in "interviewer"

With the exception of the reinterview panel design of sequence 3, each of the above combinations has proven very effective in increasing the response rate. Indeed, sequence 1 is virtually mandatory for personal interviews with executives as we noted in the previous chapter. The virtues of the other sequences are not quite so obvious.

The *telephone prenotification approach* is essentially a phone call to ask permission to mail a questionnaire. The key is the telephone presentation, which must not only gain an agreement to participate but make sure the prospective respondent is serious about cooperating. In one study in which 300 households were phoned, 264 households (88 percent) agreed to the mailing and 180 (60 percent) returned usable questionnaires.[41] If the return rate is not acceptable, a follow-up phone call can be made.

[41]Marvin A. Jolson, "How to Double or Triple Mail-Survey Response Rates," *Journal of Marketing, 41* (October 1977), 78–81.

The **lockbox approach** is designed to circumvent the screens set up by receptionists and secretaries around busy executives. The mail is used to deliver a small locked metal box containing a questionnaire and other interviewing materials such as flashcards, exhibits, and pictures. A covering letter, attached to the box, explains the purpose of the survey and tells the prospective respondent that an interviewer will conduct a telephone interview in a few days. The letter also tells the respondent that the box is a gift but that the combination to the lock will not be provided until the time of the interview. Ostensibly this is so the respondent will not be biased by seeing the interview materials in advance. However, it is clear that the value of the gift depends on participation in the survey. Also, the locked box stimulates respondent curiosity. As a result the originator of this technique has been able to obtain response rates of 50 percent to 70 percent, even with notoriously difficult respondents such as attorneys in private practice who sell time for a living and are loath to participate in "free interviews."[42]

The **drop-off approach** is an illustration of sequence 5, which is particularly well suited to studies within compact geographic areas. For public transit studies the questionnaire can be hand delivered to sampling points, such as every 25th house within areas that have access to a transit line. It also can be used for subjects living in designated political precincts or within a given radius of a specific retail outlet or other service. The major advantages are (1) only lightly trained interviewers are required to gain the cooperation of the respondents, deliver the questionnaires, and arrange a return visit; (2) response rates are high, generally between 70 and 80 percent, in part because of the initial commitment to cooperate coupled with the realization that the survey taker will be returning to pick up the completed questionnaire; (3) several questionnaires can be left in each household, if all adults are part of the sample; (4) lengthy questionnaires can be used without affecting the response rate; and (5) it is a very cost-effective method.[43]

Choice of Survey Method for HMO Study

The HMO study described in earlier chapters successfully used a modification of the drop-off method. The changes were made so advantage could be taken of the availability of a complete address list of all faculty, staff, and married students. This population was scattered over an area with a 20-mile radius, so it was not practical for the survey assistant to make unannounced personal visits. The specific procedure was as follows:

1   A telephone contact was made with each household named in the sample, to determine the head of household and obtain that person's agreement to participate. To minimize nonresponse bias, at least five telephone call-backs were made.

2   During the telephone call, arrangements were made to deliver the questionnaire and a pick-up time was set.

[42]David Schwartz, "Locked Box Contains Survey Methods, Helps End Some Woes of Probing Industrial Field," *Marketing News,* January 27, 1978, 18.

[43]Christopher H. Lovelock, Ronald Stiff, David Cullwick, and Ira M. Kaufman, "An Evaluation of the Effectiveness of Drop-Off Questionnaire Delivery," *Journal of Marketing Research, 13* (November 1976), 358–364.

3 Before the pick-up, a reminder phone call was made to see if the questionnaire was finished.

4 If the questionnaire was not ready at the promised time, arrangements for a second pick-up time were made.

Only three percent of the sample of 1500 persons refused to participate on the first contact. Fourteen percent were ineligible, not at home after calls, or had disconnected phones. Another nine percent refused to complete the questionnaire they had received, usually citing lack of time (this is not surprising, as the questionnaire had 14 pages and more than 200 variables). The overall response rate of 74 percent reflected the interest of most respondents in the subject and the subtle pressure to respond from the knowledge that someone was calling to pick up the questionnaire.

SUMMARY

The choice of a data collection method involves a series of compromises in matching the often conflicting requirements of the situation with the strengths and limitations of the available methods.

While each situation is unique to some degree, the following represent the major constraints to be satisfied:

- The available budget
- The nature of the problem and the complexity of the information that is required
- The need for accuracy
- The time constraints

Part of the skill of research design is adapting a basic data collection method—whether personal or telephone interview or mail survey—to those constraints. This process of adaptation means exploiting the advantages as well as blunting the limitations, which to some extent makes generalizations suspect. Nonetheless, it is useful to summarize the relative merits of the basic survey methods, as in Table 6–3, to put the methods into perspective. Of course these summary judgments do not reflect the myriad of special factors that may be influential in specific cases, such as availability of a sampling frame, need to ask sensitive questions, and the rarity of the population to be sampled.

The greatest potential for effective adaptation of method to situation lies with combinations of methods, or specialized variants of basic methods. The latter include omnibus surveys and mail panels, which are particularly good for tracking studies, or where limited responses from specific populations are required and budget constraints are severe. Some combinations of methods, such as the drop-off methods, similarly confer impressive advantages by combining some of the advantages of personal interview and mail surveys. As with specialized variants, however, their usefulness often is restricted to certain settings.

TABLE 6–3

Advantages and Limitations of the Basic Methods of Data Collection

	Personal Interview	Telephone Interview	Mail Survey
1. Accuracy of data that is collected from individual respondent	Fair to very good	Fair to very good	Very good
2. Amount of data that can be collected	Excellent	Fair to very good	Fair
3. Flexibility	Excellent	Good	Poor
4. Sample bias (response rate)	Excellent	Good	Poor to good
5. Direct cost per completed interview	Poor to fair	Good	Excellent
6. Time requirements	Poor to fair	Good to excellent	Fair
7. Administrative problems	Poor	Good	Very good

QUESTIONS AND PROBLEMS

1 Is the biasing effect of an interviewer more serious in a personal or telephone interview? What steps can be taken to minimize this biasing effect in these two types of interviews?

2 People tend to respond to surveys dealing with topics that interest them. How would you exploit this fact to increase the response rate to a survey of attitudes toward the local urban transit system in a city where the vast majority of people drive to work or to shop?

3 You have been given a mail survey of industrial purchasing agents to analyze. Although the response rate was only 16 percent, there are evidently no funds available to collect further data. What would you do?

4 What problems would you anticipate in designing a survey to establish the kind of paint used by the "do-it-yourself" market when the members of this sample last redecorated a room?

5 Why do most researchers using the personal or telephone interview method insist on having 10 to 15 percent of all the completed interviews validated?

6 What are the characteristics of a good interviewer? Can training improve an interviewer's performance?

7 What biases, if any, might be introduced by offering to give respondents $5.00 when they return a mail questionnaire? Would these biases be different if a gift with retail value of $5.00 were included with the questionnaire?

8 What can an interviewer do during the first 30 seconds of an interview to maximize the cooperation rate of (a) a personal interview, and (b) a telephone interview? Assume the appropriate respondent is a head of the household.

9 What are the advantages of the telephone prenotification approach over a conventional mail survey?

10 Write a cover letter to a mail survey of householders that contains a number of questions regarding the utilization of various kinds of burglary protection devices.

11 If you were a marketing research manager would you permit the following if they were important to the usefulness of a study:

a telling the respondent the interview was only 2 or 3 minutes when it usually took 4 minutes and a follow-up ten minute interview was employed

b telling the respondent the questionnaire would be anonymous but coding it so that the respondent could be identified (so that additional available information about the respondent's neighborhood could be used).

c secretly recording (or videotaping) a focus group interview.

d saying the research was being conducted by a research firm instead of your own company.

CASE 6–1
Essex Markets (A)[44]

Essex Markets was a chain of supermarkets in a medium-sized California city. For six years, they had provided for their customers unit pricing of grocery products. The unit prices were provided in the form of shelf tags that put forth the price of the item and the unit price (the price per ounce, for example). The program was costly. The tags had to be prepared and updated. Further, because they tended to become dislodged or moved, considerable effort was required to make sure that they were current and in place.

A study was proposed to evaluate unit pricing. Among the research questions were the following:

- What percentage of shoppers was aware of unit pricing?
- What percentage of shoppers used unit pricing?
- With what frequency was unit pricing in use?
- What types of shoppers used unit pricing?

[44]Prepared by Bruce McElroy and David A. Aaker as a basis for class discussion.

- For what product classes was it used most frequently?
- Was it used to compare package sizes and brands or to evaluate store-controlled labels?

It was determined that a five-page questionnaire completed by around 1000 shoppers would be needed. The questionnaire could be completed in the store in about 15 minutes, or the respondent could be asked to complete it at home and mail it in.

QUESTIONS FOR DISCUSSION

Specify how the respondents should be approached in the store. Write out the exact introductory remarks that you would use. Should the interview be in the store, or should the questionnaire be self-administered at home and mailed in, or should some other strategy be employed? If a self-administered questionnaire is used, write an introduction to it. What could be done to encourage a high response rate?

CASE 6–2

Project DATA: An Urban Transportation Study

The Downtown Agency for Transportation Action project (Project DATA) was a collaborative approach to the problem of improving the high-density movement of people and goods within downtown Cleveland.[45] In August 1968, the survey researcher employed by Project DATA was wondering how to collect downtown origin and destination (DOD) data for input to a comprehensive model of traveler behavior in downtown Cleveland. His problems had been compounded by a poor response rate during a recent test of his preferred method of data collection, a mail-back questionnaire distributed to rapid-transit users, bus patrons, and automobile travelers. Consequently, he had to decide in a short time whether to stay with the mail-back questionnaire method or try some other, more costly, procedure. If he did not change, he would have to persuade the other members of the research team that the problems encountered in the pretest could be overcome and that the mail-back method would yield sufficiently accurate results.

BACKGROUND

Downtown Cleveland represented one of the most important concentrations of people in the Midwest. It gen-

erally was defined as an area encircled by the Cuyahoga River Valley, the Innerbelt Freeway, and Lake Erie. For the purposes of Project DATA, this definition was modified slightly to include the downtown-oriented activity centers adjacent to the southeast corner of the area outside the Innerbelt Freeway. These centers include the future location of Cuyahoga Community College and the St. Vincent Hospital and its parking area.

There had been considerable progress in making downtown Cleveland more accessible through rail rapid transit and freeways; however, facilities to expedite the movement of people and goods within the downtown area were being installed at a much slower rate. Transportation planners had tended to treat downtown Cleveland as a terminus point for regional line-haul transportation. Yet, the downtown covered a broad land area with several separate activity centers and a solid network of business, commercial, and entertainment facilities. Except for a downtown loop bus system, there was little transportation among these centers.

The lack of transportation was regarded as a contributing factor in the deterioration of downtown Cleveland and many other urban areas. After the Hough riots, Cleveland was chosen by the U.S. Department of Transportation as the site of the first large-scale effort to design a comprehensive central urban transportation network. A number of systems were under consideration, including: (1) Train-type systems, (2) small automatic taxis, and (3) continuous systems. Each was to

[45]Funds and assistance on the project were provided by Case Western Reserve University, Battelle Memorial Institute, City of Cleveland, Cleveland-Seven County Transportation–Land Use Study, Cleveland Transit System, Cuyahoga County, and U.S. Department of Housing and Urban Development.

be evaluated by a model that would simulate the decision processes of different user segments. The model would consider where and how users move from one place to another for various trip purposes within the downtown area. The DOD data being collected by Project DATA were to be the base for the calibration of the simulation model. In addition the data would be used in the development of interim projects to improve the existing downtown transportation system. Thus there was considerable urgency behind the request for the data.

DESIGNING THE DOD STUDY

The first step was to establish the purpose of the study. After extensive discussions it was agreed that the following types of information were needed:

1 The numbers and socioeconomic characteristics of people who move to, from, and within downtown Cleveland

2 The locations of the activity centers within downtown Cleveland to which these people are moving

3 The methods of travel used to move these people to, from, and within downtown

4 The trip purposes of the people movements

5 The time distribution of the people-movement patterns throughout a 24-hour period

A number of alternative methods for collecting the DOD information were considered. These included mail-back questionnaires distributed to people at key locations within the downtown area, personal interviews conducted at these same key locations, telephone surveys, trip diaries distributed to people to complete over extended periods of time, mail-back questionnaires sent to houses, personal home interviews, newspaper coupons to be completed and returned by mail, and a system of distributing and collecting precoded computer cards to reflect origins and destinations of trips within the downtown area.

An evaluation of the various survey designs was

made by the Project DATA staff. It decided that a mail-back questionnaire distributed at key locations within the downtown area was the most realistic approach to collecting the needed information, taking into account the time and financial constraints of the project. To test this decision, a pilot survey was conducted. The objectives were

1 To evaluate the ability of the survey forms and questions to obtain the required data

2 To determine the approximate survey-response rates that could be expected from the various categories of people so that a proper data-sampling frame could be formulated

3 To ascertain where in the downtown area the survey questionnaires should be distributed

4 To determine the best procedures for distributing the questionnaires to the users of various modes of transportation

The pilot survey utilized the questionnaire shown in Figure 6–3. Four hundred were distributed to rapid-transit users as they went through the turnstiles in Terminal Tower. Another 600 were given to bus riders as they passed an imaginary downtown cordon line. Those questionnaires were distributed only during the A.M. and P.M. peak traffic periods. A final 400 questionnaires were distributed within two major parking lots by placing them under windshield wipers after the automobiles had been parked. The results of the pilot survey are summarized in Figures 6–4, 6–5, and 6–6.

QUESTIONS FOR DISCUSSION

1 Critique the questionnaire. Does it provide the required data?

2 Evaluate the overall research design with respect to possible sources of bias in the results and the reasons for the poor response rate.

3 Specify how you would improve this mail-back survey.

4 Suggest an alternative design and cite its advantages and shortcomings.

Downtown
Agency for
Transportation
Action

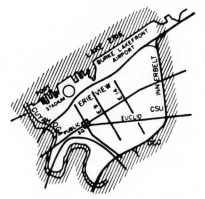

Project Data
University Circle Research Center
11000 Cedar Avenue
Cleveland, Ohio 44106

Project DATA needs to know how people travel to, from, and, especially, <u>within</u> downtown Cleveland. "Downtown" is the open area in this map.

Our goal is a better transportation system--including improved pedestrian facilities--for the downtown. We would appreciate your assistance in completing the questions on the other side of this form according to the instructions below. THANK YOU.

Case Western Reserve University · Battelle Memorial Institute · Cleveland Institute Of Art · Cuyahoga County · City Of Cleveland
Cleveland Seven County Transportation Land Use Study · Cleveland Transit System · Greater Cleveland Growth Association

BUSINESS REPLY MAIL
No Postage Stamp Necessary if Mailed in the United States

Postage Will Be Paid By

Case Western Reserve University
Cleveland, Ohio   44106
University Circle

Attention: **Dr. James B. Reswick, Project DATA**

INSTRUCTIONS:

1. Please complete the questions on the other side of this form. Only a small number of these forms are being distributed at this time. We need this information in order to design a large-scale survey that will be conducted this summer and fall. Your cooperation will make a significant difference to the project.

2. After completing the questionnaire, please fold it tightly along the dotted lines so that the address in the center of the page above is showing.

3. Please drop it into any mailbox--no postage is required.

THANK YOU FOR PARTICIPATING IN PROJECT DATA

FIGURE 6-3 Project DATA transportation questionnaire

1. Please list ALL trips you made downtown TODAY. We are especially interested in short walking trips such as: going to lunch, coming from lunch, a walk from the parking lot to the office, etc.

	Name of Place Where Trip Starts and Address If Possible	Time Trip Starts	Name of Place Where Trip Ends and Address If Possible	Time Trip Ends	Purpose of Trip (Please use codes below)	Method of Travel
Trip TO the downtown area					☐	☐
First Trip IN downtown area					☐	☐
Second Trip in downtown area					☐	☐
Third Trip						
Fourth Trip						
Fifth Trip						
Sixth Trip						
Trip FROM the downtown area					☐	☐

2. How many persons accompanied you downtown today? ☐

How many of these persons were children under 12? ☐

"Purpose of Trip"
1. work
2. personal business
3. shopping
4. social-recreation
5. school
6. eat
7. medical or dental
8. serve passenger
9. to home
10. other

"Method of Travel"
1. auto driver
2. auto passenger
3. bus
4. rapid transit
5. taxi
6. walk
7. other

3. How often do you usually come downtown? (Please Check One)

1. Every Weekday (Mon-Fri) ☐
2. Several Times a Week ☐
3. Once a Week ☐
4. Once a Month ☐
5. Other (Please Specify) ☐ _____

4. Home Address _____
(Number)   (Street)   (City)   (Zip)

5. Male ☐ Female ☐ ; Number of Persons in Your Household? ☐ Your Age? ☐ No. of Autos in Household? ☐

6. Approximate Family Yearly Income: (Please Check One)
Under $3500 ☐ ; $3500-6500 ☐ ; $6500-9500 ☐ ; $9500-12500 ☐ ; $12500-15500 ☐ ; Over $15500 ☐

7. What could be done to make your trips within downtown Cleveland easier, faster, or more pleasant?
_____
_____

8. We would appreciate any suggestions you may have for making this questionaire clearer or easier to answer. For instance, were any of the questions confusing? Why?
_____
_____

Mode	Number of Questionnaires Returned	Number of Questionnaires Handed Out	Percent Return
CTS Rapid Transit	20 (A.M.)	100	20
	19 (P.M.)	100	19
Shaker Rapid Transit	23 (A.M.)	100	23
	16 (P.M.)	100	16
CTS Bus Route 32	23 (A.M.)	100	23
(suburban express)	15 (P.M.)	100	15
CTS Bus Route 9	22 (A.M.)	100	22
(suburban local)	16 (P.M.)	100	16
CTS Bus Route 14 (low-	5 (A.M.)	100	5
income inner-city	1 (P.M.)	100	1
area local)			
Department Store Parking Lot (relatively high parking turnover rate)	10	200	5
Muny Parking Lot (caters primarily to all-day parkers)	16	200	8
Totals	186	1,400	

FIGURE 6–4 Distribution and response of pilot survey

1. A common error for rapid transit respondents was that they failed to record Terminal Tower as their first destination in the central business district (CBD).
2. A common error for all respondents was that they often failed to record return trips, especially the return lunch trip.
3. It appears that a relatively large number of people (especially bus riders) do not leave the building they work in during the day. Or, these people did not understand how to fill out the form.
4. The people that returned the questionnaire can be generally categorized into two major groups: (a) those that completely understood how to fill out question 1, and (b) those that completely misunderstood how to fill out question 1.

FIGURE 6–5 Analysis of problems by Project DATA staff

5. A few people recorded "work," "restaurant," and so on as their origin and destination points, rather than an address or the specific name of the place or location.

6. Several people did not record the number of their home address; only street, city, and Zip Code.

7. A relatively large number of respondents failed to answer question 2.

8. For the majority of the respondents, filling the trip purpose and method of travel codes presented no problems. In fact, many people improvised on the questionnaire to provide additional data.

9. In a few instances, people did not record trip times. Again, it appears that these cases were oversights. Generally, people recorded this information quite accurately. For example, walking trips lasting two or three minutes were being recorded. The longer the trip—usually the trips to and from the CBD—the more tendency there was to round off the trip time to 15- or 30-minute intervals.

10. The majority of respondents filled out the income question with no comments. However, several people residing in higher income areas questioned the necessity of the information in relation to transportation. Eleven of the 180 respondents failed to answer this question.

11. There is some confusion on the income question. For example, there were many 20- and 21-year-olds making over $15,000 annually based on the result of the survey.

12. A few respondents (seven) did not record their age.

13. Public transportation respondents receiving the questionnaire on the outbound trip (P.M.) had a tendency to record only that trip. In addition, the P.M. return rate of the questionnaire was considerably less than the A.M. (inbound) trip.

14. Several bus-rider respondents obviously failed to record their first trip in the CBD between the bus stop and their first CBD destination. In other cases, this error was difficult to identify since it is unknown to us how far it is from the bus stops to their first CBD destinations on Euclid Avenue. (Bus routes surveyed were Euclid Avenue routes.)

15. Many bus respondents misunderstood question 2 and recorded the total number of people on the bus.

16. A surprisingly large number of people enter the CBD via one mode and exit using another mode.

17. Bus riders are very concerned about trips to and from the CBD and wonder why we are concerned with only downtown transportation needs.

1. Question #1 refers to "today," while #3 refers to "usual" habits. I go downtown everyday, but I do not always drive. Also, times of leaving and arriving vary.
2. I think this questionnaire is easily followed.
3. Good questionnaire—easy to answer.
4. The first group of questions could be made more explicit.
5. They were confusing on many trips because I don't do the same thing everyday at lunch time.
6. Question #2.
7. Everything is clear.
8. Very good—not confusing.
9. If answers must be confined to the blocks, it might be well to point this out.
10. Questionnaire seems clear enough.
11. Not confusing.
12. Add a few more lines for #7 and place a line for the date.
13. Could not be made any clearer.
14. No provision for alternates—sometimes walk/bus; no space allowed for total trip home as buses connecting with rapid for suburbs cannot be included in "downtown area" trips. I need two bus trips plus rapid to get home.
15. Understand as is.
16. Question #4 is revelatory; you should ask for nearest intersection.
17. Question #2a could be reworded—glad you're interested!
18. Question #2 doesn't make it possible to answer if a bus trip and one is unaware of survey. Question #7—why discuss only downtown? The trip to town is depressing.
19. All questions clear enough.
20. No clearcut place for occasional trips.
21. It was difficult for me to answer Question # 1.
22. It is fine.
23. Clarify Questions #1 and #2—add extra part to "from downtown area" for intermediate trip, e.g., Terminal-Windemere-home (one trip or two?)
24. Home address—why necessary?
25. Use of "grid" and block number instead of address would make the form easier and more meaningful.
26. The questionnaire was very simple to fill out. I hope you get as many back as you gave out.
27. My family does not reside in Cleveland, therefore, perhaps question #6 is irrelevant.
28. You didn't provide for combined bus and rapid or car and rapid use.
29. No confusion.
30. Questionnaire was clear.
31. Upper right-hand corner should have more blocks for more than one method of travel or purpose of trip.
32. Method of travel does not indicate if more than one method is used; i.e., bus, transfer to rapid, transfer to bus again, or walk.

33. Provide a way of indicating more than one method of travel for the same trip, such as transfers to and from a bus or rapid transit.
34. Why worry about short walking trips? Alleviate the problems of getting into and out of the downtown area from the suburban residential sections.
35. I should like to know the purpose of this questionnaire and whether something constructive will come of it. I think the questionnaire is clear—I hope useful.
36. Believe inquiry as to whether or not service from home to downtown was frequent enough at hour necessary to leave would be pertinent.
37. Referring back to Question #1—List trips within downtown area for a 30-day period giving people more of an opportunity to use "Purpose of Trip" and "Method of Travel."
38. Much more time could be spent in the organization of this questionnaire.
39. What does the yearly family income have to do with the transportation problem?
40. Very specific and clear.
41. Why income of family?
42. Not confusing, but embarrassing and totally unnecessary, i.e., why the question of sex (male or female) necessary? Also, why the interest about incomes? Or if a person is alone or how many in the household? These, to me, seem totally irrelevant questions.
43. I found the questionnaire clear enough.
44. It seems a much better questionnaire than the usual.
45. Perfectly clear.
46. No distinction between going to work and business calls during day.
47. Method of travel and purpose should indicate that more than one answer is okay. Also more space for multiple answers.
48. Complication where two travel modes are used—see Question #1 "Trip"—definition not immediately clear.
49. Design a way to emphasize that you are only interested in a certain part of downtown.
50. Question #7 might be worded as below to eliminate unwanted responses. This may, however, confuse your strictly ambulatory respondents. (Question #7 reworded: What could be done *to our transportation system* to make your trips within downtown Cleveland easier, faster, and more pleasant?)
51. Extremely amateurish from a professional standpoint—too detailed, too time-consuming, too personal (address, identify with income).
52. Question #4 is not necessary.
53. Question #1 doesn't indicate whether you mean total trip or first or second leg—to my office is two steps.
54. It would seem easier to ask approximately how long a trip took than the times. I never pay much attention to timing my trips by the clock—especially shopping.
55. Questions were all clear.
56. Good questionnaire—okay.

CASE 6-3
Roland Development Corp.

Roland Development was a leading builder of homes in the Western United States. Their emphasis was on condominiums and townhouses, which were forecast to have an attractive future in these markets. These housing types lent themselves to standardization and cost reduction possibilities. Further, rising land costs were causing the share of single family detached houses to decline significantly. Meanwhile the share of market for single family attached houses (houses with common walls, floors or roofs) was expected to double in the next five years. Roland was well positioned to exploit these trends by following a strategy that differed from competition in three areas:

- Market segmentation. Roland typically segmented the market more finely than other home builders, and then designed homes to meet the specific needs of these groups.

- Direct selling. Shoppers in some department stores could find full scale, fully furnished Roland homes on display.

- Low prices for a complete housing package (including all the furnishings and necessary financing).

The company had begun to expand its limited line of condominiums and townhouses to provide design and square footage combinations that would appeal to higher income households. The management was especially pleased with the elegance, convenience and durability of the four new models they were planning to launch. Several problems remained to be solved. The first was the identification of a creative strategy that would position the new models and attract the largest number of purchases. That is, the company wanted to know what main ideas and themes should be used in the advertising of the new models. Another problem was to identify those segments of the market with the highest probability of purchasing the new models. The company asked the YKG Group, a large national research firm, to sub-

mit a written proposal for research which would provide Roland management with information useful in solving these two problems. Their proposal is summarized below.

RESEARCH PROPOSAL

The recommended research design would use a consumer panel and employ both telephone interviews and mail questionnaires. The research firm felt that the needed information could only be obtained from that very small proportion of the population who might buy such a home. Each of several different market segments would be studied to determine how they positioned the new models in relation to competing homes already on the market. The likelihood of purchasing a Roland model would also be determined during the study for each of the three market segments and also for each of several different advertising themes. This information would help Roland identify the most promising market segments for the new models, as well as the creative advertising strategy that would most appeal to them.

The proposed research design consisted of three phases: (1) the members of a large consumer mail panel would be screened to locate qualified prospects for the new models; (2) a relatively small sample of qualified prospects would be interviewed ''in-depth'' to identify possible advertising themes; and (3) a large sample of qualified respondents would be surveyed by mail to test their response to alternative creative strategies.

Phase 1. The YKG Group maintained a bank of over 200,000 families who agreed to cooperate in research projects undertaken by this firm. Considerable information existed about each family, including geographical location, occupation and age of male and female heads of family, total family income, presence and age of children, and so on. Roland managers felt that the four new models would most likely appeal to middle and upper-income families of size two, three, or four, with a household head 30 years of age or over. For this reason, the first phase of the proposed research involved mailing a short questionnaire to all panel members with those characteristics. The questionnaire asked panel members to indicate the likelihood of their purchasing a home in the next two to three years and also to report their attitude toward buying a townhouse or condominimum.

It was expected that this screening process would locate some 3000 to 5000 families who would be prospects to buy the new models over the next few years. To be considered a prospect, a family had to report being likely to purchase a home in the next two to three years, as well as having a favorable attitude toward a condominium or townhouse. Among these prospects three market segments would be identified. A high-income family would be a ''very good'' prospect if it was ''very likely'' to buy a home; a medium-income family would be a ''good'' prospect if it was ''very likely'' to buy a new home; and a high-income family would be a ''fair'' prospect if it was ''somewhat'' likely to buy a new home. All other responses were considered to indicate nonprospects.

Phase 2. In this phase about 200 qualified prospects would be interviewed using a combination of telephone and mail. These families would be mailed pictures, specifications, and line drawings of the company's new models of condos and townhouses, although they would not be identified by the Roland name. The line drawings would include front and rear views of each unit's exterior as well as sketches of each room. The specifications would include the number of square feet, wall thickness, heating and cooling equipment capacities, appliance brands and models, slab thickness, type of roof covering, and other features.

After reviewing these materials, respondents' reactions and impressions would be obtained through telephone interviews using open-ended questions. Interviewers would be told that the objective was to obtain qualitative data useful for ascertaining how potential buyers perceived the new models with respect to appearance, comfort, elegance, convenience, durability, ease and economy of maintenance, and other criteria. Interviewers would be instructed to record verbatim responses and were told that it was very important to do so because none of the responses would be tabulated or analyzed statistically. Responses to the open questions would then be studied to identify four or five ideas of themes that might be considered for use as creative strategies in advertising the new models.

Phase 3. This phase would be undertaken after four of the best advertising themes had been identified. Some 2400 families would be selected from the list of prospects obtained from Phase 1—approximately 800 ''very good'' prospects, 800 ''good'' prospects, and 800 ''fair'' prospects.

All of the families in each of the three market segments would be sent pictures, line drawings, and specifications (including prices) of the new Roland models as well as those of major competing models, all identified by brand name. Each of these three groups of prospects would then be randomly divided into four subsamples of 200, each of which would receive one, and only one, of the four advertising themes identified for the new models. Thus, the study design would consist of three samples of 800 families each. In turn, each sample would be broken into four subsamples, each of which would receive a different advertising theme.

Analysis. The effect of each advertising theme on each prospect segment would be evaluated on three measures—the degree to which it (1) resulted in the new line being rated as ''most appealing,'' (2) led respondents to request further information about the company's products, and (3) led respondents to indicate that they would be most likely to select one of the company's homes if they were to make such a purchase in the near future. For each advertising theme–prospect segment combination the research would yield three percentages. For example, for theme #1 and the ''very good'' prospects, the research might show that 38 percent of the respondents found a model in the new line ''most appealing'' among all the models reviewed; that 26 percent requested further information about the Roland models; and that 17 percent indicated that they ''most likely would purchase'' one of the new Roland models. By comparing these three percentages for each advertising theme–prospect segment combination, it would be possible to identify the most promising combinations. These results could be weighed by the relative size of each prospect segment to decide which creative strategy would be most effective in generating sales interest in the new models.

QUESTIONS FOR DISCUSSION

1 Would you recommend that Roland accept the YKG Group proposal?
2 If yes, what conclusions can be drawn from the data in Phase 3 of the research?
3 If the proposal is not accepted, what alternative designs should be considered?

7

DESIGNING THE QUESTIONNAIRE

Questionnaire construction is properly regarded as a very imperfect art. There are no established procedures that will lead consistently to a ''good'' questionnaire. One consequence is that the range of potential error contributed by ambiguous questions may be as much as 20 or 30 percentage points.[1] Fortunately, such extreme errors can be reduced sharply by common sense and the insights from experience of other researchers. A major objective of this chapter is to present systematically the ''rules of thumb'' that have been acquired with experience.

A good questionnaire is much more than a collection of unambiguous questions. First, the scope of the questionnaire should be no more or no less than is necessary to satisfy the objectives of the study. This seems a banal statement, but is no less difficult to achieve because it is obvious. A further condition is imposed by the prior choice of data collection method. While this choice is the result of the push and pull of many factors, it does set definite limits on the number, form, and ordering of the specific questions. A final condition is imposed by the respondent's willingness and ability to answer. Although the wording and sequence of questions can facilitate recall and motivate more accurate responses, there are definite limits to what can be done.

The process of designing a questionnaire to satisfy these conditions consists of the following steps:[2]

1 Plan what to measure

2 Formulate questions to obtain the needed information

3 Decide on the order of questions and on the layout of the questionnaire

4 Using a small sample, test the questionnaire for omissions and ambiguity

5 Correct the problems (and pretest again, if necessary)

We will use this sequence to organize the remainder of this chapter.

[1]Stanley L. Payne, *The Art of Asking Questions* (Princeton, N.J.: Princeton University Press, 1951).
[2]This sequence of steps was proposed by Paul B. Sheatsley, ''Questionnaire Design and Wording,'' Chicago: National Opinion Research Corp., 1969.

PLANNING WHAT TO MEASURE

The most difficult step is specifying exactly what information is to be collected from each respondent. Poor judgment and lack of thought at this stage may mean that the results are not **relevant** to the research purpose or that they are incomplete. Both problems are expensive, and may seriously diminish the value of the study.

Lack of relevance frequently results when someone has an idea that a particular piece of information would be ''interesting'' to collect, although there is no specific purpose in mind. This can lead to inflated questionnaires, increased costs of analysis, and lower-quality responses. To combat this problem, it is necessary to ask constantly, ''How will this information be used?'' and ultimately to anticipate the specific analyses that will be made.

When a questionnaire is incomplete in important respects and is sent into the field, the error is irreversible. To avoid this awful eventuality, careful thought is required, which is facilitated by

1   Clear research objectives, which describe as fully as possible the kind of information needed by the decision maker, the hypotheses, and the scope of the research

2   Exploratory research, which will suggest further relevant variables and help the researcher absorb the vocabulary and point of view of the typical respondent

3   Experience with similar studies

4   Pretesting of preliminary versions of the questionnaire

Translating Research Objectives into Information Requirements

At the end of Chapter 2 we saw how the research objectives for the HMO study were established. These objectives are summarized in Table 7–1. Before individual questionnaire items can be written, these objectives have to be translated into specific information requirements. Here is where the hypotheses play an especially important role. Since hypotheses suggest possible answers to the questions implied by the research objectives, there must be questionnaire items that could elicit those possible answers. For example, the HMO study included specific hypotheses as to which characteristics or features of a health plan would influence the choice of plan. Each of these characteristics needed to be represented by a question, so the hypotheses could be tested. From the information requirements specified on the right-hand side of Table 7–1, one can see how the process proceeded.

TABLE 7–1
Research Objectives for HMO Study

Research Objectives	Information Requirements
1. What is the probable demand for the proposed HMO?	1. General attitudes and awareness with respect to health care and the concept of prepaid plans, and specific attitudes and knowledge regarding existing health plans.
2. Which market segments will be most interested in the proposed HMO?	2. Process by which the present plan was selected; sources of information and influences.
3. What will be the probable rate of utilization of medical services by the most interested segment?	3. Satisfaction with present plan (a) overall (b) with respect to specific characteristics of the plan, and (c) intentions to change.
4. Which aspects of health plans have the greatest influence on the choice process?	4. Reaction to proposed HMO design (a) overall evaluation (b) evaluation of specific characteristics (c) preference, compared to present plan (d) likelihood of adoption (e) influence of changes in price and benefits
	5. Classification variables including demographics; distance from HMO; time in area; expected stay in area; and utilization of medical services by individual family members.

FORMATTING THE QUESTION

Before specific questions can be phrased, a decision has to be made as to the degree of freedom to be given respondents in answering the question. The alternatives are (1) open-ended with no classification, where the interviewer tries to record the response verbatim, (2) open-ended, where the interviewer uses precoded classifications to record the response, or (3) the closed or structured format in which a question or supplementary card presents the responses to be considered by the respondent. These options can be illustrated with the following brief sequence of questions from a personal interview survey:

Q. 10. Is there any particular type of information about life insurance that you would like to have, that you do not now have or don't know enough about?

       1 YES
       2 NO
       3 DON'T KNOW

If "YES" in Q. 10, ask:

_____

Q. 11. What kind of information?
PROBE: What else?

_____

_____

_____

The first question uses a precoded classification since a "yes" or "no" answer is strongly implied. The second question is completely open-ended, and the goal is to achieve an exact transcription. Only 20 percent of a national sample said "Yes" to question 10, and 44 percent of these responded only in very general terms to the follow-up question. This meant that only 11 percent of the total sample said they had a need for specific information, such as rate or family benefits in case of disability or accident. It is likely that different results would have been obtained if either Q10 or Q11 had been converted to a closed-end response, such that respondents were handed a card describing many different kinds of information and asked to indicate which they would like to have or didn't know enough about.

Open-Response Questions

The *advantages* of open-response questions stem from the wide range of responses that can be obtained and the lack of influence on the responses from prespecified categories. Respondents often appreciate this freedom, as illustrated by the surprising frequency with which people write marginal comments in mail surveys when they don't feel the response categories adequately capture their feelings. Because of these advantages, open-ended questions are useful in the following circumstances:[3]

- As an introduction to a survey or to a topic. A question such as, "In general, how do you feel about (color TV, this neighborhood, the bus service in this area)" will acquaint

[3]Sheatsley, *op. cit.*

the respondent with the subject of the survey, open the way for more specific questions, and make the respondent more comfortable with the questioning process.

- When it is important to measure the saliency of an issue to a respondent. (Asking "What do you think is the *most* important problem facing this country today?" will give some insight into what currently is bothering the respondent.)
- When there are too many possible responses to be listed, or they cannot be foreseen, for example, "What were some of the reasons why you decided to pay cash (for a major appliance purchase?)" or "What do you especially like about living in this neighborhood?"
- When verbatim responses are desired to give the flavor of people's answers or to cite as examples in a report.

Usually the *disadvantages* of open-ended questions overwhelm the advantages. The major problem is that variability in the clarity and depth of responses depends to a great extent on (1) the articulateness of the respondent in an interview situation, or the willingness to compose a written answer to a mail survey and (2) the personal or telephone interviewer's ability to record the verbatim answers quickly—or to accurately summarize—and to probe effectively. A third area arose in the previous chapter where we saw that the interviewer's expectations will influence what is selected for recording or when to stop probing. Open-ended questions are also time-consuming, both during the interview and during tabulation. Classifications must be established to summarize the responses, and each answer must be assigned to one or more categories. This involves subjective judgments that are prone to error. To minimize this source of error it may be desirable to have two editors independently categorize the responses and compare their results. This adds further to the cost.

In view of the disadvantages and the lack of convincing evidence that open-ended questions provide more meaningful, relevant, and nonrepetitive responses,[4] it is advisable to close up as many questions as possible in large-scale surveys.

Closed-Response Questions

There are two basic formats for closed-end questions. The respondent can be asked to make one or more choices from a list of possible responses. The second possibility is a rating scale where the respondent is given a continuum of labeled categories that represents the range of responses. Research organizations, such as McCollum/Spielman, use both formats to ask diagnostic questions about commercials—both the message (theme, basic idea, unique selling point, etc.) and the presentation (setting, demonstration devices,

[4]Stanley L. Payne, "Are Open-Ended Questions Worth the Effort?" *Journal of Marketing Research, 2* (November 1965), 417–418.

music, and so forth). The following sample of ad testing questions illustrates what can be done:

Choice from a list of responses

"Which of the following words or phrases best describes the kind of person you feel would be most likely to use this product—based on what you saw and heard in this commercial? (Check as many as apply)

☐ Young   ☐ Single

☐ Old   ☐ Married

☐ Modern   ☐ Homemaker

☐ Old-fashioned   ☐ Career woman
                                 (add further response
                                 categories as appropriate)

Single-choice rating on a scale

Please tell us your overall reaction to this commercial.

☐ A great commercial, would like to see it again

☐ A pretty good commercial

☐ Just so-so, like a million others

☐ Another bad commercial

Based on what you saw and heard in this commercial, how interested do you feel you would be in buying the product?

☐ Definitely would buy

☐ Probably would buy

☐ May or may not buy

☐ Probably would not buy

☐ Definitely would not buy

Regardless of the type of closed-response format, the *advantages* are the same. Such questions are easier to answer, in both an interview and a mail survey; require less effort by the interviewer; and make tabulation and analysis easier. There is less potential error due to differences in the way questions are asked and responses recorded. Normally, a closed-response question takes less time than an equivalent open-ended question. Perhaps the most significant advantage of these questions in large-scale surveys is that the answers are directly comparable from respondent to respondent (assuming each interprets the words the same way). Comparability of respondents is an essential prelude to the use of any analytical methods.

There are significant *limitations* to closed-response questions that one must constantly work to overcome. First, such questions are harder to develop—especially of the type illustrated by the multiple-choice question in the advertising survey. Good exploratory work is necessary to ensure that all potentially important response alternatives are included.

In one experiment, respondents were asked first, Who should manage company benefit funds, the company, the union or government? When these three alternatives were given, only 15 percent of the respondents suggested combinations. However, when the combinations were mentioned explicitly, the number choosing these alternatives jumped to 52 percent.[5] Second, the very nature of rigid closed responses provides fewer opportunities for self-expression or subtle qualifications, and they are not nearly so involving for the respondent.

Finally, the list of alternative response categories provides answers that might not have been considered by respondents, who are often reluctant to admit their ignorance of an issue or problem and easily can avoid such an admission by selecting a "reasonable" answer from the list. In awkward or sensitive situations the "reasonable" answer may be the one that is most socially acceptable. The opposite result will occur if the respondent tries to avoid a difficult choice or judgment by selecting the easiest alternative, such as "don't know." Where there is a distinct possibility of such biasing occurring in a personal or telephone interview survey, it may be desirable to precede the closed-response question with an open-response question. This is done often in brand-name awareness studies. The respondent is asked first what brands are associated with the product (unaided recall) and then is given a list of brands and asked to choose those that are known (aided recall).

The Number of Response Categories.　The number of *categories* can range from two all the way to a 100-point scale. Some questions—especially those dealing with points of fact—admit only two possible answers (Did you purchase a new car in the past year? Did you vote in the last election?). However, in most situations a dichotomous question will yield misleading results. Sometimes an either/or choice is not possible, and the correct answer may be both. In a survey of shaving habits, the question was asked, "Do you shave with an electric razor or a safety razor?" Some men apparently use both, the specific choice depending on the situation.[6] Attitudinal questions invariably have intermediate positions. A simple question such as "Are you considering changing your present health insurance plan?" found that 70 percent were not, 8 percent definitely were, and the remaining 22 percent were uncertain or might consider a change in the future. These subtleties are very important in interpreting such a question.

As a general rule the range of opinion on most issues can be captured best with five or seven categories. Five categories are probably the minimum needed to discriminate effectively among individuals. One popular 5-point scale is (1) strongly agree; (2) probably agree; (3) probably disagree; (4) strongly disagree, and (5) neutral or no opinion. This number of categories can be read by the interviewer and understood by the respondent. A seven- or nine-category scale is more precise but cannot be read to respondents with the assurance that they won't get confused.

Multiple-choice questions present special problems. Ideally, the response categories provided for such questions should be mutually exclusive and exhaust the possibilities.

[5]Stanley L. Payne, *The Art of Asking Questions, op. cit.,* p. 87.
[6]Boyd, Westfall, and Stasch, *Marketing Research,* 4th ed., Homewood, Ill.: Irwin, 1980.

Sometimes it is neither possible nor desirable to include all the possible alternatives. A listing of all the brands in a housewares product category, such as hand mixers, might include 50 or more names if all distributor-controlled and import brands were included. Since this is impractical, only the top five or six are listed and the rest are consigned to an "other" category, which is accompanied by a "please specify" request and a space to enter the brand name.

A common type of question requires numerical data in response: What is your annual income? How far is it to your work? How many stores did you visit? Usually it is preferable to group the possible answers into categories, for example, under $4000, $4000 to $7000 . . . $20,000 and over. This is a somewhat less sensitive way of asking an income question and facilitates coding. If the numbers falling in the response categories are not known or it is important to know the exact number (of children, pets, and so forth) for later analysis, this does not apply.

The Order of Response Categories. The order of presentation of categories to respondents in personal or telephone interview situations sometimes can have a big influence on results. For example, one way of asking a person's income over the telephone is to start low by asking, "Is your income *more* than $2000?" and increasing the figure in increments of $2000 until the first "no" response. Alternatively, one can start with the highest income category and drop the figure until the first "yes" response. A study in 1974 found that the median income when the first category was $2000 was $12,711; however, when the income question started with the high category, $17,184 was the median income.[7] One explanation for this remarkable difference is that respondents find the question threatening and try to get it out of the way by making a premature terminal response. A much better approach is to begin with the median income figure and use a series of branching questions, such as "Is it over (the median income)?" and if the answer is "no," then asking, "Is it under (half the median income)? and so forth. This gives a relatively unbiased measure of income and the lowest proportion of refusals.

Another ordering problem is encountered with mail survey questions in which respondents tend to select categories that are in the middle position of a range of values. This is especially prevalent with questions of fact, such as the number of checkouts at a local store. Respondents who do not know the answer will choose the center position as a safe guess. This also can happen with questions about information that is unique to the respondent, such as the distance to the nearest department store. When the question is constructed with multiple categories, with the middle category representing an estimate of the average distance, the natural tendency to choose the middle position may lead to inaccurate responses. One solution is to place the average or expected distance at various positions in the sequence of categories.

[7]W. B. Locander and J. P. Burton, "The Effect of Question Form on Gathering Income Data by Telephone," *Journal of Marketing Research, 13* (May 1976), 189–192.

Handling Uncertainty and Ignorance.   One awkward question concerns the handling of "don't know" and neutral responses. There are many reasons why respondents do not know the answer to a question, such as ignorance, forgetting, or an inability to articulate. If an explicit "don't know" response category is provided, it is an easy option for those in the latter group. But often "don't know" is a legitimate response and may yield very important insights.[8] Thus, the option always should be provided as a response to questions about knowledge or opinions when there is some likelihood of ignorance or forgetting. Sometimes this response category is used by those who are unwilling to answer a question. In personal and telephone interviews, it may be advisable to provide the interviewer with an additional "no answer" category to correctly identify these people. A neutral response category such as "not sure" or "neither like nor dislike" also may be desirable for those people who genuinely can't make a choice among specific opinion statements.

If there is likelihood of both ambivalence and ignorance, then both a neutral category and a "don't know" category are appropriate.

*"I'm undecided, but that doesn't mean I'm
apathetic or uninformed."*

Drawing by Barsotti; © 1980. The New Yorker Magazine, Inc.

---

[8]Indeed, Leo Bogart, in *Silent Politics: Polls and Awareness of Public Opinion* (New York: Wiley, 1972), argues that the most important and accurate thing that polls can tell us is the extent of public ignorance and knowledge.

QUESTION WORDING:
A PROBLEM OF COMMUNICATIONS

Our knowledge of how to phrase questions that are free from ambiguity and bias is such that it is easier to discuss what *not* to do rather than give prescriptions. Hence, the following guidelines are of greatest value in critically evaluating and improving an existing question.

1 *Is the vocabulary simple, direct and familiar to all respondents?* The challenge is to choose words that can be understood by all respondents, regardless of education level, but do not sound patronizing. The most common pitfall is to use technical jargon or specialized terms. Many respondents will not be able to identify their "marital status," but can say whether they are married, single, divorced, and so forth.

Special care must be taken to avoid words that have different meanings for different groups. This can be readily appreciated in cross-cultural studies, where translation problems are profound, but also is applicable within a country. One socioeconomic group may refer to the evening meal as dinner, while others call this meal supper and have their dinner at noon.

Mail surveys have a special problem with vocabulary because of the low levels of reading comprehension. A 1970 Harris poll found a very dismal picture:

- Thirteen percent of a sample of the U.S. population over 16 years of age (estimated at 24 percent if refusals were prorated) had serious literacy problems that impaired daily life

- Thirty-four percent of the sample could not fill out a simplified *Medicaid* application

- Eight percent of those with some college training had serious literacy problems

2 *Do any words have vague or ambiguous meanings?* A common error is not giving the respondent an adequate frame of reference in time and space for interpreting the question. Words such as "often," "occasionally," and "usually" lack an appropriate time referent, so each respondent chooses his own, with the result that answers are not comparable. Similarly, the appropriate space or locale often is not specified. Does the question, "How long have you lived here?" refer to this state, county, city, neighborhood, or particular house or apartment? Some words have many interpretations; thus, a respondent might interpret income to mean hourly pay rate, weekly salary, or monthly income, either before or after taxes and deductions, and could include or exclude sources of income other than wages and the incomes of other family members.

3 *Are any questions "double-barreled"?* There are questions in which a respondent can agree with one part of a question but not the other, or cannot answer at all without accepting a particular assumption. In either case, the answers cannot be interpreted. For example, what can be learned from such questions as, "Do you plan to leave your job and look for another one during the coming year?" or, "Are you satisfied with the cost and convenience of this (service)?" The second type of error is a bit more elusive to find, as the following example from a Harris poll demonstrates. The question was, "Have you often, sometimes, hardly ever, or never felt bad because you were unfaithful to your wife?" One percent said often, 14 percent said sometimes or hardly ever, and 85 percent said they never felt bad because of this.[9]

4 *Are any questions leading or loaded?* A leading question is one that clearly suggests the answer or reveals the researcher's (or interviewer's) opinion. This can be done easily by adding "don't you agree?" or "wouldn't you say?" to a desired statement.

A loaded question introduces a more subtle bias. A common type of loading of possible responses is through failure to provide a full range of alternatives, for example by asking, "How do you generally spend your free time, watching television, or what?" Another way to load a question is to provide the respondent with a reason for one of the alternatives: "Should we increase taxes in order to get more housing and better schools, or should we keep them about the same?"

A second form of loading results from the use of emotionally charged words. These are words or phrases such as "fair profits," "radical," or "luxury items" that have such strong positive or negative overtones that they overshadow the specific content of the question. Organizations and groups also have emotional associations, and using them to endorse a proposition will certainly bias the response: "A committee of experts has suggested . . . ; Do you approve of this, or do you disapprove?" For this reason it is also risky to reveal the sponsor of the study. If one brand or company is identified as the sponsor, the respondents will tend to exaggerate their positive feelings toward the brand.

Questions that involve appeals or threats to the respondent's self-esteem may also be loaded.[10] A question on occupations usually will produce more "executives," if the respondent chooses from one of a small number of occupational categories, than if it asks for a specific job title.

5 *Are the instructions potentially confusing?* Sheatsley counsels against lengthy questions that explain a complicated situation to a respondent and then ask for an opinion.[11] In his experience, "If the respondent is not aware of these facts, you have probably confused or biased him more than you have enlightened him, and his opinion won't mean much in either case." The question should be directed more toward measuring the respondent's knowledge or interest in the subject.

6 *Is the question applicable to all respondents?* Respondents may try to answer a question even though they don't qualify or may lack an opinion. Examples of such questions are, "What is your present occupation?" (assumes respondent is working), "Where did you live before you moved here?" (assumes a prior move), or, "For whom did you vote in the last election?" (assumes that respondent voted). The solution to this is to ask a qualifying or filter question and limit further questioning to those who qualify.

---

[9]Example cited by Sheatsley, *op. cit.*
[10]Such questions are vulnerable to the prestige seeking and social desirability response bias discussed in Chapter 6.
[11]Sheatsley, *op. cit.*

7 *Split ballot technique.* Whenever there is doubt as to the appropriate wording, it is desirable to test several alternatives. For instance, the responses to a question may vary with the degrees of personalization. The question, "Do you think there should be government-run off-track betting in this state?" is different from, "Is it desirable to have government-run off-track betting in this state?" Sometimes the choice can be resolved by the purpose of the study; the impersonal form being preferred if the study aims at measuring the general tenor of public sentiment. Where the choice is not obvious, the best solution is to use one version in half the questionnaire and the other version in the remaining half. Any significant differences in the results can be helpful in interpreting the meaning of the question.

SEQUENCE AND LAYOUT DECISIONS

The order or sequence of questions will be determined initially by the need to gain and maintain the cooperation of the respondent and make the questionnaire as easy as possible for the interviewer to administer. Once these considerations are satisfied, attention must be given to the problem of **order bias**—the possibility that prior questions will influence answers to subsequent questions.

The basic guidelines for sequencing a questionnaire to make it interesting and logical to both interviewer and respondent are straightforward:

1 Open the interview with an easy and nonthreatening question. This helps to establish rapport and build the confidence of the respondent in his or her ability to answer.[12] For most routine interviewing it is better to start this way than offer a lengthy explanation of the survey. It may even be desirable to design a throwaway question for this purpose: "We're doing a survey on medical care. The first question is, what do you usually do when you have a cold?"

2 The questionnaire should flow smoothly and logically from one topic to the next. Sudden shifts in topic are to be avoided, as they tend to confuse respondents and cause indecision. When a new topic is introduced, a transition statement or question should be used, explaining how the new topic relates to what has been discussed previously or to the purpose of the study.

3 For most topics it is better to proceed from broad, general questions to the more specific. Thus, one might ask, "What are some of the things you like about this community? What things don't you like?" and proceed to, "How about the transportation facilities generally?" and finally, "Should they add another bus or widen the highway?"[13] This funnel approach helps the respondent put the specific question in a broader context and give a more thoughtful answer.

[12]R. L. Kahn and C. F. Cannell, *The Dynamics of Interviewing* (New York: Wiley, 1957).
[13]Sheatsley, *op. cit.*

4 Sensitive or difficult questions dealing with income status, ability, and so forth should not be placed at the beginning of the questionnaire. Rather, they should be introduced at a point where the respondent has developed some trust and confidence in the interviewer and the study. In short interviews they can be postponed until the end of the questionnaire.

The physical layout of the questionnaire also will influence whether the questionnaire is interesting and easy to administer. For self-administered questionnaires the quality of the paper, the clarity of reproduction, and the appearance of crowding are important variables. Similarly, the job of the interviewer is considerably eased if the questionnaire is not crowded, if precise instructions are provided, and if flow diagrams with arrows and boxes are used to guide the interviewer through filter questions.

Order Bias: Does the Question Create the Answer?

We have indicated already that it is usually preferable to ease a respondent into a subject by beginning with some general, orienting questions. However, when the topic is unfamiliar to the respondents—or their involvement with the subject is low—the nature of the early questions will impact significantly on subsequent answers.

A new product concept test is the most prevalent example of an unfamiliar subject. Respondents typically are given a description of the new product and asked to express their degree of buying interest. As one study showed, however, this interest will depend on the sequence of preceding questions.[14] The new product was described as a combination pen-and-pencil selling for 29¢. Four different types of questions were asked of four matched sets of respondents before the buying-interest question was asked:

Questions Preceding Buying Interest Question	Percentage of Respondents "Very Much Interested" in Buying New Product
1. No question asked	2.8
2. Asked only about advantages	16.7
3. Asked only about disadvantages	0.0
4. Asked about both advantages and disadvantages	5.7

The nature of the preceding questions definitely establishes the frame of reference to be used by the respondent. The issue for the questionnaire designer is to decide which is the most valid frame of reference; that is, which corresponds most closely to the type of

---

[14]Edwin J. Gross, ''The Effect of Question Sequence on Measures of Buying Interest,'' *Journal of Advertising Research, 4* (September 1964), 41.

thinking that would precede an actual purchase decision in this product category. The same problem confronts survey researchers dealing with social issues that are not of immediate relevance to the respondent. The "cautionary tale" by Charles Ramond in the accompanying box shows how questions create answers in these settings.[15]

WHEN QUESTIONS CREATE ANSWERS

Suppose I were to call you on the telephone as follows: "Hello, this is Charles Ramond of the XYZ Poll. We are trying to find out what people think about certain issues. Do you watch television?"

Whatever your answer, the next question is, "Some people say that oil tankers are spilling oil and killing the fish and want to pass a law against this, do you agree or disagree?" Your answer is duly recorded and the next question is, "Have you ever read or heard anything about this?"

Again, your answer is recorded and finally I ask "Do you think anyone should do anything about this? Who? What?"

And now the main question. "I'd like you to rate some companies on a scale from minus five to plus five, minus five if you totally dislike the company, plus five if you totally like it and zero if you are in between or indifferent. First, U.S. Steel." You give a number and I say "The gas company." You give another number and I say "Exxon."

You see what is happening. Or do you. Suppose I now tell you that this form of questioning is given only to a random half of a large sample called the experimental group. To the control group, the interview is as follows: "Hello, this is Charles Ramond from XYZ Poll. We are trying to find out what people think about certain things. Do you ever watch TV?" You answer and then I ask, "Now I'd like you to rate some companies on a scale from minus five to plus five. . . ." Any difference in average rating between the experimental and control group can be attributed to them having thought about tankers spilling oil and killing the fish, for that is the only difference in the way the two groups were treated.

Questions Shape the Attitudes

I think you can see for yourselves, merely by following this interview pattern, how you might very well rate companies differently after having rehearsed your "attitude" toward oil pollution than without having done so. In case it is difficult for you to imagine how you would respond under these two conditions, I can assure you that random halves of well drawn samples of certain elite publics rated large companies very differently, depending on whether they were in the experimental or control group. They did so in survey after survey, consistently over time, thereby showing the reliability of the phenomenon.

---

[15]Charles Ramond, "When Questions Create Answers," Speech to the Annual Meeting, *Advertising Research Foundation*. New York, May 1977.

COMPUTER-CONTROLLED TELEPHONE INTERVIEWING

Computers are being used increasingly to control the administration and sequence of questions asked by an interviewer seated at a terminal equipped with a cathode ray display. This use of computers provides researchers with a way to prevent many interviewer errors, such as choosing the wrong respondent in a household, failing to ask a question that should be asked, or asking a series of questions that isn't appropriate for a particular respondent. If the respondent selection procedure or the skip patterns in a questionnaire are complicated, these interviewer errors are more likely to happen. When control of the question sequence is turned over to the computer, the interviewer is theoretically free to concentrate fully on reading the questions, recording the answers, and establishing rapport with the respondent.

There are some limitations to computer-controlled telephone interviewing. It is generally more expensive to use the computer than to administer the traditional paper-and-pencil questionnaire. For that reason, use of a computer-controlled system is recommended when a large number of surveys must be done or when the questionnaire will be used many times in a tracking study.

A second limitation relates to the problems involved in using a mechanical system and to human error in its programming and operation. A program must be written and carefully debugged for each questionnaire. The computer system must be able to handle the demands of a large number of interviewers. At the worst, several days of interviewing may pass before someone notices that a mistake has been made and the questionnaire program is incorrectly skipping over a crucial series of questions. Valuable interviewing time and money may be lost if the computer system becomes overloaded and "crashes." At its best, computer-controlled telephone interviewing can produce faster, more complete, data to the researcher.

The following are some of the features built into many computer systems that are used for marketing research.[16]

1 *Control of skip patterns or branching.* A skip occurs whenever the presentation of a question depends on the answer to a previous question. The computer ensures that the correct path is followed through the questionnaire, accomplishing this faster and more accurately than can an interviewer.

2 *Random respondent selector.* The interviewer types in the identities of all members of the household, and the computer randomly selects the person to be interviewed. This helps ensure a representative sample.

3 *"Customized" questionnaires.* The entire questionnaire can be tailored to a respondent on the basis of key information given early in the interview. For example, a respondent may indicate that only a few product attributes from a long list are judged to be

[16]Tyzoon Tyebjee, "Telephone Survey Methods: The State of the Art," *Journal of Marketing, 43* (Summer 1979), 66–78.

important. After this point, the questioning would be limited to these important attributes.

4 *Question and answer category rotation.* The computer rotates the order of questions in a series and of answer categories within a question when these are read to a respondent. This removes the bias that may occur because questions or answers at the start of a list are favored compared to those at the end.

5 *Personalization and consistency check.* The computer is able to incorporate responses to previous questions into the text of succeeding questions. For example, "When your oldest son, Greg, borrows the car, does he usually take the Chevrolet or the Toyota?" This personalization helps improve the rapport between the interviewer and the respondent. A related feature is that of a consistency check. If the respondent says he and his wife made three trips in the past year and then names four such occasions, the computer prompts the interviewer to probe for the correct number, three or four.

Developments such as these do represent advances over the traditional method of telephone interviewing. The researcher should, however, think about the potential misuse of this new technology and how to avoid it. In particular, there is a tendency to design longer and more complicated surveys. These surveys may lead to increased frustration or boredom for interviewers and respondents, the end result being more terminations and a decline in the quality of the data.

Self-Administered Computer Interviewing. The next stage in the development of computer-controlled interviewing is to bypass the interviewer entirely.[17] Increased computer literacy, improved software, and the rapidly declining cost of personal computers have made it feasible to provide respondents with a PC and have them enter their responses on the keyboard in response to instructions on the video screen. These portable interviewing systems have been used to collect data at trade shows, professional conferences, product clinics, and shopping malls. For example, Levi Strauss surveyed the trade's opinions of trends in active wear at a National Sporting Goods Show. The Borg-Warner Acceptance Corp. conducted an image and media-usage study about trade inventory financing at a National Association of Music Merchants Show.

The best results have been obtained at trade and professional shows where there is a highly concentrated pool of qualified respondents. The benefits are considerable: speed, accuracy (as the data is only entered once) and visual prescreening of qualified respondents by using conference badges. The costs are reasonable: ten minute, custom interviews with 500 respondents would cost between $8,000 and $10,000. Costs can be reduced further if there are several clients sharing the same interview. The experience of the Chevrolet Division of General Motors illustrates just how much time can potentially be saved:

---

[17]Bernie Whalen, "On-Site Computer Interviewing Yields Research Data Instantly," *Marketing News* (November 9, 1984), 1–17.

ON-SITE COMPUTER INTERVIEWING

Chevrolet used to hire interviewers to ask attendees at new model showings a series of questions. After the show the completed questionnaires were coded and the results tabulated. The results would be available in a research report between four and eight weeks later. This time lag made it difficult for the designers to act on the findings.

At the 1984 Chicago Auto Show, Chevrolet used portable computers to survey auto owners about a prototype of a new minivan that was on display. Nearly 800 prospective customers were recruited and then asked to complete a questionnaire displayed on the monitor of an IBM-PC. As they tapped in their answers on the keyboard, the results were transmitted by phone lines to a computer time-sharing bureau which processed the data and returned summary reports to a printer located at the auto show.

One day after the show the complete results were available. Among the findings was a perceived problem with the location of the fuel-filler door in the middle of the side body panel. This suggested a design modification that was later implemented.

PRETESTING AND CORRECTING PROBLEMS

First drafts of questionnaires tend to be too long, often lacking important variables, and subject to all the hazards of ambiguous, ill-defined, loaded, or double-barreled questions. The objective of the questionnaire pretest is to identify and correct these deficiencies.

Effective pretesting demands that the researcher be open to criticism and have a willingness to pursue the deficiencies. Thus, a good starting point is for the researcher to take the respondent's point of view and try to answer the questions.

As a pretest is a pilot run, the respondents should be reasonably representative of the sample population. However, they should not all be "typical," for much can be learned from those at the extremes of the sample. Will the questions work with those who have a limited education, strong negative opinions, or little understanding of the subject? Only small samples are necessary—15 is sufficient for a short and straightforward questionnaire, while 25 may be needed if the questionnaire is long and complex with many branches and multiple options. Even when the field survey is to be done by mail the pretest should be done with a personal or telephone interview to get direct feedback on problems. Only the best, most insightful, and experienced interviewers should be used for this work.

A personal interview pretest can use either a debriefing or protocol approach. In the *debriefing* approach the questionnaire is administered first, just as it would be in the full-scale study. For example, a mail survey would be filled out without assistance from the interviewer; however, the interviewer should be instructed to observe and note reactions of confusion, resistance, or uneasiness. When the interview is completed, the interviewer should debrief the respondent by asking what he or she was thinking about when forming each answer, whether there were any problems of understanding, and whether any aspects of the subject were not covered by the questions.

In the *protocol* method the subject is asked to "think aloud" as he or she is filling out the questionnaire. The interviewer records these thoughts, and at the end of the pretest asks for further clarification of problems where necessary. The latter approach seems to work better when the pretest is being done by telephone rather than face-to-face. Respondents offer more frequent and extensive comments over the telephone because they lack nonverbal means of communication.

There are limits to how well a pretest can detect errors. One study found that pretest respondents were virtually unable to detect loaded questions, and most did not recognize when response alternatives were missing or questions were ambiguous.[18] For example less than ten percent of a pretest sample pointed out the ambiguity of the following question: "Do you think things will be better or worse next summer than they are now?" Five response options were provided ranging from much better to much worse.

Although it only requires one perceptive or confused respondent to identify problems or improvements, they are not the only source of insights. Interviewers are equally important to the pretesting process. Once the interviewers have reported their experiences, they also should be asked for their suggestions. There is a danger that some interviewers will make changes in the field on their own initiative if they believe it will make their job easier. This can create serious problems if some interviewers make the change and others do not.

Finally, the pretest analysis should return full-circle to the first step in the design process. Each question should be reviewed once again and asked to justify its place in the questionnaire. How will the answer be used in the analysis? Is the pattern of answers from the pretest sensible, or difficult to interpret? Does the question add substantial new information or unnecessarily duplicate the results from another question? Of course the last step in the process may be another pretest, if far-reaching changes have been necessary.

SUMMARY

As with most steps in the research process, the design of the questionnaire is highly iterative. Because it is an integral part of the research design, the objective is to seek consistency with the other elements of the design, notably the research purpose, the budget, and the methods of analysis. Additional constraints are imposed by the data collection method and the respondent's ability and willingness to answer questions about the subject.

Within these constraints the questionnaire writer practices this art through the adroit choice of wording, response format, sequencing of questions, and layout of the ques-

[18]Shelby Hunt, Richard D. Sparkman and James B. Wilcox, "The Pretest in Survey Research: Issues and Preliminary Findings," *Journal of Marketing Research*, (May 1982), 269–273.

tionnaire. Success in this activity comes from experience, an ability to look at the subject and the wording of the questions from the respondent's perspective, and a good understanding of the objectives of the research. Guidelines for writing and organizing questionnaires have been presented in this chapter. Since they are a distillation of the experience of many researchers, adherence to these principles will narrow further the range of problems. Ultimately, a good questionnaire is one that has been thoroughly pretested. There can be no substitute for this step in the process.

QUESTIONS AND PROBLEMS

1 Open-response questions sometimes are used to establish the saliency or importance of issues, such as irritation from clutter due to excessive advertisements and station announcements during TV programs. Why would you want to use this type of response format rather than a closed-response question?

2 How do the responses from an unaided recall question on brand awareness compare to those from an aided recall question?

3 One general rule for sequencing questions in a questionnaire is to proceed from the general to the specific. What is the reason for this rule? Can you think of circumstances where the rule should be ignored?

4 Since a researcher cannot control the order in which respondents answer mail survey questions, is sequencing of those questions important?

5 Use the formula for the randomized response model to estimate the percentage of respondents who indicated they did not report all their income to the federal tax authorities in a survey in which a total of 16 percent answered "yes." Also, 10 percent of the sample were estimated to have their birthdays in June (and so would have answered "yes" to the innocuous question) and a coin toss was used to choose which of the two questions to answer.

6 Evaluate the following questions and suggest improvements:

a Please check the following activities in which you participate *as a private citizen* interested in environmental protection:

Read books and articles on the subject ☐
Belong to an environmental group ☐
Attend lectures, meetings on the subject ☐
Write letters to legislators, newspapers, or government officials ☐
Make speeches, published articles ☐
Other (please specify) ☐

b When you eat dinner out do you usually eat at the same place:
Yes ☐   No ☐

c Is the current level of government regulation of automobile safety features adequate or inadequate?

Adequate ☐   Inadequate ☐

d Where do you buy most of your groceries? _____

e Do you think that Con Edison is doing everything possible to reduce air pollution from their electricity generating stations?

Yes ☐   No ☐

f Please indicate how much of an average issue of *Sunset* magazine you usually read:

1. Less than 1/3   ☐
2. 1/3 to 1/2   ☐
3. over 1/2   ☐

g Those in favor of setting up an additional federal consumer protection agency on top of the other agencies say it is needed because the agencies we have are not getting the job done themselves. Those who oppose setting up the additional agency say we have plenty of government agencies to protect consumers and it's just a matter of making them work better. How do you feel?

h Do you often attend the theater?

i Do you think taxes are too high now?

j Everybody knows that teenagers and their parents have lots of arguments. What are some of the things you and your parents have argued about lately?

7 A large automobile manufacturer has asked you to develop a questionnaire to measure owners' satisfaction with the servicing of their vehicles. One sequence of questions will deal with satisfaction with the design, construction, operating costs, performance, and amount of service required. In order to interpret these results it has been decided to ask further questions to isolate the responsibility for car problems. That is, do car owners tend to blame the manufacturers, the service work by the dealer, or poor upkeep and driving habits of car owners?

APPENDIX
ASKING SENSITIVE QUESTIONS

One virtually can guarantee meaningless responses by directly asking such questions as, "Have you ever defaulted on a credit account?" "Do you smoke pot at least once a week?" or, "Have you ever been involved in an unreported automobile accident?" However, sometimes a research question will involve sensitive areas. There are a variety of approaches that can be used to attempt to get honest answers. For example, long, open-ended questions with familiar wording have been found effective when asking threatening questions that require quantified responses. The only limit is the creativity of the researcher. Alan Barton made this point best when in 1958 he composed the following parody on ways to ask the question, "Did you kill your wife?"[19]

1 The Casual Approach:
"Do you happen to have murdered your wife?"

2 The Numbered Card:
"Would you please read off the number on this card which corresponds to what became of your wife?" (*Hand card to respondent.*)
    1. Natural death
    2. I killed her
    3. Other (what?)
    (GET CARD BACK FROM RESPONDENT BEFORE PROCEEDING!)

3 The Everybody Approach:
"As you know, many people have been killing their wives these days. Do you happen to have killed yours?"

4 The "Other People" Approach:
  a "Do you know any people who have murdered their wives?"
  b "How about yourself?"

5 The Sealed Ballot Technique:
In this version you explain that the survey respects people's right to anonymity in respect to their marital relations, and that they themselves are to fill out the answer to the question, seal it in an envelope, and drop it in a box conspicuously labelled "Sealed Ballot Box" carried by the interviewer.

6 The Kinsey Technique:
Stare firmly into respondent's eyes and ask in simple, clear-cut language such as that to which the respondent is accustomed, and with an air of assuming that everyone has done everything, "Did you ever kill your wife?"

The Randomized Response Technique

There is good evidence that accurate answers to sensitive questions sometimes can be obtained with the randomized response technique. The respondent is asked to answer one of two randomly selected questions without revealing which question has been answered. One of the questions is sensitive, the other is innocuous, such as, "Does your birthday occur during the month of October?" The respondent selects which of the two questions

[19]A. J. Barton, "Asking the Embarrassing Question," *Public Opinion Quarterly,* Spring 1958, 67–68.

to answer by flipping a coin or looking at the last number of his or her driver's license or Social Security card to see if it is odd or even. Since the interviewer records a "yes" or "no" answer without knowing which question has been answered, the respondent feels free to answer honestly.[20]

Suppose a sample of 1000 respondents has been given a card with two possible questions:

1 Have you smoked marijuana during the past year?
2 Is the last digit of your driver's license equal to seven?

After flipping a coin to choose which question to answer, 30 percent, or 300, respond "yes." How can the proportion who responded "yes" to Question A be determined from this information? First, we know that each question has an equal probability of being chosen, because a coin flip was used. Therefore (p(Question A is chosen) = p(Question B is chosen) = 0.5. In other words $0.5 \times$ (total sample of 1000) = 500 respondents answered question A, and 500 answered question B. We also can estimate that 10 percent of those answering question B would have said "yes," because they would have had a seven as the last digit of their license. This also means that only 50 of those choosing question B would have answered yes, since $0.10 \times 500 = 50$. This formula is presented in the following table:

	Question	Estimated Sample Size	×	Estimated Percentage "Yes"	=	Estimated Responses "Yes"
A.	Have you smoked marijuana during the past year?	500	×	?	=	?
B.	Is the last digit of your driver's license equal to seven?	500	×	10	=	50
	The total population	1000	×	30	=	300

We also know, however, that 300 respondents actually answered "yes." In order for this to have happened, there must have been 250 respondents who answered "yes" to the sensitive question. Thus we can estimate that $250 \div 500 = 50$ percent of the sample

[20]Cathy Campbell and Brian L. Joiner, "How to Get the Answer without Being Sure You've Asked the Question," *The American Statistician, 27* (December 1973), 229–231; and James E. Reinmuth and Michael D. Guerts, "The Collection of Sensitive Information Using a Two-Stage Randomized Response Model," *Journal of Marketing Research, 12* (November 1975), 402–407.

had smoked marijuana in the past year. To summarize, the unknown proportion, x, answering ''yes'' to a sensitive question, can be determined from the following formula.

$$p(\text{Yes}) = p(\text{Question A is chosen}) \times p(\text{yes answer to Question A})$$
$$+ p(\text{Question B is chosen}) \times p(\text{yes answer to Question B}); \text{therefore,}$$
$$.30 = (0.5)(x) + (0.5)(0.1)$$
$$0.5x = .3 - 0.05 = .25$$
$$x = .25 \div 0.5 = .5$$

CASE 7–1
Essex Markets (B)[21]

Essex Markets, a small chain of supermarkets, was planning a study to evaluate their program of supplying unit price information on shelf tags. Among the research questions were:

What percentage of the shoppers were aware that unit pricing was being supplied?

What percentage of the shoppers used unit pricing and with what frequency?

Assume that shoppers will be intercepted in checkout lines. Write a series of questions that will allow you to answer the research questions.

[21]Prepared by Bruce McElroy and David A. Aaker as a basis for class discussion.

CASE 7–2
Smith's Clothing (A)

John Simpson, the head of Simpson Research, was attempting to design a marketing research study that would address the research questions posed by Jim Andrews, the president of Smith's Clothing, during their morning meeting. The research questions seemed rather well defined:

1 Which women's clothing stores compete with Smith's?

2 What is the image of Smith's, and how does this image compare with that of its competitors? In other words, how is Smith's positioned with respect to its competitors?

3 Who is the Smith customer and how does she differ from that of Smith's competitors?

Although no final judgment had been made, Andrews was leaning toward an in-home, self-administered questionnaire. He was not certain, however, whether a questionnaire could be developed that would be responsive to the research questions. The population of interest was operationally defined to be those women whose family income exceeded the median income. Simpson's immediate task was to draft a questionnaire and to develop a tentative sampling plan.

Smith's was a six-store chain of women's clothing stores located in Bayview, a large, growing city in the Southwestern United States. The chain had provided fine clothing for the upper class of Bayview for over 40 years. Twenty years previously, Smith's had opened its first suburban store. Having closed its downtown store ten years ago, it now had five suburban stores and one in a nearby community of 60,000 people. Smith's had avoided trendy fashions over the years, in favor of classic, lasting designs. During the last ten years a set of five or six aggressive, high-fashion retailers had expanded into or within Bayview. Thus, despite the fact that the market for fine women's clothes had expanded enormously during the past decade, the competition had grown much more intense.

Andrews was justifiably concerned about the performance of his stores. Profits at five of the six stores had fallen during each of the past four years. The sixth store had been opened only 18 months before and had not achieved its target growth rate. Although the chain was still profitable, if the existing trend continued it would soon be losing money.

This performance had stimulated Andrews to engage in serious reappraisal of the whole operation. In particular, he was reviewing the chain's rather conservative policy toward the product line, advertising, store decor, and store personnel. He felt that it might be time to consider stocking some trendy fashions and attempting to increase the store's appeal to women in their teens and twenties. A working hypothesis was that Smith's had a higher appeal relative to other stores to women over 40 and was less attractive to younger women. He realized that any such move was risky in that it would jeopardize the existing customer franchise without any guarantee that new customers would compensate. Before making any such move he felt that it was critical to learn exactly how Smith's was now positioned. He also felt that he needed a much more reliable fix on the current Smith customers in terms of their age, stores in which they shop, their preferences, and their purchase profile. With such information he would be in a much better position to identify alternatives and evaluate them.

ASSIGNMENT

Develop a research design including:

1 The type of survey to be employed

2 A questionnaire

CASE 7–3
Match-Mate

Bob Johnson, a marketing research staff member, has been asked to estimate the demand for a new product concept, tentatively called Match-Mate, before final development begins. The concept involves packaging 10 regular (Winston) and 10 menthol (Salem) cigarettes in the same pack for those who switch back and forth between regular and menthol. Technical development is not yet complete, since the menthol odor permeates most wraps. Research and development believes this problem is solvable, but before investing research effort in it a preliminary demand estimate is required.

Johnson has on his desk a research proposal for a telephone survey. A national random sample of 600 cigarette smokers would be phoned via a WATS line. The sample would be drawn from telephone directories and a screening question would be used to determine whether they were smokers. If he makes a positive decision on this proposal it will cost $8000. He is wondering (1) whether the proposed questionnaire will deliver the necessary information, and (2) what improvements could be made.

Sample Questionnaire for Telephone Survey

1 Do you smoke cigarettes? ☐ Yes ☐ No (If no, ask for someone in household who does; if none, end interview)

2 Which brands do you smoke, from most to least?

_____   _____
            Most   Least

3 How many, on the average, do you smoke each day of each brand?

☐ Over 1 pack   ☐ Over 1 pack   ☐ Over 1 pack
☐ 1/2 to 1 pack   ☐ 1/2 to 1 pack   ☐ 1/2 to 1 pack
☐ Less than 1/2 pack ☐ Less than 1/2 pack ☐ Less than 1/2 pack

4 How often do you change brands?

☐ Several times a day   ☐ Every few weeks
☐ About every day   ☐ Rarely
☐ Every few days   ☐ Never

5 Do you ever carry 2 packs so you'll have different brands for yourself?

☐ Yes ☐ No (If yes:) Which two brands? _____

6 (If smoke more than one brand:) Why do you smoke more than one brand?

_____

_____

_____

7 Do you ever carry 2 packs so you'll have another brand for someone else?

☐ Yes ☐ No (If yes:) Who?
☐ Wife   ☐ Girlfriend
☐ Husband   ☐ Boyfriend
☐ Friend   ☐ Other

8 Do you like menthol cigarettes?

☐ Yes ☐ No

9 (Describe Match Mates) Do you like this idea?

☐ Yes ☐ No ☐ Don't know

Why?

_____

_____

_____

10 (If yes or don't know:) Which 2 brands would you like?

_____ _____

Would you like menthol with regular? ☐ Yes ☐ No
Would you buy it with Winston & Salem? ☐ Yes ☐ No
If you bought Match-Mate, what brands would it be instead of?

_____ _____

11 [Demographic questions—age, sex, location, etc.]

8

ATTITUDE
MEASUREMENT

The majority of questions in marketing research surveys **are designed to measure attitudes.** For example, each of the following situations involves the measurement of some aspect of a respondent's attitude:

- An appliance manufacturer wants to know how many potential buyers are *aware* of his brand name (what brand names do they think of in connection with dishwashers?)

- Administrators concerned with formulating an energy policy want to know what proportion of the voters agree that car buyers should pay an extra tax of several hundred dollars on cars that get poor gasoline mileage.

- A food manufacturer is interested in the *intentions* of a sample of consumers to buy a possible new product after a description of the concept has been shown to them.

- Operators of an urban transit system want to know whether an aggressive advertising campaign has improved the attitudes of nonriders toward the reliability, safety, and economy of bus travel for work trips.

Common to each of these examples is a need to learn something about the basic orientation or attitude of present or prospective customers. Included within their attitudes is the information they have, their feelings of liking and disliking, and their intentions to behave.

What management really wants to understand—and ultimately influence—is behavior. For many reasons, however, they are likely to use attitude measures instead of behavior. First, there is a widely held belief that attitudes are precursors of behavior. If someone likes a brand, they are more likely to choose that brand over one that is less preferred. Second, it is generally more feasible to ask attitude questions than to observe and interpret actual behavior. Where attitude measures offer the greatest advantage over behavior measures is their capacity for *diagnosis* or *explanation*. Attitude measures can be used to help learn which features of a new product concept are acceptable or unacceptable, as well as the perceived strengths and weaknesses of competitive alternatives. Insights can be gained into the process by which choice decisions are made: What alternatives are known and considered? Why are some rejected? What problems are encountered with the products or services that are used?

In this chapter we are concerned primarily with the measurement of attitudes. Some measurement approaches have been encountered in earlier chapters. Projective techniques and physiological methods discussed in Chapter 5 are indirect methods for inferring a person's attitude. By far the most popular approach is the direct self-report, in which the respondent is asked a series of questions. The two previous chapters describe the survey methods appropriate for such self-reports. This chapter and the next are devoted specifically to attitude measurements, in recognition of their importance to marketing and of the special problems of specifying and identifying attitudes.

WHAT ARE ATTITUDES?

Attitudes are mental states used by individuals to structure the way they perceive their environment and guide the way they respond to it. There is general acceptance that there are three related components that form an attitude: a cognitive or knowledge component, a liking or affective component, and an intentions or actions component. Each component provides a different insight into a person's attitude.

The Cognitive or Knowledge Component

This represents a person's information about an object. This information includes *awareness* of the existence of the object, *beliefs* about the characteristics or attributes of the object, and judgments about the relative *importance* of each of the attributes.

Consider the knowledge a person could bring to the planning of a ski vacation in the Rockies. They might remember the names of several ski areas without prompting: Aspen, Snowmass, Alta, and Park City, for example. This is *unaided recall awareness.* The names of additional ski areas are likely to be remembered when the travel agent mentions them. This is *aided recall awareness.*

Knowledge of ski areas is not limited to awareness, however. From the experience of friends, brochures, magazine articles, and other sources, the person would have formed beliefs or judgments about the characteristics or attributes of each of these ski areas. These attributes might range from the difficulty of the slopes to the type of social life and cost of accommodation. Often these beliefs incorporate explicit comparative judgments, such as which ski area is the most difficult or the cheapest, within a set. Another kind of belief is an overall *similarity judgment:* Are Aspen and Snowmass more similar than Aspen and Alta, for example?

The Affective or Liking Component

This summarizes a person's overall feelings toward an object, situation, or person, on a like–dislike, or favorable–unfavorable scale. When there is a number of alternatives to choose among, then liking is expressed in terms of *preference* for one alternative over another. Preferences can be measured by asking which is "most preferred" or the "first choice," which is the "second choice," and so forth. Affective judgments also can be made about the attributes of an object, such as a ski area. Someone may like all other aspects of an area but dislike the location because it requires too much traveling.

The Action or Intentions Component

This refers to a person's expectations of future behavior toward an object. Is she "very," "somewhat," or "not at all" likely to go to Aspen for a ski week next winter? Intentions are usually limited to a distinct time period that depends on buying habits and planning horizons. The great advantage of an intentions question is that it incorporates information about a respondent's ability or willingness to pay for the object or otherwise take action. One may prefer Aspen over all other ski areas in the Rockies but have no intention of going next year because of the cost.

PROPERTIES OF ATTITUDE MEASUREMENT SCALES

Attitude variables—such as beliefs, preferences, and intentions—are measured with rating scales. These scales provide respondents with a set of numbered categories that represent the range of possible judgments or positions. An attitude scale involves measurement in the same sense that a thermometer measures temperature or a ruler measures distance. In each case measurement means the assignment of numbers to objects or persons to represent quantities of their attributes. For example, the attributes of a person include his income, social class, attitude, and so forth.

The assignment of numbers is made according to rules that should correspond to the properties of whatever is being measured. The rule may be very simple, as when a bus route is given a number to distinguish it from other routes. Here the only property is identity, and any comparisons of numbers are meaningless. This is a **nominal scale**. At the other extreme is the *ratio* scale, which has very rigorous properties. In between the extremes are **ordinal** and **interval scales**, as shown in Table 8–1. It is very important to understand the differences among the types of scales and to be able to identify them in practice, for their properties put significant restrictions on the interpretation and use of the resulting measurements.

TABLE 8–1
Types of Scales of Measurement

Scale	Rules for Assigning Number	Typical Application
Nominal	Objects are either identical or different	Classification (by sex, geographic area, social class)
Ordinal or Rank Order	Objects are greater or smaller	Rankings (preferences, class standing)
Interval	Intervals between adjacent ranks are equal	Index numbers, temperature scales, some attitude measures
Ratio	There is a meaningful zero point so comparisons of absolute magnitude are possible	Sales, incomes, units produced, costs, age

SOURCE: Adapted from S. S. Stevens, "On The Theory of Scales of Measurement," *Science* (June 7, 1946), 677–680.

Nominal Scales

Objects are assigned to mutually exclusive, labeled categories, but there are no necessary relationships among the categories; that is, no ordering or spacing are implied. If one entity is assigned the same number as another, they are identical with respect to a nominal variable. Otherwise, they are just different. Sex, geographic location, and marital status are nominally scaled variables. The only arithmetic operation that can be performed on such a scale is a count of each category. Thus we can count the number of automobile dealers in the state of California or the number of buses seen on a given route in the past hour.

Ordinal Scale

This scale is obtained by ranking objects or by arranging them in order with regard to some common variable. The question is simply whether each object has more or less of this variable than some other object. The scale provides information as to how much difference there is between the objects.

Because we don't know the amount of difference between objects, the permissible arithmetic operations are limited to statistics such as the median or mode (but not the mean). For example, suppose a sample of 1000 consumers ranked five brands of frozen mixed vegetables according to quality. The results for Birds-Eye brand were as follows:

Quality Rank	Number of Respondents Giving Ranking to Birds-Eye
Highest	150
Second	300
Third	250
Fourth	200
Lowest	100
Total	1000

The "second" quality category is the mode; the "third" category is the median; however, it is not possible to compute a mean ranking because the differences between ordinal scaled values are not necessarily the same. The finishing order in a horse race or class standing illustrates this type of scale. Similarly, brands of frozen vegetables can be ranked according to quality, from highest to lowest.

Interval Scale

Here the numbers used to rank the objects also represent equal increments of the attribute being measured. This means that differences can be compared. The difference between 1 and 2 is the same as between 2 and 3, but is only half the difference between 2 and 4. However, the location of the zero point is not fixed, since zero does not denote absence of the attribute. Fahrenheit and Celsius temperatures are measured with different interval scales and have different zero points. Interval scales have very desirable properties because virtually the entire range of statistical operations can be employed to analyze the resulting number, including addition and subtraction. Consequently it is possible to compute an arithmetic mean from interval-scale measures.

A recurring question regarding most attitude measures is whether or not they are interval scales. Usually it is doubtful that the intervals between categories are exactly equal, but they may not be so unequal as to preclude treating the whole as an interval scale.[1] A good example is a "willingness to buy" scale with 10 categories labeled from 1 to 10. If this were an interval scale we could say that two people, with scores of 2 and 4 respectively, differed by the same degree of "willingness" as two other people with scores of 8 and 10.

[1]G. Albaum, R. Best, and D. Hawkins, "The Measurement Properties of Semantic Scale Data," *Journal of the Market Research Society* (January 1977) 21–26.

Ratio Scale

This is a special kind of interval scale that has a meaningful zero point. With such a scale—of weight, market share, or dollars in savings accounts, for example—it is possible to say how many times greater or smaller one object is than another. This is the only type of scale that permits us to make comparisons of absolute magnitude. For example, we can say that an annual income of $15,000 is two times as large as an income of $7,500.

Interpreting Attitude Scales

The conclusions that can be obtained from attitude-scale measurements are strictly limited by the properties of the scale that is used. Failure to recognize these limits can lead to serious misinterpretation, as we see from the example in the boxed insert. The problem was created by assuming a ratio scale, where there was really only an interval scale.

INTERPRETING ATTITUDE SCALES: A PROBLEM FOR THE ADVERTISING REVIEW BOARD

The Phoenix Drug Co. currently sells the leading brand of tranquilizers, known as Restease. A competitor, Montfort Drug Co., has recently announced a tranquilizer brand called Calm, which they claim to be 50 percent more effective in reducing tensions than the leading brand.

As product manager for Restease you are concerned and also angry because you don't believe there is a significant difference in effectiveness. Your first action is to complain to the National Advertising Review Board, an advertising industry sponsored body that investigates advertising claims and can put considerable pressure on advertisers to change their claims.

As part of the investigation of your complaint, the research director from Montfort Drug is asked by the NARB to present the research findings that support the claim. Among the findings are the results of an apparently well-designed comparison test with large sample sizes. In the test, one group of product users was given Restease capsules. After a month, each user was asked to rate the effectiveness of the brand as follows:

For easing tension I found Restease to be:

Very effective	Effective	Neither effective nor ineffective	Ineffective	Very ineffective
☐	☐	☐	☐	☐

Another group of product users, identical in all respects to the first group, was given Calm capsules and asked to rate the effectiveness of this brand on the same scale.

The research director for Montfort Drug coded the scale with a $+2$ for "very effective," $+1$ for "effective," 0 for "neither effective nor ineffective," -1 for "ineffective," and -2 for "very ineffective." In his comments, he correctly points out that this is a well-accepted coding convention. When the data for the two groups are summarized, the average response for the Calm user groups is calculated to be $+1.2$, while the average for Restease is $+0.8$. Because the 0.4 difference is 50 percent more than the $+0.8$ level achieved by Restease, he concludes that the claims of superior effectiveness are valid.

While you are listening to this argument, the research director from your company has taken the same data and calculated that Calm is only 10.5 percent more effective, rather than 50 percent as claimed. Immediately you examine his figures. The only difference is that the "very effective" category has been coded $+1$, and "very ineffective" assigned $+5$, with the middle category assigned $+3$. He argues that this is an equally acceptable coding procedure. The two different coding schemes are as follows:

Very effective	Effective	Neither effective nor ineffective	Ineffective	Very ineffective
☐	☐	☐	☐	☐
$+2$	$+1$	0	-1	-2
$+1$	$+2$	$+3$	$+4$	$+5$

Soon you will be asked to present the basis of your complaint to the Review Board. What do you say about the capacity of the data presented by your competitor to support their claim of superiority?

SOURCE: Adapted from, B. Venkatesh, "Unthinking Data Interpretation Can Destroy Value of Research," *Marketing News*, January 27, 1978, 6,9.

TYPES OF ATTITUDE RATING SCALES

There are many ways to present a respondent with a continuum of numbered categories that represent the range of possible attitude judgments. The itemized-category scale is the most widely used by marketing researchers. In some situations, comparative scales, rank-order scales or constant-sum scales have advantages. Each of these major types of rating scales will be discussed in turn.

Itemized-Category Scale

The following scale from the HMO study uses itemized categories. There are four categories from which respondents can choose to indicate their overall level of satisfaction with their present health insurance plan:

Very satisfied	Quite satisfied	Somewhat satisfied	Not at all satisfied
☐	☐	☐	☐

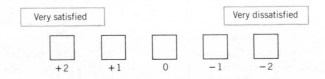

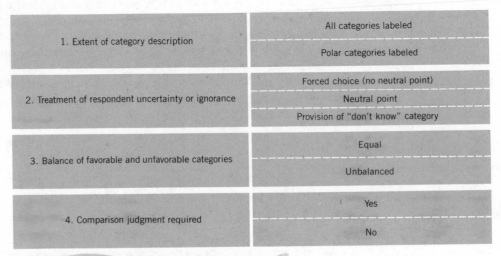

FIGURE 8–1   Types of itemized-category scales

This satisfaction scale has the following characteristics:

1   All categories are labeled

2   The respondent is forced to make a choice; there is no provision for neutral opinion or ''don't know'' responses

3   There are more favorable than unfavorable categories, so the scale is unbalanced

4   There is no explicit comparison of the respondents' present plan with other health insurance plans

The design of the satisfaction scale requires decisions along several dimensions, as shown in Figure 8–1. Another feature of this scale is that there is no attempt to make the intervals between categories even approximately the same. A quite different scale would have resulted had the decision been to label only the polar or end categories, balance the favorable and unfavorable categories, and provide an obvious neutral category. A numerical scaling of the response categories from $+2$ to -2, as presented in the following chart, could help to achieve a quasi-interval scale. While evidence is mixed, it appears that an adequate approximation of an interval scale can be achieved with this procedure.[2]

Yet another set of choices is illustrated by the following scale, which was used to ask respondents in the HMO study about the various medical services (including private clinics, private doctors, and an existing HMO) on a number of attributes, one of which was quality of care provided:

Q28 *". . . we are interested in your opinions about the medical services offered in this area . . .*
(a) Quality of medical care provided: (check one for each provider)"

	Excellent	Very good	Average	Below average	Don't know
Private doctors in area	☐	☐	☐	☐	☐
Private clinics	☐	☐	☐	☐	☐
Health organizations in the area	☐	☐	☐	☐	☐

The scale used for this question is unbalanced, with all categories labeled and a "don't know" category provided, and implies a comparison with other health care providers. The decision to use an unbalanced scale was based on an assumption of positively skewed attitudes toward all health care providers. This assumption was borne out by the results, which showed that only 15 percent rated private doctors as average or below average. However, 31 percent replied "don't know" to this question, indicating they did not have sufficient experience to form a judgment. This could be thought of as a form of awareness question. In general, a "don't know" category should be provided whenever respondents have insufficient experience to make a meaningful attitude judgment.

Comparative Scale

Another version of the preceding scale would label the categories "excellent," "very good," "good," "fair," and "poor," thereby eliminating the implicit comparison. The problem with such a scale is that the reference point is unclear and different respondents may use different reference points or standards. Are private doctors rated "excellent" or "very good" because they are superior to the existing alternatives, or because they measure up to an ideal form of medical care provider? In marketing studies where competitive

[2]C. E. Osgood, G. Suci, and P. Tannenbaum, *The Measurement of Meaning* (Urbana, Ill.: University of Illinois Press), 1957.

alternatives are being evaluated, some form of explicit or implicit comparison should be built into the scale, for example:

Compared to private clinics in the area the doctors
in private practice provide a quality of medical care which is:

Very superior		Neither superior nor inferior		Very inferior
☐	☐	☐	☐	☐

A recent review of research[3] on the question of the appropriate number of response categories concluded:

- "Scales with two or three response alternatives are generally inadequate in that they are incapable of transmitting very much information and they tend to frustrate and stifle respondents"
- There is little to be gained from using more than nine categories
- An odd rather than an even number of categories is preferable, when the respondent legitimately can adopt a neutral position

Rank-Order Scale

These scales require the respondent to arrange a set of objects with regard to a common criterion: students in terms of performance on an exam, advertisements in terms of interest, or new-product concepts with regard to willingness to buy in the future. The result is an ordinal scale with the inherent limitations of weak scale properties. Because ranking is such a familiar activity, it is easy to explain to respondents, takes relatively little time, and hence is used widely in surveys. The ranking task also corresponds to the choice process in those shopping environments where a buyer can make direct comparisons among the available alternatives (brands, flavors, product variations, etc.).[4]

It is doubtful that respondents can meaningfully rank more than five or six objects. The problem is not with the rankings of the first and last objects but with those in the undifferentiated middle. One solution, when there is a number of objects, is to break the ranking task into two stages. With nine objects, for example, the first stage would be to rank the objects into classes: top three, middle three, and bottom three. The next stage would be to rank the three objects within each class.

When using paired comparisons, the objects to be ranked are presented two at a time and the respondent has to choose between them according to some criterion such as overall preference or willingness to buy. Before a ranking of all objects can be obtained, all possible combinations of pairs have to be presented. This means that for n objects

---

[3]Eli P. Cox, "The Optimal Number of Response Alternatives for a Scale: A Review," *Journal of Marketing Research, 17* (November 1980), 407–422.

[4]G. Brown, T. Copeland, and M. Millward, "Monadic Testing of New Products—An Old Problem and Some Partial Solutions," *Journal of Market Research Society, 15* (April 1973), 112–113.

there are $[n(n - 1) \div 2]$ comparisons. This is very manageable for five objects (10 comparisons), but with more objects, the task can get out of hand. With 10 brands, for example, there are 45 paired comparisons. Paired-comparisons data have some potential analytical advantages, which will become apparent in Chapter 19 when we discuss multidimensional scaling.[5] A serious problem, however, is that the comparison of two objects at a time is seldom the way choices are made in the marketplace; thus, an item may do well in a paired comparison situation, but perform poorly in an actual market situation.[6]

Constant-Sum Scale

This scale requires respondents to allocate a fixed number of rating points (usually 100) among several objects, to reflect the relative preference for each object.[7] It is widely used to measure the relative importance of attributes, as in the following example:

> *Please divide 100 points among the following characteristics so the division reflects the relative importance of each characteristic to you in the selection of a health care plan.*

Ability to choose a doctor	_____
Extent of coverage provided	_____
Quality of medical care	_____
Monthly cost of the plan	_____
Distance to clinic or doctor from your home	_____

The most attractive feature of this scale is the quasi-interval nature of the resulting scale. Just how close it comes to a true interval scale has not been fully established, however. The scale is limited in the number of objects or attributes it can address at one time. Respondents would have difficulty allocating points accurately among more than a few categories.

Guidelines for Designing Scales

Attitude rating scales are widely used to test the effectiveness of advertising copy, compare the performance of new product concepts, and segment markets. Despite years of experience with these applications, the design of the rating scale is usually an ad hoc judgment based on the researcher's preferences and past experiences in similar situations.

There is little argument on the criteria a rating scale should ideally satisfy; the results should be reliable and valid, there should be sharp discrimination among the objects being rated, and a sensitivity to advertising or product stimuli. These criteria are seldom em-

[5]H. A. David, *The Method of Paired Comparisons* (London: Griffin, 1963).

[6]A. B. Blankenship, "Let's Bury Paired Comparisons," *Journal of Advertising Research, 6* (March 1966), 13–17.

[7]J. P. Guilford, *Psychometric Methods* (New York: McGraw-Hill, 1954).

ployed in practice. Part of the reason is the sheer variety of rating scales. The real problem is the absence of empirical evidence on the performance of the various rating scales on these criteria. However, one study[8] of 13 different scales did shed some useful light on the subject, and can help us narrow down the set of acceptable scales.

Respondents in the study were given various subsets of the 13 scales, and asked to rate six brands in each of six package goods categories such as coffee, analgesics, detergents, and toothpaste. Three criteria were used to compare the performance of the scales: (1) response distribution—which is the ability to avoid having responses pile up in the end categories, (2) discrimination among brands in the category, and (3) concurrent validity—how well the ratings related to current brand usage. This latter criterion is not the same as predictive power, for it may only tell us about consistency with reported usage behavior and not what the person would do in the future.

Three scales were found to be particularly attractive:

Brand Awareness. This question asked: "When I mention detergents, what brand do you think of? Any others? Have you heard of (interviewer mentions other brands of interest that were not reported)?

_____ First unaided mention
_____ Second unaided mention
_____ Other unaided mention
_____ Aided recall
_____ Never heard of

This scale was consistently the best discriminator among brands, and had high concurrent validity. By design it yielded uniform distributions of responses.

Verbal Purchase Intent. The question asked: "What is the chance of your buying (*brand*) the next time you purchase this product?

Definitely will buy	Very likely will buy	Probably will buy	Might or might not buy	Definitely will not buy
☐	☐	☐	☐	☐

This unbalanced scale made efficient use of the five categories, distributing the responses quite uniformly. The labels were easy for the respondents to handle. On average it discriminated well.

The Paired Comparison. The brands to be rated were presented two at a time, so each brand in the category was compared once to each other brand. In each pair the

[8]Russell I. Haley and Peter B. Case, "Testing Thirteen Attitude Scales for Agreement and Brand Discrimination," *Journal of Marketing,* 43 (Fall 1979), 20–32.

respondents were asked to divide 10 points among the brands on the basis of how much they liked one compared to the other. A score was then totaled for each brand. Although this scale performed well on the criteria, it is cumbersome to administer. Another possible limitation is that the frame of reference is always the other brands in the set being tested. These brands may change over time.

There are several features shared by all three of the most effective scales.

- They restrict the numbers of highly positive ratings that could be given, either by forcing a choice or directly comparing brands.

- They provide a limited number of categories which have verbal anchors. Respondents prefer words to numbers, and especially avoid negative numbers. Also, the inclusion of more than seven categories may actually reduce the power of the scale to discriminate.

- The stimulus to the respondent is simple and unambiguous. One of the worst performing scales presented a picture of a thermometer with 10 categories of liking, each of which was labeled by a number from zero to 100, as well as an assortment of verbal anchors. For example, 80 was labeled ''like very much'' while 50 was ''indifferent'' and 30 was ''not so good.''

Although these guidelines are useful, and should be carefully heeded, the best guidance still comes from a careful tailoring of the scale to the research objectives followed by thorough pretesting for comprehension and discrimination.

METHODS OF SCALING ATTITUDES: MULTIPLE ITEM BATTERIES

Attitudes toward complex objects such as health plans, automobiles, credit instruments, or transportation modes have many facets. Thus it is often unrealistic to attempt to capture the full picture with one overall attitude-scale question. For example, the public appears to support the general idea of income tax reform but opposes the elimination of the most popular tax loopholes. While beliefs in any specific issue, aspect, or characteristic are useful indicators of the overall attitude, there may be unusual reasons that make the single belief unrepresentative of the general position.[9] To cope with this problem, a variety of methods have been developed to measure a sample of beliefs toward the attitude objects (such as agreement or disagreement with a number of statements about the attitude object) and combine the set of answers into some form of average score. The most frequently employed of these methods are Likert, Thurstone, and semantic-differential scales. An adaptation of these methods with particular relevance to marketing problems is associative scaling.

[9]C. A. Moser and G. Kalton, *Survey Method in Social Investigation*, 2nd ed. (London: Heinemann, 1971).

Likert Scale

A Likert scale requires a respondent to indicate a degree of agreement or disagreement with a variety of statements related to the attitude object. It is also called a summated scale, for the scores on the individual items are summed to produce a total score for the respondent. An important assumption of this scaling method is that each of the items (statements) measures some aspect of a single common factor; otherwise the items cannot legitimately be summed. In other words, the resulting scale is unidimensional. The Likert scaling method, then, refers to the several steps in the procedure for culling out the items that don't belong. The result is a series of 5 to 20 or more statements and questions, of which the following are illustrative:

	Agree strongly	Agree somewhat	Neither agree nor disagree	Disagree somewhat	Disagree strongly
1. There needs to be much improvement in the health insurance available for people like me.	☐	☐	☐	☐	☐
2. I have a variety of very good health plans from which to choose.	☐	☐	☐	☐	☐
3. I haven't heard of a health insurance plan that will protect me against a disastrous illness.	☐	☐	☐	☐	☐

The first step in developing a Likert scale is to generate a number of statements relevant to the attitude. They should be either clearly favorable or unfavorable. Since this step is common to several other methods, it is useful to quote Oppenheim's advice on how to tell when useful statements are being produced:

> *We are on the wrong path when many of our respondents start to quibble or want to change the items or add to them; when items are skipped or crossed out; when respondents do not seem interested in discussing the scale or, if they want to discuss it, do so chiefly in order to explain how it fails to cater to their own attitudes. We are on the right path when respondents seem to recognize the statements ("I'll bet you got that from my brother-in-law; he's always saying things like that"); when they make free use of the "strongly agree" or "strongly disagree" response categories; when they seem excited or angered by some of the statements that they disagree with, or show signs of satisfaction that their own views are well represented; then they seem eager to provide us with more examples.*[10]

Once the items are written, they are given to a screening sample, which is reasonably representative of the population being studied. Their responses are scored by assigning values from 1 (strongly unfavorable responses) to 5 (for strongly favorable responses) to each item. A strongly favorable attitude would be either a "strongly disagree" response

---

[10]A. N. Oppenheim, *Questionnaire Design and Attitude Measurement* (New York: Basic Books, 1966), p. 114.

to a negative statement (i.e., the first question in the preceding chart), or a "strongly agree" response to a positive statement, such as the second question in the chart.

The next step is an *item analysis,* with the objective of choosing the subset of items that best discriminates among those with favorable and unfavorable attitudes.[11] This is usually done by examining the correlation between responses to each item and a total score obtained by summing the responses to all other items. This assumes that the total score generated by the response to the complete set of items is a good proxy for the attitude being studied, even though it includes some items that eventually will be eliminated—items that have little relationship to the overall score, either because they are ambiguous or because they are measuring something else.

Item analysis also can be conducted by first dividing the respondents into two groups according to their total score and then comparing the average score for each item across the two groups. Usually the two groups are defined respectively as the 25 percent of the respondents with the most favorable total score and the 25 percent with the least favorable total score. A good single item is one for which the mean scores for the two groups are very different. Items with small mean differences would be eliminated. For example, using these criteria, we can test whether the following item is a good measure.

> *There needs to be much improvement in the health insurance available for people like me.*

This item is part of a set of 20 items. Suppose we used the total score on these 20 items to divide a sample of 400 into a favorable group of 100 and an unfavorable group of 100. The first step in the test is to correct for the scoring direction, since the "strongly agree" answer actually represents a very unfavorable attitude. Thus, "strongly agree" is assigned a scale value of one. The next step is to compare the distributions of scores on this item for both groups. This is done in Table 8–2. It is evident that this item does a good job of discriminating among those with favorable versus unfavorable scores. Just how well it discriminates depends on the difference in mean scores for the other 19 items in the set.

Finally, the subset of items is ready to be administered. The results, when obtained, are utilized first by examining the distribution of total scores. This raises the question of what score constitutes a favorable attitude. The maximum summated score for a 15-item Likert scale is $(15 \times 5) = 75$. But suppose that the maximum total score obtained by any respondent is 58. Is this a strongly favorable attitude? The answer depends on the standard against which the score is compared. Here, the average score for all respondents would be a more appropriate standard than the maximum score. Although the initial focus of the analysis is on the total score, the responses to individual items can have considerable diagnostic value. Thus, referring to the earlier example, it is very useful to know that 45 percent are in agreement with the statement that they have a variety of very good health plans to choose from.

[11]C. Selltiz, M. Jahoda, M. Deutsch, and S. W. Cook, *Research Methods in Social Relations* (New York: Holt Rinehart, 1959).

TABLE 8–2
Item Analysis

| | | Distribution of Response | |
| | | Favorable | Unfavorable |
Response Category	Scale Value	Group	Group
Strongly agree	1	2%	34%
Agree	2	8	23
Neither agree nor disagree	3	27	28
Disagree	4	41	11
Strongly disagree	5	22	4
		100%	100%

$$\text{Average score} \qquad \overline{X}_f = 3.7 \qquad \overline{X}_u = 2.2$$
$$\overline{X}_f - \overline{X}_u = 1.5$$

The popularity of this scale is due to its relative ease of construction and administration. The major reservations are with the scale properties and the lack of reproducibility. Despite a widespread treatment of the total score as an interval scale, there is no evidence to suggest that it has more than ordinal properties. Reproducibility, which is the ability to reproduce an individual's answers to each item from knowledge of the total scale, is less of a concern to most researchers. Just because many response patterns can result in the same total score does not alter the interpretation of the aggregate distribution of responses.

Thurstone Scale

This procedure also is known as the *method of equal-appearing intervals*, since the objective is to obtain a unidimensional scale with interval properties.

The first step is to generate a large number of statements or adjectives reflecting all degrees of favorableness toward the attitude objects. Then, a group of judges is given this set of items (as many as 75 to 100 in all) and asked to classify them according to their degree of favorableness or unfavorableness. This is usually done with an 11-category bipolar scale, with "very favorable" at one end and "very unfavorable" at the other and a neutral position in the middle. The judges are instructed to treat the intervals between categories as equal and make evaluations of each item without expressing their own attitudes. The scale value of each item is the median position to which it is assigned by the judges. Items that have been placed in many different categories are discarded as ambiguous because there was no consensus among the judges. The resulting scale consists of 10 to 20 items that are distributed uniformly along the scale of favorability. The scale then is administered as part of a survey by asking each respondent to select those statements which best reflect her feelings toward the attitude object. The respondent's attitude score is the average of the scale scores of the chosen statements.

Because of the two-stage procedure, a Thurstone scale is both time consuming and expensive to construct; however, the scale itself is easy to administer and requires a minimum of instructions. But because there is not an explicit response to each item in the scale, there is not as much diagnostic value as in a Likert scale. Thurstone scales also have been criticized because the scale values themselves may be dependent on the attitudes of the original judges. This seems to be a problem only with topics that elicit strong feelings, such as abortion and school integration.

Semantic-Differential Scale

This scaling procedure is widely used to describe the set of beliefs that comprise a person's image of an organization or brand. It is also an insightful procedure for comparing the images of competing brands, stores, or services.[12] Respondents are asked to rate each attitude object in turn on a number of five- or seven-point rating scales bounded at each end by polar adjectives or phrases. Some researchers prefer *monopolar* scales such as "sweet—not sweet," while others use *bipolar* scales such as "sweet—sour." In either case, the respondent chooses the end point only if that adjective is closely descriptive of that object. However, the midpoint of the scale has two different meanings, depending on the type of scale.[13] With monopolar scales, the midpoint is simply a step on the scale from "sweet" to "not sweet," whereas on a bipolar scale, it is a neutral point indicating "neither sweet nor sour."

There may be as many as 15 to 25 semantic-differential scales for each attitude object. The scales in the following chart were used in a beer brand image study in a U.S. regional market. (Only four of a total of 10 scales are shown.) Each of 10 brands was evaluated separately on the same set of 10 scales for comparison.

Low price	⌐_⌐	⌐_⌐	⌐_⌐	⌐_⌐	⌐_⌐	High price
Consistent quality	⌐_⌐	⌐_⌐	⌐_⌐	⌐_⌐	⌐_⌐	Spotty quality
Tangy	⌐_⌐	⌐_⌐	⌐_⌐	⌐_⌐	⌐_⌐	Smooth
Bitter	⌐_⌐	⌐_⌐	⌐_⌐	⌐_⌐	⌐_⌐	Not bitter

[12]W. A. Mindak, "Fitting the Semantic Differential to the Marketing Problem," *Journal of Marketing, 25* (April 1961), 28–33.

[13]Jean Morton-Williams, "Questionnaire Design," in Robert M. Worcester, *Consumer Market Research Handbook* (London: McGraw-Hill, 1972), p. 87.

This set of scales is characteristic of most marketing applications of the semantic differential.

1 The pairs of objects or phrases are selected carefully to be meaningful in the market being studied and often correspond to product/service attributes.[14] Exploratory research generally is required to ensure that important attributes are represented and described in words that are familiar to respondents.[15]

2 The negative or unfavorable pole is sometimes on the right side and sometimes on the left. This rotation is necessary to avoid the halo effect in which the location of previous judgments on the scale affects subsequent judgments because of respondent carelessness.

3 The category increments are treated as interval scales so group mean values can be computed for each object on each scale. As with Likert scaling, this assumption is controversial, but is adopted because it permits more powerful methods of analysis to be used.

The semantic differential also may be analyzed as a summated rating scale. Each of the seven scale categories is assigned a value from −3 to +3 or 1 to 7, and the scores across all adjective pairs are summed for each respondent. Individuals then can be compared on the basis of their total scores. Summation is not usually advisable, however, for a good deal of specific information is lost in the aggregate score, which may be distorted if there are several scales that measure roughly the same thing.

Profile Analysis. Visual comparisons of the images of different objects can be aided by plotting the mean ratings for each object on each scale. To show what can be done, Figure 8–2 compares the ratings for two well-known national brands of beer and a regional brand, on six of the 10 scales. Even with three brands and only six of 10 attributes, the interpretation of the profiles is not easy. With more brands and attributes, the overall comparisons of brands are even harder to grasp. A second difficulty is that not all attributes are independent; that is, several of the attributes may be measuring approximately the same dimension. For example, there is not likely to be much difference in the meaning of the ''tangy—smooth'' and ''bitter—not bitter'' scales to most beer drinkers. This is borne out by the similarity of the scores of the three brands on these two scales in Figure 8–2. Fortunately there are several procedures using multidimensional scaling techniques that can deal effectively with these problems and yield easily interpreted spatial maps that describe the overall image of a brand. These are discussed in detail in Chapter 17, which deals with methods for analyzing interdependencies among variables.

[14]The scale was developed originally by Osgood et al., *op. cit.*, as a method for measuring the meaning of an object to an individual. They explored a wide variety of adjective pairs that were sufficiently general to be applicable to diverse concepts and objects. From their results they identified three dominant dimensions along which judgments are made and labeled them the evaluative, potency, and activity dimensions.

[15]Several methods for eliciting attributive descriptors are described in John Dickson and Gerald Albaum, ''A Method for Developing Tailormade Semantic Differentials for Specific Marketing Content Areas,'' *Journal of Marketing Research, 14* (February 1977), 87–91.

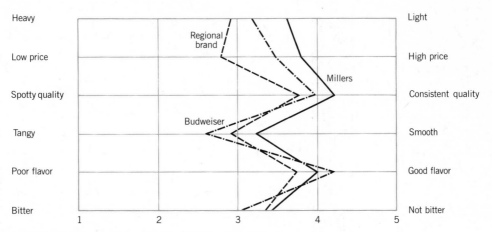

FIGURE 8–2   Profile analysis of three beer brands

	Coors Beer		
	+3	+3	+3
	+2	+2	+2
Heavy	+1	Consistent +1	Tangy +1
	−1	Quality −1	−1
	−2	−2	−2
	−3	−3	−3

Stapel Scales.   This is a simplified version of the semantic-differential scale,[16] which uses only one pole rather than two opposite poles. Respondents are asked to indicate the object by selecting a numerical response category. The higher the positive score, the better the adjective describes the object. A typical format for this scale is shown in the following table, as it would be adapted to the measurement of beer brand attitudes.

The main virtues of this scale are that it is easy to administer and is especially suited to telephone interviewing. Also, this scale is easier to construct, for there is no need to provide adjectives or phrases to assure bipolarity.

Associative Scaling

Although the semantic-differential and Stapel scales are used widely for image studies, they have substantial limitations in markets where the average respondent is likely to be knowledgeable only about a small subset among a large number of choice alternatives.

[16]J. Stapel, "Predictive Attitudes," in L. Adler and I. Crespi, eds., *Attitude Research on the Rocks* (Chicago: American Marketing Association, 1968) pp. 96–115.

Which store	Eaton's Store or Catalog	The Bay	Simpsons	Sears Store or Catalog	Horizon	Sayvette	Towers	Woolco	Zellers	Any Other	None DK	More Than One Answer
1. Has the lowest overall prices?	1	2	3	4	5	6	7	8	9	0	B	X
2. Has the highest overall prices?	1	2	3	4	5	6	7	8	9	0	B	X
3. Is the easiest one to get to from your home?	1	2	3	4	5	6	7	8	9	0	B	X
4. Has the most knowledgeable, helpful sales clerks?	1	2	3	4	5	6	7	8	9	0	B	X
5. Has the highest-quality products?	1	2	3	4	5	6	7	8	9	0	B	X
6. Has the lowest-quality products?	1	2	3	4	5	6	7	8	9	0	B	X
7. Gives you the best overall value for the money?	1	2	3	4	5	6	7	8	9	0	B	X
9. Gives you the worst overall value for the money?	1	2	3	4	5	6	7	8	9	0	B	X
9. Has the best advertising?	1	2	3	4	5	6	7	8	9	0	B	X
10. Is the best for the latest, most fashionable merchandise?	1	2	3	4	5	6	7	8	9	0	B	X
11. Has the largest overall merchandise selection or assortment?	1	2	3	4	5	6	7	8	9	0	B	X
12. Do you shop at most often?	1	2	3	4	5	6	7	8	9	0	B	X

FIGURE 8–3 Retail store image questions (Telephone Questionnaire)

They also can be cumbersome and time consuming to administer when there are a number of attributes and alternatives to consider. An alternative approach, designed to overcome these limitations, asks the respondent simply to associate one alternative with each question. The questions in Figure 8–3 illustrate how this approach is employed in a telephone survey of retail-store images.

The technique is argued to be particularly appropriate to choice situations that involve a sequential decision process.[17] For example, supermarkets have to be within a reasonable distance to be considered, and within that set the choice is made on the basis of which chain is best in satisfying their needs. Of course the technique does not answer the questions of how consumers make trade-offs when there are several important dimensions and no alternative is superior across the board. Thus the benefits of low cost and ease of telephone administration are purchased at a possible cost of reduced validity in representing the market structure. For this reason the associative technique is best suited to market tracking where the emphasis is on understanding shifts in relative competitive positions.

CHOOSING AN ATTITUDE SCALE

The choice of an appropriate scale is complicated by two problems:

1 There are many different techniques, each with its own strengths and weaknesses.

2 Virtually any technique can be adapted to the measurement of any one of the attitude components.

While these problems are significant impediments to broad generalizations, it is also true that all techniques are not equally suitable for all purposes. Table 8–3 summarizes some useful rules of thumb as to which scale types are likely to be best suited to the various components of attitudes. What is most evident from this table is the versatility of the itemized-category scale, which itself has many variations. Ultimately, the researcher's choice will be shaped by (1) the specific information that is required to satisfy the research objectives, (2) the adaptability of the scale to the data collection method and budget constraints, and (3) the compatibility of the scale with the structure of the respondent's attitude.

The value of careful selection and adaptation of scales will be demonstrated here by a study of attitudes toward automobile dealers. The data came from a mail survey of people who had purchased a new car from an automobile dealer between one and two years earlier.[18] Each respondent rated 14 attributes of the dealer's service department on two separate scales. The first scale asked how *important* the attribute was (on a four-

---

[17]Douglas J. Tigert, Sylvia Ma, and Terry Cotter, *Los Angeles Wave I: Consumer Attitudes Towards and Shopping Habits at Major Supermarket Chains*. Toronto, Canada: University of Toronto, December 1, 1976.

[18]John A. Martilla and John C. James, "Importance—Performance Analysis," *Journal of Marketing*, January, 1977, 77–79.

TABLE 8–3

Appropriate Applications of Various Attitude Scales

Attitude Component	Type of Scale				
	Itemized-Category	Rank-Order	Constant-Sum	Likert	Semantic-Differential
Knowledge					
awareness	**				
attribute beliefs	**	*	*	*	**
attribute importance	**	*	**	*	
Affect or liking					
overall preferences	**	*	**	*	*
specific attributes	**	*	*	*	**
Action					
intentions	**	*	**	*	

** = Very appropriate.
* = Sometimes appropriate.

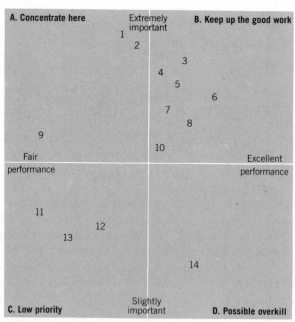

FIGURE 8-4 Importance-performance grid with attributable ratings for automobile dealer's service department.

Attribute	Median Importance Rating	Illustrative Constant-Sum Scale	
		Customer *A*	Customer *B*
1. Job done right the first time	3.8	35	25
2. Fast action on complaints	3.6	15	20
3. Prompt warranty work	3.6	10	15
4. Able to do any job needed	3.6	10	10
5. Service available when needed	3.4	15	20
6. Courteous and friendly service	3.4	15	10
		100	100

point scale ranging from "extremely important" to "not important"). The second scale asked how well the service department *performed* (on a four-point scale from "excellent" to "poor"). Each attribute was located in the grid shown in Figure 8–4, according to its median score on the two scales.

To illustrate how the grid can be used, quadrant A includes those attributes, such as "low prices on service" (attribute 9), which are very important and where performance is rated only fair. By contrast, in quadrant B, customers place a high value on "courteous and friendly service" (attribute 6) and "prompt warranty work" (attribute 3) and are pleased with the dealer's performance. In quadrant C, the dealer's performance is rated low in terms of providing courtesy buses and rental cars, but fortunately these are not perceived as important services.

While the importance–performance grid yields useful insights, this application suffered from the inability of the four-point rating scale to discriminate. Ten of the 14 attributes had median ratings between 3.3 and 3.8 on this scale, where 4 means "extremely important" and 3 is "important." A constant-sum scale, on the other hand, might have resulted in sharper distinctions among attributes, as shown in the following table giving two possible patterns of responses of service customers thinking hard about which of six attributes were really important.

SUMMARY

This chapter has dealt with attitudes, defined as the mental orientation of individuals that structures the way they respond to their environment. This concept is useful to marketers only to the extent that the various components of attitudes can be measured "accurately."

Measurement was defined here as the assignment of numbers to objects or persons to represent quantities of their attributes. The problem is to establish how to assign numbers. This leads to an examination of the properties of different scales of measurement—nominal, ordinal, interval, ratio—and establishes a useful basis for evaluating various attitude scales, including itemized-category, rank-order, semantic-differential, Thurstone, and Likert scales. Each of these methods involves a direct self-report, which means that they should be supplemented with the behavioral and indirect measures discussed in Chapter 5.

To this point we have not been explicit as to what is meant by an "accurate" measurement of any kind. Intuitively it means freedom from error. More formally, an accurate measure is both valid and reliable. The nature of these concepts and the special issues involved in their application are discussed in the appendix to this chapter.

QUESTIONS AND PROBLEMS

1 Advertising is an expenditure that ultimately must be justified in terms of an effect on sales and profits, yet most evaluations of advertising are in terms of the effects on attitudes. How do you account for this apparent mismatch?

2 In what ways could a product manager for a branded food product use the data from regular attitude surveys? How could the value of these surveys be enhanced by including information on media exposure probabilities, as well as socioeconomic and demographic variables, for individual respondents?

3 How would you select a set of phrases or adjectives for use in a semantic-differential scale to be used to evaluate the image of banks and other consumer financial institutions? Would the procedure differ if you were going to use a Likert scale?

4 Develop an attitude scale, or a battery of attitude items, to be used by an urban transit system wishing to know whether an aggressive advertising campaign has improved the attitudes of nonriders toward the reliability, safety, and economy of bus travel for work trips.

5 Suppose paired comparison choices of most-preferred brand were made among three brands (A, B, and C), by a sample of 100 respondents. The results of 25 choosing A and 75 choosing B would be represented as $A_{25}B_{75}$. One possible set of results from the three paired comparisons might be $A_{50}B_{50}$, $B_{50}C_{50}$, and $A_{50}C_{50}$. Is this set of results consistent with any one of the following results of the choice of most-preferred brand from an array of the three brands? Why?

$$A_{25}B_{25}C_{50}$$
$$A_{33}B_{33}C_{33}$$
$$A_{50}B_{0}C_{50}$$

6 Under what circumstances can attitude measures be expected to be good predictors of subsequent behavior? Is there any value to measuring attitudes in situations where attitudes are likely to be poor predictors?

7 In March of 1977 the U.S. Federal Energy Administration conducted a personal interview survey of a sample of homes where there was a heating load (that is, the outside temperature was below 65°F). The average indoor temperature of these homes, as measured by a calibrated thermometer was 70° ± 2°F during the day and 69° ± 2°F at night. This represented little or no change from the previous two years; yet, during an independent telephone survey the FEA found that people said they were keeping their homes at 66°F during the day and 64°F at night.

    a What are some of the possible hypotheses for this difference between stated and actual?

    b What questions would you ask during a telephone survey to clarify the stated house temperature and learn about people's attitudes toward reducing the house temperature?

8 In February 1975, the Gallup poll asked, ''Do you approve or disapprove of the way Ford is handling his job as President?'' and found 55 percent approved and 28 percent disapproved. A poll by Harris at the same time asked, ''How do you rate the job President Ford is doing as President—excellent, pretty good, only fair, or poor?'' Forty-six percent gave ''positive'' responses (excellent or pretty good), and 52 percent were negative (only ''fair'' or ''poor''). How do you explain the differences? What are the implications of your explanation for public opinion polls as guides to political leaders?

APPENDIX
THE ACCURACY OF ATTITUDE MEASUREMENTS

Attitude measures, in common with all measures used in marketing, must be both accurate and useful. In this appendix, the focus is on those aspects of attitude measures that contribute to accuracy: validity, reliability, and sensitivity.

Validity

An attitude measure is valid if it measures what it is supposed to measure. If this is the case, then differences in attitude scores will reflect differences among the objects or individuals on the characteristic being measured. This is a very troublesome question; for example, how is a researcher to know whether measured differences in the attitudes of managers, consumer activists, and consumers toward marketing practices, regulation, and the contribution of the consumer movement are true differences? There have been three basic approaches to this question of validity assessment.

Face or consensus validity is invoked when the argument is made that the measurement so self-evidently reflects or represents the various aspects of the phenomenon that there can be little quarrel with it. For instance, buyers' recognition of advertisements is usually accepted at face value as an indication of past ad exposure. This faith typically is supported by little more than common sense, despite evidence that recognition scores are influenced by reader interest.[19]

Criterion validity is more defensible, for it is based on empirical evidence that the attitude measure correlates with other ''criterion'' variables. If the two variables are measured at the same time, **concurrent validity** is established. Better yet, if the attitude measure can predict some future event, then **predictive validity** has been established. A measure of brand preference or buying intentions is valid if it can be shown through sales records to predict future sales. This is the most important type of validity for decision-making purposes, for the very nature of decisions requires predictions of uncertain future events.

While face, concurrent, and predictive validity provide necessary evidence of overall validity, they are often not sufficient. The characteristic of these three approaches is that they provide evidence on **convergent validity**. That is, an attitude measure can represent adequately a characteristic or variable if it correlates or ''converges'' with other supposed measures of that variable. Unfortunately, an attitude measure may converge with measures of other variables in addition to the one of interest. Thus, it is also necessary to establish **discriminant validity** through ''low correlations between the measure of interest and other measures that are supposedly not measuring the same variable or concept.''[20] Advertising recognition measures often fail this second test. While they correlate or converge with past ad exposure, which is what we want, they also are correlated with number of magazines read and product interest.

Construct validity can be considered only after discriminant and convergent validity have been established. It is achieved when a logical argument can be advanced to defend a particular measure. The argument aims first to define the concept or construct explicitly and then to show that the measurement, or operational definition, logically connects the empirical phenomenon to the concept. The extreme difficulty of this kind of validation lies in the unobservable nature of many of the constructs—such as social class, personality, or attitudes—used to explain marketing behavior. For example, is occupation a good operational definition of social class, or does it measure some other characteristic? One way to assess construct validity is to test whether or not the measure confirms hypotheses generated from the theory based on the concepts. Since theory development is at a youthful

---

[19]Roger M. Heeler and Michael L. Ray, ''Measure Validation in Marketing,'' *Journal of Marketing Research, 9* (November 1972), 361–370.

[20]Heeler and Ray, *op. cit.*, p. 362. See also Donald T. Campbell and Donald W. Fiske, ''Convergent and Discriminant Validation by the Multitrait–Multimethod Matrix,'' *Psychological Bulletin, 56* (1959), 81–105.

stage in marketing, the theory itself may be incorrect, making this approach is hazardous. This is one reason why little construct validation is attempted in marketing. A more significant reason is the lack of well-established measures that can be used in a variety of circumstances. Instead, marketing researchers tend to develop measures for each specific problem or survey and rely on face validity.

Reliability

So far we have been talking about systematic errors between an observed score (X_0) and a true score (X_t), which will determine whether or not a measure is valid. However, the total error of a measurement consists of this systematic error component (X_s) and a random error component (X_r). Random error is manifested by lack of consistency (unreliability) in repeated or equivalent measurements of the same object or person. As a result, any measurement can be expressed as a function of several components:

$$X_0 = X_t + X_s + X_r$$
Observed score = true score + systematic error + random error

To interpret this equation, remember that a valid measure is one that reflects the true score. In this situation, $X_0 = X_t$ and both X_s and X_r are zero. Thus, if we know the measure is valid, it has to be reliable. The converse is not necessarily true. A measure may be highly reliable, $X_r = 0$, and still have a substantial systematic error that distorts the validity. But, if the measure is not reliable, it cannot be valid since at a minimum we are left with $X_0 = X_t + X_r$. In brief, reliability is a necessary but not a sufficient condition for validity.[21]

Although reliability is less important, it is easier to measure, and so receives relatively more emphasis. The basic methods for establishing reliability can be classified according to whether they measure stability of results over time or internal consistency of items in an attitude scale.

Stability over time is assessed by repeating the measurement with the same instrument and the same respondents at two points in time and correlating the results. To the extent that random fluctuations result in different scores for the two administrations, this correlation and hence the reliability will be lowered. The problems of this test–retest method are similar to those encountered during any pretest–posttest measurement of attitudes. The first administration may sensitize the respondent to the subject and lead to attitude change. The likelihood of a true change in attitude (versus a random fluctuation) is increased further if the interval between the test and the retest is too long. For most topics, this would be more than two weeks. If the interval is too short, however, there may be

---

[21]George W. Bohrnstedt, "Reliability and Validity Assessment in Attitude Assessment and Attitude Measurement," in Gene F. Summers, ed. *Attitude Measurement* (Chicago: Rand McNally, 1970). Also, J. Paul Peter, "Reliability: A Review of Psychometric Basics and Recent Marketing," *Journal of Marketing Research,* 16 (February 1979), 6–17.

a carryover from the test to the retest: attempts to remember the responses in the first test, boredom or annoyance at the imposition, and so forth. Because of these problems, a very short interval will bias the reliability estimate upward, while longer periods have the opposite effect.

The equivalence approach to assessing reliability is appropriate for attitude scales composed of multiple items that presumably measure the same underlying unidimensional attitude. The split-half method assumes that these items can be divided into two equivalent subsets that then can be compared. A number of methods have been devised to divide the items randomly into two halves and compute a measure of similarity of the total scores of the two halves across the sample. An average split-half measure of similarity—coefficient alpha—can be obtained from a procedure that has the effect of comparing every item to every other item.

Sensitivity

The third characteristic of a good attitude measure is sensitivity, or the ability to discriminate among meaningful differences in attitudes. Such sensitivity is achieved by increasing the number of scale categories; however, the more categories there are, the lower the reliability. This is because very coarse response categories, such as "yes or no," in response to an attitude question can absorb a great deal of response variability before a change would be noted using the test–retest method. Conversely, the use of a large number of response categories when there are only a few distinct attitude positions would be subject to a considerable, but unwarranted, amount of random fluctuation.

CASE 8–1
Wine Horizons

Wine Horizons was a medium-sized New York State winery that emphasized sparkling wines. The company was not known to the public as a producer of good-quality domestic champagne because all of their output was sold to well-known hotels and restaurants that put their own labels on the bottles. However their still (non-sparkling) wines were sold under the Wine Horizons label and were moderately well known.

The management of the company had been planning for some time to launch a line of champagnes under their own brand name. They were seriously considering whether the launch should be based on a packaging innovation. The specific proposal was to package their champagne in six-packs of 7-ounce bottles in an easy-to-carry container, at a retail price of approximately $9.00. The 7-ounce quantity was chosen as it was the equivalent of two average-sized champagne glasses, thus making one bottle a convenient serving for one or two people. This size and price were expected to make the champagne an attractive alternative to imported beers in a variety of social situations.

Before a decision could be made the management team had to be satisfied that there was an adequate market for the new packaging. They also wanted to know the occasions during which the target market would be likely to use the product, and whether these people would expect to find it in the imported beer or wine section of their retail outlet. To answer these questions the firm of Ritchey and Associates was retained to conduct a market study. A meeting to review their attitude questionnaire was just beginning.

DEVELOPMENTS IN THE WINE INDUSTRY

The wine industry had enjoyed significant growth in recent years. The growth of white wines had been especially strong, but sparkling wines had also experienced an upward trend. Champagne sales had grown, but less than sparkling wines in general. The reason for the increased popularity of white wines was not known, but many in the industry believed it was due to a general trend toward "lightness" on the part of consumers, as reflected in their increased use of light beers, light wine, bottled mineral water, health foods, and low-tar cigarettes. Whatever the reason, wine was being chosen more frequently as a beverage alternative to beer and liquor in various formal and informal social situations. It was also believed that champagne was not sharing in wine's growth because of the difficulty in keeping champagne fresh after the bottle was opened—a large, opened bottle of champagne would lose all its carbonation in a few hours and "go flat."

Two wineries had recently begun test marketing wine in small packages. One winery was offering Chablis, Rosé, and Burgundy in six-packs of cans, with each can containing six ounces of wine. Another winery was test marketing Chablis in six-packs of 6.5-ounce bottles. The new packaging seemed to be selling reason-

ably well in test areas, and retailers reportedly had a favorable attitude toward the new packaging. Compared with "single" small bottles or cans of wine—which were considered a nuisance—retailers felt that the six-packs were more profitable and more convenient to stack and display.

THE RESEARCH STUDY

The objectives of the study were to (1) measure consumers' acceptance of wine in six-packs, (2) identify the type of person who was a potential purchaser and user of champagne in six-packs, (3) determine where in the store they would expect to find such champagne, and (4) determine the size of the potential market. The sample would be champagne drinkers who were 21 years of age or older. Also, the research would be limited to markets where the six-packs of wine were already being tested. It was further decided that the data would be collected with personal interviews using a shopping mall intercept method. This would permit the interviewer to show a picture of the proposed six-pack, and use cards to list answer categories in complex questions. Only malls that contained liquor stores would be selected. The interviewers would be located in the vicinity of the liquor store, and attempt to interview adults leaving the stores.

A six-part questionnaire (see Exhibit 1), was designed to obtain the desired information. The major issues to be resolved were whether this questionnaireand the mall intercept design would identify potential users, and yield a valid estimate of the potential market for the six-packs.

QUESTIONS FOR DISCUSSION

1 Will the proposed questionnaire and research design achieve the research objectives?

2 What alternative questions could be used to assess attitudes and intentions-to-buy? Which approach would yield the most valid responses?

EXHIBIT 1

Hello! My name is _____ . I'm an interviewer with the marketing research firm of Ritchey and Associates, and we are conducting a study concerned with certain alcoholic beverages. Would you please take a few minutes to answer some questions? I assure you that your answers will be kept *completely confidential*.

1. Are you 21 years of age or older? (ASK ONLY IF NECESSARY)
   _____ Yes   _____ No (TERMINATE)

2. Do you drink any alcoholic beverages?
   _____ Yes   _____ No (TERMINATE)

3. What different kinds of alcoholic beverages do you drink?
   _____ Beer   _____ Liquor (any kind)
   _____ Wine   _____ Other
   _____ Champagne (to Q5)

4. Do you drink champagne?
   _____ Yes   _____ No (TERMINATE)

5. About how often you drink champagne? (CLARIFY RESPONSE IF NECESSARY)
   _____ Once a week or more often   _____ About once in 2–3 months
   _____ About twice a month   _____ About twice a year
   _____ About once a month   _____ About once a year
                                              _____ DK

6. On what types of occasions do you drink champagne?
   _____ Dinner for two   _____ Picnics
   _____ Small dinner party   _____ After athletic activities
   _____ Parties   _____ Just relaxing
   _____ Special holidays   _____ Other (specify) _____
   _____ Dinner

7. Do you consider champagne to be an appropriate beverage to serve at informal occasions, or is it only for formal occasions?
   _____ Appropriate for informal occasions
   _____ Only for formal occasions   _____ For both occasions

EXPLAIN: I'm now going to ask you some questions about wine, not champagne. These are questions about some new packaging that has recently been used by some brands of wine.

8. Are you aware that some wine is now being sold in packages consisting of six small cans and bottles, each containing about 6 ounces?
   _____ Yes   _____ No (to Q10)   _____ DK (to Q10)

EXHIBIT 1 (continued)

9. Have you ever purchased wine sold in such packaging or drunk wine from one of these small containers?

_____ Purchased   _____ Both

_____ Drank   _____ Neither

10. Do you think it's a good idea to sell wine in packages consisting of six small cans or bottles—that is, are you in favor of it?

_____ A good idea, in favor of   _____ Indifferent (to Q12)

_____ Not a good idea   _____ Undecided (to Q12)

11. Why?

EXPLAIN: Wine Horizons is one of the largest private label bottlers of champagnes in the United States. For example, it supplies well-known hotel chains and restaurants with their own brand of champagne. Wine Horizons is planning to market this package (SHOW PICTURE) of six small bottles of champagne.

12. Do you think it's a good idea to sell champagne in packages consisting of six small bottles—that is, are you in favor of it?

_____ A good idea, in favor of (to Q14)   _____ Indifferent (to Q14)

_____ Not a good idea   _____ Undecided (to Q14)

13. Why not?

14. Would you consider purchasing such a package of champagne at the retail price of $9.00?

_____ Yes (to Q16)   _____ No

_____ Maybe, possibly (to Q16)   _____ DK

15. Why not?

16. For what kinds of occasions would you use these small bottles of champagne?

_____ Dinner for two   _____ Picnics

_____ Small dinner party   _____ After athletic activities

_____ Parties   _____ Just relaxing

_____ Special holidays   _____ Other (specify) _____

_____ Dinner

17. Would you use them for any of the occasions shown on this list? (SHOW CARD)

_____ Dinner for two   _____ Picnics

_____ Small dinner parties   _____ After athletic activities

_____ Parties   _____ Just relaxing

_____ Special holidays

_____ Dinner

EXHIBIT 1 (continued)

18. In what types of retail stores would you expect to find this product being sold?
    _____ Liquor stores   _____ Other (specify) _____
    _____ Supermarkets

19. In what section of the store would you expect to find this package of champagne, that is, what other products would you expect to find alongside it?
    _____ Other champagnes   _____ Beer
    _____ Wine   _____ Other (specify) _____

CASE 8–2
National Kitchens

For several years the management of National Kitchens, a diversified packaged foods manufacturer, had been watching the rapid growth in sales of microwave ovens. They were particularly interested in the prospects for ready-to-eat soup in glass jars. The attraction of glass packaging was that the soup could be heated in a microwave oven in its original container. However, ready-to-eat soup in glass jars was expected to cost one or two cents more per serving than canned soups—which at the time cost ten cents per serving. While the price premium for glass was thought to be excessive, there was some new data on the acceptability of this price premium that had just been provided by a glass manufacturer.

THE MICROWAVE OVEN MARKET

In 1979, approximately 11.5 percent of U.S. households owned microwave ovens. This penetration was expected to expand to 19 percent by 1984 and grow faster than the population for the foreseeable future. The growth was due to improved oven performance, better cooking equipment and recipes, consumer education, and changing life styles that created a need for labor-saving devices.

Cooking with a microwave was a problem because metal utensils were impervious to microwaves and could not be placed in the oven. Even metal pigments on printed or glazed dinnerware could result in a damaged oven. Many microwave oven owners used special ovenware, but this resulted in extra dishes to clean.

THE RESEARCH STUDY

The glass manufacturer had designed a brief questionnaire to evaluate consumer attitudes to glass packaging for a variety of microwave oven cooking jobs. This questionnaire was mailed to 600 names obtained from the warranty cards returned to one microwave oven manufacturer. The results had just been tabulated and were being shown to National Kitchens.

Of the 20 questions, numbers 15 and 20 most directly addressed the issue of ready-to-eat soup in glass:

15. Would you purchase ready-to-eat soup in a single-serving container (approximately 10 ounces) that could be put directly into your microwave oven and poured into a bowl after heating? Assume the same price per serving as canned soup.

    ☐ Yes About how many individual servings per month? _____

    ☐ No   Why not? _____

20. Please review questions 15 to 19 and, for each one, indicate below whether or not you would be willing to pay 1¢ or 2¢ more per individual serving for the product described. (Enter an x beside each question, under the appropriate column.)

Question Number	Would pay 1¢ or 2¢ more per serving	Would not pay 1¢ or 2¢ more per serving
15		
16		
17		
18		
19		

Of the 600 questionnaires, 312 were returned. The responses to question 15 and that part of question 20 that related to soup in glass are summarized in Table 1.

QUESTIONS FOR DISCUSSION

1 What have you learned about the potential market for soup in glass jars?

2 What else would you like to know?

3 How else would you assess people's attitudes toward this concept?

TABLE 1
Summary of Question Responses

Number of servings per month	Q. 15: No. of Responses	Q. 20: No. responding that they would pay 1¢ or 2¢ more per serving
0("No")	103	185 = would not pay 1¢ or 2¢ more
1	8	3
2	12	7
3	5	3
4	26	19
5	9	6
6–10	31	14
11–15	19	9
16–20	56	38
21–30	11	9
31–40	17	8
41–50	14	10
50+	1	1

section C
Causal Research

9

EXPERIMENTATION

A utility company wants to encourage people to insulate their homes. It is recognized that insulation will conserve energy, reduce utility bills, improve living comfort, and retard fires. A decision is needed as to which of these appeals should be used in the campaign. More particularly, an advertisement using both the utility bill and comfort appeals has been developed and a decision is needed as to whether the advertisement should be the basis of a statewide promotion.

In previous chapters several research approaches have been discussed, such as the use of secondary data, small-sample interviewing, observation, and surveys. All these can provide helpful insights into these questions and others. However, they are primarily useful as elements of exploratory or descriptive research efforts. They are not well suited to making definitive judgments about which appeal, if any, will work or about how much impact an advertisement will have. To determine the answer to these more demanding causal questions, experimentation, the subject of this chapter, is employed.

Experiments are defined as studies in which implementation involves an intervention by the observer beyond that required for measurement.[1] Thus, the simplest experiment would be to run the advertisement and then measure its impact. The act of running the advertisement would be the experimental intervention or treatment. Ultimately, there is no substitute for actually trying the advertisement to see how it works. As we shall see, such a simple experiment has limitations, and it usually would be useful and worthwhile to consider other research designs.

There are two types of experiments. The first, laboratory experiments, as the name suggests, are experiments in which the experimental treatment is introduced in an artificial or laboratory setting. For example, a shopper might be exposed to a new product in a simulated supermarket, or two groups of hospital users might be asked to react to two different pricing plans for delivery of medical services. The second, field experiments, are conducted in the "field." For example, one television advertisement is run in Omaha and another in Dayton. The next day viewers in the two cities are called to determine their response. A field experiment is the experimental treatment or intervention introduced

---

[1] Ronald E. Frank, William F. Massy, and Alfred Kuehn, *Quantitative Techniques in Marketing Analysis* (Homewood, Ill.: Richard D. Irwin, 1962), p. 33.

in a completely natural setting. The respondents usually are not aware that an experiment is being conducted; thus, the response tends to be natural.

The laboratory experiment tends to be *artifical*. Furthermore, there is a **testing effect** in that respondents are usually aware of being in a test and therefore are sensitized and tend not to respond naturally. Thus, the question always arises: What will happen outside the laboratory? Are the results projectable to the real world? Does the result have **external validity**? External validity refers to the applicability of the experimental results to situations external to the actual experimental context. Field experiments tend to have much greater external validity than laboratory experiments. Laboratory experiments, however, tend to be much less costly and allow the experimenter greater control over the experiment, thus reducing alternative explanations of the results and increasing "*internal validity*." **Internal validity** refers to the ability of the experiment to unambiguously show relationships. Field experiments are difficult to control; often, competing explanations for the results exist. For example, a large response to the Omaha advertisement could be caused by the number of people in Omaha, the weather when the advertisement was run, or the scheduling of civic activities. Although it is possible, by improving the experimental design, to reduce the number of competing explanations of the results of field experiments, they still tend to have less internal validity than laboratory experiments.

The purpose of an experiment is usually to detect or confirm causal relationships and to quantify them. The validity issue is, thus, extremely important. Of course, enhanced validity has associated costs and, as with other research approaches, the goal is not to maximize validity regardless of cost. The goal, rather, is to make the appropriate trade-off between validity and cost. The design of an experiment allows considerable room for making such trade-offs.

Whether one is evaluating the validity of completed experiments or considering or designing an experiment to address a research question, two types of perspectives on experimental design are useful. First, it is important to understand some of the design alternatives available. A knowledge of alternative experimental designs can lead to a more effective experiment and can also improve the understanding of the power and limitations of the various designs. Until one design is contrasted with others, it is difficult to understand fully its potential threats to validity. Second, it is important to know what types of validity threats, both external and internal, exist so that experimental results can be interpreted in a more sophisticated manner and the possibility of design improvements can be identified.

Because experimental design is concerned with detecting and quantifying causal relationships, it is appropriate to start with a discussion of causation. The following sections describe several types of experimental design. In the context of describing the various designs, the threats to validity are introduced. In the second section the concept of experimental control is introduced. In the third, the use of more than one experimental treatment is considered, along with the concept of interactions between treatments. The fourth section discusses the use of "before" measures and their associated problems. The fifth section summarizes the threats to validity and evaluates a commonly used advertising test. The final section provides a short discussion of the limitations of experiments.

WHAT ARE CAUSAL RELATIONSHIPS?

A concern with causality appears throughout marketing decision making. For example:

Market Analysis:	What effect have recent price increases had on product class sales?
Marketing Program Development:	Does the number of sales calls per month affect the size of the order placed?
	Can a new three-class airfare (including a budget or "no-frills" category) generate sufficient new passengers to offset the revenue loss of existing passengers switching to the cheaper category?
Peformance Evaluation:	What effect has the new sales training program had on sales performance?
	Has the new nutritional information disclosure requirement changed consumer purchasing habits?

The Limitations of Descriptive Designs

Underlying each of the research questions just given is the need to understand a causal *relationship* between an action and a probable outcome. These could be actions taken in the past (if we are in an evaluative or problem solving mode) or predictions about future actions. If the focus is on the future, then the primary interest is in comparing the outcomes of decision alternatives.

Why can't a descriptive research design answer these needs for causal insights? In the first place, most descriptive research does exactly as it says—it provides a snapshot picture of some aspect of the market environment at a specific point in time. Thus we use surveys, store audits, observation studies, analyses of financial records, and so on to give us information about such variables as brand shares, distributive coverage, and demographic characteristics of heavy buyers. There is no hint of a causal insight to be obtained from such data. Yet under some circumstances descriptive information can be used to infer—but rarely to establish—the presence of causal relationship.

The first step toward causality is usually a calculation of the strength of association of two or more variables measured during the descriptive study. If a causal link exists between two variables, they would be expected to be associated. Thus, we might find that a high quality of service is associated with health maintenance organizations that have small staffs. Does that show that a causal link exists and if staff sizes were reduced that the quality of service would increase? Hardly. What is probably happening is that a third (spurious) causal variable is involved. It may be that instead of

Reduced staffs *cause* Quality service

a more appropriate causal chain might be

Small facilities *cause* Quality service
Small facilities *cause* Reduced staffs

The association between reduced staffs and quality service was thus due to the existence of a third variable that causes both, namely facility size.

Another way is to measure association with data over time. For example, historical data may show an association between advertising expenditures and sales. Does this finding mean that advertising causes sales? Unfortunately this question is not easily answered. There is still the possibility of a third causal variable, like distribution, being involved. Increased distribution might require more advertising support and may generate sales. There is also a direction of a causation issue. It could be that the advertising expenditures are budgeted as a fixed percent of sales. Thus, a forecast of sales increases may lead to increases in advertising expenditures, so the more correct model could be

Sales change *causes* Advertising expenditure change

instead of

Advertising expenditure change *causes* Sales change

Clearly, what is needed is some idea of the time sequence of events; that is, did the change in advertising activity actually precede the observed change in sales? With a positive answer to this question we get closer to the characteristics of a proper causal design.

Conditions for Valid Causal Inferences

As this discussion of descriptive studies suggests, the following types of evidence are relevant to evaluating causal relationships:

- Evidence that a strong association between an action and an observed outcome exists
- Evidence that the action preceded the outcome
- Evidence that there is no strong competing explanation for the relationship—that a high level of internal validity exists

In addition, if the resulting causal inference is to be useful to management, it should be

- Generalizable beyond the particular setting in which it was found; that is, it should have a high level of external validity
- Persistent in that it will hold long enough to make management action worthwhile

Useful information that has one or more of these characteristics can be obtained via descriptive studies. Parts III and IV of this book, covering data analysis, will present techniques such as cross-tabulations and regression analysis, which aid in overcoming the interpretation problems of descriptive studies. In addition, Chapter 14 presents a more extensive discussion of causal inference and the interpretation problems in descriptive research.

Although useful information can be obtained from descriptive research, experiments are the research approach that is more directly applicable to making causal inferences. In the balance of this chapter experimental designs will be presented and discussed in terms of their ability to make valid causal inferences.

EXPERIMENTATION WITH CONTROL GROUPS

"Try It Out" Design

The simplest experiment is simply to apply the experimental treatment to a subject or group and measure the results. The utility company could run a two-week advertising campaign in Modesto, California during January, advocating insulation. They then could measure the number of requests for price quotations received by insulation firms. A high number of requests would serve to justify the advertising expenditure and support a decision to expand it to other cities.

This experimental design can be described with the following notation:[2]

$$X \qquad O$$

Where: X represents the exposure of a group to an experimental treatment whose effect is to be observed, and

O represents the observation or measurement taken on the group.

Thus, an observation is made after a group has been exposed to an experimental treatment.

One problem with this design is that it leaves open the possibility that the results could be explained by events external to the design. For example, insulation requests could be due to the fact that California was unseasonably cold during the test period, that utility bills are always high during January and high bills prompt interest in insulation,

[2]This system of notation was introduced by Donald T. Campbell and Julian C. Stanley, *Experimental and Quasi Experimental Designs for Research* (Chicago: Rand McNally, 1963).

or that *Time* magazine had a cover story on energy during the period. Such a possibility of confounding effects that are external to the design are termed **history effects**. In marketing studies, a prime source of history effects are the actions, retaliatory or otherwise, of competitors. In some situations competitors deliberately run special promotions into markets in which others are experimenting to foul them up. The longer the time period involved, the greater the likelihood that history will account for observed results. A one-year trial run of a marketing program in a single city probably would generate many history effects.

Another problem analogous to history is **maturation**, which refers to changes within respondents that are a consequence of time, including aging, growing tired, or becoming hungrier. For example, suppose the experimental treatment is a one-year delinquency prevention program. At the year's end the program is evaluated by measuring the number of subjects who have jobs and the incidence of crime. If 18-year-olds are more likely than 17-year-olds to hold jobs and avoid crime, then the findings may be the result of the young men's maturing during the year and not because of the delinquency program.

Nonmatched Control Group Design

One approach to control for history and maturation effects is to introduce a control group. Data on insulation requests might be readily available for Reading, California. Thus, the number of requests obtained in Reading could be compared with that of Modesto. Presumably many history effects, such as unusual California weather or a *Time* cover story, would influence Reading as well as Modesto. This design would be

$$X \quad O_1$$
$$\cdots \cdots \cdots$$
$$O_2$$

The top line refers to the Modesto group and the bottom line to the Reading group, which, of course, receives no experimental treatment. The results of interest would then be $O_1 - O_2$. A dotted horizontal line means that the groups are separate, that the experimental treatment does not reach the control group. If people in Modesto read the Reading newspaper, such would not be the case.

Another major problem that existed in the first design and is not solved by the second is termed **selection bias**. It may be that the response to the experiment is strictly a function of the city selected, Modesto. Modesto has many characteristics that could influence the experiment, including its location, its income, its quality of insulation firms, and its climate. If two, three, or more test cities and a like number of control cities were used, the selection bias very likely would be reduced, but it still would be there. Perhaps all of the test cities would be in the northern part of the state and the control cities in the southern part.

Selection bias is particularly severe when self-selection occurs, as when the test group consists of those who volunteered to participate in a program or research study. For example, suppose a group of students agreed to participate in a physical fitness program.

To evaluate the program, the number of pushups that the group can do is compared to those who did not volunteer to be part of the experimental group. Those who did volunteer are likely to be in better condition before the program, and the results simply might reflect this selection bias.

Matched Control Group Design

One approach to reducing selection bias is to match the experimental and control groups. Thus, if average temperature is expected to effect a community's reaction to insulation advertising, cities are matched as to their average temperature. A control city is picked that would be similar to Modesto in terms of temperature. Of course, another city may be found that would match Modesto in other dimensions besides temperature, like the percentage of homes not insulated, or demographic variables. The design can be denoted as

$$
\begin{array}{ccc}
M & X & O_1 \\
\hdashline
M & & O_2
\end{array}
$$

where M indicates that the two groups are matched with respect to some variable of interest.

The use of matched control groups is very beneficial when the sample design and cost considerations limit the size of the sample. It is very costly to run a test marketing program with subsequent measurement in a city or a small group of cities, and the researchers are often constrained to a single test city or at most two or three. In such cases, attempting to match the control city or cities with the test city or cities may be appropriate.

Randomized Control Group Design

The problem with matching is that test units cannot be matched on all relevant dimensions. They can be matched on one, two, and sometimes several dimensions, but in most contexts there are many dimensions that potentially could influence the results. Further, some or even most of these might be unknown or ones for which information is not available. For example, response to insulation might be due to people's attitude toward home improvement. If no information existed on people's attitudes it would not be possible to develop sets of matched cities on this dimension.

Randomly assigning test units or subjects to test and control groups provides a mechanism that when the sample size is sufficient, serves to match test and control groups on all dimensions simultaneously. Suppose we had 50 cities to use in our test. We randomly assign 25 to the test condition and the remaining 25 we use as control. Because of the randomization it would be unlikely that the test cities were larger, colder, or of higher income than the control cities. All of these factors should tend to average out. Of course, as the sample size increases, the degree of matching achieved by randomization also will increase.

Randomization is really a powerful device and is associated closely with the development and use of experimental methods. In fact, experimental designs that use randomization sometimes are called true experimental designs. A randomized design can be denoted as

$$
\begin{array}{ccc}
R & X & O_1 \\
\hline
R & & O_2
\end{array}
$$

where R indicates that the test units are randomly assigned to test and control. Randomization is particularly appropriate whenever the sample size is large enough so that the randomization will tend to cause the test and control groups to be similar.

Direct mail tests of advertising appeals are an ideal setting for this design. The mailing list can be sampled randomly to obtain the experimental and control groups. Suppose, for example, three different promotion pieces to a series of plays are to be tested. The question is which will deliver the most orders. A mailing list of 20,000 people is available. A random sample of 1200 is selected and divided randomly into three groups of 400 each. The experiment would appear as:

$$
\begin{array}{cccl}
R & X_1 & O_1 & n = 400 \\
\hline
R & X_2 & O_2 & n = 400 \\
\hline
R & X_3 & O_3 & n = 400
\end{array}
$$

where the X_1 refers to the first experimental treatment "level," namely the first of the three promotional pieces; X_2 refers to the second level; and so on. Here there is no separate control group. Each of the three treatments acts as a control for the others. The point of the experiment is to compare the three experimental treatments.

A variant of this design combines the treatment and the observation in the same questionnaire. In fact, this is the preferred method of obtaining reactions to different marketing options using surveys. For example, a study was conducted to determine the demand for a bus service at various price levels. One approach would be to ask prospective patrons if they would ride if the fare were 25¢, 50¢, or $1. However, it may be unrealistic to ask a respondent to make a judgment on a 50¢ fare after he or she has just considered a 25¢ fare. To avoid this problem, each respondent was given only one price. Each pricing alternative was presented to a randomly chosen third of a representative sample from the service area of the new bus route. Once the nature of the service and the fare level was described to each respondent, a measure of intentions or preferences relative to present modes of transportation was obtained as follows:

$$
\begin{array}{cc}
R & (X_1, O_1) \\
\hline
R & (X_2, O_2) \\
\hline
R & (X_3, O_3)
\end{array}
$$

Randomized Block Design

A randomized control group design controls by the randomization process for all variables, since there should be no tendency for an experimental group to differ systematically from the others on any dimension. However, there will be differences as long as the sample size is not extremely large. For example, even with 1200 in the sample the group receiving the first promotion piece could happen to be wealthier, more interested in the plays selected, or more urban than suburban. Thus, it could be argued that a superior performance by the first promotional piece actually could have been caused by these characteristics of the sample. Matching ensures that on the matched variable or variables there is no difference between test samples. Randomization controls for all variables, not just the matched ones, but only ensures that the groups will *tend* to be similar.

Randomization and matching are combined in the randomized block design. The research identifies which of the variables is the most important and controls for it by adding a block effect, which means that the control variable is used to define groups and to conduct the randomized experiment within each group. Symbolically the randomized block design might be

$$
\begin{cases} R & X & O_1 \\ R & & O_2 \end{cases}
$$
$$
\begin{cases} R & X & O_3 \\ R & & O_4 \end{cases}
$$

The solid line separates the two experiments.

For example, suppose that the urban respondents were expected to react more favorably than suburban respondents to a promotion for subscriptions to a series of plays; therefore, it was felt important to ensure that the experimental groups did not differ on this dimension. When a block effect is added, the experiment simply is repeated for both urban respondents and suburban respondents. Thus 600 randomly selected urban respondents would be divided randomly into three test groups. Similarly, 600 randomly selected suburban subjects would be divided randomly into three groups. This experiment could be represented as follows:

$$
\text{Urban} \begin{cases} R & X_1 & O_1 & N = 200 \\ R & X_2 & O_2 & n = 200 \\ R & X_3 & O_3 & n = 200 \end{cases}
$$
$$
\text{Suburban} \begin{cases} R & X_1 & O_4 & n = 200 \\ R & X_2 & O_5 & n = 200 \\ R & X_3 & O_6 & n = 200 \end{cases}
$$

The results might be presented as in Table 9–1.

TABLE 9–1

Percentage Who Ordered Tickets

Treatment	Urban	Suburban	Means
A	11	4	7.5
B	24	11	17.5
C	24.5	15.5	20
Means	20	10	15

If in the original experiment, which did not block the urban–suburban factor, the group that received promotion B happened to have a higher percentage of urban respondents than the other group, it could have appeared superior to treatment C. However, when the blocked design is used, treatment C is superior.

The results provide evidence that treatment C is the best; however, it is not much better than treatment B. The difference is close enough that it might be due to chance. The treatment C respondents might just happen to be better prospects, and if the sample size were increased tenfold, promotions B and C actually might be the same. Hypothesis testing provides precise answers to such considerations and will be discussed in Chapter 14.

Another separate motivation for matching on the urban–suburban dimension might be to see if there were differences in reaction to the three promotions. Perhaps a segmentation strategy might emerge that would indicate that one promotion was best for urban dwellers and another for suburban. The analysis of such **interactive effects** will be presented in a later section when factorial designs are discussed. It should be emphasized that this motivation is completely distinct and different from the experimental design motivation, to ensure that the respondents' location does not confound the results.

There is no reason why several control variables cannot be used. To the urban–suburban control variable, a prior-attendance control variable (attended frequently, attended, did not attend) and an age-control variable (older, middle-aged, and younger)

TABLE 9–2

Sales in an Experiment Involving Advertising and Price

	High Price	Low Price	Average Sales
High advertising	105	133	119
Low advertising	103	124	113.5
No advertising	101	112	106.5
Average sales	103	123	113

could be added. The experiment then simply is repeated for each cell. For example, a group of respondents who are urban, attended frequently in the past, and who are middle-aged will be divided into three groups and the three experimental treatments will be applied to each group. The problem is, of course, that as the number of control variables increases so do the number of cells and the required sample size. In our example there are two times three, times three, or 18 cells. The usual solution to this problem is the Latin square design, described in the appendix to this chapter.

COMBINING EXPERIMENTAL TREATMENTS

Only one experimental variable was involved in all the designs presented thus far. In some of the illustrations, several treatment levels were included, for instance, in the three types of promotions tested in the randomized-block illustrative example. However, only one experimental variable, promotion effects, was tested. In this section the use of two or more experimental variables in factorial designs will be considered, and the concept of interaction will be introduced.

Factorial Designs

In the randomized control group design, a single experimental variable was involved. In the factorial design, two or more experimental variables are considered simultaneously. Each combination of the experimental treatment levels applies to randomly selected groups.

Suppose that a consumer product was to be tested in 36 cities. Three levels of advertising were to be tested, a high level, a low level, and no advertising. In addition, two price levels are to be considered, a high price and a low price. The resulting factorial experiment could be denoted as

R	X_1 (Hi Adv–Hi Price)	O_1	$n = 6$
R	X_2 (Hi Adv–Low Price)	O_2	$n = 6$
R	X_3 (Low Adv–Hi Price)	O_3	$n = 6$
R	X_4 (Low Adv–Low Price)	O_4	$n = 6$
R	X_5 (No Adv–Hi Price)	O_5	$n = 6$
R	X_6 (No Adv–Low Price)	O_6	$n = 6$

The output of the experiment will provide not only the effects of advertising but also the effects of the price variable. Suppose the findings were as shown in Table 9–2. Thus, in one experiment the effects of two variables are determined. The real power of a factorial design, however, is that it provides the ability to determine interactive effects.

Interactive Effects

Figure 9–1a shows the results in graphical form. The judgment about advertising can be refined now. When the product is priced high the advertising effect almost disappears, whereas when the product is priced low the advertising effect is much larger. This illustrates an interaction effect between two experimental variables. The effect of the advertising level is termed a *main effect*, the main effect due to advertising. Similarly, the effect of price is termed the main effect of price. The main effect is distinguished from the **interactive effect** of pairs of experimental variables.

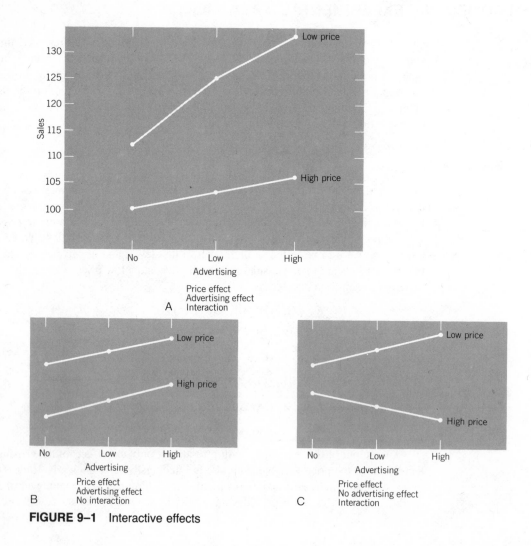

FIGURE 9–1 Interactive effects

In Figure 9–1*a*, there is a price effect because the low-price results are higher on the average than the high-price results. There is also an advertising effect, as the average results for the various advertising levels differ. As has been noted already, there is also an interaction effect. Figure 9–1*b* is an example of the case where there is both an advertising and price effect but no interaction. The two main effects are additive here. The absence of interactions results in additive effects, and the price effect is simply added to the advertising effect to get the total result. Figure 9–1*c* shows a case where there is a price main effect but no advertising main effect. The average sales for each level of advertising are the same. There is, however, an interactive effect between advertising and price, an effect that is even more pronounced than that of Figure 9–1*a*.

The factorial design could be expanded to have three or more variables. Each then would generate a main effect and each pair would generate a possible interactive effect. Of course, there needs to be an experimental group for each combination of experimental treatment levels. Thus, if three levels of advertising, two levels of price, and three promotion alternatives were involved, a total of 12 possible conditions would have to be tested. That would require a sample size of at least 12, which might be expensive if test cities were involved. Further, if each cell is to provide a reliable estimate of that treatment combination, several test cities might be desired. If the respondents were people instead of cities, several hundred might be required in each experimental group. Thus, one of the problems of factorial designs is that the number of experimental groups can get large rather quickly. Of course, the Latin square concept (described in the appendix) can be employed to reduce the number somewhat, if interactions can be neglected.

The makers of Budweiser beer conducted a set of experiments, beginning in 1961 and continuing for many years, that are probably the most well-known and influential of all marketing experiments to date.[3] One of their first experiments was a factorial design involving three advertising levels (normal, 25 percent under normal, and 50 percent over normal), three levels of sales effort, and three levels of expenditure on point-of-purchase displays and signs. The company did not wish to risk experimenting with any of their major markets. They feared that a 25-percent reduction of advertising could cause lasting harm to an important market. After excluding the major markets from the 198 marketing areas, 27 were selected for the experiment and assigned randomly to one of the 27 experimental groups. The experiment was conducted and the results measured for a 12-month period (since advertising is thought to have important lagged effects). The experiment's results showed that a reduction in advertising did not decrease sales; in fact, it increased them. This, and subsequent experiments, led Budweiser to reduce considerably their level of advertising.

Factorial designs also could be expanded to include block effects. Thus, either the experiment of advertising and price or the Budweiser experiment could have been duplicated, once for large cities and once for small ones, for example. Furthermore, factorial designs could be created using matching instead of randomization to develop the experimental groups.

[3]James R. Emshoff and Russel L. Ackoff, "Advertising Research at Anheuser-Busch, Inc. (1963–1968)," *Sloan Management Review* (Winter 1975), 1–15.

THE USE OF "BEFORE" MEASURES

The Before–After, "Try-it-Out" Design

One of the problems with the "try-it-out" design is selection bias. For example, Pacific Telephone ran an experimental advertising campaign in Fresno, California aimed at reducing the number of directory assistance calls. The number of calls after the campaign could be caused by the size of the test city, its ethnic composition, or any other characteristic. Among the ways to help provide some control for such characteristics is to add a matched control city or to add several cities to the test and assign them randomly to test and control groups. Another approach to improving the control is to add a "before measure":

$$O_1 \quad X \quad O_2$$

The before measure acts as a control because if the city were large the O_1 measure also would be large. The interest is then in the change from O_1 to O_2. Pacific Telephone measured the number of directory assistance calls before the test campaign was run and after the test campaign and compared the two after correcting for seasonal patterns.

The designs considered thus far have been "after only" designs because they had no before measure. The before measure can be added to any design already presented. It will add sensitivity by adding another method to control for confounding variables. If the observations are unobtrusive and available, like the number of directory assistance calls or store or brand sales, then a before measure is routinely used. In some situations, as when a new product or service is involved, a before measure may simply not be available.

When the observation is not unobtrusive, then the before measure still is used often, but several potential threats to internal validity then emerge. Consider, for example, a laboratory experiment to test an advertisement aimed at reducing the incidence of smoking among teenage women. Attitudes and perceptions toward smoking are measured, the group is exposed to the advertisement, and the attitudes are measured again, immediately or perhaps after several days. The before measure in such an experiment may produce the following validity threats:

1 *Before Measure Effect.* The before measure may alert the respondents to the fact that they are being studied. The result can be a tendency to give more socially desirable responses and behavior, such as reducing the claimed and actual smoking frequency. Of course, subjects in any laboratory experiment usually will know, to some extent, they are being studied (the testing effect), but the existence of a before measure can heighten this feeling and associate it with the subject matter of the observation. Further, the before measure can stimulate or enhance an interest in the subject of the study. It can, therefore, generate heightened curiosity and attention and even lead to discussing the topic with friends and changing behavior. Thus, the mere fact that a prior measurement was taken can have an effect on any measurement taken after the treatment. The before measurement also can affect the respondent's reaction to the experimental treatment.

2 *Mortality Effect.* This is due to the possibility that some subjects may stop participating in the experiment, or may not respond when sought out for a follow-up interview. This drop-out effect is usually not uniform across the sample being studied. Busy people, high-income households, and urban area residents are always more difficult to reach.

3 *Instrumentation Effect.* This is the result of a change in the measuring instrument. Such an effect may be as simple as a change in question wording between interviews or the use of a different interviewer for the follow-up interview. A more subtle problem is a consequence of interviewers changing as they gain experience and literally becoming different instruments.

Before–After Randomized Control Group Design

The addition of a control group in the randomized case generates the following design:

$$R \quad O_1 \quad X \quad O_2$$
$$R \quad O_3 \qquad O_4$$

This design provides a control group that helps control for history and maturation effects and in addition controls for the reactive effect of O_1 on O_2 (part of the before measure effect). The output of interest would be the difference obtained by subtracting O_2 from O_1 and O_4 from O_3. However, the design fails to control for the effect of the before measure upon X, the experiment treatment (the other part of the before measure effect). It may be that the before measure will sensitize the respondents so that their reaction to the experimental treatment will be distorted. The teenage women subjects might, after giving their attitudes about smoking, react quite differently to an antismoking advertisement than if they had not given their attitudes.

The Solomon Four-Group Design

A solution to the previous problem is to augment the design with an "after only" design as follows:

$$R \quad O_1 \quad X \quad O_2$$
$$R \quad O_3 \qquad O_4$$
$$R \qquad X \quad O_5$$
$$R \qquad\qquad O_6$$

This design is usually prohibitively expensive, but it does provide the power to control for the before measure effect of O_1 on both X and O_2. This design provides several measures of the experimental effect [*ie.*, $(O_2 - O_4)$, $(O_2 - O_1) - (O_4 - O_3)$, $(O_6 - O_5)$].

If there is agreement among these measures the inferences about X can be much stronger. If there is no agreement, it is still possible to measure directly the interaction of the treatment and before measure effects $[(O_2 - O_4) - (O_5 - O_6)]$.

The Separate-Sample Before–After Design

There are many circumstances—such as a national introduction of a new product or service, or implementation of federal legislation—that make it impossible to find an unaffected subgroup to use for a control. When, for example, the truth-in-lending bill was passed it applied to all. Thus, it is not possible to identify any control subgroup. The use of a one-group before–after design might be unacceptable because of the reactive effect of the before observation. In such cases a separate random sample is sometimes interviewed for the before measure:

$$R \quad O_1 \quad (X)$$
$$\cdots\cdots\cdots\cdots\cdots\cdots\cdots$$
$$R \quad\quad\quad X \quad O_2$$

The bracket (X) indicates that all groups are exposed to the treatment but only one is interviewed after the treatment. The major shortcoming of this design is an inability to say anything about history, that is, concurrent events that might account for O_2. There is also a possible instrumentation problem if the observations come from sample surveys. Even though the interviewers in the before and after measurements are the same people, they will have gained experience as the study progressed and perhaps have learned about the reasons for the experiment, so their expectations of the proper responses may have changed also. Because of the weakness of this design it is desirable that it be tried repeatedly, at different times and in different settings.

Time-Series Designs

Time-series designs are similar to the before–after "try-it-out" design except that a series of measurements are employed during which an experimental treatment occurs:

$$O_1 \quad O_2 \quad O_3 \quad O_4 \quad X \quad O_5 \quad O_6 \quad O_7$$

There are two variants of this design, depending on whether the measurements are all from the same sample or from separate samples.

Trend Studies.   Here the measures come from a succession of *separate* random samples from the same population and yield much of the basic information on which marketing decisions are made. There is virtually no limit to the kinds of series that can be measured.

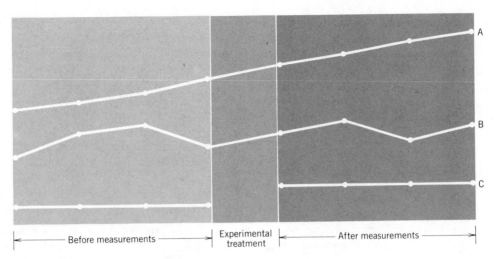

Before measurements ⟵⟶ Experimental treatment ⟵⟶ After measurements

FIGURE 9–2 A time-series design

For example:

- Aggregate economic series (gross national product, employment rates, consumer prices)
- Social indicators (United Fund contributions, infant mortality, cost of housing, air pollution level)[4]
- Records of sales or patronage (from accounting data, reservations systems, or store audits)
- Continuous market monitoring studies (involving bimonthly or quarterly surveys of awareness, attitudes, media exposure, and purchase satisfaction and intentions)[5]

The data from trend studies can be analyzed only in the aggregate form in which they are collected. The question is whether the measures following the experimental treatment are a continuation of earlier patterns or whether they mark a decisive change. In Figure 9–2, a decisive change is apparent only in case C.

The insights from trend studies can be expanded considerably if several trends can be analyzed simultaneously. For example, an estimate of the price elasticity of demand for a product can be obtained if parallel trends of prices and market shares or sales are available.

The availability of data spanning a number of time periods means that *maturation*

---

[4]Leslie D. Wilcox, Ralph M. Brooks, George M. Beal, and Gerald M. Klonglan, *Social Indicators and Societal Monitoring* (San Francisco: Jossey-Bass, 1972).

[5]An example of this type of study is reported in John C. Maloney, ''Attitude Measurement and Formation,'' a paper presented to the Test Market Design and Measurement Workshop, American Marketing Association, Chicago, April 1966.

is unlikely to be a possible cause of the observed effect. *History* and *instrument* changes remain as possible threats to validity. Of the two threats, the possibility that a simultaneous event produced the change is clearly the most difficult to rule out. If one is to use this design there must be continuing sensitivity to plausible competing explanations.[6] Ideally this should be done prior to the experimental treatment, so that the data needed to confirm or disconfirm the competing hypotheses are available. This may entail recording the weather, prices of related products, and so forth.

Continuous Panel Studies.[7]   These collect a series of measurements on the same sample of test units over an extended period of time. The term usually is applied to

- Reinterview panels, in which the same questions are asked of the same people—usually with a long interval between reinterviews to minimize before-measure effects
- Diary panels, in which large samples of households record (1) the details of their purchases (brands, package sizes, prices paid, coupons used, etc.) in a variety of product categories or (2) their media viewing/reading behavior

Both types of panels offer insights into choice behavior that cannot be obtained from any other source. Each person whose behavior or attitude changed can be identified, instead of being buried in the aggregation of a time series. This is especially important in product categories where stable sales often obscure large, but compensating, gains and losses of individual buyers.

Since panel data normally are collected directly from an individual, there is a significant threat to internal validity from the before-measure effect. When a person is asked about a subject and knows that further interviews will be made, the result is an unusual degree of awareness and sensitivity. Fortunately, this seems to decay over time, and within three to five months the preceding interview usually is forgotten. Other threats to validity include history, changes in instrumentation, and nonrandom selection.

SUMMARY

Table 9–3 summarizes the 11 designs that have been introduced. A distinction is made in Table 9–3 between designs that involve randomization and designs that do not. If a commerical is to be tested, one approach is to run it in Fresno and measure subsequent sales. The persistent question, of course, is to what extent the subsequent sales are caused

---

[6]For a stimulating discussion of this method of strengthening causal inferences, see Eugene J. Webb, Donald T. Campbell, Richard D. Schwartz and Lee Lechrest, *Unobtrusive Measures: Nonreactive Research in the Social Sciences,* (Chicago: Rand McNally, 1966).

[7]The term "panel" sometimes refers to a consumer jury, whose members provide a reaction to some proposed product on a one-shot basis.

TABLE 9–3
Summary of Experimental Designs

Nonrandomized Designs	
No "Before" Measure	Includes "Before" Measure

1. "Try-it-out" design

   $X \quad O$

   where X = run a TV commercial
   O = observe sales

2. Nonmatched control group design

   Test city $X \quad O_1$
   ....
   Other city O_2

3. Matched control group design

   Test city $M \quad X \quad O_1$
   ....
   Matched city $M \quad\quad\quad O_2$

7. Before–After "Try-it-out" design

   $O_1 \quad X \quad O_2$

11. Time-series design

   $O_1 \quad O_2 \quad O_3 \quad O_4 \quad X \quad O_5 \quad O_6 \quad O_7 \quad O_8$

Randomized Designs	
No "Before" Measure	Includes "Before" Measure

4. Randomized control group design:
   Randomly selected test & control cities

   $R \quad X \quad O_1$
   ....
   $R \quad\quad\quad O_2$

5. Randomized block design: Experiment
   repeated in two contexts thought to
   have different reactions to X

   $R \quad X \quad O_1$
   ....
   $R \quad\quad\quad O_2$
   ———————
   $R \quad X \quad O_3$
   ....
   $R \quad\quad\quad O_4$

6. Factorial designs: Multiple
   experimental treatments:

   $R \; X$(Hi Adv, Lo Price) O_1
   $R \; X$(Hi Adv, Hi Price) O_2
   $R \; X$(Lo Adv, Lo Price) O_3
   $R \; X$(Lo Adv, Hi Price) O_4

8. Before–after randomized control
   group design

   $R \quad O_2 \quad X \quad O_2$
   ....
   $R \quad O_3 \quad\quad\quad O_4$

9. Solomon four-group design

   $R \quad O_1 \quad X \quad O_2$
   ....
   $R \quad O_3 \quad\quad\quad O_4$
   ....
   $R \quad\quad\quad X \quad O_5$
   ....
   $R \quad\quad\quad\quad\quad O_6$

10. Separate-sample before–after design

   $R \quad O_1 \quad (X)$
   ....
   $R \quad\quad\quad X \quad O_2$

by the commercial and not by such other factors as the size of Fresno and competitor price changes. In nonrandomized designs, there are two methods of controlling for influences on sales other than the experimental treatment. One is the use of control or comparison cities, where the commercial is not being run. The other is to compare subsequent sales with a before measure of sales.

Because there are so many influences on sales, a powerful way to control for all of them is to split test units randomly, such as by dividing test cities into those receiving the experimental treatment and those acting as control or comparison cities. The theory is that the other influences on sales would tend to be equally prevalent in the test cities and in the control cities. As the number of test units increases, the theory will be more likely to hold. If the advertising test involved 40 test cities randomly split between test cities and control cities, we would be more confident of the results than if only two cities were available for the test. The use of randomization is considered so basic to experimentation that some people refer to experiments involving randomization as "true" experiments, as opposed to "quasi-experiments" not using randomization.

THREATS TO VALIDITY

An experiment is intended to provide information regarding the causal influence of an experimental treatment on the measure of interest. The internal validity of the experiment depends upon the extent to which competing explanations for the results are avoided. The external validity of the experiment refers to the extent that the causal inferences can be generalized from the experimental environment to the environment of the decision maker. Although most of the threats to internal and external validity have been mentioned, it is useful to recap them.

Threats to Internal Validity

1 History: events external to the experiment that affect the responses of the people involved in the experiment

2 Maturation: changes in the respondents that are a consequence of time, such as aging, getting hungry, or getting tired

3 Testing effect: awareness of being in a test, which can sensitize and bias respondents

4 Before-measure effect: the before measure also can sensitize and bias respondents, therefore influencing both the after observation and the respondent's reaction to the experimental treatment

5 Instrumentation: the measuring instrument may change, as when different interviewers are used

6 Mortality: respondents dropping out of the experiment

7 Selection bias: an experimental group is systematically different in some relevant way from the population being studied

Threats to External Validity

Laboratory experiments have the greatest external validity problem because of the *artificiality* of the setting and arrangements. The exposure to an experimental treatment, such as a mock-up of a new product in a laboratory, can be so different from conditions in the real world that projections become very difficult and risky.[8] Consider the plight of a researcher seeking to design a laboratory experiment to yield quick feedback on the effect of a company rebuttal to adverse publicity. (An example is a government report on Alka-Seltzer, which contended that because it contained aspirin it was damaging to some of the stomach conditions it was designed to treat.) Since "bad news" is thought to have superior attention-getting ability, a valid laboratory experiment would make provision for selective exposure, attention, or perception of the attack and the rebuttal. This problem has defeated several ingenious researchers.

In addition to the artificiality problem of laboratory experiments, most of the previous list of seven internal validity threats also apply to external validity. In particular, selectivity bias can be very serious. In field experiments the test market site, the stores chosen to test, and the people interviewed as part of the experiment are sometimes not representative of the entire market or population. In a laboratory experiment the respondents are often not a good representation of the population, especially if the experiment requires considerable effort and if self-selection is involved. As Banks notes, "the greater the demand upon respondents in terms of either the effort expended or the period of time covered by the experiment, the greater the likelihood that the subject who cooperates throughout the study is atypical."[9]

Also, a significant before measure effect may diminish external validity. If the before measure increases respondent sensitivity to the treatment, then the results will not be typical of the "real world." This problem can be severe in experiments that ask respondents to record purchases in a diary. These consumer panel members invariably pay closer attention to the choices in the categories being recorded, and they may buy greater than usual quantities in order to have something to record. The novelty does wear off, and purchase behavior is thought to return to normal, but that can occur after the experiment is over.

This enumeration of sources of invalidity is bound to be incomplete. Some threats are too specific to a given setting to be generalized easily. For example, the likelihood that competitors will distort the results of market tests (by aggressive promotional activity, additional salesforce effort, or even doing nothing when they certainly would take action

---

[8]The magnitude of these problems is well illustrated in Jack A. Gold, "Testing Test Market Predictions," *Journal of Marketing Research* (August 1964) 8–16.

[9]Seymour Banks, *Experimentation in Marketing* (New York: McGraw-Hill, 1965), p. 33.

if the new product were launched into a regional or national market) is an ever-present "history" problem in this particular setting.

What is important is not the completeness of the checklist of threats but a heightened sensitivity to the possibility of threats so that

1 The extent and the direction of the bias in results can be considered when it becomes time to use the relationship obtained from the experiment to make a decision.

2 The possibility of design improvements can be anticipated.

3 Other methods of measurement with different restraints on validity can be employed. The virtue of multiple measures of approaches to the same phenomena is that the biases of each may cancel each other.

To show how the checklist of possible threats can be used to guide the thinking of a researcher or manager who wants to make a judgment about the quality of results of an experiment, we turn to the example of an advertising testing method.

Theater Testing of Television Commercials

The theater testing procedure pioneered by the Schwerin Research Corporation is representative of an approach now employed by the advertising research firms ASI, ARS and McCollum/Spielman:

1 About 1000 names are selected randomly from residential telephone directories in a metropolitan area.

2 Each person on the list is sent four to eight invitations to attend a preview of a television program. They are told they have a chance to win a prize if they come. Usually 300 to 400 respond.

3 Prior to the film, the participant is given a list of brands and asked to select the one in each of three product categories that he or she would prefer to receive in a lottery drawing, which is then held.

4 The audience is exposed to a 30-minute pilot television film that includes test commercials for one brand in each of the three product categories.

5 Immediately after the program, the audience members record what they recalled from the commercials. Then they are given another list of brands and are asked to check the brand they now want. Another drawing is held.

The effectiveness of each television advertisement is evaluated by the size of the difference or change between the before and the after measure of brand preference. But is this a valid evaluation? Can an observed change be attributed solely to exposure to the advertisement? If so, can the results be generalized to the market environment?

A review of the checklist of threats to validity reveals a major competing explanation for the observed change in preference. A significant before-measure effect probably results when the audience members are given the list of brands in three product categories. Not only does the before measure signal the topic of the research, it also produces—together with the test effect—atypical behavior such as thinking and talking about the brand beforehand and paying unusual attention to the advertisements as they appear. These behaviors will influence both the appeals recalled and the response to the second request for brand preferences. Internal validity is compromised further by "game playing" in reaction to the lottery. The extent and direction of these biases is very difficult to assess.

Both internal and external validity are threatened by a **selection bias**. Those who attend are self-selected and unlikely to be representative of any target audience. In addition to being residents of the New York City area in most cases, they are curious about television programs, perhaps because they are heavy television watchers, and they have half a day to spend. The ticket distribution method raises the possibility that the audience is composed of an unusual proportion of affinity groups with shared interests. A further threat is the artificiality of both the viewing environment and the choice situation—where no cost or search effort is involved.

Another problem might be the instrumentation effect. The before measure might reflect brand preference, whereas the after measure might reflect, in part, the respondent's desire for variety.

In light of these problems, why does the theater testing method remain a popular means of testing television commercials? First, there aren't many attractive, economical alternatives to this method. Second, the biases are well known to the users and are thought to apply rather uniformly to all low-price consumer products. This bears on the third and most important reason: the objective of the research is to *compare* the effects of copy alternatives in a standardized setting, not to make absolute estimates of effects. This is true of a large proportion of marketing research and accounts for many of the compromises encountered in marketing experiments.

Ultimately, the argument that less rigorous procedures are required for the comparison of alternatives is more defensible if there is parallel validation activity. In the advertising-copy-testing context this means on-air field testing of the same advertising alternatives for comparison with the results of the theater test.

THE LIMITATIONS OF EXPERIMENTS

Experimentation is a powerful tool in the search for unambiguous relationships that we hope may be used to make valid predictions about the effects of marketing decisions and to develop basic theories. The laboratory experiment is the preferred method because of its internal validity; however, because of acute external validity problems in the laboratory setting, managers are reluctant to rely upon it. Unfortunately, the field experiment is beset by a number of problems whose net effect has been to limit the vast majority of marketing experiments to short-run comparisons across stores, home placements of product variations, and so forth. Relatively few large-scale experiments with social programs, marketing programs, or advertising campaigns are conducted in any given year. What are the reasons?

Cost

Cost and time pressures are the first hurdle. Even "simple" in-store tests require additional efforts to gain cooperation; to properly place the display, price, or promotion; to measure the uncontrolled variables; and then to audit the resulting sales differences. The measurement costs alone are often substantial. When larger interventions, such as comparing alternative advertising themes in multiple geographic areas, are contemplated, management may be very wary that the benefits will exceed the costs. These costs are likely to be considerable if any amount of reinterviewing or special manipulation of advertising, product, or other controllable variables is required.

Another cost is the fact that management decisions are delayed by the research. For some experiments the impact of the experimental treatment can extend over a long time period, as much as a year or even longer. Consider the Budweiser advertising experiments, which were run for a full year. The researcher is often placed in a difficult position. If the experiment, especially the after observation, is not allowed sufficient time, the validity of the results might suffer. On the other hand, if the experiment is too lengthy the resulting delays in making and implementing policy might be unacceptably long. One way to avoid the constraint of time pressure is to conduct an ongoing program of experimentation in anticipation of recurring decisions. Thus, some companies are building up data files of responses to marketing programs in a variety of contexts.

Security

Still another cost is that of security. A field experiment naturally involves exposing a marketing program in the marketplace, so it is difficult to hide from competitors who are in contact with their own field salesforce, store personnel, research suppliers, and trade sources. For example, one consumer products company constructed product displays in several stores in one city for one eight-hour period on one Friday. At the end of the day all traces of the test had been removed. By Monday the major trade magazine and most competitors knew of the test and the details of the test product.

Implementation Problems

Implementation problems abound in the conduct of experiments. First, it may not be easy to *gain cooperation* within the organization. Proposals to experiment with varying the size and call frequency of a salesforce are resisted by regional managers, who do not want their market area to receive a reduction in sales effort. Administrators of social programs may resist efforts to assign people randomly to treatments. They want to decide the assignments according to who can benefit most from the service and which service is most suitable. A second problem to which experiments involving market areas are especially susceptible is *contamination*, because of an inability to confine the treatment to the designated experimental area. Buyers from one geographic area may visit an adjacent area or receive media messages that overflow from that area. It is seldom possible to partition geographic market areas so that the sales measurements and treatments exactly coincide. Experiments involving people as test units may become contaminated because people in the control group associate with people assigned to the program and learn what they have been doing. A third problem is that the variability in behavior across test units can be so large that it is difficult to detect experimental effects. Of course, some of the variability can be removed by adding blocking or by matching, but it will not be eliminated. The question is: Can it be reduced enough so that the experimental effects can be discerned?

The ultimate problem, however, is that there may be no person or geographic area available to serve as a control. This is the case with industrial markets composed of a few large buyers who communicate among each other or are geographically dispersed. Any effort to limit a new-product introduction to a subset of such a market would be unsuccessful. The same problem occurs in attempting to assess the effects of federal legislation, which goes into effect in all parts of the country at the same time. Also, practitioners may be unwilling to deny access to a social program because they believe that it is counter to their professional obligation.

Uncertain **Persistency of Results**

This is the final category of the problems that limit the acceptance and usage of field experiments. For an experimental result to be useful it must hold long enough to be acted on to advantage. The two factors most damaging to an assumption of persistency are high rates of technological, economic, or social change in the market environment; and aggressive competitive behavior. During the experiment the competition may elect to monitor the test independently and learn as much as possible—or take unusual action, such as a special consumer promotion, to confound the results. Similarly, when the test is expanded to a regional or national market the competitors may either do nothing or retaliate. This means that there are at least four combinations of circumstances, each with different implications for the nature of the causal relationship being studied:

		POSSIBLE COMPETITIVE RESPONSES After experiment	
		No response	Retaliation
During Experiment	No response	1	3
	Retaliation	4	2

To the degree that the decision maker cannot assess, (1) the probability of each of the four possible events, (2) the magnitude of the retaliatory action, if any, or (3) the number of direct competitors taking action, then the persistency—and hence the value—of the experimental results will be uncertain.

SUMMARY

Experiments are conducted to identify and quantify causal relationships. Laboratory experiments are often relatively inexpensive and provide the opportunity to exercise tight control. In a laboratory, for example, an exposure to a concept can be controlled; whereas in the more realistic field context there are many factors that can distort an exposure, such as weather, competitive reactions, and family activities. However, the laboratory experiment suffers from the testing effect and from the artificiality of the situation. Thus, the external validity (the ability to generalize from the experiment) is limited. Field experiments have greater external validity but are more costly to run (in expense, time, and security), are difficult to implement, and lack the tight control possible in the laboratory. As a result their internal validity is often a problem.

There are several experimental design alternatives to consider. The use of a control group can serve to help control for history and maturation effects. With small sample sizes, as in the use of test cities, it is useful to match the test and control groups to reduce selection bias. The large-sample randomization, which can effectively "match" on all variables (known and unknown), is preferred. Blocking can add further control, and the Latin square provides a way to reduce the number of cells introduced by considering several control or blocking variables. Several experimental variables can be tested at once using factorial designs. Such designs provide not only main effects but also allow the analysis of interactions between experimental treatments. For example, a promotion might be very effective among urban residents but ineffective among suburban residents.

The use of a before measure increases the sensitivity of the experiment by adding another form of control; however, a before measure can serve to sensitize and bias the respondents, therefore having an effect on the after measure and on the respondent's reaction to the experimental treatment.

QUESTIONS AND PROBLEMS

1 When would a laboratory test market (used to test new brands—see p. 621) be preferred over a full market test in two test cities? (See p. 625.) In a laboratory test market, people are exposed to advertisements for a new brand and then are asked to buy a brand from that product class from a supermarket aisle that has been set up as realistically as possible. After they use the brand, they are asked if they would like to repurchase it.

2 A blind taste was responsible in part for the decision by Coca-Cola to introduce the "new Coke," a product that ran into resistence by those loyal to "old Coke" (now Coke Classic). In a blind taste test, unlabeled colas would be tasted and the respondent would report tast preferences. Evaluate the validity of this experiment.

3 Contrast the following pairs of concepts by defining and illustrating each:

    a History vs. Instrumentation effects.

    b Maturation vs. Mortality effects.

    c Testing vs. Before-measure effects.

    d Selection Bias vs. Self-selection.

    e Randomized Block Design vs. Factorial Design

4 To evaluate an advertising campaign designed to stimulate transit usage, a survey was designed. A sample of 200 transit riders was contacted while riding on the transit system. An additional 200 people who do not ride the transit system were contacted by phone. All respondents were asked about transit usage and whether they recalled seeing the advertising campaign. A total of 70 percent of those recalling the advertisement rode the transit system last week, whereas only 20 percent of those who had not recalled the advertisement rode the system during the last week. It was thus concluded that the advertising had made a dramatic impact upon transit usage. Critique this conclusion. Design an experiment to address this issue.

5 What type of design was the Schwerin commercial test? How might the design be improved so as to reduce the validity problems?

6 Consider Figure 9–1 and Table 9–2. Explain interaction in the context of the figure. In Table 9–2 the average sales are given for each advertising level. Plot these numbers on Figure 9–1a, and use these plots to show the main effect of advertising. Average to two lines in Figure 9–1b and 9–1c to obtain the overall effects of advertising. Why are the effects of advertising and price additive in Figure 9–1b.

7 Design a Latin square experiment (described in the appendix) to test the effect of self facings upon the sales of Tang drink. Six facings are to be tested; 2, 4, 6, 8, 10, and 12. Six stores are to be used. In each store a facing will be employed for one week. The test is to last six weeks.

8 Consider Question 7 in Chapter 21 (p. 589).

APPENDIX
LATIN SQUARE DESIGN

The Latin square design is a method to reduce the number of groups involved when interactions between the treatment levels and the control variables can be considered relatively unimportant. We will use a laboratory nutritional labeling experiment to describe and illustrate the Latin square design.

    The goal of the experiment was to contribute to the judgment of those proposing and evaluating several public policy nutritional labeling alternatives. In particular, the research goal was to determine the impact upon shopper perceptions and preferences of variations in nutritional information on labels of canned peas. Four levels of information were tested. The first provided only a simple quality statement. The second listed some major nutrient components and whether the product was high or low on them. The third provided the

	Stores			
	1	2	3	4
Private Brand A 21 cents	III	IV	I	II
Private Brand B 22 cents	II	III	IV	I
Major Brand A 25 cents	I	II	III	IV
Major Brand B 26 cents	IV	I	II	III

FIGURE 9–3 A Latin square design: The treatment levels I, II, III, and IV

Source: Adapted from Edward H. Asam and Louis P. Bucklin, "Nutritional Labeling for Canned Goods: A Study of Consumer Response," *Journal of Marketing, 37* (April 1973), 36.

amounts of each nutrient. The fourth listed all nutritional components and was the most complete.

There were two control or block variables, the store and the brand. Four brands of canned peas, each with associated prices, were used. Four locations, each adjacent to a supermarket, were used and 50 shoppers were interviewed in each. It was felt that interactions among the nutritional information treatments and the brands or stores would be insignificant, so the Latin square could be used. The design is shown in Figure 9–3. Note that treatment level I appears with each store once and only once, and with each brand once and only once. Thus, the results for treatment level I should not benefit from the fact that one of the brands is rated higher than the others or that shoppers from one of the stores are more sensitive to nutrition.

TABLE 9–4

Mean Scores for Attitudes and Preference Scales for Four Different Levels of Nutritional Information on Can Labels

Nutritional Treatment	Scale					
	Like	Good Buy	Tasty	Tender	Wholesome	Preference
Level I	4.73	4.88	5.05	5.78	4.86	2.47
Level II	4.49	4.38	4.87	5.39	4.90	2.28
Level III	4.63	4.71	4.87	5.65	5.13	2.55
Level IV	4.86	4.91	5.07	5.99	5.32	2.69

Adapted from Edward H. Asam and Louis P. Bucklin, "Nutritional Labeling for Canned Goods: A Study of Consumer Response," *Journal of Marketing, 37* (April 1973), p. 36.

Each respondent was exposed to four cans of peas. For example, at store 1 respondents were exposed to Private Brand A at 21¢ with the treatment III label information, to Private Brand B at 22¢ with treatment II, and so on. After being exposed to the four cans, the respondents were asked to evaluate each on six different nine-point scales. Thus, this experiment illustrates the use of multiple measures of the results. The mean score for each treatment level is shown in Table 9–4. Again, the issue as to whether the results are "statistically significant" will be deferred until Chapter 13.

In a randomized block design, each cell would require four experimental groups, one for each treatment level. In the Latin square design each cell requires only one treatment level so that a minimum of 16 groups is required instead of 64. The Latin square normally would have a separate sample for each cell. In this study, the same 50 respondents from store 1 were used for all the cells in the first column. Each respondent reacted to four brands. Thus, the store block served effectively to control for not only the store but many other characteristics of the sample. As a result the experiment was more sensitive. However, the experience of rating one brand may have had a carryover effect on the task of rating another, which could generate a bias of some kind.

The Latin square design allows one to control two variables without requiring an expanded sample. It does require the same number of rows, columns, and treatment levels, so it does impose constraints in that respect. Also, it cannot be used to determine interaction effects. Thus, if nutritional information should have a different effect on private-label brands than major brands, this design could not discern such differences.

CASE 9–1

Evaluating Experimental Designs

A description of a variety of experimental designs follows. For each design: (1) indicate the type of experiment that is being used, (2) briefly discuss the threats to **internal** and **external validity** and identify those you regard as the most serious, and (3) describe how you would improve the design to overcome the problems you have identified.

1 In the Bayer deceptive advertising case an issue was whether people were influenced by some Bayer advertisements to believe that Bayer was more effective in relieving pain than other aspirins. In an experiment designed to address that issue a Bayer print advertisement was shown to 428 people projectable to the U.S. adult population, and two television advertisements were shown to 240 people recruited from local organizations (which received $1.00 for each participant) in nine communities in Massachusetts, Missouri, and Georgia. After being exposed to the advertisements, respondents were asked to identify the main points of the advertisement, what the adver-

tisement meant by its major claim, and whether the advertisement suggested that Bayer is more effective at relieving pain than any other brand of aspirin. The percentage of respondents were tabulated who, in response to the open-ended questions, said (1) that Bayer is best and (2) that Bayer is better than other aspirins. Whether the respondents made explicit reference to effectiveness also was noted. These percentages were used to address the issue. For example, across all surveys it was found that 10 percent felt that a main point of the advertisement was that Bayer is best or better than other aspirins *in effectiveness*. Also across all surveys, 71 percent felt that the advertisement suggested that Bayer works better than any other aspirin.

2 In 1982, the instrument group of National Chemical decided to change from a modest advertising effort aimed at generating leads for its salesforce to a more substantial program aimed at increased awareness and preference. A major vehicle for this campaign was *Chemical Process Instrumentation*, a leading trade magazine. To evaluate the advertising a survey was made of the readers of that magazine before and after the one-year campaign. In each case a systematic sample of 2500 readers was sent questionnaires that included these items:

List the companies you consider to be the leading manufacturers of the following products.
Check the one manufacturer (for each product) that you would first consider when purchasing the item.

	Before	After
Returned questionnaires	572	513
Percentage aware of National Chemical	23%	46%
Percentage prefer National Chemical	8%	11%

The results were averaged across the major products carried by National Chemical.

3 An account executive notices that his client is sponsoring a program that will be shown on about three-fourths of the network's station lineup. He sees a possibility for testing the effectiveness of the new commercials being used. His letter to the research supervisor reads, in part: "What if we picked several markets that will receive the program and several that won't? Then within each of these we can measure attitudes and purchasing among a randomly selected group of consumers. After the broadcast we

The results showed:

can interview other randomly selected groups on the same questions."

4 A manufacturer of products sold in food stores wished to find out whether a coupon good for 10¢ off the purchase price of its product could win new users. Coupons were mailed to half the households in the city's upper-80-percent income groups. Ten days before mailing, phone interviews were conducted with 200 randomly selected households scheduled to receive the coupon and 200 randomly selected who would not receive it. Whoever answered the phone was questioned about his awareness of brands and past purchasing within the product category. One month later callbacks were made to 400 households. Of the original group, 165 coupon receivers and 160 nonreceivers were asked the awareness and purchase questions again. In addition, 100 coupon recipients and 100 nonrecipients who were not previously questioned were interviewed on this occasion. The latter also were picked randomly from the receiver and nonreceiver populations.

CASE 9–2
Barrie Food Corporation

Al Blankenship (of Carter-Wallace) has just given an enthusiastic account of a new technique for evaluating television commercials. Your boss—the marketing research manager for a large food manufacturer—who is in the audience with you, wants you to analyze the technique carefully and make a recommendation on the use of the technique. The transcript of Blankenship's remarks follows:

Jim stopped in my office one day early this year, bursting with an idea he had to test the effectiveness of television commercials. He told me that in fall, 1976, WCAU-TV had telecast a pro-

gram which discussed the pros and cons of the proposed roofed-over sports stadium for the city. Viewers were asked to telephone their reactions to a special number to indicate whether they were in favor of or opposed to the sports palace. Jim and his group had been assigned the job of keeping a running total of the vote.

He had become intrigued, he said, that this sort of approach might be used to measure the effectiveness of television commercials. In a balanced experiment, you could have an announcer, immediately following the test commercial, ask people to telephone in to request a sample of the product. Differences in rate of response between different commercials would measure their effectiveness.

My reaction was immediate and positive. This was really getting close to a behavioral measurement of response to advertising. But it lacked a crucial control. How could you be sure that the same number of people had been exposed to each commercial? The technique required a measurement of the size of audience exposed to each test commercial.

In this situation, I thought of C. E. Hooper, since one of Hooper's specialties is measurement of audience size. If audience size could be built in as a control, it seemed to me that the technique was solid. I got Jim together with Bruce McEwen, Executive Vice President of Hooper. Bruce was just as excited as I had been.

However, following our discussion, I began to cool off. I was afraid that the audience size measurement made the whole thing too cumbersome, and that the cumbersomeness might somehow introduce error. There was something a bit sloppy about the methodology. I did not warm up to the idea, the more I thought about it, that the viewer was going to get a free sample merely by a telephone call. This was not real life. I was afraid that the free offer bit would result in such a high level of response that it would be impossible to differentiate between commercials.

Several weeks later it hit me. What we needed was an easy method of controlling audience size and who received the special offer and a way to make the viewer pay at least something for his product. Couponing, properly designed, could provide the solution.

A simple method was devised, and pretesting was conducted on the couponing aspects to make sure that the price level was right. The entire test procedure required four steps: a screening telephone call, a coupon mailout, a telephone postcall, and measurement of coupon redemption.

The precall is made within a stated time period in advance of the television show that is to carry the test advertising. The respondent is asked about his or her viewing plans for the forthcoming period. The last brand purchased of each of several product groups is asked about. The product group for the brand of the test commercial is included.

Immediately following screening, each person stating that he or she intended to watch the test vehicle is sent a special coupon, good for the product advertised at a special, low price. This coupon is sent in the manufacturer's envelope, and so far as the recipient knows, has no connection with the survey. This is not a store coupon. To be redeemed, it must be sent to the manufacturer. However, it is made as easy as possible to redeem. A postage-paid return envelope is included, and all the recipient must do is to insert the proper coins in a card prepared for this purpose, which includes his name and address. The coupon has an expiration date of one week from date of mailing, to prevent responses that are meaningless trickling in over a long time period. The procedure makes it possible to consider coupon responses only from those who viewed the program, which is crucial.

The day following the telecast, a call is made to each person who has said that he or she expected to view the particular program. The only purpose of the call is to determine whether the person has actually viewed the particular show. No question about advertising or about brands is asked.

**section D
Sampling**

10

SAMPLING FUNDAMENTALS

Marketing research often involves the estimation of a characteristic of some population. For instance, the average usage level of a park by community residents might be of interest, or information on the attitudes of a student body toward a proposed intramural facility could be needed. In either case, it would be unlikely that all members of the population would be surveyed. Contacting the entire population, that is, the entire census list, simply would not be worthwhile from a cost–benefit viewpoint. It would be both costly and, in nearly all cases, unnecessary, since adequate reliability usually can be obtained from a sample. Further, it often would be less accurate since nonsampling errors like nonresponse, cheating, and data-coding errors are more difficult to control.

There are many ways of obtaining a sample. Some are informal and even casual. Passersby may be queried as to their opinions of a new product. If the response of everyone in the population is uniform—they all either love it or hate it—such an approach may be satisfactory. If you want to determine if the water in a swimming pool is too cold, it isn't necessary to take a random sample; you just have to test the water at any one place, because the temperature will be constant throughout.

In most cases, however, the situation is more complex. There are several questions to be answered and a wide variability in responses. It is then necessary to obtain a representative sample of the population consisting of more than a handful of units. It is possible, even necessary in some cases, to obtain a sample representative of the population just by using judgment and common sense. The preferred approach, however, is usually to use probability sampling to obtain a representative sample. In probability sampling, all population members have a known probability of being in the sample.

Probability sampling has several advantages over nonprobability sampling. First, it permits the researcher to demonstrate the representativeness of the sample. Second, it allows an explicit statement as to how much variation is introduced because a sample is used instead of a census of the population. Finally, it makes possible the more explicit identification of possible biases.

TABLE 10–1

Issues in Probability Sampling

Identifying the target population
Selecting the probability sample
    Simple random sampling
    Stratified sampling
    Cluster sampling
    Multistage sampling
Determining the sample size
Handling the nonresponse problem

In this chapter, probability sampling will be described first, followed by a description and comparison of nonprobability sampling methods.

Probability sampling involves four considerations, as summarized in Table 10–1. First, the target population—the group about which information is being sought—must be specified. Second, the scheme for selecting the sample needs to be developed. As Table 10–1 indicates, there are several kinds of schemes to consider. Third, the sample size must be determined. The sample size will depend upon the accuracy needs, the variation within the population, and the cost. Finally, the nonresponse problem must be addressed.

THE TARGET POPULATION

Sampling is intended to gain information about a population. Thus, it is critical at the outset to identify the population properly and accurately. If the population is defined in a fuzzy way, the results also will be fuzzy. If the population is defined improperly, the research probably will answer the wrong question as a result. For example, if some research questions involve prospective car buyers and the population contains all adults with driver's licenses, the research output will be unlikely to provide the relevant information.

Although the definition of the target population is important, it often is neglected because it seems obvious and noncontroversial. But considerable effort in identifying the target population usually will pay off. The following guidelines should be considered.

Look to the Research Objectives

If the research objectives are well thought out, the target population definition will be clear as well. Recall from Chapter 2 that the research objectives include the research question, the research hypothesis, and a statement of the research boundaries. Each of these elements contribute to refining the definition of the target population. For example, the research question might involve how business firms in Chicago would react to a particular pricing method for advertising in the yellow pages of the telephone directory. The hypothesis might indicate that retailers of different types needed to be sampled. The consideration of the research boundary could restrict the population to metropolitan Chicago. Thus, the target population would be retail business firms in metropolitan Chicago.

Consider Alternatives

It is a rare study for which there are no alternative, reasonable, target population definitions. The task is really to identify and evaluate several of the alternatives instead of simply assuming that the first one mentioned is appropriate. For example, suppose the task was to determine the relative importance of such features as compactors, saunas, patios, and the like in medium-priced homes. The target population could be present owners of medium-priced homes, shoppers in middle-income shopping centers, those in a region that might upgrade their homes, or clients of real estate firms. The choice will depend upon the research objectives. The key point is to recognize that alternative definitions exist.

Know Your Market

If the research objective is to learn about the market response to some element of the marketing program, it is necessary to know something about the market. One may hope that some previous research will provide this type of information. Without it, the population definition will have to be unnecessarily broad and, therefore, unnecessarily expensive. For example, if a shopping center were considering whether restaurants should be added to the center, the opinions of customers and potential customers would be desired. A key question for the population definition, especially if potential customers were to be reached, would be how large an area the shopping center draws. If previous studies show, for instance, that the center draws from a three-mile radius, that information will help in defining the target population.

Consider the Appropriate Sampling Unit

The target population consists of sampling units. A sampling unit may contain people, stores, households, organization transactions, products, or whatever. One task is to specify which sampling unit is appropriate. Is the interest in museums or in museum directors? Sometimes the choice is not clear. Should a study of banking activity or of leisure time activities use individuals or households? The choice will depend upon the purpose of the study and perhaps upon some judgments about consumer behavior. For example, if decisions about banking or leisure activities are thought to be family decisions, then the household might be the appropriate sampling unit. A respondent would report for the family. The assumption would be that family members are enough alike that responses within a family would tend to be similar. If, however, the decisions are assumed to be relatively independent among household members, then the sampling unit would be individuals instead of households.

Specify Clearly What Is Excluded

The specification of the target population should make clear what is excluded. A study of voting intentions on certain candidates and issues might restrict the sampling population to those of voting age and even to those who intend to vote or those who voted in the last election. If the election were in Cook County, for instance, it would be reasonable to restrict the population to those eligible to vote in Cook County.

Don't Overdefine

The population, of course, should be compatible with the study purpose and the research questions; however, the researcher should not arbitrarily overdefine the population. For example, a population of working wives between the ages of 25 and 30, earning more than $15,000 may be artificially restrictive. Such a restrictive population can generate a very costly design, because so many people need to be screened out to obtain the desired sample.

Consider Convenience

When there is a choice, preference should be given to populations that are convenient to sample. Suppose that the population was to include those who are bothered by airplane noise. One population compatible with the research purpose might be those who live within one mile of an airport. This population would be easy and convenient to sample. Of course, the population should not be distorted for the sake of creating a convenient sample. A population of subscribers to *Sports Illustrated* may be convenient to sample, but it may not be appropriate for the research purpose.

The Sampling Frame

It is important to distinguish between the population and the sampling frame. The sampling frame is usually a list of population members used to obtain a sample. There might be a list of magazine subscribers, retail hardware stores, or college students. Actually, the description of a sampling frame does not have to enumerate all population members. It may be sufficient to specify the procedure by which each sampling unit can be located. For instance, a member of a probability sample of school children could be obtained by randomly selecting a school district, a school, a classroom, and, finally, a pupil. The probability of picking any given pupil could be determined, even if a physical list were not created that included all students in the population.

Sometimes it is possible to define the population to match exactly the sampling frame. Usually, however, an exact match is not possible and the task is to consider what portions of the population are excluded by the sampling frame and what biases are therefore created. For example, a list of residents of a city will exclude those in new housing developments. The question is: How many are in this category, and will their responses to the survey be different than the others? The existence of such biases usually will not affect the usefulness of the study, as long as they are identified and the interpretation of the results takes them into consideration.

SELECTING THE PROBABILITY SAMPLE

There are a variety of methods that can be used to select a probability sample. The simplest, conceptually, is termed "simple random sampling." It not only has practical value, but it is a good vehicle for gaining intuitive understanding of the logic and power of random sampling.

Simple Random Sampling

Simple random sampling is an approach in which each population member, and thus each possible sample, has an equal probability of being selected. The implementation is straightforward. Put the name of each person in the population on a tag and place the tags in a large bowl. Mix the contents of the bowl thoroughly and then draw out the desired number for the sample. Such a method was, in fact, used to select the order in which men would be drafted for military service during the Vietnam War, using birth dates. Despite the fact that the bowl was well mixed, the early drawing revealed a much higher number of December dates than January dates, indicating that the randomizing process can be more involved than it seems. The apparent reason was that the December tags were put in last, and the mixing was not sufficient to create a random draw. The solution was to randomize the order in which the dates were placed in the bowl.[1]

The use of a table of random numbers is usually much more practical than the use of a large bowl. A random-number table is a long list of numbers, each of which is computer generated by randomly selecting a number from 0 to 9. It has the property that knowledge of a string of ten numbers gives no information about what the eleventh number is. Suppose a sample is desired from a list of 5000 opera season-ticket holders. A random-number table such as that shown in Table 10–2 might provide the following sets of numbers:

7659|0783|4710|3749|7741|2960|0016|9347

Using these numbers, a sample of five would be created that would include these ticket holders:

0783|4710|3749|2960|0016|

[1]Seymour Sudman, *Applied Sampling* (New York: Academic Press, 1976), p. 50.

TABLE 10–2

A Set of Random Numbers

55	38	32	99	55	62	70	92	44	32
87	63	93	95	17	81	83	83	04	49
11	59	44	39	58	81	09	62	08	66
82	93	67	50	45	60	33	01	07	98
31	40	45	33	12	36	23	47	11	85
24	38	77	63	99	89	85	29	53	93
57	68	48	78	37	87	06	43	97	48
44	84	11	59	73	56	45	65	99	24
65	60	59	52	06	03	04	79	88	44
98	24	05	10	07	88	81	76	22	71
59	67	80	91	41	63	18	63	13	34
76	59	07	83	47	10	37	49	54	91
77	41	29	60	00	16	93	47	54	91
28	04	61	59	37	31	66	59	97	38

The numbers above 5000 are disregarded, because there are no season-ticket holders associated with them.

The researcher can start anywhere in the random-number table, as long as the choice is made before looking at the numbers. It isn't fair to discard some numbers from the table because "they don't look random" or because they are not "convenient" for some reason or other.

If the original list of season-ticket holders were arranged in a random fashion, then a result equivalent to the computer-generated list could be obtained by taking the first ticket holders in the list. However, there is always the danger that the list may have some subtle deviations from a random order. Perhaps it was prepared according to the order in which the tickets were purchased. Thus, the more interested and organized patrons would be early on the list. The use of random numbers eliminates such concerns.

Systematic Sampling. Another approach, termed "systematic sampling," involves systematically spreading the sample through the list of population members. Thus, if the population contained 10,000 people and a sample size of 1000 were desired, every tenth person would be selected for the sample. Although in nearly all practical examples such a procedure would generate a sample equivalent to a simple random sample, the researcher should be aware of regularities in the list. Suppose, for example, that a list of couples in a dance club routinely placed the woman's name first. Then selecting every tenth name would result in a sample of all males.

One situation in which systematic sampling is risky is the sampling of time periods. Suppose the task was to estimate the weekly traffic flow on a certain street. If every twelfth 10-minute period were selected, then the sampling point would be the same each day, and periods of peak travel or low usage easily could be missed.

A common use of systematic sampling is in telephone surveys. A number like 17 could be obtained from a random-number table. Then the seventeenth name on each page of a telephone directory would be a sample member. (Actually, a random number of inches from the top of the page would be used, so that names would not have to be counted.) Of course, more than one name could be selected from each page if a larger sample were needed, or every other (or every third or fourth) page could be used if a smaller sample were desired.

Creating Lists.   The biggest problem in simple random sampling is to obtain appropriate lists. The Donnelley Company maintains a list drawn from telephone directories and automobile registrations that contains around 88 percent of U.S. households. Such a list can be used to get a national sample for a mail survey. Within a community, the local utility company will have a fairly complete list of the households.

The problem, of course, is that lists do not exist for specialized populations. There is no list of high-income people, mothers, tennis players, or cyclists, for example. A solution for this problem that is usually unsatisfactory is to use a convenient list. For example, for tennis players, a list of subscribers to *Tennis World* or membership lists in tennis clubs might be available. Obviously, neither would be representative of the entire tennis-playing population but still might be useful for some purposes. When such lists are used that do not match the population, biases are introduced that should be considered. For instance, readers of *Tennis World* will be much more involved and knowledgeable than the average tennis player. A list of residents of a given community will not include new arrivals nor people living in dwellings built since the list was created. Thus, whole new subdivisions can be omitted. If such omissions are important, it can be worthwhile to identify new construction areas and design a separate sampling plan for them.

Sometimes several lists are combined in the hope of obtaining a more complete representation of the population. For example, subscribers to *Tennis World* and *Tennis Today* might be combined with a list of those who had purchased tennis equipment through a mail-order catalog. This approach, however, introduces the problem of duplication. Those appearing on several lists will have an increased chance of being selected. Removing duplication can be expensive and must be balanced against the bias that is introduced.

Another problem with lists is that of simply keeping them current. Many industrial firms maintain lists of those who have expressed interest in their products, and these are used in part for the mailing of promotional material. Similarly, many organizations, such as charities, symphonies, and art galleries, have lists of various types; but these lists can become outdated quickly as people move and change jobs within an organization.

Telephone Interviewing.   The use of telephone directories as a basis for generating a sample is extensive, as might be expected. The concern with the use of directories is the population members who are omitted because they have changed residences, requested an unlisted number, or simply do not have a telephone.

It is estimated that, in California, about 10 percent of the total subscribers still having telephones during the last month of a directory's one-year lifespan cannot be reached by their listed number. Thus, the average for the year is around 5 percent.[2] Since Californians are relatively mobile, the national average may be a bit less.

A more serious problem is the voluntarily unlisted telephones. Table 10–3 shows the percentage of unlisted telephones in the Pacific Telephone area and in the total Bell System. Clearly, the Pacific area has a much higher incidence of unlisted phones than the rest of the United States. There is also a great deal of variation within the Pacific area. The percentage of unlisted numbers in 1975 ranged from 18 percent in San Diego to 37 percent in Los Angeles. The extent of the problem will obviously depend upon the geographic area involved.

Table 10–3 indicates that the number of unlisted telephones is not only substantial, but it is growing. A big reason is apparently the increase in the number of crank or prank calls. A 1975 survey of 175 households with unlisted phones revealed that more than 50 percent gave the avoidance of crank or prank calls as the reason, a percentage more than twice that of a 1964 survey.[3] Other reasons given were:

Avoid salesmen	30%
Avoid unwanted calls—gave occupation, business, or position as reason	27%
Didn't want to be bothered—by ex-spouse, family, friends, etc.	13%

Several studies have been conducted that show that those requesting unlisted telephones do differ from other telephone subscribers. A study done in 1974 of 36,000 new Pacific Telephone subscribers found that those requesting an unlisted number tended to be female, divorced or separated, middle-aged, employed in the clerical or service field, and without an automobile.[4] However, the overall differences were not huge. The largest difference reported was with respect to sex. Of those requesting unlisted telephones, 42 percent were female, whereas 32 percent of the other subscribers were female. Another study showed that radio listening differed between those with listed telephones and others.[5]

If an area with a high incidence of unlisted telephones is involved, or if there is a special need to include all respondents with telephones, there are methods to reach both listed and unlisted subscribers. One approach is to dial numbers randomly. However, because large banks of numbers have not been assigned, such an approach is very costly. It is possible to ask the telephone company to identify blocks of unused number segments, which will reduce the cost somewhat.

Another approach starts from a sample of listed telephone numbers. The number called is then the number drawn from the directory, plus some fixed number like ten. Of course, this method will still result in reaching some nonworking numbers. A study using

---

[2]Clyde L. Rich, "Is Random Digit Dialing Really Necessary?," *Journal of Marketing Research, 14* (August 1977), 301.
[3]*Ibid.*, 301.
[4]*Ibid.*, 304.
[5]Sydney Roslow and Lawrence Roslow, "Unlisted Phone Subscribers Are Different," *Journal of Advertising Research, 12* (August 1972), 35–38.

TABLE 10–3
Percentage of Unlisted Telephones

Year as of January 1	Pacific Telephone	Total Bell System
1977	28.1	n.a.[a]
1976	28.0	n.a.
1975	27.8	n.a.
1974	27.2	n.a.
1973	26.9	16.5
1972	26.7	16.1
1971	25.2	15.7
1970	24.0	14.7
1969	22.7	14.0
1968	20.8	12.6
1967	19.9	11.6
1966	19.8	11.0
1965	18.0	10.0
1964	16.8	9.2

[a]n.a. = not available.
SOURCE: Adapted from Clyde L. Rich, "Is Random Digit Dialing Really Necessary?", *Journal of Marketing Research,* 14 (August 1977), p. 301.

this approach, conducted in two Colorado communities (Sterling and Boulder) resulted in 10 percent nonworking numbers in Sterling and 29 percent in Boulder.[6]

The method of adding a fixed number to a listed telephone number will not include those who are in a new series of numbers being activated by the telephone company. Seymour Sudman of The Survey Research Laboratory of the University of Illinois, a researcher long interested in sampling issues, therefore suggests that the last three digits in a listed telephone number be replaced by a three-digit random number. He indicates that the coverage will then increase and that half of the resulting numbers will generally be nonworking numbers.[7]

Stratified Sampling

In simple random sampling, a random sample is taken from a list (or sampling frame) representing the population. Often some information about subgroups within the sample frame can be used to improve the efficiency of the sample plan, that is, to obtain estimates with the same reliability with a smaller sample size. Reliability refers to the estimate variation caused by the fact that a sample is used instead of a population.

[6]E. Laird Landon, Jr. and Sharon K. Banks, "Relative Efficiency and Bias of Plus-One Telephone Sampling." *Journal of Marketing Research, 14* (August 1977), 294–299.

[7]Sudman, *op. cit.,* 65.

Suppose information on the attitudes of students toward a proposed new intramural athletic facility is needed. Further, suppose that there are three groups of students in the school—off-campus students, dormitory dwellers, and those living in fraternity and sorority houses. Suppose, further, that those living in fraternities and sororities have very homogeneous attitudes toward the proposed facility—the variation or variance in their attitudes is very small. Assume, also, that the dormitory dwellers are less homogeneous and that the off-campus students vary widely in their opinions. In such a situation, instead of allowing the sample to come from all three groups randomly, it will be more sensible to take fewer members from the fraternity/sorority group and to draw more from the off-campus group. We would separate the student body list into the three groups and draw a simple random sample from each of the three groups.

The sample size of the three groups will depend upon two factors. First, it will depend on the amount of attitude variation in each group. The larger the variation, the larger the sample. Second, the sample size will tend to be inversely proportional to the cost of sampling. The smaller the cost, the larger the sample size that can be justified. (Sample-size formulas for stratified sampling are introduced in the next chapter.)

In developing a sampling plan, it is wise to look for natural subgroups that will be more homogeneous than the total population. Such subgroups are called "strata"; hence, the term **stratified sampling.**

Cluster Sampling

In cluster sampling, the population again is divided into subgroups, here termed **clusters** instead of strata. This time, however, a random sample of subgroups is selected and all members of the subgroups become part of the sample. This method is useful when subgroups can be identified that are representative of the whole population.

Suppose a sample of high-school sophomores who took an English class was needed in a midwestern city. There were 200 English classes, each of which contained a fairly representative sample with respect to student opinions on rock groups, the subject of the study. A cluster sample would select randomly a number of classrooms, say 15, and include all members of those classrooms in the sample. The big advantage of cluster sampling is lower cost. The subgroups or clusters are selected so that the cost of obtaining the desired information within the cluster is much smaller than if a simple random sample were obtained. If the average English class had 30 students, a sample of 450 would be obtained by contacting only 15 classes. If a simple random sample of 450 students across all English classes were obtained, the cost probably would be significantly greater. The big question, of course, is whether the classes are representative of the population. If the classes from the upper-income areas have different opinions about rock groups than classes with more lower-income students, the assumption underlying the approach would not hold.

Multistage Designs

It is often appropriate to use several stages in developing a sample. Perhaps the most common example is in the case of area samples, in which a sample is desired of some area such as the United States or the state of California.

Suppose the need was to sample the state of California. The first step would be to develop a cluster sample of counties in the state. Each county would have a probability of being in the cluster sample proportionate to its population. Thus, the largest county—Los Angeles County—would be much more likely to be in the sample than a rural county. The second step would be to obtain a cluster sample of cities from each selected county. Again, each city is selected with a probability proportionate to its size. The third step is

*"And don't waste your time canvassing the whole building,
young man. We all think alike."*

Drawing by Stevenson; © 1980. The New Yorker Magazine, Inc.

to select a cluster sample of blocks from each city, again weighting each block by the number of dwellings in it. Finally, a systematic sample of dwellings from each block is selected, and a random sample of members of each dwelling is obtained. The result is a random sample of the area, in which each dwelling has an equal chance of being in the sample. Note that individuals living alone will have a larger chance of being in the sample than individuals living in dwellings with other people.

To see how a cluster sample of cities is drawn so that the probability of each being selected is proportionate to its population, consider the following example. Suppose there are six cities in Ajax County. In Table 10–4, the cities, plus the rural area, are listed together with their population sizes and the "cumulative population." The cumulative population serves to associate each city with a block of numbers equal in size to its population. The total population of Ajax County is 100,000. The task is to select one city from the county, with the selection probability proportionate to the city population. The approach is simply to obtain a random number between 1 and 100,000. Taking the fourth row of Table 10–2 and starting from the right we get the number 89,701. The selected city would be the one with a cumulative population corresponding to 89,701: Austin. Clearly, the largest city, Filmore, would have the best chance of being drawn (in fact, a 60-percent chance), and Cooper the smallest chance (only 2 percent).

The large marketing research firms develop a set of clusters of dwellings after each U.S. census. The clusters may be counties or some other convenient grouping of dwellings. Perhaps 100 to 300 such areas are selected randomly. Each area will have a probability of being selected proportional to the population within its boundaries. This set of clusters then would be used by the marketing research firm for up to 10 years for their national surveys. For each area, data are compiled, on blocks and on living units within blocks. For rural areas, these firms hire and train interviewers to be available for subsequent surveys. Respondents from each area are selected on the basis of a sampling scheme such as stratified sampling or on the basis of a multistage scheme.

TABLE 10–4

Cities in Ajax County

City	Population	Cumulative Population
Concord	15,000	1– 15,000
Mountain View	10,000	15,001– 25,000
Filmore	60,000	25,001– 85,000
Austin	5,000	85,001– 90,000
Cooper	2,000	90,001– 92,000
Douglas	5,000	92,001– 97,000
Rural area	3,000	97,001–100,000

DETERMINING THE SAMPLE SIZE: *AD HOC* METHODS

How large should the sample be? This question is simple and straightforward, but to answer with precision is not so easy. Statistical theory does provide some tools and a structure with which to address the question which will be described in more detail in Chapter 11. In this chapter several *ad hoc* but practical approaches are discussed.

Rules of Thumb

One approach is to use some rules of thumb. Sudman suggests that the sample should be large enough so that when it is divided into groups, each group will have a minimum sample size of 100 or more.[8]

Suppose the opinions of citizens regarding municipal parks, was desired. In particular, an estimation was to be made of the percentage who felt that tennis courts were needed. Suppose, further, that a comparison was desired among those who (1) used parks frequently, (2) used parks occasionally, and (3) never used parks. Thus, the sample size should be such that each of these groups had at least 100 people. If the frequent park users, the smallest group, were thought to be about 10 percent of the population, then under simple random sampling a sample size of 1000 would be needed to generate a group of 100 subjects.

In almost every study, a comparison between groups provides useful information and is often the motivating reason for the study. It is therefore necessary to consider the smallest group and to make sure that it is of sufficient size to provide the needed reliability.

In addition to considering comparisons between major groups, the analysis might consider subgroups. For example, there could be an interest in breaking down the group of frequent park users by age and comparing the usage by teenagers, young adults, middle-aged persons, and senior citizens. Sudman suggests that for such minor breakdowns the minimum sample size in each subgroup should be 20 to 50.[9] The assumption is that the accuracy needed for the subgroups is less. Suppose that the smallest subgroup of the frequent park users, the senior citizens, is about one percent of the population and it is desired to have 20 in each subgroup. Under simple random sampling, a sample size of about 2000 might be recommended in this case.

If one of the groups or subgroups of the population is a relatively small percentage of the population, then it is sensible to use *disproportionate sampling*. Suppose only 10 percent of the population watches educational television, and opinions of this group are to be compared with others in the population. If telephone interviewing were involved, people might be contacted randomly until 100 people were identified who do not watch educational television. The interviewing then would continue, but all respondents would be screened, and only those who watch educational television would be interviewed. The result would be a sample of 200, half of which watch educational television.

[8]*Ibid.*, 30.
[9]*Ibid.*, 30.

Budget Constraints

Often a strict budget constraint exists. A museum director can spare $500 for a study and no more. If data analysis will require $100 and a respondent interview is $5, then the maximum affordable sample size is 80. The question then becomes whether a sample size of 80 is worthwhile or if the study should be changed or simply not conducted.

Comparable Studies

Another approach is to find similar studies and use their sample sizes as a guide. The studies should be comparable in terms of the number of groups into which the sample is divided for comparison purposes. They also should have achieved a satisfactory level of reliability.

Table 10–5, which is based upon a summary of several hundred studies, provides a very rough idea of typical sample size. Note that the typical sample size tends to be larger for national studies than for regional studies. A possible reason is that the national studies generally address issues with more financial impact and therefore require a bit more accuracy. Note, also, that samples involving institutions tend to be smaller than those involving people or households. The reason is probably that insitutions are more costly to sample than people.

Factors Determining Sample Size

Sample size really depends upon four factors. The first is the number of groups and subgroups within the sample that will be analyzed. The second is the value of the information in the study in general and the accuracy required of the results in particular. At one extreme, the research need not be conducted if the study is of little importance. The third is the cost of the sample. A cost-benefit analysis must be considered. If sampling costs are low, a larger sample size can be justified than if sampling costs are high. The final factor is the variability of the population. If all members of the population have

TABLE 10–5

Typical Sample Sizes for Studies of Human and Institutional Populations

Number of Subgroup Analyses	People or Households		Institutions	
	National	Regional or Special	National	Regional or Special
None or few	1000–1500	200–500	200–500	50–200
Average	1500–2500	500–1000	500–1000	200–500
Many	2500+	1000+	1000+	500+

SOURCE: Seymour Sudman, *Applied Sampling* (New York: Academic Press, 1976), p. 87.

identical opinions on an issue, a sample of one is satisfactory. As the variability within the population increases, the sample size also will need to be larger. Chapter 11 will provide the interested reader with another perspective on sample size determination.

NONRESPONSE PROBLEMS

The object of sampling is to obtain a body of data that is representative of the population. Unfortunately, some sample members become nonrespondents because they (1) refuse to respond, (2) lack the ability to respond, (3) are not at home, or (4) are inaccessible.

Nonresponse can be a serious problem. It means, of course, that the sample size has to be large enough to allow for nonresponse. If a sample size of 1000 is needed and only a 50-percent response rate is expected, then 2000 people will need to be identified as possible sample members. Second, and more serious, is the possibility that those who respond differ from nonrespondents in a meaningful way, thereby creating biases.

The seriousness of nonresponse bias depends upon the extent of the nonresponse and the nature of the bias it creates. If the percentage involved is small, the bias is small. Unfortunately, however, the percentage can be significant. A 1976 study that involved interviews with over 12,000 grocery shoppers revealed that during the course of the year over 55 percent of this group received a request for an interview. Refusal rates were reported to range from 41 percent for store intercept interviews to 47 percent for telephone interviews.[10] Obviously, however, response rates can vary enormously. It would not be uncommon to face a nonresponse rate of over 80 percent in a mail survey. The nature of the bias rarely can be ignored, because the very act of being a nonrespondent often implies a meaningful difference. Further, nonrespondents for in-home interviews tend to be urban dwellers, single or divorced, employed, and from the higher social classes.

Although it is impossible to generalize about the extent of nonresponse, a study by Ognibene, a researcher at the BBD&O advertising agency, illustrates this problem.[11] He contacted by telephone a group of 200 men, randomly selected from the New York telephone directory and asked them questions on number of years of schooling, family size, readership of a newspaper, and awareness of several advertisements. Three months later, a four-page questionnaire, with a cover letter and a stamped return envelope, was sent to the sample. A total of 12 percent of the questionnaires was returned for incorrect address; of the balance, 34 percent responded and 66 percent did not. Two of the seven test questions resulted in nonresponse bias. The estimate of newspaper readership exceeded the actual readership by 27 percent. This bias could be partly because the question on newspaper readership appealed more to newspaper readers than nonreaders, thus increasing the likelihood of their returning the questionnaire.

[10]"Shoppers Grant 91 Million Interviews Yearly," *Survey Sampling Frame* (published by Survey Sampling, Inc.), Spring 1978, 1.

[11]Peter Ognibene, "Correcting Nonresponse Bias in Mail Questionnaires," *Journal of Marketing Research, 8* (May 1971), 233–235.

What can be done about the nonresponse problem? A natural tendency is to replace each nonrespondent with a "matched" member of the sample. For example, if a home is included in the sample but the resident is not at home, a neighbor may be substituted. The difficulty is that the replacement cannot be matched easily on the characteristic that prompted the nonresponse, such as being employed or being a frequent traveler. Three more defensible approaches are (1) to improve the research design to reduce the number of nonresponses, (2) to repeat the contact one or more times (callbacks) to try to reduce nonresponses, and (3) to attempt to estimate the nonresponse bias.

Improving the Research Design

In Chapter 6, the refusal problem was discussed in some detail, along with suggestions on how to improve the research design to reduce the incidence of refusals. The challenge in personal and telephone interviewing is to gain initial interest and to generate rapport through interviewer skill and the design and placement of questions. In mail surveys, the task is to motivate the respondent, through incentives and other devices, to respond. The number of not-at-homes can be reduced by scheduling calls with some knowledge of the respondents' likely activity patterns. For example, midday is obviously a bad time to reach employed homemakers. Sometimes it is useful to make a telephone appointment for an in-home interview, although one study found that this tactic tended to increase the refusal rate.[12]

Callbacks

Callbacks refer to overt new attempts to obtain responses. The use of callbacks is predicated on the assumption that they will generate a useful number of additional responses and that the additional responses will reduce meaningfully a nonresponse bias. If the nonresponse is due to refusals or the inability to respond, callbacks may not reduce significantly the number of nonrespondents. It is most effective for the not-at-home nonrespondent. For some surveys, it may be worthwhile to use as many as six callbacks to reduce the number of nonrespondents to acceptable levels, although the first and second callbacks are usually the most productive.[13] The efficiency of the callbacks will be improved by scheduling them at different times of the day and week.

In a mail survey, the callback is particularly important, because the nonresponse level can be so high. As was noted in Chapter 6, it is common practice to send the questionnaire to prompt nonrespondents at regular intervals.

[12]G. Allen Bruner and Stephen J. Carroll, Jr., "The Effect of Prior Telephone Appointments on Completion Rates and Response Contact," *Public Opinion Quarterly, 31* (Winter 1967), 652–654.

[13]In the late sixties the Survey Research Center (University of Michigan) found, when they made six or more calls, they reached 25 percent of the final sample on the first call, 33 percent on the first callback, and 17 percent on the second callback. The remaining 25 percent were reached on subsequent callbacks. (William C. Dunkelberg and George S. Day, "Nonresponse Bias and Call-backs in Sample Surveys," *Journal of Marketing Research, 10* (May 1973), 160–168.)

Estimating the Effects of Nonresponse

One approach is to make an extra effort to interview a subsample of the nonrespondents. In the case of a mail survey, the subsample might be interviewed by telephone. In a telephone or personal survey, an attractive incentive, such as a worthwhile gift, might be employed to entice a sample of the nonrespondents to cooperate. Often, only some of the critical questions thought to be sensitive to a nonresponse bias are employed in this stage.

The Politz approach is based upon the fact that not-at-homes can be predicted from a knowledge of respondents' frequency of being away from home.[14] The respondents are asked how many evenings they are usually at home (if the interviewing is to be done in the evening). This information serves to categorize them into groups that can serve to represent the not-at-home respondents. For instance, if a respondent is usually at home only one night a week, it might be assumed that there are six more like him among the nonrespondents. On any given night, there would be only one chance in seven of finding him home. Thus, on the average, six homes with people with this tendency to be away would have to be contacted to find one person at home. This respondent is therefore assumed to represent six of the nonrespondents. There are uncertainties introduced by this approach, but it does provide a way to proceed, especially when callbacks are costly.

NONPROBABILITY SAMPLING

In probability sampling, the theory of probability allows the researcher to calculate the nature and extent of any biases in the estimate and to determine what variation in the estimate is due to the sampling procedure. It requires a sampling frame—a list of sampling units or a procedure to reach respondents with a known probability. In nonprobability sampling, the costs and trouble of developing a sampling frame are eliminated, but so is the precision with which the resulting information can be presented. In fact, the results can contain hidden biases and uncertainties that make them worse than no information at all. These problems, it should be noted, are not alleviated by increasing the sample size. For this reason, statisticians prefer to avoid nonprobability sampling designs; however, they often are used legitimately and effectively.

It is worthwhile to distinguish among four types of nonprobability sampling procedures: judgmental samples, snowball designs, convenience samples, and quota samples.

Judgmental Sampling

In judgmental sampling, an "expert" uses judgment to identify representative samples. For example, patrons of a shopping center might serve to represent the residents of a city, or several cities might be selected to represent a country.

Judgmental sampling usually is associated with a variety of obvious and not-so-

---

[14]Alfred N. Politz and Willard R. Simmons, "An Attempt to Get 'Not-At-Homes' into the Sample Without Callbacks," *Journal of the American Statistical Association, 44* (March 1949), 9–31, and *45* (March 1950) 136–137.

obvious biases. For example, shopping-center intercept interviewing can oversample those who shop frequently, who appear friendly, and who have extra time. Worse, there is no way of really quantifying the resulting bias and uncertainty, because the sampling frame is unknown and the sampling procedure is not well specified.

There are situations where judgmental sampling is useful and even advisable. First, there are times when probability sampling is either infeasible or prohibitively expensive. A random sample of homosexuals may be impossible to obtain, and a judgmental sample of those frequenting bars and other gathering places is used. A list of sidewalk vendors might be impossible to obtain, and a judgmental sample might be appropriate in that case.

Second, if the sample size is to be very small–say, under 10— a judgmental sample usually will be more reliable and representative than a probability sample. Suppose one or two cities of medium size were to be used to represent 200 such cities. Then it would be appropriate to pick judgmentally two cities that appeared to be the most representative with respect to such external criteria as demographics, media habits, and shopping characteristics. The process of randomly selecting two cities could very well generate a highly nonrepresentative set. If a focus-group interview of eight or nine people were needed, again, a judgmental sample might be a highly appropriate way to proceed.

Third, it sometimes is useful to obtain a deliberately biased sample. If, for example, a product or service modification were to be evaluated, it might be possible to identify a group that, by its very nature, should be disposed toward the modification. If it were found that they did not like it, then it could be assumed that the rest of the population would be at least as negative. If they liked it, of course, more research probably would be required.

The Snowball Design

A snowball design is a form of judgmental sampling that is very appropriate when it is necessary to reach small, specialized populations. Suppose a long-range planning group wanted to sample people who were very knowledgeable about a new specialized technology, such as the use of lasers in construction. Even specialized magazines would have a small percentage of readers in this category. Further, the target group may be employed by diverse organizations, like the government, universities, research organizations, and industrial firms. Under a snowball design, each respondent, after being interviewed, is asked to identify one or more others in the field. The result can be a very useful sample. This design can be used to reach any small population, such as deep-sea divers, people confined to wheelchairs, owners of dunebuggies, families with triplets, and so on. One problem is that those who are socially visible are more likely to be selected.

Convenience Sampling

To obtain information quickly and inexpensively, a convenience sample can be employed. The procedure is simply to contact sampling units that are convenient—a church activity group, a classroom of students, women at a shopping center on a particular day, the first

50 recipients of mail questionnaires, or a few friends and neighbors. Such procedures seem indefensible, and, in an absolute sense, they are. The reader should recall, however, that information must be evaluated, not ''absolutely,'' but in the context of a decision. If a quick reaction to a preliminary service concept is desired to determine if it is worthwhile to develop it further, a convenience sample may be appropriate. It obviously would be foolish to rely on it in any context where a biased result could have serious economic consequences, unless the biases could be identified. A convenience sample often is used to pretest a questionnaire.

Quota Sampling

Quota sampling is judgmental sampling with the constraint that the sample include a minimum number from each specified subgroup in the population. Suppose a 1000-person sample of a city is desired and it is known how the population of the city is distributed geographically. The sample could be dispersed in the same manner, as shown in Table 10–6. Thus, interviewers might be asked to obtain 100 interviews on the east side, 300 on the north side, and so on.

Quota sampling often is based on such demographic data as geographic location, age, sex, education, and income. As a result, the researcher knows that the sample ''matches'' the population with respect to these demographic characteristics. This fact is reassuring and does eliminate some gross biases that could be part of a judgmental sample; however, there are often serious biases that are not controlled by the quota-sampling approach. The interviewers will contact those most accessible, at home, with time, with acceptable appearance, and so forth. Biases will result. Of course, a random sample with a 15-to-25-percent or more nonresponse rate will have many of the same biases. Thus, quota sampling and other judgmental approaches, which are faster and cheaper, should not always be discarded as inferior.

TABLE 10–6

A Quota Sample

Area of the City	Percentage of the Population	Sample Size
East side	10	100
North side	30	300
Inner city	20	200
Southwest side	40	400
Total	100	1000

SHOPPING-CENTER SAMPLING

Shopping-center studies in which shoppers are intercepted present some difficult sampling problems. As noted in Chapter 6, well over 20 percent of all questionnaires completed or interviews granted were store-intercept interview.[15] One limitation with shopping-center surveys is the bias introduced by the methods used to select the sample. In particular, biases that are potentially damaging to a study can be caused by the selection of the shopping center, the part of the shopping center from which the respondents are drawn, the time of day, and the fact that more frequent shoppers will be more likely to be selected. Sudman suggests approaches to minimize these problems and, in doing so, clarifies the nature of these biases.[16]

Shopping-Center Selection

A shopping-center sample usually will reflect primarily those families who live in the area. Obviously, there can be great differences between people living in a low-income neighborhood and those in a high-income, professional neighborhood. It is usually good policy to use several shopping centers in different neighborhoods, so that differences between them can be observed.

Sampling Locations within a Center

The goal is usually to obtain a random sample of shopping-center visits. Because of traffic routes and parking, one entrance may draw from very different neighborhoods than another. A solution is to stratify by entrance location and to take a separate sample from each entrance. To obtain an overall average, the resulting strata averages need to be combined by weighting them to reflect the relative traffic that is associated with each entrance.

Suppose that a survey is employed to determine the average purchase during a shopping trip. Assume that there were two shopping-mall entrances. Entrance A, which drew from a working-class neighborhood, averaged 200 shoppers per hour; while Entrance B, which drew from a professional suburb, averaged 100 shoppers per hour. Thus, 67 percent of shoppers used Entrance A and 33 percent of shoppers used Entrance B. Assume further that the Entrance A shoppers spent $60 on the average, while the Entrance B shoppers averaged $36. These statistics are tabulated as follows:

Entrance	Hourly Traffic	Proportion of Shoppers	Sample Size	Average Purchase ($)
A	200	.67	100	60
B	100	.33	100	36

[15]Shoppers Grant 91 Million Interviews Yearly," *op. cit.*

[16]Seymour Sudman, "Improving the Quality of Shopping Center Sampling," *Journal of Marketing Research, 17* (November 1980), 423–431.

The estimate of the average dollar amount of the purchase made by a shopping-center visitor would be the Entrance A average purchase plus the Entrance B average purchase, weighted by the proportion of shoppers represented, or:

$$(.67 \times 60) + (.33 \times 36) = \$52$$

Sometimes it is necessary to sample within a shopping center because the entrances are inappropriate places to intercept respondents. The location used to intercept shoppers can affect the sample. A cluster of exclusive women's stores will attract a very different shopper than the Sears store at the other end of the mall. A solution is to select several "representative" locations, determine from traffic counts about how many shoppers pass by each location, and then weight the results accordingly.

Time Sampling

Another issue is the time period. For example, people who work usually shop during the evening, on weekends, or during lunch hours. Thus it is reasonable to stratify by time segments—such as weekdays, weekday evenings, and weekends—and interview during each segment. Again, traffic counts can provide estimates of the proportion of shoppers that would be in each stratum, so the final results can be weighted appropriately.

Sampling People *vs.* Shopping Visits

Obviously, some people shop more frequently than others and will be more likely to be selected in a shopping-center sample. If the interest is in sampling shopping-center visits, then it is appropriate to oversample those who shop more. If the goal is to develop a sample that represents the total population, however, then it becomes important to adjust the sample so that it reflects the infrequent as well as frequent shoppers.

One approach is to ask respondents how many times they visited the shopping center during a specified time period, such as the last four weeks. Those whose current visit was the only one during the time period would receive a weight of one. Those who visited two times would have a weight of one-half; those who visited three times would have a weight of one-third; and so on.

Another approach is to use quotas, which serve to reduce the biases to levels that may be acceptable. One obvious factor to control is the sex of the respondent, since women shop more than men. The interviewers can be instructed simply to sample an equal proportion of men and women. Another factor to control would be age, as those aged 25 to 45 tend to make more visits to shopping centers than do either younger or older shoppers.[17] Still another would be employment status, as unemployed people spend more time shopping than those employed.[18] The quotas would be set up so that the number sampled would be proportional to the number in the population. If 55 percent of the

[17]Sudman, *op. cit.*, 430.
[18]*Ibid*, 430.

people were employed, then the quota should ensure that 55 percent of the sample was employed.

SUMMARY

There are four main considerations in developing a probability sample. First, the target population must be defined. In doing so, the researcher should look to the research objectives for guidance and consider alternative definitions.

Second, the mechanism for selecting the sample needs to be determined. The simple random sampling, cluster sampling, stratified sampling, and multistage designs are among the available choices. It is important to consider the differences that may exist between the population list or sampling frame from which the sample is drawn and the target population. Potential biases should be identified. For example, in telephone interviewing, the telephone directory will not include those with unlisted numbers.

The third consideration is sample size. Several *ad hoc* methods are available, such as insuring that there are at least 100 sample members for each group within the population that is of interest. In the next chapter we will examine analytical approaches to determining sample size. Regardless of the method chosen, four factors must be considered: the number of subgroups to be analyzed, the accuracy desired, the cost of sampling, and the amount of variation within the population.

The fourth consideration is nonresponse bias. Nonresponse bias can be reduced by improving the research design to reduce refusals and by using callbacks. Sometimes the best approach is to estimate the amount of bias and adjust the interpretation accordingly.

Nonprobability sampling methods, such as judgmental sampling, snowball sampling, and quota sampling, are appropriate in the right context, even though they can be biased and lack precise estimates of sampling variation. Shopping-center sampling is widely used, in part because it is relatively inexpensive. Biases in shopping-center samples can be reduced by adjusting the sample to reflect shopping-center characteristics, the location of the shoppers within the shopping center, the time period of the interviewing, and the frequency of shopping.

It is true that judgmental sampling does contain potential biases; however, the reality is that there are many sources of bias in research, and the biases associated with judgmental sampling may be small in terms of the total overall design. In particular, as the previous chapters have indicated, bias and uncertainty can be caused by:

1 Nonresponse bias in probability sampling. In fact, many of the biases mentioned with respect to judgmental sampling also occur when there is substantial nonresponse in a probability sampling scheme.

2 The way questions are worded. Questions can be ambiguous, hard to understand, and biased.

3 The questionnaire structure. The questionnaire can be too long or badly organized and motivated; the result can be fatigue and resentment.

4 Interviewer bias. The way the interviewer follows the sampling plan, introduces the survey, asks the questions, and interprets the answers all can create both bias and uncertainty in the data.

5 Data analysis. The data-analysis phase, to be discussed in upcoming chapters, can involve coding errors and errors in interpretation.

Thus, sampling errors need to be kept in perspective. It is silly but common to create a sampling design that has less than a one-percent sampling error but may have a 30-percent incidence of errors from other sources.

QUESTIONS AND PROBLEMS

1 Develop a population list or sampling frame for an attitude study when the target population is:

    a All those who rode on a public transit system during the last month

    b Retail sporting goods stores

    c Stores that sell tennis rackets

    d Watchers of evening television

    e High-income families

    f Adults over 18 years of age in California

    g Dwelling units with compactors

    h Users of unit pricing during the past week

2 In question 1, consider how the various populations might be stratified.

3 A manufacturer wanted to get opinions from 4000 hardware-store managers on a new type of lawnmower. An associate provided a list of such stores, divided into 400 large and 3600 small stores. He drew a random sample of 200 stores and was disappointed to find only 19 large stores in the sample, since they represented more than 30 percent of the potential volume. A friend suggested that he draw a second sample. What do you recommend? What other pieces of information would you like to have?

4 A telephone survey is planned to determine the day-after-recall of several test commercials to be run in Fargo, North Dakota. Design a telephone sampling plan.

5 The owners of a seven-store drugstore chain want to sample shoppers of their chain and shoppers of a competing chain so that they can administer a 10-minute questionnaire. Develop alternative sampling plans. Recommend one and defend your recommendation.

6 A town planning group was concerned about the low usage of a library by its citizens. To determine how the library could increase its patronage, they planned to sample all holders of a library card. Comment.

7 Assume that you have a list of 80 managers of Research and Development departments that are numbered from 1 to 80. Further, you want to talk to a random sample of seven of them. Use the following random numbers to draw a sample of seven. Draw four additional samples. Calculate the average number in each case.

6031l428243730443968059455937559496776391450608085041765794444744l288200

8 A concept for a new minicomputer designed for use in the home is to be tested. Because a demonstration is required a personal interview is necessary. Thus, it has been decided to bring a product demonstrator into the home. The city of Sacramento has been selected for the test. The metropolitan area map has been divided into a grid of 22,500 squares, 100 of which have been selected randomly. Interviewers have been sent out to call on homes within the selected square until five interviews are completed. Comment on the design. Would you make any changes?

9 The U.S. Department of Energy would like a census of power generating windmills. How could such a census be obtained?

10 Use the random numbers in Table 10–2 to select a city from the set in Table 10–4.

11 A shopping-center sample was used to evaluate a new product. Given the following data, what is your estimate of the proportion of people that say they will buy the product?

Time Period	Location of Shopping Center	Normal Store Traffic	Sample Size	Proportion of Sample Saying They Will Buy It
Weekdays	A	500	100	50
Evenings	A	200	100	25
Weekends	A	400	100	20
Weekdays	B	600	100	60
Evenings	B	250	100	30
Weekends	B	550	100	35

CASE 10–1
Exercises In Sample Design

In each of the following situations you are asked to make recommendations as to the type of sample to be used, the method of selecting the sample, and the sample size:

1 The manager of the appliance department of a local full-line department store chain is planning a major one-day nonprice promotion of food processors, supported by heavy advertising in the two local newspapers. She has asked you to recommend a method of sampling customers coming into the department. The purpose is to assess the extent to which customers were drawn by the special advertisement, and the extent to which the advertisement influenced their intentions to buy. A pretest of the questionnaire indicates that it will take about three minutes to administer. The manager is especially interested in learning whether there are significant differences in the response to the questionnaire among (a) males versus females, (b) gift buyers versus other buyers, and (c) age groups.

2 A major airline wants to run a preliminary study on the attitudes of university students toward air travel. The company's research director already has submitted an interview plan and has estimated that, on the average, each interview will require an hour to an hour and a half to administer. It is estimated that

the cost of interviewing and interpretation of the interview will be roughly $75.00 per respondent.

3 A small Caribbean island relied heavily upon tourist income. There was a need to develop a study so that an estimate could be provided each month as to:

a The number of tourists

b The length of stay

c Their activities

d Their attitudes toward some programs and acitivities

The plan was to conduct a short interview with each respondent and to leave with them a short questionnaire to be completed and mailed after returning home.

Several sampling plans were considered. One would be to generate a random sample of hotel rooms and to interview each occupant. Another involved sampling every nth person that passed a predetermined point in the city. Still another was to sample departing planes and ships. There were about six plane departures and three ship departures per day. Design a sampling plan so that each month 500 tourists are obtained in the sample.

4 A sample of homeowners in the state of Illinois is desired for a major segmentation study conducted by a large financial institution. A lengthy personal interview lasting over one hour will be conducted with each respondent. A sample size of 3000 is targeted.

CASE 10–2
Talbot Razor Products Company

One of the products marketed by Talbot was an after-shave lotion called Enhance. This brand was sold through drugstores, supermarkets, and department stores. Sales exceeded $30 million per year but were barely profitable

because of advertising expenses that exceeded $9 million. For some time the company and its advertising agency had felt the need to undertake a study to obtain more data on the characteristics of their users as contrasted to those of other leading brands. Both the company and the agency believed that such information would help them find better ways to promote the Enhance brand.

Preliminary discussions between the advertising department and the research department of the advertising agency resulted in the following study objectives:

1 To determine the characteristics of Enhance users versus competitors by such factors as age, income, occupation, marital status, family size, education, social class and leisure time activities.

2 To determine the image of the Enhance brand versus competitors on such attributes as masculinity, expensiveness, and user stereotypes (such as young men, factory workers, young executives, and men living in small towns).

3 To discover the meaning to consumers of certain words which were used to describe after-shave lotions.

4 To examine the media habits of users by television programs, magazines, and newspapers.

In discussing the sampling universe, the advertising manager stated that he thought the study results should be broken down by heavy versus light users of Enhance. In his opinion, as few as 15 to 20 percent of the users might account for 60 percent of the total purchases. He had no idea how many containers a user would have to buy during a specified time period to qualify as a heavy or a light user. The research director and the advertising manager disagreed on a definition of user: the research director thought that anyone who had used the Enhance product within the past year should qualify as a user, and therefore, be included in the study, while the advertising manager thought that a user should be defined as one who had purchased the product within the past three months. In fact, the advertising manager went on to say, "I am really interested only in those people who say that the Enhance brand is their favorite brand or the brand that they purchase more than any other."

After much discussion about what constituted or should constitute a user, the research director pointed out that, in his opinion, the advertising manager was being unrealistic about the whole sampling problem. He had conducted a pilot study to determine how many qualified users he could obtain out of every 100 persons interviewed in Sacramento, California. While he did not feel that the findings were completely representative, he did think that they provided a crude estimate of the sampling problem and the costs which would result from using any kind of a probability sample. The research director said:

In the Sacramento study we were interested only in finding out how many males 18 years of age or older used after-shave, what brands they had purchased during the past year and the past 3 months, and what brand they bought most frequently. All interviewing took place during the evening hours and over the weekend. The findings revealed that only about 70 percent of the male respondents were at home when the interviewer made the call. Of those who were home and who agreed to cooperate, only 65 percent were users of after-shave: that is, affirmatively answered the question: "Do you ever use after-shave?" Of those who used after-shave, only 7 percent had purchased the Enhance brand within the past three months, while 15 percent reported having purchased it within the past year. The costs of the Sacramento job figured out to about $6.00 per contact including the not-at-homes, refusals, and completed interviews, all as contacts. The sample size for the Sacramento pilot study was 212 male respondents and the field costs were $1272. These costs will be increased substantially if the sample includes smaller towns and farm interviews.

The research director believed that the best sample size they could hope for would be one which provided about 100 interviews with Enhance users plus 100 interviews with users of other brands in each of 10 to 15 metropolitan areas. This would provide a total sample size of 2000 to 3000 and would require contacts with between 40,000 and 50,000 respondents. The research director indicated that this size sample would permit breakdown of the results for the United States by heavy versus light users.

The advertising manager did not think this would be an adequate national sample. He said:

> *I can't present these results to my management and tell them that they are representative of the whole country, and I doubt if the sample in each of the 10 to 15 metropolitan areas is big enough to enable us to draw reliable conclusions about our customers and noncustomers in that particular area. I don't see how you can sample each metropolitan area on an equal basis. I would think that the bigger areas such as New York and Chicago should have bigger samples than some of the smaller metropolitan areas.*

The research director explained that this way of allocating the sample between areas was not correct since the size of the universe had no effect on the size of the sample. He said:

> *If we do it the way you are suggesting, it will mean that in some of the big metropolitan areas we'll end up with 150 to 200 interviews while, in some of the smaller ones, we'll have only 50 or 75 interviews. Under such conditions it would be impossible to break out the findings of each metropolitan area separately. If we sample each area equally, we can weigh the results obtained from the different metropolitan areas so as to get accurate U.S. totals.*

When the discussion turned to costs, the advertising manager complained:

> *I can't possibly tell my management that we have to make 40,000 to 50,000 calls in order to get 2000 to 3000 interviews. They're going to tell me that we're wasting an awful lot of money just to find users. Why can't we find Enhance users by selecting a sample of drugstores and offering druggists some money for getting names and addresses of those men who buy after-shave. We could probably locate Enhance users for maybe 35 to 50 cents each.*

The research director admitted that this would be a much cheaper way, but pointed out that he would not have any idea what kind of sample would result, and therefore it would be impossible to tell anything at all about the reliability of the survey. The advertising manager thought management would provide no more than $30,000 for the study. The research director estimated that the results could be tabulated, analyzed, a report written, and the results presented to management for about $7000, thus leaving around $23,000 for fieldwork.

QUESTIONS FOR DISCUSSION

1 How should the sampling universe be defined?

2 How large a sample should be collected?

3 How should the sample be distributed geographically?

11

SAMPLE SIZE AND STATISTICAL THEORY

A practical question in much of marketing research involves the determination of sample size. A survey cannot be planned or implemented without knowing the sample size. Further, the sample-size decision is related directly to research cost and therefore must be justified.

In the previous chapter, several practical approaches to obtaining sample size were presented. These approaches are extremely sensible, will lead to reasonable sample-size decisions, and in fact are used often in marketing research. There is, however, a formal approach to determining sample size using statistical theory. It is useful to understand this formal approach—the subject of this chapter—for several reasons. First, in some contexts it can be applied directly to make more precise sample-size decisions. Second, it can provide worthwhile guidance even when it may not be easy to apply the statistical theory. Finally, the discussion serves to introduce some important concepts and terms of sampling that, together, will generate a deeper understanding of the process. Among these terms and concepts are *population characteristics, sample characteristics, sample reliability,* and *interval estimation.* Each of them will be introduced, and then the sample-size question will be considered.

POPULATION CHARACTERISTICS

Let us assume that we are interested in the attitudes of symphony season-ticket holders toward changing the starting time of weekday performances from 8:00 P.M. to 7:30 P.M. The population is comprised of the 10,000 symphony season-ticket holders. Their response to the proposal is shown in Figure 11–1. Of these ticket holders, 3000 responded "definitely yes" (which is coded as +2). Another 2000 would "prefer yes" (coded as +1), and so on. The needed information is the average or mean response of the population (the 10,000 season-ticket holders), which is termed

$$\mu = \text{the population mean} = 0.3$$

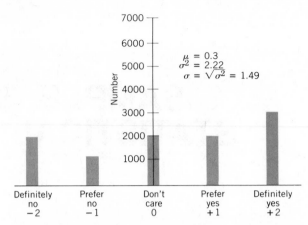

FIGURE 11–1 The population opinion on symphony starting time of 7:30 P.M. on weekdays

This population mean is one population characteristic of interest. It normally is unknown, and our goal is to determine its value as closely as possible by taking a sample from the population.

Another population characteristic of interest is the population variance, σ^2, and its square root, the population standard deviation, σ. The population variance is a measure of the population dispersion, the degree to which the different season-ticket holders differ from one another in terms of their attitude. It is based upon the degree to which a response differs from the population average response, μ. This difference is squared (making all values positive) and averaged across all responses.[1] In our example, the population variance is

$$\sigma^2 = \text{the population variance} = 2.22$$

and

$$\sigma = \text{the population standard deviation} = 1.49$$

[1]Here follows one method for calculating the population mean and variance. Note the responses are weighted by the response frequency. Thus, the response $+1$ is weighted by 0.20, because it occurs 0.20 of the time in the population. For a further discussion, see any introductory statistics book.

Response R	Response Frequency f	Weighted Average Rf	Population Mean μ	Difference Between Response and μ $R - \mu$	Difference Squared $(R - \mu)^2$	Weighted Average $(R - \mu)^2 f$
$+2$	.3	.6	.3	1.7	2.89	.87
$+1$	.2	.2	.3	.7	.49	.10
0	.2	0	.3	.3	.09	.02
-1	.1	$-.1$	.3	1.3	1.69	.17
-2	.2	$-.4$	.3	2.3	5.29	1.06
Total		$0.3 = \mu$				$2.22 = \sigma^2$

SAMPLE CHARACTERISTICS

The problem is that the population mean is not known but must be estimated from a sample. Assume that a simple random sample of size 10 is taken from the population. The 10 people selected and their respective attitudes are shown in Figure 11–2.

$$\bar{X} = \frac{1}{10} \sum_{i=1}^{10} X_i = 0.5$$

$$s^2 = \frac{1}{n-1} \sum (X_i - \bar{X})^2 = \frac{14.50}{9} = 1.61$$

$$s = \sqrt{s^2} = 1.27$$

Just as the population has a set of characteristics, each sample also has a set of characteristics. One sample characteristic is the sample average or mean:

$$\bar{X} = \frac{1}{n} \sum_{i=1}^{n} X_i = 0.5$$

Two means now have been introduced, and it is important to keep them separate. One is the population mean (μ), a population characteristic. The second is the sample mean ($\bar{X}$), a sample characteristic. Because the $\bar{X}$ is a sample characteristic, it would change if a new sample were obtained. The sample mean ($\bar{X}$) is used to estimate the unknown population mean (μ).

Another sample characteristic or statistic is the sample variance (s^2), which can be used to estimate the population variance (σ^2). Under simple random sampling, the sample variance is

$$s^2 = \text{sample variance} = \frac{1}{n-1} \sum_{i=1}^{n} (X_i - \bar{X})^2 = 1.61$$

	Attitude
1. John T.	$X_1 = +1$
2. Lois M.	$X_2 = +2$
3. Steve K.	$X_3 = +2$
4. Paul A.	$X_4 = 0$
5. Carol Z.	$X_5 = +1$
6. Judy D.	$X_6 = +1$
7. Tom E.	$X_7 = -1$
8. Sharon P.	$X_8 = +1$
9. Jan K.	$X_9 = -2$
10. Ed J.	$X_{10} = 0$

FIGURE 11–2 A sample of symphony season-ticket holders

Note that s^2 will be small if the sample responses are similar and large if they are spread out. The corresponding sample standard deviation is simply[2]

$$s = \text{sample standard deviation} = \sqrt{s^2} = 1.27$$

Again, it is important to make a distinction between the population variance (σ^2) and the sample variance (s^2).

SAMPLE RELIABILITY

Of course, all samples will not generate the same value of $\bar{X}$ (or s). If another simple random sample of size 10 were taken from the population, $\bar{X}$ might be 0.3 or 1.2 or 0.4 or whatever. The point is that $\bar{X}$ will vary from sample to sample.

Intuitively, it is reasonable to believe that the variation in $\bar{X}$ will be larger as the variance in the population, σ^2, is larger. At one extreme, if there is no variation in the population, there will be no variation in $\bar{X}$. It also is reasonable to believe that, as the size of the sample increases, the variation in $\bar{X}$ will decrease. When the sample is small, it takes only one or two extreme scores to substantially affect the sample mean, thus generating a relatively large or small $\bar{X}$. As the sample size increases, these extreme values will have less impact when they do appear, because they will be averaged with more values. The variation in $\bar{X}$ is measured by its standard error,[3] which is

$$\sigma_{\bar{X}} = \text{the standard error of } \bar{X} = \frac{\sigma_X}{\sqrt{n}} = \frac{1.49}{\sqrt{10}} = .47$$

(σ_X can be written simply as σ). Note that the standard error of $\bar{X}$ depends on n, the sample size. If n is altered, the standard error will change accordingly, as Table 11–1 shows.

The variable X has a probability distribution, reflected in Figure 11–1. The sample mean, $\bar{X}$, also has a probability distribution. It is customary to assume that the variation of $\bar{X}$ from sample to sample will follow the normal distribution.[4] Figure 11–3 shows the familiar bell-shaped normal probability distribution. In other words, it indicates that $\bar{X}$

---

[2]The term $n - 1$ appears in the expression for the sample variance so that s^2 will be an unbiased estimate of the population variance. The reader need not be concerned about this fact; it has little practical significance. If the population size, termed N, is small relative to the sample size, n, a "finite population correction factor" of $N - n/N - 1$ should be added. Thus, if N is 1000 and n is 100, the correction factor would be 0.9. If N is more than 10 times the sample size, the correction factor is rarely of significance.

[3]We also could use the term population standard error of $\bar{X}$. The word "population" is omitted in this context to make the discussion less cumbersome.

[4]Such an assumption is not as extreme as it may seem. The $\bar{X}$ distribution will be normal if the distribution of the underlying population is normal, or if the sample size gets large. The last condition is due to the central-limit theorem. In practice, if the population distribution is fairly symmetrical in appearance, a "large" n can be 30, 20, or even smaller, depending upon the accuracy required by the situation. Even with a sample size of 10, the error introduced by assuming that $\bar{X}$ is distributed normally is often not of practical importance, and the reality is that there is often no practical alternative.

TABLE 11–1

Increasing Sample Size

Sample Size	σ_x	$\sigma_{\bar{x}} = \sigma_x / \sqrt{n}$
10	1.49	0.470
40	1.49	0.235
100	1.49	0.149
500	1.49	0.067

usually will be close to the population mean (μ) and that it is just as likely to be larger than μ as smaller. The top drawing in Figure 11–3 shows how the area under the normal curve is divided. The area corresponds to probability; that is, the area under the curve between two points is the probability that $\bar{X}$ will be between those two points. For example, in the middle figure, 95 percent of the area is shown. Thus, the probability that $\bar{X}$ lies within $2\sigma_{\bar{x}}$ of the population mean (μ) is 0.95. Similarly, the bottom figure shows 90 percent of the area under the normal curve. Its interpretation is that the probability is 0.90 that $\bar{X}$ is within $5/3 \ \sigma_{\bar{x}}$ of the population mean (μ).[5]

Thus, the concept of a standard error now can be illustrated in the context of Figure 11–3. There is a 0.95 probability that $\bar{X}$ will fall within ± 2 standard errors of the population mean. In our symphony example from Figure 11–1, suppose we drew 100 different samples of 10 people. About 95 percent of the resulting sample means ($\bar{X}$) would be within ± 2 standard errors ($\sigma_{\bar{x}} = .47$) of the population mean ($\mu = 0.3$). Figure 11–3 is sometimes called a sampling distribution, since it indicates the probability of getting a particular sample mean.

Table 11–1 illustrates how the standard error of X decreases as the sample size gets larger. Thus, with a large sample, $\bar{X}$ will tend to be close to μ, and the distribution of $\bar{X}$ will change accordingly. Figure 11–4 shows the effect of a sample-size change from 10 to 40 on the distribution of $\bar{X}$. If the sample size were increased further, the $\bar{X}$ probability distribution would get taller and more narrow.

A source of confusion is the fact that two probability distributions are being discussed. It is very important to keep them separate. The first is the distribution of response over the population, as illustrated by Figure 11–1. The population standard deviation, σ, reflects the dispersion of this distribution. The second is the distribution of $\bar{X}$, illustrated by Figures

[5]Actually, the numbers 2 and 5/3 are approximations. The correct numbers from a normal distribution table are as follows:

Number of σ_x	Probability
2.575	0.99
1.96	0.95
1.64	0.90
1.282	0.80

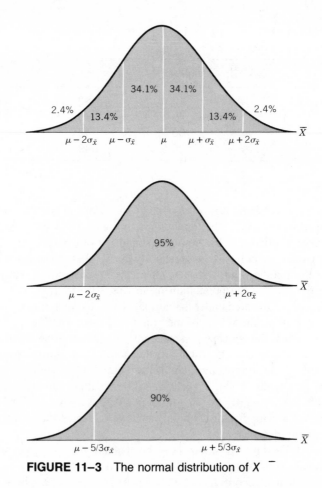

FIGURE 11–3 The normal distribution of $\bar{X}$

11–3 and 11–4 (the dispersion of which is reflected by $\sigma_{\bar{x}}$). To conceptualize the $\bar{X}$ distribution, it is necessary to conceive of many replications of the sample.

INTERVAL ESTIMATION

The sample mean, $\bar{X}$, is used to estimate the unknown population mean (μ). Because $\bar{X}$ varies from sample to sample, it is not, of course, equal to the population mean (μ). There is a sampling error. It is useful to provide an interval estimate around $\bar{X}$ that reflects our judgment of the extent of this sampling error:

$$\bar{X} \pm \text{sampling error} = \text{the interval estimate of } \mu$$

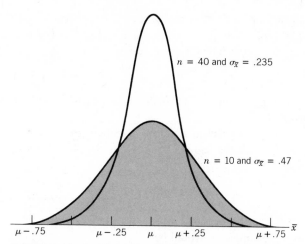

FIGURE 11–4 The effect of increasing sample size on the normal distribution of $\bar{X}$

The size of the interval will depend on how confident we want to be that the interval contains the true unknown population mean. If it were necessary to be 95 percent confident that the interval estimate contained the true population mean, the interval estimate would be

$$\bar{X} \pm 2\sigma_{\bar{x}} = \bar{X} \pm \frac{2\sigma_X}{\sqrt{n}} = 95 \text{ percent interval estimate of } \mu$$

(recall that $\sigma_{\bar{x}} = \sigma_X/\sqrt{n}$). The interval size is based on $2\sigma_{\bar{x}}$ because, as Figure 11–3 shows, the probability that $\bar{X}$ will be within $2\sigma_{\bar{x}}$ of the population mean is 0.95. In our example, the interval would be

$$\bar{X} \pm 2\sigma_{\bar{x}} = 0.5 \pm 2 \times .47 = 0.5 \pm .94$$

since $\sigma_{\bar{x}} = \dfrac{\sigma_X}{\sqrt{n}} = .47$. Note that this interval includes the true population mean (recall from Figure 11–1 that $\mu = 0.3$). About 95 percent of samples will generate an interval estimate that will include the true population mean.

If the desire were to be 90 percent confident that the interval estimate included the true population mean, then the interval estimate would be

$$\bar{X} \pm \tfrac{5}{3}(\sigma_{\bar{x}}) = \bar{X} \pm \frac{\frac{5}{3}\sigma_X}{\sqrt{n}} = 90 \text{ percent interval estimate of } \mu$$

Again, the interval is based upon $\frac{5}{3}$ ($\sigma_{\bar{X}}$) because, as shown in Figure 11–3, there is a 0.90 probability that $\bar{X}$ is within $\frac{5}{3}$ ($\sigma_{\bar{X}}$) of the true population mean, μ. In our example, the 90 percent interval estimate is

$$\bar{X} \pm \tfrac{5}{3} (\sigma_{\bar{X}}) = 0.5 \pm \tfrac{5}{3} (.47) = 0.5 \pm .78$$

Note that the interval is smaller, but that we are less confident that it would include the true population mean.

If the population standard deviation ($\sigma_{\bar{x}} = \sigma$) is not known, it is necessary to estimate it with the sample standard deviation, s.[6] Thus, the 95 percent interval estimate would be

$$\bar{X} \pm \frac{2s}{\sqrt{n}} = 95 \text{ percent interval estimate with } \sigma \text{ unknown}$$

In our example, it would be

$$.5 \pm 2\left(\frac{1.27}{\sqrt{10}}\right) = .5 \pm .80$$

since from Figure 11–2, s was determined to be 1.27.

To summarize, the interval estimate of the population mean, μ, can be written as

$$\bar{X} \pm \text{ sampling error, or } \bar{X} \pm \frac{z\sigma_X}{\sqrt{n}}$$

where

$$z = 2 \text{ for a 95-percent confidence level}$$
$$z = 5/3 \text{ for a 90-percent confidence level}$$
$$\sigma_X = \text{population standard deviation (s is used if σ_X is unknown)}$$
$$n = \text{the sample size}$$

Thus, the size of the interval estimate will depend upon three factors. The first is the confidence level. If we are willing to be less confident that the interval estimate will include the true unknown population mean, then the interval will be smaller. The second factor is the population standard deviation. If there is little variation in the population, then the interval estimate of the population mean will be smaller. The third is the sample size. As the sample size gets larger, the sampling error is reduced and the interval will get smaller.

---

[6]Actually, the use of s adds a bit more uncertainty to the interval estimate. If the sample size is small, and if it is important to be extremely precise in the confidence interval estimate, this uncertainty can be accounted for explicitly by replacing the normal distribution with the t-distribution, which makes the interval larger. For example, using the t-distribution, the 95 percent interval estimate would involve a factor of 2.23 for a sample size of 10, a factor of 2.06 for a sample size of 20, and a factor of 2.00 for a sample size of 60. As n gets larger, the t-distribution approaches the normal distribution.

THE SAMPLE-SIZE QUESTION

Now, we are finally ready to use these concepts to help determine sample size. To proceed, the analyst must specify:

1 The size of the sampling error that is desired
2 The confidence level, for example, the 95-percent confidence level

This specification will depend upon a trade-off between the value of more accurate information and the cost of an increased sample size. For a given confidence level, a smaller sampling error will "cost" in terms of a larger sample size. Similarly, for a given sampling error, a higher confidence level will "cost" in terms of a larger sample size. These statements will become more tangible in the context of some examples.

Using the general formula for the interval estimate (recall that σ and σ_X are the same)

$$\bar{X} \pm \text{sampling error, or } \bar{X} \pm \frac{z\sigma}{\sqrt{n}}$$

we know that

$$\text{Sampling error} = \frac{z\sigma}{\sqrt{n}}$$

Dividing through by the sampling error and multiplying by $\sqrt{n}$

$$\sqrt{n} = \frac{z\sigma}{(\text{sampling error})}$$

and squaring both sides, we get an expression for sample size:

$$n = \frac{z^2\sigma^2}{(\text{sampling error})^2}$$

Thus, if we know the required confidence level, and therefore z, and also know the allowed sampling error, then the needed sample size is specified by the formula.

Let us assume that there is a need to be 95 percent sure that our sampling error in estimating the population mean does not exceed 0.3. In this case, sampling error = 0.3, and, since the confidence level is 95 percent, $z = 2$. In our example, from Figure 11–1, the population standard deviation is 1.49, so the sample size should be

$$n = \frac{2^2(1.49)^2}{(.3)^2} = 99$$

Changing the Confidence Level. If the confidence level were changed from 95 percent to 90 percent, the sample size could be reduced because we do not have to be as certain of the resulting estimate. The z term would then be 5/3 and the sample size would be

$$n = \frac{(z\sigma)^2}{(\text{sampling error})^2} = \frac{(5/3)^2(1.49)^2}{(.3)^2} = 65.5$$

Changing the Allowed Error.   If the allowed error were increased, the sample size also would decrease, even if a 95-percent confidence level were retained. In our example, if the allowed error were increased to 0.5, then the sample size would be

$$n = \frac{(z\sigma)^2}{(\text{sampling error})^2} = \frac{4(1.49)^2}{(0.5)^2} = 35.5$$

The Population Size.   It should be noted that the sample-size calculation is completely independent of the size of the population. A common misconception is that a "good" sample should have a relatively high percentage of the sampling frame included. Actually, the size of the sample will be determined in the same manner, whether the population is 1000 or 1,000,000.

Determining the Population Standard Deviation

The procedure just displayed assumes that the population standard deviation is known. In most practical situations it is not known and it must be estimated by using one of several available approaches.

One method is to use a sample standard deviation obtained from a previous comparable survey or from a pilot survey. Another approach is to estimate σ subjectively. Suppose the task is to estimate the income of a community. It might be possible to say that 95 percent of the people will have an income of between $4000 and $20,000. Assuming a normal distribution, there will be four population standard deviations between the two figures, so that one population standard deviation will be equal to $4000.

Another approach is to take a "worst-case" situation. In our example, the largest population variance would occur if half the population would respond with a $+2$ and the other half with a -2.[7] The population variance would then be 4, and the recommended sample size, at a 95-percent confidence level and a 0.3 allowable error, would be 178. Note that the sample size would be larger than desired, and thus the desired accuracy would be exceeded. The logic is that it is all right to err on the side of being too accurate.

---

[7]The population variance would be $0.5(2 - 0)^2 + 0.5(-2 - 0)^2 = 0.5 \times 4 + 0.5 \times 4 = 4$, since 0.5 of the population responded with a $+2$, and the population mean, or average, would be zero. See footnote 1 for a calculation formula.

Proportions

When proportions are to be estimated (the proportion of people with negative feelings about a change in the starting time of the symphony, for example), the procedure is to use the sample proportion to estimate the unknown population proportion, π. Because this estimate is based on a sample, it has a population variance, namely

$$\sigma_p^2 = \frac{\pi(1 - \pi)}{n}$$

where

$$\pi = \text{the population proportion}$$
$$P = \text{the sample proportion (corresponding to } \bar{X}\text{),}$$
$$\quad \text{used to estimate the unknown population}$$
$$\quad \text{proportion}$$
$$\sigma_p^2 = \text{the population variance of } P$$

The formula for sample size is then

$$n = \frac{z^2\pi(1 - \pi)}{(\text{sampling error})^2}$$

As Figure 11–5 shows, the worst case, where the population variance is at its maximum, occurs when the population proportion is equal to .50:

$$\pi(1 - \pi) = .25$$
$$\pi = .50$$

Because the population proportion is unknown, a common procedure is to assume the worst case. The formula for sample size then simplifies to

$$n = \frac{z^2(.25)}{(\text{sampling error})^2}$$

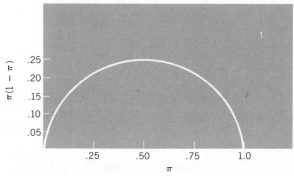

FIGURE 11–5   A graph of $\pi(1 - \pi)$

In general,

$$\text{Sample size} = n = z^2\sigma^2 \div (\text{sampling error})^2$$

where

> $z = 2$ for a 95-percent confidence level
> $z = 5/3$ for a 90-percent confidence level
> $\sigma = $ the population standard deviation

and

> sampling error $ = $ the allowed sampling error

For proportions,

$$\text{Sample size} = n = z^2(.25) \div (\text{sampling error})^2$$

FIGURE 11–6 Some useful sample-size formulas

Thus, if the population proportion is to be estimated within an error of 0.05 (or 5 percentage points) at a 95-percent confidence level, the needed sample size is

$$n = \frac{2^2(.25)}{(.05)^2} = 400$$

since z equals 2, corresponding to a 95-percent confidence level, and the allowed sampling error equals 0.05. Figure 11–6 summarizes the two sample size formulas.

Several Questions

A survey instrument or an experiment usually will not be based upon just one question. Sometimes hundreds can be involved. It usually will not be worthwhile to go through such a process for all questions. A reasonable approach would be to pick a few representative questions and determine the sample size from them. Included should be the most crucial ones with the highest expected variance.

STRATIFIED SAMPLING

In stratified sampling, the population is divided into subgroups or strata and a sample is taken from each. Stratified sampling is worthwhile when one or both of the following are true:

1 The population standard deviation differs by strata

2 The interview cost differs by strata

Income Stratum (i)	Proportion (π_i)	Standard Deviation (σ_i)	Interview Cost (c_i)	$\pi_i\sigma_i/\sqrt{c_i}$	n_i
Low	.3	1	25	.06	177
Medium	.5	2	25	.20	588
High	.2	4	100	.08	235
				$.34 = \Sigma_i\pi_i\sigma_i \div \sqrt{c_i}$	$1000 = n$

FIGURE 11-7 Allocating sample size to strata

Suppose we desired to estimate the usage of electricity to heat swimming pools. The population of swimming pools might be stratified into commercial pools at hotels and clubs and individual home swimming pools. The latter may have a small variation and thus would require a smaller sample. If, however, the home-pool owners were less costly to interview, that would allow more of them to be interviewed than if the two groups involved the same interview cost.

How does one determine the best allocation of the sampling budget to the various strata? This classic problem of sampling was solved in 1935 by Jerzy Neyman.[8] His solution is represented by the following formula:

$$n_i = \frac{\pi_i\sigma_i/\sqrt{c_i}}{\Sigma_i\,(\pi_i\sigma_i/\sqrt{c_i})}n$$

where

n = the total sample size
π_i = the proportion of the population in stratum i
σ_i = the population standard deviation in stratum i
c_i = the cost of one interview in stratum i
Σ_i = the sum over all strata
n_i = the sample size for stratum i

Figure 11-7 presents information on a survey of the monthly usage of bank teller machines. The population is stratified by income. The high-income segment has both the highest variation and the highest interview cost. The low- and medium-income strata have the same interview cost but differ with respect to the standard deviation of bank teller usage. The column at the right shows the breakdown of the 1000-person sample into the three strata. Note that the high-income stratum is allocated 235 people. If a simple random

[8]Jerzy Neyman, "On the two different aspects of the representative method: The method of stratified sampling and the method of purposive selection," *Journal of the Royal Statistical Society*, 1934, 97, 558–606.

sample of size 1000 had been taken from the population, around 200 would have been taken from the high-income group, since 20 percent of the population is from that stratum.

The formula shows how to allocate the sample size to the various strata; however, how does one determine the sample size in the first place? One approach is to assume that there is a budget limit. The sample size is simply adjusted upward until it hits the budget limit. The budget should be figured as follows:

$$\text{Budget} = \Sigma_i \, c_i \, n_i$$

The second approach is to determine the sampling error and decide whether or not it is excessive. If so, the sample size would be increased. The sampling error formula is

$$\text{Sampling error} = z\sigma_{\bar{x}}$$

and is based on the standard error of $\bar{X}$, which is found as follows:

$$\text{Standard error of } \bar{X} \text{ or } \sigma_{\bar{x}} = \sqrt{\Sigma_i \, \pi_i \, \sigma_i^2 / n_i}$$

It is based upon the variances of the individual strata. In the example given in Figure 11–7,

$$\sigma_{\bar{x}} = .07$$

As was illustrated in the last chapter, the estimate of the population mean under stratified sampling is a weighted average of the sample means found in each stratum sample:

$$\text{Estimate of the population mean} = \Sigma_i \, \pi_i \, \bar{X}_i$$

where

$$\bar{X}_i = \text{the sample mean for stratum } i$$

MULTISTAGE DESIGNS

If other sampling designs are employed, the logic used to generate the optimal sample size will still hold; however, the formula can get complicated. For example, in an area design the first step might be to select communities at random. Then the procedure could be to select census tracts, then blocks, and finally households. In such a design the expression for determining the standard error of $\bar{X}$ becomes hopelessly complex. The solution is to replicate the entire sampling plan and obtain two, three, or four independent estimates of $\bar{X}$. These different estimates can be used to estimate the standard error of $\bar{X}$.

SEQUENTIAL SAMPLING

Sometimes a researcher may want to take a modest sample, look at the results, and then decide if more information, in the form of a larger sample, is needed. Such a procedure is termed sequential sampling. If a new industrial product were being evaluated, a small probability sample of potential users might be contacted. Suppose it were found that their average annual usage level at a 95-percent confidence level was between 10 and 30 units, and it was known that for the product to be economically viable the average would have to be 50 units. This is sufficient information for a decision to drop the product. If, however, the interval estimate from the original sample were from 45 to 65, then the information would be inadequate for making that decision and an additional sample might be obtained. The combined samples then would provide a smaller interval estimate. If the resulting interval were still inadequate, the sample size could be increased a third time. Of course, although sequential sampling does provide the potential of sharply reducing costs, it can result in increased costs and a delayed decision.

The concept of sequential sampling is useful because it reminds the researcher that the goal of marketing research is to provide information to aid in decision making. The quality of the information must be evaluated in the decision-making context. Too often, information tends to be evaluated absolutely (it is intellectually comfortable to be "certain"). Instead, it should be judged with respect to its use.

SUMMARY

This chapter has introduced some useful concepts and applied them to the problem of determining the sample size. A population characteristic, such as the attitude of symphony season-ticket holders, is to be estimated by the sample. A sample statistic, such as the average attitude of a sample of season-ticket holders, is used to estimate the population characteristic. The sample statistic will have a variance (it will not be the same each time a sample is drawn), and this will be a measure of its reliability. The estimate, based upon the sample statistic, has an interval associated with it that reflects its variance and the confidence level of the researcher. The sample size then is determined by the confidence level desired, the allowed estimate error, and the variance of the population as per the following formula:

$$n > \frac{(z\sigma)^2}{(\text{sampling error})^2}$$

In stratified sampling, the sample size of each stratum will depend on the variance and the interviewing cost within each stratum.

QUESTIONS AND PROBLEMS

1 A group of 25,000 design engineers was asked a series of questions concerning the importance of various attributes of a milling machine. The group had the following response to the question, "How important is it that the machine be capable of working with both hard and soft metals?"

Scale	Description	Frequency	Percentage
5	Extremely important	5000	20
4	Important	8000	32
3	Desirable	6000	24
2	Only a small plus	2000	8
1	Of no consequence	4000	16
		25,000	100

a What is the average response of this population?

b What is the variance and standard deviation? (See footnote 1.)

c A sample of size 25 yielded the following numbers: 4, 4, 1, 2, 3, 5, 4, 2, 3, 3, 3, 4, 4, 4, 1, 1, 5, 5, 4, 1, 3, 4, 4, 5, 2. Determine the sample mean, the sample variance, and the sample standard deviation.

d Calculate the standard error of the sample mean, $\sigma_{\bar{X}}$. How would your calculation change if the sample size were 100 instead of 25? Why? Estimate the $\sigma_{\bar{X}}$ using s instead of σ.

e Repeat parts (a) and (b) assuming that half the population of 25,000 engineers had responded "extremely important" and half had responded "of no consequence."

2 A sample of size 100 was taken from the population represented in Figure 11–1. The results showed that

$$\bar{X} = 0.52$$
$$s^2 = 2.62$$

a Determine a 90 percent interval estimate for μ. (Recall from Figure 11–1 that $\sigma = 1.49$.)

b Determine a 95 percent interval estimate for μ.

c Repeat (a) and (b) using s^2 instead of σ^2.

d What sample size would be needed to reduce the sampling error to 0.10 if a confidence level of 95 percent were desired? Use the fact that $\sigma = 1.49$.

3 If the proportion of people who intend to vote Democratic were to be estimated at a 95-percent confidence level, what sample size should be taken

   a If the accuracy is to be ±0.01 (or one percentage point)?

   b If the accuracy is to be ±0.03?

   c If the accuracy is to be ±0.06?

   d Repeat the above for a 90-percent confidence level.

4 A promotion campaign is being planned to encourage people to reduce heat in their houses at night. In order to measure the campaign's impact, we desire to determine the proportion of people who reduce their heat at night, π. A telephone sample will be taken before and after the campaign.

   a What sample size is required if an accuracy of ±0.03 is desired at a 90 percent confidence level?

   b At a 95 percent confidence level?

   c How would your answer to part (b) change if you knew that the proportion would not exceed 0.3? What if it would not exceed 0.1?

   d Assume that a before-measure was taken with a sample size of 400 and the sample proportion was 0.3. Generate a 90 percent confidence level estimate for the population proportion. (Hint: recall that $\sigma_p^2 = [\pi(1 - \pi)/n]$.)

5 A new consumer product is proposed. It is thought that 25 percent of the population will buy it. A critical question is how frequently buyers will use it. A judgment has been made that 95 percent of them will use it between one and 17 times per month. On that basis, the population standard deviation is estimated to be 4.

   a Explain how the standard deviation estimate was obtained.

   b What sample size is required if an accuracy of ±1 is needed at the 90 percent level? At the 95 percent level? (The sampling error should not exceed 1.)

   c Repeat (b) for an accuracy of ±0.4.

   d What considerations should be introduced in selecting the confidence level and desired accuracy?

6 The problem is to estimate the sales for the coming year for a maker of industrial equipment. The forecast is based upon asking customers how much they are planning to order next year. To use the research budget efficiently, the customers are stratified by the size of their orders during the past year. The following is some relevant information based on the past year:

Strata Customer Size (i)	Proportion (π_i)	Standard Deviation (σ_i)	Interview Cost (c_i)
Large	.1	40	64
Medium	.2	3	64
Small	.7	2	64
Number of customers: 5,000			

a Assume that a total of 300 interviews are to be conducted. How would you allocate those interviews among the three strata?

b If a simple random sample of size 300 were obtained from the population, about 10 percent, or 30 interviews, would be from the large customer stratum. Why did you recommend in part (a) that more than 30 interviews be conducted from this stratum?

c The survey was conducted, and the average values (in thousands) for each stratum were as follows:

$$\bar{X}_1 = 100$$
$$\bar{X}_2 = 8$$
$$\bar{X}_3 = 5$$

What would your estimate be of the population mean, the average sales that will be received from all customers next year?

d Given the context of part (c), what would be the variance of your estimate of the population mean? Do you think that this variance would be larger or smaller than the variance of your estimate of the population mean if you had taken a simple random sample of size 300 from the total population? Why?

e What is the total interviewing cost, given a cost per interview of $64 and 300 interviews?

f Assume now that it has been decided that the small customers can be contacted by telephone, making their cost per interview only $9 each. Repeat the analysis that you did for part (a). How would you allocate 300 interviews now?

g Under part (f), what is now the total interviewing cost?

h How many interviews could you conduct, assuming that you had the same amount of money determined under part (e), that you allocated the interviews according to your answer in part (f), and that the costs were as in part (f)?

CASES FOR PART II

DATA COLLECTION

CASE II–1 PACIFIC GAS & ELECTRIC (A)[1]

In the Spring of 1977, Pacific Gas & Electric (PG&E) was interested in determining what could be done to encourage the installation of solar water heaters. As a first step it was decided that some exploratory marketing research should be conducted. As a result, a research proposal for a telephone survey to determine homeowners' knowledge, attitudes, and intentions toward solar water heaters was on the desk of John Glenning, a marketing research analyst of PG&E. John needed to decide whether the methodology, including the sampling plan and the questionnaire, was sound. He further needed to decide whether a telephone interview was the appropriate research approach. Focus-group interviews had been very helpful in developing a home insulation program several years earlier, and he felt that a real alternative was to commission several focus groups.

Solar Water Heaters

Solar water heaters have been in use for a long time. In fact, they were very popular in Florida during the early thirties. They are extremely simple, as Exhibit II–1 illustrates. Cold water is pumped onto the roof of a house, where it circulates through "collector panels" that are heated by the sun. Hot water then returns to a storage tank. A conventional gas or electric water heater will raise the water temperature, if necessary, on cloudy days. The water heater application of solar energy is attractive because solar water heaters are much more economical than solar space (house) heaters and because the market potential for solar swimming pool heaters is limited.

The expected rate of return that a homeowner can expect from the installation of a solar water heater will depend upon a set of assumptions about how the unit is financed and what energy source it will replace. Generally, the investment is unattractive if gas currently is used, but it can be attractive if water is now heated with electricity. If a utility were to install and lease units to homeowners, the investment's attractiveness might

[1]Written by Darrell R. Clarke and David A. Aaker as a basis for class discussion.

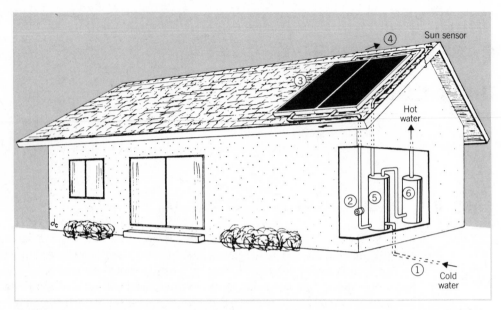

EXHIBIT II–1   Solar hot-water heating system. Cool water is drawn from supply line (1), and pump (2) circulates water through collector panels (3). Hot water leaving panels (4) is transferred to storage tank (5). Preheated water circulates to backup heater (6) for additional heating, if necessary, before distribution through hot water outlets.

improve since the payments could be stretched out and since the utility probably would have lower installment costs than a conventional dealer. One possibility to be explored is whether PG&E should be involved in leasing and installing solar water heaters.

PG&E's Solar Program

PG&E's solar program, budgeted at over half a million dollars, had two primary objectives. The first was to gather and analyze information on available solar energy systems' cost-effectiveness, dependability, and acceptability to PG&E customers. The second was to inform customers of the information obtained.

Projects undertaken toward these objectives included solar demonstration homes, monitoring of other solar installations, product testing, and customer information programs. Three demonstration solar houses were built, and five more were planned. A part of PG&E advertising had been devoted to solar applications. An energy conservation trailer was displayed at fairs and shopping centers. Over 90,000 copies of a booklet entitled *Sun Energy* were distributed.

Two approaches toward encouraging homeowner installation of solar water heaters had been proposed. The first, now under active consideration by PG&E, was the use of advertising and other customer information programs to communicate information regarding solar water heaters and to get homeowners to consider installing them. One purpose of the proposed research was thus to determine who should be the target audience, what their characteristics and their information needs were, and what appeals would be most effective. The second approach was to involve PG&E in the solar heating business. This involvement could take a variety of forms. One possibility was to develop a pilot program in which PG&E would install and lease solar water heaters to homeowners. Another purpose of the research was to evaluate the practicality of such a pilot program. At the time, the only known solar leasing program was operated by the Municipal Utility of Santa Clara, which installed plastic solar swimming-pool heaters for a $200 installation fee and a monthly fee payable during the six-month swimming season.

Research Objectives

Several specific types of research information were desired. First, a knowledge of home-owners' awareness, knowledge, attitudes, and intentions concerning residential applications of solar energy, particularly water heaters was needed to determine appropriate objectives of customer information programs. Second, knowing what information was desired by consumers and from what sources would guide customer information programs. Third, an estimate of the effect on intentions of alternative financing methods in general and a PG&E leasing program in particular had to be developed. Fourth, descriptions of the different customer groups on the basis of awareness, knowledge, attitudes, and intentions were required.

Several specific hypotheses were developed, based in part upon some marketing research conducted by the San Diego Gas and Electric Company. The hypotheses were intended to make the issues represented by the research questions more specific and to summarize current thinking about customers' positions toward solar energy.

1 Interest in and general awareness of solar energy is high, but knowledge of specific applications, including solar water heaters, is rather low.

2 Solar energy is regarded as expensive and not yet fully perfected.

3 Attractions of solar energy include saving money, conserving energy, helping the environment, and being innovative. Cost payback is a very important consideration in any solar energy decision.

4 Utilities are generally perceived as reliable sources of information and equipment.

5 Solar leasing by utilities will be attractive to one segment because less investment is required and because a utility company would be trusted to assure performance. Another segment will be opposed to utility involvement with solar programs.

6 There should be a positive association between knowledge and intention, because information should influence intentions and because interested people seek out information.

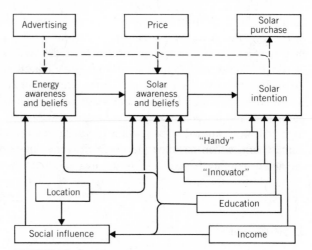

EXHIBIT II–2 Hypothesized model

7 People interested in installing solar water heaters tend to be young, affluent, well-educated, concerned about energy, "handy" people who enjoy trying new things, and owners or friends of owners of swimming pools.

These hypotheses, together with other opinions, served as the basis for a tentative model of the decision process associated with solar water heaters. This model is shown in Exhibit II–2.

Methodology

The research approach was a telephone interview of a sample of 200 homeowners in the San Francisco Bay Area. The questionnaire is shown in the next section. A telephone survey was selected because it is relatively free of bias, economical, and fast.

The target population for the survey was all PG&E customers in the San Francisco Bay Area who own their own detached homes. The sample was obtained from the telephone directories of the six Bay Area counties. The sample was divided among the Bay Area counties on the basis of the county populations. Thus, there were to be 70 respondents in the largest county and 14 in the smallest. Within each county a sample was drawn by systematically sampling from the telephone directory. If a telephone interviewer needed 25 respondents and the directory allocated to her or him contained 250 pages, then one respondent would be obtained from every tenth page. On each selected page the interviewer would measure a fixed amount, such as three inches from the top of the first column. The interviewer would then begin calling people starting at that point and continue until a completed interview was obtained.

Telephone Interview Format

Appendix
Respondent No. ＿＿＿ ＿＿＿＿＿ (1–3)
City ＿＿＿＿＿＿＿ ＿＿＿＿＿＿ (4)

SOLAR ENERGY SURVEY

Hello, I'm ＿＿＿＿ from Drexel Research Corporation, a national consumer research firm. We're taking a survey in your area about home energy use and would like to ask you a few questions. May I please speak to the head of the household? (*IF THE HEAD OF THE HOUSEHOLD IS NOT AVAILABLE, THANK THE PERSON ON THE PHONE AND TERMINATE THE INTERVIEW. IF THE HEAD OF THE HOUSEHOLD IS REACHED, REINTRODUCE YOURSELF AND PROCEED.*)

1. Do you own or rent the home in which you live?

Own ＿＿(CONTINUE)＿＿＿＿＿＿＿ ☐
Rent ＿＿(TERMINATE)

1a. Is that home a single family dwelling?

Yes ＿＿(CONTINUE)＿＿＿＿＿＿＿ ☐
No ＿＿(TERMINATE)

2. I'm going to read you a few statements about energy conservation and for each one I'd like you to tell me whether you agree or disagree with it. (READ STATEMENTS BELOW)
(FOR EACH STATEMENT "AGREE" WITH, ASK:)
Do you agree completely or somewhat?
(FOR EACH STATEMENT "DISAGREE" WITH, ASK:)
Do you disagree somewhat or completely?

| | AGREE | | DISAGREE | |
	Completely	Somewhat	Somewhat	Completely
a. It is important for the United States to have an energy conservation program	＿＿1	＿＿2	＿＿3	＿＿4 (6)
b. What an individual consumer does or does *not* do to save energy has a meaningful effect on the energy shortage	＿＿1	＿＿2	＿＿3	＿＿4 (7)

    c. New supplies of
natural gas will be
discovered before
any serious
shortages develop   _____1   _____2   _____3   _____4   (8)

3. I'd like to know how well the following statements describe you. Please tell me whether
you agree completely, agree somewhat, disagree somewhat or disagree completely
with . . . (READ LIST)

I generally like to try
new ideas at work and
in my life   _____1   _____2   _____3   _____4   (9)

I like to experiment
with new ways of
doing things   _____1   _____2   _____3   _____4   (10)

	Agree Completely	Agree Somewhat	Disagree Somewhat	Disagree Completely	
I like to build things for my house	_____1	_____2	_____3	_____4	(11)
I like to fix things around the house	_____1	_____2	_____3	_____4	(12)
I wait for new things to be proven before trying them	_____1	_____2	_____3	_____4	(13)

4. Now I'd like to talk about solar energy. Please tell me all the ways that you can think
of that solar energy can be used in the home. (PROBE AND CLARIFY)

_____ (14)

_____ (15)

_____ (16)

_____ (17)

5a. Have you seen any advertisements or brochures about solar energy devices recently?

                    (18)

         Yes ___(CONTINUE) _____   1

         No ___(SKIP TO Q. 5c) _____   2

5b. Who was the advertisement or brochure from?

_____ (19)

_____

5c. Have you read any articles about solar energy recently in magazines or newspapers?

                    (20)

         Yes _____   1

         _____   2

6a. Have you seen any displays of solar equipment?

(21)

Yes ____(CONTINUE) _____ 1

No ____(SKIP TO Q. 7a) _____ 2

6b. Where did you see this display?

_____ (22)

7a. Have you ever seen a solar heating unit on a house or building?

(23)

Yes ____(CONTINUE) _____ 1

No ____(SKIP TO Q. 8) _____ 2

7b. Where was that?

_____ (24)

_____

8. Have you ever discussed solar energy with your friends?

(25)

Yes _____ 1

No _____ 2

9a. Have you ever considered buying a solar water heater for your home?

(26)

Yes ____(CONTINUE) _____ 1

No ____(SKIP TO Q. 10) _____ 2

9b. What kind was that? (PROBE AND CLARIFY)

_____ (27)

_____

_____ (28)

10a. What would be the main *advantage* of having a solar water heater in your home? (PROBE:)
What other advantages?

_____ (29)

_____

_____ (30)

10b. And what would be the main *disadvantage* of having a solar water heater? (PROBE:)
What other disadvantages?

_____ (31)

_____

_____ (32)

11a. About how much would you estimate your average monthly utility bill is for gas and electricity?

$ _____ (33)

11b. About how much per month do you think you might save on your gas and electricity bill if you had a solar water heater?

$ _____ (34)

12a. As you may know, water in a solar water heater is pumped through solar collector panels on the roof and stored in a tank. This water is then heated additionally by the existing water heater if it isn't hot enough—say on a cloudy day. A solar water heater costs around $1,500 installed, and can save $4 to $5 per month on your gas bill. How interested do you think you might be in buying and installing a solar water heater in your home? Would you say you would be . . . (READ LIST)

(35)

Definitely interested in buying one _____(CONTINUE) _____	1
Somewhat interested in buying one ____(SKIP TO Q. 13a) _____	2
or Not at all interested in buying one ____(SKIP TO Q. 13a) _____	3

12b. If you did purchase a solar water heater, would you pay cash for it or finance it?

(36)

Pay cash _____	1
Finance _____	2

13a. Have you heard that you can deduct 10% of the cost of any solar equipment you buy from your state income tax?

(37)

Yes _____	1
No _____	2

13b. Would this tax deduction make you more likely to buy a solar water heater, less likely to buy one, or wouldn't make any difference one way or the other?

(38)

More likely _____	1
Less likely _____	2
No difference _____	3

14a. If you could lease a water heater for a lower monthly charge than a loan payment, would you rather lease one than buy one?

(39)

Yes ____(CONTINUE) _____		1
No _____	SKIP TO	2
No difference _____	Q. 15a	3

14b. Who would you prefer to *lease* a solar water heater from . . . (READ LIST)

(40)

A utility company _____(ASK Q. 14c, THEN SKIP TO Q. 15a)		1
The government _____	SKIP TO	2
or Some other company _____	Q. 14d	3

14c. Why would you prefer to lease from a utility company? (PROBE AND CLARIFY)

_____ (41)

_____

_____ (42)

14d. Why wouldn't you want to lease it from a utility company? (PROBE AND CLARIFY)

_____ (43)

_____

_____ (44)

15a. What information would you need to have before deciding on buying a solar water heater? (PROBE AND CLARIFY)

_____ (45)

_____ (46)

_____ (62)

15b. Which of the following would you consider to be the most reliable source of information on solar water heaters . . . (READ LIST)

	(47)
A solar heater company _____	1
The government _____	2
A utility company _____	3

16a. Do you have a swimming pool?

	(48)
Yes ____(CONTINUE) _____	1
No ____(SKIP TO Q. 17) _____	2

16b. Is your pool heated?

	(49)
Yes ____(CONTINUE) _____	1
No ____(SKIP TO Q. 16d) _____	2

16c. How is your pool heated?

	(50)
Gas heater _____	1
Solar heater _____	2
Other (specify) _____	x

16d. Do you have a pool cover?

	(51)
Yes _____	1
No _____	2

Now I need to ask some questions about you and your home so we can classify your answers with those of the others on this survey.

17. What is the total number of rooms in your home, excluding bathrooms?

_____ (52)

18. Approximately how old is your home? (DO NOT READ LIST)

Years	(53)
1 or less _____	1
2 _____	2
3 _____	3
4–7 _____	4
8–10 _____	5
11–15 _____	6
16–20 _____	7
Over 25 _____	8
Don't know _____	9

19. How many people are living in your home, including yourself?

_____ (54)

20. Are you—(READ LIST)

	(55)
Married _____	1
Single, widowed, or divorced _____	2

21. Are there any children under the age of 18 living at home with you?

	(56)
Yes _____	1
No _____	2

22. Into which of the following groups does your age fall? (READ LIST)

	(57)
Under 25 _____	1
25–35 _____	2
36–49 _____	3
50–64 _____	4
65 and over _____	5
(DO NOT READ) Refused _____	0

23. Which of the following best describes the amount of formal education you had the opportunity to complete? (READ LIST)

	(58)
Grade school _____	1
Some high school _____	2
Graduated high school _____	3
Some college _____	4
Graduated college _____	5

24. Which of the following categories best describes the approximate market value of your home? (READ LIST)

(59)

Under $25,000 _____	1
$25,000–$34,999 _____	2
$35,000–$49,999 _____	3
$50,000–$59,999 _____	4
$60,000–$75,000 _____	5
Over $75,000 _____	6
(DO NOT READ) ⊣ ⌈ Don't know _____	0
⌊ Refused _____	0

25. Which of the following groups best represents your total annual family income before taxes? (READ LIST)

(60)

Under $10,000 _____	1
$10,000–$14,999 _____	2
$15,000–$19,999 _____	3
$20,000–$24,999 _____	4
$25,000–$35,000 _____	5
Over $35,000 _____	6
(DO NOT READ) Refused _____	0

26. (RECORD ONLY:) Sex

(61)

Male _____	1
Female _____	2

CASE II–2 BELLBOY[1]

The Southwestern Bell Telephone Company (SWB) has applied to the FCC for permission to initiate a new service known as BELLBOY in the Dallas/Fort Worth area. As a regulated monopoly, SWB is under the control of the FCC with respect to new services. (See Exhibit II–2 for a recent ruling). The proposed BELLBOY system is a compact, lightweight, one-way signaling device about the size of a candy bar. It is carried when the user is away from the office telephone. Someone can contact the user by simply dialing a special number which gives a "beep" signal from the BELLBOY. The user then would call the office from any nearby phone.

[1]This case is used with the permission of Associate Professor A. Bruno and Assistant Professor S. G. McIntyre, Santa Clara University.

In order to be granted a permit to operate the service in the new area, SWB must submit to the FCC evidence of a "substantial unmet demand" for the service in the relevant market. If the evidence submitted is not contested and seems reasonable to the FCC, then the permit will be granted. Exact procedures have not been established yet as to what constitutes acceptable demonstration of "unmet demand," except for the fact that in one similar case New York Telephone used a survey technique to secure a license.

Accordingly, SWB has hired a consultant who has conducted the following survey (Exhibit II–3).

Two companies that already provide a similar one-way signaling service in the Dallas/Fort Worth area are very disturbed by the impending competition from the telephone monopoly; these companies view the market as small but well served at present. Therefore, lawyers have been hired to contest the SWB application before the FCC. These lawyers, in turn, have called upon you, as an expert in survey techniques, to criticize the SWB survey. The following information is provided:

Exhibit II–1   Internal memorandum from the lawyers
Exhibit II–2   Quote from a recent and relevant FCC ruling
Exhibit II–3   The survey report done for SWB by Peters Marketing Research

EXHIBIT II–1
Memorandum

October 7, 1976

To: PBP File No. 1498
2230

From: AB

Re: Southwestern Bell's amendment dated September 29,
     1976 to the Dallas-Fort Worth guardband application
     which has been protested by Page A Fone and FWS

On October 4 we transmitted to you a copy of the referenced amendment which includes what in effect amounts to a further survey of need. I believe that this survey should be critically evaluated or refuted or at least weakened to the full extent possible so that we will establish a complete record for a possible court appeal. It seems to me that the survey is a sort of a theoretical exercise which does not demonstrate in any practical sense that there is a need for Bell's paging service. Nevertheless, the Commission may be inclined to accept it uncritically unless we attack it successfully; and *in view of the New York Telephone Company holding that a survey of need will be accepted unless the existing carriers raise substantial and material questions regarding it,* we have no choice but to contest it if at all possible.

One thought that has occurred to me with respect to the three price levels used in the survey is that *there has been no showing that any one of these prices is just and reasonable as it must be under the accepted common carrier pricing standards.*

Thus, a response by any member of the public to any one of the three prices does not establish a valid basis for determining the need because any one of the three prices might be unrealistic, meaning that the proposed service could not actually be offered at those prices. Also, as you pointed out in one of the recent pleadings, *this type of a survey merely establishes the existence of a continuing market, not the existence of a need or demand for additional services.*

Finally, perhaps we should ascertain from Page A Fone and FWS what efforts they have been making recently to aggressively promote their paging services. If such promotion has not resulted in an upsurge of orders, this would suggest that there is no *unsatisfied* demand, regardless of what the survey shows. This would also constitute a "substantial and material question" about the validity of the survey.

AB: ln

EXHIBIT II–2
Quote from FCC Ruling

Statement by the Federal Communications Commission in the matter of Application of New York Telephone Co. for Permit for a new one-way signaling Base Station on 152.84 MH in Buffalo, N.Y. (June 19, 1974)

"We shall apply the following policy in consideration of applications by common carriers in this service: If the applicant for a new frequency can *demonstrate substantial unsatisfied need* for service by one or more of the alternative methods set forth in Long Island Paging and existing carriers fail to raise *substantial and material questions* regarding that need showing, then no hearing will be required on this issue. Where a prospective carrier surveys a particular market and demonstrates that substantial unsatisfied demand exists despite the presence of other carriers offering the same or similar services, his application will be granted."

EXHIBIT II–3
Bellboy Attitudinal Evaluation Survey (Dallas/Fort Worth)

---

1. *TEST SUMMARY*

   A. *Objectives*

   The objectives of this study were to determine:

   The interest in BELLBOY service among businesses in the Dallas/Fort Worth metropolitan area.

   Among those interested it was further desired to determine:
   - The types of companies and types of jobs in those companies that could benefit most from BELLBOY service; and,
   - Reaction to three possible monthly charges.

B. Method And Sample Selection

Three hundred and eighty-two telephone interviews were conducted with the *individual in charge of communication needs* at businesses throughout the Dallas/Fort Worth metropolitan area.

The telephone numbers of the businesses were supplied by Southwestern Bell Telephone Company and sample selection was implemented by Southwestern Bell Telephone Company on a systematic random basis selecting every Nth number and included all business listings as of July 1975.

Each business contacted was selected from the lists provided on a systematic random basis to comprise the primary sample. In addition, total remaining listings were randomly selected to form the sub-sample to be used as necessary for substitution to the primary sample.

A primary listing was replaced with a subsample listing only after one of the following circumstances was encountered which would have precluded a 'completed' interview:

- Three unsuccessful attempts had been made to contact the 'key' individual on three different days, or three times a day;
- A refusal on the part of the respondent;
- Unavailability of the 'key' person throughout the alloted calling time;
- Disconnected/not in service telephone numbers; and,
- A Southwestern Bell Telephone number selected as part of the sample.

All telephoning was conducted by Peters Marketing Research personnel during late July and early August, 1975.

C. Interview Procedure

Upon reaching the randomly pre-selected company, an attempt was made to speak with the person at that company who handled communications. If that person were not available a callback was made at a later time.

Upon reaching the desired individual, it was explained that we were conducting a survey for the telephone company about a new service called BELLBOY, and wanted to obtain their opinions concerning this new service.

Next, BELLBOY service was briefly explained and the respondent indicated their general interest in the service, assuming it would be reasonably priced.

Those not interested were questioned concerning their reasons for lack of interest. The interview was then concluded.

Those interested in BELLBOY service were asked to briefly describe their company's business and to indicate anticipated benefits from the BELLBOY service.

Reaction to the number of potential users at three price levels was then determined.

2. MANAGEMENT SUMMARY

A. In total, approximately one-fourth of all companies contacted indicated an interest in using the BELLBOY service, assuming the price was reasonable.

Projecting this response pattern to the entire Dallas/Fort Worth Metropolitan area which consists of 74,789 (approximate) business customers/potential customers can be derived as follows:

Low Estimate:

11,218—composed of those indicating a "yes" response.

High Estimate:

14,210—composed of those indicating a "yes" response and one-half of those indicating a "maybe" response.

Respondents Interested or Not Interested in Using This Service

	Percentage of Sample[a]	Projected Number of Customer Companies
Yes	15%	11,218.35
Maybe	8	5,983.12
No	77	57,587.53
Total	100%	74,789
Base	(382)	(74,789)

[a]See Table 1.

B. Those companies that indicated yes or maybe were asked to indicate the number of employees who could be possible users of "BELLBOY" at specified prices.

As seen from the following table, potential usage of "BELLBOY" service by more employees increases as the alternative prices decrease at all but one level.

Potential Usage by Price[a]

NUMBER OF EMPLOYEES	At $24			At $20			At $16		
	Total %	Yes %	Maybe %	Total %	Yes %	Maybe %	Total %	Yes %	Maybe %
1–3	36	36	35	47	50	42	54	64	35
4–5	5	4	7	7	5	11	9	7	14
6–10	5	5	4	6	7	3	11	8	14
11–25	2	2	3	2	2	3	1	—	3
26–75	—	—	—	—	—	—	1	2	—
Over 75	1	—	3	1	—	3	1	—	3
Don't know	1	—	3	1	—	3	1	—	3
None	50	53	45	36	36	35	22	19	28
Total	100	100	100	100	100	100	100	100	100

[a]See Tables 6, 7, 8.

C. In an effort to evaluate the effect of the monthly charge on company usage and subsequent revenues, the following two projected monthly revenue tables have been developed. Figures shown are percentages developed in the previous table and applied to the 74,789 Dallas/Fort Worth metropolitan business customers.

It is apparent from the tables regarding the high (yes + 1/2 maybe) estimate that, with increased market penetration brought about by price reduction, total revenues at first decrease (at the $20.00 per unit level) and then increase (at the $16.00 per unit level). Total revenues increase for each lower price schedule when considering the low (yes only) estimate.

Also apparent, in terms of our customer mix at the prices evaluated, is the relatively small size of the average customer, and the importance in terms of revenue of the very large customer.

D. As indicated by Table 9, those companies by type of business most interested in "BELLBOY" were service, retailing, construction and professional organizations.

E. As might be expected, the jobs in which companies indicated the primary needs were those where employees were consistently away from the office or where a key employee would need to be contacted. See Table 4.

F. Those companies not interested in the BELLBOY service often indicated that they were 'always in the office' and did not need to contact anyone outside. Other companies indicated that there was 'just no need' for the service. Some companies also stated their business was 'too small' and did not have enough employees to warrant the service. See Table 3.

It should be remembered that no sales effort was employed as part of this project. Obviously, it could be anticipated that many companies expressing a lack of interest might alter their opinion if the advantages of BELLBOY were made more apparent through personal sales contact.

Projected Monthly Revenues
High Estimate of Potential Market (14,210 companies)

At $24.00 Per Month, Per Unit			
Number Of Companies	Average Number Of Employees	Number Of BELLBOY Units	Monthly Revenue
5086	2	10,172	$244,128
658	4.5	2,961	71,064
681	8	5,448	130,752
314	18	5,652	135,648
90	100	9,000	216,000
Total 6829	—	33,233	$797,592

Average number of BELLBOY units per customer—4.87

At $20.00 Per Month, Per Unit			
Number Of Companies	Average Number Of Employees	Number Of BELLBOY Units	Monthly Revenue
6866	2	13,732	$274,640
890	4.5	4,005	80,100
875	8	7,000	140,000
314	18	5,652	113,040
90	100	9,000	180,000
Total 9035	—	39,389	$787,780

Average number of BELLBOY units per customer—4.36

Projected Monthly Revenues
High Estimate of Potential Market (14,210 companies)

| | At $16.00 Per Month, Per Unit | | |
Number Of Companies	Average Number Of Employees	Number Of BELLBOY Units	Monthly Revenue
8227	2	16,454	$263,264
1204	4.5	5,418	86,688
1316	8	10,528	168,448
90	18	1,620	25,920
224	50.5	11,312	180,992
90	100	9,000	144,000
Total 11,151	—	54,332	$869,312

Average number of BELLBOY units per customer—4.87

Projected Monthly Revenues
Low Estimate of Potential Market (11,218 companies)

| | At $24.00 Per Month, Per Unit | | |
Number Of Companies	Average Number Of Employees	Number Of BELLBOY Units	Monthly Revenue
4039	2	8,078	$193,872
449	4.5	2,020.5	48,492
561	8	4,488	107,712
224	18	4,032	96,768
Total 5273	—	18,618.5	$446,844

Average number of BELLBOY units per customer—3.53

| | At $20.00 Per Month, Per Unit | | |
Number Of Companies	Average Number Of Employees	Number Of BELLBOY Units	Monthly Revenue
5609	2	11,218	$224,360
561	4.5	2,524.5	50,490
785	8	6,280	125,600
224	18	4,032	80,640
Total 7179	—	24,054.5	$481,090

Average number of BELLBOY units per customer—3.35

Projected Monthly Revenues
Low Estimate of Potential Market (11,218)

At $16.00 Per Month, Per Unit			
Number Of Companies	Average Number Of Employees	Number Of BELLBOY Units	Monthly Revenue
7180	2	14,360	$229,760
785	4.5	3,532.5	56,520
897	8	7,176	114,816
224	50.5	11,312	180,992
Total 9086	—	36,380.5	$582,088

Average number of BELLBOY units per customer—4.00

TABLE 1

Respondents Interested or Not Interested in Using This Service (Base: 382)

Base	(382)
	(%)
Yes	15
Maybe	8
No	77
Total	100

Based on answers to the question: (Q.3) "If the monthly rate for this service was reasonable from your standpoint, would you be interested in using this service in the operation of your business?"

TABLE 2

Respondents Who Are or Are Not Familiar with a One-Way Pocket Signaling Unit

	Companies Interested (Base: 87)	Companies Not Interested (Base: 295)
	%	%
Yes	62	50
No	38	50
Total	100	100

Based on answers to the question: (Q.2) "Are you familiar with a one-way pocket signaling unit?"

TABLE 3

Reasons Respondents Are Not Interested in BELLBOY service (Base: 295)

Reason	% Giving This Reason
Always in office/no need to contact anyone outside	29
Just don't need/not interested	24
Business too small/not that many employees	11
Always able to reach/keep close contact	10
Have own communications system	6
Have two-way radios/mobile phones/car radios	5
System has too short a range/doesn't cover enough territory	5
Have system like this	4
Don't want interruptions when away from office	3
Salespeople call in/employees call us	3
Other	4
Total	104

Based on answers to the question: (Q.4) "You probably have a good reason why you feel BELLBOY service would not interest you. Would you mind telling me what it is?"

TABLE 4

Types of Jobs That Might Benefit from the BELLBOY service

		Total %	Yes %	Maybe %
	Base:	(87)	(58)	(29)
Employees in the field/salespeople/ people on the road		51	52	48
Supervisor/manager/owner/president		40	45	31
Service people		15	16	14
Professional		9	9	10
Administrative/office personnel		5	7	—
Total		120	129	103

Based on answers to the question: (Q.5) "What types of jobs do the people have that might benefit from BELLBOY service?"

TABLE 5

Number of Employees Who Work at Jobs That Might Benefit from BELLBOY service

		Total %	Yes %	Maybe %
	Base:	(87)	(58)	(29)
One		20	21	21
Two		14	16	10
Three		20	24	14
Four		10	12	7
Five		12	12	10
Six		5	3	7
Seven–nine		5	7	—
Ten–twenty		6	3	10
Twenty-one and over		7	2	17
Refused		1	—	4
Total		100	100	100

Based on answers to the question: (Q.6) "About how many employees do you have in these types of jobs?"

TABLE 6

Number of Employees Who Could Be Possible Users of the Service for $24.00 per Month

	Total %	Yes %	Maybe %
Base:	(87)	(58)	(29)
One–three	36	36	35
Four–five	5	4	7
Six–ten	5	5	4
Eleven–twenty-five	2	2	3
Twenty-six–seventy-five	—	—	—
Over seventy-five	1	—	3
Don't know	1	—	3
None	50	53	45
Total	100	100	100

Based on answers to the question: (Q.7) "If the price for each BELLBOY unit was about $1.15 per business day or about $24.00 per month, how many employees could be possible users of this service?"

TABLE 7

Number of Employees Who Could Be Possible Users of the Service for $20.00 per Month

	Total %	Yes %	Maybe %
Base:	(87)	(58)	(29)
One–three	47	50	42
Four–five	7	5	11
Six–ten	6	7	3
Eleven–twenty-five	2	2	3
Twenty-six–seventy-five	—	—	—
Over seventy-five	1	—	3
Don't know	1	—	3
None	36	36	35
Total	100	100	100

Based on answers to the question: (Q.8) "If the price were lowered to $.95 per business day, or about $20.00 per month per unit, how many employees would be possible users of this service?"

TABLE 8

Number of Employees Who Could Be Possible Users of the Service for $16.00 per Month

	Base:	Total % (87)	Yes % (58)	Maybe % (29)
One–three		54	64	35
Four–five		9	7	14
Six–ten		11	8	14
Eleven–twenty-five		1	—	3
Twenty-six–seventy-five		1	2	—
Over 75		1	—	3
Don't know		1	—	3
None		22	19	28
Total		100	100	100

Based on answers to the question: (Q.9) "If the price were lowered to $.75 per business day, or about $16.00 per month per unit, how many employees would be possible BELLBOY users?"

TABLE 9

Type of Company Business

	Base:	Total % (87)	Yes % (58)	Maybe % (29)
Service		34	34	35
Retailing		30	31	28
Construction		10	9	14
Professional		9	10	17
Real Estate		6	5	7
Manufacturing		3	5	—
Other		14	12	17
Total		106	106	118

Based on answers to the question: (Q.10) "It would be helpful if you could briefly describe your company's business."

TABLE 10

Number of Employees in Company

		Total %	Yes %	Maybe %
	Base:	(87)	(58)	(29)
One		2	3	—
Two		2	2	3
Three		7	10	—
Four		11	15	3
Five		10	9	14
Six		6	7	4
Seven		5	5	4
Eight		5	5	4
Nine–Twenty		25	26	24
Twenty-one–thirty		6	9	—
Thirty-one–forty		2	2	3
Forty-one–fifty		1	—	3
Fifty-one–ninety-nine		4	—	10
One hundred and over		13	5	28
Don't know		1	2	—
Total		100	100	100

Based on answers to the question: (Q.11) "About how many employees does your company have in (CITY NAME _____)?"

BELLBOY Telephone Interview

RESPONDENT NAME _____

TELEPHONE

COMPANY _____ AREA CODE _____ PHONE _____

CALLS: DATE/TIME   1st _____ 2nd _____ 3rd _____

INTRODUCTION

Hello, I'm _____ of Peters Marketing Research. We are conducting a study for the TELE-PHONE COMPANY and I would like to talk with the person that handles _____ (CO. NAME) communications needs. Have I reached that person?

Yes (_____)
No (_____)

   *IF YES, GET NAME AND GO TO "AGREEMENT"
  **IF NO, GET NAME, ASK TO BE CONNECTED, AND GO BACK TO "INTRODUCTION"
***IF NO, AND THE PERSON CANNOT BE CONTACTED, GET NAME AND CALL BACK

AGREEMENT

Mr./Ms. _____, as I mentioned, the TELEPHONE COMPANY has asked us to conduct a study and gather information about a new service that might be offered. This new service is entitled BELLBOY.

1. Would you mind if I asked a few questions to get your opinion concerning this service?
   Okay   (_____)-GO TO Q.2
   Not okay   (_____) TERMINATE INTERVIEW

2. Are you familiar with a one-way pocket signaling unit?
   Yes   (_____)
   No   (_____)-GO TO EXPLANATION

EXPLANATION OF BELLBOY SERVICE

Well, briefly, Southwestern Bell's BELLBOY is a compact, lightweight, one-way signaling device about the size of a candy bar. There are others that are similar but the BELLBOY unit fits easily into your pocket. BELLBOY is carried whenever you are away from your office. Your people can contact you simply by dialing a number which gives you a "beep" signal from your BELLBOY. The "beep" tells you someone wants to reach you. You then would call your office from any nearby telephone.

3. If the monthly rate for this service was reasonable from your standpoint, would you be interested in using this service in the operation of your business?
   Yes   (_____)-GO to Q.5
   Maybe   (_____)
   No   (_____)-GO to Q.4, THEN
                                   TERMINATE

4. You probably have a good reason why you feel BELLBOY service would not interest you; would you mind telling me what it is?

_____

_____

_____

_____

_____

_____

_____

5. What types of jobs do the people have that might benefit from the BELLBOY service?

6. About how many employees do you have in these types of jobs? _____.

7. If the price for each BELLBOY unit was about $1.15 per business day or about $24.00 per month, how many employees could be possible users of this service?

0	(_____)
1–3	(_____)
4–5	(_____)
6–10	(_____)
11–25	(_____)
26–75	(_____)
Over 75	(_____)
Don't know	(_____)

    ENTER ACTUAL ANSWER

8. If the price were lowered to $.95 per business day, or about $20.00 per month per unit, how many employees would be possible users of this service?

0	(_____)
1–3	(_____)
4–5	(_____)
6–10	(_____)
11–25	(_____)
26–75	(_____)
Over 75	(_____)
Don't know	(_____)

    ENTER ACTUAL ANSWER

9. If the price were lowered to $.75 per business day, or about $16.00 per month per unit, how many employees would be possible BELLBOY users?

0	(_____)
1–3	(_____)
4–5	(_____)
6–10	(_____)
11–25	(_____)
26–75	(_____)
Over 75	(_____)
Don't know	(_____)

    ENTER ACTUAL ANSWER

10. It would be helpful if you could briefly describe your company's business.

    _____

    _____

    _____

11. About how many employees does your company have in (CITY NAME) _____?

part III

DATA ANALYSIS

12

FUNDAMENTALS OF DATA ANALYSIS

The HMO study introduced in Chapter 2 resulted in a survey from which 1145 usable questionnaires were obtained. This represents a stack of paper literally over 10 feet high. Data analysis plays an important role in turning this quantity of paper into defensible, actionable sets of conclusions and reports. It is actually a set of methods and techniques that can be used to obtain information and insights from the data.

An understanding of the principles of data analysis is useful for several reasons. First, it can lead the researcher to information and insights that otherwise would not be available. Second, it can help avoid erroneous judgments and conclusions. Third, it can provide a background to help interpret and understand analysis conducted by others. Finally, a knowledge of the power of data analysis techniques can constructively influence the research objectives and the research design.

Although data analysis can be a powerful aid to gaining useful knowledge, it cannot rescue a badly conceived marketing research study. If the research purpose is not well conceived, if the research questions are irrelevant, or if the hypothesis is nonviable or uninteresting, then the research will require an abundance of good fortune to be useful. Further, data analysis rarely can compensate for a bad question, an inadequate sampling procedure, or sloppy fieldwork.

On the other hand, data analysis has the potential to ruin a well-designed study. Inappropriate or misused data analysis can suggest judgments and conclusions that are at best unclear and incomplete and at worst erroneous. It thus can lead to decisions inferior to those that would have been made without the benefit of the research. One important reason for studying data analysis, therefore, is to avoid the pitfalls associated with it.

The purpose of parts 3 and 4 of this book is to describe data analysis techniques so that when the appropriate situation arises the researcher can draw upon them. Another goal is to provide an understanding of the limitations of the various techniques, so that the likelihood that they will be misused or misinterpreted will be minimized. The techniques and approaches exposed in this chapter are used routinely by nearly all descriptive and causal research. It is, therefore, important for the reader to understand them.

The type of data analysis required will be unique to each study; however, nearly all studies involving data analysis will require the editing and coding of data, will draw upon one or more data analysis techniques, and will have to be concerned with presenting the results effectively.

1 Data editing and coding—Chapter 12
2 Data analysis techniques
    a Question tabulation—Chapter 12
    b Question tabulation among subgroups in the sample—Chapter 12
       • Difference between means
       • Cross-tabulations
    c Correlation analysis—Chapter 12
    d The analysis of three questions—Chapter 14
    e Multivariate analysis—Part IV
       • Factor analysis
       • Multidimensional scaling
       • Cluster analysis
       • Conjoint analysis
       • Regression analysis
       • AID
       • Discriminant analysis
3 Presenting the results—Chapter 15

In this chapter the data editing and coding phase will be discussed first. Basic ways to tabulate individual questions from a questionnaire then will be developed. Next the focus will turn to question tabulation among sample subgroups and correlation analysis. Hypothesis testing is introduced in this chapter, although it is treated more completely in Chapter 13. Subsequent chapters examine the other data analysis techniques.

EDITING AND CODING

Editing

The role of the editing process is to identify omissions, ambiguities, and errors in the responses. It should be conducted in the field by the interviewer and field supervisor, as well as by the analyst just prior to data analysis. Among the problems to be identified are the following:

1 *Interviewer error*. Interviewers may not be giving the respondent the correct instructions.

2 *Omissions.* Respondents often fail to answer a single question or a section of the questionnaire, either deliberately or inadvertently.

3 *Ambiguity.* A response might not be legible or it might be unclear which of two boxes is checked in a multiple response system.

4 *Inconsistencies.* Sometimes two responses can be logically inconsistent. For example, a respondent who is a lawyer may have checked a box indicating that he or she did not complete high school.

5 *Lack of cooperation.* In a long questionnaire with hundreds of attitude or image questions, a respondent might rebel and check the same response (in an agree–disagree scale, for example) for a long list of questions.

6 *Ineligible respondent.* An inappropriate respondent may be included in the sample. For example, if a sample is supposed to include only women over 18, others should be excluded.

When such problems are identified, there are several alternatives available. The preferred alternative, where practical, is to recontact the respondent. This is often quite feasible and should be done by the interviewer if the questions involved are important enough to warrant the effort. Another alternative, to throw out the whole questionnaire as not usable, might be appropriate if it were clear that the respondent either did not understand the survey or was not cooperating. A less extreme alternative is to throw out only the problem questions and retain the balance of the questions. Some respondents will bypass questions like income or age, for example, and cooperate fully with the other questions. When the analysis involves income or age, only those respondents who answered those questions will be included, but in the rest of the analysis all respondents could be included. Still another alternative is to code illegible or missing answers into a category such as ''don't know'' or ''no opinion.'' Such an approach may simplify the data analysis without materially distorting the interpretation.

A byproduct of the editing process is to provide evaluation and guidance to the interviewers. A tendency of an interviewer to allow a certain type of error to occur should be detected by the editing process.

Coding

Coding the closed-ended questions is fairly straightforward. In this process, we specify exactly how the responses are to be entered. Figure 12–1 shows three of the questions for the HMO study introduced in Chapter 2. Question 18 is to be entered in column 46. The responses are coded as 1 through 5. Thus, if ''I am not sure now'' were checked, a ''3'' would be entered in column 46. Similarly, the next question would be entered in column 47. Question 20 will be entered in columns 48 and 49.

Coding for open-ended questions is much more difficult. Usually a lengthy list of possible responses is generated and then each response is placed into one of the list items. Often the assignment of a response involves a judgment decision if the response does not

18. As a general guess, do you think you or your family would now enroll in a plan similar to the one we have described, should it be available?
    1. ☐ Yes, I would enroll
    2. ☐ I would probably enroll
    3. ☐ I am not sure now   46
    4. ☐ I would probably not enroll
    5. ☐ No, I would not enroll
19. What approximately was your total family income for last year? (Before tax and deductions).
    1. ☐   Below $4000
    2. ☐ $4000–$6999
    3. ☐ $7000–$9999
    4. ☐ $10,000–$12,999   47
    5. ☐ $13,000–$15,999
    6. ☐ $16,000–$20,000
    7. ☐   More than $20,000
20. What is the age of the head of household? ☐☐   48,49

FIGURE 12–1 Coding questions

exactly match a list item. For example, a question such as, "Why did you select your instrument from Ajax Electronics?" might elicit literally hundreds of different responses, such as price, delivery, accuracy, reliability, familiarity, doesn't break down, can get it repaired, features, includes spare parts, a good manual, appearance, size, and shape. Decisions must be made about the response categories. Should "reliability" and "doesn't break down" be in the same category, or do they represent two different responses? The difficulty of coding and analyzing open-ended responses provides a motivation to avoid them in the questionnaire whenever possible.

TABULATING EACH QUESTION

Usually the first step in data analysis is to analyze each question or measure by itself. There is a variety of ways in which responses to a question can be presented. The most common are a frequency distribution and an average (or percentage).

Frequency Distribution

A frequency distribution simply reports the number of responses that each question received. Figure 12–2 provides a frequency distribution for two of the questions from the HMO study. A key question is the enrollment plan question in which the respondents are

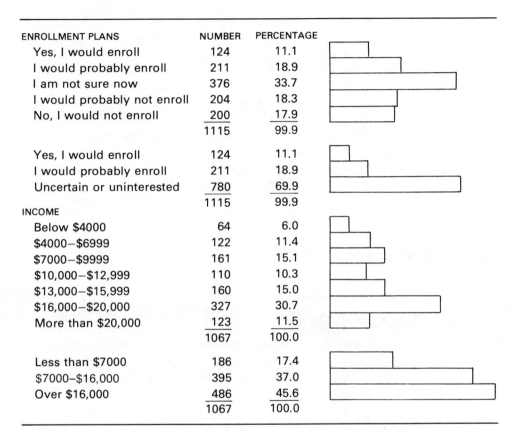

ENROLLMENT PLANS	NUMBER	PERCENTAGE	
Yes, I would enroll	124	11.1	
I would probably enroll	211	18.9	
I am not sure now	376	33.7	
I would probably not enroll	204	18.3	
No, I would not enroll	200	17.9	
	1115	99.9	
Yes, I would enroll	124	11.1	
I would probably enroll	211	18.9	
Uncertain or uninterested	780	69.9	
	1115	99.9	
INCOME			
Below $4000	64	6.0	
$4000–$6999	122	11.4	
$7000–$9999	161	15.1	
$10,000–$12,999	110	10.3	
$13,000–$15,999	160	15.0	
$16,000–$20,000	327	30.7	
More than $20,000	123	11.5	
	1067	100.0	
Less than $7000	186	17.4	
$7000–$16,000	395	37.0	
Over $16,000	486	45.6	
	1067	100.0	

FIGURE 12–2   Frequency distribution

asked if they would enroll in the described plan. The number of people in each response category is shown. Thus, 124 responded ''Yes, I would enroll.'' The figure shows two other methods of presenting the frequency distribution. One is the percentage breakdown of the various categories. The percentage is often easier to interpret than the actual numbers. Rounding errors cause the percentage total to differ from 100 percent. The other is a visual bar-graph presentation. The bottom of the figure shows the same type of presentation for the income question. Note that the sample size is smaller, as some respondents did not answer the income question.

For many questions it is useful to combine some of the question categories. For example, in Figure 12–2 the enrollment question is shown with three of the responses combined into an ''uncertain or uninterested'' category. The logic is that a response of ''I am not sure now'' probably means that the respondent will not enroll. Responses to a new concept usually need to be discounted somewhat to correct for initial curiosity and a desire to please the survey sponsor. Decisions to combine categories should be supported by some kind of logic or theory. Resulting combinations also should result in categories that contain a worthwhile number of respondents. It usually is not useful to work with categories with only a few respondents. In fact, one purpose of combining categories is to develop larger respondent groups. Note that the two lowest income categories had relatively small respondent groups before they were combined.

Why not start with only three categories in each case? The questionnaire then would be shorter and easier to complete. One reason is that before the study is conducted there may be no knowledge as to how the respondents are distributed. If too few categories are planned, then all the respondents may end up in one of them and none in the others. Furthermore, extra categories might make responses more realistic. In the enrollment plan question in Figure 12–2, if there were not five responses available, people might have a greater tendency to check the "I would probably enroll" category.

Means and Percentages

In some situations it is desirable to use a single number to describe the responses to a question. In such circumstances the sample mean or percentage is used.[1] The sample mean is simply the average number, obtained by dividing the sum of the responses to a question by the sample size (the number of respondents to that question). The percentage is the proportion who answered a question a certain way, multiplied by 100.

Table 12–1 illustrates a study of the reaction of members of a community to a transit system. As part of the study, four lifestyle and attitude questions were asked, using a seven-point, agree–disagree scale. The first column of Table 12–1 gives the mean or average score among the 62 respondents. They indicate that the sample in general is concerned with gasoline costs and is not excited about jogging. When the response is based upon two alternatives, or when a single alternative is the focus of the analysis, then the percentage is used. For example, question 5 in Table 12–1 reports that 36 percent of the shoppers live close to a transit station. The balance of Table 12–1 will be discussed shortly.

When to Use What

There is an obvious trade off between the use of the frequency distribution and the use of a single number. The frequency distribution can be unwieldy but does provide more information. For example, Table 12–2 shows the response to an attitude question. The

---

[1]Another candidate is the median, which is simply the middle number. The average income, for example, may be distorted by a few millionaires, while the median income would be a more representative number. The percentage is actually an average itself. Suppose that the percentage of business-people who read *Forbes* is desired. If we code all readers as "1" and all nonreaders as "0" and add up all the ones and divide by the sample size we have the proportion who are readers. The procedure is the same as obtaining an average.

TABLE 12–1

The Rapid Transit User

| | Mean Score | Transit System | | Difference Between Sample Means $\bar{X}_U - \bar{X}_N$ |
		User[a] $\bar{X}_U$	Nonuser[b] $\bar{X}_N$	
Agreement on a 7-point (7 is strongly agree; 1 is strongly disagree) scale to the statements:				
1. I dislike driving	3.7	4.3	2.9	1.4
2. I like to jog	3.9	3.8	4.0	−0.2
3. I am concerned about gasoline costs	5.3	6.1	4.4	1.7[c]
4. I am concerned about air pollution	4.6	4.6	3.9	0.7
Percentage who answer affirmatively to the question:				
5. Do you live within three miles from a transit station?	36%	50%	25%	25%[d]
Sample size	62	28	34	

[a]Average score over the 28 respondents using the transit system.
[b]Average score over the 34 respondents not using the transit system.
[c]Significant at the 0.01 level.
[d]Significant at the 0.10 level.

TABLE 12–2

A Question Response[a]

	Response	Frequency	Percentage
Disagree	−3	300	30
	−2	120	12
I prefer abstract art exhibitions to nonabstract art exhibitions	−1	50	5
	0	50	5
	+1	100	10
	+2	300	30
Agree	+3	80	8

[a]Mean response = −0.3.

average response indicates that the sample is fairly neutral about abstract art. Underlying that mean response, however, is the frequency distribution that indicates that a substantial group likes abstract art, a larger group dislikes it, and, in fact, very few people actually are neutral. In situations where the population is not likely to be clustered around the mean, the frequency distribution can be useful.

When nominal scales are involved, frequency distributions must be employed. Recall from Chapter 8 that a nominal scale is one in which numbers merely label or identify categories of objects. For example, suppose respondents were asked if they lived in an urban area, a suburban area, or a rural area. There would be no way to determine an average number to represent that sample (although the percent who live in rural areas could be used).

THE DIFFERENCE BETWEEN MEANS OR PERCENTAGES

The second step in most data analysis procedures is to repeat the analysis of a single question for various subgroups of the population. Thus, the interest might be in the heavy user, and the analysis would be done for this group. More likely, it would be done for the heavy user, the light user, and the nonuser; and the results would be compared. Responses are usually much more meaningful and useful when a comparison is involved.

There is a variety of variables besides usage that can be used to identify subgroups of interest. In a segmentation study we might focus upon

- Loyal buyers versus nonloyal buyers
- Those interested in abstract art versus those not interested
- Customers of a competing store versus others
- Those aware of our art gallery versus others
- High-income versus moderate-income versus low-income groups

If our initial analysis involved means (or percentages), then the focus would turn to the difference between means (or percentages). If the initial analysis involved frequency distributions then cross-tabulation, the subject of the next section, would be the focus.

Let us return to Table 12–1. It might be of interest to determine how those who use the transit system differ from those who do not use it. Table 12–1 presents the sample means of the five questions for the users and the nonusers. The sample percentages answering positively to the location question also are presented for each group.

The differences between the responses for the two groups provide some interesting insights. The difference between sample means for question 1, for example, indicates that the transit user tends to dislike driving more than the transit nonuser. The question 2 difference indicates that the user shows only a small tendency to enjoy jogging more than the nonusers. The other comparisons suggest that the user is more concerned about gasoline costs and air pollution and lives closer to a transit station.

The difference between means is concerned with the association between two questions, the question defining the groups (transit usage in this case) and another question (question 1 on disliking driving, for example). In terms of the scale definitions introduced in Chapter 8, the question defining the groups would be considered a nominally scaled question and the question upon which the means are based would be considered an intervally scaled question. Of course, the analysis could use three, four, or more groups instead of just two. For example, comparisons could be made among nonusers of the traffic system, light users, medium users, and heavy users.

Hypothesis Testing

Suppose in Table 12–1 that when all community members were surveyed, the mean response to question 3 on gasoline costs was the same for the transit nonusers as for the transit users. However, we have responses only from a sample of all community members. The resulting sample means will depend on which sample is drawn. Thus, if a sample of transit users and nontransit users has been obtained, the sample means usually will differ (because of sampling error) even if the population mean values do not. A reasonable question is how likely it is for there to be a difference in sample means as large as the 1.7 shown in Table 12–1 if the two population groups have the same mean. Footnote c in Table 12–1 indicates the likelihood is under 0.01. Thus, the differences between sample means for question 3 are said to be significant at the 0.01 level. The differences found in question 5 also are significant, although at a lesser level. Thus, the result cannot be dismissed easily as a sampling variation. In many of our analyses we will want to check for statistical significance before proceeding. It would not be wise to spend much time on a result that was simply an accident of sampling. This subject matter and its logic is termed hypothesis testing and will be covered in more detail in the following chapter.

CROSS-TABULATIONS

The objective is still to repeat the analysis of a single question for various subgroups. However, if the initial analysis is based on a frequency distribution instead of sample means, then the appropriate analysis is termed cross-tabulation. It also is called cross-tabs, cross-classification, and contingency table analysis.

Figure 12–3 illustrates cross-tabulation with two examples from the HMO study. The focus here is on the enrollment intentions question. Often a usage or intentions question is the key question in a study. We wish to determine if various groups differ in their intentions. One way to define groups is by using the income question or variable. The top of Figure 12–3 shows an intentions-by-income cross-tabulation. It presents the frequency distribution breakdown for intentions within each of the three income groups. If

INTENTIONS TO ENROLL—BY INCOME

	Less than $7000	$7000—$16,000	Over $16,000	
Most interested	20.4% (38)	11.6% (46)	7.6% (37)	11.3% (121)
Moderately interested	19.4% (36)	11.9% (47)	17.9% (87)	16.0% (170)
Uncertain or uninterested	60.2% (112)	76.5% (302)	74.5% (362)	72.7% (776)
	100% (186)	100% (395)	100% (486)	100% (1067)

(The differences between income groups are significant at .01 level)

INTENTIONS TO ENROLL—BY AGE

	Under 30 Years	30—40 Years	Over 40 Years	
Most interested	14.0% (60)	12.5% (40)	6.6% (24)	11.1% (124)
Moderately interested	21.9% (94)	20.0% (64)	14.5% (53)	18.9% (211)
Uncertain or uninterested	64.1% (276)	67.5% (216)	78.9% (288)	70.0% (780)
	100% (430)	100% (320)	100% (365)	100% (1115)

(The differences between age groups are significant at .01 level)

FIGURE 12–3 Cross-tabulations—the HMO Study (number of respondents in brackets)

the three groups were similar, then each of their frequency distributions should be expected to be similar to that of the total sample (shown at the right). In fact, the higher-income people are less likely to be interested than the middle-income groups, and the low-income group is the most interested. More than 20 percent of the low-income group was classified as "most interested," as contrasted with only 7.6 percent of the high-income group.

The bottom of Figure 12–3 shows the intentions by age cross-tabulation. Again the frequency distribution within each of the subgroups must be compared to the frequency distribution for the total sample, shown at the right. The youngest group has somewhat more interest than the middle group, and both have considerably more interest than the older group.

Cross-tabulation is the analysis of association between two variables that are nominally scaled. Of course, any interval-scaled variable can be used to define groups and therefore form a nominal-scaled variable. For example, income and age are intervally scaled (actually, ratio scaled), but in the context of Figure 12–3, they are used to define categories and thus are nominally scaled.

Hypothesis Testing

Again, at issue is whether the difference observed, between income groups for example, is simply due to sample variations. If different samples were drawn, the results surely would differ. Thus, even if all income groups in the *population* were identical with respect to their enrollment intentions, some differences between the enrollment intentions between the income groups in our *sample* would be natural and expected. The question is: What is the probability that the observed differences are as large as those shown in the top of Figure 12–3? The fact that they are significant at the 0.01 level indicates that this probability is less than 0.01 and that it is very unlikely that the differences are caused by sampling variations. This hypothesis test, termed the chi-square test, will be described in more detail in the next chapter.

SAMPLE CORRELATION

The correlation measures the degree to which there is an association between two intervally scaled variables. A positive correlation will reflect a tendency for a high value of one variable to be associated with a high value in the second. A negative correlation reflects an association between a high value on one variable and a low value on the second variable. Of course, one or both of the intervally scaled variables could be used to define categories such as age and income in Figure 12–3, but that would sacrifice information. If the data base included an entire population, such as all adults in California, the measure would be termed the population correlation. If, however, it is based upon a sample, it is termed a sample correlation.

If two variables are plotted on a two-dimensional graph, termed a scatter diagram, the sample correlation reflects the tendency for the points to cluster systematically about a straight line rising or falling from left to right. The sample correlation is termed "*r*" and always is between −1 and +1. An *r* of +1 indicates a perfect positive association between the two variables, whereas if *r* is −1 there is perfect negative association. An *r* of 0 reflects the absence of any linear association.

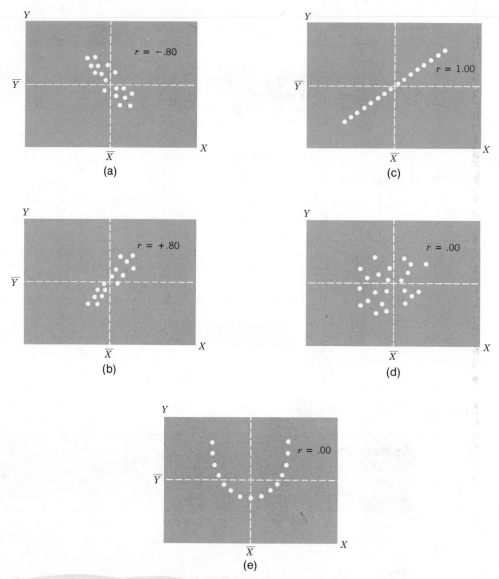

FIGURE 12–4 Some scatter diagrams

Figure 12–4 illustrates five scatter diagrams. In Figure 12–4 (a), there is a rather strong tendency for a small Y to be associated with a large X. The sample correlation is $-.80$. In Figure 12–4 (b), the pattern slopes from the lower left to the upper right, and thus the sample correlation would be $+.80$. Figure 12–4 (c) shows an example of a sample correlation of $+1$. It is a straight line running from the lower left to the upper right. Figure 12–4 (d) shows an example in which there is no relationship between X and Y. Figure 12–4 (e) shows a plot in which there is a clear relationship between the two variables, but it is not a linear or straightline relationship. Thus, the sample correlation is .00.

A more detailed conceptual explanation of the sample correlation and its calculation is presented in the appendix to this chapter. Further, when regression analysis is discussed in Chapter 19, a rather useful interpretation of the square of the sample correlation (r^2) will be presented that will provide additional insights into its interpretation.

The correlation provides a measure of the relationship between two questions or variables. The underlying assumption is that the variables are intervally scaled (recall the discussion in Chapter 8), such as age or income. At issue is to what extent a variable must satisfy that criterion. Does a seven-point agree–disagree scale qualify? The answer depends in part upon the researcher's judgment about the scale. Is the difference between -2 and -1 the same as the difference between $+2$ and $+3$? If so, it qualifies. If not, a correlation analysis may still be useful but the results should be tempered with the knowledge that one or both of the scales may not be intervally scaled. In most cases insights gained and judgments made as a result of correlation analysis will not be affected by departures from intervally scaled data. Of course, if one or both of the variables are 0–1 variables, then the more appropriate approach is the difference between means or cross-tabulation. (0–1 variables only take on the values 0 or 1, such as user = 1 and nonuser = 0.)

An example of the use of sample correlations comes from a study of donations toward a charitable health organization conducted by Stephen Miller. The organization studied contributions solicited by mail. A sample of 97 ZIP codes was selected for study. For each, the percentage of mail requests that resulted in donations of $5 or more was determined. The interest is in what characteristics of the ZIP code area would be correlated with donation behavior. Table 12–3 shows the paired correlations between the percent of families who donated and five other variables. The ZIP code areas that have a high percentage of families who receive interest income (from savings accounts, for example) have the highest correlation with mail solicitation response.

Hypothesis Testing

The appropriate hypothesis test in this situation is whether the sample correlation (the correlation based upon the sample) would be as large as it is if the population correlation (the correlation using data from the total population) were zero. The hypothesis tested is that the population correlation is zero. If the sample correlation is significant at the 0.10 level, then the probability of getting a sample correlation that large is below 0.10. In

TABLE 12–3

Correlations with the Percentage of Families Who Are Donors

	Sample Correlation
Average adjusted gross income per household	.186
Percentage of households with dividend income	.451[a]
Average dividend dollar income per household	.205
Percentage of households with interest income	.589[a]
Average interest dollar income per household	.304

SOURCE Adapted from Stephen J. Miller, "Source of Income as a Market Descriptor," *Journal of Marketing Research*, XV (February 1978), p. 131.

[a]The difference between these correlations is statistically significant at the .01 level.

Table 12–3, however, another test is mentioned. The footnote in that table indicates that the cited correlations are significantly different, that is, the differences are unlikely to be due to a sampling accident. The hypothesis tested in Table 12–3 is that the two population correlations are the same.

MEASURING ASSOCIATION—A RECAP

A basic procedure in data analysis is determining whether or not two variables are associated. Three methods for exploring association have just been presented. Which is used depends on the nature of the variables involved. Figure 12–5 summarizes the methods of measuring association. If both of the variables are nominally scaled—in that they serve to label or identify categories such as heavy users, light users, or nonusers—then the approach is cross-tabulation. If one of the variables is intervally scaled, such as age or income (that is, scales objects and has a constant unit of measurement), then the difference between means is employed. If both variables are intervally scaled, then the appropriate association measure is the sample correlation.

MULTIVARIATE ANALYSIS

The analysis usually starts with a tabulation of each question. It then moves to a consideration of pairs of questions. The next step is to consider questions in groups of three, as is discussed in Chapter 14. Multivariate analysis techniques allow the analysis of three or more questions simultaneously and are covered in Part 4 of this book.

Why use multivariate analysis anyway? Clearly, substantial information can be obtained without using such a complex technique; however, there are several reasons why multivariate analysis is useful.

One reason is to group variables or people. In an image study of an electronics company, for example, firms might be rated in reference to innovativeness, number of

	NOMINAL-SCALED VARIABLES	INTERVAL-SCALED VARIABLES
Nominal-scaled variables	Cross-tabulation	Difference between means
Interval-scaled variables	Difference between means	Correlation

FIGURE 12–5 Measurements of association

plants, financial strength, capacity, size of research and development, production efficiency, service capability, and so on. Several of these variables might be measuring the same firm attribute. For example, number of plants, financial strength, and capacity might all reflect a size dimension. One role of factor analysis, discussed in Chapter 16, is to group variables. Another problem, often addressed by cluster analysis, which is described in Chapter 17, is to group people. In this chapter we have contrasted groups of people defined by a single question. Cluster analysis allows the researcher to define groups of people using many questions.

Another reason for multivariate analysis is to improve the ability to predict variables such as usage or to understand relationships between variables such as advertising and usage. A start toward both prediction and understanding is provided by the analysis of questions in pairs, which can identify associations that, in turn, provide evidence of causation. The problem is that relationships between two variables can be confounded by a third variable. The third variable can cause the other two. Wealth may be associated with the use of nursing homes only because older people tend to have accumulated more money than younger people. Thus, it is useful to consider several explanatory or predictor variables simultaneously. Among the techniques for doing so are conjoint analysis (Chapter 18) and regression analysis and the other techniques discussed in Chapter 19. In Chapter 14, the introduction of a third variable in cross-tabulation will be presented and an overview of causal inference and data analysis will be provided; thus, many of the basic concepts of multivariate analysis will be introduced there.

PRESENTING THE RESULTS

Eventually the researcher must develop some conclusions from the data analysis and present the results. The presentation, whether oral, written, or both, can be critical to the ultimate ability of the research to influence decisions. We will address this in Chapter 15, where we provide several guidelines that will lead to effective presentations and where we also offer some special tips for making oral presentations.

SUMMARY

The first data analysis phase is to edit and code the data. Editing involves identifying omissions, ambiguities, inconsistencies, lack of cooperation, and ineligible respondents. Coding involves deciding how the responses are going to be entered.

There are a variety of data analysis techniques available. The most basic is to analyze each question by itself. A frequency distribution provides the most complete information and often leads to decisions to combine response categories. Reporting only the sample means or percentages is the other principal approach.

The usual next step is to tabulate questions among subgroups and involves two of the questions from the questionnaire. Thus, the sample mean or the frequency distribution is obtained for subgroups such as transit users and transit nonusers. Another technique involves the association between two intervally scaled variables and is termed correlation analysis. The sample correlation is a number between $+1$ and -1 that reflects the degree to which two variables have a linear or straight-line relationship. In all these two-question analyses, the concept of hypothesis testing—the subject of the next chapter—is relevant.

The simultaneous analysis of three questions or variables is the subject of Chapter 14. Multivariate analysis, which involves techniques used to analyze three or more questions simultaneously, is covered in Part 4. The final data analysis phase involves the presentation of the results, the subject of Chapter 15.

QUESTIONS AND PROBLEMS

1 Code the questionnaire developed in the Match-Mate Case. Alter questions if you feel coding and data analysis considerations warrant.

2 A poll of just over 1000 Californians selected by an area sampling plan were asked early in Governor Brown's tenure whether they felt that Governor Brown was doing a good, fair, or poor job as governor. They were then asked why they held those opinions. The results were coded into 35 response categories. Each respondent's answer was coded in from one to six of the categories. A total of 1351 responses were coded. The most frequently used categories (besides ''No Answer,'' given by 135 of the respondents) were the following:

a Not bad or good, OK so far, too soon to tell (253)

b Doing his best (123)

c Trying to help people, cares about people (105)

d Cutting down government expenses (88)

e Like or agree with his ideas (69)

f Not afraid to take a stand (61)

Do you think the responses are being analyzed properly? Those giving a lengthy reply that includes as many as six coded responses will have more weight than a respondent that gives a short direct response which is coded into only one category.

Is that appropriate? Are there any alternatives? Code the following responses into those categories listed above and into others you feel are appropriate.

a I like his position on welfare. It's probably the most critical problem facing the state. On the other hand he is not helping the business climate. All the regulations are making it impossible to bring in industry. It's really too soon to make a judgment, however.

b He's reducing unemployment, improving the economy. I like his ideas about welfare and cutting down government expense. However, I don't like his position on the smog device bill. On balance, he's doing OK.

c He's too much of a politician. He will swing with the political currents. He has started some needed government reorganization, however.

d I dislike his stand on education. He is really not interested in education perhaps because he has no children. He's young and immature. He takes strong stands without getting his facts straight.

e He's concerned about the farm workers. He's doing a good job. I like him.

3 Analyze Figure 12–3. What conclusions can you draw? What are the implications? What additional data analysis would you recommend, given your conclusions?

4 In the HMO study the "Intentions to enroll" by "Intentions to have more children" cross-tabulation is shown in the following table. Interpret it in the context of Figure 12–3.

INTENTIONS TO ENROLL   By Intentions to Have More Children

	Yes, Intend To Have Children	Not Sure	Do Not Intend To Have Children	Total
Most interested	14.1% (39)	14.9% (97)	9.1% (13)	11.1% (121)
Moderately interested	25.6% (71)	17.6%(114)	16.8% (25)	18.9% (170)
Uncertain or uninterested	60.3%(167)	67.5%(438)	74.1%(110)	70.0% (776)
	100%(277)	100%(649)	100%(148)	100%(1,067)

5 Consider the PG & E (*A*) case. Plan an analysis strategy. What cross-tabulations would you run? What difference-between-means calculations? What correlations would be useful? Identify some questions for which you would use means (or percentages) and others for which you might consider the entire frequency distribution in your analysis. Identify two key questions and determine the frequency distribution using the case data.

APPENDIX
SAMPLE CORRELATION

The sample correlation is best understood in terms of a three-step logical development. As part of the first step, the points could be plotted in a scatter diagram. In the sample shown in Figure 12–6, the Y axis indicates the sales in thousands of dollars per day of stores in a retail chain, and the X axis indicates the distance in travel time to the nearest competing store. Six stores are located on the scatter diagram. A reasonable measure of association would be

$$\Sigma(X - \overline{X})(Y - \overline{Y})$$

Points in quadrants I and III would suggest a positive association, so large values of X would be associated with large values of Y. For store E, for example, the $(X - \overline{X})$ $(Y - \overline{Y})$ term equals five times six, or 30.

Refer to Table 12–4 for a summary of this calculation. If the data point had been higher (farther away from Y) or farther to the right (farther from $\overline{X}$), then the value of $(X - \overline{X})(Y - \overline{Y})$ term for store E would have been greater. On the other hand, a point near one of the dotted axes would contribute little to the association measure. Store D is located on the $\overline{X}$ line and, as shown in Table 12–4 contributes zero to the association measure. Similarly, points in quadrants II and IV suggest a negative association. Thus, store B, which is in quadrant II, has a negative contribution to the association measure. Table 12–4 shows this contribution to be -2.

The second step in the logical development of the sample correlation is to divide the association expression by the sample size:

$$\frac{1}{n - 1} \Sigma(X - \overline{X})(Y - \overline{Y})$$

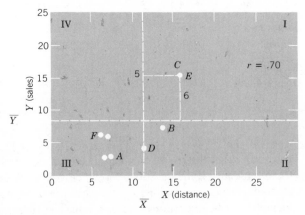

FIGURE 12–6 A scatter diagram

TABLE 12–4

Determining the Sample Correlation Coefficient

	Daily Sales (Thousands)		Distance to Nearest Competing Store (Min.)		
	Y	$Y - \bar{Y}$	X	$X - \bar{X}$	$(X - \bar{X})(Y - \bar{Y})$
Store A	3	−6	7	−4	24
Store B	8	−1	13	2	−2
Store C	17	8	13	2	16
Store D	4	−5	11	0	0
Store E	15	6	16	5	30
Store F	7	−2	6	−5	10
Total	54	0	66	0	$78 = \Sigma(X - \bar{X})(Y - \bar{Y})$
Average	$\bar{Y} = 9$		$\bar{X} = 11$		$15.6 = \dfrac{1}{n - 1}\Sigma(X - \bar{X})(Y - \bar{Y})$

$$r_{YX} = \frac{1}{n - 1}\frac{\Sigma(X - \bar{X})(Y - \bar{Y})}{s_X s_Y} = \frac{78}{5(3.85)(5.76)} = .70$$

$$s_X = 3.85 = \frac{1}{n - 1}\Sigma(X - \bar{X})^2$$

$$s_Y = 5.76 = \frac{1}{n - 1}\Sigma(Y - \bar{Y})^2$$

This will insure that the measure does not increase simply by increasing the sample size. The association between retail store sales volume and distance to competitive stores should not get larger simply because the association measure is calculated using data from 20 stores instead of 10. Thus, we divide by the sample size. The fact that $n - 1$, the degree of freedom, is used instead of n can be considered a minor technical point with no practical significance. Table 12–4 shows that this association measure would then be 15.6.[2]

One problem remains. A researcher could alter dramatically the size of the association measure simply by changing the units of one of the variables. For example, if the sales were measured in dollars instead of thousands of dollars, then the association measure would be 15.6 million instead of 15.6. Such a dependence upon the units of measure makes the measure difficult to interpret. The solution is to divide the measure by the sample standard deviations for X and Y.[3] The result is the sample correlation coefficient,

[2]This measure is actually termed the sample covariance.

[3]The sample standard deviation was discussed in Chapter 11; the formula is

$$s_X = \sqrt{\frac{1}{n - 1}\Sigma(X_i - \bar{X})^2}$$

which will not be affected by a change in the measurement units of one or both of the variables:

$$r_{XY} = \frac{1}{n-1} \Sigma \left(\frac{X - \overline{X}}{s_X} \right) \left(\frac{Y - \overline{Y}}{s_Y} \right)$$

The sample correlation has several important properties. First, as the logical development has demonstrated, it is independent of sample size and units of measurement. Second, it lies between -1 and $+1$. Thus, the interpretation is intuitively reasonable.

CASE 12–1
American Conservatory Theatre[4]

The American Conservatory Theatre (ACT), a major repertory theater located in San Francisco, was completing its tenth season in March 1976. The management team at ACT decided to conduct a major research study, intended to help their planning effort. A questionnaire was developed and mailed to their approximately 9000 season subscribers. A return rate of 40 percent was obtained. A sample of 982 of these returned questionnaires was selected for analysis.

One of the major interests of ACT management was in developing an understanding of the dynamics of the process whereby individuals became ACT subscribers. To assist in this process the sample was divided into four groups according to their behavior pattern over the past five seasons:

1 Continual subscribers (32 percent)—subscribed all five seasons

2 Gradual subscribers (31 percent)—one or more seasons of attendance followed by becoming a subscriber

[4]Prepared by Adrian B. Ryans, Charles B. Weinberg, and David A. Aaker as a basis for class discussion.

3 Sudden subscribers (21 percent)—became a subscriber without attending prior performances

4 Miscellaneous patterns (16 percent)

The existence of a substantial "sudden subscriber" group was surprising and ran counter to conventional belief among theater managers that people were first enticed to attend a few performances at a particular theater and only after they had had some positive experiences with this theater would they become subscribers.

The next step in the research study was to attempt to identify characteristics of the continual, gradual, and sudden subscriber groups that might be of use in understanding the segment differences and as inputs in the development of audience building and retention programs. Five variables appeared to be useful in this regard:

1 Years resident in the San Francisco Bay Area, measured on a scale ranging from 1 = two years or less, to 5 = more than 20 years.

2 Age of subscriber, measured on a scale ranging from 1 = 25 years old or less, to 5 = more than 65 years old.

TABLE 12–5
Subscriber Groups

	Mean Scores		
	Continual	Gradual	Sudden
Years resident (1 to 5 scale)[a]	4.32	3.68	3.53
Age (1 to 5 scale)[a]	3.34	2.74	2.86
Income (1 to 4 scale)	2.54	2.39	2.38
Cultural activities (0 to 6 scale)[a]	2.84	2.95	2.08
Twenty hours of TV (0–1 dummy variable)	0.31	0.26	0.38
Sample size	314	304	206

[a]Indicates that the differences between means are significant at the .01 level.

3. Household income, measured on a scale ranging from 1 = $15,000 per year or less, to 4 = more than $50,000 per year.

4 Whether the subscriber spent more than 20 hours a week watching TV, measured as a dummy variable; 1 if yes, 0 if no.

5 Attendance at six other cultural institutions (i.e., ballet, Civic Light Opera, DeYoung Museum, Museum of Modern Art, opera, and symphony) in San Francisco. The attendance score is the number of the six different activities that the respondent attended at least once in the previous year.

Table 12–5 shows the differences between the mean scores for the three groups for these five variables.

Each respondent was asked which two benefits from a list of eight were the best reasons for purchasing a subscription. One of the benefits listed was the subscription price discount (ACT offered subscribers seven plays for the price of six). The percentage of each subscriber group that mentioned each benefit is shown in Table 12–6.

QUESTIONS FOR DISCUSSION

1 Does it surprise you that there are so many ''sudden subscribers''? Why would a person subscribe (at a cost that could be as high as $50 per person) instead of first trying it out? After reviewing Table 12–5, in what aspects would you say that such a person differed from other subscribers? Interpret the footnote in Table 12–5.

2 What does Table 12–6 say about the difference between the three groups? What are the other implications of Table 12–6 for ACT?

TABLE 12-6
Benefits Obtained by Subscribing to ACT

Subscriber Group	Ease Of Ordering (%)	Guaranteed Ticket (%)	Price Discount (%)	Priority Seating (%)	Discount On Special Plays (%)	More Certain To Attend (%)	New Play Series (%)	Support For Act (%)	Total Mentions
					Benefit[a]				
Continual subscriber	7.5	16.4	12.4	22.0	1.1	25.9	2.9	11.8	549
Gradual subscriber	8.2	16.5	12.5	22.2	1.1	28.5	3.0	7.9	558
Sudden subscriber	11.0	13.9	10.4	25.7	1.6	30.7	1.6	5.1	374
Total Sample	8.6	15.8	12.0	23.0	1.2	28.1	2.6	8.6	1481

[a]Each respondent could check a maximum of two benefits. Percentages are based on total number of benefits checked.

CASE 12–2
The Seafood Grotto[5]

A study involving 158 families, selected randomly from a large New England city, was designed to help The Seafood Grotto, operators of several fine seafood restaurants, to determine who their customers were. Four segmentation variables were explored: age, income, social class, and life cycle. Social class was determined using Warner's Index of Status Characteristics, which uses the variables of occupation, income source, house type, and dwelling area. Life cycle was based upon four categories: under 40 without children, under 40 with children, 40 and over with children in the household, and 40 and over without children in the household.

Each segmentation variable was correlated with

[5]Prepared by Robert D. Hisrich, Michael P. Peters, and David A. Aaker as a basis for class discussion.

frequency-of-use descriptions of various entertainment activities, ranging from about once a year to more than once a week, and with a variable that simply noted whether the selected entertainment activities were used during the past year. Using Table 12–7, answer the following questions.

QUESTIONS FOR DISCUSSION

1 Can you say which segmentation variable is the most relevant for expensive restaurants?

2 Looking at the data across activities, which variables are the most relevant?

3 Explain the statistical test that is reported.

TABLE 12–7

Correlation Coefficients for the Use/Nonuse and Frequency of Use of an Entertainment Activity

Entertainment Activity	Use/Nonuse				Frequency of Use			
	Income	Social Class	Age	Life Cycle	Income	Social Class	Age	Life Cycle
Bowl	-.08	-.15[b]	.28[a]	.38[a]	.12	-.04	.35[b]	.25[b]
Movies	.25[b]	.01	.38[a]	.46[a]	-.14	.35[a]	-.44[a]	-.49[a]
Ski	.18[b]	-.02	.27[a]	.36[a]	-.05	-.25[b]	-.08	-.07
Golf	.43[a]	.06	-.08	.04	.06	.32[b]	.15	.15
In-state travel	-.20[a]	-.02	.26[a]	.25[a]	.09	.06	.14	.05
Out-of-state travel	-.24[a]	.10	-.07	.06	.13	-.05	-.03	-.07
Foreign travel	.14	.09	-.01	.01	—[c]	—[c]	—[c]	—[c]
Dine at expensive restaurant	.27[a]	.02	.08	.17[b]	.12	.23[a]	.13	.17[b]
Dine at moderately priced restaurant	-.22[a]	-.03	.17[b]	.20[a]	.19[b]	-.12	.17[b]	.08
Dine at inexpensive restaurant	-.14	-.16[b]	.25[b]	.31[a]	.10	-.25[a]	-.07	-.07
Nightclubs	.12	.08	.32[a]	.41[a]	.28[a]	.11	-.42[a]	-.34[a]
Cocktail parties	-.23[a]	.03	.03	.16[b]	.15	-.02	.05	.01
Professional athletic events	-.32[a]	.01	.21	.33[a]	-.13	.07	-.09	-.12
College/high school athletic events	-.25[a]	-.06	.11	.17[b]	.35[a]	.23[b]	-.12	-.22[b]

[a]Significant at .01 level or better
[b]Significant at .05 level or better
[c]Foreign travel was excluded from this part of the analysis because it rarely occurs more than once a year.

13

HYPOTHESIS TESTING

When an interesting, relevant, empirical finding emerges from data analysis based on a sample, a simple yet penetrating hypothesis test question should occur to every manager and researcher as a matter of course: Does the empirical finding represent only a sampling accident? For example, suppose a study was made of wine consumption. Data analysis revealed that a random sample of 100 California residents consumes more wine per family than a random sample of 100 New York residents. It could be that the observed difference was only caused by sampling error; in actuality, there may be no difference between the two populations. If the difference found in the two samples could be caused by sampling fluctuations, then it makes little sense to spend additional time on the results or to base decisions on them. If, on the other hand, the results are not simply caused by sampling variations, then there is reason to consider the results further. The hypothesis test question is thus a screening question. Empirical results should pass that test before the researcher spends much effort considering them further. Although the screening question implied by a hypothesis test is primarily used only to discard or discount results, the concept and its accompanying machinery are still an important part of analysis.

A primary objective of this chapter will be to provide a real understanding of the logic of hypothesis testing. The hope is that the reader will become conditioned to asking whether the result was an accident. Just thinking of the question at the appropriate time is half the battle. Further, an effort will be made to help the reader think in terms of a model or set of assumptions (such as there is no difference between California and New York in per capita wine consumption) in very specific terms. Hypothesis testing provides an excellent opportunity to be rigorous and precise in thinking and in presenting results.

The calculations will be presented for several hypothesis tests, although they need not be memorized. They can be looked up when needed, and, in any case, a computer usually provides them. However, a knowledge of the specific calculations of some representative tests can increase understanding substantially.

In the first section, the four steps of hypothesis testing are developed in the context of an example. This is followed by sections describing two of the most important hypothesis tests used in marketing research. The second section discusses the hypothesis test used in cross-tabulations. Here the chi-square statistic, which is useful in interpreting a cross-tabulation table, is developed. The third section presents the hypothesis test used when differences between means are involved. The difference between means was one of the association measures used in the last chapter. It also appears in most experiments, as the material in Chapter 9 illustrated.

THE FOUR STEPS OF HYPOTHESIS TESTING

An Illustrative Example

To guide the development and control of wilderness areas and national parks, a large-scale survey was conducted. A total of nearly 10,000 people participated and answered a series of questions about their usage of wilderness areas and their opinions on public policy alternatives regarding them. One key question was how to control the number of people requesting use of some of the popular rafting rivers. At one extreme, a very restrictive policy was proposed using a permit system that would preserve the ''wilderness'' characteristic but deprive many people of the opportunity to use the national resource. At the other extreme, there would be unrestricted access. One question asked for opinions about this policy spectrum as it applied to several wilderness areas. The scale was as follows:

HIGHLY								No	
RESTRICTIVE								RESTRICTIONS	
0	1	2	3	4	5	6	7	8	9

The average response of the 10,000 respondents was 5.6.

A theory to be explored was that those who did white-water rafting would be in favor of fewer restrictions. Twenty-five such people were identified in the study, with an average response rate of 6.1. Thus, the evidence supports the contention that those engaging in white-water rafting did tend to support a no-restrictions policy more than did the rest of the population. This contention will be termed the alternate hypothesis.

But how convincing is the evidence? After all, we only know the opinions of a sample of 25 rafters. The difference between 5.6 (the 10,000 respondent average) and 6.1 (the white-water rafters' average) might be more a case of luck than proof that the white-water rafters had different opinions. To evaluate the evidence statistically, the probability that the result was an accident is determined.

Assume—just for argument—the null hypothesis that the opinions of white-water rafters do not differ from those of the general population (the 10,000 respondents), and that if all the white-water rafters were contacted their average response would be 5.6 instead of 6.1. If a sample of twenty-five white-water rafters were obtained, their average response might be 5.6, 5.4, 5.8, or 5.2. The question is: With what frequency would the sample response be 6.1 or more?

---

1. Evidence is generated that supports a position, termed the alternate hypothesis. Thus in a 25-person sample, the average response was 6.1, which indicates that the white-water rafters favor fewer restrictions than the general population.
2. Conceptualize the null hypothesis. Thus, the average response of all white-water rafters is actually 5.6, the same as the general population.
3. Ask: What is the probability of obtaining such evidence if the null hypothesis were true? That is, what is the probability that the average response of 25 white-water rafters will exceed 6.1 if the average response for all white-water rafters is 5.6?
4. Calculate the probability, the *p*-value. In this example, the probability is 0.16.

FIGURE 13–1 Hypothesis test steps

Formally, what is the probability that the white-water rafters' average response, which will be termed $\overline{X}$ (the sample mean), will be 6.1 or more, given that the population response is 5.6 (μ = the population mean = 5.6)? Using some probability calculations, it is found that the probability is just over .15.[1] Thus, there is more than a 15-percent chance that the average response of a sample of 25 white-water rafters would exceed 6.1 even if the average for all white-water rafters were 5.6. There are more than 15 chances out of 100 that the difference found (between 6.1 and 5.6) was simply due to a sampling accident. This probability is termed the *p*-value. It is the result of testing the hypothesis that the white-water rafter population mean response is 5.6.

Thus, the four basic steps in a hypothesis test are as illustrated in Figure 13–1. The first step is to develop and analyze data, which usually involves some measure of association to prove or support a position (termed an alternate hypothesis). For example, a position could be that the response of all white-water rafters exceeds 5.6. Second, a null hypothesis is conceptualized. For example, a null hypothesis is that the average response of all white-water rafters is 5.6, the same as that of the general population. The third and most important step is to raise the question of the probability that the empirical "evidence" supporting the original judgment could have been a statistical accident. Suppose that the null hypothesis is true. What is the probability that the evidence could be created by chance? The fourth step is to actually calculate that probability, termed the *p*-value.

---

[1]To proceed, it is necessary to obtain an estimate of the sample standard error of $\overline{X}$ as was done in Chapter 11:

$$s_{\overline{x}} = s/\sqrt{n} = 2.5/\sqrt{25} = 2.5/5 = .5$$

since s, which is $= \sqrt{\dfrac{1}{n-1}\Sigma(X-\overline{X})^2}$, was determined to be 2.5 in this example. The next step is to obtain the *t*-statistic:

$$t = (\overline{X} - \mu)/s_{\overline{x}} = (6.1 - 5.6)/.5 = 1$$

The *t*-statistic reflects the number of sample standard errors of $\overline{X}$ that the sample mean, $\overline{X}$, differs from our hypothesized population mean ($\mu = 5.6$). Our probability question now can be phrased in terms of that statistic. What is the probability that the *t*-statistic would exceed 1? The assumption is made that the *t*-statistic is normally distributed. Using a normal table, the probability is found to be 0.16.

Interpretation

The hypothesis test reminds the researcher and the manager of the possibility of a statistical accident that lurks behind almost all data analyses. Furthermore, it serves to quantify the reliability, indicating the extent to which the data support the empirical finding. If the p-value is low 0.01, for example, then it is unlikely that a sampling accident is involved. A high p-value, 0.25, for example, means that the probability is high that the empirical results are simply sampling fluctuations and, therefore, the evidence is not impressive.[2] To summarize:

EVIDENCE THAT THE NULL HYPOTHESIS IS FALSE IS:

Impressive	if the p-value is low (i.e., 0.01)
Unimpressive	if the p-value is high (i.e., 0.25)

Sometimes it is inconvenient to report the actual p-value. Instead, the significance level is noted. A significance level of 0.01 indicates that the p-value was smaller than 0.01. Similarly, a significance level of 0.05 or 0.10 indicates that the p-value was smaller than 0.05 or 0.10, respectively.

The Effect of Sample Size

The consideration of sample size is important to the interpretation of hypothesis tests. The p-value is generally sensitive to sample size, in that if the sample size increases, the p-value usually will become smaller (will be more significant). For example, suppose that the white-water rafter sample size was 900 instead of 25 and that the average response was 5.8. The p-value then would be less than 0.01.[3] Thus, it could be concluded that the white-water rafters' response was indeed significantly more (at the 0.01 level) than 5.6. If it were 5.6, there would be less than a one-percent chance of getting an average response of 5.8 or more with a sample of 900.

[2]A very low p-value (e.g., 0.01) provides strong support for the empirical finding but it does not *prove* that the null hypothesis is false. One chance out of 100 is unlikely, but not impossible. Thus even a very low p-value does not provide proof that the null hypothesis is untrue, only strong evidence in that direction. Conversely, if the p-value is relatively high (0.25, for example), there is a 25-percent chance that the evidence could be this strong or stronger, even if the null hypothesis were true. Thus, the evidence is not impressive. However, it still is evidence supporting the alternative hypothesis. The fact that the sample of white-water rafters had a response of 6.1 does provide evidence that the average response of all white-water rafters exceeds 5.6. The p-value of 0.15 indicates only that the evidence is not overwhelming in that there is a 15-percent chance it could represent only a statistical accident. But it is evidence, nevertheless. The absence of a low p-value certainly does not indicate that the alternative hypothesis is wrong, only that the evidence supporting it is relatively weak.

[3]If the sample standard error again was found to be 2.5, then

$$t = \frac{\overline{X} - \mu}{s/\sqrt{n}} = \frac{5.8 - 5.6}{2.5/\sqrt{900}} = 2.4$$

A t-value of 2.4 would have associated with it a p-level less than 0.01.

However, it may well be of no interest if the response of white-water rafters differs only slightly from the response of others. The hypothesis test does not provide information as to whether the evidence put forth is meaningful—only whether it is likely to have been a statistical accident. If the sample size becomes large, the probability of getting "lucky" or "unlucky" with the sample becomes small. Conversely, if the sample size is small, the probability of a statistical accident will be higher. The p-value can be conceived as a mechanism to report the impact of the sample size on the reliability of the results. If the sample size is large, a low p-value should be expected; if the sample size is small, a high (insignificant) p-value is more likely.

Figure 13–2 summarizes how the p-value is interpreted. It includes the concept that a hypothesis test really reflects whether the sample size is adequate to discern that the null hypothesis is false. The null hypothesis will always be false in the sense that there will always be at least an infinitesimal departure from the null hypothesis. If the sample size is large enough, this infinitesimal departure will be discerned.

Definition
p-value is the probability of obtaining sample evidence against the null hypothesis given that the null hypothesis is true.

Interpretation

	Low p-value (i.e., 0.01)	High p-value (i.e., 0.25)
Evidence that the null hypothesis is false is _____	impressive	not impressive
The sample size is _____ to discern that the null hypothesis is false	large enough	too small

What is a "low" p-value?
It depends on the context. In some contexts it could be .01 and in others it could be 0.20. The most common definition of "low" is 0.10.

Does a "low" p-value prove a null hypothesis to be false?
No, only that the evidence against it is impressive.

Some vocabulary—the following have identical meanings
The p-value is less than .10.
The sample evidence is *significant* at the .10 level.
The null hypothesis would be *rejected* at the .10 level.

FIGURE 13–2 Interpreting the p-value

CROSS-TABULATION AND CHI-SQUARE

In the previous chapter the data analysis technique of cross-tabulation of two questions was presented. The appropriate hypothesis that was tested was that there was no relationship between the questions. That test was based upon a measure of the relationship between the questions of a cross-tabulation table termed the chi-square statistic. In this section, the chi-square and its associated test will be introduced more formally. In addition to leading to a useful hypothesis test, the chi-square statistic provides a measure of association.

Consider Table 13–1, which shows the results of a survey of 200 opera patrons who were asked how frequently they attended the symphony in a neighboring city. The frequency of attendance was partitioned into the categories of never, occasionally, and often; thus it became a nominally scaled variable. The respondents also were asked whether they regarded the location of the symphony as convenient or inconvenient. The resulting cross-tabulation shows the percentage breakdown of attendance in each location category.

TABLE 13–1

A Cross-Tabulation of Opera Partrons

		Location (L)			
		Convenient	Not Convenient	Row Total	p_A
Attendance at symphony (A)	Often (more than 6 times a season)	1 27.5% $O_1 = 22$	2 15% $O_2 = 18$	20% (40)	.20
	Occasionally	3 60% $O_3 = 48$	4 43.3% $O_4 = 52$	50% (100)	.50
	Never	5 12.5% $O_5 = 10$	6 41.7% $O_6 = 50$	30% (60)	.30
	Column total	100% (80)	100% (120)	100% (200)	1.00
	p_L	.40	.60	1.00	

$$\chi^2 = \Sigma \frac{(O_i - E_i)^2}{E_i} = 20$$

NOTE: E_i equals the expected cell values and O_i equals the observed cell values.

The observed number of respondents in cell i, termed O_i, is also shown. Thus, 22 people in cell 1 attended the symphony often and felt that the location was convenient ($O_1 = 22$).

The row totals and column totals and the proportions (P_A and P_L) are tabulated in the margin. Note that they are the frequency distribution for the respective variables. For example, the column total indicates that 80 respondents (0.40 of all the respondents) felt the location was convenient and 120 (0.60 of all the respondents) felt it was inconvenient. The frequency distribution is termed a "marginal" here because it appears in the margin. If an analyst computes marginals, she simply means frequency distributions for the individual questions.

Independence

Before introducing the (sample) chi-square statistic as a measure of association between the two nominally scaled variables, it is useful to develop and illustrate the notion of statistical independence. The concept of independence is really central not only to the chi-square statistic but to all association measures.

Two variables are statistically independent if a knowledge of one would offer no information as to the identity of the other. Consider the following experiment, illustrated in Table 13–2. Suppose that a coin was bent in such a manner that it would come up heads 0.40 of the time. Suppose, further, that we have a deck of cards that is a bit unusual in that it has 20 percent spades and 30 percent clubs and the rest either hearts or diamonds. The experiment consists of flipping the coin and drawing a card from the shuffled deck. The outcome of the coin flip is independent of the draw from the card deck. Before the experiment begins the chance of getting a spade is 0.20. After the coin is flipped and heads appears, the probability of getting a spade is still 0.20. The knowledge of the

TABLE 13–2
An Experiment and Its Expected Outcome

| | | Flip Coin | | Outcomes | |
		Heads	Tails	Expected	Probability
Drawing a card	Spade	$E_1 = 16^a$	$E_2 = 24$	40	.20
	Heart or Diamond	$E_3 = 40$	$E_4 = 60$	100	.50
	Club	$E_5 = 24$	$E_6 = 36$	60	.30
	Outcomes Expected	80	120	200	
	Probability	.40	.60		

$^a E_i$ = expected cell size under independence

outcome of the coin flip does not affect our information as to the outcome of the card draw; therefore, the coin-flip outcome is statistically independent of the card draw.

Expected Value

If the previous experiment were repeated many times, we would expect 20 percent of the outcomes to include a spade draw. The number of "spade" outcomes that we would expect would be $0.20n$, where n is the number of experiments conducted. We also would expect 0.40 of these experiments to involve a head and 0.60 to involve a tail. Then the number of experiments resulting in a spade and a head would be "expected" to be

$$(0.40) \ (0.20n)$$

If n is equal to 200 and E_i is the number of outcomes expected in cell i, then for cells 1, 2, and 3 we have

$$E_1 = (0.40) \ (0.20n) = 16$$
$$E_2 = (0.60) \ (0.20n) = 24$$
$$E_3 = (0.40) \ (0.50n) = 40$$

The reader should determine E_4, E_5, and E_6. The expected number of outcomes in cell i, E_i, is the number that would be expected, on average, if the experiments involving independent variables were repeated many times. Of course, cell 1 will not have 16 entries; sometimes it will have more and sometimes fewer. However, on average, it will have 16.

In Table 13–1, the two variables are location and attendance. If the two variables were independent, then the expected frequencies in each cell would be

$$E_i = p_L p_A n$$

where p_L and p_A are proportions defined in the table. Thus, for cell 6 we would have

$$E_6 = (0.3) \ (0.6)200 = 36$$

The Chi-Square Statistic

The chi-square statistic is a measure of the difference between the actual numbers observed in cell i, termed O_i, with the number expected under the assumption of statistical independence, E_i. The chi-square statistic is defined as

$$\chi^2 = \Sigma \ \frac{(O_i - E_i)^2}{E_i} \ \text{with} \ (r - 1)(c - 1) \ \text{degrees of freedom}$$

where

$$O_i = \text{the observed number in cell } i$$
$$E_i = \text{the number in cell } i \text{ expected under independence}$$
$$r = \text{the number of rows}$$
$$c = \text{the number of columns}$$

If the variables are statistically independent, the χ^2 value will still be nonzero because the observed cell values very probably will not be exactly E_i, but the χ^2 value should be relatively small. If, however, the variables are not independent—if they are associated or related—then the χ^2 value should be relatively large. Thus, if there is an increased tendency for a spade to be drawn when a head appears, then the χ^2 value will tend to get large. The chi-square statistic has an associated number of degrees of freedom that will be used when hypothesis testing is discussed. It is determined by the formula $(r - 1)$ $(c - 1)$ and is not of conceptual importance.

The expected frequencies are shown in Table 13–2. The chi-square statistic for Table 13–1 is calculated as 20, a relatively large value, which suggests that the two variables may not be statistically independent. At least in this particular instance, a sample association was found between the two variables.

Limitations As an Association Measure

The chi-square statistic provides a measure of association between two questions, but it has several limitations. First, it is basically proportional to sample size, which makes it difficult to interpret in an absolute sense and to compare cross-tabulations with unequal sample sizes. However, in a given analysis, it is often necessary to compare different cross-tabulations with the same sample size. Second, unlike correlation analysis, it has no upper bound. Thus, it is difficult to obtain a feel for its value.[4] A further discussion of the use of chi-square as an association measure and some alternatives are presented in the appendix to this chapter.

The Hypothesis Test

The null hypothesis associated with the sample chi-square statistic is that the two (nominally scaled) variables are statistically independent. Under this null hypothesis the expected size of each cell would be the E_i term. Departures of O_i from the E_i predictions would increase the chi-square statistics and provide evidence that the null hypothesis is incorrect. The alternate hypothesis is that the two variables are not independent.

[4]Furthermore, the chi-square value does not indicate how the two questions are related. Some cells may contribute more than others to the chi-square value. The table could be partitioned into subtables, such as a 2 × 2 table obtained by excluding the ''never'' group. A systematic exploration of the sample chi-square statistics associated with such subtables can help suggest which cells are responsible for the departure from independence.

The hypothesis test is based upon the fact that the chi-square statistic is distributed as the chi-square distribution with $(r - 1)(c - 1)$ degrees of freedom, assuming the null hypothesis is true.[5] Again the concept of degrees of freedom, although needed to use the chi-square distribution tables, is not conceptually important and can be provided by a computer program or by reference to a statistics book.[6]

Given a knowledge of the chi-square statistic value and the number of degrees of freedom, it is relatively easy to use a chi-square distribution table to determine the p-value. For two degrees of freedom the table provides the following:

χ^2 STATISTIC	p-VALUE
2.77	0.25
4.61	0.10
5.99	0.05
9.21	0.01
13.80	0.001

In Table 13–1 the chi-square statistic was 20, so the p-value would be considerably below 0.001. Thus, the probability of getting a chi-square statistic of 20 or larger, if the two variables were actually independent, is under 0.001. The results are thus significant at the .001 level. The evidence therefore suggests that the two variables are not independent.

To summarize, evidence that there is a relationship between two nominally scaled variables is developed—the nonzero chi-square value of 20. Second, the hypothesis that the two variables are independent is conceptualized. Third, the question is posed: What is the probability of obtaining such evidence, given the null hypothesis? Finally, the probability is determined—the p-value is under 0.001.

The hypothesis test logic now will be applied to the difference between means.

THE DIFFERENCE BETWEEN MEANS

To illustrate the hypothesis test appropriate for the difference between sample means, consider the following pricing experiment. Three prices are under consideration for a new product: 39¢, 44¢, and 49¢. To determine the influence that the various price levels will

---

[5] In working with chi-square distribution, it is desirable that the E_i values all be more than 5. One or two could be lower, but if several are low it is usually wise to combine cells so that the E_i values are increased.

[6] The degrees of freedom are the number of pieces of information (in this case $r \cdot c = 6$), less the number of information pieces needed to calculate the E_i terms. In calculating the E_i terms, $r + c$ proportions are needed but the fact that the proportions add to 1.0 can be exploited so that only $r + c - 1$ information pieces are needed. Thus the degrees of freedom are

$$rc - (r + c - 1) = (r - 1)(c - 1) = 2$$

have upon sales, three samples of five supermarkets are randomly selected from the geographic area of interest. Each sample is assigned one of the three price levels. Figure 13–3 shows the resulting sales levels in both graphic and tabular form. The 39¢ stores, the first row, had sales of 8, 12, 10, 9, and 11, averaging 10 units. The 44¢ stores, the second row, averaged 8 units; and the 49¢ stores, the third row, averaged 7 units. Obviously, the determination of the optimal price will require an extensive analysis involving a host of considerations. However, before the analysis begins, it is appropriate to consider the hypothesis that price levels have no effect on sales. Under the null hypothesis, differences between sample means could be caused by the fact that only a sample of five was employed for each price level. The alternate hypothesis is that there is a price effect, that sales would not be the same for each of the price levels if they were applied to all stores.

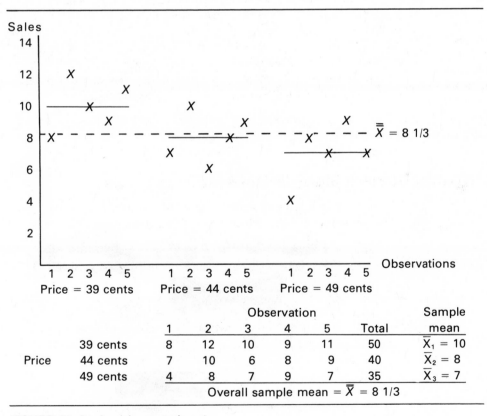

| | | Observation | | | | | | Sample |
		1	2	3	4	5	Total	mean
	39 cents	8	12	10	9	11	50	$\bar{X}_1 = 10$
Price	44 cents	7	10	6	8	9	40	$\bar{X}_2 = 8$
	49 cents	4	8	7	9	7	35	$\bar{X}_3 = 7$
					Overall sample mean = $\bar{\bar{X}}$ = 8 1/3			

FIGURE 13–3 A pricing experiment

Variation Between Stores

If the new product were placed in all stores in the population, the sales would vary from store to store. This variation is captured by the population variance.[7] One estimate of the population variance can be derived from the variation among the stores in the sample:

$$\frac{1}{14} \sum_{i=1}^{15} (X_i - \overline{\overline{X}})^2 = 3.8$$

where

$-1 \leftarrow$

X_i = the sales of store i

14 = the sample size, less one

$\overline{\overline{X}}$ = the average sales of the stores in the sample ($= 8\frac{1}{3}$)

Two other estimates of the population also are available and provide the basis for the test of the hypothesis that price levels have no effect on sales. The first is to focus upon the variation between stores at different price levels ($\overline{X}_1 = 10$, $\overline{X}_2 = 8$, and $\overline{X}_3 = 7$). The second is to consider the variation between stores at the same price level (for example, the stores with the 39¢ price level had sales of 8, 12, 10, 9, and 11). Under the null hypothesis that price levels have no effect on sales, each of these estimates should be similar. If the estimate based upon variation between stores of different price levels is inflated, then doubt will be cast upon the null hypothesis.

Variation Between Stores at Different Price Levels

The first variance estimate is based upon the variation between the sample mean values of each row (price level), which is calculated as follows:

SS_r = sum of squares between rows (price level)

= variation explained by the row (price level)

$$= n \left[\sum_{p=1}^{r} (\overline{X}_p - \overline{\overline{X}})^2 \right]$$

$$= 5[(10 - 8\tfrac{1}{3})^2 + (8 - 8\tfrac{1}{3})^2 + (7 - 8\tfrac{1}{3})^2] = 23.3$$

[7]The population variance is

$$\sigma^2 = \frac{1}{N} \sum_{i=1}^{N} (X_i - \mu)^2$$

N = the number of stores in the population (as opposed to the number of stores in the sample)

X_i = the sales of store i

μ = the average sales of all stores in the population

where

$$\overline{X}_p = \text{the mean sales at price level } p \ (\text{i.e., } \overline{X}_1 = 10)$$
$$\overline{\overline{X}} = \text{the overall mean } (\text{i.e., } \overline{\overline{X}} = 8\tfrac{1}{3})$$
$$n = \text{the number of observations at each price level } (n = 5)$$
$$p = \text{the price level } (p = 1, 2, 3)$$
$$r = \text{the number of rows (price levels) } (\text{i.e., } r = 3)$$

Clearly, as the difference between means gets larger so will the sum of terms $(\overline{X}_p - \overline{\overline{X}})^2$.

The first variance estimate is termed MSS_r and is obtained by dividing the SS_r by its associated degrees of freedom (d.f.), which here is the number of rows less one:

$$\text{MSS}_r = \text{mean sum of squares between rows (price levels)}$$
$$= \text{an estimate of the variance among stores}$$
$$= \text{SS}_r/\text{d.f.}$$
$$= (23.3)/2 = 11.65$$

Again, the determination of the degrees of freedom need not concern us here. In fact, the actual calculation formula for SS_r and the other terms is also of little consequence. As a practical matter, the computer program or a reference statistics text can provide the appropriate formula for degrees of freedom, sum of squares, and other terms.[8] The intent here is to provide a feel for the terms and expressions that will be encountered in this rather commonly used statistical hypothesis test and to provide a conceptual understanding of the test itself, rather than to teach the reader to actually make the raw calculations.

Variation Within Price Levels

The second variance estimate is based upon the variation within each row (price level), which is

$$\text{SS}_u = \text{sum of squares unexplained by the row (price level}$$
$$= \text{variation within the rows (price levels)}$$
$$= \sum_{i=1}^{n} \sum_{p=1}^{r} (X_{ip} - \overline{X}_p)^2$$
$$= (8 - 10)^2 + (12 - 10)^2 + \ldots + (9 - 7)^2 + (7 - 7)^2 = 34$$

where X_{ip} equals the sales of observation i at price level p. Note that SS_u is based upon the squared deviation from the row mean.

[8]An exceptionally clear and accessible text is Geoffrey Keppel, *Design and Analysis: A Researcher's Handbook* (Englewood Cliffs, N.J.: Prentice-Hall, 1973).

The second variance estimate is termed MSS_u and is generated by dividing SS_u by its associated degrees of freedom, which is here equal to $r(n - 1)$ or 12:

$$MSS_u = \text{mean sum of squares unexplained by the row (price level)}$$
$$= \text{an estimate of the variance among stores}$$
$$= SS_u/\text{d.f.}$$
$$= 34/12 = 2.8$$

The ANOVA Table

These expressions are summarized in Table 13–3, which presents an analysis of variance and is termed an ANOVA table. The ANOVA table is a conventional way to present a hypothesis test regarding the difference between several means. The table indicates, at the left, the source of the variation. The first row summarizes the determination of MSS_r, which is based upon the variation between rows (the explained variation, or the variation explained by the price level).

The second row summarizes the determination of MSS_u, which is based on the within-row variation (variation unexplained by the price levels). The third row represents the total variation based upon the deviations of the individual sales results from the overall mean. Notice that the total variation (53.3) is equal to the sum of SS_r and SS_u. All the variation is accounted for.[9]

The *F*-statistic and *p*-value

We now consider the ratio of the two estimates of the (population) variance of the store sales.[10] This ratio is termed an F-ratio or F statistic:

$$F = \frac{MSS_r}{MSS_u} = \frac{11.65}{2.8} = 4.16$$

If the null hypothesis that price levels have no effect on sales is true, then our variance estimates using the difference between the sample means, MSS_r, should be the same as that based upon the within-row (price level) variations. The F-ratio should then be close to one. If, however, the hypothesis is not true and the different price levels generate different sales levels, the MSS_r term will have two components. One component will reflect the variance among stores; the other will reflect the different price effects. As a result, the F-ratio will tend to become large.

The p-value is the probability that the F-ratio would be larger than 4.66, given the null hypothesis. To generate the p-value, the F-probability distribution is used. Associated

---

[9]The reader also might note that the total degrees of freedom, which is the total sample size of 15 less one, or 14, is equal to the sum of the degrees of freedom associated with the first two rows of the ANOVA table.

[10]The estimate of population variance introduced at the outset was the total variation divided by its degrees of freedom. In this case, it was 3.8, which is in between the other two estimates.

TABLE 13–3
Price Experiment ANOVA Table

Source of Variation	Variation Sum Squares (SS)	Degrees of Freedom (df)	Variance Estimate Mean Sum Squares (MSS)	F-Ratio
Between rows—explained variation	$SS_r = 5 \sum_{p=1}^{3} (\bar{X}_p - \bar{\bar{X}})^2$ $= 23.3$	$r - 1 = 2$	$MSS_r = \dfrac{SS_r}{2} = 11.65$	$\dfrac{MSS_r}{MSS_u} = 4.16$
Within rows—unexplained variation	$SS_u = \sum_{i=1}^{5} \sum_{p=1}^{3} (X_{ip} - \bar{X}_p)^2$ $= 34$	$r(n - 1) = 12$	$MSS_u = \dfrac{SS_u}{12} = 2.8$	
Total	$SS_t = \sum_{i=1}^{5} \sum_{p=1}^{3} (X_{ip} - \bar{\bar{X}})^2$ $= 57.3$	14		

with each F-ratio are the numerator (MSS$_r$) degrees of freedom (2), and the denominator (MSS$_u$) degrees of freedom (12). Knowing this pair of degrees of freedom, a table of the F-distribution (Table III at the back of the book) can be used to determine, at least approximately, the p-value. The F-distribution table provides the following p-values for our case, in which the degrees of freedom are 2 and 12.

F-STATISTIC	p-VALUE
1.46	0.25
2.81	0.10
3.89	0.05
6.93	0.01

Thus, the p-value associated with 4.66 is not in the table but would be about 0.04. If the null hypothesis were true, there would be a 0.04 probability of getting an F-statistic of 4.66 or larger. Therefore, the evidence that the null hypothesis is not true is fairly substantial. The observed difference between sample means could have occurred by accident even if the null hypothesis were true, but the probability is low (1 chance in 25). Since the p-value is less than 0.05, we can say that the F-statistic is significant at the .05 level.

When possible, it is always useful to plot the data and get a graphic perspective. Figure 13–3 showed such a plot. The null hypothesis is that all points come from the same population and that there is no difference between the three price levels. The p-value denotes the probability of getting the difference between the three sample means, given the null hypothesis.

The Significance Level

Sometimes it is convenient to report only the significance level. Recall Table 12–1, which reported the difference between the transit user and nonuser. One footnote indicated that the difference between sample means for question 3 was significant at the 0.01 level.[11] That means that the p-value was below 0.01. Therefore, under the hypothesis that the population means are the same on this question, the probability of getting sample means differing by that much or more is less than 0.01. Another Table 12–1 footnote indicated that the difference found in question 5 is significant at the 0.10 level. This means that under the null hypothesis that the population percentages are the same, the probability of getting sample percentages that differ by .25 or more is less than 0.10. The evidence thus suggests—but of course does not prove—that the null hypotheses are not true for questions 3 and 5.

The reader should note that the evidence similarly does not prove that the null hypothesis is true for questions 1, 2, and 4 in Table 12–1. The evidence merely suggests

[11]Actually, when only two groups are involved, an equivalent test uses the t-statistic instead of the F-statistic. For further details see an introductory statistics text.

that the hypothesis *could* be true, that it is consistent with the data. Thus, the hypothesis test is a very limited although useful preliminary step in the analysis. It really identifies those pieces of evidence that are so unimpressive (in that they could be due just to the luck of the sample) that more detailed analysis is simply not worthwhile.

Expanding the ANOVA Table

In Chapter 9 we saw how an experiment involving a treatment variable such as price could be expanded. It is possible to control experimentally for one or more variables, such as store size or city, by adding one or more "block effects." In essence, the experiment is repeated for each block (i.e., large stores and small stores). It also is possible to add more treatment variables. In either case, more than one nominally scaled variable is introduced, and there exist several "difference between sample means" relationships. To handle such experiments, the ANOVA table is expanded.

To illustrate, consider the experiment conducted by Keith Hunt on corrective advertising, which is advertising required by the FTC to "correct" a previous advertisement deemed deceptive.[12] The advertisement in question was one introducing F-310, a gasoline additive. The FTC claimed, in part, that the product did not significantly reduce pollution as claimed and that the demonstration involving a balloon attached to the exhaust emissions of two cars was rigged, in that one car had a dirty engine and the other emitted invisible pollutants. The effect of various "corrective advertisements" had policy implications for the FTC, which wanted a fair and effective remedy for deceptive advertising but did not want to be harsh and punitive.

Three types of corrective advertisements were tested:

1 *Explicit.* A specific statement explicitly pointing out the deceptive characteristics of the advertisement in question

2 *General.* A general statement about the deception of the advertisement

3 *No corrective advertisement.* A bland statement by the FTC on gasoline additives with no mention of the company

Prior to being exposed to one of the corrective advertisements, the respondents were exposed to one of three "inoculation" advertisements. An inoculation advertisement is hypothesized to mitigate the effect of the corrective advertising, either by giving high levels of support (supportive inoculation) or by giving weak doses of the corrective advertisement, which are refuted (refutational inoculation). Three inoculation treatments were used:

1 *Refutational.* This advertisement warned of the upcoming corrective ad and refuted it. "If every motorist used F-310 for 2000 miles, air pollutants would be reduced by

[12]H. Keith Hunt, "Effects of Corrective Advertising," *Journal of Advertising Research, 13* (October 1973), 15–22.

Type of Inoculation	Type of Corrective Advertising			
	Explicit	General	No corrective advertising	Sample means
Refutational inoculation	(1)	(2)	(3)	16.7
Supportive inoculation	(4)	(5)	(6)	16.9
No inoculation	(7)	(8)	(9)	15.4
Sample means	10.1	18.2	20.4	

Cell size = 22

FIGURE 13–4 A factorial design

thousands of tons per day. The FTC doesn't seem to think that is significant. We think it is.''

2 *Supportive.* This contains no mention of the FTC or the upcoming corrective advertisement but does restate the positive arguments.

3 *No inoculation.* This advertisement makes no mention of the positive arguments.

A 3 × 3 factorial design was used, as outlined in Figure 13–4. Each of the 9 cells had 22 respondents, each of which was exposed to the ''deceptive'' advertisement, the inoculation treatment, and the corrective advertisement. The criterion measure was the degree of agreement or disagreement, on a 28-point scale (where larger numbers indicate greater agreement), with the statement, ''I like Chevron with F-310.'' Figure 13–4 shows the sample means for each of the nine cells. The hypothesis test involves determining the probability of obtaining the observed differences between the sample means, under the hypothesis that the population means were the same.

The expanded ANOVA table is shown in Table 13–4. Notice that each of the two treatments, inoculation and corrective advertising, now has an associated variation (sum of squares) and variance estimate (mean sum of squares). Consider first the inoculation treatment. The F-ratio for inoculation is

$$F\text{-ratio} = \frac{\text{MSS}_{Inoculation}}{\text{MSS}_{Unexplained}} = \frac{35.2}{34.4} = 1.02$$

The associated p-value would be approximately 0.36. Thus, the evidence against the null hypothesis of no inoculation effect is not impressive. The evidence is the fact that the

TABLE 13–4

Expanded ANOVA Table

Source of Variation	Variation (SS)	Degrees of Freedom (df)	Mean Sum of Squares (MSS)	F-Ratio	p-Value Less Than
Inoculation	70.5	2	35.2	1.02	.36
Corrective advertising	3,882.4	2	1,941.2	56.43	.001
Interaction between treatments	503.7	4	125.9	3.66	.007
Unexplained variation	6,496.6	189	34.4		
Total	10,953.2	197			

three sample means found in Figure 13–4 (16.7, 16.9, and 15.4) are not equal. However, although they are not equal, they are close enough so that we cannot reject the null hypothesis that the population means are equal.

Consider next the corrective advertising. The F-ratio is calculated for the corrective advertising treatment in the same manner:

$$F\text{-ratio} = \frac{\text{MSS}_{Corrective\ Advertising}}{\text{MSS}_{Unexplained}} = \frac{1941.2}{34.4} = 56.43$$

The associated p-value is less than 0.001. Thus, the evidence is extremely impressive against the null hypothesis that there is no corrective advertising effect. The evidence is the fact that the three sample means found in Figure 13–4 (10.1, 18.2, and 20.4) are not equal. Thus, the null hypothesis that there is no corrective advertising effect can be rejected at the 0.001 level. A closer look at the three sample means in Figure 13–4 reveals that it is the explicit corrective advertising that is effective at changing attitudes. This finding is potentially important in designing remedies for deceptive advertising.

There is an advantage to analyzing the two treatments in the same analysis-of-variance table. By including both, the unexplained variation is reduced, as is the associated mean sum of squares (MSS_u). As a result, there will be less "noise" in the data, the results will be more sensitive, and the F-ratios will be larger.

Interaction

There is a third term in Table 13–4, the interaction between the two treatments. An interaction effect means that the impact of one treatment, such as inoculation, will not be the same for each condition of the other treatment. Figure 13–5 shows the results graphically. Note that inoculation affects the attitude created by explicit corrective ad-

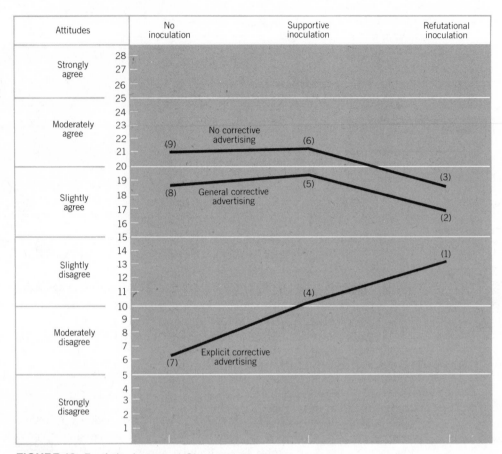

FIGURE 13–5 Attitude toward Chevron with *F*-310

Source: Adapted from H. Keith Hunt, "Effects of Corrective Advertising," *Journal of Advertising Research, 13* (October 1973), 15–22.

vertising, but it really has little effect under the "no corrective advertising" and the "general corrective advertising" conditions. There is thus an interaction effect present. If there were no interaction, the shape of the three lines shown in Figure 13–5 would be the same. Their levels would differ, but their shapes would be the same.

The hypothesis of no interaction can be tested in the ANOVA table given in Table 13–4 by determining the appropriate *F*-ratio for interaction:

$$F\text{-ratio} = \frac{\text{MSS}_{Interaction}}{\text{MSS}_{Unexplained}} = \frac{125.9}{34.4} = 3.66$$

The associated *p*-value is approximately .007. Thus, the evidence against the null hypothesis of no interaction is very impressive.

SUMMARY

Hypothesis testing involves four steps: (1) develop evidence supporting a judgment; (2) conceptualize the null hypothesis; (3) determine the probability of obtaining the evidence if the null hypothesis were true; and (4) calculate the probability—that is, the p-value—of the hypothesis test. There are several points worth remembering about hypothesis testing:

1 Hypothesis testing is a screening test. If the evidence does not pass this test, it may not be worth much attention. If it does pass this test, then it might at least be worth further analysis.

2 Hypothesis testing really measures the sample size. A large sample nearly always will yield "statistically significant" results, and a small enough sample probably will not be statistically significant. Thus, the test really does no more than provide a measure of sample size.

3 Hypothesis testing does not establish whether the null hypothesis is true or false; it only quantifies how persuasive the evidence is against it. A low p-value indicates impressive evidence, and a high p-value indicates the evidence is not impressive.

A cross-tabulation has associated with it a chi-square test of the relationship between the two variables. The null hypothesis is that the two variables are statistically independent, that is, knowledge of one provides no information about the other. The resulting p-value represents the probability under the null hypothesis of getting a chi-square statistic as large or larger than the one observed. If the p-value is low, then the evidence is rather impressive that the independence assumption is not true. If it is high, then the evidence is very weak that the independence assumption is not true.

The difference between means is a commonly used statistic in data analysis, particularly when experimentation is involved. The appropriate null hypothesis in this context is that there is no difference between means in the population. The p-level then represents the probability that the observed differences between means could have been that large if, in fact, the null hypothesis that all means are the same were true. The test is based upon the F-statistic and the accompanying F-distribution. The extended ANOVA table provides the ability to conduct several difference-between-means tests at the same time.

QUESTIONS AND PROBLEMS

1 In Table 12–1, the statement concerning gasoline costs generated a larger difference (1.7) than the other three statements. Could you therefore conclude that it was the statement that best distinguished the unit-price user from the unit-price nonuser? What assumptions are involved in that conclusion? Interpret footnote c.

2 The Consumer Fraud Council claims that Skippy Foods does not put the required weight of peanut butter in its 10-ounce jar. For evidence a sample of 400 jars are randomly selected, weighed, and found to average 9.9 ounces. The p-value, 0.07, is associated with the hypothesis that the population mean (μ) is actually 10 ounces and the production process is not generating "light" bottles. Has the council proved the point? Evaluate the evidence. Is the evidence statistically significant at the 0.10 level? At the 0.05 level? Should the Consumer Fraud Council recommend a boycott?

3 A new product was tested in Fresno with a 25¢ coupon and in Tulsa with a 50¢ coupon. A sample of 100 people was contacted in each test city. A total of 40 percent of those contacted in Tulsa had tried the new product, whereas only 30 percent of those contacted in Fresno had tried it, a 10-percent difference. Prior to making the decision as to which coupon to use in the marketing program, a hypothesis was suggested.

a What should the null hypothesis be?

b What should the step 1 position, or alternate hypothesis, be?

c The probability of obtaining this result under the null hypothesis, namely, that the trial level in Tulsa was 10 percent higher than that in Fresno, was determined to be 0.06. What is the p-value?

d Is the result significant at the 0.10 level? At the 0.05 level? Would you reject the null hypothesis at the 0.10 level? At the 0.05 level?

e Does the hypothesis show that there will be more trials with a 50¢ coupon? Do you feel that a 50¢ coupon should be used?

4 A study was conducted to determine the relationship between usage of a library and age of users. A sample of 400 was polled and the following cross-tabulation was generated. The numbers in parentheses are the observed cell sizes (O_i).

Age of library users

		Under 25	25 to 45	Over 45	Row total	Prop.
	Heavy	$\dfrac{26.2\% \ (21)}{E_1 = 17.8}$	$\dfrac{19.5\% \ (41)}{E_4 =}$	$\dfrac{24.5\% \ (29)}{E_7 =}$	22.3% (89)	.223
Library usage	Medium	$\dfrac{32.5\% \ (26)}{E_2 =}$	$\dfrac{18.1\% \ (38)}{E_5 =}$	$\dfrac{31.8\% \ (35)}{E_8 =}$		
	Light	$\dfrac{41.3\% \ (33)}{E_3 =}$	$\dfrac{62.4\% \ (131)}{E_6 =}$	$\dfrac{43.6\% \ (48)}{E_9 =}$		
	Column total	100% (80)			100% (400)	1.00
	Proportion	.20			1.00	

    a Complete the table.

    b Interpret the term $E_1 = 17.8$

    c Calculate the χ^2 value.

    d Is the χ^2 value significant? At what level? What exactly is the null hypothesis?

    e This data set proves that the usage of the library differs by age. True or false? Why?

5 Determine the p-value and the significance level of a hypothesis test on the table presented in problem 4 of Chapter 12. What is the null hypothesis? Interpret the p-value.

6 An experiment was conducted to determine which of three advertisements to use in introducing a new personal computer. A total of 120 people who were thinking of buying a personal computer was split randomly into three groups of 40. Each of the groups was shown a different advertisement and each person was asked his or her likelihood of buying the advertised brand. A scale of 1 (very unlikely) to 7 (very likely) was used. The results showed that the average likelihood of purchase was:

Advertisement A	5.5
Advertisement B	5.8
Advertisement C	5.2

The ANOVA table was as follows:

Source of Variation	SS	df	MSS	F-ratio	p-value
Due to advertisements	12	2	6.0		
Unexplained	234	117	2.0		
Total	246	119			

    a What is the appropriate null hypothesis? The alternate hypothesis?

    b What is the F-ratio? The p-value?

    c Is the result significant at the 0.10 level? The 0.05 level? The 0.01 level?

    d Are there any differences among the impacts of the three advertisements?

7 Using problem 6, assume that each of the three groups of respondents had been divided into two groups: younger (under 30) and older (over 30). The revised ANOVA table was as follows:

Source of Variation	SS	df	MSS	F-ratio	p-value
Due to advertisements	12	2	6.0		
Due to age	24	1	24.0		
Unexplained	210	116	1.81		
Total	246	119			

    a What are the F-ratio and p-value associated with the hypothesis test that there is no advertisement effect? Why is it different than that in problem 6? Notice that the total SS and the advertisement SS have not changed.

    b Test the hypothesis that there is no age effect.

8 Recall Case 12–1, the American Conservatory Theater. Calculating from Table 12–5, the F-statistics for the difference between means for the five variables are 27.9, 27.7, 2.4, 14.3, and 2.4. The number of degrees of freedom for the numerator is 2 (three minus one). The total degrees of freedom are 823. Why? Thus the degrees of freedom for the denominator are 821. Determine the significance level to be associated with each variable. What is the null hypothesis? Calculating from Table 12–6 of the same case, the chi-square value is 23.9. What is the significance level of the appropriate hypothesis test? What is the appropriate null hypothesis?

APPENDIX
MEASURES OF ASSOCIATION
FOR NOMINAL VARIABLES

We saw earlier in this chapter that the chi-square statistic is seriously flawed as a measure of the association of two variables. The nub of the problem is that the computed value of chi-square can tell us whether there is an association or a relationship but gives us only a weak indication of the strength of the association. The principal purpose of this appendix is to describe a measure, Goodman and Kruskal's Tau, which overcomes many of the problems of chi-square. First we look at some efforts to correct the problems of the chi-square measure. To illustrate these measures we return to Table 13–1, which is reproduced here. According to the chi-square test ($\chi^2 = 20$), the relationship between location and attendance in Table 13–1 is highly significant. That is, there is a probability of less than .001 that the observed relationship could have happened by chance. Now we wish to know whether there is a sufficiently strong relationship to justify taking action.

		Location (X)		Row Total
		Convenient	Not Convenient	
Attendance at Symphony (Y)	Often	22	18	40
	Occasionally	48	52	100
	Never	10	50	60
	Column total	80	120	200

Measures Based on Chi-Square

The most obvious flaw of chi-square is that the value is directly proportional to the sample size. If the sample were 2000, rather than 200 in the previous table, and if the distribution of responses were the same (i.e., all cells were 10 times as large) the chi-square would be 200 rather than 20. Two measures have been proposed to overcome this problem:

(1) Phi-squared: $\phi^2 \quad = \chi^2/n = \dfrac{20}{200} = 0.10$

(2) Contingency coefficient: $\phi = \sqrt{\dfrac{\chi^2}{n + \chi^2}}$

$$= \sqrt{\dfrac{20}{200 + 20}} = 0.31$$

Both measures are easy to calculate but unfortunately are hard to interpret. On the one hand, when there is no association they are both zero. But when there is an association between the two variables, there is no upper limit against which to compare the calculated values. (There is a special case, when the cross-tabulation has the same number of rows r and columns c, that an upper limit of the contingency coefficient can be computed for two perfectly correlated variables as $\sqrt{(r - 1)/r}$.)

Goodman and Kruskal's Tau

This is one of a class of measures that permit a "proportional reduction in error" interpretation. That is, a value of Tau between zero and one has a meaning in terms of the contribution of an independent variable—such as location—to explaining variation in a dependent variable such as attendance at the symphony.

The starting point for the calculation is the distribution of the dependent variable. Suppose we were given a sample of 200 people and, without knowing anything more about them, were given the task of assigning them to one of the three categories, as follows:

		Number in Category	
Attendance	1. Often	40	(20%)
at	2. Occasionally	100	(50%)
Symphony	3. Never	60	(30%)
(Y)		200	

The only way to complete the task is to randomly draw 40 from the 200 for the first category, and then 100 for the second category, and so forth. The question is, how many of the 40 people who actually belong in the first category would wind up in that category if this procedure were followed? The answer is 40 times (40 ÷ 200), or 8 people. This is because a random draw of any size from the 200 will on average contain 20 percent who are attending the symphony regularly.

For the purpose of computing Tau, our interest is in the number of errors we would make by randomly assigning the known distribution of responses. For the first category this is $40 - 8 = 32$ errors. Similarly, for the second ("occasionally") category we would make $100 (100 ÷ 200) = 50$ errors, and for the third category there would be $60 (140 ÷ 200) = 42$ errors. Therefore, we would expect to make $32 + 50 + 42 = 124$ errors in placing the 200 individuals. Of course, we do not expect to make exactly 124 errors, but this would be the best estimate if the process were repeated a number of times.

The next question is whether knowledge of the independent variable will significantly reduce the number of errors. If the two variables are independent we would expect no reduction in the number of errors. To find out we simply repeat the same process we went through for the total sample *within each category of the independent variable* (that is, within each column). Let us start with the 80 people who said the location of the symphony was convenient. Again we would expect an average, when randomly assigning 22 people from the "convenient location" group to the "often attend" category, to have $22 (58 ÷ 80) = 16$ errors. In total, for the "convenient location" group we would expect $16 + 48 (32 ÷ 80) + 10 (70 ÷ 80) = 44$ errors. We next take the 120 in the "not convenient" group and randomly assign 18 to the first category, 52 to the second category, and 50 to the third category of the dependent variable. The number of errors that would result would be

$$18 (102 ÷ 120) + 52 (68 ÷ 120) + 50 (70 ÷ 120) = 74 \text{ errors}$$

With knowledge of the category of the independent variable X to which each person belonged, the number of errors is $44 + 74 = 118$. This is six errors fewer than when we didn't have that knowledge. The Tau measure will confirm that we haven't improved our situation materially by adding an independent variable, X:

$$\text{Tau} = \frac{\left(\begin{array}{c}\text{number of errors} \\ \text{not knowing } X\end{array}\right) - \left(\begin{array}{c}\text{number of errors} \\ \text{when } X \text{ is known}\end{array}\right)}{\text{number of errors not knowing } X}$$

$$= \frac{124 - 118}{124} = 0.05$$

We now have a measure that is theoretically more meaningful, since a value of 0 means no reduction in error and a value of 1.0 indicates prediction with no error. However, a value of 1.0 can be achieved only when all cells but one in a column are empty, and such a condition is often impossible given the marginal distributions. Thus, most tables have a ceiling on Tau which is less than 1.0. For example, for the tables on symphony attendance the best relationship we would expect to get—given the marginal distributions of the table—is as follows:

		Location (X)		Total
		Convenient	Not Convenient	
Y	Often	40	0	40
	Occasionally	40	60	100
	Never	0	60	60
		80	120	200

The Tau for this table is 0.19. This value helps put our calculated value in perspective. The ceiling value of 0.19 for Tau, in a table that satisfies the known marginals, indicates that there is little basis for expecting a strong relationship in this table.

CASE 13–1

Medical Systems Associates: Measuring Patient Satisfaction[13]

Between 1950 and 1969 per capita consumer expenditures for nursing home services grew at a faster rate than any other health service category. During this period serious doubts were raised as to the quality of nursing home care and service. These concerns were confirmed by an HEW investigation in 1971 that lead to substantial adverse publicity. Ray Baxter of Medical Systems Associates (MSA) felt that most of the problems stemmed from the "product-orientation" of the nursing homes; that is, they were "more concerned with selling the services and facilities they had than with providing a service mix designed to satisfy the needs and wants of the patients." A study grant was received from HEW to test this broad proposition, and in particular (1) to study the process by which patients chose nursing homes and (2) to identify the determinants of

patient satisfaction. In early 1972 Baxter had completed the fieldwork and was wondering what he could conclude about the latter objective from the relationships he had observed in the data.

STUDY DESIGN

The primary vehicle for data collection was a twelve-page personal interview questionnaire containing more than 200 variables. The questionnaire was generally divided into six major conceptual areas as follows:

1 Socioeconomics

2 Lifestyle measures (past and present)

3 Attitudes, interests, and opinions

4 Nursing home selection process

5 Evaluation of nursing home environment

6 Perceived health

Questionnaire development required considerable trial and revision. Questions had to be worded to be compatible with low educational levels because the median school grade attained by patients was under eight years. Five-point rating scales did not work because the respondents rejected the supplied category descriptions and substituted broader descriptions of favorable, neutral, and negative. Standard projective techniques did not work well, apparently because many of the respondents were highly introspective.

The final questionnaire was administered in late 1971 to a stratified random sample of 122 patients in 16 nursing homes in Wisconsin. These homes were selected from a universe of 93 homes. The sampling plan was designed to insure representativeness along the following dimensions:

1 Type of ownership (individual, partnership, corporate, nonprofit)

2 Level of care (skilled, limited, personal)

3 Type of assistance approval (Medicare *and* Medical Assistance, Medical Assistance *only,* and no assistance)

4 Size (small—less than 100 patients; medium—100 to 200 patients; and large—more than 200 patients)

In order to maintain approximate proportionate representativeness of the sample with the universe, the number of patients randomly selected from each sample-member nursing home was based on the size of the home.

Prior to the contact of respondents by the field interviewers, telephone calls or visits to the administrators of each nursing home in the sample were made, eliciting their cooperation. In general, administrators proved to be highly cooperative.

In contacting respondents, the interviewer was provided with a prearranged random sampling procedure which she was instructed to follow. Upon completion of the basic interview, the interviewer requested that the respondent sign two ''release forms'' permitting the researchers subsequently to obtain financial data and to discuss medical details with the respondent's doctor.

ANALYSIS

The issue of the measurement of patient satisfaction and identification of determining variables was complicated by the special nature of the respondents. As Baxter noted, ''Very few persons not in nursing homes want to be in a nursing home. And how satisfied is any person with a nursing home when he has given up an established lifestyle because he now needs services he would prefer to not need? Most persons, in and out of nursing homes would opt for good health and independence. Because a nursing home represents an undesired portion of a life cycle, the problem, then, is to measure the satisfaction level of people who are, in an important sense, dissatisfied.''

Three approaches were used to measure ''conditional satisfaction,'' as it was termed. One was the *acceptance* of the necessity of entering a nursing home. The second was their *adjustment* to the disruption of established routines. The third was the patient's direct *evaluation* of his physical (medical), attitudinal, and environmental satisfaction. Each of the elements in the evaluation measure was represented by a separate index, based upon combinations of responses to various questions, as follows:

1 An Environmental Rating Index (ERI) was based upon answers to 14 questions involving satisfaction with such aspects of the nursing home as room size, physical layout, staff courtesy, medical care, cleanliness of facilities, food preparation, and so forth.

2 A Psychological Adjustment Index was based upon a series of attitudinal questions involving such issues as perceived self-usefulness, self-perceived level of activity, perceived lifestyle change, self-perceived reaction of others to nursing home patients, perceived difficulty in adjusting to nursing home life (upon arrival), desire to relocate, and so on.

TABLE 13–5

Cross-Classification Results: Environmental Rating Index
versus Selected Variables[a]

| Variable | Environmental Rating Index | | |
	Low	Medium	High
NURSING HOME RELIGIOUS AFFILIATION			
Church-supported	15.8%	34.1%	45.9%
Nonsectarian	84.2	65.9	54.1
	100.0	100.0	100.0
Sample Size	(19)	(41)	(61)
"HAVE YOU MADE ANY NEW FRIENDS HERE?"			
Yes	84.2	71.8	96.7
No	15.8	28.2	3.3
	100.0	100.0	100.0
Sample Size	(18)	(39)	(60)
NUMBER OF FRIENDS			
"Just a couple"	31.2	21.4	5.1
"Just a few"	31.2	14.3	20.3
"Quite a few"	37.6	64.3	74.6
	100.0	100.0	100.0
Sample Size	(16)	(28)	(59)

[a]All variables are associated with the ERI at a level of .05 or greater using the χ^2 test of significance.

3 A Physical Well-Being Validity Index was based upon a comparison of patients' self-perceived level of health with that indicated by medical records.

The focus of the initial analysis was on the determinants of the Environmental Rating Index (ERI). Cross-classification analyses with chi-square tests of significance were run for combinations of many variables with the ERI. Only three of the variables showed any statistical significance. (These variables, and the strength of the relationships, are summarized in Table 13–5). None of the other variables, such as the modernity of the home, the size of the home, the reasons for being in the nursing home, the selection process, or patient mobility, were found to be significantly associated with the ERI. As Ray Baxter reviewed these results he was wondering what conclusions he could draw, and whether other analyses would be required to examine the basic "product orientation" hypothesis with the ERI.

CASE 13–2

Apple Appliance Stores

An experiment using a randomized design was conducted by the Apple Appliance chain of 300 retail stores. Four levels of advertising provided the experimental treatment: none, low, medium, and high. In addition, the stores were divided by store size into small, intermediate, and large. A random sample of eight stores was taken from each of the three store-size groups. Each set of eight stores was divided randomly into four groups of two stores for the experimental treatment, as summarized by the following figure:

Store sales were measured during the six-month period after the experiment started. Sales also were determined during the same period in the previous year. The difference between the sales during the two periods was the variable of interest. A plot of the sales change is shown in Figure 13–6.

In Table 13–6, an analysis of variance is shown. Exactly what statistical questions are answered by the table? What additional, unanswered questions may be of interest?

		Store size			
		Small	Medium	Large	Total
Advertising level	None	2	2	2	6
	Low	2	2	2	6
	Medium	2	2	2	6
	High	2	2	2	6
	Total	8	8	8	

TABLE 13–6

Analysis of Variance of Sales Changes

Source of Variation	Sum of Squares	Degrees of Freedom	Mean Sum Squares	F-Ratio
Advertising	360	3	120	3.0[a]
Store size	88	2	44	1.1
Interaction	984	6	164	4.1[b]
Unexplained variation	480	12	40	
Total	1912	23		

[a]Significant at the 0.10 level.
[b]Significant at the 0.05 level.

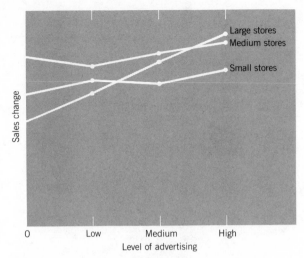

FIGURE 13–6 Effect of advertising on sales

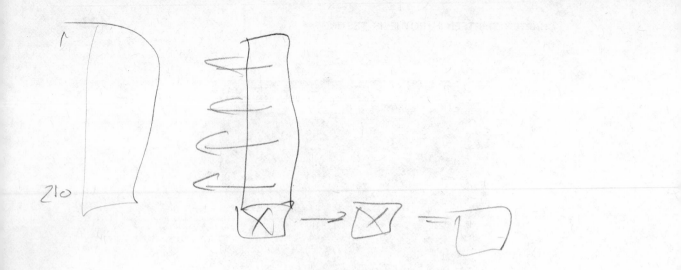

210

14

INTRODUCING A THIRD VARIABLE

In the HMO study it was found that the greatest interest in the proposed HMO was among the low-income respondents (see Figure 12–3 in Chapter 12). An appropriate question concerns why this association was found. Perhaps it was because higher-income people are more satisfied with their existing medical programs. They may be satisfied because they can afford good health care or because they eat better and are healthier. Or perhaps the interest in the HMO by the low-income respondents might be because the low-income people are students, who have needs and characteristics other than income that make them want the HMO. In fact, maybe the association between income and intentions to enroll has nothing to do with income but was just due to occupation.

Data analysis, particularly in descriptive studies, should be guided by such inquiries. Each analysis and potential analysis should be exposed to penetrating questions. The process involves mental effort, attempting to generate and explore hypotheses that are as rich and sophisticated as possible. It should not be satisfied with findings that are naive and simple if theory, common sense, and directed analysis can show otherwise.

Hopefully as much of this mental effort as possible will be exerted long before the data analysis starts. Recall the discussion in Chapter 2 about developing research questions with accompanying hypotheses that are as specific as possible. It is rare in a descriptive study, however, to have all the hypotheses (or even all the research questions) fully developed before the data analysis stage. Thus, the process needs to continue throughout the data analysis. Data analysis is not a set of computer techniques that provide a nice output if someone pushes a button.

A primary goal of this chapter is to open the reader's mind to the possible logical explanation of an association (or the lack of an association) found between two variables. Hopefully a richer and more sophisticated thought process will emerge. Methodologically, the chapter will introduce a third variable into the analysis. In Chapter 12, associations between two variables were discussed. In this chapter, relationships among three variables will be considered. Thus, this is the first of the "multivariate analysis" chapters. Many of the concepts and issues of multivariate analysis can be considered best in the three-variables context. Conceptually, this chapter will deal with causal relationships and with the problems of inferring causality in a descriptive study where experimental controls have not been employed.

Much of marketing research is concerned with identifying and understanding causal relationships. What influence will a price change have upon attendance? Do lifestyle patterns affect the use of regional shopping centers? The problem of research design and data analysis is to provide evidence relevant to making judgments about causal relationships.

As the discussions on causal inference presented in Chapter 9 indicated, there are three types of evidence relevant to evaluating casual relationships:

- Evidence that a strong association exists between an action and an observed outcome
- Evidence that action preceded the outcome
- Evidence that there is no strong competing explanation for the relationship

The strongest type of evidence comes from experimental design studies where competing explanations for associations are reduced or eliminated by the design. The question is: How can competing explanations be identified and explored when experimental controls are not present? The first step in addressing that question is to provide an overview of the type of competing explantions that should be considered.

CAUSAL RELATIONSHIPS

Causation, strictly speaking, means that a change in one variable will produce a change in another. In this context, the definition will be broadened somewhat to include the concept of a precondition influencing a variable of interest. Thus, we could conceive that credit-card usage is partly determined by a persons's sex. In this case, sex could be conceptualized as causal in nature, despite the fact that it would be impossible to take a group of people and change their sex to observe if a change in credit-card usage was "produced." The weaker term, "influence," often will be used when it is more appropriate than the term "cause," but the logic of the analysis normally will remain the same.

Given the causation concept, that a change in one variable will produce a change in another, it is reasonable to conclude that, if two variables are causally linked, they should be associated. Thus, an obvious data analysis procedure to identify or confirm causation is to measure the association between two variables. If association provides evidence of causation, then, conversely, the lack of association suggests the absence of causation. Thus, an association between attitude (A) and behavior (B) is evidence of:

$$\text{A Causal Relationship}$$
$$A \rightarrow B$$

If a third variable is introduced into the analysis, however, at least five other causal explanations for the association become possible. The association could be due spuriously to a third variable, C (such as income—a high-income explains a person's attitude toward the Republican party's positions and the person's voting behavior):

SPURIOUS ASSOCIATION BETWEEN A AND B

But there are other possibilities as well. Three of the most interesting are:

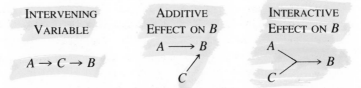

| INTERVENING VARIABLE | ADDITIVE EFFECT ON B | INTERACTIVE EFFECT ON B |

The first is that the third variable intervenes in the causal link between variables A and B. The second is that variable C is an independent cause of variable B. The third is that there is an interactive effect of variables A and C on variable B.

Even when a third variable is not involved in the analysis, the direction of causation could still be in doubt. It could be that we have:

A CAUSAL RELATIONSHIP
IN THE REVERSE DIRECTION
$B \rightarrow A$

In the following five sections, each of the five causal interpretations will be discussed. It should be noted that the discussion could apply to any association measurement introduced in Chapter 12.

SPURIOUS ASSOCIATION

Association measures, by themselves, do not demonstrate causation. This statement merits repeating because it is so easy to forget or suppress in the context of data analysis. Association measures do not demonstrate causation because they can be the result of extraneous variables. For example, the number of churches in a community is associated with the number of liquor stores. Yet, few would maintain that churches tend to spawn liquor stores (or the reverse). The fact is that the association is spurious because of the third variable, community size, which influences both the number of churches and the number of liquor stores. Another example is the fact that the amount of damage at a fire is associated with the number of fire trucks, only because a large fire both attracts fire trucks and causes substantial damage. If you add fire trucks, you don't increase the damage.

A major task of data analysis is to help the researcher identify such spurious associations, determine their nature and extent, and attempt to correct for them. Actually, the term "spurious association" is misleading, since the association is usually real enough. It is the causal interpretation that is spurious. However, the phrase has grown to mean an inappropriate causal interpretation of associations.

Association measures can be useful in prediction even if no causal analysis is involved. If a researcher needs to know the number of liquor stores in a community, a knowledge of the number of churches will be helpful, even though there is no causal link between the two. Often, however, there is a desire to gain a deeper understanding of the relationship. Even if prediction is the primary objective, a better understanding of the relationship may suggest the conditions under which the association can be used for predictions and the likely conditions under which the prediction might err. Sometimes, however, the desire is not only to predict the dependent variable but to influence it. Thus, an organization may want to influence the number of churches in a community—to increase their number, for example. Then there is a need to identify variables that influence the number of churches so that effective programs can be developed and implemented.

The Transit Study[1]

The possibility that a third variable is a source of spurious association will be considered first in the context of an example. Table 14–1 shows an analysis of a study of advertising for a transit system. The system had not done any previous media advertising. To test the effectiveness of getting people to use the system more, a series of television advertisements were run with the appeal that money, time, and aggravation could be saved by riding the transit system. A survey of people in the area just after the test period generated 360 responses. Three variables were isolated for analysis:

I: Whether the respondent intended ($I = 1$) or did not intend ($I = 0$) to use the system during the coming four-week period

A: Whether the respondent could ($A = 1$) or could not ($A = 0$) recall the transit advertising

U: Whether the respondent had ($U = 1$) or had not ($U = 0$) used the system during the four-week period preceding the test advertising

The objective was to determine if the advertising was successful in generating intentions to use the system. Thus, the analysis starts by looking at the relationship between advertising and intentions. The first cross-tabulation in Table 14–1 explores this relationship. Notice that the percentage is based on intention, which is assumed to be the variable

[1]This discussion is based in part on Hans Zeisel, *Say It With Figures* (New York: Harper & Row, 1968), pp. 105–226.

Table14-1
Intentions to Use versus Advertisement Recall and Previous Usage

| | ALL RESPONDENTS —A— | | TRANSIT USER —A— | | —U— | TRANSIT NONUSER —A— | |
	RECALL ADV.	NOT RECALL ADV.	RECALL ADV.	NOT RECALL ADV.		RECALL ADV.	NOT RECALL ADV.
Intended to use —I—	63%(95)	36%(75)	85%(85)	80%(48)		20%(10)	18%(27)
Not intend to use	37%(55)	64%(135)	15%(15)	20%(12)		80%(40)	82%(123)
	100%(150)	100%(210)	100%(100)	100%(60)		100%(50)	100%(150)
χ^2	25		0.66			0.416	
χ^2 test	Sig. at .001 level		Not sig. at 0.25 level			Not sig. at 0.25 level	
Logical implication	$A \rightarrow I$				$A \overset{I}{\underset{U}{\nwarrow\nearrow}}$		

409

to be influenced, the dependent variable. The advertising recall variable (*A*) is thus the causal or independent variable. Table 14–1 shows that the association between advertising (*A*) and intentions (*I*) is high. The association can be determined by comparing the percent who intend to use the system. It is confirmed by the size and statistical significance of the chi-square statistic, here a measure of association. Thus an implication could be that advertising influences intentions via:

A Causal Relationship

$A \rightarrow I$

The next step in the analysis was to introduce the usage variable. When the analysis of the relationship between advertising and intention to use is repeated for transit users and nonusers, the association between advertising and intention virtually disappears. Note that the chi-square statistic is small and statistically insignificant. The association disappears because it was spurious, caused by the fact that advertising recall and intentions were both influenced by usage.

A Spurious Relationship

between *A* and *I*

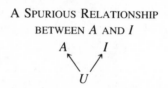

When the association between two variables is explained by the identification of a third variable influencing both, the association is termed spurious. The extent to which an association provides evidence of a causal relationship is largely based upon the confidence that the association is not spurious. Thus, an effort to discover measured or unmeasured extraneous variables is an important task of analysis.

Figure 14–1 shows the association between advertising recall and intentions in graphic

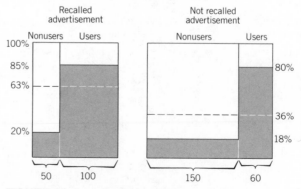

FIGURE 14–1   Intentions to buy

form. It shows that the 63 percent of those with positive intentions who recalled the advertising represented an average of 50 nonusers and 100 users. Further, the 36 percent of those not recalling the advertising but who intended to use represented an average of 150 nonusers and 60 users. The reason that the association between advertising and intentions was explained by the usage variable was because of the difference between the composition of the "recalled-advertising" group and the "didn't-recall-advertising" group. The users tended to notice and recall the advertising whereas the nonusers were not as interested in the transit system or its advertising. If the composition has been identical, the association between advertising and intentions would not have been affected by the introduction of the usage variable.

Experimental Control

To understand this logic completely, it is necessary to recall the concept of experimental control introduced in Chapter 9. Suppose an experiment was designed to test the effect of advertising on intentions by selecting a group of 100 users and another group of 100 nonusers. Half of each of these groups would be selected randomly and exposed to the advertisements. Thus, a user subgroup of size 50 would be exposed to the advertisement and the remaining 50 users would not be exposed. Intentions would then be measured for all 200 subjects. The result would be a randomized block design:

| | Block effect | |
Treatment	Nonusers	Users
Advertising exposure	50	50
No advertising exposure	50	50

Here, the usage variable is controlled by being introduced as a block. Using the notation of Chapter 9, the symbolic representation is:

$$
\text{Nonusers} \begin{cases} R & X & 0_1 & n = 50 \\ \cdots\cdots\cdots\cdots \\ R & & 0_2 & n = 50 \end{cases}
$$

$$
\text{Users} \begin{cases} R & X & 0_3 & n = 50 \\ \cdots\cdots\cdots\cdots \\ R & & 0_4 & n = 50 \end{cases}
$$

An experiment also can control for variables without introducing them as a block in the design. Assume that the experiment is conducted on 200 randomly selected people, including users and nonusers. The advertisement-exposure treatment is given to half, who are selected randomly. The result would be a simple randomized design:

$$R \qquad 0 \quad n = 100$$
$$\cdots\cdots\cdots\cdots$$
$$R \quad X \quad 0 \quad n = 100$$

Any resulting association between advertising and intentions then could be assumed to be devoid of any spuriousness. It might be that, by accident, the exposed group had an abnormally high representation of nonusers, or users. Although that possibility might have to be considered (and could be considered), the fact that the exposed group was selected randomly acts to minimize that possibility, as well as the possibility that other variables besides usage were generating (spuriously) the association between advertising and intentions. This randomization is a way of controlling extraneous variables, such as usage and others that may be unknown.

In the "test" represented in Table 14–1, the exposed and unexposed groups were self-selected. People were assigned randomly to the two groups, and therein lies the possibility that other factors caused the self-selection to occur. One of these factors, as has been illustrated, was usage. There may be others.

Statistical Control

A second method to control for variables that are a source of spurious association is termed "statistical control." An example is the process of introducing usage in Table 14–1 as a control variable. The association between A and I for the nonuser group then could be interpreted as association with usage held constant—all are nonusers. The association for the user group has the same interpretation.

Another illustration comes from a chain of retail book stores. Suppose store sales were thought to be influenced by store advertising. Suppose, however, that the association between advertising and sales was caused spuriously by store size. The large stores tended to have higher sales and to advertise more. A solution might be to control statistically for store size by determining the association between store sales and advertising for large stores and the association for small stores. In Chapter 19 the use of regression analysis to accomplish statistical control will be presented.

Statistical control provides a way to proceed when a true experiment is not conducted, and it often will control adequately for the identified variable. The problem is that there might be other variables that are unmeasured and even unknown. These will remain uncontrolled and will be a source of misinterpretation. The analyst should draw upon existing theory and common sense to attempt to identify possible sources of spurious association and to determine the extent to which they may be affecting the analysis. The advantage of randomization in experimental control is that it will control for both known and unknown variables.

A Combination of Causal Paths

There are times when the association between two variables is completely explained by the introduction of a third variable; however, the more common situation is where the association is reduced but not eliminated by the introduction of the control variable. In Table 14–1 the association was still positive, although small, after the introduction of the control variable. If it were a bit larger, it might have been reasonable to conclude that the original association represented partly a causal link and partly a spurious association:

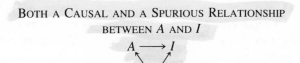

BOTH A CAUSAL AND A SPURIOUS RELATIONSHIP
BETWEEN A AND I

We now turn to the three other ways in which a third variable can be introduced into the analysis: as an intervening variable, as an additive cause, and as an interactive cause.

INTERVENING VARIABLES

An intervening variable is conceptually very different from a variable causing spurious association:

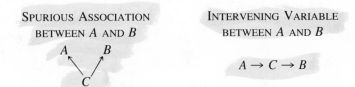

SPURIOUS ASSOCIATION
BETWEEN A AND B

INTERVENING VARIABLE
BETWEEN A AND B

$$A \rightarrow C \rightarrow B$$

However, from a data analysis viewpoint the two cases are indistinguishable. In each case, the association between A and B will disappear if the analyst controls for C. In the first case, it is because C caused both A and B or is associated with both A and B. In the second, it is because C intervened between A and B; that is, A causes C, which in turn causes B.

The two cases can be distinguished by determining the direction of causation between A and C. If it runs from A to C, then an intervening variable is involved. In the example of Table 14–1, the interpretation is actually rather clear. It is impossible for the advertising during the test period to influence behavior before that period. Further, it is very possible that past usage did influence attention to, and readership of, the advertisements and, thus, advertising recall. It is not unusual for the advertising exposure to be higher among those in the audience who use and are thus involved with the advertisement. Thus, it was concluded that the most appropriate model was

A SPURIOUS ASSOCIATION
BETWEEN *A* AND *I*

A   *I*

U

If the third variable seemed to intervene between the two variables, the association—even though eliminated by the third variable—would not be deemed spurious, because the link between the two variables still would be meaningful. Suppose that three variables of interest were:

A = advertising expenditures
O = the attitude of opinion leaders
G = the attitude of the general population

If the association between *A* and *G* were eliminated when the analysis controlled for *O*, the interpretation might be that advertising influenced general attitudes by influencing opinion leaders, thus we would have

AN INTERVENING VARIABLE
BETWEEN *A* AND *G*
$A \rightarrow O \rightarrow G$

and the association of *A* and *G* would not be regarded as spurious.

Of course, there could be a causal path directly between the two variables *A* and *B* and also an indirect influence from *A* to *B* operating through variable *C*:

BOTH DIRECT AND INDIRECT CAUSAL
RELATIONSHIPS BETWEEN *A* AND *B*

AN ADDITIVE CAUSAL RELATIONSHIP

The introduction of a third variable also can have an additive causal effect. The diagram depicting such a relationship would be:

AN ADDITIVE EFFECT ON *B*
$A \longrightarrow B$

C

For example, Figure 14–2 indicates that there is an association between people's concern for the environment in general (E) and their concern about air pollution (A). In addition, the method of commuting (C) also influences their attitudes toward air pollution. Thus, it might be reasonable to hypothesize that there is

AN ADDITIVE EFFECT ON A

$$E \longrightarrow A$$
$$\nearrow$$
$$C$$

The lower line in the graphical representation in Figure 14–2 shows the relationship between A and E for those who commute by car. The upper line is the relationship between A and E for those who commute without using a car. The effect of the commute method has been *added* to the effect of E. The fact that the two lines are parallel is characteristic

	Environmental Concern (E)					
			E_1-Low Commute (C)		E_2-High Commute (C)	
	E_1-Low	E_2-High	C_1-Car	C_2-Other	C_1-Car	C_2-Other
Attitude toward air pollution (A)[a]	4.1	5.6	3.7	4.8	5.2	6.3
Sample size	75	90	30	45	60	30

[a] On a 1–7 (low to high concern) scale.

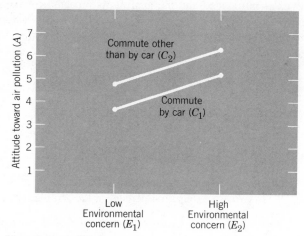

FIGURE 14–2 Air pollution attitudes

of an additive relationship. Recall the examples in the discussion of Figure 9–1. Unless an interactive term is included, the assumption in an experiment is that the treatment and block effects are additive. Similarly, most of the techniques to be introduced in Part IV also will employ the additive assumption.

INTERACTIVE CAUSAL RELATIONSHIPS

The introduction of a third variable also might suggest some interactions. Sales (S) might be influenced by distribution (D), but only if the packaging and display (P) is appealing and capable of attracting the shoppers' attention. The causal relationship, then, might be:

AN INTERACTIVE EFFECT ON S

Interactions, which are present when associations between two variables are affected by the presence or absence of a third variable, were explored in the context/of factorial experimental designs (recall Figures 9–1 and 13–5). In the context of cross-tabulations this possibility is explored by developing cross-tabs for subgroups defined by the third variable.

Suppose that a segmentation study is attempting to identify the heavy users of a certain library. In Figure 14–3 it is shown that 28 percent of those below age 40 use it, while only 20 percent of those over age 40 use it. To explore the relationship further the variable of sex is introduced and the analysis is repeated for men and for women. The age and usage relationship is much stronger for men than it is for women. Thus, the addition of the sex variable has permitted the analysis to be more refined. As Figure 14–3 shows, the two lines are not parallel, since an interaction is present. This is depicted as follows:

AN INTERACTIVE EFFECT
ON USAGE

Age
⟩⟶ Usage
Sex

In another case the relationship appeared to be zero until a third variable was introduced.[2] In two age groups, 64 percent of the sample listened to classical music. However,

[2]Hans Zeisel, *Say It With Figures* (New York: Harper & Row, 1968), pp. 123–124.

	Below 40	40 and Over	Below 40		40 and Over	
			Men	Women	Men	Women
Library usage	28%	20%	36%	20%	23%	17%
Sample size	1,224	952	619	605	480	472

Source: Adapted from Hans Zeisel, *Say It with Figures* (New York: Harper & Row, 1968), p. 21.

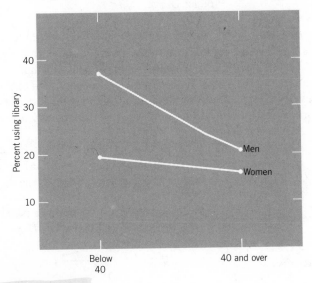

FIGURE 14–3 Library usage

among the college-educated people, the older group tended to listen more, while among noncollege-educated people, the younger group tended to have a higher percentage of listeners. Again, the addition of the interactive variable, education, helped refine the analysis.

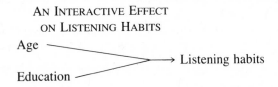

An Interactive Effect
on Listening Habits

The conclusion occasionally can be clouded by the existence of a portion of the sample that is not responsive to one of the variables. For example, in a study of the impact of advertising exposure, it was found that product users, the bulk of the sample, were not responsive to the advertising. When only nonusers were examined, this hypothesized effect emerged:

AN INTERACTIVE EFFECT
ON IMPACT ON AUDIENCE

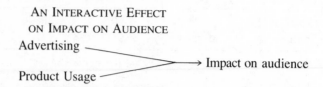

In taste tests, there may be a substantial group who simply are not taste-sensitive. When these people are removed from the analysis, the conclusions can be more pronounced.

The soundest way to identify interactions is to employ theory, previous findings, and common sense. However, when there are many variables involved and theory is underdeveloped, it is useful to identify interactions that are present in the study without performing all conceivable cross-tabs (sometimes literally infeasible). An appropriate method is AID, to be described in Chapter 19.

Again, a combination of relationships can exist. For example, an interactive effect might be found in addition to an independent effect. Perhaps distribution (D) will influence sales (S), but its influence will be larger when the packaging and display (P) are effective:

AN INTERACTIVE AND DIRECT CAUSAL
RELATIONSHIP BETWEEN D AND S

THE DIRECTION OF CAUSATION ISSUE

If a causal link between two variables is thought to exist, a reasonable question is: Which variable is the causal (or independent) variable and which is the "caused" (or dependent) variable? Such a question arose when the task was to distinguish between

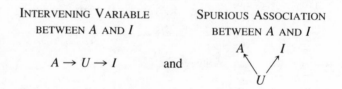

INTERVENING VARIABLE
BETWEEN A AND I

$A \rightarrow U \rightarrow I$ and

SPURIOUS ASSOCIATION
BETWEEN A AND I

In some situations there is a reciprocal causal relationship. Attitudes can influence purchase, for example. However, the act of purchasing and using a product or service can affect the attitude, which again affects purchase. Even when a reciprocal causal relationship exists, it might be useful to determine the direction of the dominant flow of influence. Does the attitude-to-purchase direction have a greater effect than the purchase-to-attitude direction, for example?

One approach to determining the direction of causation is to draw upon logic and previous theory, as was done in arguing that the usage variable was a common cause of advertising recall and intentions:

SPURIOUS ASSOCIATION BETWEEN A AND I

In this context it is useful to observe whether one of the variables is relatively fixed and unalterable. Variables like sex, age, and income are relatively permanent. If, for example, an association is found between age and attendance at rock concerts, it would be unrealistic to claim that attendance at rock concerts causes people to be young. In this case age could not be a "caused" variable because it is fixed in this context. However, it could be that age is an important determinant of who attends rock concerts.

A second approach is to consider the fact that there is usually a time lag between cause and effect. If such a time lag can be postulated, the causal variable should have a positive association with the effect variable lagged in time. When intervally scaled variables are involved, the approach is termed *cross-lag correlation.*[3]

SUMMARY[4]

In Chapter 12, we introduced measures of association between two variables, which can provide evidence of causal relationships. The task for the analyst in a descriptive study is to exert the mental effort required to employ theory, common sense, and data analysis to explore competing explanations for associations. This chapter explores four explanations that become possible when a third variable is introduced.

The first, termed spurious association, involves the possibility that two variables—such as advertising and intention—are both caused by a third variable, usage. Spurious association can be detected by developing association measures for subgroups defined by

---

[3]Discussed in D. T. Campbell and J. C. Stanley, "Experimental and Quasi-Experimental Designs for Research on Teaching," in N. L. Gage, ed., *Handbook of Research on Teaching,* (Chicago: Rand McNally, 1963). For an example, see Terrence O'Brien, "Stages of Consumer Decision Making," *Journal of Marketing Research, 8* (August 1971), 283–289.

[4]The interested reader who would like to pursue further the ideas contained in this chapter is referred to Norris Rosenberg, *The Logic of Survey Analysis* (New York: Basic Books), 1968.

the spurious variable (i.e., users and nonusers). The problem is to identify the spurious variable.

Three other possibilities exist when a third variable is introduced:

INTERVENING VARIABLE   ADDITIVE EFFECT   INTERACTIVE EFFECT

$$A \rightarrow C \rightarrow B$$

$$A \searrow \atop C \nearrow B$$

$$A \atop C \searrow\!\!\!\!\nearrow \rightarrow B$$

The latter two were introduced in Chapter 9.

QUESTIONS AND PROBLEMS

1   When does association imply causation? Under what conditions? Could there ever be a causal relationship without association present?

2   Does the discussion surrounding Table 14–1 indicate that the following causal relationships hold?

$$U \rightarrow A \qquad \text{and} \qquad U \rightarrow I$$

Using the data in Table 14–1, generate a cross-tabulation of U vs. A and U vs. I. Determine the χ^2 value and its associated significance level for both.

3   What is a spurious association? Explain spurious association in the context of the Table 14–1 example. How do you distinguish between spurious association and the existence of an intervening variable? Why was the following model rejected in Table 14–1?

$$A \rightarrow U \rightarrow I$$

4   Two randomized experimental designs were described in the chapter, a randomized block design and a randomized design. If the Table 14–1 data were based on these designs how would the structure of Figure 14–1 differ?

5   Explain the difference between experimental control and statistical control. Give examples.

6   How would you distinguish among the following?

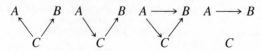

7 How would you distinguish between the following?

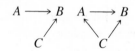

8 How would you distinguish between the following?

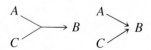

9 There were two competing hypotheses in a study of instant coffee. The first was that attitude change caused behavior change as measured by market share. The other was that behavior change precipitated attitude change as people adjusted their attitudes to match their behavior. Bimonthly data on market share and attitudes were obtained for a three-year period for several brands. The correlation between market share and lagged attitude was 0.70. The correlation between attitude and lagged market share was 0.46. Can you make any judgment about the direction of causation?

10 In the HMO study, the intentions-to-enroll question was described in Chapter 12 as a five-point scale ranging from "Yes, I would enroll" (1) to "No, I would not enroll" (5). The average response was 3.12. The following shows the response by income and by the response to a question asking whether the distance to the proposed HMO was satisfactory.

	ALL	INCOME OVER $13,000	INCOME UNDER $13,000	DISTANCE SATIS- FACTORY	DISTANCE UNSATIS- FACTORY
Average enrollment intentions	3.12	3.32	2.85	3.00	3.62
Sample size	1132	655	477	930	202

	INCOME UNDER $13,000		INCOME OVER $13,000	
	DISTANCE SATISFACTORY	DISTANCE UNSATISFACTORY	DISTANCE SATISFACTORY	DISTANCE UNSATISFACTORY
Average enrollment intentions	2.77	3.39	3.20	3.72
Sample size	416	61	514	141

Consider intentions as the caused or dependent variable. What is the nature of the causal relationships? Plot intentions by the "distance satisfactory" question. Replot it for both income levels.

11 A study of homemakers' usage of detergent involved three variables:

U 1 Heavy user of detergent
  0 Light user of detergent

H 1 Orientated toward the home
  0 Oriented outside the home

C 1 Bought detergent brands primarily for their cleaning power
  0 Evaluated detergents on other grounds

Analyze the data using two- and three-variable cross-tabs, with U as the dependent variable, and determine the nature of the causal links between the three variables. The number of respondents in the various categories is as follows:

$H = 1$				$H = 0$			
$C = 0$		$C = 1$		$C = 0$		$C = 1$	
$U = 1$	$U = 0$	$U = 1$	$U = 0$	$U = 1$	$U = 0$	$U = 1$	$U = 0$
50	40	400	20	220	150	90	5

15

PRESENTING THE RESULTS

It is difficult to exaggerate the importance of the role that communication skills play in effective management. Along with the related skill of working with and motivating people, the ability to communicate effectively is undoubtedly the most important attribute a manager can have. There is also little doubt that managers are dissatisfied with the level of communication skills that now exists. Business schools are criticized routinely and justifiably for focusing upon techniques and neglecting communication skills. Further, managers frequently make harsh judgments about themselves and their colleagues with respect to communication skills. A senior advertising executive concluded that "advertising people are bright, presentable, usually articulate—but most of them are duds when it comes to making presentations."[1] A special *Business Week* report indicated that "so appalling is the quality of written reports in some companies that senior executives are sending their managers through writing courses intended to put some point back into the reports that cross their desks and to eliminate the extraneous material that increasingly obscures the point."[2]

Effective communication between the research user or users and the research professionals is extremely important to the research process. The formal presentation usually will play a key role in the communication effort. There are really two points on the research process where a presentation is used. First, there is the presentation of the research proposal, discussed in Chapter 3, where the audience members will need to decide to accept, change, or reject. Second, there is the presentation of the research results, where decisions associated with the research purpose are addressed and the advisability of conducting further research is often considered. This chapter will focus upon the presentation of research results, but much of the material will apply to the research proposal presentation as well.

---

[1] Ron Hoff, "What's Your Presentation Quotient?" *Advertising Age*, (January 16, 1978) 93.
[2] "Teaching the Boss to Write," *Business Week*, (October 25, 1976), 56.

GUIDELINES TO SUCCESSFUL PRESENTATIONS

The objective of this chapter is to help readers avoid making presentations that are ineffective because they are dull, confusing, or irrelevant. Have you been exposed lately to any that hit the jackpot, that are all three? Presentations can be written, oral, or both. Later in the chapter, some tips on making oral presentations will be offered. First, however, several guidelines will be presented and discussed that apply to both types of presentations. In general, a presenter should:

1 Communicate to a specific audience
2 Structure the presentation
3 Create audience interest
4 Be specific and visual
5 Address validity and reliability issues

Each of these guidelines will be discussed in turn.

Communicate to a Specific Audience

The first step is to know the audience and its background and objectives. Most effective presentations seem like a conversation or a memo to a particular person, as opposed to an amorphous group. The key to obtaining that feeling is to identify the audience members as precisely as possible.

Audience identification will affect presentation decisions such as selecting the material to be included and the level of presentation. Excessive detail or material presented at too low a level can be boring or patronizing. However, the audience can be irritated or lost when material perceived as relevant is excluded or the material is presented at too high a level. In an oral presentation, the audience members can be asked whether they already know some of the material.

Frequently, there will be two or more different audiences to which a presentation must be addressed. There are several ways to deal with such a problem. In a written presentation, an executive summary at the outset can provide an overview of the conclusions for the benefit of the audience that is not interested in details. The presentation should respect the time constraints of the audience members. An appendix also can be used to reach some selectively without distracting the others. Sometimes in the introduction to a chapter or a section the reader can be told the nature of the contents and that it may be bypassed by certain audiences. In an oral presentation, the existence of multiple audiences should be recognized with a statement such as, "I need to provide some information on instrumentation next. You engineers in the audience could help by making sure that I don't miss anything." With such an acknowledgment, the engineers probably will be flattered and helpful rather than bored and restless.

Structure the Presentation

Each piece of the presentation should fit into the whole, just as individual pieces fit into a jigsaw puzzle. The audience should not be muttering, "What on earth is this person talking about?" or "How does this material fit in?" or "I'm lost." The solution is to provide a well-defined structure. As Figure 15–1 illustrates, the structure should include an introduction, a body, and a summary. Further, each of the major sections themselves should be structured in a similar manner. The precept is to tell the audience what you are going to say, say it, and then tell them what you said. Sometimes you want to withhold the conclusion to create interest. In that case the audience could then be told—"The objective here will be to come to a recommendation as to whether this new product should go into test market and, if so, with what type of pricing strategy."

The Introduction. This should play several roles. First, it should provide audience interest, a task that will be discussed in detail in the next section. A second function is to identify the central idea or objective of the presentation. A third role is to provide a road map to the rest of the presentation so that the audience can picture the organization and flow. Sometimes the only way to develop such a road map is to say something like, "This presentation has four parts. The research purpose and objectives will be discussed first. In the second section the research design will be described. . . ." However, with a little effort and luck it is sometimes possible to develop and use a flowchart that will

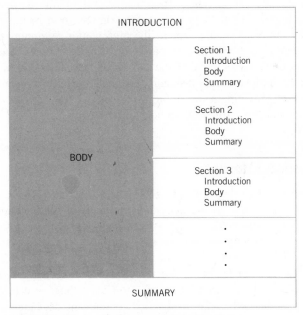

FIGURE 15–1 The presentation structure

provide the structure in a more interesting way. For example, in this book such a structural role was played by Figures 1–1, 2–2, 3–1, and 4–1 (the reader should attempt to identify other figures so used). When such a device is used, the audience should be clear when each section is to be addressed. The label for the section should use identical wording throughout, and the start of the section should be made clear: "Having finished the second section, we now move to the third section."

The Body.   Usually it is best to divide the body of the presentation (or the major section) into two to five parts. The audience will be able to absorb only so much information. If that information can be aggregated into chunks, it will be easier to assimilate. Sometimes the points to be made are not combined easily or naturally. In that case, it is sometimes necessary to use a longer list: "There are 12 problems with this new product concept." However, the presentation should never drift through the body with no structure at all.

One way to structure a presentation is by the research questions: "This research was conducted to address four research questions. Each of these will be considered in turn." Another method that is often useful when presenting the research proposal is to base it upon the research process, as was illustrated in Chapter 3.

The most useful presentations will include a statement of implications and recommendations relevant to the research purpose. However, when the researcher lacks information about the total situation because the research study only addresses a limited aspect of it, then the ability to generate recommendations may be limited.

The Summary.   The purpose of the presentation summary is to identify and underline the important points of the presentation and to provide some repetition of their content. The summary should support the presentation communication objectives by helping the audience to retain the key parts of the presentation content. The audience usually will perk up when they realize the end is near and an overview of the presentation is coming, so the summary section should be signaled clearly. A section summary has the additional task of providing a transition to the next section. The audience should feel that there is a natural flow from one section to the next.

Create Audience Interest

The audience should be provided with a motivation to read or listen to the presentation's major parts and to the individual elements of each section. The audience should know why the presentation is relevant to them and why each section was included. A section that cannot hold interest probably should be excluded or relegated to appendix status.

The research purpose and objectives are a good vehicle to provide motivation. The research purpose should specify decisions to be made and should relate to the research questions. A presentation that focuses upon those research questions and their associated hypotheses will naturally be tied to relevant decisions and hold audience interest. In contrast, a presentation that attempts to report on all questions that were included in the survey and in the cross-tabulations often will be long, uninteresting, and of little value.

The researcher should point out those aspects of the results that are important and interesting. Suppose a chart is used that contains 10 descriptors of customers in 13 different markets. The presenter should circle three or so of those 130 numbers and be prepared to observe: "Look at this number. We had hypothesized it to be higher than the others and it is actually lower. Let's look at the possible reasons and implications." The presenter should not have a compulsion to wade through every detail of the questionnaire and the analysis.

As the analysis is proceeding and as the presentation is being prepared, the researcher should be on the lookout for results that are exceptionally persuasive, relevant, interesting, and unusual. Sometimes the deviant respondent with the strange answers can provide the most insight if she is pursued and not discarded. For example, in Figure 13–3, more respondents answered the age question than the income question. Of the 48 respondents who did not answer the income question, almost all of them were "moderately interested" in the new health plan. Why? Are there any implications? Sometimes a few or even one deviant respondent can provide useful ideas and insights.

The best way to provide interest is to make the content so relevant that the audience will be interested; however, you will not always be blessed with absorbing content. Especially in those cases, it is very useful to make the presentation a lively and interesting experience. One way is to interject humor. The best humor is that tied to the subject matter or to the presentation, as opposed to memorized jokes that really do not fit. It is good to reward the audience periodically, however, and humor often works. Another tactic is to use a change of pace in the presentation. Break up the text with graphs, pictures, or even cartoons. In an oral presentation, try a variety of visual aids and some audience-involvement techniques. For example, the audience can be asked a question periodically and given a chance to talk and become involved.

Be Specific and Visual

Avoid talking or writing in the abstract. If different members of the audience have different or vague understandings of important concepts, there is a potential problem. Terms that are ambiguous or not well known should be defined and illustrated or else omitted. Thus, in a segmentation study, an "active saver" might be unambiguously defined as one who added at least $500 to savings each of the last two years.

The most interesting presentations usually use specific stories, anecdotes, studies, or incidents to make points. They will be much more interesting and graphic than a generalization, however accurate and scientific. Instead of "studies have shown that . . . ," it is more effective to say, "in the Topeka test market the 69¢ price had far less trial than the 89¢ price for product X when the bright blue package was used." A utility company conducted a focus-group study to learn homeowners' motivation to conserve energy and their attitudes toward adding insulation. The marketing research director, in presenting the results to top management, played a 20-minute edited videotape recording of the focus groups, in which the key segments were illustrated graphically. The impact on the audience was greater than otherwise would have been possible. They actually heard specific customers, representative of the emerged segments, forcefully put forth their views.

The adage, ''A picture is worth a thousand words,'' applies to both written and oral presentations. A mass of data often can be communicated clearly with graphs. A wide variety is available, such as bar graphs, line graphs, pie charts (see Figure 15–2). Color can be employed to add interest, to highlight findings, and to help deal with complexity.

Address Issues of Validity and Reliability

The presentation should help the audience avoid misinterpreting the results. Throughout Part II of this book countless potential research design issues have been raised that can affect the validity and interpretation of the results. The wording of the questions, the ordering of the questions, and the sampling design are among the design dimensions that can lead to biased results and misinterpretations. The presentation should not include an exhaustive description of all the design considerations. Nobody is interested in a text discussion of the advantages of telephone over mail surveys or how you located homes in an area sampling design. However, when the wording of a question or some other design issue can affect an interpretation and ultimately a research conclusion, then that issue should be raised and its possible affect upon the interpretation discussed. For example, in a product concept test, the method of exposing respondents to the concept may be crucial. Some discussion of why the method used was selected and its affect on the interpretation may be very useful. Try to identify those design issues that will affect interpretation and raise them in the context of the interpretation.

The presentation should include some feel for the reliability of the results. At a minimum, it always should be clear what sample size was involved. The key results

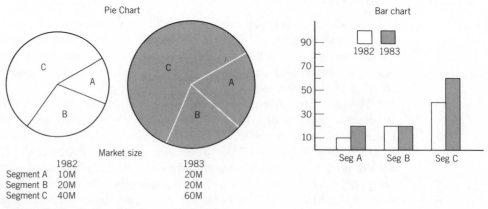

FIGURE 15–2 Graphically portraying data

should be supported by more precise information in the form of interval estimates (discussed in Chapter 11) or by a hypothesis test. The hypothesis test basically indicates, given the sample size, what probability exists that the results were merely an accident of sampling. If the probability (or significance level) is not low, then the results probably would not be repeated. Do not imply more precision than is warranted. If 15 out of 52 respondents answered positively, do not give the percentage as 28.846. Rather, use 29 percent or "nearly 30 percent." Consider the following exchange:

Speaker:	27.273% favored version B of the product.
Audience Member:	What was the sample size?
Speaker:	Around 11.
Audience Member:	Really? As large as that!

THE ORAL PRESENTATION

The ability to communicate orally is extremely important to effective management in general and to the marketing research function in particular. What can be done to insure the oral presentation is as effective as possible? The following five suggestions will be discussed in this section.

1 Don't read.
2 Use visual aids.
3 Make sure the start is positive.
4 Avoid distracting the audience.
5 Involve the audience.

Don't Read

Not everyone will agree with this first suggestion; however, it is the firm conviction of these authors that the risks and disadvantages of reading overwhelm the advantages. The biggest problem with reading is that it is usually boring for the reader and for the audience. Very few can make a script sound interesting, and those few usually do even better without a script. Further, it is necessary to develop the ability to communicate orally in front of a group without a script, in preparation for those occasions when there is no time to prepare a script or when the presenter must adapt to new developments in the middle of a presentation. If someone relies too heavily upon a script and uses it in what may be limited opportunities to give presentations, this important capability will not be developed as rapidly and completely as possible.

The advantages of a script are that the time of the presentation and the choice of words are not left to chance and the presenter is protected from an attack of stage fright. The alternative is good preparation, a set of notes, and rehearsal. The notes should provide (1) an outline so that the proper flow is maintained, and (2) a list of items that should be included. The presenter sometimes will want to consult the notes only occasionally to make sure that something has not been omitted. More detailed notes can be consulted more frequently. So that they do not distract, the notes should be on a lectern or on cards or a clipboard, positioned so that they can be managed easily with one hand. Especially when the length of the presentation needs to be carefully controlled, rehearsal is essential. Often, five or more rehearsals can be worthwhile. It is even better if feedback is available in the form of a practice audience or from a videotape. Stage fright can be combatted with deep breathing, pauses, and experience. There is no substitute for experience.

Use Visual Aids

Visual aids perform several functions. First, they provide a way to give impact to information and to focus attention upon important points. Second, ideas that are extremely difficult to express in words often can be communicated easily with visual aids. Finally, they help to provide variety to the presentation. Visual aids include transparencies, charts, handouts, slides, videotapes, films, samples, demonstrations, and role playing. Transparencies, charts, slides, and handouts are probably the most widely used.

"Gentlemen, I have good news and bad news."

© 1977 Henry R. Martin.

Transparencies are easy to make and can be carried in a file folder. They provide the advantage of controlling the audience's attention. The transparency can be exposed one line at a time by covering the rest with a piece of paper. The audience thus focuses upon what is being uncovered at the moment and does not wander ahead of the presentation. The presenter can write on the transparency to make a point during the presentation. The key to successful use of transparencies is to use readable, large type and to minimize the number of words or numbers used. Experienced and skilled users of transparencies often use only five or fewer lines per transparency, with each line containing only a few words or numbers. One rule of thumb is that a single transparency should contain no more than 30 words or items of data.

Similar guidelines apply to charts and slides, which share most of the characteristics of transparencies. Charts are more versatile than transparencies but are less convenient to make and carry. Slides are better for large audiences, since they can be seen more easily, but they require time to prepare and are not easily modified. Thus, they are not suitable for a presentation that is still being developed and refined.

The use of handouts provides the audience with something to take notes on and to take with them. As a result, the burden of taking notes is greatly reduced. Sometimes when transparencies are used, the audience's note-taking task is so difficult that it becomes distracting. Handouts free the audience to attend and participate more fully in the presentation. Their disadvantages are that they must be prepared physically and the audience is tempted to look ahead. There is always the distraction of making sure everyone is on the right page (numbering the pages helps).

Make Sure the Start is Positive

The start should be positive, confident, and involving. Sometimes a period of silence can be used effectively to get attention. It is useful to stimulate and involve the audience immediately, perhaps by a provocative question or statement. Absolutely never apologize at the outset, even in jest. If you tell the audience you are nervous, unprepared, or unknowledgeable, even in the context of a humorous line, they will tend to believe you.

Avoid Distracting the Audience

The presenter needs to be conscious that the audience is easily distracted. The following dos and don'ts address some common causes of distraction:

1 Take everything out of your pockets and make sure there is nothing on the lectern other than your notes. Remove pens, pointers, keys, clips—everything. It often happens, without your even being aware of it, that you will pick up objects and manipulate them until the audience is severly distracted, if not driven bananas.

2 Try to avoid the extremes of either obvious pacing or hiding behind a lectern. It can be as distracting to see a speaker clutch a lectern for support as to see someone pace

back and forth. The speaker's movements should be purposeful and natural, such as stepping aside to point to a chart, standing or sitting beside the lectern, or moving closer to the audience for a short portion of the presentation.

3 Maintain good eye contact. This provides audience feedback, stimulates trust and confidence in what you are saying, and involves the audience. A speaker who avoids eye contact by looking up or down or somewhere else risks distracting the audience.

4 Be concerned with the sound of your voice. Listen to a tape of your presentation if possible. A presentation can be distracting if it is too soft, loud, fast, slow, or monotoned. Be sure to use pauses to break up the presentation and to allow the audience time to digest material.

Involve the Audience

An involved audience will be more interested. An effective technique is to intersperse questions throughout. If time does not permit a discussion, a pause at least will give the audience members a chance to reflect. Sometimes it is useful to ask each person to write down his or her opinion on a piece of paper, for instance, personal judgment of a key value in the data analysis. Another technique is to refer to the ideas of people in the audience, saying, for example, ''As John mentioned last week. . . .''

Of particular importance is the question-and-answer part of the presentation. This often concludes the talk, but it can be permitted to occur during the presentation. Pause and make sure that the question is understood; then, if possible, give a short positive or negative response and as compact an explanation as possible. If you do not know, say so, adding (if appropriate) that you will get the answer by the next day. A good technique is to write the question down so you do not forget it. Equally as important, the audience sees that you are taking them seriously. Anticipate questions beforehand, and rehearse answers. Sometimes it is even effective to leave things out of the presentation if they could be covered more effectively in the context of the question-and-answer section.

SUMMARY

Communication skills are important to the marketing research process, which involves the presentation of the research proposal and the research results. An effective presentation involves several elements. The audience should be clearly identified so that the presentation will be on target. The presentation should include an introduction with an overview of the presentation structure, a body, and a summary. Motivation can be provided by relating the presentation to the research objectives and purpose, by focusing on the most interesting findings, and by having an interesting presentation style. The use of specific examples and visual material can communicate the presentation more effectively and interestingly. The presenter should discuss those elements of methodology that affect interpretation.

Several guidelines can help improve oral presentations. Reading tends to be boring and should be avoided. Visual aids such as transparencies and handouts can add punch and improve communication. Make sure the start is positive. Try to involve the audience and avoid distracting mannerisms.

QUESTIONS AND PROBLEMS

1 By what criteria would you evaluate a written presentation? Develop an evaluation form. Would it differ depending on whether the research proposal or the research results were being presented?

2 By what criteria would you evaluate an oral presentation? Develop an evaluation form.

3 Observe three specific oral presentations outside of class. Consider the following:

a Were there any distracting mannerisms?

b What did the presenters do with their hands?

c How was the audience involved, if at all?

d Evaluate the visual aids used. Would you recommend the use of other visual aids?

e Did you ever become confused or bored? Was there anything the presenter could have done differently to counteract that tendency?

CASES FOR PART III

DATA ANALYSIS

CASE III–1 PACIFIC GAS & ELECTRIC (B)[1]

The research proposal described in the Pacific Gas & Electric (A) case (Case II-1) was implemented. The resulting data are available on floppy disks.[2] The coding information for the open-ended questions follow. First, develop a data analysis strategy. Second, conduct the analysis. Third, present your conclusions and insights. Fourth, what additional research, if any, would you conduct? It can be useful to combine responses. For example, "solar awareness" could be defined as "high" if at least one application was named and $1–$10 was given as the range of expected monthly savings, "low" if no applications were named and a different savings rate was specified, and "medium" otherwise.

CITY		Q4 SOLAR USES		Q5b AD. SOURCE	
CATEGORY	CODE	CATEGORY	CODE	CATEGORY	CODE
Walnut Creek	0	Water	1	PG&E	1
Novato	1	Pool	2	Home or news	
Marin	2	House	3	magazine	2
San Francisco	3	Cooling	4	TV	3
San Mateo	4	Electric	5	Environ.	
Palo Alto	5	Plants	6	magazine	4
San Jose	6	Windows	7	Newspaper	5
Fremont	7	Not proven	8	Display	6
Oakland	8	Everything	9	Company	7
Richmond	9	No response	0	Popular science	
				magazine	8
				Several	9
				No response	0

[1]Written by Darrell R. Clarke and David A. Aaker as a basis for class discussion.
[2]The floppy desks are available from your professor.

Q6b DISPLAYS		Q7b SOLAR HEATING UNIT		Q9b	
CATEGORY	CODE	CATEGORY	CODE	CATEGORY	CODE
PG&E	1	Media	1	Unnamed company	1
Show	2	Local house	2	Undecided	2
Display house	3	Display house	3	Looked at cost	4
Store	4	Relative- friend	4	Water	5
Media	5	Out of area	5	Build himself	7
School	6			Pool	7
Friend	7			No response	0
Company	8				
No response	0				

Q10a ADVANTAGES		Q10b DISADVANTAGES		Q11 COST/SAVINGS	
CATEGORY	CODE	CATEGORY	CODE	CATEGORY	CODE
Cheaper	1	Weather	1	1–10	1
Conserve energy	2	Cost	2	11–20	2
Safer	4	Performance	3	21–30	3
Uses	5	Needs back-up	4	31–40	4
Utility independent	6	Unproved	5	41–50	5
Performance	7	Ugly or bulky	6	51–60	6
Wrong	8	Unneeded	7	61–70	7
Are none	9	Future uncertain	8	71–80	8
No response	0	No response	0	81 +	9
				No response	0

Q14c WHY UTILITY		Q14d WHY NOT UTILITY		Q15a DESIRED INFORMATION[a]	
CATEGORY	CODE	CATEGORY	CODE	CATEGORY	CODE
In the business	1	Charge too much	1	Cost	1
Reliable	2	Too big	2	Performance	2
Less bureaucracy	3	Dislike private	3	Appearance-size	3
Dislikes government	4	Shouldn't	4	Durability	4
Pay with bill	5	Keep utility out	5	Technical	5
Husband works for	6	Private better	6	Installation	6
No response	0	No response	0	General	7
				Authority	8
				Why need	9
				No response	0

[a]*Note:* Column 62, the last column in the data presentation, is the last response to Q15a.

435

CASE III–2 RALSTON DEVELOPMENT COMPANY

As the researchers from Acton Associates left his office, Joe Ralston felt he had been given the means to win a battle but he still wasn't sure he could win the war. While a survey of Beaverdale residents, conducted by Acton, had clearly supported his concept of a regional shopping center over a competitive proposal, the results were less convincing as a demonstration of citizen support for a major shopping center development. He had to decide quickly whether to introduce the results into the planning commission hearing scheduled the following week. While the main item on the agenda was whether to provide for a regional shopping center in the Beaverdale general plan, a choice of location also would be made. For five months he had been working full time to influence these decisions in favor of his company.

Joe Ralston had an enviable record as a developer of large regional shopping centers across Canada. His record had never been quite so threatened as by the situation he now faced. The basic problem was the absence of opportunities for new centers, as a result of weak economic conditions, oversaturation of retail selling space in most major markets, and an acute shortage of prime sites for development. Indeed, current business was so weak that Ralston Development would have to dismantle a substantial portion of the organization if a big center were not started within six months.

The only live prospect on the horizon was in Beaverdale, a prosperous suburban town of 40,000 residents that was part of a major metropolitan area. Five months earlier the Beaverdale Planning Commission had agreed to a staff feasibility study of a development proposal by Ralston Development. The effect of the proposal would be to expand a small local shopping center, with one existing department store, into a regional center with four department stores and numerous specialty shops, all connected by a covered mall. There would be enough selling space to attract shoppers from a radius of six to seven miles. A major advantage of the site was the proximity to the arterial freeway passing through the town. The attraction to the planning commission was the opportunity for substantial local employment, plus tax revenues of more than a million dollars a year.

Unfortunately for Joe Ralston, a local family holding undeveloped farmland near the freeway decided they had an equally good site for a regional shopping center. Their site was one mile from the site Ralston wanted to develop. Since the Santini family was highly visible in the local government, the planning commission was in no position to deny their request for equal consideration.

During a series of public meetings to discuss the competing proposals, a great deal of local opposition surfaced. Some opposition came from a loose coalition of environmental groups with previous success in thwarting large developments in the area. They were joined, somewhat uneasily, by a group of local residents anxious about the strain that the traffic from the shopping center would put on the congested local roads. Joe Ralston was sure these opposition groups were not representative of the community; however, he had to concede that this was only intuition. In the meantime, the opposition was becoming more strident and much more active, with the evident encouragement of at least one and possibly two of the five planning commissioners. It was this situation that led him to decide that the best way to blunt the opposition was to conduct a survey of the residents in the portion of the town adjacent to the proposed developments.

While the principal research objective was to measure the support for a regional shopping center, Ralston also expected the results to show the superiority of his proposal over the Santini's. A further objective was to clarify the sources of opposition and support to help develop a campaign to mobilize support for his project.

The Residential Survey

The consultants were well aware that the results of their study would be subject to hostile cross-examination by the opposition groups and the other developer. (They also knew that Joe Ralston would have to use either the entire study or none of it.)

During a series of focus-group interviews it became clear that many people were badly informed about the issues and consequently had very shaky opinions. Thus it was decided that respondents should be given complete descriptive information to insure they had a proper basis for a choice. This meant a personal interview study of heads of households.[3] Respondents were to be given a map showing each proposed shopping center, and a lengthy written description would be read by the interviewer. Great care was taken in writing these descriptions to eliminate any bias that would favor one proposal over the other, or provide anything other than purely objective information. Descriptions were simply labeled R or S (corresponding to Ralston or Santini), to minimize the effect of the sponsor. The description for Proposal R is shown in Exhibit III–2. The order of presentation would be randomized to avoid bias. To insure maximum response, three callbacks were to be used and a supervisor would attempt to convert refusals.

Interpreting the Results

The study was conducted under great pressure in less than three weeks. A 68-percent response rate and a final sample size of 407 were achieved. Because of the urgency of the project, the Acton Associates project director delivered the key results from the computer as soon as they were available. A set of the tables was reviewed with Joe Ralston and left for him to digest. The following summarizes the results of immediate interest to Ralston and his associates. (Because of rounding error, percentage breakdowns may not sum to 100%.)

---

[3]The sample was drawn randomly from a list of utility customers in Beaverdale. Apartment dwellers paid their bills directly to the utility company.

EXHIBIT III–1

Description of Proposal R. Given Verbally to Respondents

Questions 1 and 3. Which newspapers were read regularly and at which shopping center was most of the shopping done?

Questions 4. Have you heard of any plans to build a large shopping center with four or five large department stores, in the nearby area?"

	$n =$	$\% =$
Yes	215	52.8
No	182	44.7
Don't know	10	2.5
Total	407	11%

Question 5. "How do you think most people in Beaverdale feel about the need for a shopping center, with four or five large department stores, in the nearby area?" (PROBE)

	$n =$	$\% =$
Haven't discussed it/never came up	92	22.0%
Others favor it/welcome it	54	12.9
Want nice-looking buildings/ quality	5	1.2
Want all in one area	2	0.5
Want for convenience/less driving/save gas	51	12.2
Like idea of more centers	26	6.2
Not needed/over-run with shopping centers	131	31.3
Mixed feelings	9	2.1
Traffic is problem/congestion	15	3.6
Oversaturation of stores	8	2.0
Want to save trees/green areas	10	2.4
Nothing/just moved to area	10	2.4
No answer	6	1.4

Question 6. "Which of these best describes your opinion of the need for such a shopping center?" (*Hand Card to Respondent*)

Answer to Q4:

	Have heard	Have not heard	Total
Very much needed	28 (13.0%)	15 (8.2%)	43
Somewhat needed	72 (33.5)	50 (27.5)	122
Not much needed	42 (19.5)	39 (21.4)	81
Not at all needed	72 (33.5)	69 (37.9)	141
No answer	1 (0.5)	9 (4.9)	10
	215 (100%)	182 (100%)	397

Question 7. HAND RESPONDENT DIAGRAM ☐ *R* or ☐ *S: Read Carefully and Consistently the Matching Statement to Respondent. Ask Questions, Then Show Other.*

(The same questions were asked for both *R* and *S*. For example: for *R* only the respondent was asked: "What do you like about the one marked *R*?" and "What do you dislike about the one marked *R*?" Then the same questions were asked about *S*. The open-ended responses are not tabulated here.)

Question 8. *Leave Both Diagrams in Front of Respondent. Hand Correct Preference Scale.*

8a. In choosing between □ *R* and *S* or □ *S* and *R* (order was random) which box says how you feel?

	Question 6		
	Shopping center needed	Center not needed	Total
Strongly prefer *R*	44 (26.3%)	45 (19.7%)	89 (22.5%)
Somewhat prefer *R*	36 (21.6)	74 (32.4)	110 (27.8)
No preference	22 (13.2)	66 (28.9)	88 (22.3)
Strongly prefer *S*	32 (19.2)	30 (13.2)	62 (15.7)
Somewhat prefer *S*	33 (19.8)	13 (5.7)	46 (11.6)
Total	167 (100%)	228 (100%)	395 (100%)

(Note *R* = Ralston Development Company proposal and *S* = Santini proposal)

8b. There are three alternatives. One of the two proposed shopping centers or no shopping center in either location: Which do you most prefer? Which do you least prefer?

		Q8b: Most prefer			
		R (Ralston)	*S* (Santini)	Neither	Total
Q8b:	*R*	—	88 (88.9%)	39 (30.0%)	127 (32.3%)
Least	*S*	145 (87.9%)	—	72 (55.4%)	217 (55.1%)
Prefer	Neither	20 (12.1%)	11 (11.1%)	19 (14.6%)	50 (12.7%)
	Total	165 (100%)	99 (100%)	130 (100%)	394 (100%)

		Q8b: Most prefer			
		R (Ralston)	*S* (Santini)	Neither	Total
Q6: Need for	Very much needed	21 (12.7%)	19 (19.2%)	3 (2.2%)	43 (10.8%)
Shopping	Somewhat needed	60 (36.1)	46 (46.5)	17 (12.6)	123 (30.5)
Center	Not much needed	38 (22.9)	15 (15.2)	28 (20.7)	81 (20.9)
	Not at all needed	43 (25.9)	16 (15.2)	85 (63.0)	144 (35.4)
	No opinion	4 (2.4)	3 (3.0)	2 (1.4)	9 (2.4)
	Total	166 (100%)	99 (100%)	135 (100%)	400 (100%)

Question 9–20. These questions dealt with

A. Preferences for department stores
B. Community involvement
C. Attitudes toward future rates of development
D. Classification variables, such as home ownership, length of time as resident of Beaverdale, education, income, and sex.

EXHIBIT III–2

Description of Proposal *R* (Ralston) Given Verbally to Respondents

The proposed shopping center on a 62-acre site fronts Harrison Road and Highway 463 and is bisected by Harrison Road.

As shown in the diagram the proposed shopping center is to contain four or five department stores including the existing Campton store[a] with two and three floor levels each and with a single-level, climate-controlled, enclosed shopping mall containing a variety of smaller convenience and specialty shops. An auto service center and a freestanding restaurant are planned.

The two halves of the site are to be joined at the center's shopping level by using the air space over Harrison Road. The shopping complex will span Harrison Road.

Primary access to the center will be immediately north of where the complex spans Harrison Road. Additional access will be from the proposed Newton Parkway, and from Fairview Boulevard through the Campton facility. Existing residential streets at the site's western edge will end at their present locations.

Parking accessible from existing or planned access roads will be provided encompassing the entire center. Lower-level parking, beneath the entire mall and mall shops area, will be provided. Approximately one-third of the total parking spaces will be covered.

Pedestrian access to the proposed center from the westerly residential neighborhood will be along existing residential streets.

Landscaping is planned throughout to define the roadway network and parking areas and to enhance the proposed center's overall aesthetics.

All exterior and pedestrian areas are proposed to be illuminated as are parking areas and the planned roadway network.

[a]Major Canadian department store chain.

part IV

SPECIAL TOPICS IN DATA ANALYSIS

16

FACTOR ANALYSIS

As Chapter 12 made clear, after editing and coding, the first data analysis step is usually to tabulate each question. Thus, the interest might be to tabulate the responses to the HMO enrollment intentions question, obtaining the average response or the frequency distribution. The next step is usually to repeat this tabulation for various subgroups of the sample, which are defined by a second question. For example, the enrollment intentions for low-, medium-, and high-income subgroups might be contrasted. Recall that, in Chapter 14, the introduction of a third question or variable was considered.

Thus far a construct or variable has been represented by a single question. Enrollment intentions, for example, were based upon a single question. However, it often will be theoretically and practically desirable to combine several questions, thereby creating a new variable that is based upon more than one question. The fact that some constructs simply require more than one question to represent them in part generates a need to combine questions or variables. Social class, for example, often is represented best by a set of questions including income, education, and occupation. The need to combine questions also is due, in part, to the fact that sets of questions measuring such complex areas as lifestyle or image often contain considerable redundancy. If questions on lifestyle or if image-question sets were not combined, the analysis would be most unwieldy and confused. A variable that is based upon a combination of questions, of course, can be tabulated, just as original questions or variables are tabulated.

Factor analysis and the subjects of Chapter 17, multidimensional scaling and cluster analysis, are techniques that serve to combine questions, thereby creating new variables. These techniques often are termed the **analysis of interdependence** techniques because they analyze the interdependence between questions, variables, or objects. The goal is to generate understanding of the underlying structure of questions, variables, or objects and to combine them into new variables. These three techniques can be illustrated by the following simple example.

Suppose that we are interested in determining how prospective students select universities. The first step might be to determine how institutions are perceived and evaluated by prospective students. To generate relevant questions, students might be asked to talk informally about schools. More particularly, the students could be asked why one school

443

is preferred or why two are regarded as similar. The result could be 100 or more terms, such as large, good faculty, expensive, good climate, dormitories, facilities, athletic program, social aspects, impersonal, and so on. A second step might be to ask a group of prospective students to evaluate the importance to them of each of these attributes. At this point the analysis can get bogged down simply because there are too many attributes or variables. Furthermore, many of these attributes are redundant, really measuring the same construct. To determine which are redundant and what they are measuring, the analyst can turn to factor analysis. One result will be a set of new variables (or factors) created by combining sets of school attributes.

In another phase of the study, groups of students could be identified according to what they are looking for in a college. We might hypothesize that one group is concerned about individual attention; another, low cost; another, proximity to home; and still another, quality education. If such groups exist and can be identified, then it may be possible to isolate several, describe them, and develop a communication program—tailored to their interests—that could be directed toward them. **Cluster analysis** can be used to identify such groupings. Cluster analysis is used to identify people, objects, or variables that form natural groupings or clusters. A new variable is defined by cluster membership.

Later in the study it might be useful to determine how schools are perceived—which ones are perceived as similar and which ones are considered different. Is Stanford more like the University of California at Berkeley because of location and educational quality, or is Stanford perceived as being more similar to Harvard or MIT, two private schools? The general problem of positioning objects such as universities in an interpretable, multidimensional space is termed **multidimensional scaling** (MDS). The resulting locations or positions on the relevant perceptual dimensions serve to define new variables. We now turn to factor analysis, the subject of this chapter.

THE BASIC CONCEPTS OF FACTOR ANALYSIS

The Function of Factor Analysis

Factor analysis can be used by researchers to do a variety of tasks, including cluster analysis and multidimensional scaling; however, it has two primary functions in data analysis. One function is to identify underlying constructs in the data. Thus, the variables "impersonal" and "large" in our school study actually may be indicators of the same theoretical construct.

A second role of factor analysis is simply to reduce the number of variables to a more manageable set. In reducing the number of variables, factor analysis procedures attempt to retain as much of the information as possible and to make the remaining variables as meaningful and as easy to work with as possible.

The basic factor analysis concepts will be introduced and illustrated in the context of several examples. The first is a (hypothetical) study conducted by a bank to determine if special marketing programs should be developed for several key segments. One of the study's research questions concerned attitudes toward banking. The respondents were asked their opinion on a zero-to-nine, agree-disagree scale, on the following questions:

1 Small banks charge less than large banks.

2 Large banks are more likely to make mistakes than small banks.

3 Tellers do not need to be extremely courteous and friendly—it's enough for them simply to be civil.

4 I want to be personally known at my bank and to be treated with special courtesy.

5 After being treated in an impersonal or uncaring way by a financial institution, I would never patronize that organization again.

For illustrative purposes, assume that a pilot study was conducted using 15 respondents. An actual pilot study probably would have a sample size of from 100 to 400. The pilot study data are shown in Figure 16–1. Also shown in this figure are the correlations among the variables. A factor analysis program usually will start by calculating the variable-by-variable correlation matrix. In fact, it is quite possible to input directly the correlation matrix instead of the raw data. In any case, the factor analysis program will provide as one of its outputs the correlation maxtrix. It is a good idea to examine these correlations to see what information and hypotheses can be obtained. Which correlations are the largest? What does this imply?

What is a Factor?

To interpret the balance of Figure 16–1, it is first necessary to understand the concept of a factor. The input variables very likely will contain redundancy. Several may be measuring in part the same underlying construct. This underlying construct is what is termed a **factor**. A factor is thus simply a variable or construct that is not directly observable but needs to be inferred from the input variables. The factor also might be viewed as a grouping of those input variables that measure or are indicators of the factor.

Factor Scores

Although a factor is not observable like the other five variables, it is still a variable. One output of most factor analysis programs is values for each factor for all respondents. These values are termed **factor scores** and are shown in Figure 16–1 for the two factors that were found to underlie the five input variables. Thus, each respondent has a factor score on each factor, in addition to the respondent's rating on the original five variables. The

INPUT DATA AND FACTOR SCORES

INDIVIDUAL		INPUT DATA VARIABLE					FACTOR SCORE FACTOR	
		1	2	3	4	5	1	2
1.	Joe E.	9	6	9	2	2	−.97	.79
2.	Mary S.	4	6	2	6	7	1.02	−.18
3.	Shirley G.	0	0	5	0	0	−.69	−2.20
4.	Jan A.	2	2	0	9	9	1.52	−.22
5.	Edward B.	6	9	8	3	3	−.80	1.35
6.	Joe W.	3	8	5	4	7	.35	.53
7.	Tom M.	4	5	6	3	6	.06	.06
8.	Heather P.	8	6	8	2	2	−.78	.42
9.	Mike T.	4	4	0	8	8	1.54	−.44
10.	Bill W.	2	8	4	5	7	.48	.58
11.	Gail L.	1	2	6	0	0	−.88	−1.55
12.	Alan B.	6	9	7	3	5	−.22	.95
13.	Richard Y.	6	7	1	7	8	1.48	−.10
14.	Alice D.	2	1	7	1	1	−.98	−.89
15.	Susan A.	9	7	9	2	1	−1.13	.92

CORRELATIONS

VARIABLE	VARIABLE 1	2	3	4	5
1	1.00	.61	.47	−.02	−.10
2		1.00	.73	.19	.32
3			1.00	−.83	−.77
4				1.00	.93
5					1.00

FACTOR LOADINGS

VARIABLE	FACTOR 1	2	COMMUNALITY
1	−.24	.72	.57
2	.06	.87	.75
3	−.94	.33	.99
4	.94	.21	.92
5	.93	.26	.93
Percentage Variation Explained	55%	36%	

FIGURE 16–1 Factor analysis of bank attitudes

factor is a derived variable in the sense that the factor score is calculated from a knowledge of the variables that are associated with it.

Factor Loadings

How is the factor interpreted if it is unobservable? Interpretation is based upon **factor loadings**, which are the correlations between the factors and the original variables.[1] At the bottom of Figure 16–1 are shown the factor loadings for our bank study. For example, the correlation between variable 1 and factor 1 is −0.24. The factor loadings thus provide an indication of which original variables are correlated with each factor and the extent of the correlation. This information then is used to identify and label the unobservable factors subjectively.

Clearly, variables 3, 4, and 5 combine to define the first factor, which might be labeled a "personal" factor. The second factor is correlated most highly with variables 1 and 2. It might be termed a "small-bank" factor.

Communality

Each of the five original input variables has associated with it a variance reflecting the variation of the 15 respondents. The amount of variable 1 variance that is explained or accounted for by the factors is the **communality** of variable 1 and is shown in Figure 16–1 to be 57 percent. Communality is the percent of a variable's variance that contributes to the correlation with other variables or is "common" to other variables. In Figure 16–1 variables 3, 4, and 5 have high communalities; therefore, their variation is represented fairly completely by the two factors, whereas variable 1 has a lower communality. Just over 50 percent of the variance of variable 1 is due to the two factors.

Variance Explained

The percentage of variance explained is a summary measure indicating how much of the total original variance of all the five variables is represented by the factor.[2] Thus, the first factor explains 55 percent of the total variance of the five variables and the second factor accounts for 36 percent more variance. The percentage-of-variance-explained statistic can be useful in evaluating and interpreting a factor, as will be illustrated shortly.

[1]Actually the factor loadings will be correlations only when (1) the input variables are standardized [each variable has its mean subtracted and is divided by its standard deviation $(X - X)/\sigma_r$] and (2) the factors are perpendicular or independent (an explanatory comment appears in footnote 4), two conditions that normally are present. As previously noted, most factor analysis programs begin by calculating a correlation matrix, a process that standardizes the variables. If either condition is not present, the factor loadings, although not correlations, still can be interpreted as indicators of the association between the variables and the factors. Further, a matrix of variable-factor correlations, termed a factor structure matrix, is provided as an output of the factor analysis program.

[2]The percentage of variance explained is proportional to the sum of squared loadings associated with that factor. Thus a factor's percent of explained variance depends in part on the number of variables on which the factor has high loadings. A variable's communality is actually equal to the sum of the squared factor loadings on that variable.

WHY PERFORM FACTOR ANALYSIS ON DATA?

One reason is to obtain insights from the groupings of variables that emerge. In particular, it often is possible to identify underlying constructs, constructs that might have practical and theoretical significance. Another reason is to reduce the number of questions or scales to a manageable number. This variable reduction can be accomplished in either of the two following ways.

1 Select one, two, or more of the input variables to represent each factor. The variables would be selected on the basis of their factor loadings and a judgment as to their usefulness and validity. In the example of Figure 16–1, question 2 might be selected to represent the second factor. If the factor analysis is based upon a pilot study, the larger study to follow then will have fewer questions to include. A set of 100 questions in a pilot study might be reduced to a group of 20 to 30 in the larger study.

2 Replace the original input variables with the factor scores. In the example represented by Figure 16–1, the result would be two interpretable factors replacing five variables. In a larger problem 50 input variables might be replaced by eight or nine factors. Subsequent data analysis would become easier, less expensive, and have fewer interpretation difficulties.

FACTOR ROTATION

Factor analysis is complicated somewhat (or made more interesting, depending upon your perspective) by the fact that it is possible to generate several factor analysis solutions (loadings and factor scores) for any data set. Each solution is termed a particular **factor rotation** and is generated by a **factor rotation scheme.** Each time the factors are rotated the pattern of loadings changes, as does the interpretation of the factors. Geometrically, rotation means simply that the dimensions are rotated. (For a geometric interpretation of factor analysis see the appendix to this chapter.) Although there are many such rotation programs, varimax rotation is the most common and will be described here.

The basic "unrotated" factor analysis usually employs principal components analysis (also termed principal factor analysis) and will be introduced first. The objective of the principal components is to generate a first factor that will have the maximum explained variance. Then with the first factor and its associated loadings fixed, principal components will locate a second factor maximizing the variance explained in this second factor. The procedure continues until there are as many factors generated as variables or until the analyst concludes that the number of useful factors has been exhausted. Determination of the number of factors to include will be considered shortly.

When principal components analysis is used, the interpretation of the factors can be difficult. The use of varimax rotation can improve greatly the interpretability. A study of the perceptions of 94 consumers of a particular brand of coffee will illustrate.[3] The consumers, after sampling the coffee, rated it on 14 semantic-differential scales. The ratings were factor analyzed by the principal components method, and the results are shown on the left side of Figure 16–2. The first factor explained nearly 75 percent of the variance and seems clearly to reflect a general like-dislike dimension. This interpretation is supported by the fact that scale 14 was, in fact, an overall preference rating and had a high loading with the first factor. The remaining three factors really contain no loadings over 0.40 and are difficult to interpret. Such interpretation difficulty is not uncommon and motivates the use of varimax rotation.

Varimax rotation, probably the most widely used rotation scheme, searches for a set of factor loadings such that each factor has some loadings close to zero and some loadings close to −1 or +1. The logic is that interpretation is easiest when the variable-factor correlations are either close to +1 or −1, indicating a clear association between the variable and the factor; or close to zero, indicating a clear lack of association.[4]

The right portion of Figure 16–2 shows a varimax rotated solution. Notice that, like the principal components solution, a total of 83.3 percent of the variance is explained by the four factors. Further, the communalities are the same. However, in the varimax rotation each of the four factors explains a substantial amount of the variance, whereas in the principal components solution the first factor explained nearly all of the variance. In this data set the varimax rotation was not successful in pushing some loadings to zero. Thus, the interpretation is still somewhat difficult. However, it is possible to provide an interpretation of the first four factors by considering the variables with the largest factor loadings. The factors might be labeled:

Factor 1 Mellow-comforting

Factor 2 Heartiness

Factor 3 Genuineness

Factor 4 Freshness

The varimax rotation thus leads to quite a different perspective, which, incidentally, is not necessarily a more correct perspective. A subjective judgment guided by theory is needed to determine which perspective, the principal components or the varimax rotation, is more valid.

The factor solution presented in Figure 16–1 also was a varimax solution and actually was fairly easy to interpret. Sometimes a varimax solution (or principal components) will generate seemingly interpretable factors even when, in actuality, there is little structure present. To guard against this eventuality it is prudent to split the data in half when possible

---

[3]This example is drawn from Bishwa Nath Mukherjee, "A Factor Analysis of Some Qualitative Attributes of Coffee," *Journal of Advertising Research, 5* (March 1965), 35–38.

[4]Both principal components and varimax rotation constrain the factors to be uncorrelated or geometrically perpendicular. They are rotation schemes that allow the factors to be correlated or geometrically oblique. They are specialized, create interpretation problems, and will not be discussed here.

COFFEE ATTRIBUTES	PRINCIPAL COMPONENTS				VARIMAX ROTATION				COMMUNALITIES
	I	II	III	IV	I	II	III	IV	
1. Pleasant flavor	.86	−.01	−.20	.04	−.63	.38	.36	.34	.78
2. Sparkling taste	.91	−.01	−.01	−.09	.48	.43	−.53	.38	.83
3. Mellow taste	.86	−.11	−.28	.00	−.70	.26	.38	.36	.83
4. Expensive taste	.91	.15	−.001	−.10	.46	−.53	.54	.29	.87
5. Comforting taste	.87	−.002	−.31	.10	−.74	.38	.30	.32	.87
6. Alive taste	.93	.03	−.02	−.16	.49	.43	−.59	.35	.90
7. Tastes like real coffee	.90	−.02	.04	−.21	.42	.38	−.64	.37	.86
8. Deep distinct taste	.77	.36	.11	.16	.31	−.74	.27	.22	.77
9. Taste just brewed	.79	−.28	.24	−.09	.23	.24	.52	−.62	.76
10. Hearty flavor	.87	.25	.22	.17	.28	−.75	.33	.39	.89
11. Pure clean taste	89	.11	−.05	.10	.51	−.55	.36	.36	.82
12. Roasted taste	.76	−.29	.04	.27	.43	.28	.16	−.67	.74
13. Fresh taste	.84	−.27	.19	.12	.33	.32	.36	−.70	.83
14. Overall preference	.90	.04	.08	−.23	.38	.43	−.65	.34	.86
Percentage of variance explained	74.6	3.4	2.7	2.6	22.9	21.3	20.4	18.7	
Accumulative variance explained	74.6	78.0	80.7	83.3	22.9	44.2	64.6	83.3	

FIGURE 16–2 Factor loadings before and after rotation

Source: Adapted from Bishwa Nath Mukherjee, "A Factor Analysis of Some Qualitative Attributes of Coffee," *Journal of Advertising Research,* 5 (March 1965) 37.

and run two factor analyses. If the same factors emerge in each, then some confidence that the factors actually exist may be warranted.

HOW MANY FACTORS?

Since factor analysis is designed to reduce many variables to a smaller number of underlying factors or constructs, a central question is: How many factors are involved in the model? It is always possible to keep generating factors until there are as many factors as original variables, but such a practice would defeat at least one of the primary purposes of the technique.

Theoretically, the answer to the question is clear. There is a certain number of constructs that the input variables are measuring. These constructs are identified before the analysis from our theory and knowledge of the situation, and then the data are factor analyzed until these constructs emerge as factors. Unfortunately, our theory is rarely that well defined. We, therefore, add some rules of thumb to the theoretical answer.

The rule of thumb most heavily relied upon in factor analysis studies is that all included factors (prior to rotation) must explain at least as much variance as an "average variable." In Figure 16–1 the average variable would explain one-fifth or 20 percent of the variance. Actually, the second factor explained 36 percent, and the third factor, which was not shown, explained only 7 percent of the variance. In Figure 16–2 this rule was violated, since with 14 variables the variance explained for an included variable should be equal to that of an average variable, which would be one-fourteenth or 7 percent. The logic is that if a factor is meaningful and capable of representing one or more of the variables then it should absorb at least as much variance as an average original input variable.

Just because there is a lot of variance explained, of course, does not mean that a factor is valid or meaningful or useful. If an irrelevant scale or question were repeated many times, each with a small modification, a factor underlying those questions would explain much of the variance but not be a very interesting construct because of the questions on which it was based were not very interesting.

A related rule of thumb is to look for a large drop in the variance explained between two factors (in the principal components solution). For example, if the variance explained by five factors (before rotation) were 40 percent, 30 percent, 20 percent, 6 percent, and 4 percent, there is a drop in variance explained in the fourth factor. This drop might signal the introduction of meaningless factors of relative unimportance. Again, in Figure 16–2 the application of this rule of thumb would result in the consideration of only one factor.

Perhaps the most appropriate rule is to stop factoring when the factors stop making sense. Eventually the smaller factors will represent random variation and should be expected to be uninterpretable. Conversely, if a factor that would be excluded by one of the two rules of thumb were theoretically interpretable and of practical interest, or resulted in varimax rotated factors with these qualities (i.e., Figure 16–2), it probably should be retained. Clearly, the determination of the number of factors, like the interpretation of individual factors, contains a large degree of subjectivity.

TWO ADDITIONAL EXAMPLES

Two additional examples will illustrate. The first, based upon a study by Dickson and Albaum, addresses the common research problem of determining how objects such as retail stores are perceived and evaluated.[5]

Measuring Discount Store Image

A list of 29 semantic-differential, seven-point scales was generated using 27 indepth interviews. In each interview respondents were asked to elicit the first word that they associated with each of four kinds of stores-a discount store, a supermarket, a shoe store, and a department store. Among their other tasks was to describe each of the four stores in paragraph form. The interviews were analyzed to obtain a list of 29 words and phrases that were mentioned by more than one respondent, which then were arranged into semantic-differential scales. Among the resulting scales were:

Crammed merchandise------------Well spaced merchandise

Low pressure salesmen------------High pressure salesmen

A total of 82 personal interviews was then completed in which respondents were asked to evaluate each of the four stores along each of the 29 bipolar seven-point scales. The responses involving the discount store were factor analyzed. The input data were comprised of the discount store rating on the 29 semantic-differential scales by each of the 82 respondents. The output is shown in Figure 16–3.

To make the interpretation easier, the variables have been grouped in terms of their factor loadings. Thus, the first variable has its highest loading on the first factor and is grouped with other variables having this same characteristic.

The first factor seems to involve both the elements of good service and friendly service and, consequently, has been labeled the "good service-friendly" factor. The second factor, labeled "price level," is remarkably unambiguous. The third factor, labeled "attractive," includes the concept of bright store and good displays and thus is less clear. Note that variable 21 has an extremely low loading and should not contribute much to the interpretation of the third factor. The fourth factor is termed spaciousness because the variable that has the highest correlation with it was "spacious shopping" and because several of

[5]John Dickson and Gerald Albaum, "A Method for Developing Tailor-made Semantic Differentials for Specific Marketing Content Areas," *Journal of Marketing Research, 8* (February 1977), 87–91.

SCALE	FACTOR					COMMUNALITY
	I	II	III	IV	V	
1. Good service	.79	−.15	.06	.12	.07	.67
2. Helpful salesmen	.75	−.03	.04	.13	.31	.68
3. Friendly personnel	.74	−.07	.17	.09	−.14	.61
4. Clean	.59	−.31	.34	.15	−.25	.65
5. Pleasant store to shop in	.58	−.15	.48	.26	.10	.67
6. Easy to return purchases	.56	−.23	.13	−.03	−.03	.39
7. Too many clerks	.53	−.00	.02	.23	.37	.47
8. Attracts upper class customers	.46	−.06	.25	−.00	.17	.31
9. Convenient location	.36	−.30	−.02	−.19	.03	.26
10. High quality products	.34	−.27	.31	.12	.25	.36
11. Good buys on products	.02	−.88	.09	.10	.03	.79
12. Low prices	−.03	−.74	.14	.00	.13	.59
13. Good specials	.35	−.67	−.05	.10	.14	.60
14. Good sales on products	.30	−.67	.01	−.08	.16	.57
15. Reasonable value for price	.17	−.52	.11	−.02	−.03	.36
16. Good store	.41	−.47	.47	.12	.11	.63
17. Low pressure salesmen	−.20	−.30	−.28	−.03	−.05	.18
18. Bright store	−.02	−.10	.75	.26	−.05	.61
19. Attractive store	.19	.03	.67	.34	.24	.66
20. Good displays	.33	−.15	.61	.15	−.20	.57
21. Unlimited selection of products	.09	.00	.29	−.03	.00	.09
22. Spacious shopping	.00	.20	.00	.70	.10	.54
23. Easy to find items you want	.36	−.16	.10	.57	.01	.49
24. Well organized layout	−.02	−.05	.25	.54	−.17	.39
25. Well spaced merchandise	.20	.15	.27	.52	.16	.43
26. Neat	.38	−.12	.45	.49	−.34	.72
27. Big store	−.20	.15	.06	.07	−.65	.49
28. Ads frequently seen by you	.03	−.20	.07	.09	.42	.23
29. Fast check out	.30	−.16	.00	.25	−.33	.28
Percent of variance explained	16	12	9	8	5	
Cumulative variance explained	16	28	37	45	50	

POSSIBLE FACTOR INTERPRETATIONS:

Factor I	Good service—friendly
Factor II	Price level
Factor III	Attractiveness
Factor IV	Spaciousness
Factor V	Size

FIGURE 16–3 Factor loadings for a discount store (Varimax Rotation)

453

the other variables with high correlation have a connotation of spaciousness. However, it would be quite possible to argue that ''well organized'' might capture the meaning of the fourth factor better. The final factor, also somewhat unclear, is termed ''size'' because the only loading over 0.50 relates to the size. There might be some consideration given to excluding the fifth factor because it is ambiguous, it really reflects only one variable, and because the variance explained is only 5 percent.[6]

Note that the variation of a number of variables is not well represented by the five factors. In particular, variables 9, 17, 21, 28, and 29 have communalities below 0.30 and thus their meaning is not really reflected by the five factors. A variable like ''convenient location'' (variable 9) may be an important perceptual dimension to consumers, but there may be no other variables in this variable set that overlap with it. Therefore, no factor is formed loading heavily on ''convenient location'' that explains a substantial percent of the total variance. If theory and management judgment leads to the conclusion that convenient location is a worthwhile variable, then it should be included in subsequent data gathering and analysis even though it did not generate high loadings on any factor. Factor analysis, like many data analysis techniques, needs to be augmented by thought, theory, and common sense.

The Performing Arts

A study of the performing arts in Champaign-Urbana, Illinois was conducted to learn what types of people were attending events.[7] Eight hundred respondents were given a questionnaire that asked, among other things, how often in the past year they attended each of 19 performing arts performances. One goal was to determine what sociodemographic and personality variables would explain attendance. However, it was difficult and inappropriate to work with 19 different attendance variables. Thus, factor analysis was employed to reduce the 19 variables to a smaller group of factors.

Figure 16–4 shows the output of the (varimax) rotated factor analysis. A total of 53 percent of the variance was explained by the three factors. The third factor explained seven percent of the variance, which is more than one-nineteenth or 5.2 percent of the variance (there being 19 variables). The communalities indicate that the factors did least well at explaining the variance of variables 9, 12, and 17. Notice that the rotation resulted

[6]A variance explained of five percent is low relative to the variance explained by the other factors and relative to that expected by one of 29 variables, which would be 3.4 percent. However, the reader should note that Figure 16–3 represents a varimax rotation. The comparable percentage of variance explained for the original principal components solution (which, of course, involved different factor loadings and, therefore, different factors) was 25 percent, 10 percent, 6 percent, 5 percent, and 4 percent. Thus, before rotation there was a substantial gap between the variance explained by the first two factors and the others. However, given that after rotation at least four factors seem interpretable and useful, the analyst would not be tempted to restrict the number of factors to two.

[7]Richard P. Nielsen and Charles McQueen, ''Performing Arts Consumer Behavior: An Exploratory Study'' in Ronald C. Curhan, ed., *The 1974 Combined Proceedings* (Chicago: American Marketing Association, 1974) p. 393.

	I MODERN MUSIC AND DANCE	II CLASSICAL MUSIC AND DANCE	III THEATRE	 COMMUNALITY
1. Jazz music	.62	.02	.23	.44
2. Folk music	.74	.08	.10	.56
3. Ethnic music	.76	.13	.05	.60
4. Symphonic music	.12	.81	.01	.67
5. Oratorio music	.53	.44	.18	.51
6. Chamber music	.07	.65	.19	.46
7. Classical opera	.41	.61	.15	.56
8. Contemporary opera	.61	.35	.17	.52
9. Band concerts	.52	.23	.03	.32
10. Choral recitals	.56	.45	.08	.52
11. Contemporary music	.66	.23	.24	.55
12. Folk/ethnic dance	.45	.16	.22	.28
13. Classical ballet	.46	.57	.11	.55
14. Modern dance	.65	.16	.28	.54
15. Serious theatre	.31	.39	.50	.50
16. Comedy theatre	.32	.31	.57	.52
17. Musical drama theatre	.16	.26	.51	.35
18. Musical comedy theatre	.01	.04	.71	.51
19. Experimental theatre	.25	.01	.68	.53
Percentage of Variance Explained	36%	10%	7%	
Cumulative Variance Explained	36%	46%	53%	

FIGURE 16–4 Performing Arts: Factor loadings

Source: Richard P. Nielsen and Charles McQueen, "Performing Arts Consumer Behavior: An Exploratory Study." Ronald C. Curhan, ed. *The 1974 Combined Proceedings* (Chicago: American Marketing Association, 1974) p. 393.

in most variables loading high on only one factor and a large percentage of relatively low and high loadings.

The first factor was termed "modern music and dance." The variables thought to represent this factor are underlined. The second factor, "classical music and dance," had heaviest loadings on variables 4, 6, 7, and 13. A careful look at the loadings for factor 2 will uncover some interpretation judgments. Note that the third factor has generally fewer variables with high loadings and the loadings are not as large. Factors that explain less of the variance have this quality.

SUMMARY

Application

Factor analysis is used to identify underlying dimensions or constructs in the data and to reduce the number of variables by eliminating redundancy.

Inputs

The input to factor analysis is usually a set of variable values for each individual or object in the sample. It is possible instead to input the matrix of correlations between the variables,[8] Actually, any type of square matrix whose components provide a measure of similarity between variables could be factor analyzed. The similarity measures does not have to be a correlation, although that is the most commonly used one.

Outputs

The most important outputs are the factor loadings, the factor scores, and the variance-explained percentages. The factor loadings, that is, the correlations between the factors and the variables, are used to interpret the factors. Sometimes an analyst will pick one or two variables that load heavily upon a factor to represent that factor in subsequent data collection or analysis. It also often is appropriate and useful to calculate the factor score and use that as a variable in the subsequent data analysis. The "percent-of variance-explained" terms help to determine the number of factors to include and the quality of their representation of the original variables.

Key Assumption

The most important assumption is that there are factors underlying the variables and that the variables indeed completely and adequately represent these factors. In practical terms, this assumption means that the list of variables should be complete, in that among them each factor is measured at least once and hopefully several times from several different perspectives. If, for some reason, the variables list is deficient from the beginning, it will take a large dose of luck to emerge with anything very useful.

---

[8]Factor analysis could be conducted on a correlation matrix between people or objects instead of a between-*variable* correlation matrix. The resulting factors would then represent groups of people instead of groups of variables. This approach is called *Q*-factor analysis. The more common focus upon relationships between variables is termed *R*-factor analysis.

Limitations

The greatest limitation is that factor analysis is a highly, subjective process. The determination of the number of factors, the interpretation of the factors, and the rotation to select (if one set of factors displeases the analyst, rotation may be continued indefinitely) all involve subjective judgment.

A related limitation is that there are really no statistical tests regularly employed in factor analysis. As a result, it is often difficult to know if the results are merely an accident or do reflect something meaningful. Consequently a standard procedure of factor analysis should be to divide the sample randomly into two or more groups and independently run a factor analysis with each group. If the same factors emerge in each analysis, then confidence that the results do not represent a statistical accident is increased.

QUESTIONS AND PROBLEMS

1 How is a factor loading interpreted?

2 What is a communality? What is the implication of low communality for a few of the variables?

3 How does principal components analysis differ from varimax rotation?

4 Why are factors rotated?

5 Identify a situation where you would expect the first factor to have high loadings on all variables and to account for almost all the variance.

6 Suppose five variables were factor analyzed and the percentage of variance explained was 80 percent, 12 percent, 5 percent, 2 percent, and 1 percent. How many factors would you include? What if the first three factors were interpretable and relevant?

7 Suppose you are conducting a large, 2000-respondent study for a bank. Among other elements the study includes:

a A 28-item image rating for three commercial banks, two savings and loans banks, and an "ideal" financial institution

b A 75-item lifestyle question set

c A 30-item set of questions to determine whether the respondents are opinion leaders, sources of product information, and so on.

d A 40-item set of questions on the importance of bank services

e A set of questions on usage of 35 bank services

Specifically, how would factor analysis be employed in this study?

8 Do you agree with the labels attached to the varimax rotated factors in Figure 16–2? Do you believe the varimax rotations are more valid than the principal components factors? More interesting?

9 Consider case 20–2. Interpret Table 20–7 and address questions 1, 3 & 4.

10 Factor analyze Q3 items in PG&E (p. 326).

APPENDIX
ADDITIONAL PERSPECTIVES
TO FACTOR ANALYSIS

In this appendix, two additional perspectives may provide further insight into the somewhat slippery subject of factor analysis. The first is a geometric perspective and the second is an algebraic or "factor model" perspective.

A Geometric Perspective

It often is helpful to consider a geometric interpretation of factor analysis. Principal components analysis, normally the first step in a factor analysis, will be described from a geometric perspective in the context of an example. Suppose a group of prospective students rated, on a -5 to $+5$ scale, the importance of "good faculty" and "program reputation" in their decision as to which school to attend. Thus, a -5 rating would mean that the individual does not really care if the school has a good faculty (rather, she or he might be more concerned about the athletic program). The respondents are plotted with respect to their ratings on the X_1 (good faculty) scale and on the X_2 (program reputation) scale. At this point, two questions arise. First, are there really two dimensions operating, or are both variables really measuring the same thing? If a person values a good faculty, it seems likely that she or he also would value program reputation. Thus, these two dimensions might be measuring the underlying construct of overall quality. Second, there is the practical question of whether the number of variables could be reduced from two to one without sacrificing information.

Principal components analysis provides an approach to these questions. It will generate a new dimension, shown as F_1 in Figure 16–5, that retains as nearly as possible the interpoint distance information or variance that was contained in the original two dimensions. The new axis is termed F_1, or the first factor. It also is termed the first principal component or the first principal factor. Each person has a "score" or projection on the new dimension, just as he or she had on the original X_1 and X_2 dimensions. For example, person 7 has a coordinate on factor 1 that is shown to be $F_{7,1}$ in Figure 16–5. This projection is termed the factor score for person 7 on factor 1.

An important statistic is the percentage of the original variance that is included in the first factor. The original variance is the variance on the X_1 axis plus the variance on

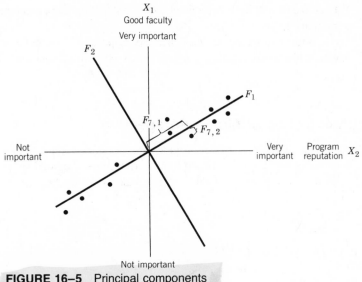

FIGURE 16–5 Principal components

the X_2 axis. In this case, the variance of the factor scores on factor 1 might be 90 percent of the total original variance.[9] This statistic provides an indication of how well the factor serves to represent the original data.

In Figure 16–5, the points do not all lie exactly on the line represented by the first factor. There is variation about the first factor. To capture this variation, a second factor, F_2, is added perpendicularly to F_1. The two factors together will represent the data completely. They will account for all the variation along the two axes, X_1 and X_2. Just as there were factor scores for the first factor, there also will be factor scores or projections on the second factor. The projection on factor 2 for person 7 is shown in Figure 16–5.

In Figure 16–5, since there are only two dimensions, the second factor is positioned automatically. However, if a third dimension such as "school size" were added to the original analysis (it would be shown coming out of the page), the position of the second factor would have to be determined. It could be a dimension tilted at any angle to the figure and still be perpendicular to the first factor.[10] With three original variables, the second factor is selected so that the variance of the factor scores on the second factor is maximized.

The analysis can continue in selecting factors until the process is stopped (using one of the rules of thumb) or until the number of factors equals the number of original variables.

[9]The variance on the X_1 axis is $\frac{1}{10} \Sigma (X_{i1} - \bar{X}_1)^2$ where $\bar{X}_1$ is the mean on the X_1 axis and X_{i1} is the value of individual i on the X_1 variable. The sample size here is 11, since there are 11 people in the sample. The variance on the X_2 axis is $\frac{1}{10} \Sigma (X_{i2} - \bar{X}_2)^2$ and the variance on factor 1 is $\frac{1}{10} \Sigma (F_{i1} - \bar{F}_1)^2$ where $\bar{X}_2$ and $\bar{F}_1$ are again the respective means.

[10]Let one pencil represent the third dimension, X_3, coming out of the page, and then see if possible positions of the second factor can be conceptualized using a second pencil.

Each factor will have associated with it a statistic, the percentage of the variance explained by that factor.

After factors have been generated by principal components they can be rotated using one of the many rotation schemes, such as varimax rotation.

An Algebraic or Factor Model Perspective

The factor analysis model provides another perspective. It shows that a basic assumption of factor analysis is that each input variable is a weighted sum of the factors plus an error term. The weights for each factor are the factor loadings:

$$x_{iv} = a_{v1}F_{i2} + a_{v2}F_{i2} + a_{v3}F_{i3} + \dots\dots + e_{iv}$$

where

i = an index for individual i

v = an index for variable v

x_{iv} = the (standardized) value of individual i on variable v

F_{if} = the (standardized) factor score of individual i upon factor f

a_{vf} = the factor loading of variable v on factor f

e_{iv} = an error term that includes all sources of variation in x_{iv} that are not accounted for by the factors

The factor model is interpreted just like the regression model, the subject of Chapter 19. Relating the factor model to the regression model generates useful insights. The reader who has not been exposed to regression analysis should skip the following, making a mental note to return to it after covering Chapter 19.

In the factor model, just as in the regression model, there is a small set of independent variables, here termed **factors**, which are hypothesized to explain or cause the dependent variable. The regression coefficients, here termed **factor loadings**, link the factors to the variables and are used to help interpret the factors. In this context the factor loadings are the correlations between the factors and the variables.[11] The error term in both the factor and regression models absorbs measurement error and variation in the dependent variable not caused or explained by the factors. It is the source of the unexplained variation in the dependent variable that is an important concept in both factor analysis (percentage of variance explained and communality) and regression analysis (r^2).

In regression analysis, the values of the independent variables (the factor scores) were known and were inputs to the analysis. In factor analysis, of course, the factor scores are

---

[11]As was noted in footnote 1, the factor loadings will be equal to the correlations only when the variables are standardized and when the factors are independent (perpendicular). When the variables are standardized, the factor coefficients become "beta coefficients" in the regression context. Unlike regression analysis, where the independent variables usually are correlated, the factors are independent. That is why a factor loading is here a correlation, whereas a beta coefficient in the regression context is not a correlation.

outputs. Just as an individual has an associated value on each of the original input variables, she or he also has a factor score for each of the factors. In subsequent analysis it may be convenient and appropriate to work with the factor scores instead of the original variables. The factor scores might be preferred because there are simply fewer factors than variables and (if the analyst is lucky) the factors are conceptually meaningful.

CASE 16–1

Barney Advertising[12]

Barney Advertising, a large advertising agency specializing in consumer products, conducted an exploratory study to determine if patterns of consumer behavior exist and if such patterns were interpretable and had managerial significance. The concept was to analyze consumer behavior by starting with behavior itself. Suppose there was a group of consumers who were heavy users of three products. It might be that such consumers had some specific set of needs, dispositions, and experiences in common. For example, if heavy users of headache remedies are also heavy users of cold tablets and stomach remedies, is there reason to suspect that this group of consumers has in common an unusual number of ailments, a particular attitude about what should be done about ailments, or both?

Groupings of products should be able to stimulate and guide research and suggest cooperative marketing or advertising programs. The approach also could work with magazines people read, the television programs people watch, or the activities in which people engage.

The Brand Rating Index questionnaire for homemakers, which contains questions about the purchase and use of 144 products, the buying plans of 21 durable items, and the exposure patterns of 54 magazines and 166 television programs provided the data base. The study focused upon the 104 products the respondent buys for his or her family. These 104 products were intercorrelated, and the resulting matrix was factored by the principal components method. The resulting factors (each of which explained more than 1/104th of the variance) were rotated by the varimax method. To guard against the possibility that factors might be formed by

[12]Prepared by William D. Wells and David A. Aaker as the basis for class discussion.

chance associations, the analysis was performed on two samples of 1000 homemakers, drawn independently and randomly from the BRI set of 12,500 homemakers. Only factors that emerged in both analyses were reported.

A factor score was computed for each respondent on each factor. The factor scores were then cross-tabulated by the demographic characteristics of the respondents. Figure 16–6 reports the factor loadings for each factor. The factor loadings in parentheses are those below 0.50 which were of interest or judged to be useful in interpreting the factors.

QUESTIONS FOR DISCUSSION

1 Comment on the study. Was it necessary to use two samples of size 1000? Why not use three samples of 500 instead?

2 How exactly would you proceed with the study to determine which demographic variables (age, sex, income, occupation, area, and type of residence) explain the heavy usage of product groups?

3 Interpret the factors. Why should heavy users of toothpaste also be heavy users of cereal (factor 1)? Shouldn't plastic bags and plastic wrap be substitutes and therefore have different signs (factor 2)? Why is the loading for cotton swabs so low (factor 3)? Why is the loading for liquid dietary low (factor 4)? What demographic variable could explain factor 6? Why is the margarine loading negative in factor 8? Why are factors 9, 10, and 11 separate?

FACTOR 1		FACTOR 8	
Laundry soap, detergent	73	Butter	74
Toothpaste	70	Margarine	−58
Toilet tissue	69		
Weekly supermarket bill	68	FACTOR 9	
Shampoo	65	Shortening	58
Cold cereal	61	Flour	58
Toilet soap	60	(Layer cake mix)	(39)
Peanut butter	58		
Frankfurters	56	FACTOR 10	
FACTOR 2		Frozen cakes, pastries	66
Plastic bags	69	Packaged cookies	63
Plastic wrap	65		
Aluminum foil	55	FACTOR 11	
(Wax paper bags)	(43)	Instant pudding	62
		Cooked pudding	57
FACTOR 3		Flavored gelatin dessert	55
Diapers purchased	84		
Strained baby food	82	FACTOR 12	
Soap for baby clothes	79	Pain reliever tablets	68
(Cotton swabs)	(47)	Relief for upset stomach	68
		Cold, allergy tablets	55
FACTOR 4			
Artificial sweeteners	70	FACTOR 13	
Diet soft drinks	69	Oven cleaner	64
(Liquid dietary)	(43)	Window spray	64
		(Liquid furniture polish)	(36)
FACTOR 5			
Canned lunch meat	66	FACTOR 14	
Canned spaghetti	65	Spray furniture polish	63
Canned beef stew	61	Liquid furniture polish	−55
Canned pork and beans	51		
(Casserole mixes)	(44)	FACTOR 15	
		Scouring powder	70
FACTOR 6		All purpose cleaner	62
Canned vegetables	75		
Canned fruit	75	FACTOR 16	
		Spray disinfectant	63
FACTOR 7		Liquid disinfectant	57
Mustard	67	Air freshener sprays	51
Catsup	62		
(Mayonnaise)	(38)		

FIGURE 16–6 Factor loadings

CASE 16–2
The Store Image Study Revisited[13]

In this chapter Figure 16–3 shows the output of a factor analysis conducted on the ratings of 82 respondents who were asked to evaluate a particular discount store using 29 semantic-differential, seven-point scales. The same respondents were asked to evaluate a supermarket. A

[13]Based on the study by John Dickson and Gerald Albaum, "A Method for Developing Tailormade Semantic Differentials for Specific Marketing Content Areas," *Journal of Marketing Research, 8* (February 1977), 87–91.

second factor analysis was conducted on the super-market data and the results are shown in Figure 16–7.

1 Label the factors. Compare these factors with those found in the discount store analysis of Figure 16–3. Why should they be different? *Hint:* It isn't because a discount store is different from a supermarket.

2 Analyze the communalities. Which are low? What are the implications? Contrast with Figure 16–3.

	SCALE	FACTORS					COMMUNALITY
		I	I	III	IV	V	
1.	Well spaced merchandise	.73	.10	−.11	.02	.12	.57
2.	Bright store	.63	−.08	.45	−.11	.06	.62
3.	Ads frequently seen by you	−.04	.08	−.02	−.12	.58	.36
4.	High quality products	.50	.32	.24	.01	−.03	.41
5.	Well organized layout	.70	.08	.05	−.00	.12	.51
6.	Low prices	−.09	.64	−.02	.19	.18	.49
7.	Good sales on products	.27	.73	−.00	−.10	−.01	.62
8.	Pleasant store to shop in	.63	.36	.09	.12	.01	.55
9.	Good store	.73	.37	.26	.19	−.06	.78
10.	Convenient location	.18	.01	.59	−.10	.36	.52
11.	Low pressure salesmen	−.15	.05	.40	−.06	−.11	.20
12.	Big store	.08	−.02	.42	−.00	.14	.20
13.	Good buys on products	.35	.73	.04	.18	−.10	.70
14.	Attractive store	.68	.28	.38	.10	−.10	.70
15.	Helpful salesmen	.43	.16	.34	.34	.45	.64
16.	Good service	.60	.19	.21	.35	.01	.56
17.	Too many clerks	−.06	.03	−.01	.62	−.08	.40
18.	Friendly personnel	.48	.11	.17	.47	.36	.62
19.	Easy to return purchases	.39	.10	.01	−.10	.43	.36
20.	Unlimited selection of						
	products	.10	.09	.48	.17	−.18	.31
21.	Reasonable prices for value	.24	.71	.04	.01	.13	.58
22.	Neat	.87	−.00	.11	.07	.04	.78
23.	Spacious shopping	.72	.02	−.26	−.01	.18	.62
24.	Attract upper-class						
	customers	.38	−.37	−.17	−.06	.06	.32
25.	Clean	.83	.11	.16	.12	.03	.74
26.	Fast check-out	.22	.12	−.07	.68	−.13	.55
27.	Good displays	.73	.19	.07	.14	.13	.61
28.	Easy to find items you want	.57	.23	−.08	.03	−.01	.39
29.	Good specials	.37	.62	.08	.06	.32	.63
Percentage of Variance Explained		26	11	6	5	5	
Cumulative Variance Explained		26	37	43	48	53	

FIGURE 16–7 Factor loadings for a supermarket (Varimax Rotation).

17

MULTIDIMENSIONAL SCALING AND CLUSTER ANALYSIS

In this chapter, discussion of the analysis of interdependence continues as multidimensional scaling (first introduced in Chapter 8) and cluster analysis are presented. Multidimensional scaling (MDS) addresses the general problem of positioning objects in a perceptual space. Much of marketing management is concerned with the question of positioning. With whom do we compete? How are we compared to our competitors? On what dimensions? What positioning strategy should be followed? These and other questions are addressed by MDS.

In data analysis, it frequently is useful to group or cluster. In factor analysis, a goal was to group variables into factors. In MDS, the goal is sometimes to group brands or objects in competitive sets. In segmentation research, it often is useful to group people by such characteristics as perceptions, attitudes, or behavior. A direct approach to grouping is cluster analysis, the subject of the second section of this chapter.

MULTIDIMENSIONAL SCALING

Multidimensional scaling basically involves two problems. First, the dimensions upon which customers perceive or evaluate objects (organizations, products, or brands) must be identified. For example, students must evaluate prospective colleges in terms of their quality, cost, distance from home, and size. It would be convenient to work with only two dimensions, since the objects could then be portrayed graphically. However, it is not always possible to work with two dimensions, since additional dimensions sometimes are needed to represent customers' perceptions and evaluations. Second, objects need to be

465

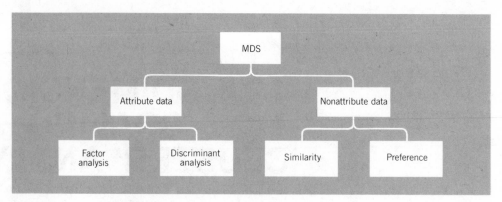

FIGURE 17–1 Approaches to multidimensional scaling

positioned with respect to these dimensions. The output of MDS is the location of the objects on the dimensions and is termed a **perceptual map.**[1]

There are several approaches to multidimensional scaling. They differ in the assumptions they employ, the perspective taken, and the input data used. Figure 17–1 provides a categorization of the major approaches in terms of the input data. One set of approaches involves object attributes. If the objects are colleges, the attributes could be faculty, prestige, facilities, cost, and so on. MDS then will combine these attributes into dimensions, such as quality. Another set of approaches bypasses attributes and considers similarity or preference relationships between objects directly. Thus, two schools could be rated as to how similar they are or how much one is preferred over the other, without regard to any underlying attribute. The attribute-based approaches will be described first. A presentation of the nonattribute-based approaches will follow. Finally, the ideal-object concept will be discussed.

Attribute-Based Approaches

An important assumption of the attribute-based approaches is that we can identify attributes upon which individuals' perceptions of objects are based. Let us start with a simple example. Suppose that the goal is to develop a perceptual map of the nonalcoholic beverage market.[2] Suppose further that exploratory research has identified 14 beverages that seem relevant and nine attributes that are used by people to describe and evaluate these beverages. A group of respondents is asked to rate, on a seven-point scale, each of the

---

[1]There is a variety of programs available to process the various input data and generate a perceptual map. For a summary, see Roger N. Shepard, "A Taxonomy of Some Principal Types of Data and of Multidimensional Methods for Their Analysis," in Roger N. Shepard, A. Kimball Romney, and Sera Beth Nerlove, eds., *Multidimensional Scaling* (New York: Seminar Press, 1972), pp. 21–44.

[2]This example is based on research reported in Thomas P. Hustad, Charles S. Mayer, and Thomas W. Whipple, "Consideration of Context Differences in Product Evaluation and Market Segmentation," *Journal of the Academy of Marketing Science, 3* (Winter 1975), 34–47.

beverages on the nine attributes. An average rating of the respondent group on each of the nine attributes, termed profile analysis in Chapter 8, would be of interest. However, it would be much more useful if the nine attributes could be combined into two or three dimensions or factors. Two approaches commonly are used to reduce the attributes to a small number of dimensions. The first is factor analysis, described in the previous chapter. A second is discriminant analysis.

Factor Analysis. Since each respondent rates 14 beverages on nine attributes, he or she ultimately will have 14 factor scores on each of the emerging factors, one for each of the beverages. The position of each beverage in the perceptual space then will be the average factor score for that beverage. The perceptual map shown in Figure 17–2 illustrates. Three factors, accounting for 77 percent of the variance, serve to summarize the nine attributes. Each of the beverages is then positioned on the attributes. Since three factors or dimensions are involved, two maps are required to portray the results. The first involves the first two factors, while the second includes the first and third factors. For convenience, the original attitudes also are shown in the maps as lines or vectors. The direction of the vectors indicates the factor with which each attribute is associated, and the length of the vector indicates the strength of association. Thus, in the left map, the "filling" attribute has little association with any factor, whereas in the right map, the "filling" attribute is strongly associated with the "refreshing" factor.

Discriminant Analysis. Whereas the goal of factor analysis is to generate dimensions that maximize interpretability and explain variance, the goal of discriminant analysis is to generate dimensions that will discriminate or separate the objects as much as possible.[3] As in factor analysis, each dimension is based upon a combination of the underlying attributes. However, in discriminant analysis, the extent to which an attribute will tend to be an important contributor toward a dimension depends upon the extent to which there is a perceived difference among the objects on that attribute.

Figure 17–3 shows a MDS solution for the Chicago beer market, based upon discriminant analysis. Each of 500 male beer drinkers described eight brands of beer on each of 35 attributes.[4] Each brand is positioned on these two dimensions by averaging over the 500 respondents. Seventeen of the attributes also are shown as vectors in the figure. As in Figure 17–2, their correlation with the two dimensions is reflected by their length and direction. The two dimensions thus can be interpreted by identifying which attribute or cluster of attributes falls closest to them. In this case, the horizontal axis represents a "price-quality" distinction and the vertical axis represents some notion of "body" (including sweetness, maltiness, etc.). The price-quality axis is the better of the two in discriminating, since the brands are much more spread out in this axis (horizontal) than on the vertical "body" axis. The brands can be evaluated relative to either the two major discriminant axes or the 17 attribute vectors by projecting the brand. The dotted lines

---

[3]The dimensions are termed discriminant functions instead of factors.

[4]The two dimensions pictured accounted for about 90 percent of the discrimination among images of these eight brands. The interpretation is analogous to the percent of variance explained in factor analysis.

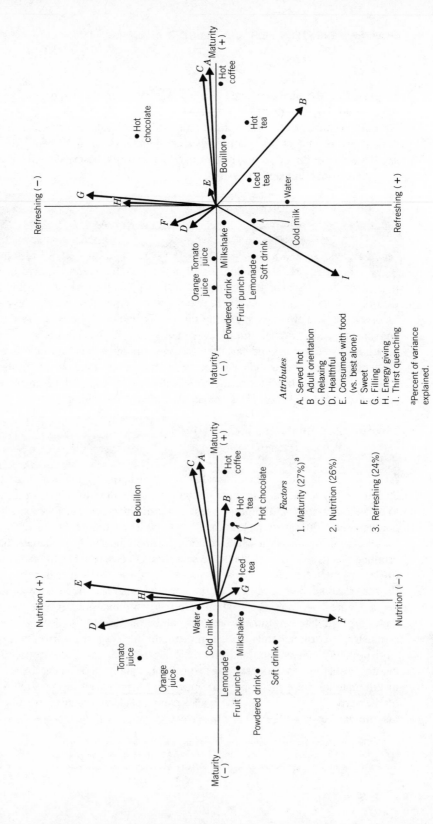

FIGURE 17–2 Perceptual maps of a beverage market

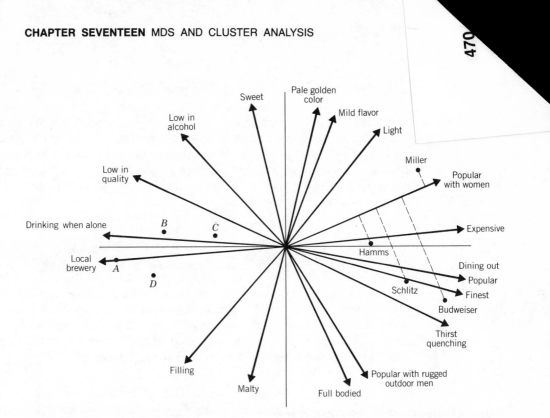

FIGURE 17–3 The Chicago beer market

Source: Richard M. Johnson, "Market Segmentation—A Strategic Management Tool," *Journal of Marketing Research, 9* (February 1971) 15.

show that Miller is perceived as being the most popular with women, followed by Budweiser, Schlitz, Hamms, and four popular-priced beers, in that order. Miller's position reflected a prior long-running "champagne of bottled beer" campaign directed at women. Similarly, Budweiser is regarded as being the most expensive beer, and so on.

Comparing Factor and Discriminant Analysis. Each of the approaches has advantages and disadvantages. Discriminant analysis identifies clusters of attributes on which objects differ. If all objects are perceived to be similar with respect to an attribute (such as the safety of an airline) then that attribute should not affect preference (such as the choice of an airline). Following that logic the discriminant analysis objective of selecting attributes that discriminate between objects seems sensible. A second useful characteristic of discriminant analysis is that it provides a test of statistical significance. The null hypothesis is that two objects actually are perceived identically. The test will determine the probability that the between-object distance was due simply to a statistical accident. A third quality of discriminant analysis is that it will identify a perceptual dimension even if it is represented by a single attribute.

In contrast, factor analysis groups attributes that are similar. If there are not several attributes representing a dimension, it will tend not to emerge in the factor analysis solution. Factor analysis is based upon both perceived differences between objects and differences between people's perceptions of objects. Thus, it tends to provide a richer solution, use more of the attributes, and result in more dimensions. All perceptual dimensions are included, whether they discriminate between objects or not. Hauser & Koppelman conducted a study of shopping centers in which they compared several approaches to multidimensional scaling.[5] They found that factor analysis dimensions provided more interpretive value than did those of discriminant analysis.

Introducing Importance Weights. Both factor analysis and discriminant analysis ignore the relative importance of the individual attributes to customers. Myers & Tauber suggest that the attribute data be multiplied by importance weights and then be subjected to a factor analysis.[6] As a result the attributes considered more important will have a greater tendency to be included in a factor analysis solution. They present a factor analysis perceptual map for snack food that included the dimensions of ''convenience'' and ''nutrition.'' When that study was repeated, this time with importance weights introduced, a ''child likes'' dimension replaced the ''convenience'' dimension.

Nonattribute-Based Approaches

Attribute-based MDS has the advantage that attributes can have diagnostic and operational value and the dimensions can be interpreted in terms of their correlations with the attributes. Further, the Hauser & Koppelman study concluded that attribute data were easier for respondents to use and that dimensions based upon attribute data predicted preference better than did dimensions based upon nonattribute data.[7]

However, nonattribute data also has several conceptual disadvantages. First, if the list of attributes is not accurate and complete, the study will suffer accordingly. The generation of an attribute list can be most difficult, especially when possible differences among people's perceptions are considered. Second, it may be that people simply do not perceive or evaluate objects in terms of underlying attributes. An object may be perceived or evaluated as a whole that is not decomposable in terms of attributes. Finally, attribute-based models may require more dimensions to represent them than would be needed by more flexible models, in part because of the linearity assumptions of factor analysis and discriminant analysis. These disadvantages lead us to the use of nonattribute data, namely, similarity and preference data.

[5]John R. Hauser and Frank S. Koppelman, ''Alternative Perceptual Mapping Techniques: Relative Accuracy and Usefulness,'' *Journal of Marketing Research, 16* (November 1979) 495–506. Hauser and Koppelman conclude that factor analysis is superior to discriminant analysis; however, many other experienced researchers prefer discriminant analysis for the reasons noted herein.

[6]James H. Myers and Edward Tauber, *Market Structure Analysis* (Chicago: American Marketing Association), 1977, pp. 48–55. The authors call this technique a *weighted covariance analysis*.

[7]Hauser & Koppelman, *op. cit.*

Similarity Data. Similarity measures simply reflect the perceived similarity of two objects in the eyes of the respondents. For example, each respondent may be asked to rate the degree of similarity of each pair of objects. The respondent is generally not told what criteria to use to determine similarity; thus, the respondent does not have an attribute list that implicitly suggests criteria to be included or excluded. In the following example, the respondent judged Stanford to be quite similar to Harvard.

The number of pairs to be judged for degree of similarity can be as many as $n(n - 1) \div 2$, where n is the total number of objects. With 10 brands, there could be 45 pairs of brands to judge (although fewer could be used). This is a large number of judgments, so it usually is desirable to have a separate card for each pair. The respondent is instructed to place the cards on a "sort board" that has locations corresponding to the similarity-of-scale categories and should check each pile to insure that all the pairs in the pile (category) have the same degree of similarity or dissimilarity.

Although it is essential that at least seven or eight objects be judged, the approach is easier to illustrate if only four objects are considered. First, the results of the pairwise similarity judgments are summarized in a matrix, as shown in Figure 17–4. The numbers in the matrix represent the average similarity judgments for a sample of 50 respondents. Instead of similarity ratings, the respondents could be asked simply to rank the pairs from most to least similar. An average rank-order position then would replace the average

Average similarity ratings

Objects	A	B	C	D
A				
B	3.2			
C	1.7	3.9		
D	5.1	3.3	4.7	

Rank by degree of similarity

Objects	A	B	C	D
A				
B	2			
C	1	4		
D	6	3	5	

FIGURE 17–4 Similarity judgments

similarity rating matrix. It should be noted, however, that rank ordering can be difficult if nine, 10, or more objects are involved.

A perceptual map could be obtained from the average similarity ratings; however, the most common procedure is to use only the ordinal or "nonmetric" portion of the data. Thus, the knowledge that objects A and C in Figure 17–4 have an average similarity of 1.7 is replaced by the fact that objects A and C are the most similar pair. The conversion to rank-order information is shown in Figure 17–4. Ordinal or nonmetric information is preferred for several reasons. First, it actually contains about the same amount of information, in that the output usually is not affected by replacing intervally scaled or "metric" data with ordinal or nonmetric data. Second, the nonmetric data often are thought to be more reliable.

Next, a computer program is employed to convert the rankings of similarity into distances in a map with a small number of dimensions, so that similar objects are close together and vice versa.[8] The computer will be programmed to locate the four objects in a space of two, three, or more dimensions, so that the shortest distance is between pair (A, C), the next shortest is pair (A, B), and the longest pair is (A, D). One possible solution that satisfied these constraints in two dimensions is the following:

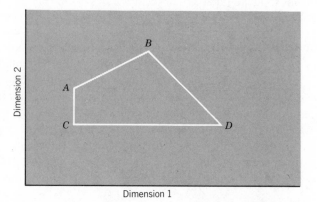

The reader might be able to relocate the points differently and still satisfy the constraints so that the rankings of the distances in the map correspond to the rankings of the pairwise similarity judgments. This is because there are only a few points to move in the space and only six constraints to satisfy. With 10 objects and 45 constraints, the task of locating the points in a two-dimensional space is vastly more difficult, requiring a computer. Once a solution is found—the points are located in the space—it is unlikely that there will be a significantly different solution that still satisfies the constraints of the similarities matrix.

[8]Lester A. Neidell, "The Use of Nonmetric Multi-dimensional Scaling in Market Analyses," *Journal of Marketing, 33* (October 1969), 37–43.

Thus, we can argue that the intervally scaled nature of the distances between points really was hidden in the rank-order input data all the time.

The power of the technique lies in its ability to find the smallest number of dimensions for which there is a reasonably good fit between the input similarity rankings and the rankings of distance between objects in the resulting space. Usually, this means starting with two dimensions and, if this is not satisfactory, continuing to add dimensions until an acceptable fit is achieved. The determination of "acceptable" is a matter of judgment, although most analysts will trade off some degree of fit to stay with a two- or three-dimensional map because of the enormous advantages of visual interpretations. There are situations where more dimensions are necessary. This happened in a study of nine different types of sauces (mustard, catsup, relish, steak sauce, dressing, etc.). Most respondents perceived too many differences to be captured with two or three dimensioins, in terms of either the types of foods the sauces would be used with or the physical characteristics of each sauce.[9]

The interpretation of the resulting dimensions takes place "outside" the technique. Additional information must be introduced to decide why objects are located in their relative positions. Sometimes the location of the objects themselves can suggest dimensional interpretations. For example, in Figure 17–3, the horizontal axis might be interpreted as a price-quality dimension because it separates the expensive "name" brands from the inexpensive store brands. Another approach is to correlate object characteristics, such as attribute ratings, with the object's position on the dimensions.

An example of rank-order similarity data is shown in Table 17–1. This could be the ranking of a single respondent or the average of a group of respondents. The resulting perceptual map is shown in Figure 17–5. In this case, the object locations serve to identify the dimensions. For example, objects 3, 6, 5, and 11 provide some insights into the horizontal dimensions labeled "luxurious." Disregard the ideal point notation for now.

Preference Data. Rank-order preference data also can be used as the basis for similarity measures and perceptual maps. Preference data contain similarity information. Objects that are ranked second and sixth in a rank-order preference should be "farther apart" or less similar than objects ranked third and fourth. In general, an individual should be expected to rank closely together those objects perceived as being similar. Preference information also can be obtained using a scale. Thus, if an individual rated one object as 7.6 on a 10-point preference scale and another as 4.4, then a reasonable similarity measure would be the difference of 3.2.

The use of preference data to develop perceptual maps introduces a different and quite important perspective into the analysis. It may be that individuals' perceptions of objects are different in a preference context than in a similarity or attribute-based context. A dimension might be very useful in describing the differences between two objects, but it is of no consequence in determining preference. Thus, two objects could be very different

[9]James H. Myers and Edward Tauber, *Market Structure Analysis* (Chicago: American Marketing Association, 1977), p. 38.

TABLE 17–1

Rank Order of Dissimilarities between Pairs of Car Models[a,b]

STIMULI	1	2	3	4	5	6	7	8	9	10	11
1	—	8	50	31	12	48	36	2	5	39	10
2		—	38	9	33	37	22	6	4	14	32
3			—	11	55	1	23	46	41	17	52
4				—	44	13	16	19	25	18	42
5					—	54	53	30	28	45	7
6						—	26	47	40	24	51
7							—	29	35	34	49
8								—	3	27	15
9									—	20	21
10										—	43
11											—

SOURCE   Paul E. Green and Frank J. Carmone, "Multidimensional Scaling: An Introduction and Comparison of Nonmetric Unfolding Techniques," *Journal of Marketing Research, 6* (August 1969), 331.

[a]The rank number "1" represents the most similar pair.
[b]See Figure 17–5 for model descriptions.

in a similarity-based perceptual map but could be regarded as very similar in a preference-based perceptual map. The analyst needs to consider such a possibility in selecting which approach is most appropriate.

Are Perceptions the Same for Different People?

In both attribute- and nonattribute-based approaches, it has been suggested that the analysis be conducted for data averaged over groups of respondents. The implicit assumption has been that individuals in the group have the same perceptions of the objects and that the observed differences in their responses represent mostly measurement error. However, there may be situations in which there are subgroups that have very different perceptions of the objects. In such cases, it usually is useful to identify those subgroups either by prior knowledge of their characteristics or by clustering them on the basis of their individual responses. Separate perceptual maps then would be developed for each of the groups with similar perceptions.

Perceptual differences can be detected by examining the standard deviations in either the attribute or ·nonattribute data. Apparent perceptual differences can be caused by respondents having a lack of knowledge; thus, it is useful to determine how familiar respondents are with the various objects. Respondents who are unfamiliar with objects should not be used to generate perceptual maps.[10]

---

[10]David A. Aaker and Peter Wilton, "Perceptual Heterogeneity: Measurement and Implications," Proceedings of the 1984 AMA Educators' Conference (Chicago: American Marketing Association), 1984.

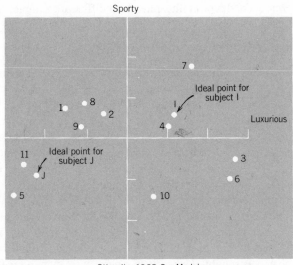

Stimuli—1968 Car Models

1. Ford Mustang 6
2. Mercury Cougar V8
3. Lincoln Continental V8
4. Ford Thunderbird V8
5. Ford Falcon 6
6. Chrysler Imperial V8

7. Jaguar Sedan
8. AMC Javelin V8
9. Plymouth Barracuda V8
10. Buick Le Sabre V8
11. Chevrolet Corvair

FIGURE 17–5   Illustration of joint space of ideal points and stimuli.

Ideal Objects

The concept of an ideal object in the space is an important one in MDS because it allows the analyst to relate object positioning to customer likes and dislikes. It also provides a means for segmenting customers according to their preferences for product attributes.

An ideal object is one the customer would prefer over all others, including objects that can be conceptualized in the space but do not actually exist. It is a combination of all the customers' preferred attribute levels. Although the assumption that people have similar perceptions may be reasonable, their preferences are nearly always heterogeneous—their ideal objects will differ. One reason to locate ideal objects is to identify segments of customers who have similar ideal objects.

There are two types of ideal objects. The first lies within the perceptual map. For example, if a new cookie were rated on attribute scales such as

Very sweet ···························· Not at all sweet
Large, substantial ················· Small, dainty

a respondent might well prefer a middle position on the scale.

The second type is illustrated by a different example. Suppose attributes of a proposed new car included

Inexpensive to buy ························· Expensive to buy
Inexpensive to operate ··················· Expensive to operate
Good handling ······························· Bad handling

then respondents would very likely prefer an end point on the scale. For instance, the car should be as inexpensive to buy and operate as possible. In that case, the ideal object would be represented by an ideal vector or direction rather than an ideal point in the space. The direction would depend upon the relative desirability of the various attributes.

There are two approaches to obtaining ideal object locations. The first is simply to ask respondents to consider an ideal object as one of the objects to be rated or compared. The problem with this approach is that the conceptualization of an ideal object may not be natural for a respondent and the result may therefore be ambiguous and unreliable.

A second approach is indirect. For each individual, a rank-order preference among the objects is sought. Then, given a perceptual map, a program will locate the individual's ideal objects such that the distances to the objects have the same (or as close to the same as possible) rank order as the rank-order preference. The preferred object should be closest to the ideal. The second most preferred object should be farther from the ideal than the preferred but closer than the third most preferred, and so on. Often it is not possible to determine a location that will satisfy this requirement perfectly and still obtain a small number of dimensions with which an analyst would like to work. In that case, compromises are made and the computer program does as well as possible by maximizing some measure of "goodness-of-fit."

Two individuals' ideal objects have been located in Figure 17–5. Figure 17–6 shows a grouping of the ideal objects in the perceptual map portrayed in Figure 17–3. The circles in Figure 17–6 are proportional in size to the number of ideal objects that they represent. Each circle represents a potential market segment.

Multidimensional Scaling—A Summary

Application.   MDS is used to identify dimensions by which objects are perceived or evaluated, to position the objects with respect to those dimensions, and to make positioning decisions for new and old products.

Inputs.   Attribute-based data involve respondents rating the objects with respect to specified attributes. Similarity-based data involve a rank order of between-object similarity that can be based upon several methods of obtaining similarity information from respondents. Preference data also can provide the basis for similarity measures and generate perceptual maps from quite a different perspective.

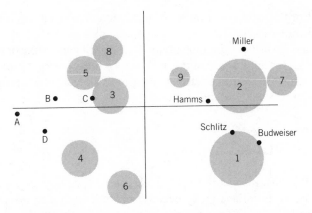

FIGURE 17–6 Distribution of ideal points in product space

Source: Richard M. Johnson, "Market Segmentation—A Strategic Management Tool," *Journal of Marketing Research,* 9 (February 1971) 16.

Ideal points or directions are based upon either having the respondent conceptualize her or his ideal object or by generating rank-order preference data and using the data in a second stage of analysis to identify ideal points or directions.

Outputs. The output will provide the location of each object on a limited number of dimensions. The selection of the number of dimensions is made on the basis of a goodness-of-fit measure (such as the percentage of variance explained in factor analysis) and on the basis of the interpretability of the dimensions. In attitude-based MDS, attribute vectors may be included to help interpret the dimensions. Ideal points or directions may be an output in some programs.

Key Assumptions. The overriding assumption is that the underlying data represent valid measures. Thus, we assume that respondents can compare objects with respect to similarity or preference or attributes. The meaning of the input data is rather straightforward; however, the ability and motivation of respondents to provide it is often questionable. A related assumption is that an appropriate context is used by the respondents. For some, a rank-order preference of beer could be based on the assumption that it was to be served to guests. Others might assume the beer was to be consumed privately.

With the attribute-based data, the assumption is made that the attribute list is relevant and complete. If individuals are grouped, the assumption that their perceptions are similar is made. The ideal object introduces additional conceptual problems.

Another basic assumption is that the interpoint distances generated by a perceptual map have conceptual meaning that is relevant to choice decisions.

Limitations. A limitation of the attribute-based methods is that the attributes have to be generated. The analyst has the burden of making sure that respondents' perceptions and evaluations are represented by the attributes. With similarity and preference data, this task is eliminated, but the analyst then must interpret dimensions without the aid of such attributes, although attribute data could be generated independently and attribute-dimension correlations still obtained.

CLUSTER ANALYSIS

All scientific fields have the need to cluster or group similar objects. Botanists group plants, historians group events, and chemists group elements and phenomena. It should be no surprise that when marketing managers attempt to become more scientific they should find a need for procedures that will group objects. Actually, the practical applications in marketing for cluster analysis are far too numerous to describe; however, it is possible to suggest by example the scope of this basic technique.

One goal of marketing managers is to identify similar segments so that marketing programs can be developed and tailored to each segment. Thus, it is useful to cluster customers. We might cluster them on the basis of the product benefits they seek. Thus, students could be grouped on the basis of the benefits they seek from a college. We might group customers by their lifestyles. The result could be a group that likes outdoor activities, another that enjoys entertainment, and a third that is into cooking and gardening. Each segment may have distinct product needs and may respond differently to advertising approaches.

We might want to cluster brands or products to determine which brands are regarded as similar and therefore competitive. Brands or products also might be grouped with respect to usage. If two brands or products are found to be bought by the same group of people, a tie-in promotion might be possible.

If a test-market experiment is planned, it might be useful to identify similar cities so that different marketing programs could be compared by trying them in different cities. To identify similar cities we might cluster them on the basis of variables that could contaminate the test, such as size or ethnic composition.

In marketing media decisions, it often is helpful to know which media have similar audiences and which appeal to different audiences.

An Example

A very simple clustering approach, termed quick clustering, will serve to introduce many of the concepts of cluster analysis.[11] In a study of gasoline brands, respondents were asked to rate each of 11 brands along a scale from seven (very favorable) to one (unfavorable). Table 17–2 shows the correlations between the brands.

[11]Joseph M. Kamen, "Quick Clustering," *Journal of Marketing Research* (July 1970), 199–204.

TABLE 17–2

Correlations between Gasoline Brands

| | STANDARD | MARTIN | SHELL | TEXACO | PHILLIPS | MOBIL | D-X | OWENS | SKELLY | CLARK | GULF |
	1	2	3	4	5	6	7	8	9	10	11
1. Standard	—	.01	.36	.38	.33	.29	.26	.11	.37	.18	(.41)
2. Martin	.01	—	.16	.09	.13	.16	.13	(.64)	.18	(.36)	.20
3. Shell	.36	.16	—	.34	.38	.34	.34	.06	.31	.26	.33
4. Texaco	.38	.09	.34	—	.43	.45	.33	.05	.36	.27	.34
5. Phillips	.33	.13	(.38)	.43	—	.44	(.48)	.17	.43	.32	.28
6. Mobil	.29	.16	.34	(.45)	.44	—	.36	.12	(.46)	.18	.32
7. D-X	.26	.13	.34	.33	(.48)	.36	—	.11	.39	.30	.23
8. Owens	.11	(.64)	.06	.05	.17	.12	.11	—	.35	.30	.18
9. Skelly	.37	.18	.31	.36	.43	(.46)	.39	.35	—	.24	.31
10. Clark	.18	.36	.26	.27	.32	.18	.30	.30	.24	—	.21
11. Gulf	(.41)	.20	.33	.34	.28	.32	.23	.18	.31	.21	—

SOURCE: Joseph M. Kamen, "Quick Cluster," *Journal of Marketing Research*, July 1970, p. 201.

In quick clustering, the highest entry in each column is circled. Then the highest number in all columns is noted (0.64) and the brands involved—two independents. Martin and Owens—form the first cluster. If another brand in either the Martin row or the Owens row has a circled coefficient, it is added to this first cluster. Clark, also an independent but which serves only premium gasoline, qualifies (Owens-Martin-Clark).

The procedure then repeats itself with Owens, Martin, and Clark omitted from the analysis. The highest remaining circled correlation is then 0.48, which pairs Phillips and D-X. In the Phillips row, we find another circled number representing the Shell-Phillips correlation. Thus our second cluster is D-X, Phillips, and Shell. Proceeding in this manner, the two remaining clusters of Mobil-Skelly-Texaco and Standard-Gulf are developed. Thus, four clusters emerge from the process.

Figure 17–7 portrays graphically the quick-clustering process. It shows the merging of the brands and the correlation level at which the merging took place. Such a figure is useful because it provides some feel for the quality of the clustering, that is, the degree to which the brands within the cluster hang together. A simple listing of the four clusters would not provide any indication that Owens and Martin are much more closely linked to each other than to Clark. Figure 17–7 also provides other diagnostic information, as the following discussion will make clear.

Cluster analysis is based upon some measure of the similarity or proximity of two objects. The clustering procedure itself must be guided by a criterion by which clusters are selected. Given a criterion, one of several methods to select clusters can be used. Each of the elements of cluster analysis will be considered next.

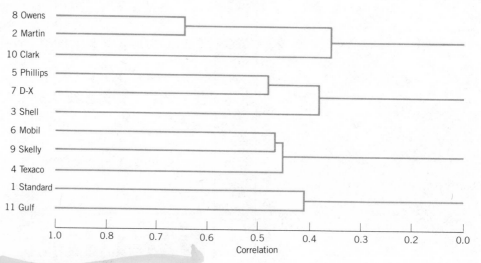

FIGURE 17–7 Hierarchy of clusters

Measures of Similarity

In Table 17–2 the measure of similarity was the familiar correlation coefficient. Actually, any measure that reflects similarity can provide the basis for a clustering program. Clearly, the clustering will be only as good as the underlying measure.[12]

The Clustering Criterion

In the quick clustering example, the clustering was based on the pairwise correlation. More typically, there exists some overall measure of the quality of the clustering that guides the program. It could be the average measure of similarity within the clusters. Thus, in the Owen-Martin-Clark cluster, it would be the average of the three involved correlations, 0.64, 0.36, and 0.30. Another measure might be the average similarity within clusters divided by some measure of the average similarity between objects in different clusters. The clustering program attempts to find sets of clusters that yield a high value of the clustering criterion.

The Clustering Method

There are two approaches to clustering, a hierarchical approach and a nonhierarchical approach. Hierarchical clustering can start with all objects in one cluster and divide and subdivide them until all objects are in their own single-object cluster. This is called the "top-down" approach. The "bottom-up" approach, in constrast, can start with each object in its own (single-object) cluster and systematically combine clusters until all objects are in one cluster. In either case, the result is an elegant hierarchical arrangement of clusters, as shown at the top of Figure 17–8. When an object is associated with another object in a cluster, it remains clustered with that object. The quick clustering approach emerged with a hierarchical structure, although it was incomplete because it stopped at four clusters and had no mechanism to combine the final four. The reader should attempt to think of such a mechanism.[13]

---

[12]A common measure of similarity to use is the simple straight-line (or Euclidean) distance. Symbolically, the distance measure is

$$d_{ij}^2 = \sum_{v=1}^{n} (x_{iv} - x_{jv})^2$$

where

d_{ij} = the distance between objects (persons) i and j

x_{iv} = the value of variable v for object i

x_{jv} = the value of variable v for object j

n = the number of variables

Thus, the difference between object i and j is determined for variable v and squared. Summing over all variables yields the squared distance between the two objects.

[13]The technique AID, which will be discussed in Chapter 19, provides one approach to hierarchical cluster analysis. The objective of AID is to keep splitting the sample to generate homogeneous subgroups.

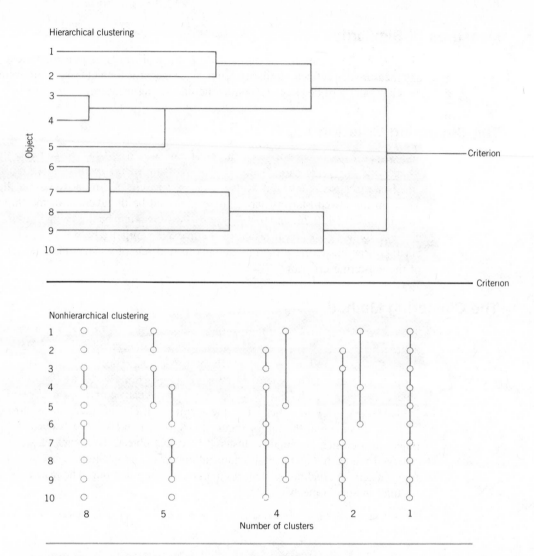

FIGURE 17–8 Hierarchical versus nonhierarchical clustering

A nonhierarchical clustering program will differ only in that it will permit objects to leave one cluster and join another as clusters are being formed, if the clustering criterion will be improved by doing so. The bottom half of Figure 17–8 shows the progress of a nonhierarchical clustering program. Note that object 2, for example, is in a cluster with object 1 when there are five clusters, but when there are only four, it is combined with object 3.

Each approach has advantages. Hierarchical clustering emerges as relatively easy to read and interpret. The output has the logical structure that theoretically always should exist. Its disadvantage is that it is relatively unstable and unreliable. The first combination or separation of objects, which may be based on a small difference in the criterion, will constrain the rest of the analysis. In the quick cluster example, the second cluster was based on the 0.48 correlation between Phillips and D-X. Yet, if the correlation between Phillips and Mobil had been only slightly higher, they would have formed the second cluster and the whole analysis would have been different. In doing hierarchical clustering, it is sound practice to split the sample into at least two groups and to do two independent clustering runs to see if the similar clusters emerge in both runs. If they are entirely different, there is an obvious cause for caution.

The advantage of nonhierarchical clustering is that it tends to be more reliable; that is, split-sample runs will tend to look more similar than hierarchical clustering. If the program makes a close decision early in the analysis that subsequently proves to be wrong with respect to the clustering criterion, it can be remedied by moving objects from cluster to cluster. The major disadvantage is that the series of clusters, as illustrated in the bottom half of Figure 17–8, is usually a mess and very difficult to interpret. The fact that it does look messy is sometimes good in that the analysis does not get any false sense of order when none exists. But the fact remains it can be very difficult to work with.

The Number of Clusters

A central question in clusters analysis is the determination of the appropriate number of clusters. There are several possible approaches. First, the analyst can specify in advance the number of clusters. Perhaps because of theoretical and logical reasons the number of clusters is known. Or, the analyst may have practical reasons for specifying the number of clusters that derive from the planned use of clusters. Second, the analyst can specify the level of clustering with respect to the cluster criterion. If the cluster criterion is easily interpretable, such as the average within-cluster similarity, it might be reasonable to establish a certain level that would dictate the number of clusters.

A third approach is to determine the number of clusters from the pattern of clusters generated by the program. For example, we might look at Figure 17–7 and conclude that there are 10 clusters with only Owens and Martin being combined. Or the correlation of 0.4, which specifies six clusters, might seem like a logical place to break the analysis. The analyst, in looking at the cluster pattern, might look for clusters that are stable over a relatively large range of the clustering criteria.

Whatever approach is used, it usually is useful to look at the total cluster pattern, such as those illustrated in Figures 17–7 and 17–8. They can provide a feel for the quality of the clustering and for the number of clusters that emerge at various levels of the clustering criterion. Usually more than one clustering level is relevant.

Cluster Analysis—A Summary

Application.   Cluster analysis is used to group variables, objects, or people. For example, people can be grouped into segments.

Input.   The input is any valid measure of similarity between objects, such as correlations. It also is possible to input the number of clusters or the level of clustering.

Output.   The output is a grouping of objects into clusters. Usually a series of such groupings is provided, such as those portrayed in Figure 17–7 and 17–8. Associated with each set of clusters will be the value of the clustering criterion. Some programs also output diagnostic information associated with each object. For example, the distances from each object to the center of its cluster and to the center of the next closest cluster are provided. This information can help determine in more depth the cluster cohesion and the level of association between an object and a cluster.

Key Assumptions.   The most important assumption is that the basic measure of similarity on which the clustering is based is a valid measure of the similarity between objects. A second major assumption is that there is theoretical justification for structuring the objects into clusters. As with other multivariate techniques, there should be theory and logic guiding and underlying cluster analysis.

Limitations.   It is usually difficult to evaluate the quality of the clustering. There are no standard statistical tests to insure that the output does not represent pure randomness. The value of the criterion measure, the reasonableness of the output, the appearance of a natural hierarchy (when a nonhierarchical method is used), and the split-sample reliability tests all provide useful information. However, it is still difficult to know exactly which clusters are very similar and which objects are difficult to assign. It is usually difficult to select a clustering criterion and program on any other basis than availability.

SUMMARY

Multidimensional scaling involves identifying dimensions by which objects are perceived and evaluated and positioning those objects and ideal objects with respect to those dimensions. The use of attribute data provides useful diagnostic information; however, it can be difficult to create a relevant and complete attribute list. The alternative is to base the perceptual map upon similarity or preference data.

Cluster analysis provides a direct approach to grouping variables, objects, or people. The clusters are based upon some kind of between-object similarity measure. Either hierarchical or nonhierarchical methods may be used to form clusters of objects on the basis of their between-object similarity.

QUESTIONS AND PROBLEMS

1 Suppose an MDS study was to be made among high-school seniors for use by the University of Indiana. The goal was to see how Indiana was positioned with respect to the 10 to 20 colleges with which it competes and to determine how students evaluate colleges.

   a How would you determine which colleges should be the object of the MDS study?

   b Generate a list of attributes that you feel should be included in the study. What methods did you use to generate the list?

   c Detail 10 different ways to generate between-object similarities. Which one would you use in the study?

   d Do you think the perceptual map would differ if preference data were used? Can you illustrate any hypothesized difference with an example?

2 How might a perceptual map like that of Figure 17–2 be used to suggest a new-product concept? Be specific. How might the concept be developed? How might it be tested?

3 The claim is made that MDS is of little help in new-product planning because most of the dimensions are "psychological" dimensions and not really actionable. The prediction of psychological reactions to physical changes is most difficult. Further-more, it is questioned how much guidance we gain from hearing that we need a "sportier" car or a more "full-bodied" beer. Comment.

4 How would you go about introducing ideal objects into Figure 17–2?

5 It is argued that people are not consciously aware of which dimensions they are employing to value similarity or even preference judgments. Further, a respondent may base judgments on attributes he or she is unwilling to admit. The use of nonattribute data in MDS is thus rather like motivation research in that it allows the researcher to make judgments about information not available by direct methods. Comment.

6 Suppose, given Figure 17–3, an advertising objective was to reposition Miller's as being more "full-bodied" and "popular with outdoor men" and closer to Budweiser instead of being "the champagne of bottled beer," a beer for women. How could MDS be used to test proposed copy and evaluate the results of a campaign? Can you think of any possible problems of this type of an application?

7 A relevant issue is whether respondents can provide directly similarity judgments that are meaningful. In particular:

   a Do consumers commonly make overall similarity judgments? If not, will their judgment be meaningful?

   b Does the perceptual map represent the internal cognitive structure, or does the nature of the task and memory limitation inhibit the full dimensionality from being recovered?

   c Do respondents share the same concept of what is meant by "similarity"?

8 Attempt to label the dimensions of Figure 17–2 using only the object location information

9 Describe why cluster analysis might be appropriate both before and after an MDS study.

10 Suppose similarity ratings for beer were cluster analyzed and three distinct clusters were found. How might those clusters differ? On what dimensions? On what characteristics?

11 When might hierarchical clustering be preferred over nonhierarchical clustering?

12 Respondents in a study were asked to indicate their activities (such as playing tennis, attending plays, attending dinner parties, etc.) on a seven-point scale (from 1 = never to 7 = frequently). A correlation between respondents was obtained. Cluster analyze these respondents.

1.	.62	.32	−.10	−.30	.01	.50	−.12	−.40	.22	−.07	.32
2.	—	.11	.02	−.45	.12	.82	.05	−.10	.32	−.15	.15
3.		—	−.60	.16	.35	.50	.87	.01	−.15	.44	.20
4.			—	.34	.71	.35	.42	−.10	.19	.49	.26
5.				—	.40	−.01	−.12	.51	.49	−.11	.35
6.					—	.08	.26	.11	.09	−.46	−.01
7.						—	−.17	.20	.03	.07	.16
8.							—	.09	.33	.32	.32
9.								—	.16	.01	−.12
10.									—	.03	.11
11.										—	.40
12.											—

13 Cluster the respondents represented by the correlation matrix in Figure 16–1 (page 446).

CASE 17–1

Nester's Foods

Nester's Foods is evaluating a group of concepts for new diet products. To evaluate the positioning of these new products, an MDS study was conducted. The respondents, women who were on a diet, were asked to group 38 food products, including 10 of the new diet concepts. The output of the MDS, based upon these similarity ratings, is shown in Figure 17–9. "L.C." stands for low calorie, and "M/S" stands for meal substitute.

QUESTIONS FOR DISCUSSION

1 Label the dimensions.

2 Group the products into clusters visually and describe the different clusters. What are the positioning implications?

3 What other information would you collect, and how would you use it in the analysis?

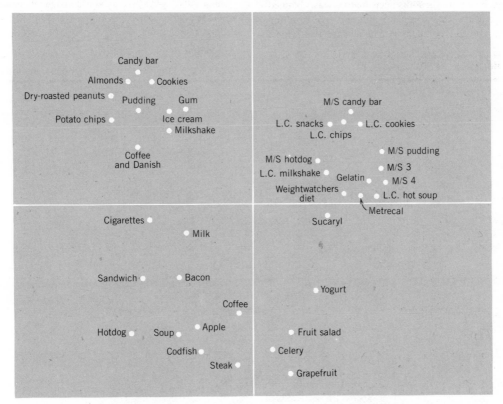

FIGURE 17–9 Two-dimensional perceptual configuration of 38 food products

Source: Adapted from Yoram Wind and Patrick J. Robinson, "Product Positioning: An Application of Multidimensional Scaling," in Russell I. Haley, ed. *Attitude Research in Transition* (Chicago: American Marketing Association, 1972).

CASE 17–2

The Toothpaste Market[14]

A panel of 73 homemakers rated eight brands of tooth-paste plus an ideal brand on nine characteristics including children like it, reduces cavities, widely available, whitens teeth, good for gums, contains fluoride, and low priced. For each individual a nine-by-nine matrix of between-object distances was obtained based upon these ratings. The 73 individuals were then cluster analyzed on the basis of the matrices of between-object distances. Clusters of sizes 46, 20, 4, and 3 members emerged. For each cluster and for the aggregate, an average between-object-distance matrix was obtained and used as the input to a MDS program. The resulting perceptual maps for the aggregate and the two largest

[14]Prepared by Lester A. Neidell, Richard D. Teach, and David A. Aaker as the basis for class discussion.

clusters are shown in Figures 17–10, 17–11, and 17–12.

QUESTIONS FOR DISCUSSION

1 Evaluate the method of obtaining the similarity matrix. What are the underlying assumptions? What alternative ways would you consider in generating the similarity matrix? Comment on the use of a common ideal point.

2 Attempt to label the dimensions.

3 Do the segments have different perceptual maps?

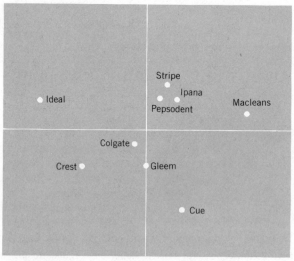

FIGURE 17–10 Aggregate perceptual map for cluster 3 ($n = 46$)

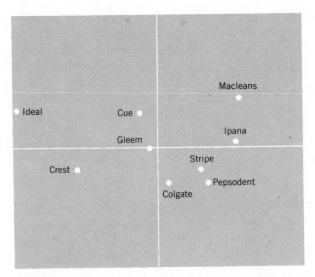

FIGURE 17–11   Aggregate perceptual map for cluster 4 ($n = 20$)

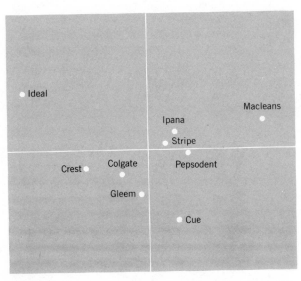

FIGURE 17–12   Aggregate perceptual map ($n = 73$)

18

CONJOINT ANALYSIS

Before beginning an examination of the technique of conjoint analysis, we first will take a look at three examples of the kind of management problems for which conjoint analysis is extremely well suited:

1 Modifying a credit card
2 Identifying land-use attitudes
3 Revamping an industrial product line

MODIFYING A CREDIT CARD[1]

A firm wanted to improve the benefits of its credit card to retailers, to get more of them to honor the card. Changes could be made to any of the following attributes:

- Discount rate (percent of billings deducted by credit card company for providing the service); the alternatives were 2.5 percent versus 6 percent
- Speed of payment after receipt of week's vouchers (one day versus 10 days)
- Whether card authorization was by computer terminal or toll-free billing number
- Extent of support payment for local advertising by retailer (either 1.0 percent or 0.75 percent of billings)
- Provision of a rebate of 15 percent of charges on all billings in excess of the retailer's quota (which would be set at 25 percent more than the previous year's sales)

Because there are two levels for each of the five factors, there were 32 possible combinations of credit cards that could be offered. The best combination would be both attractive to the retailers and profitable to the company.

[1]Paul E. Green, ''A New Approach to Market Segmentation'' *Business Horizons* (February 1977), 61–73.

491

IDENTIFYING RESIDENTIAL LAND-USE ATTITUDES

Most suburban land development follows a "spread" or "urban sprawl" pattern with large home lots and uniformly low population densities. Is this what home buyers want, or do they accept this alternative because it is the only one offered by land developers? Specifically, would buyers be willing to sacrifice some elements of private space to gain a better view from their yard? More importantly, would they accept cluster developments—groups of small lots surrounded by large areas of open land that may be scenically valuable or ecologically vulnerable? The answer to these questions depends on the importance that potential home buyers attach to attributes such as the view from the back or front yard, versus measures of lot size such as back-yard size, distance between houses, and distance to the front sidewalk.[2]

REVAMPING AN INDUSTRIAL PRODUCT LINE

The Brazilian subsidiary of the Clark Equipment Company was considering the replacement of their largest-selling forklift truck with two new models. One new model was to have slightly less performance than the current model but sell at a five-percent lower price. The other new model would offer an automatic transmission for the first time, plus better performance and reliability, but at a five-percent higher price. For this move to be profitable the company would have to gain and hold an additional three percent of the market.[3]

OVERVIEW OF CONJOINT ANALYSIS

Conjoint analysis is an extremely powerful and useful analysis tool. Its acceptance and level of use have been remarkably high since its appearance around 1970. One study concluded that over 1000 conjoint studies were undertaken between 1971 and 1978.[4]

As the previous examples indicate, a major purpose of conjoint analysis is to help select features to offer on a new or revised product or service, to help set prices, to predict the resulting level of sales or usage, or to try on a new-product concept. Conjoint analysis

[2]Robert L. Knight and Mark D. Menchik, "Conjoint Preference Estimation for Residential Land Use Policy Evaluation." Institute for Environmental Studies, University of Wisconsin, July 1974.

[3]*Clark Material Handling Group—Overseas: Brazilian Product Strategy* (A), HBS Case Services, 1981.

[4]Phillipe Cattin and Richard R. Wittink, "Commercial Use of Conjoint Analysis: A Survey," *Journal of Marketing,* Fall, 1982.

provides a quantitative measure of the relative importance of one attribute as opposed to another. In Chapter 8, other methods to determine attribute importance weights were introduced. The most direct was simply to ask people which attribute is important. The problem is that respondents usually indicate that all attributes are important. In selecting a car, they want good gas mileage, sport appearance, lots of room, a low price, and so forth. In conjoint analysis the respondent is asked to make trade-off judgments. Is one feature desired enough to sacrifice another? If one attribute had to be sacrificed, which one would it be? Thus, the respondent provides extremely sensitive and useful information.

Some of the characteristics of situations where conjoint analysis has been used productively are

1   Where the alternative products or services have a number of attributes, each with two or more levels (e.g., automatic versus manual transmission)
2   Where most of the feasible combinations of attribute levels do not presently exist
3   Where the range of possible attribute levels can be expanded beyond those presently available
4   Where the general direction of attribute preferences probably is known (travelers want less noise, faster travel, more comfort, and so on)

The usual problem is that preferences for various attributes may be in conflict (a large station wagon cannot get into small parking spaces) or there may not be enough resources to satisfy all the preferences (a small price tag is not compatible with certain luxury features). The question usually is to find a compromise set of attribute levels.

The input data are obtained by giving respondents descriptions of concepts, which represent the possible combinations of levels of attributes. For example, one of the credit card concepts for retailers to evaluate would be:

1   Six-percent discount rate
2   Payment within 10 days
3   Credit authorization by telephone
4   0.75 percent of billings to support payments for local retailer advertising
5   No rebates

Respondent retailers then evaluate each concept in terms of overall liking, intentions to buy, or rank order of preference compared to other concepts.

The computer program then assigns values or "utilities" for each level of each attribute. When these utilities are summed for each of the concepts being considered, the rank order of these total value scores should match the respondents' rank ordering of preference as closely as possible. This process can be illustrated with the utilities from the credit card study shown in Figure 18–1. The combination with the highest total utility should be the one that originally was most preferred, and the combination with the lowest total utility should have been least preferred:

Attribute	Most Preferred Combination		Least Preferred Combination	
	Level	Utility	Level	Utility
Discount rate	2.5%	0.9	6%	−0.9
Speed of payment	1 day	0.2	10 days	−0.3
Credit authorization	Computer	0.3	Telephone	−0.3
Marketing support	1.0%	0.05	0.75%	−0.05
Rebate	15.0%	0.1	None	−0.1
Total utility for Combination		1.55		−1.65

Interpreting Attribute Importance

The greater the difference between the highest and the lowest valued levels of an attribute, the more important the attribute. Conversely, if all the possible levels have the same utility, the attribute is not important, for it has no influence on the overall attitude. In the credit card study, the size of the discount was clearly the most important attribute. While this is not a surprising finding it should be kept in mind that the magnitude of the difference in utilities for the two discount levels is strongly influenced by the choice of extreme levels. Had the chosen discount levels been 2.5 percent and 4 percent, the difference in utilities would have been much less. For this reason it is often desirable to use three or even four levels of a complex attribute.

Usually the measures of attribute importance obtained from a trade-off study are only a means to an end. The real pay-off comes from using the results to identify optimal combinations of levels of attributes for new products, services, or policies. To see how this is done we first need to look more closely at the way the trade-off data are collected from respondents, analyzed, and interpreted.

COLLECTING TRADE-OFF DATA

Respondents can reveal their trade-off judgments by either considering two attributes at a time, or by making an overall judgment of a full profile of attributes.

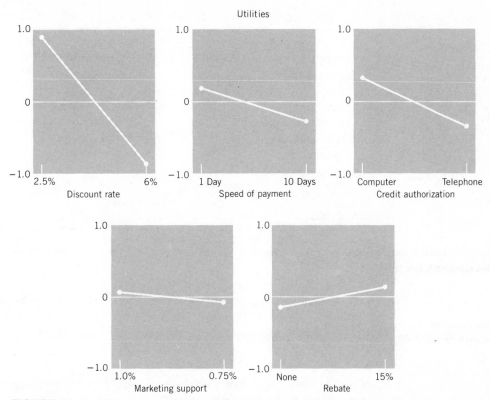

FIGURE 18–1 Utilities for credit card attributes (each of the separate interval scales is measured in terms of a common unit)

Source: Paul E. Green, "A New Approach to Market Segmentation," *Business Horizons* (February 1977).

The Full-Profile Approach

Respondents are given cards that describe complete product or service configurations. For example, two possible full-profile descriptions of package tour holidays are shown in Figure 18-2. Not all possible combinations of attribute levels have to be presented in order to estimate the utilities. For example, in Figure 18–2, even with six attributes, each described at three levels, there are 18 profiles to compare.[5] Respondents can be asked either to rank-order the profiles in order of preference, or assign each of the 18 cards to a category of a rating scale measuring overall preference or intentions to buy. The ad-

[5]In fact there are $(3 \times 3 \times 3 \times 3 \times 3 \times 3) = 729$ possible combinations. Fortunately it is possible to use an experimental design, known as an *orthogonal array*, in which a small set of combinations is selected such that the independent contributions of all six factors are balanced, to reduce this to 18 combinations. See Paul E. Green, "On the Design of Choice Experiments Involving Multifactor Alternatives," *Journal of Consumer Research, 1* (September 1974), 61–68.

Card 1	Card 2
Water temperature	Water temperature
Just warm enough to swim	Comfortably warm
Hotel location	Hotel location
Five-minute walk to beach	Facing beach
Size of nearest town	Size of nearest town
Fishing village	Major country town
Flight schedule	Flight schedule
Weekend	Weekday
Local entertainment	Local entertainment
Bars	Bars, nightclubs, theaters
Price	Price
$250	$300

[a] This illustration is adapted from Dick Westwood, Tony Lunn, and David Bezaley, "The Trade-Off Model and Its Extensions," paper presented at the Annual Conference of the British Market Research Society, March 1974.

FIGURE 18–2   Sample package tour holidays

Source: This illustration is adapted from Dick Westwood, Tony Lunn, and Davod Bezaley, "The Trade-Off Model and Its Extensions," paper presented at the Annual Conference of the British Market Research Society, March 1974.

vantage of the rating scale is that it can be administered by mail, whereas a ranking task usually entails a personal interview.

The Trade-Off Approach (Two Attributes Simultaneously)

Respondents are asked to rank each combination of levels of two attributes from most preferred to least preferred. The matrix shown in Figure 18–3 illustrates this approach, with the numbers in the cells representing one respondent's rankings. In this matrix, there are nine possible alternatives to be ranked. (The best and the worst alternatives are obvious. The interesting evidence is that the respondent doing the ranking in this example is willing to walk five minutes to find comfortably warm water.) However, there are nine attributes in all, so potentially there could be

$$n(n - 1) \div 2 = 9(8) \div 2 = 36$$

such matrices for each respondent to fill in. Fortunately, it is not necessary to present all pairs in order to extract statistically the utilities without confusing the contributions of the various attributes.

		Facing beach	5 minutes walk to beach	More than 5 minutes walk to beach
	Comfortably warm	1	2	5
Water temperature	Just warm enough to swim	3	4	6
	Too cold to swim	7	8	9

FIGURE 18–3 Two-attribute trade-off approach

Comparing Data Collection Approaches[6]

The arguments in favor of the full-profile approach are that (1) the description of the concepts is more realistic since all aspects are considered at the same time, (2) the concept evaluation task can employ either a ranking or rating scale, and (3) fewer judgments have to be made by the respondent than if the two-attribute trade-off approach were used. Unfortunately, as the number of attributes increases the task of judging the individual profiles becomes very complex and demanding. With more than five or six attributes there is a strong possibility of information overload, which usually leads respondents to ignore variations in the less important factors. To get the flavor of this problem, look back to Figure 18–2 and see how difficult it is to choose one package holiday over another.

The pairwise trade-off approach is not a panacea either. Because more judgments are required, the task can be tedious and time consuming. Consequently, respondents may lose their place in the matrix or develop a standardized response pattern just to get the job done. Since only two attributes are being considered there is a potential loss of realism. This problem is most troublesome when there is substantial environmental correlation among attributes for technological or other reasons. For example, the 0-to-55-mph acceleration time, gas mileage, horsepower rating, and top speed of an automobile are not independent attributes. When only two of these four attributes are being considered, respondents may be unclear as to what should be assumed about the other factors. This problem also is encountered with price, because it may be used as an indicator of quality. Of course, if environmental correlations are high it may be possible to create a composite factor. This means losing information about the component attributes.

Studies comparing the two methods typically find that the estimated utilities are roughly similar and that, for large numbers of factors which are not environmentally correlated, the trade-off approach yields somewhat higher predictive validity. In part because it is difficult to find factors that are not correlated, the full-profile approach has become increasingly preferred. Almost 70 percent of recent studies used this approach, and another 15 percent used a combination of full-profile and two factors at a time.[7]

[6]This section draws on Paul E. Green and V. Srinivasan, "Conjoint Analysis in Consumer Research: Issues and Outlook," *Journal of Consumer Research*, 5 (September 1978), 103–123.

[7]Cattin and Wittink, *op. cit.*

Analyzing and Interpreting the Data

The analysis of conjoint or trade-off studies, like all other marketing research, is guided by the research purpose. As an illustration, a manufacturer of automobile batteries with a lifetime guarantee wanted to know how much emphasis to place on the fact that the batteries never need water. A conjoint study was conducted in which respondents were asked to evaluate full-concept profiles made up of combinations of three attributes and three levels:

ATTRIBUTE	LEVELS
Price	$30, $45, $60
Length of guarantee	Lifetime, 60 months, 48 months
Maintenance required	No water needed, add water once a year, add water as needed

The input to the analysis was a ranking of these stimulus profiles by preference. The data analysis problem is first to estimate a set of utilities (sometimes called part-worths) for the nine attribute levels such that

1 The sum of the attribute level utilities for each specific profile equals the total utility for the profile

2 The *derived* ranking of the stimulus profiles, based on the sum of estimated attribute level utilities, corresponds as closely as possible to the *original* ranking by the respondent.

While the details of the techniques used to achieve this are beyond the scope of this discussion, the elements are straightforward. The part-worth utilities can be obtained with an iterative procedure which starts with an arbitrary set of utilities and systematically modifies them until the total utility of each profile correlates maximally to the original ranks. The procedure continues until no change in the utility of an attribute level will improve the correlation. As a practical matter most analysts use regression analysis (Chapter 19) to obtain the attribute weight utilities since it provides very similar results and is much easier and cheaper to use than an iterative procedure.[8]

Once the utilities are estimated, they are displayed and the relative importance of each attribute is determined. In the case of automobile batteries, the following graph displays the results. According to these utility values, both price and length of guarantee are more important than the maintenance attribute. However, the relative difference in the total utility from a change in the level of maintenance $(0.6 - 0.2 = 0.4)$ is greater

---

[8]In the regression approach the rank ordering is the dependent variable and the independent variables are 0-1 variables for each level on an attribute less one. Thus, for the price attribute there would be a 0-1 variable for $45 (coded as "1" only if the profile had a $45 price) and a 0-1 variable for $60 (coded as "1" only if the profile had a $60 price). The profile with a $30 price would be the reference level and therefore would not have its own 0-1 variable. If the $45 variable is coded "0" and the $60 variable is coded "0" then the level must be $30.

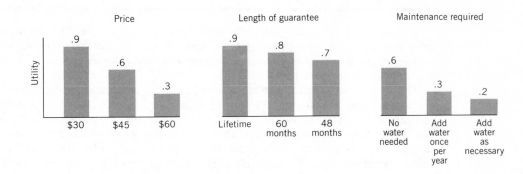

than for a change in the length of guarantee (0.9 − 0.7 = 0.2). Clearly, the fact that the battery doesn't need water should be emphasized as an advertising appeal, especially if potential buyers are not aware of this benefit.

APPLICATION ISSUES

Three areas of application appear especially promising. First, the insights that are gained into how consumers make choices within an existing market, coupled with information on the perceptions of the competitive alternatives, are valuable for guiding communications programs. Second, the analysis can suggest new product or service configurations with significant consumer appeal relative to competitive alternatives. Finally, the utility measurements can be used to develop strategic marketing simulations.[9] These are used to evaluate the volume and profit implications of changes in marketing strategies. The following is a typical application, taken from Green & Wind.[10]

> As a case in point, a large-scale study of consumer evaluations of airline services was conducted in which consumer utilities were developed for some 25 different service factors such as on-ground services, in-flight services, decor of cabins and seats, scheduling, routing, and price. Moreover, each utility function was developed on a route (city-pair and purpose-of-trip basis).
>
> As might be expected, the utility function for each of the various types of airline service differed according to the length and purpose of the flight. However, in addition to obtaining consumers' evaluations of service profiles, the researchers also obtained information concerning their perceptions of each airline (that is, for the ones they were familiar with) on each of the service factors for which the consumers were given a choice.

[9] Paul E. Green, J. Douglas Carrol, and Stephen M. Goldberg, "A General Approach to Product Design Optimization via Conjoint Analysis," *Journal of Marketing, 45* (Summer 1981), 17–37.

[10] Paul E. Green and Yoram Wind, "New Way to Measure Consumers' Judgments," *Harvard Business Review* (July–August 1975), 107–117.

The Reserves have been facing declining strength because of an inability to attract and retain people. The question was, what actions should be taken to modify the "product" or the "communications" to increase enlistments among civilians as well as the likelihood of reenlistment?

The overall objective of the study was to examine in detail motivational factors in enlistment and retention. More specific objectives were to (1) measure young men's propensity to serve or reenlist, (2) determine current perceptions of the Reserves, (3) "determine the relative importance of the 12 key job attributes that may provide the basis for influencing young men to join and remain in the Reserves," and (4) indicate what configurations of job characteristics, benefits, and incentives will enhance accessions and reenlistment intentions among various target groups.

These objectives were tailor-made for a trade-off analysis. Separate samples of 17- to 26-year-old males without prior service, and current reservists were studied. A computer-based interactive interview was used, with respondents responding on a keyboard to questions presented on a cathode-ray tube. The trade-off questions were in the form of preferences for pairs of attributes. A typical question appeared as follows:

"Which would you prefer . . .

A 4-year enlistment term and a $1000 bonus	OR	A 6-year enlistment term and a $3000 bonus?

Other attributes investigated included starting pay, educational assistance, hair regulations, retirement benefits, and hours of meeting each month.

The output of the study included the measurement of the relative importance of various attributes, and estimates of actual recruitment levels which would occur given any change in the attributes of the military "job."

FIGURE 18–4   Trade-off analysis of the attributes of the Reserves and the National Guard

These two major pieces of information provided the principal basis for developing a simulation of airline services over all major traffic routes. The purpose of the simulation was to estimate the effect on market share that a change in the service configuration of the sponsor's services would have, route by route, if competitors did not follow suit. Later, the sponsor used the simulator to examine the effect of assumed retaliatory actions by its competitors.

Although the large majority of applications have been in the private sector, conjoint and trade-off analyses also are well suited to conduct cost-benefit analyses of public policy decisions. A recent application (see Figure 18–4) to the problem of recruiting for the Armed Services Reserves, shows what can be done.[11]

[11]Public Sector Research Group of Market Facts, Inc., "Conjoint Analysis of Values of Reserve Component Attributes," a report prepared for the Department of Defense (Washington, D.C.: U.S. Government Printing Office, November 1977).

There are constraints on application, however. The most useful applications have been in complex, expensive, or risky product or service categories such as remote computer terminals, transportation modes, and major appliances; or with problems such as retail branch site selection. Even in these categories, the requirement that each attribute be divided into discrete levels is a potential limitation. The difficulty is with such attributes as durability or styling, which are difficult to divide sensibly into levels because there are no objective standards to define "very safe" or "smart styling." The value of trade-off analysis is limited further when used with products or services having only one or two important attributes or where little explicit attention is paid to trade-offs because the costs or risks are low.

THE ANALYSIS OF DEPENDENCE

Factor analysis, multidimensional scaling, and cluster analysis, the subjects of Chapters 16 and 17, are termed *analysis of interdependence* techniques because they analyze the interdependence between questions, variables, or objects. The goal is to group or position variables or objects. In contrast, when there is a single variable that is the focus, such as a person's preference for a new concept, the goal is to predict this preference level or to understand what influences it. Such a variable is termed a *dependent variable*. The variables that are used to predict or explain the dependent variable are termed *independent variables*. The techniques employed to help analysts predict or explain are termed *analysis of dependence* techniques.

Conjoint analysis is an analysis of dependence technique. The dependent variable is the preference judgment that a respondent makes about a new concept. The independent variables are the attribute levels that were specified. Thus, one motivation is prediction. What sales or usage level will a new concept achieve? A second is understanding relationships. What is the effect on preference of changing one of the attribute levels? In the next chapter, several more analyses of dependence techniques will be introduced including regression analysis, discriminant analysis, and AID and a data analysis overview will be presented in which the various data analysis techniques will be positioned.

SUMMARY

Applications

Conjoint analysis is used to predict the buying or usage of a new product, which still may be in concept form. It also is used to determine the relative importance of various attributes to respondents, based upon their making trade-off judgments.

Inputs

The primary input is a list of attributes describing the concept. For each attribute the various levels need to be described. Respondents make judgments about the concept either by considering two attributes at a time (the trade-off approach) or by making an overall judgment of a full profile of attributes (the full-profile approach).

Outputs

A value of relative utility is assigned to each level of an attribute. Each respondent will have her or his own set of utilities, although an average respondent can be created by averaging the input judgments. The percent of respondents that would most prefer one concept from among a defined set of concepts can be determined.

Assumptions

The basic assumption is that people evaluate concepts by adding up their evaluation of the individual attribute levels of the concept. It is assumed that the individual attributes are not excessively redundant and that there are no interactions between attributes.

Limitations

In the trade-off approach the problem is that the task is too unrealistic. It's difficult to make trade-off judgments about two attributes while holding all the others constant. In the full-profile approach the task can get very demanding, even for a motivated and conscientious respondent. There is a very real limit on the number of attributes that can be used, especially in the full-profile approach.

QUESTIONS AND PROBLEMS

1 In either the full-profile or the trade-off approach the respondent can rank order the alternative choices or can arrange them on some scale, such as extremely desirable, very desirable, desirable, neutral, and undesirable. What are the advantages and disadvantages to using a rank-order approach?

2 Explain how conjoint analysis is used to determine attribute importance. Is the resulting attribute importance sensitive to the selection of levels for an attribute? Illustrate by using Figure 18–1.

3 Compare the full-profile approach to the trade-off approach. What are the advantages of each? Which would you use in the example of automobile batteries? If price were one of the attributes, would you be more likely to use the full-profile approach?

4 Do purchasers of major appliances, such as refrigerators and room air conditioners, treat price as an attribute in an additive model of preference that underlies conjoint analysis? That is, do they arrive at an overall judgment by summing the evaluative rating of each attribute (including price)? How would you test whether this model applied to this situation?

5 Do the following:

    a Reflect on the last airplane flight you took. What attributes did you consider in your choice of airline?

    b To learn more about the trade-offs you made in your choice of airline, conduct a trade-off analysis on yourself. Start with the attributes and then establish two or three feasible levels for each attribute. Prepare trade-off matrices of 10 or more possible pairs of attributes, and fill in the cells according to a criterion that seems appropriate. What have you learned?

6 Interview the manager of a local "quick copy" shop or an individual who recently bought or specified a copy machine to learn which attributes were used to choose the copying machine they acquired most recently. Can the buyer describe which features trade-offs were made? Are there logical levels to the attributes that were used?

CASE 18–1

The Electric Truck Case[12]

John Hirsch of Central Utility was attempting to develop conclusions from a conjoint analysis study of electrically powered trucks. The study objectives were (1) to determine the number of commercial applications that were compatible with the limitations of electric vehicles and (2) to assess the perceived importance of those technical requirements as compared to other vehicle characteristics, such as initial costs and pollution levels.

In the first phase of the study a sample of truck owners was interviewed and the nature of their applications was determined. They found that 11 percent of commercial truck applications could get along with the

[12]Prepared by George Hargreaves, John D. Claxton, Frederick H. Siller, and David A. Aaker as a basis for class discussion.

electric vehicle limitations of a 40-mile range, a maximum of 40 stops, a load limit of 1500 pounds payload, and "seldom" freeway travel. The most sensitive dimension was freeway travel. If that limitation were removed, the electric vehicle could be used for 19 percent of applications. In the second phase of the study, people responsible for purchases of commercial trucks were invited to an "electric vehicle seminar at which an operating electric truck was available for inspection and test driving." During the seminar they discussed the advantages and disadvantages of electric vehicles and participated in a conjoint analysis study.

As Table 18–1 indicates, the conjoint study involved five attributes, each of which had two levels associated with it. For example, the initial price was

TABLE 18–1
Relative Utilities of Conventional versus Electric Vehicles

Attribute	Conventional Vehicle	Utility	Electric Vehicle	Utility
Speed and range	Unlimited	+1.426	40 mph and 40 miles	−1.426
Operating costs	Standard: 10¢/mile	−0.928	Reduced: 5¢/mile	+0.928
Initial price	Standard: $5000	+0.901	Premium: $8000	−0.901
Pollution levels	Standard: Gasoline engine	−0.544	Zero	+0.544
Propulsion system	Conventional: Gasoline engine	−0.019	New propulsion system	+0.019
	Net utility	+0.836	Net utility	−.836

either $5000 or $8000. The respondents were those attending the electric vehicle seminars. Each respondent was asked to rank 16 alternative truck designs, based upon the attributes shown in Table 18–1. The rankings of the respondents were averaged and provided the inputs to a conjoint analysis program. The output utilities also are shown in Table 18–1.

QUESTIONS FOR DISCUSSION

Evaluate the study. Do you feel the attributes and the attribute levels were well selected? Interpret Table 18–1. What information does it contain? What are the underlying assumptions? What additional analysis might be useful to do?

CASE 18–2
Fargo Instruments

Ed Heedam was an account executive for the marketing research firm, Boyle Research, and was designing a study for Fargo Instruments, makers of private label calculators for major retailers. One of Fargo's retail chain customers wanted to review its line of calculators. The need was to determine what types of features to offer in the next generation of models. Among the features that could be included in a model were rechargability, financial functions, statistical functions, warranty, and algebraic parentheses to assist calculation. The study needed to estimate how much the target customer group, college students, would pay for the various features. The tentative plan was to use a telephone interview.

One option was clearly conjoint measurement. If conjoint was used, there would need to be a decision as to whether two-by-two trade-off or the full profile

approach should be used. However, Ed wondered if there might be alternatives to conjoint that may work in this case, alternatives that may be more amenable to telephone interviewing and provide the same information. In particular, he was considering two alternatives, a constant sum approach and a dollar metric approach.

In the constant sum the respondent would allocate ten points over the five attributes proportional to the attribute's importance to him or her. In the dollar metric, the respondent would be asked to indicate what attribute level would be least preferred (unless the answer was obvious) and how much he or she would pay to receive another attribute level. Both would force the respondent to chose between attributes and would thus address the "I like all the features" problem of simply asking directly for the importance of each attribute.

QUESTIONS FOR DISCUSSION

1 What are the similarities and differences between the constant sum and dollar metric approaches to conjoint? Which are best suited to telephone interviewing? Which would you select in this case? Under what circumstances would conjoint tend to be pre-ferred? What about the dollar metric? What about the constant sum?

2 Would you select the full profile or the trade-off approach?

3 What other changes would you consider making in the design?

19

REGRESSION ANALYSIS AND A DATA ANALYSIS OVERVIEW

In data analysis there is often one or a small number of key variables that become the focus of the study. When a new product or concept is being explored, for example, one of the key variables is usually the respondent's attitude or intentions toward it. Is it something that the respondent would consider buying and/or using? The goal may be to predict the ultimate usage of the product or concept under a variety of conditions. Another goal might be to understand what causes high intentions so that when the product does emerge the marketing program can be adjusted to improve the success probability.

Consider the HMO study. In this study, the intention to enroll was one of the variables of interest. One motivation was prediction: to predict the enrollment if the plan were implemented. Thus, the intention question was analyzed to help predict the acceptance of the concept among the sample of respondents.

However, it would be desirable to determine how the intentions to enroll were related to distance to the HMO. If such a relationship were known it might be possible to predict intentions for neighborhood areas just by knowing the distance to the HMO. Similarly, if the relationship between enrollment intentions and the health plan now used were known, then some knowledge would be available about the possible intentions of others just by knowing their health plan. Furthermore, if the relationship between the coverage of the HMO (what services are included) and people's intentions were known, then the prediction could be adjusted depending upon the coverage actually used when the plan was implemented.

Regression analysis provides a tool that can quantify such relationships. Further, unlike cross-tabs and other association measures, which deal only with two variables, regression analysis can integrate the relationship of intentions with two, three, or more variables simultaneously. Thus, a regression analysis could generate a model that could address the following question: If there is a group of people who now live five miles from the proposed HMO and who now belong to Blue Cross, what enrollment intention level with this group have regarding the HMO plan if the coverage is comprehensive? Since nearly all management decisions depend upon accurate predictions of key variables, regression analysis can be an extremely practical and powerful tool.

Prediction is not the only reason that a knowledge of the relationship between intentions and other variables is useful in the HMO study. Another motivation is to gain understanding of the relationship so that the marketing program can be adjusted. If the relationship between intentions and the distance to the HMO is known, then a decision as to where to focus the marketing program geographically can be made more intelligently. It would make little sense to expend marketing effort upon groups with little potential. Further, the relationship of intentions to the health plan of participants might provide information as to what competitive health plans are most vulnerable and could help guide the development of the marketing program. The relationship between intentions and an HMO characteristic such as coverage could influence the exact type of plan introduced. A ''product feature'' such as coverage should be specified so that the costs of the feature can be balanced with its impact upon enrollment.

Regression analysis not only quantifies individual relationships but it also provides statistical control. Thus, it can quantify the relationship between intentions and distance while statistically controlling for the health plan and coverge variables.

Regression analysis, like conjoint analysis, is an analysis of dependence technique, since it involves a dependent variable as the focus of the analysis. The dependent variable is predicted by or explained by the remaining ones, the independent variables. For example, in the HMO study the enrollment intentions would be the dependent variable. The distance to the HMO, the existing health plan, and the HMO planned coverage would be three independent variables. The independent variable sometimes is called the *predictor* variable because, when prediction is the goal, it helps to predict values of the dependent variable. It also sometimes is called the *explanatory* variable because it might explain variation in the dependent variable. The analysis of dependence is oriented toward either prediction or gaining understanding of the relationships between a set of independent variables and a dependent variable.

Regression analysis will be described in detail in this chapter. The chapter will also include a brief description of two regression analysis extensions, simultaneous equation regression analysis and unobservable variables in regression analysis, and two other analysis of dependence techniques, discriminant analysis, and AID. The chapter will conclude with an overview of data analysis. A variety of techniques have been covered in the data analysis chapters in Part III and Part IV. It will be useful to position these techniques within the total data analysis process. In doing so, the steps of data analysis presented in Chapter 12 will be expanded and modified.

In describing regression analysis, special emphasis will be placed upon identifying the inputs that are required, the outputs that are generated, and the important assumptions and limitations that are associated with it. The outputs are generally of two types: (1) a measure of how well prediction is accomplished and (2) the measurement of the relationship between the various explanatory variables and the dependent variables. The outputs often will have associated with them some statistical tests of significance.

THE REGRESSION MODEL

The construction of a regression model usually starts with the specification of the dependent variable and the independent variable or variables. Suppose that our organization, Midwest Stereo, has 200 retail stores that sell hi-fi and related equipment. Our goal is to determine the impact of advertising upon store traffic, that is, the number of people who come into the store as a result of the advertising. More specifically, we are concerned with the number of people entering the store on a Saturday as a result of advertising placed the day before. The following regression model might then be hypothesized:

$$Y = \alpha + \beta X + e$$

where

Y = the number of people entering the store on Saturday
X = the amount of money the store spent on advertising on Friday
e = an error term
α, β = model parameters

There are several aspects of the model worth emphasizing. First, the hypothesized relationship is linear; it represents a straight line, as shown in Figure 19–1. Such an assumption is not as restrictive as it might first appear. Even if the actual relationship is curved, as illustrated by the dotted arc in Figure 19–1, the relationship still may be close to linear in the range of advertising expenditures of interest. Thus, a linear relationship still may be very adequate.[1]

The error term is central to the model. In reality store traffic is affected by variables other than advertising expenditures. It also is affected by store size and location, the weather, the nature of what is advertised, whether the advertising is in newspapers or on radio, and other factors. Thus, even if advertising expenditures are known, and our hypothesized linear relationship between advertising expenditures and store traffic is correct, it will be impossible to predict store traffic exactly. There still will be a margin of error. The error term explicitly reflects the error.[2]

---

[1]Further, a simple transformation of the independent variable can change some types of nonlinear relationships into linear ones. For example, instead of advertising, we might replace the advertising term with its square root or with the logarithm of advertising. The result would be a model such as

$$Y = \alpha + \beta \log X + e$$

$$\text{or } Y = \alpha + \beta \sqrt{X} + e$$

[2]There are several assumptions surrounding the error term. First, we assume that it is, on average, zero. The line is hypothesized to be positioned so that errors are as likely to occur above the line as below. Second, we assume that the error is not larger for large values of X than for small values of X. Third, for some of the judgments, subsequent analyses will assume that the error has a normal distribution. These three assumptions actually are of minor practical concern. A fourth assumption is that errors are independent of each other. This assumption can fail when time-series data are used, and a model underprediction at one time period is more likely to be followed by another underprediction that an overprediction. For a more complete discussion of this fourth assumption, including tests and remedies, see Ronald J. Wonnacott and Thomas H. Wonnacott, *Econometrics* (New York: John Wiley, 1970), pp. 136–145. Finally, the fifth assumption is that the errors are independent of the X term. This last assumption will be explained in more detail later.

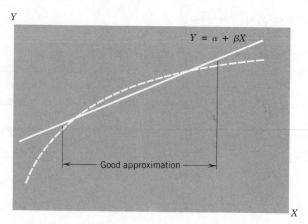

FIGURE 19–1 The linear approximation

THE MODEL PARAMETERS

Estimating the Parameters

The parameters, α and β, are the characteristics of the relationship between X and Y that are of prime interest. One of the goals of the regression analysis is to determine what they are. The procedure is to obtain a random sample of stores and to use the information from this random sample to estimate α and β. For example, assume that a random sample of 20 stores was selected. For each store in the sample, the number of people entering the store on a given Saturday was determined. Further, for each store the expenditure on advertising for the previous day was recorded. The results are plotted in Figure 19–2.

The next step is to obtain a line that has the best "fit" to these points. Of course, a line could be drawn freehand; in practice, however, a computer program is used. The computer program generates a line that has the property that the squared vertical deviations from the line are minimized. Examples of vertical deviations from the line are shown in Figure 19–2 as brackets. Such a line is termed a *least-squares line* and is denoted by the following expression:

$$Y = a + bX = 275 + 0.74X$$

The least-squares criterion is used because it is convenient (for the computer) and because it is logical.

The value a (275) is an estimate of the parameter α and the value b (0.74) is an estimate of the parameter β. These estimates, a and b, are termed *regression coefficients* and are based upon the random sample.

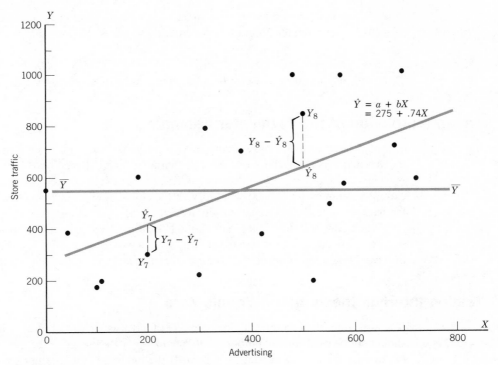

FIGURE 19–2 Advertising versus store traffic

The term $\hat{Y}$ (read as "Y hat" since it appears as a Y with a hat) indicates the points on the line and is an estimate of store traffic based upon the regression model. For example, when X is 600, then

$$\hat{Y} = 275 + 0.74X = 719$$

Thus, if advertising expenditures of 600 were planned, our store traffic estimate would be 719, the point on the line corresponding to an X value of 600. In contrast, Y is the actual sales level. For example, for one store the advertising expenditure (X) was 500, the store traffic (Y) was 870, and the store traffic estimate ($\hat{Y}$) was 645.

If another random sample of 20 stores were obtained, it undoubtedly would contain different stores. As a result, the plot of X and Y would differ from Figure 19–2, and the regression coefficients, a and b, would be different. Every random sample would have associated with it a different a and b. A measure of this variation of the parameter estimates, a and b, is given by their standard errors. Thus, just as the sample mean, $\bar{X}$, has a standard error, which is estimated by $s_{\bar{x}}$, so do a and b have a standard error associated with each of them.[3] The computer program will output these terms. In our example:

$$s_a = 100 \text{ and } s_b = 0.23$$

They will play a role in a useful hypothesis test to be discussed shortly.

The Interpretation of the Parameter Estimates

The parameter estimates have a very precise meaning. The parameter β indicates that if the variable X is changed by one unit, the variable Y will change by β units. Thus, if \$1 is added to the advertising budget, regardless of the level at which the budget is set, an extra β customers will be expected to visit the store. Similarly, the parameter α reflects the number of customers expected, on average, if no advertising is run the previous day.

When understanding is the motivation behind the data analysis, the prime interest is in b, the estimate of the β parameter. The size of b will be a reflection of the influence of advertising upon store traffic. The parameter α is frequently of little interest.

Testing the Hypothesis that β Equals Zero

If β were zero, then there would be no effect of advertising on store traffic and the model should not be used for any purpose with a nonzero b. Before using the model, it is useful to consider the hypothesis that β is zero. If the evidence that β is nonzero (namely the nonzero estimate b) is unimpressive, we may want to discard the model.

As indicated previously, the estimate b has a variation associated with it (measured by s_b) because it is based upon a sample of stores. Thus, it could happen that b is nonzero even if the parameter β is actually zero. In fact, it would be highly likely that, even if there were no relationship between advertising (X) and store traffic (Y), any given random sample would produce a nonzero value for b. One way to evaluate the magnitude of b, taking into account its variation, is to use a statistical hypothesis test. The test, like any hypothesis test, is based upon a probability question. What is the probability, the p-value, that the absolute value of b would be as large as it is if, in fact, the parameter β were equal to zero?[4] If the p-value is high (i.e., 0.25) then the evidence that β is nonzero is unimpressive and the model may well be discarded. Conversely, a hypothesis that the β is actually zero should be viewed with suspicion if the p-value were low.

To determine that probability (the p-value) we calculate t, the number of standard errors, s_b, represented by b:

$$t = b \div s_b$$

---

[3] The term $s_{\bar{x}}$ is equal to the sample standard deviation s divided by $\sqrt{n}$:

$$s_{\bar{x}} = s \div \sqrt{n}$$

[4] A two-sided test is involved.

TABLE 19–1

The Normal Curve[a]

t	p-value
1.0	.317
1.5	.134
1.65	.100
2.0	.046
2.5	.012
3.0	.003

[a]The probability that the absolute magnitude of t is larger than a particular value is shown by the shaded areas under the curves.

We assume that t is distributed normally.[5] Various probabilities are given in Table 19–1. This table shows that if t is equal to 1.0 the probability is 0.317, a relatively high p-value; whereas if t is above 1.65 then the p-value is below 0.10.

In our example the t-value is

$$t = b \div s_b = 3.2$$

The probability (the p-value) that t would be that large if β were zero is less than 0.01 (in fact it is shown in Table 19–1 to be below .003). Thus, we say that the independent variable is significant at the 0.01 level (which means that the p-value is less than 0.01) and that the evidence suggests that β is not zero. Since the model "passed" the hypothesis test it is appropriate to make judgments based upon it.

PREDICTION

The regression model, of course, can be used as a predictive tool. Given an advertising expenditure, the model will predict the store traffic that will be generated. For example, if an advertising expenditure level of $200 is proposed, a model-based estimated store traffic would be

$$\hat{Y} = a + bX = 275 + 0.74(200) = 423$$

[5]As noted in Chapter 11, it is actually distributed as a t distribution, a distribution similar in shape to a normal distribution that approaches the normal as the sample size gets larger.

Two cautionary comments. First, prediction using extreme values of the independent variable (such as $X = 2000$) can be risky. Recall Figure 19–1, which illustrated that the linearity assumption may be appropriate for only a limited range of the independent variables. Further, the random sample provided no information about extreme values of advertising. Second, if the market environment changes, such as a competitive chain opening a series of stores, then the model parameters probably will be affected. The data from the random sample were obtained under a set of environmental conditions. If they change then the model may well be affected.

How Good is the Prediction, r^2?

A natural question is: How well does the model predict? Consider store 8 in Figure 19–2, which reported an advertising expenditure of $500 and a store traffic of 870. Applying the model to store 8, a model-based prediction results:

$$\hat{Y}_8 = a + b(500) = 275 + 0.74(500) = 645$$

The difference between this estimate and the actual store traffic for store 8 is 870 less 645, or 225. If this difference is squared for each store (which converts all errors to positive numbers) and then summed over all 20 stores, a measure of model performance is obtained that is termed the variation in Y, which is unexplained by the regression model:

$$\text{Unexplained variation in } Y = \sum_{i=1}^{n} (\hat{Y}_i - Y_i)^2$$

To evaluate the predictive ability of the model, some standard of comparison is needed. The standard that is used is the best prediction that could be generated in the absence of any knowledge of the independent variable. In that case, the best estimate of store traffic would be $\bar{Y}$, the sample-store traffic average, or 540. Thus, our best guess of store traffic for store 8 would be 540 if we had no information about the advertising expenditures. Our error then would be 870 less 540, or 330, which is greater than the error obtained when the advertising expenditure was known and the model was applied. On the average, the error should be less when the model is used, if the model has any value at all. A measure of the quality of estimates without the model is obtained by summing the squared deviations from $\bar{Y}$ and is termed the total variation in Y:

$$\text{Total variation of } Y = \sum_{i=1}^{n} (Y_i - \bar{Y})^2$$

The difference between the total variation of Y and the variation that remains unexplained by the regression model is termed the variation explained by the regression model.[6]

[6]The explained variation is

$$\sum_{i=1}^{n} (\hat{Y}_i - \bar{Y})^2$$

It can be shown that the total variation is equal to the explained variation plus the unexplained variation.

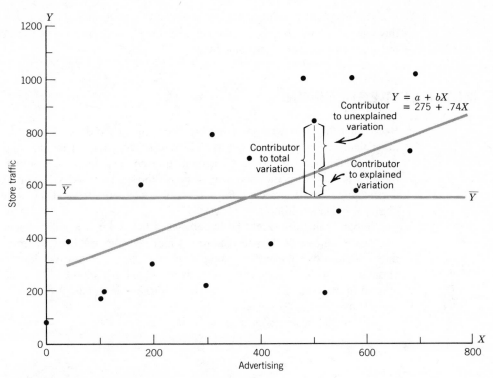

FIGURE 19–3 Explaining the variation in Y

Figure 19–3 illustrates. The measure of the regression model's ability to predict is termed r^2 and is the ratio of the explained variation to the total variation:

$$r^2 = \frac{\text{total variation} - \text{unexplained variation}}{\text{total variation}} = \frac{\text{explained variation}}{\text{total variation}}$$

For our example, in Figure 19–2, r^2 is equal to 0.35. Thus, 35 percent of the total variation of Y is explained or accounted for by X. The variation in Y was reduced by 35 percent by using X and applying the regression model.[7]

The r^2 term is the square of the correlation between X and Y.[8] Thus, it lies between zero and one. It is zero if there is no linear relationship between X and Y. It will be one

---

[7]When a regression line is found that best "fits the data," it seems a bit strange to evaluate its predictive power by determining r^2, which is really a measure of how well the model fits the data. This measure applied to the data used to estimate the model parameters is of interest, but it is hardly a reliable measure of the model's ability to predict. The r^2 measure is appropriate but it should be applied to different data, in this case stores not in the original sample of 20, if it is to represent a true test of the model's ability to predict. The r^2 for new data usually will be lower than the r^2 for data used to estimate model parameters.

[8]It is also the square of the correlation between Y and $\hat{Y}$.

if a plot of X and Y points generates a perfectly straight line. A good way to interpret r, the sample correlation, is instead to interpret r^2, which has a very natural percentage reduction in variation interpretation.

MULTIPLE REGRESSION

Recall that the error term included the effects upon the dependent variable of variables other than the independent variable. It may be desirable to include explicitly some of these variables in the model. In a prediction context, their inclusion will improve the model's ability to predict and will decrease the unexplained variation. In terms of understanding, it will introduce the impact of other variables and therefore elaborate and clarify the relationships.

In our example it might be hypothesized that store size will influence store traffic. The larger stores usually will tend to get more customers. Thus, if store size is known, the prediction of store traffic should improve. Also, it might be desirable to include a variable that would be one if the store were located in a suburban area and zero if it were located in an urban area. Such a zero-one variable is termed a **dummy variable** and is often convenient and useful.

Our model now becomes

$$Y = \beta_0 + \beta_1 X_1 + \beta_2 X_2 + \beta_3 X_3 + e$$

where

$X_1 =$ advertising expenditures on the previous day

$X_2 =$ size of the store in thousands of square feet

$X_3 =$ dummy variable taking on the value one if the store is suburban and zero if it is urban

TABLE 19–2

Regression Coefficients in the Store Traffic Model

Variable	Parameter	Regression Coefficients b_i	Standard Errors s_{b_i}	t-value (b_i/s_{b_i})	Beta Coefficients
Intercept	β_0	$b_0 = -38$	230	-0.2	
Advertising	β_1	$b_1 = 0.44$	0.26	1.7	0.36
Store size	β_2	$b_2 = 240$	120	2.0	0.41
Urban/ suburban	β_3	$b_3 = -39$	110	-0.4	-0.06

NOTE   Beta coefficients are the regression coefficients adjusted so that they are free of the original units of measurement. As a result, their values directly reflect the explanatory power of their associated independent variable.

As before, the first logical step is to obtain data from the random sample on the independent variables and the dependent variable and use this information to estimate the four model parameters. With three independent variables, it is no longer possible to illustrate the process as was done in Figure 19–2; however, the logic is the same. Parameter estimates, also termed regression coefficients, are derived by a computer program that will minimize the resulting unexplained variation in Y, thus

$$\text{Unexplained variation in } Y = \sum_{i=1}^{n} (\hat{Y}_i - Y_i)^2$$

where

$$\hat{Y} = b_0 + b_1 X_1 + b_2 X_2 + b_3 X_3$$

and

b_0, b_1, b_2, and b_3 are regression coefficients selected to minimize the
    unexplained variation in Y

$\bar{Y} = $ the regression model estimate of store traffic for store i

$Y_i = $ the actual store traffic for store i

$n = $ the number of stores in the random sample

The regression coefficients will be unique to the random sample that happened to be selected. If another random sample were taken, the regression coefficients would be slightly different. This sampling variation in the regression coefficients is measured by the standard error associated with each of them. The computer calculates this standard error and provides it as one of the outputs:

s_{b_0}, s_{b_1}, s_{b_2}, s_{b_3} are the standard errors of the regression coefficients

As in the single-variable model, each independent variable will have associated with it a t-value. For example, the store size t-value is b_2 divided by s_{b_2} and is used to test the hypothesis that β_2 is zero. Table 19–2 shows the regression coefficients and their associated errors and t-values for our example.

Parameter Interpretation in Multiple Regression

Parameters of the multiple regression model are interpreted identically to those of the single-variable model, with one important qualification. The parameter β_1 is interpreted as the change in store traffic that would be expected to be obtained if advertising expenditures were increased one unit and if the X_2 and X_3 variables were not changed (or if X_2 and X_3 were held constant). The added qualification that the remaining independent variables remain unchanged is an important one.

If X_2 and X_3 were not included, the interpretation of β_1 would be less clear. It could be that an apparent positive impact of advertising upon store traffic was due only to the fact that larger stores tend to advertise at higher levels and that a larger advertising expenditure meant that a larger store was involved. However, in the multiple regression context, the analysis has controlled for the store size and the β_1 coefficient reflects the advertising effect with store size held constant.

The major assumption of multiple regression is that all the important and relevant variables are included in the model. If an important variable is omitted the predictive power of the model is reduced. Further, if the omitted variable is correlated with an included variable the estimated coefficient of the included variable will reflect both the included variable and the omitted variable.[9] In our example the coefficient of advertising in the single-equation model was inflated (0.74) because it reflected not only the impact of advertising but also the impact of store size. Since larger stores tend to advertise more heavily than smaller stores, store size was correlated with advertising expenditures.

Evaluating the Independent Variables

When regression analysis is used to gain understanding of the relationships between variables, a natural question is: Which of the independent variables has the greatest influence upon the dependent variable? One approach is to consider the t-values for the various coefficients. The t-value, already introduced in the single-variable regression case, is used to test the hypothesis that a regression coefficient (i.e., β_1) is equal to zero and a nonzero estimate (i.e., b_1) was simply a sampling phenomenon.[10] The one with the largest t-value can be interpreted to be the one that is the least likely to have a zero β parameter. In Table 19–2, that would mean the store size variable (X_2) closely followed by the advertising variable (X_1).

A second approach is to examine the size of the regression coefficients; however, when each independent variable is in different units of measurement (store size, advertising expenditures, etc.), it is difficult to compare their coefficients. One solution is to convert the regression coefficients to "beta coefficients." Beta coefficients are simply the regression coefficients adjusted by expressing each variable by its estimated standard deviation instead of by its original measurement.[11] The beta coefficients can be compared to each other: the larger the beta coefficient, the stronger the impact of that variable upon the

---

[9]Recall the assumption that the error term is not correlated with the independent variables. If the error term includes an omitted variable that is correlated with an independent variable, this assumption will not hold.

[10]Three qualifications. First, like any hypothesis test, the t-test is sensitive to sample size. A small but non-zero regression parameter (i.e., β_1) can generate a low "p-level" if the sample size is large enough (and therefore s_b is small enough). Second, if the independent variables are intercorrelated (multicollinearity exists) the model will have a difficult time ascertaining which independent variable is influencing the dependent variable and small t-values will emerge (the s_b terms will get large). Thus, small t-values can be caused by intercorrelated independent variables. Third, in addition to testing each independent variable using the t-test, it is possible to test (using an F-test) the hypothesis that all regression parameters are simultaneously zero. If such a hypothesis test is not "passed," the entire model might be dismissed.

[11]The beta coefficients are obtained from the regression coefficients by the formula

$$\text{Beta coefficient for variable } i = b_i \, (s_{X_i}/s_Y).$$

It is interpreted as the change in terms of the standard deviation of Y that would be expected if X_i were increased by one standard deviation of X_i and the other independent variables were unchanged.

dependent variable. In Table 19–2, an analysis of the beta coefficients indicates that the store size and the advertising variables have the most explanatory power, the same conclusion that the analysis of t-values showed.

r^2 Revisisted

The r^2 term has the same definition and interpretation in multiple regression as it has in single-variable regression.[12] It is still the ratio of the explained variation to the total variation:

$$r^2 = \frac{\text{explained variation}}{\text{total variation}} = \frac{\text{total variation} - \text{unexplained variation}}{\text{total variation}}$$

In the example reported in Table 19–2, the r^2 value is 0.49.

THE HMO EXAMPLE

Table 19–3 presents a regression analysis applied in the HMO study. The dependent variable is the intentions-to-enroll question. There are 24 independent variables in the regression analysis.

The r^2 value is 0.20, meaning that 20 percent of the variation in intentions is explained by the independent variables. This level sounds low and perhaps is somewhat low given the large number of independent variables. However, the task of explaining an attitude or behavior of individuals is a very demanding task. It is much easier to explain the attitude or behavior of groups of individuals where individual idiosyncracies average out. For an analysis that is concerned with explanation or prediction at the individual level, a value of 0.20 might be considered moderate.

The primary interest of this analysis is to identify the independent variables that are most effective at explaining the variation in the dependent variable. Variable 19, the perceived distance to the HMO, had the largest beta coefficient. It was closely followed by variable 20, the satisfaction with available health plans, and variable 21, the desired coverage of health plans. The identity of these three variables provides considerable insight into explaining why some respondents are attracted to the HMO plan.

This type of regression is exploratory. The goal is to identify independent variables. In contrast, when the theory is better developed, the relevant independent variables would be specified in advance and hypotheses might be developed as to their regression coefficients. A useful technique is to split the sample into two groups. Exploratory regression analysis with the first group could help refine independent variable selection. The more refined model then could be tested on the rest of the sample.

[12]The square root of r^2 would be the correlation between Y and $\hat{Y}$.

TABLE 19–3

A Regression Analysis—the HMO Study (dependent variable is intentions to enroll: 1 = yes . . . 5 = no)

Independent Variables	Regression Coefficient	Beta Coefficient	Level of Significance[a]
1. Price HMO plan	−0.14	−0.06	—
2. Preference: Insurance vs. Prepaid form of plan[b]	−0.11	−0.12	**
3. Blue Cross Member (1 = yes, 0 = No)	−0.05	−0.02	—
4. Kaiser Member (1 = Yes, 0 = No)	−0.25	−0.08	*
5. United Medical Clinic (1 = Yes, 0 = No)	−0.27	−0.07	—
6. Student Health Service (1 = Yes, 0 = No)	−0.25	−0.04	—
7. Time with present plan (years)	−0.06	−0.06	—
8. Cost Defrayment	−0.15	−0.07	—
9. Education (head of household)	−0.02	−0.02	—
10. Income (annual family income, in $)	−0.06	−0.10	*
11. Marital Status	−0.10	−0.08	*
12. Children planned	−0.08	−0.04	
13. Planned stay in Bay Area (years)	−0.03	−0.03	—
14. Chronic Conditions in the Family (1 = Yes, 0 = No)	−0.10	−0.03	—
15. Age (of head of household) (years)	0.10	0.10	
16. Family size (total number of members)	−0.06	−0.08	*
17. Payments to Health Plans Last Year ($)	0	0	—
18. Uninsured Medical Expenses Last Year ($)	0	0	—
19. Perceived Distance to HMO (1 = satisfactory, 5 = unsatisfactory)	0.17	0.16	**

TABLE 19–3 (continued)

Independent Variables	Regression Coefficient	Beta Coefficient	Level of Significance[a]
20. Satisfaction with Health Plans Available (4 = Yes, 0 = No)	0.13	0.14	**
21. Desired Coverage in Health Plan (4 = High, 0 = Low)	−0.18	−0.14	**
22. Importance, attachment to a Family Doctor (4 = Low, 0 = High)	−0.07	−0.05	—
23. Importance, Need of Well Checks (3 = High, 0 = Low)	0.03	0.01	—
24. Ethnic: White (1 = Yes, 0 = No)	0.14	0.04	—

NOTE $r^2 = 0.20$
Sample size: 990

[a]Level of Significance Code: — = Not significant.
       * = Significant 5 percent level.
     ** = Significant 1 percent level

[b]An insurance plan allows the participant to select any clinic whereas a prepaid group commits the participant to a single clinic.

SUMMARY

Applications

Regression analysis is used (1) to predict the dependent variable, given knowledge of independent variable values and (2) to gain an understanding of the relationship between the dependent variable and independent variables.

Inputs

The model inputs required are the variable values for the dependent variable and the independent variables (although actually only the intervariable correlations are enough).

Outputs

The regression model will output regression coefficients—and their associated beta coefficient and t-values—that can be used to evaluate the strength of the relationship between the respective independent variable and the dependent variable. The model automatically controls statistically for the other independent variables. Thus, a regression coefficient represents the effect of one independent variable with the other independent variables held constant. Another output is the r^2 value, which provides a measure of the predictive ability of the model.

Statistical Tests

The hypothesis that the regression parameter is zero and the parameter estimate is nonzero only because of sampling is based upon the t-value.

Assumptions

The most important assumption is that the selected independent variables do, in fact, explain or predict the dependent variable, that there are no important variables omitted. In creating and evaluating regression models the following questions are appropriate: "Do these independent variables influence the dependent variable? Do any lack any logical justification for being in the model? Are any variables omitted that logically should be in the model?" A second assumption is that the relationship between the independent variables and the dependent variable is linear and additive. A third assumption is that there is a "random" error term that absorbs the effects of measurement error and the influences of variables not included in the regression equation.

Limitations

First, a knowledge of a regression coefficient and its t-value can suggest the extent of association or influence that an independent variable has upon the dependent variable. However, if an omitted variable is correlated with the independent variable, the regression coefficient will reflect the impact of the omitted variables on the dependent variables. A second limitation is that the model is based upon collected data that represent certain environmental conditions. If those conditions change, the model may no longer reflect the current situations and can lead to erroneous judgments. Third, the ability of the model to predict, as reflected by r^2, can become significantly reduced if the prediction is based upon values of the independent variables that are extreme in comparison to the independent variable values used to estimate the model parameters. Fourth, the model is limited by the methodology associated with the data collection, including the sample size and measures used.

AN OVERVIEW OF DATA ANALYSIS

Additional Analysis of Dependence Techniques

Two analysis of dependence techniques have been presented in detail, conjoint analysis and regression analysis. Two extensions to regression analysis and two additional techniques will be briefly described before presenting an overview of data analysis.[13]

Simultaneous Equation Regression Analysis. Consider a regression model with price, advertising, and perceived product quality (the three independent variables) influencing sales (the dependent variable). Suppose that sales also influenced advertising because the advertising budget was in part set as a percent of sales and that advertising (which emphasized workmanship and quality) and price also affected perceived product quality. Instead of a single regression equation, it would then be more appropriate to work simultaneously with three regression equations and three associated dependent variables (sales, advertising, and product quality). A single regression equation, for example, would not reflect the indirect impact of advertising through its impact upon product quality and would confuse the sales to advertising influence with the advertising to sales influence.

Unobservable Variables in Regression Analysis. In single or simultaneous regression analysis, there could be several indicators of one of the key variables. For example, the performance of salespeople, the dependent variable, could be based upon ratings of supervisors, ratings of customers, sales gain over last year, and sales gain over plan. The question is how to combine the four indicators (the observables) to provide a measure of salesperson performance (the unobservable). The answer, provided by the model, is to weight each indicator according to its relationship to the independent variables.

If there is only one regression equation involved, and the unobservable variable is the dependent variable, the approach is termed canonical correlation. In the more usual case in which multiple dependent variables and thus multiple equations are involved, the approach is often termed causal modeling since the interest is in causal relationships or LISERAL analysis. LISERAL is the name of the computer program which is used to estimate the parameters of such models.

Discriminant Analysis. Discriminant analysis is similar to regression analysis except that the dependent variable, the variable to be predicted or explained, is nominally scaled. For example, the interest might be in determining how a user of a service differs from a nonuser. Or what product characteristic or introduction strategy distinguishes a successful new product from a failure? Or can a prediction be made if a new product will be a success knowing its characteristics and details about its introduction strategy. Or can a prediction be made of whether a customer will repay or loan or not?

[13]For a description and illustrative applications of these and other data analysis techniques see David A. Aaker, *Multivariate Analysis in Marketing*, 2nd ed., Stanford, CA: Scientific Press, 1981.

AID. AID, which stands for automatic interaction detection, identifies interactions in the data. An interaction occurs when the effect of one variable (such as advertising) on the dependent variable (sales) is conditional upon a third variable (advertising has a high impact on sales only when low prices are employed).

AID locates a variable that creates two groups that differ as much as possible with respect to the dependent variable. Thus, sales of a soft drink, the dependent variable, may differ the most between the two groups defined with respect to whether calories are important to brand choice. The program then attempts to again divide each of these two groups. Suppose the "calories are important" group is again divided by attitudes toward taste. The "taste is important" group had much higher sales than the "taste is not important" group. If the taste variable did not appear in the analysis of the "calories are not important" group, we would say that an interaction was found between calories and taste, taste is important but only for the "calories are important" group, not for others. AID, which requires large samples, is useful in exploratory studies. For an example of an AID output see Figure 20–3.

An Overview of the Data Analysis Process

In Chapter 12, it was suggested that the data analysis process often involves six steps. Since Chapter 12, a wide variety of techniques and concepts have been presented. It now is possible and appropriate to expand and modify the portrayal of the data analysis process presented at the outset of Chapter 12. Figure 19–4 presents an overview of data analysis that serves to position the various techniques covered in the data analysis chapters.

The first step is the editing and coding process discussed in Chapter 12. The second step was not mentioned explicitly in Chapter 12. It involves the identification and creation of constructs and their associated measures. Before relationships between constructs can be explored, it is necessary to select and develop those constructs. Sometimes constructs are conceptualized and generated subjectively by simply combining variables by using their sum or by employing a more complex formula. Such subjective variable creation, of course, should be guided by theory. In this phase, factor analysis is used routinely to help develop combinations of variables on the basis of their intercorrelations. Similarly, cluster analysis is used to identify groups of respondents, such as respondents who are most concerned with convenience.

In most marketing research studies, a summary analysis of each variable provides a basic "top line" analysis. Even if such an analysis is not the primary focus of the study, useful insights often are provided.

The analysis then usually moves in one of three directions. The first is association analysis, which includes cross-tabulation, the difference between means, and correlation analysis. Sometimes it is important to include a third variable when conducting association analysis to control for spurious association or to identify intervening or interactive relationships.

When one of the variables is identified as one to be predicted or explained by the other variables, it is termed a dependent variable and the analysis of dependence is

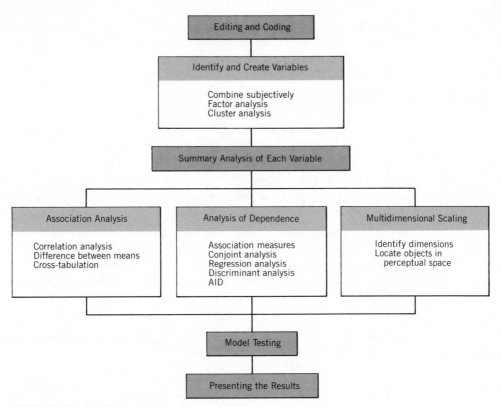

FIGURE 19–4 Data analysis: An overview

involved. The measures of association can be interpreted in this context. Of course, the techniques of conjoint analysis, regression analysis, discriminant analysis, and AID are among the analysis of dependence techniques.

In some studies, an objective is to learn how objects such as brands or organizations are perceived and evaluated by groups of people. The interest might be in determining how objects are positioned with respect to other objects and with respect to the dimensions used to perceive and evaluate. The appropriate tools are those of multidimensional scaling.

Usually, the data analysis focuses upon model building. It often is necessary to test the models and hypotheses that result from the various analyses. The testing can involve using a ''hold-out'' sample. For example, data from one-third of the respondents could be set aside and used to test the model. If a regression model were involved, the interest might be on the regression coefficients and r^2 when the model is employed on the hold-out data. Testing, however, may require another study. For example, a hypothesis or model may be suggested by exploratory or descriptive research that can be tested best by conducting an experiment.

The final step, covered in Chapter 15, is development of the final judgments and the presentation of those judgments and the supporting analysis.

QUESTIONS AND PROBLEMS

1 Some regression models are used to predict, some to gain understanding, and some to do both. Consider a product manager for Betty Crocker Cake Mix. Give an example of each of the three types of models in the context of this product manager.

2 In Table 19–2 the estimate of β_0 is negative. That means that, if the values of X_1, X_2, and X_3 are zero, we would have store traffic of—38 people. What is a minus person, anyway? Explain this strange result.

3 Consider the problem of predicting sales for each store in a chain of 220 bookstores. The model will have two functions. First, it will be used to generate norms that will be used to evaluate store managers. Second, it will be used to evaluate new site locations. What independent variables would you include in the model? How would you measure them?

4 What model would you hypothesize, given the results of Table 19–3?

5 The following table represents two other regression analyses completed in the HMO study. The dependent value of the first is the respondent's overall evaluation of the

Independent Variables	Proposed HMO Beta Coefficient	Respondent's Present Plan Beta Coefficient
Ability to choose doctor	.18[a]	.02
Coverage provided	.21[a]	.45[a]
Distance to doctor or hospital	.12[a]	.01
Participation	.13[a]	.08[a]
Efficiency in operations	−.03	.15[a]
Quality of care	.28[a]	.17[a]
Personal attention	.04	.09[a]
r^2	.38	.47
Dependent variable	Overall evaluation of proposed HMO	Overall evaluation of respondent's present plan

[a]Significant at the .01 level.

proposed HMO. The independent variables were responses to the question: "How satisfactory does this plan appear to you with respect to the following factors?" The scale was 1 to 5. The second analysis was the same except the focus was on the respondent's present plan instead of the HMO. Provide an interpretation of the results. What does a beta coefficient of 0.18 for the first variable mean? Interpret the table footnote. What do the two regressions show? What are the management implications?

6 If an estimated regression model $Y = a + bX$ yielded an r^2 of .64, we could say (choose one):

   a 64 percent of the variation in the dependent variable was explained by the independent variable

   b The sample correlation between Y and X was .80

   c 64 percent of the data points lie on the regression line

   d Two of the above

   e None of the above

7 An analyst for an oil company has developed a formal linear regression model to predict the sales of 50 of their filling stations. The estimated model is

$$Y = b_0 + b_1 X_1$$

where

$$Y = \text{average monthly sales in gallons}$$
$$X_1 = \text{square foot area of station property (difference from mean)}$$

Some empirical results were:

VARIABLE	MEAN	RANGE OF DATA	REGRESSION COEFFICIENT	t-VALUE
Y		5000–80,000 gal	$b_1 = 3.1$	
X_1	10,000	3000–20,000 sq ft	$b_0 = 10,000$	2
$r^2 = .30$				

   a What does r^2 mean?

   b Interpret the parameter estimates b_1 and b_0.

   c Is the X_1 variable significant? At what level?

   d A new station is proposed with 30,000 sq ft. What would you predict sales to be? What assumptions underlie the estimate?

8 Two additional variables now are added to the model of question 7:

$$Y = b_0 + b_1 X_1 + b_2 X_2 + b_3 X_3$$

where

$$X_2 = \text{average daily traffic flow—cars}$$
$$X_3 = \text{number of competing filling stations}$$

The empirical results now are:

Variable	Variable Mean	Variable Range	Regression Coefficient	t-Value
Y	10,000			
X_1	10,000	3000–20,000	$b_1 =$ 4.0	1.3
X_2	6000	2500–12,500	$b_2 =$ 4.0	1.0
X_3	12	0–25	$b_3 = -1000$	1.0
$r^2 = .45$			$b_0 = 10,000$	

a Which independent variable seems now to be the most significant predictor?

b Are X_1, X_2, and X_3 significant at the 0.05 level?

c How might you explain why b_1 is now larger?

d Interpret b_2.

e Provide a prediction of sales given the following inputs:

$$X_1 = 5,000$$
$$X_1 = 2,000$$
$$X_3 = 0$$

How might you qualify that prediction? What model assumptions may be violated?

f A skeptic in upper management claims that your model is lousy and cites as evidence a station in Crosby, North Dakota, where

$$X_1 = 5,000$$
$$X_2 = 2,000$$
$$X_3 = 0$$

yet sales are 50,000, which is far more than predicted by the model. How would you answer this attack?

CASE 19-1

Ajax Advertising Agency

As a model builder in the marketing services group in a large advertising agency, you are pondering your latest assignment. The task is to develop a model that will predict the success of new frequently purchased consumer products. Many clients rely heavily on new products and need to be able to predict the likelihood of success before undertaking expensive test markets. They also need guidance in developing products and marketing programs that will be successful in the test market and ultimately in national distribution.

Preliminary discussions with a set of client representatives and other agency people already have provided some tentative conclusions:

1 It has been decided that to support the model developing and testing process, a panel of 1200 households would be established in a city often used as a test market. Thus, as new products were introduced into this city, the panel could be used to monitor their performance. Over a period of three years it was expected that 50 or 60 products could be observed.

2 It was suggested that product success depends on obtaining consumer knowledge of the product, enticing people to try the product, and then achieving respectable levels of repurchase. Thus, it was concluded that a useful model would be one that was capable of predicting and explaining the following three variables: (a) product knowledge, (b) trial, and (c) repeat purchase.

Operationally, these variables would be measured by taking a consumer survey covering 250 homemakers randomly selected from the 1200-member panel. These homemakers would be contacted by telephone. The variables would be defined as follow:

1 *Product knowledge*: Percentage who were able to recall advertising claims accurately at the end of 13 weeks

2 *Trial*: Percentage who made one or more purchases of the product during the first 13 weeks

3 *Repeat purchases*: Percentage who had purchased and used the product who repurchased it or planned to do so

The immediate task was to develop three sets of explanatory or independent variables that would explain and predict the three dependent variables. In addition, it would be necessary to specify the nature of the causal relationship—whether it would be, for example, additive or multiplicative and/or linear or nonlinear.

One variable seemed obvious. Product knowledge should depend on the level of advertising. Advertising could be measured in several ways. It would be possible, by monitoring local and national media, to estimate the average number of media impressions (advertisement exposures) per household. It was not clear, however, if advertising's impact on product knowledge was linear.

Several other tasks must be faced eventually. For instance, the model will need to be tested and validated. The data base to be collected could be used for this purpose. The variables to be included in the data base will need to be specified soon. Also, thought will have to be given to how and when managers should use the model.

ASSIGNMENT 1

Develop a model of product knowledge. Specify variables, indicating precisely how they should be measured in any test application of the model. Indicate how such a model could be tested. Prepare a one-page paper summarizing your model.

ASSIGNMENT 2

Develop a model of trial purchase and one of repeat purchase. Indicate how you would use such a set of models if you were coming out with a new type of packaged cake mix.

CASE 19–2

Election Research, Inc.[14]

Election Research, a marketing research firm specializing in political campaigns, did an analysis on the 1972 California state legislature elections. Data were obtained for 72 districts and included the total number of registered voters by district, their party affiliation, the number of votes received by each candidate, the campaign expenditures of each candidate, and the identity of the incumbent, if one existed.

Of the 72 districts used, 27 had Republican winners and 45 had Democratic winners. There were 55 incumbent winners and 17 nonincumbent winners. The winners received an average of 66.6 percent of the votes cast and incurred 63.2 percent of the advertising expenses. The winner's advertising expenditure averaged $18,031 per district ($22,805 without an incumbent and $10,710 with an incumbent).

The following are the results of three regression runs (the numbers in parentheses are the t-values):

All districts:
$$WSV = .240 + .174WSTE + .414WSRV + .075I \quad r^2 = .535, N = 72$$
$$\qquad\qquad (4.82) \qquad\quad (7.01) \qquad\quad (4.60)$$

Incumbent districts:
$$WSV = .329 + .157WSTE + .409WSRV \qquad\qquad r^2 = .440, N = 55$$
$$\qquad\qquad (3.67) \qquad\quad (6.07)$$

Nonincumbent districts:
$$WSV = .212 + .234WSTE + .399WSRV \qquad\qquad r^2 = .615, N = 17$$
$$\qquad\qquad (3.39) \qquad\quad (3.21)$$

where: WSV = the winner's share of total votes cast
$WSTE$ = the winner's share of total advertising expenditures
$WSRV$ = the proportion of registered voters that are registered to the winner's political party
I = the winner's incumbency dummy variable. A dummy variable is a 0-1 variable. In this case $I = 1$ for an incumbent district and $I = 0$ for a nonincumbent district.

QUESTIONS FOR DISCUSSION

Interpret the regression coefficients. What exactly does the coefficient .174 mean? Interpret the coefficients .414 and .075 as well. Why is the coefficient for the WSTE variable different in the three equations?

Explain exactly what the t-value means. Determine the p-value associated with each. Interpret r^2. Why is r^2 different for each equation?

Why does the incumbency dummy variable appear only in the first equation?

Could this model be used productively to predict? What insights could a candidate get from the model?

[14]Prepared by Scott Vitell and David A. Aaker as the basis for class discussion.

CASES FOR PART IV

SPECIAL TOPICS IN DATA ANALYSIS

CASE IV-1   SMITH'S CLOTHING (B)

In the Smith's Clothing (A) case a research project was developed in which the following types of information were gathered:

1   Image data using 20 attributes for four different stores, including Smith's
2   Patronage data: where respondents shopped and where they last bought
3   A bank of 30 lifestyle questions relating to shopping and women's clothing
4   A 10-question scale that measures opinion leadership in women's fashions and tendency to discuss women's fashions
5   A set of importance weights on the 20 attributes used in the image question bank
6   Demographic variables

Develop an analysis strategy using the various multivariable techniques that have been covered. The sample size is 1000.

CASE IV-2   NEWFOOD[1]

Mr. Conrad Ulcer, newly appointed New Products Marketing Director for Concorn Kitchens, was considering the possibility of marketing a new highly nutritional food product with widely varied uses. This product could be used as a snack, a camping food, or as a diet food. The product was to be generically labeled Newfood.

Because of this wide range of possible uses, the company had great difficulty in defining the market. The product was viewed as having no direct competitors. Early product and concept tests were very encouraging. These tests led Mr. Ulcer to believe

---

[1]Reproduced with permission from Prof. Gerald Eskin, and the Board of Trustees, Leland Stanford Junior University.

that the product could easily sell 2 million cases (24 packages in a case) under the proposed marketing program involving a 24¢ package price and an advertising program involving $3 million in expenditures per year.

The projected P & L for the first year national was:

Sales	2.00 million cases
Revenue	$8.06 million (assumes 70% of the retail price is revenue to the manufacturer)
Manufacturing Costs	$3.00 million ($1 million fixed manufacturing costs plus $1 per case variable)
Advertising	$3.00 million
Net Margin	$2.06 million

There were no capital expenditures required to go national, since manufacturing was to be done on a contract pack basis. These costs were included in the projected P & L. Concorn has an agreement with the contract packer requiring that once a decision to go national is made, Concorn was obligated to pay fixed production costs ($1 million per year) for three years even if the product was withdrawn from the market at a later time.

Even though there are no capital requirements, it was the company's policy not to introduce new products with profit expectations of less than $.5 million per year (a three-year planning horizon was usually considered).

Because there was considerable uncertainty among Concorn management as to either probable first year and subsequent year sales, or the best introductory campaign, it was decided that a six-month market test would be conducted. The objectives of the test were to:

- Better estimate first year sales.
- Study certain marketing variables in order to determine an optimal—or at least better—introductory plan.
- Estimate the long-run potential of the product.

These objectives were accomplished through the controlled introduction of the product into four markets. Conditions were experimentally varied within the grocery stores in each of the four markets. Sales were measured with a store audit of a panel of stores. Preliminary results had been obtained. Now it was up to Mr. Ulcer to decide what they meant for the introductory strategy of Newfood.

Design of Experimental Study

The three variables included in the experimental design were price, advertising expenditures and location of the product within the store. Three prices were tested (24 cents, 29 cents, 34 cents), two levels of advertising (a simulation of a $3 million introduction plan and a $6 million plan), and two locations (placing the product in the bread section versus the instant breakfast section). Prices and location were varied across stores within cities while advertising was varied across cities. The advertising was all in the form of spot TV. The levels were selected so that they would stimulate on a local basis the impact that could be achieved from national introduction programs at the $3 million and $6 million expenditure levels. Due to differential costs between markets and differential costs between spot and network (to be used in national introduction), an attempt was made to equate (and measure) advertising inputs of gross advertising impressions generated, normalized for market size. Unfortunately, it was not possible to achieve exactly the desired levels. This was due to the problem of nonavailabilities of spots in some markets and discrepancies between estimates of TV audiences made at the time the test was being planned and the actual audiences reached at the time the commercials were actually run.

The advertising plan and actual GRP's achieved by city are as follows:

City	Desired GRP'S—Simulation of First Year National Program	Desired GRP'S per Week	Actual GRP'S Achieved
3	$3.0 million	100	105
4	$3.0 million	100	110
1	$6.0 million	200	165
2	$6.0 million	200	190

Complete information is not available on the distribution of spots over the 6-month period, but it is known that about as many spots were run in the first 2 months as in the next 4 months combined.

The test design is summarized below. Treatment was held constant over the entire 6-month period. Each cell contained 3 stores; each store was audited monthly.

CITY	ADV LEVEL	P = 24¢		P = 29¢		P = 34¢	
		L1	L2	L1	L2	L1	L2
3	Low	*					
4	Low						
1	High						
2	High						

P = Price.
L = Location.
*3 stores per cell.

The design generated the following sample sizes:

	Per Month	Total for 6 Months
Per Price	24	144
Per Location	36	216
Per Adv Level	36	216
Per City	18	108
Total	72	432

The data were analyzed on a bimonthly basis. The response measure used in the analysis was average unit sales per month per experimental cell.

Control Measures

In the selection of cities and stores for the tests, attempts were made to match cells and cities on such variables as store size, number of checkout counters, and characteristics of the trading area. Because it was not certain that adequate matches had been achieved, it was decided to obtain measurements on some of these variables for possible use in adjusting for differences in cell characteristics. It was also felt that it might be possible to learn something about the relationships between these variables and sales, and that this information would be of assistance in planning the product introduction into other markets.

The data are listed in Exhibit IV-1. Exhibit IV-2 presents a matrix of simple correlation coefficients. Thus the correlation between the first two months sales (S1) and price was $-.70$.

QUESTIONS FOR DISCUSSION

1 The correlation between price and sales is large and negative for all three time periods. What does this say about how price works?

2 Explain the correlations between advertising and sales? What is happening to the advertising effect over time?

3 Note that the intercorrelations between advertising location and price are all zero. Why?

4 Run regressions for each of the three sales variables (S1, S2, and S3) using P, A and L as independent variables. What do these regressions imply about the effect of price? Of advertising? Of location?

EXHIBIT IV–1

Ave Unit Sales Per Month				Adv (1 if High, 0 Other- wise)	Location (1 if Instant Break- fast 0 Other- wise)			
First 2 Months s1	Second 2 Months s2	Last 2 Months s3	Price P	A	L	Income (000) I	Store $ Vol (000) V	City #
225,	190,	205,	24,	0,	0,	7.3,	34	3
323,	210,	241,	24,	0,	0,	8.3,	41	4
424,	275,	256,	24,	1,	0,	6.9,	32	1
268,	200,	201,	24,	1,	0,	6.5,	28	2
224,	190,	209,	24,	0,	1,	7.3,	34	3
331,	178,	267,	24,	0,	1,	8.3,	41	4
254,	157,	185,	24,	1,	1,	6.9,	23	1
492,	351,	365,	24,	1,	1,	6.5,	37	2
167,	163,	145,	29,	0,	0,	6.5,	33	3
226,	148,	170,	29,	0,	0,	8.4,	39	4
210,	134,	128,	29,	1,	0,	6.5,	30	1
289,	212,	200,	29,	1,	0,	6.2,	27	2
204,	200,	175,	29,	0,	1,	6.5,	37	3
288,	171,	247,	29,	0,	1,	8.4,	43	4
245,	120,	117,	29,	1,	1,	6.5,	30	1
161,	116,	111,	29,	1,	1,	6.2,	19	2
161,	141,	111,	34,	0,	0,	7.2,	32	3
246,	126,	184,	34,	0,	0,	8.1,	42	4
128,	83,	83,	34,	1,	0,	6.6,	29	1
154,	122,	102,	34,	1,	0,	6.1,	24	2
163,	116,	116,	34,	0,	1,	7.2,	32	3
151,	112,	119,	34,	0,	1,	8.1,	36	4
180,	100,	75,	34,	1,	1,	6.6,	29	1
150,	122,	101,	34,	1,	1,	6.1,	24	2
MEAN 236	164	171	29	.5	.5	7.0	32	

EXHIBIT IV–2
Matrix of Simple Correlation Coefficients

		(S1)	(S2)	(S3)	(P)	(A)	(L)	(I)	(V)
(S1)	1	1							
(S2)	2	.88	1						
(S3)	3	.92	.90	1					
(P)	4	−.70	−.73	−.77	1				
(A)	5	.12	.03	−.16	0	1			
(L)	6	.01	−.04	.04	0	0	1		
(I)	7	.18	.00	.34	−.13	−.75	0	1	
(V)	8	.39	.30	.54	−.18	−.74	−.04	.81	1

5 Rerun the regressions adding the variables I and V. Do your judgements about the effects of price, advertising and location change? Why.

6 If possible, obtain an output of residuals (differences between the model predicted Y and the actual Y). Check the residuals to identify observations that do not seem to fit the model. Why don't they fit? For example, the residual for the second observation of the S1 variable would be the difference between 323 (the observed value) and the prediction made by the model, the intercept

plus P (24) times the price regression coefficient
plus A (0) times the advertising regression coefficient
plus L (0) times the location regression coefficient
plus I (8.3) times the income regression coefficient
plus V (41) times the store regression coefficient.

7 What additional regression runs, if any, should be made to complete the analysis of this data?

part V

APPLICATIONS

20

MARKET ANALYSIS

An essential prerequisite for effective marketing action is a thorough understanding of the dimensions and structure of the market. In this chapter, the focus will be largely upon the present market. Chapter 23 will deal with the question of forecasting future demand in new-product contexts.

Two parts of the market analysis task will be discussed in turn. The first is market segmentation, which involves the identification of managerially meaningful market segments, or subgroups within the market. The second is the estimation of potential demand for the product or service within the total market and specific segments. Central to both is the issue of market definition, an issue to which we turn first.

WHAT IS THE MARKET?

A market for a product, service, or idea consists of all those people with an actual or potential interest in the product, as well as the right resources for exchanging the product.[1] This definition is helpful, for it raises a number of questions that will have to be dealt with if useful measures of the market for a product or service are to be obtained.

The first question is: What is meant by "interest?" Degree of interest depends on the closeness of the match between a person's needs and the ability of the product (service, idea, etc.) to meet those needs. As Figure 20–1 indicates, if there is a close match, a purchase will result. In Chapter 8 we discussed how to measure judgments of product attributes. The next step is to identify which segments have wants and the resources that make them current or potential buyers of the products.

A most relevant question in market analysis involves the definition of the product, for this affects both the size and the composition of the market. Consider the product definitions that could have been used in the HMO study: (1) health service, in which case the market is potentially all those in the state, (2) HMOs which have a smaller market consisting of those who would consider a clinic approach and who have access to an

[1]Philip Kotler, *Marketing for Nonprofit Organizations* (Englewood Cliffs, N.J.: Prentice-Hall, 1975).

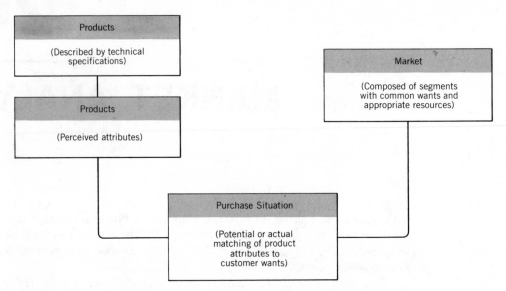

FIGURE 20–1 A purchase situation

HMO, and (3) an HMO in a specific geographic location. Recall that the product actually was defined very narrowly at the outset. The market thus included only those who would find the concept, location, and fees acceptable, *and* were employed by a large organization in the area.

Two problems substantially complicate the definition of the product, for purposes of measuring both present and potential size of the market. First, we have implicitly defined a product as a physical entity or service that has a capacity to satisfy a customer need. This means that products do not have to be physically similar to be competitive. For many automotive applications, high-performance engineered plastics and metals are directly substitutable for each other because they can be used in the same way and hence can satisfy the same needs. Great care must be taken in deciding which closely related substitute will be included in the definition of the product, for this will have a pronounced effect on its potential.[2] Indeed, one way of looking at potential is to ask what would be the size of the plastics market if everyone switched from zinc die-casting to plastics.

In general, the market is largest for the *generic* product class, which describes the fundamental utility the user expects from the product: nutrition, speed control, health care, and so on. A second problem with product definition is that within a generic product class there is usually a hierarchy of products:

1 Entirely different product or service *types* or subclasses that exist to serve significantly different patterns beyond the generic need, e.g., hot versus cold cereals.

[2]George S. Day, Allan D. Shocker, & Rajendra Srivastava, "Customer-Oriented Approaches to Identifying Product Markets" *Journal of Marketing 43* (Fall, 1979) 8–19.

2 Different product or service *variants* exist within the same overall type, for example, nutritional versus presweetened cold cereals

3 Competitive brands are produced within a specific product variant

The choice of the level in the product hierarchy to choose will depend on (1) the management problem and (2) the judgment of actual or potential buyers as to which products are substitutes within usage situations in which similar patterns of benefits are sought. The question of perceived substitutability can be illustrated with the perceptual mapping techniques discussed in chapters 8 and 17. With the product or service defined to the satisfaction of the manager and the researcher, it then is possible to proceed with an analysis of the market. We now turn to market segmentation research, which is natural and useful for any organization interested in understanding its customers and their differences.

MARKET SEGMENTATION

Market segmentation is the development and pursuit of marketing programs directed at subgroups or segments of the population that the organization could possibley serve. A variety of marketing tools can be used to implement a segmentation strategy. Products and services can be developed and positioned for particular segments of the population. Distribution channels can be selected to reach certain groups. Promotional programs can be designed to appeal to certain types of consumers.

A segmentation strategy can involve "concentration" upon only one segment and the development of a marketing program directed to it. Organizations often are more effective at concentrating upon a single segment, even if it is small, than in attempting to serve large segments that are diverse in their needs. Thus, a retail clothier might specialize in serving those who need very large sizes. A maker of cookies might specialize in a local market. A computer company might attempt to compete with IBM by focusing upon a single application area.

A segmentation strategy also can involve two or more segments where a "differentiated" marketing program is developed for each. Under such a strategy, the organization does not restrict its efforts to a single segment but rather develops several marketing programs tailored to individual segments. Perhaps the classic case of a differentiated marketing program is that of General Motors. Early in the life of the company, General Motors decided to develop a prestige product line (Cadillacs), an economy product line (Chevrolets), and several other offerings to fill the gap between the two. The company thus covered the entire market by dividing it into segments and developing a line for each segment. However, a differentiated segment strategy could involve just the advertising campaign. The advertising could stress one brand attribute to one segment and a different one to another. Thus, a bicycle manufacturer might stress the recreational uses of its product in the United States and the transportation value of the product in such countries as the Netherlands.

Market Segmentation Research

The goal of a segmentation strategy is the development of effective marketing programs directed to segments. Marketing research can help toward this end in several ways. First, it can help identify segments by suggesting operational ways to define them. Second, it can help evaluate segments by estimating their size. Finally, it can provide rich descriptions of segments that will be helpful in attempting to conceive and develop creative, effective marketing programs.

A researcher designing a segmentation study, which usually involves a survey, will need to consider all the steps of the research process introduced in Chapters 2 and 3; however, it is useful to highlight five steps that are or should be associated specifically with a segmentation study:

1 Determine the research purpose and objectives.
2 Identify survey questions to provide the bases for defining and describing segments.
3 Select the basis or bases upon which to define segments.
4 Describe the target segments in terms of other variables or descriptors.
5 Develop effective marketing programs directed at target segments.

These five steps will be discussed in turn.

Segmentation research, like all marketing research, starts with the identification of the research purpose and objectives. It is particularly important to emphasize the role of the purpose in the context of segmentation research. Segmentation research all too often becomes a descriptive study that is not linked to any decision. The result is usually an interesting profile of an organization's customers that gets quickly relegated to a dusty shelf. The key to effective segmentation research is to determine at the outset exactly what decisions are to be affected by the research. What elements of the marketing program potentially can be tailored to segments? Research objectives also are important, particularly specific hypotheses. For example, how do those who donate blood differ from those who do not? The intent is to generate hypotheses that will guide the development of the questionnaire and subsequent analyses.

The second step is the operational choice of which sets of questions to include in the study. Among the possibilities that can be considered are product usage, benefits sought from the product or service, lifestyle descriptors, and demographic variables. The third step is to select a basis (or small number of bases) for defining segments. Perhaps the most common basis is the usage of the product or service or the intentions to use it. The fourth step, the heart of data analysis, is to describe the segments as completely as possible. The richer and deeper the knowledge of a segment the easier it will be to develop effective marketing programs directed at that segment. The final step closes the loop by refocusing attention upon the development of the marketing program.

Possible Bases for Segmenting Markets

The list of possible bases in Table 20–1 is not exhaustive; however, it gives the flavor of the important variables that can be used to define and describe different segments of the market. Each will be described briefly so that the important distinctions are evident. More comprehensive listings and descriptions can be found elsewhere.[3] In many segmentation studies, most of these variables will be included. In the data analysis phase, one variable will be selected to define the segments. Each segment then will be described in terms of the other variables. If usage is the segment-defining variable, a profile of the heavy user will be obtained by using the other variables included in the survey.

The main feature of Table 20–1 is the classification of segmentation variables into those which are *identifying* or labeling characteristics of the person or organization, and *product-specific* measures of behavior or attitudes within the product category being analyzed. This distinction will be valuable in the search for the "best" basis for segmentation.

Segmentation by Identifying Characteristics

Geographic Location.   This is a widely used basis for segmentation and is the principal organizing basis for census statistics. It is a critical consideration in the public sector where governmental jurisdictions influence resources, laws, and other determinants of program success. Aggregate product demand, tastes, and preferences are significantly different between regions and countries. In all markets, it is necessary to recognize that costs and market potential vary with market location.

Demographic Characteristics.   These are the variables that describe the vital statistics of birth, death, family formation, and aging in society, as well as the religious affiliations and racial and national origins of the population. For a good deal of marketing work it has been useful to consider jointly marital status and the presence and ages of children in a family life-cycle variable. Overall lifestyles and consumer purchasing rates in categories such as insurance, appliances, and houses are significantly influenced by this variable. Typical breakdowns of the family life-cycle variable are:[4]

• Bachelor stage, young singles not living at home
• Newly married couples, no children
• Full nest I, youngest child under 6 years

---

[3]Ronald Frank, William Massy, and Yoram Wind, *Market Segmentation* (Englewood Cliffs, N.J.: Prentice-Hall, 1972).
[4]W. D. Wells and G. Gubar, "Life Cycle Concept in Marketing Research," *Journal of Marketing Research, 3* (November 1966), 362.

TABLE 20–1

Possible Bases for Segmentation

IDENTIFYING CHARACTERISTICS
  Geographic Location

Demographic	— age
	— stage of family life cycle
	— sex
	— race
	— national origin
	— religion
	— family size
Socioeconomic	— income
	— occupation
	— education
	— social class
Psychological	— personality traits
	— psychographics (activities, interests, opinions, and life styles)
Organizational	— size
	— type (sic)
	— profit margin
	— decision processes

  Usage or application situation
  Other: media habits, political party affiliation

PRODUCT-SPECIFIC RESPONSE CRITERIA

(**A**) Behavioral	— participation record (voting)
	— user status
	— usage rate or frequency
	— loyalty status
	— time of purchase
(**B**) Attitudinal	— stage of readiness (awareness, knowledge, attitude, intentions)
	— benefits sought
	— image
	— responsiveness to marketing variables
	— confidence in ability to make judgments

- Full nest II, youngest child over 6 years
- Full nest III, older married couples with dependent children
- Empty nest I, older married couples, no children at home
- Empty nest II, head of household retired
- Solitary survivor in labor force
- Solitary survivor retired

Socioeconomic Characteristics.   There are four closely interrelated characteristics in this category: income, occupation, education, and social class. Each has a significant influence on the spending and usage patterns of individuals, as well as on other characteristics. Education is associated closely with income and occupation. Occupation, in turn, is a major component of social class, along with such variables as income, residential area, and type of dwelling. A social class is a group (such as lower-upper, upper-middle, lower-middle, and upper-lower) with similar values, interests, and behavior patterns.

Psychological Characteristics.   There is a continuum from very *general personality* characteristics, which describe an individual's orientation and response to their environment (e.g., aggressiveness and needs for achievement and dominance) to specific *lifestyle* and *activity, interest, and opinion* (AIO) measures. These latter measures sometimes are lumped together into the category of psychographic characteristics. A lifestyle is a distinctive mode of orientation of an individual or segment toward consumption, work, and play (e.g., swingers, straights, etc.). Activities, interests, and opinions are, by contrast, fairly specific to the purchase and use of the product category. However, they are sufficiently general and person-oriented that they can be used in a number of product categories. The questions are typically in a Likert-scaled agree–disagree form, for example,[5]

Price conscious

I shop a lot for specials.

I usually watch the advertisements for announcements of sales.

A person can save a lot of money by shopping around for bargains.

Fashion conscious

I usually have one or more outfits that are of the very latest styles.

I often try the latest hairdo styles when they change.

Although lifestyle and psychographic variables have had their greatest application to such high-imagery or differentiated consumer products as cosmetics and financial protection, there is considerable potential for use in the public sector. For example, clients of welfare agencies are said to consist of at least two lifestyle groups: one group accepts the culture

---

[5]Thomas P. Hustad and Edgar A. Pessemier, "The Development and Application of Psychographic Life Style and Associated Activity and Attitude Measures," in William D. Wells, *Life Style and Psychographics* (Chicago: American Marketing Association, 1974).

of poverty, while the other works hard to save to escape from poverty. Each group requires different programs and handling.

Organizational Characteristics. Just as individuals have distinctive features that influence their behavior as buyers and users, so do organizations. Businesses and some governmental organizations can be classified according to *type* or *activity* (using the SIC described in Chapter 4) and *size,* and in terms of sales by value added or number of employees. Other possible variables are *profitability* and *growth,* since slow-growth and unprofitable organizations have very different responses to new products. One electrical products manufacturer has found it can classify the organizations it sells to, such as utilities, by their characteristic *purchasing practices:*

1 Equal split: does not recognize any value differentiation among offerings
2 Evaluation: business apportioned on basis of evaluation of each supplier across all attributes
3 Winner-take-all: all of each item awarded on basis of price and terms
4 Fixed share: business awarded on habitual pattern of share division
5 Arbitrary: no discernible pattern

Application or Usage Situation. Products or services ultimately are acquired because of their utility; therefore, it frequently is preferable to segment directly according to the usage situation. For example, in segmenting the market for long-distance telephone services, the type of organization may mask different uses of the phone. One industrial distributor may use Outward WATS for calling customers; another may use Inward WATS for the convenience of suppliers calling distributor purchasing agents.

Product-Specific Measures

Behavioral Measures. Product-specific measures of behavior are associated closely with the situation or setting surrounding the study. Among the most widely used measures of behavior are

- User status (is the person or organization a nonuser, a potential user, a former user, or a regular user?)
- Usage rate or frequency (this will distinguish among light and medium versus heavy users or patrons)
- Time of first purchase relative to other buyers (innovator, early adopter, late majority, etc.)
- Loyalty status (loyalty toward the store, brand, or organization)
- Brand choice (user of Brand X versus nonusers)
- Voting record (did or did not vote in one or more past elections)

Perhaps the most powerful segmentation variable is usage. Consider a symphony director who wants to increase attendance. Usage segmentation might be well worth considering. The heavy-user segment is the backbone of the symphony. Programs might be designed to insure that heavy users are satisfied and that their support continues. The season could be expanded providing more opportunities for attendance. The light users might be converted to more regular attendance by special ticket plans. Promotions aimed at stimulating increased attendance might be aimed at this segment. The nonuser might be attracted with special "pops" concerts or the special outdoor concerts.

Product-Specific Attitudinal Measures. In many situations, notably with new products or programs, there is no past record of specific behavior in the category. Here the attitudinal variables discussed in Chapter 8 are valuable. One of the most useful is the stage-of-readiness variables that correspond to the following hierarchy of effects:

- Unaware of the product or program
- Aware that it exists
- Informed about its characteristics
- Interested
- Intend to buy, use, or participate in

In the introduction of any new product or program it is important to identify those that are unaware of its existence. No product or program can precipitate action until awareness has been achieved. The unaware segment might require a special informational marketing program. Segments at other levels of the hierarchy also are of interest and often will merit a special distinct marketing effort.

Another powerful segmentation basis is "benefit segmentation," where the benefits that people seek from products serve as bases for defining segments. Thus, one group of stereo buyers might be interested in styling, another in high performance, and still another in economy. Each segment thus defined would require different marketing programs. For example, the style segment would require a very different product line and marketing programs than the other two segments. The power of benefit segmentation is that it usually is implemented easily, in that benefit segments tend to suggest marketing programs. Consider segmenting the art market according to those seeking aesthetic experience, cultural edification, and social status, or short-term diversion. Each segment would require a different marketing program.

Choosing the "Best" Basis for Defining Segments

Clearly, there is an infinite number of ways to segment any market. Which one (or two or three) should be selected in any given context? The overriding criterion is that the segmentation basis define segments for which marketing programs can be developed that will generate high market response relative to program cost. Thus, the segmentation basis cannot be evaluated independently of the marketing program. There must be a chemistry between the marketing program and the choice of the basis for defining the segments. Theoretically, what is needed is the detailed performance analysis of each segmentation basis, given the marketing programs that are to be associated with the segments. Of course, such an analysis is difficult, especially when the goal of the segmentation study is to identify productive segments and to stimulate the development of effective marketing programs. There are several guidelines that can be used to help evaluate the various segmentation bases when the marketing programs have not yet been conceived.

First, the basis for segmentation should be capable of stimulating ideas for promising marketing programs. Some ways to segment—using age or income, for example—are convenient to use but do not always help the manager conceive marketing programs. Thus, it often is useful to work with a less convenient segment, defining variables such as lifestyle, benefits, or usage. Such variables often lead more directly to effective marketing programs.

Second, the identified segments should be worthwhile. If a segment is deemed to be too small, it is unlikely that any marketing program will generate a market response that will be profitable for the organization. Thus, an important output of segmentation research study is to estimate the sizes of the various segments. A survey of the population might determine, for example, that only 3.5 percent of the population is unaware of a new product. Such a segment may be too small to warrant the development of a marketing program. The "largest" segments, of course, are not always the most worthwhile. The problem is that several competitors, employing the same logic, may be fighting aggressively for the "attractive" segment, while all are ignoring a smaller segment. The smaller segment, perhaps with specialized needs, actually might be the more attractive.

Third, the resulting segments must be accessible at reasonable cost. The target segments usually will need to be reached through a distribution channel and via an informational program. If these or other elements of the marketing program are too costly to implement, then the payoff from the segmentation strategy will be low, even if the segment response to the marketing program is high.

Fourth, although each situation is unique, it is true that some segmentation bases have tended to reappear as effective segment-defining variables. Usage is probably the most frequently used segmentation basis. Most segmentation studies at least consider segments defined by usage. Another is benefit segments, which often lead to effective, focused marketing programs.

Describing the Target Segments

Data analysis in a segmentation study has two primary objectives. The first is to specify the target segments and estimate their size. The second is to describe as completely as possible the target segments.

The specification of the target segments can involve more than simply identifying the basis upon which they will be defined. If usage is the basis, for example, the researcher still will have to decide the number of segments. At one extreme, for instance, symphony patrons could be divided into users and nonusers. At the other extreme, they could be divided into, say, 10 groups, based upon their frequency of attendance. Even a "user" category needs clarification. How recent does the last usage experience have to be, for example?

Usage may be based upon one question. Sometimes, however, it will be useful to segment on the basis of a set of questions describing product image, benefits sought, or a lifestyle. Suppose it was desired to segment on the basis of individuals' perceived image of our bank. Cluster analysis might be appropriate to group people into clusters on the basis of their responses to a set of 20 or 30 image questions. Again the issue as to how many clusters or segments to retain must be addressed.

The second part of data analysis is to provide a description of the defined segments. This can be accomplished in several ways. The most simple is to profile each of the defined segments in terms of the other variables. The result will be a series of "difference between means" observations or a series of cross-tabulations. The analysis of dependence techniques, which allow the consideration of more than one descriptive variable at a time, also can be employed. The segment-defining variable then would be the dependent variable.

An example of a segment profile is shown in Table 20–2. The segments are defined

TABLE 20–2
Profile of Traditional–Modern Married Women

	Traditional	Modern
DEMOGRAPHIC PROFILE (Percentage having characteristic)		
Age —Under 25	32%	51%
Age —Over 55	35	12
Education —Some college	40	50
Employed	26	56
Income —Under $10,000	30	27
Income —Over $20,000	20	22
Dwelling unit—Apartment	5	11
LIFE-STYLE PROFILE (Percentage agreeing)		
1. A woman's place is in the home	68	30
2. The working world is no place for a woman	28	9
3. The father should be the boss in the house	81	59
4. I think the women's liberation movement is a good thing	41	61
5. There is too much emphasis on sex today	90	81
6. I would like to spend a year in London or Paris	25	39

TABLE 20–2 (continued)

	Traditional	Modern
7. We will probably move at least once in the next five years	32	41
8. I like sports cars	30	47
9. I have somewhat old-fashioned tastes and habits	91	81
10. I went to the movies at least once in the past year	68	79
11. I visited an art gallery or museum at least once last year	45	52
12. I went bowling at least once last year	30	39
13. I went to a pop concert at least once last year	7	18
14. I like to feel attractive to members of the opposite sex	79	89
15. I want to look different from others.	66	72
MEDIA DIFFERENCES (Percentage exposed)		
Radio —Heavy rock	8	20
Radio —Popular music	44	56
Television —Waltons	42	32
Television —Little House on the Prairie	33	24
Television —Happy Days	16	20
Television —Daytime game shows (in general)	12	8
Magazines —Cosmopolitan	10	16
Magazines —Glamour	7	13
Magazines —Playboy	9	19
Magazines —Redbook	27	34
PRODUCT USAGE (Percentage using weekly or more often)		
Lipstick	87	80
Hair spray	62	56
Eye make up	48	62
Suntan lotion (summer)	28	40
Artificial sweetener	33	8
Beer	9	12
Menthol filter cigarettes	8	12
Gasoline	78	83

SOURCE Adapted from Fred D. Reynolds, Melvin R. Crask, and William D. Wells, "The Modern Feminine Life Style," *Journal of Marketing*, 41 (July 1977), 38–45.

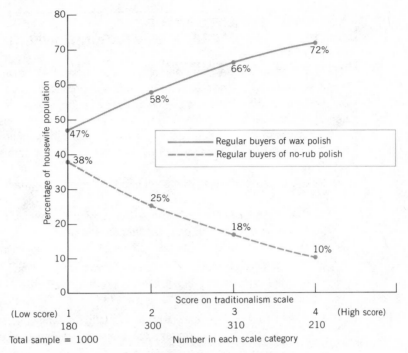

FIGURE 20–2 Buyers of polish: wax versus no-rub

Source: Tony Lunn, "Segmenting and Constructing Markets," in R. M. Worcester, ed. *Consumer Market Research Handbook.* (London: McGraw-Hill (UK), Ltd., 1973.)

in terms of respondents' views of the role of women in the marriage context. The example is based upon a mail survey in which 2000 questionnaires were sent to members of a mail panel, a group of people who had agreed to participate in a mail survey and who received modest compensation for doing so. The question that served to define the segments asked which of the following two ways of life was best for the respondent:

1 A traditional marriage, with the husband assuming the responsibility for providing for the family and the wife running the house and taking care of the children

2 A modern marriage, where husband and wife share responsibilities more—both work and both share homemaking and child responsibilities

Forty-five percent of the respondents preferred a traditional arrangement and approximately 55 percent selected the "modern" alternative.

This kind of analysis also can proceed, one explanatory variable at a time, with cross-tabulations. An illustration is a study some years ago of the British floor polish market.[6]

---

[6]Tony Lunn, "Segmenting and Constructing Markets," in R. M. Worcester, ed., *Consumer Market Research Handbook* [London: McGraw-Hill (UK), Ltd., 1973].

A BENEFIT SEGMENTATION OF THE
UNITED STATES MARKET FOR VACATION TRAVEL TO CANADA*

In our study we classified persons on the basis of 45 vacation benefits that they might have sought on their last trip. In the final analysis, we managed to group fully 92 percent of potential visitors into segments based on the relative rating they gave to these benefits. Once we could distinguish distinct segments on the basis of benefits sought on the last vacation trip, we could then try to understand the vacationers in each segment, not only in terms of the vacation benefits desired but also in terms of what they do and who they are.

By the time the analysis was completed, six benefit segment groups emerged:

1 The "Nonactive Visitor," who seeks familiar surroundings where he has been before and where he can visit friends and relatives. He is not very inclined to participate in any activity (29 percent of possible visitors).

2 The "Active City Visitor," who seeks familiar surroundings. This segment is more inclined to participate in activities, especially city sightseeing, shopping, cultural, and other entertainment (12 percent of possible visitors).

3 The "Family Sightseers," who are looking for a new vacation place that would be a treat for the children and that would be an enriching experience (6 percent of possible visitors).

4 The "Outdoor Vacationer," who seeks clean air, rest and quiet, and beautiful scenery. Many are campers and the availability of recreation facilities is important. Children are an important factor (19 percent of possible visitors).

5 The "Resort Vacationer," who is most interested in water sports (e.g., swimming) and good weather, and who prefers a popular place with a big-city atmosphere (8 percent of possible visitors).

6 The "Foreign Travel Vacationer," who wants to vacation in a place he has never been before with a foreign atmosphere and beautiful scenery. Money is not a major concern but good accommodations and service are. He wants an exciting, enriching experience (26 percent of possible visitors).

*B. M. Rusk and Marian Schott, "Marketing Canada as a Vacation Nation, Evaluating the Creative Implementation of a Benefit Market Segmentation Study" in Yoram Wind and Marshall Greenberg, eds., *Moving Ahead with Attitude Research* (Chicago: American Marketing Association, 1977).

There were two main product types in the market: wax polish, which demanded a good deal of effort; and liquid, no-rub polish, which was easier to use and was gaining in market share. A segmentation study, using demographic variables, failed to show any differentiation between segments defined by which of the two types were used. However, a specially designed "traditionalism" scale was able to discriminate clearly between buyers of the two types, as Figure 20–2 shows. Wax polish users were much more inclined to give traditional responses.

Multivariable techniques are often helpful in explaining differences in segment groups. The results of an AID study to describe segments defined by average monthly long-distance billing are shown in Figure 20–3. A set of 15 demographic characteristics and four telephone equipment descriptors was used as possible descriptive or explanatory variables. Thus, the largest difference in billings ($11.11 vs. $4.96) was found by dividing the total sample (n = 1750) into a high income group (15.4 percent of the sample) and a low income group. The AID program next split the low income group into those with an extension (average billings of $6.20) and those without.

Designing Marketing Programs

In summary, the mechanics of a segmentation study are quite straightforward. Respondents are asked several sets of questions that can reveal information on usage, loyalty, image, attitudes, benefits sought, lifestyle, demographics, media habits, location, or organizational characteristics. Each analysis starts by identifying one question or set of questions to define a set of segments. Then each of the defined segments is described in terms of the other questions that are included on the questionnaire. A rich description of the defined

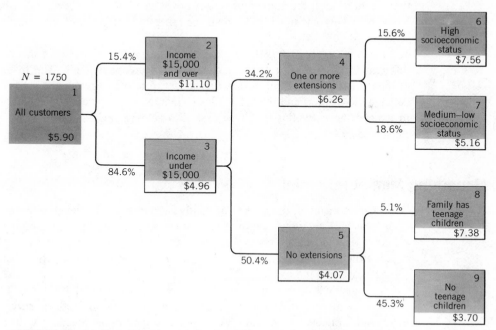

FIGURE 20–3 Segmentation of the long-distance market by average monthly long-distance expenditures in 1972: AID analysis.

segments is desired so that effective marketing programs can be tailored to those segments. The bottom line is whether the segmentation research eventually will emerge with proposals for marketing programs that will be effective with respect to the individual segments.

The analysis, of course, can be repeated for several segment-defining variables. One analysis might employ usage, another benefits, and still a third might be based upon lifestyle questions. However, there is obviously a practical limit as to the number of segmentation schemes that can be considered. The most valuable segmentation studies will be those that are based upon segment-defining variables, that are appropriate for the situation at hand. We now turn to the problem of evaluating a market or a market segment by determining its potential.

ESTIMATION OF MARKET POTENTIAL

Before market potential can be estimated, it must be defined and the definition is not always obvious.

What is market potential? The word *potential* implies *existing in possibility* or *capable of being developed;* therefore, market potential refers to the sales for the product or service that would result if the market were fully developed—that is, if everyone who could buy, would buy. This potential ideally should be expressed in terms of demand during a specified time period.

Potential refers to a *limiting* value for industry demand. It is in this sense that it is different from current or forecasted industry or company sales. The magnitude of the difference will depend on the newness of the product (whether there has been time to develop the market) and the economics of market development. It may not be profitable to expend the marketing effort necessary to achieve the potential. These concepts are illustrated in Figure 20–4.

Measuring Market Potential

As a market matures, the current demand (the industry sales level) approaches the maximum feasible, and industry growth rates slow. As a result, the current product sales level, if known, is often a good proxy for the market potential of a mature product. If the market is still growing, however, then the potential market may be much larger than the existing sales level would indicate.

Two methods commonly used to measure market potential are labeled **top-down** and **bottom-up**, to recognize the differences in their starting point. Both use survey information extensively, either to establish specific purchase and usage levels or to determine future purchases and usage intentions.

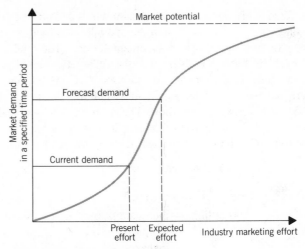

FIGURE 20–4 Market potential

Bottom-Up Measurement.   The starting point of a bottom-up approach is to identify the situations or applications in which the product is used or could be used. The next step is to identify the major market segments in which the usage situation exists or will likely occur. In industrial marketing these are often SIC classes. At this point it is necessary to go into the field to estimate the potential for each of the segments. A sample is drawn for each segment. Each respondent then is asked questions concerning present usage of the product and its close substitutes and possible applications or future applications of the product.

In industrial markets, segments sometimes are defined best by firm size. For example, a company with a new log-handling device determined from a survey the size of lumber mills that could afford to use one, two, three, or a maximum of four of these devices.[7] The company then obtained from various lumber mill associations a complete listing of all mills of each size within the geographic areas in which it was interested. The final step was to "build up" or accumulate the results into an overall estimate of market potential.

The bottom-up approach is straightforward if a list of all potential buyers is available, together with a good estimate of what each will buy. Unfortunately, one or both frequently is lacking. It then is necessary to start from the top and work down.

Top-Down or Chain-Ratio Approach.   The logic of this approach can be illustrated through its application to the estimation of the market potential for a new banking service

[7]Morgan B. McDonald, "Estimating Market Potential," in *Appraising the Market for New Industrial Products* (New York: Conference Board, 1967).

offered to organizations with pension funds and profit-sharing plans. The specific question concerned what proportion of the $90 billion in funds would be switched to banks offering this financial portfolio-management service. The total market is $90 billion in invested funds. Because it is estimated that 0.9 of the organizations use outside managers, the available market is reduced to $90 × .9, or $81 billion. Since only 0.22 of organizations are believed to be interested in switching, the available market is further reduced to $81 × .22, or $17.8 billion. The proportion who actually will switch in a given year, 0.25, and the proportion that would consider a bank as a fund manager, 0.43, are then introduced. The final potential, then, is the product of four proportions, as follows:

$$\$90 \text{ billion} \times 0.9 \times 0.22 \times 0.25 \times 0.43 = \$2 \text{ billion}$$

where

$\$90 \text{ billion} = $ the quantity of invested funds
$0.9 = $ the proportion of organizations using outside managers
$0.22 = $ the proportion interested in switching managers
$0.25 = $ the proportion who actually would switch managers in a given year
$0.43 = $ the proportion of those who would consider a bank for managing a large fund
$\$2 \text{ billion} = $ available potential

The data to perform this series of computations came from secondary sources, published surveys, and a special survey of the market.

Relative Market Potential

Most marketing resources, but especially sales effort, service coverage, and communications activity, are allocated by geographic region or territory. The key to efficient allocation is knowledge of the potential of each geographic segment relative to other segments. Very simply, a geographic market with 10 percent of the total potential should receive 10 percent of the total efforts, other factors being equal. Similarly, if geographic market A has twice the potential of market B, the former should get twice the resources. In general, this principle is followed when establishing sales quotas, which represent reasonable targets for salespeople to strive to exceed. Territories with large potentials will get large quotas; however, relative potential is seldom the only determinant of a sales quota. Other factors such as historical sales levels, actual marketing expenditures in the territory, newness of the salesperson to the territory, territory workload, and travel time all will influence the quota. Nonetheless, potential is usually the critical determinant. In the remainder of this section we will examine several methods for estimating relative potential, starting with methods that will yield a potential directly and then turning to indirect or corollary data methods for situations where direct data are not available.

Direct Data Methods. The bottom-up approach to estimating total market potential is equally applicable to relative market potentials. The only difference is the degree of aggregation. Recall that this approach requires a list of all potential buyers and an estimate of what each will buy. If that list of buyers can be grouped into geographic segments, then it is easy to accumulate the potential within the segment.

An even more direct approach is based on a disaggregation of *total industry sales*. The sales information may come from government sources, industry surveys, or trade associations. For example, the National Electrical Manufacturers Association reports shipments of refrigerators to retailers. Now, such data is useful for establishing relative market potentials only if the sales can be broken down by the organization's sales or operating territories. Fortunately, industry refrigerator-shipment data are available by trading area. This permits a direct comparison of the share of company sales and industry sales in each territory. In the example shown in Table 20–3, this comparison indicates that the company is weak (in relative terms) in sales territories, 1, 2, and 5.

The virtue of this direct approach is that it is straightforward and easy to implement. On the negative side, the data are often not available, either because total sales are not available or, when available, can be broken down only into geographic units such as states or provinces that do not correspond to sales territories.

A further limitation of this method of estimating potentials is that it can be very misleading. First, as we discussed in Chapter 4, all secondary data are prone to error. Even if these errors are small in the aggregate, they may be pronounced in small geographic subdivisions. Second, industry *sales* are not necessarily a good indicator of market *po-*

TABLE 20–3

Determining Sales Potential by Territory

Company Sales Territory	(1) Share of Total Industry Refrigerator Sales in Territory (%)	(2) Share of Company Refrigerator Sales In Territory (%)	(3) Expected Company Sales	(4) Actual Company Sales
1	3.2	2.5	$165,000	$129,100
2	4.7	4.0	242,900	206,700
3	8.1	9.0	418,500	466,000
4	2.8	5.1	144,600	263,500
5	6.7	6.3	346,200	325,500
—	—	—	—	—
—	—	—	—	—
Etc.	—	—	—	—
	100	100	$5,167,000	$5,167,000

tential, especially in small geographic areas. The degree to which the current sales level approximates the market potential depends on the maturity of the product or service and the level of marketing effort. However, level of effort—as measured on a per capita basis—is likely to be more intense in a concentrated urban area than in an outlying suburban area; hence, the geographic areas are not comparable in terms of the development of their potential.

Corollary Data Methods. One solution to the absence of industry sales data for each territory is to use another variable which is (1) available for each sales territory or region and (2) is correlated highly with the sales of the product. For example, the territory demand for childcare services or baby food is correlated highly with the number of births in the area during the previous three years. Thus, the share of births in all geographic areas within the territory of interest would be a good proxy for the relative market potential within that territory.

Seldom is a single variable an adequate indicator of the relative market potential within a territory. For example, territory potential for drug products will depend not only on population but also on per capita income and perhaps the number of physicians and pharmacists per 100,000 population in the area. A furniture manufacturer might find it necessary to consider the number of marriages in the area. Manufacturers of consumer goods that are neither low-priced staples or high-value luxury goods find that the multiple-variable "buying power" index published annually by *Sales Management* magazine is a good reflection of the relative buying power of the different counties and cities in the United States and Canada. The relative buying power (*RBP*) of an area i, is given by

$$RBP = .5Y_i + .3R_i + .2P_i$$

where

Y_i = percentage of national *disposable income* in area i
R_i = | percentage of national *retail* sales in area i
P_i = percentage of national *population* in area i

The *RBP* of a county with 0.125 percent of national income, 0.15 percent of national retail sales, and 0.16 percent of national population would be 0.5 (0.125) + 0.3 (0.15) + 0.2 (0.16) = 0.139.

Two problems face the researcher attempting to construct a multiple-variable index. First, there is the question of which variables to use; this will be conditioned by what is available at the territory level. Then weights have to be assigned to each of the variables to reflect their relative influence on the sales of the products or services of interest. Ideally, a regression analysis could answer this question, but this requires a satisfactory substitute for industry sales for each territory to serve as the dependent variable. The standardized regression coefficients would provide direct estimates of the weights.

Sometimes, industry sales data, as well as data for the corollary variables, are available at the state or provincial level, but not at the territory level. In this situation, a regression analysis using observations at the state level will provide an approximation for the weights that is probably better than a subjective judgment.

Relative Sales Potentials. What can be done if a reliable estimate of total industry sales is not available, the customers cannot provide a good estimate of their purchases of the product, and the product is used in many industries so there are no obvious corollary variables? This was the situation confronting the Hansen Company, a manufacturer of quick connective couplings for air and fluid power transmission systems, who distributed these products through a national network of 31 industrial distributors. The company badly needed data on the relative performance of their distributors to be able to evaluate and control their activity. Their approach was based on the only reliable data that were available to them—sales of company products by distributor. To utilize these data, they made the assumption that it should be possible for Hansen distributors to attain the same *sales-per-employee ratio* in noncustomer establishments as in customer establishments. To establish the sales-per-employee ratio that would serve as a performance standard, the following steps were taken:

1 A random sample of 178 accounts was drawn from a census of all customer accounts buying $2000 or more from the seven best distributors (where "best" was defined in terms of perceived effectiveness of management and utilization of an up-to-date data processing system).

2 Each account was assigned to a two-digit SIC group on the basis of its principal output or activity.

3 Data on the number of employees in each account were obtained primarily from industrial directories.

4 Sales-per-employee ratios were computed for each SIC group within the set of seven distributors.

5 Sales-per-employee ratios for each SIC group were multiplied by the total employment in all establishments in each of the 31 distributor territories. The employment data came from the 1973 *County Business Patterns* publication of the United States Census.

The output of these five steps was a table for each distributor, patterned after Table 20-4, which gives the results for distributor *A*.

The resulting sales potential was compared with actual sales, which for distributor *A* amounted to $86,218 in 1973. That is, actual sales performance was 52.6 percent of sales potential. The sales performance for all distributors ranged from 125.0 percent to 15.4 percent, with an average of 50.3 percent. It is not surprising that the distributor with sales of only 15.4 percent of potential was subjected to a very careful review, which revealed that the salespeople did not really know how to sell the product to major accounts in the area.

TABLE 20–4
1978 Sales Potential—Distributor A

Two-digit Sic Group	1978 Hansen Sales Per Employee	Total Employees	Sales Potential
33	$1.56	4,113	$ 6,416
34	2.53	14,792	37,424
35	3.28	15,907	52,175
36	1.93	32,677	63,067
37	1.71	2,024	3,461
38	3.48	409	1,423
Total		69,922	$163,966

SUMMARY

A first step in market analysis is to consider exactly how the market is to be defined. In particular, the set of products that compete can be defined very broadly (i.e., all beverages) or very narrowly (i.e., diet sodas).

Market segmentation is the development and pursuit of marketing programs directed at subgroups or segments of the population that the organization could possibly serve. Segmentation research should attempt to help the managers create effective segmentation strategies. It usually involves a survey in which respondents provide such information as product usage or intentions to use, image, attitudes, lifestyle, media habits, demographic characteristics, and organizational characteristics. One of these variables, such as usage or benefits sought, serves to define a set of segments. These segments then are described in terms of the rest of the information obtained. The concept is to obtain a complete understanding of the segments so that effective marketing programs can be developed.

Markets and market segments often need to be evaluated in terms of their potential, which is defined as the level of sales that would result if the market were fully developed. Bottom-up and top-down methods can be used to assess potential. A related problem is to determine relative market potentials of an organization's territories or regions.

QUESTIONS AND PROBLEMS

1 How would you determine the relevant product class for the following:
  a TAB soda
  b The Oakland Symphony

    c AMTRAK

    d Nissan Maxima

    e Carte Blanche

2 A study is to be designed to determine the characteristics of those attending the Chicago Bulls basketball games.

    a Develop a question(s) that would identify attendance level. Indicate how the responses would be analyzed to identify groups of people based upon their attendance.

    b What other questions would be in the study? In answering this question, be sure to attempt to develop specific hypotheses as to what descriptors would distinguish among the various attendance-level-defined groups.

3 In this chapter, it was postulated that usage and benefit variables are the best segment-defining variables in many situations. In what specific context would you expect the following variables to be effective segment defining variables?

    a Image measures

    b Attitude

    c Knowledge of product attributes

    d Lifestyle

    e Age

    f Income

4 Consider Table 20–2. Assume you are a product manager for a line of women's cosmetics and that you are interested in developing a line of cosmetics aimed at the "modern" segment.

    a Using the data in Table 20–2, describe the modern segment.

    b How might you use these data to develop a marketing program aimed at the modern segment?

    c What additional information would you have liked to see included in the study that was not included?

    d What additional lifestyle questions would you include? Be specific.

5 Summarize the findings of Figure 20–3, the segmentation of the long-distance telephone market. How might these findings be used to develop a marketing program? What alternative ways are there to analyze the data? Which would you recommend?

6 Consider the benefit segmentation of the U.S. market for vacation travel to Canada.

    a What additional variables would you include in the study?

    b Outline an analysis strategy.

7 Distinguish between market potential and company sales potential. Given that the former is available, how would you obtain the latter for the following situations?

   a A new HMO

   b A new semiconductor memory device

   c A new parcel delivery service

8 How would you improve the top-down estimate of market potentials for the new financial-portfolio-management method that was described in this chapter?

9 The application of the relative sales potential method to the sales performance of the 31 distributors of Hansen Company products revealed that one of them was performing at 125 percent of potential. How do you account for this result? What other limitations of the approach should be considered in interpreting the sales potential results?

CASE 20–1

Barkley Foods (B)

Barkley Foods had purchased an established line of gourmet frozen dinners only a few months ago. John Stevenson, the manager of marketing research for Barkely, was somewhat surprised to learn that virtually no consumer research had been done on the market for gourmet frozen foods, although a considerable amount of concept and product testing had been done. He believed that the best way to learn about the market would be to conduct a benefit segmentation study. Further, because the market was very dynamic, it would be important to track the segment structure over time so that any changes could be observed. The task was to design the study. In preparation, John was reviewing some basics about segmentation research and some recent research about segmentation.

   Benefit segmentation is aimed at identifying segments that value different product benefits. Thus, dog food buyers might be partitioned into five groups according to whether the product benefit most valued is visual appeal, aroma, nutrition, convenience, or cost. A benefit segmentation study involves:

1 Developing a list of benefits.

2 Clustering people into segments on the basis of their valuation of benefits.

3 Describing the segments in terms of other variables such as demographics, life style, brand usage, uses or applications, and brand perceptions.

   A recent article by Russell Haley, who developed benefit segmentation in the late 1960s, suggested that it is sometimes better to do backward benefit segmentation as opposed to the more conventional forward benefit segmentation. The backward approach begins with behavior. People are clustered on the basis of their behavior patterns, and the resulting behavioral segments are then described in terms of their benefit preferences, demographics, lifestyles, and so on.

   The two approaches do not generally end up with the same segment structure. A study focusing on the changing attitudes and behavior towards food and eating illustrates. NPD Research maintains panels of consumers who report on in-home consumption of individual products and brands in 52 food and beverage categories. A set of 21 groups of foods such as salad vegetables and dressings, sodas, and candies, was identified. People from this database were clustered on the basis of the food they eat into four segments:

1 Child-Oriented (i.e. hot dogs, pop, pizza)

2 Diet Concerned (i.e. skim milk, salads, fruit)

3 Meat and Potatoes (i.e. whole milk, pork, gravy)

4 Sophisticated Consumers (i.e. wine, butter, bagels)

Four benefit segments emerged when people were clustered on 56 items that included some life style and general attitude questions as well as benefit questions:

1 A taste segment

2 An exercise and nutrition segment

3 A sophisticated segment that enjoys alcoholic beverages

4 A segment of avoiders—people who avoid calories and other unwanted elements in their foods and beverages

There actually was little overlap between the two segmentation schemes. For example, knowing if a person was an avoider provided little information as to which behavior segment he or she was in.

QUESTIONS FOR DISCUSSION

1 How would you go about developing lists of benefits? What about a list of "behavioral" items?

2 How could you reduce the list to a manageable size?

3 What would be the best segment defining variable, benefits or behavior?

4 Of what value would such a segmentation study be? How could you improve its chances of being useful?

CASE 20–2
Johnson's Department Stores[9]

Johnson's Department Stores is a chain of department stores generally located in small- and medium-sized towns throughout the Southwest. They noted that in-home shopping had been estimated at over 10 percent of general merchandise sales; yet, their catalog buying business continued to be disappointing.

To help them develop a better marketing program, they sent a mail questionnaire (of 1099 sent, three mailings generated 302 usable responses) to a random sample of female home-makers in a Georgia community of 18,000 persons. The questionnaire included 85 general lifestyle statements and 22 specific trade area statements, to which respondents indicated agreement or disagreement on a six-point scale. The variables were

[9]Written by Fred Reynolds and David A. Aaker as a basis for class discussion.

reduced, as shown in Table 20–5, to nine more fundamental variables or factors. Also shown are the correlation or factor loadings with original variables to the factors.

Table 20–6 indicates the profiles of three catalog buying groups along these factors.

QUESTIONS FOR DISCUSSION

1 What is the statistical test reported?

2 How would you further analyze this data?

3 What judgments would you make from Table 20–6?

4 What recommendations for marketing strategy do you see?

TABLE 20–5

Lifestyle Scales

Scale Titles and Statements	Factor Loading
1. Time Conscious	
—It takes too much time to shop out of town.	.77
—When you consider travel time, it costs too much to shop out of town.	.63
—I always shop where it saves me time.	.61
—I usually buy at the most convenient store.	.61
2. Gregarious Community Worker	
—I am an active member of more than one social or service organization.	.68
—I like to work on community projects.	.70
—I have personally worked on a project to better our town.	.50
—I often visit friends in the evening.	.55
3. Attitude Toward Local Shopping Conditions	
—Local prices are out of line with other towns.	.66
—Local merchants offer good selections.	.59
—Local merchants don't offer the latest styles.	.66
—Local stores try to sell you old stock.	.61
—Local stores offer you good quality for the price.	.69
—Local stores are never open when I want to shop.	.55
—Local stores are attractive places to shop.	.69
—It is hard to get credit in local stores.	.51
—Local salesclerks are poorly trained.	.54
4. Attitude Toward Small City Shopping Conditions	
—Small City merchants really know their jobs.	.74
—The latest styles are always available in Small City.	.73
—Salespeople in Small City are well trained.	.71
5. Attitude Toward Large City Shopping Conditions	
—I like to shop in Large City and frequently do.	.76
—I get more for my money in Large City.	.69
—Parking is a problem in Large City.	.48
—It isn't worth the extra effort to shop in Large City.	.69
—It is more fun to shop in Large City than locally.	.58
6. Shopping Center Oriented	
—I enjoy going to big shopping centers.	.54
—Shopping centers are the best places to shop.	.76
—I prefer shopping centers over downtown shopping areas.	.70

TABLE 20–5 (*continued*)

Scale Titles and Statements	Factor Loading
7. Price Conscious	
—I shop a lot for specials.	.83
—I find myself checking the prices in the grocery store even for small items.	.72
—I usually watch the advertisements for announcements of sales.	.81
—A person can save a lot of money by shopping around for bargains.	.55
8. Venturesome	
—When I see a new brand on the shelf, I often buy it just to see what it is like.	.79
—I like to try new and different things.	.61
—I enjoy doing new things.	.52
9. Self-Confidence	
—I think I have more self-confidence than most people.	.74
—I am more independent than most people.	.55
—I think I have a lot of personal ability.	.50
—I like to be considered a leader.	.67

TABLE 20–6

Descriptive Profiles of Catalog Buying Groups

Descriptive Variable	Groups		
	Nonbuyer (N = 75)	Infrequent Buyer (N = 186)	Frequent Buyer (N = 41)
Family income level[a]	4.933	5.565	6.488
No. children < 12 Years Old[a]	0.547	0.758	1.098
Time conscious	15.800	15.640	14.781
Gregarious community worker	13.227	13.936	14.439
Attitude toward local shopping conditions[a]	40.360	39.269	34.829
Attitude toward small city shopping[a]	11.667	11.726	12.951
Attitude toward large city shopping[a]	14.160	15.570	16.756
Shopping center orientation[a]	12.213	13.339	13.463
Price conscious	16.120	17.048	17.244
Venturesome[a]	10.827	12.086	12.463
Age group[a]	4.027	3.543	2.951
Self-confidence[a]	15.680	16.108	17.805

[a]p-value $\leq .10$ based on F-tests

21

Advertising Research

Roger is the product manager for King Cola, a product with a $22 million media budget. Last year half was spent on television, 30 percent in magazines and the rest was used to support retailer newspaper advertising. Roger, like most product managers, will need research help to set advertising objectives and to make three types of tactical advertising decisions that are the focus of this chapter: the creative decision, the budget decision and the media decision.

Setting advertising objectives involves a host of questions. How should the brand be positioned? Should taste or a fun, active use experience be emphasized? What should the target audience be? Should the focus be on attracting new customers or keeping old ones? Is there a brand awareness problem? Almost any research that provides insights into the market, customer motivation, and brand performance will help to set objectives.

Much of advertising research is termed copy-testing and is directed at the creative decision—whether an advertisement should be run and, if not, how it should be changed. It involves exposing an audience to the advertisement and observing their response. The bulk of this chapter will be devoted to describing this type of research. A key issue introduced in the first section of the chapter is how advertising should be evaluated. In the four sections that follow, four criteria will be introduced and research approaches based upon each criteria will be examined. An overview of copy test validity will then be provided. Tracking studies where the impact of advertising campaigns are monitored continuously over time is then described and discussed. A description of diagnostic research that provides detailed information for the creative team as to how the audience is reacting and the underlying reasons follows.

The budget decisions relates to how many exposures over what time period is needed to achieve the objectives. Roger, of course, can consider increasing or decreasing the advertising budget, or perhaps shifting some portion of it to promotions. The media decision involves the selection of the media class (i.e., television vs. magazines vs. radio vs. billboards) and the media vehicle (i.e., 60 Minutes vs. Cagney and Lacy, or *Vogue* vs. *New Yorker*). Research approaches to address budget and media decisions will be presented in the final two sections of the chapter.

CRITERIA

What separates an effective advertisement from a dud? The criteria will depend, of course, upon the brand involved and its advertising objective. However, there are four basic categories of responses that are used in advertising research in general and copy testing in particular: (1) advertisement recognition, (2) recall of the commercial and its contents, (3) measure of commercial persuasion, and (4) impact on purchase behavior. Each of these measures will be illustrated and discussed.

Its useful to distinguish between the pretesting of mock-ups of proposed advertisements, pretests of finished advertisements, and posttests of running advertisements or campaigns. Each has a role to play in the process. Pretesting helps advertisers make judgments as to whether the advertisement should be used and, if not, how it might be improved. Posttests, which measure the actual performance of a placed advertisement, can help determine whether to continue with the commercial type being run or, if not, what types of changes are needed. Some of the following copy test procedures will be more suitable to posttesting of running advertisements, but most can be adapted to the pretesting context as well. Others are designed to be used as pretests.

RECOGNITION

One level of testing is whether a respondent can recognize the advertisement as one that he or she has seen before. An example of recognition testing is the Bruzzone Research Company (BRC) tests by mail of television commercials.[1] Questionnaires, such as the one shown in Figure 21–1, are mailed to 1000 households. The sample is drawn from the Donneley list of all households that either have a registered automobile or listed telephone. Interest in the subject matter and a dollar bill payment usually generates a sample of 500. The recognition question is shown at the top. At the bottom is the brand association question, a critical dimension of most campaigns. On the average 60 percent recognize the commercial and 73 percent of these can correctly select the correct brand from the list of three. Test-retest correlations of .98 have been reported.

Another firm, Communicus, determines similar recognition measures of both television and radio commercials by showing respondents brief (10 seconds) edited portions of the commercial (excluding advertiser identification). Respondents are asked if they had seen or heard it before, to identify the advertiser, and to play back other identifying copy points. The percentage of those who can recognize the commercial and identify the sponsor has been decreasing. It fell from 59 percent in 1974 to 50 percent in 1980, perhaps because of increased clutter.[2]

[1]Donald E. Bruzzone, "The Case for Testing Commercials by Mail" presented at the 25th Annual Conference of the Advertising Research Foundation, New York, October 23, 1979.

[2]Lewis C. Winters, "Comparing Pretesting and Posttesting of Corporate Advertising" *Journal of Advertising Research* 23 (February/March 1983) 25–32.

Please look over these pictures and words from a TV commercial and answer the questions on the right.

(Boy #1) What's this stuff?

(Boy #2) Some cereal. Supposed to be good for you.

(Boy #1) Did you try it?

(Boy #2) I'm not going to try it. You try it.

(Boy #1) I'm not going to try it.

(Boy #2) Let's get Mikey.

(Boy #1) Yeah.

(Boy #2) He won't eat it. He hates everything.

He likes it! Hey, Mikey!

(Announcer) When you bring [brand name] home, * don't tell the kids it's one of those nutritional cereals you've been trying to get them to eat. You're the only one who has to know.

Do you remember seeing this commercial on TV?

☐ Yes　☐ No　☐ Not sure-I may have

How interested are you in what this commercial is trying to tell you or show you?

☐ Very interested　☐ Somewhat interested　☐ Not interested

How does it make you feel about the product?

☐ It's a good product　☐ It's OK　☐ It's bad　☐ Not sure

Please check any of the following if you feel they describe this commercial.

☐ Amusing　　　☐ Irritating
☐ Appealing　　☐ Lively
☐ Clever　　　　☐ Original
☐ Confusing　　☐ Phony
☐ Convincing　　☐ Pointless
☐ Dull　　　　　☐ Repetitious
☐ Easy to forget　☐ Sensitive
☐ Effective　　☐ Silly
☐ Gentle　　　　☐ Uninteresting
☐ Imaginative　☐ Warm
☐ Informative　☐ Well done
☐ Interesting　☐ Worth remembering

* We have blocked out the name. Do you remember which brand was being advertised?

☐ Life
☐ Total
☐ Special K
☐ Don't know

Does anyone in your household use this type of product?

☐ Regularly
☐ Occasionally
☐ Seldom or never

FIGURE 21-1　Measuring recognition with the BRC mail questionnaire

In print, Starch has been measuring advertisement recognition since 1923. In the Starch survey, respondents are taken through a magazine and, for each advertisement, asked if they saw it in the issue. The *noted* score is the percentage who answer affirmatively. Two companion measures are *seen-associated* (note the name of the advertiser) and *read-most* (read more than 50 percent of the copy). Studies using the Starch data indicate that advertisement recognition will depend upon the product class, the involvement of the segment in the product class, and on such media-option variables as the advertisement size, color, position, and copy approach. Although Starch scores are highly reliable in a test-retest sense, there is concern about their validity. The respondent can claim readership where none exists to please or impress the interviewer, or because of confusion with prior advertising for the brand. Further, this bias can be difficult to predict for a particular advertisement.

Logically, recognition is a necessary condition for effective advertising. If the advertisement cannot pass this minimal test it probably will not be effective. In one study of inquiries received by an advertiser of electronic instrumentation, those with low Starch scores were also low in inquiries received. Of course, high recognition does not guarantee effectiveness.

RECALL

Day-After-Recall

The day-after-recall (DAR) measure of a television commercial, first used in the early 1940s by George Gallup, then with Young & Rubican, is closely associated with Burke Marketing Research.[3] "How did the ad Burke out?" is a common question. The procedure is to telephone 150 to 300 program viewers the day after a television commercial appears. They are asked if they can recall any commercials the previous day for a particular brand. They are then asked for anything they can recall about the commercial, what was said, what was shown, and what the main idea was. DAR is the percent of those in the commercial audience, who were watching the show before and after the commercial was shown, who recalled something specific about the commercial such as the sales message, the story line, the plot, or some visual or audio element.

The DAR is an "on-air" test in that the commercial exposure occurs in a natural, realistic, in-home setting. It is well established and has developed extensive norms over the years. The average DAR is 24. One fourth of all commercials score under 15 and one-fourth score over 31. It also provides diagnostic information about what elements of the commercial are impacting and what are not.

Gallup & Robinson and Mapes & Ross provide a similar measure for print media.

---

[3]Benjamin Lipstein, "An Historical Perspective of Copy Research" *Journal of Advertising Research 24* (December 1984) 11–15.

They place a magazine with 150 of its regular readers and ask that it be read in a normal manner. The next day the readers are asked to describe ads for any brands of interest.

Recall measures have generated controversy over the years and, as a result, are not as influential as they once were. One concern is that they are an inappropriate measure of emotional commercials. Foote, Cone & Belding measured both masked recognition (where the brand name is blocked out) and DAR for three "feeling" commercials and three "thinking" commercials.[4] The DAR was much lower for the "feeling" commercials (19 versus 31), whereas the recognition scores were only marginally lower (32 versus 37). They concluded that recognition is a better measure of the ability of a feeling commercial's memorability than DAR, which requires the verbalization of the content.

A more basic concern with DAR is that it simply is not a valid measure of anything useful.[5] First, its reliability is suspect. Extremely low test/retest correlations (below .30) have been found when commercials from the same product class have been studied. Second, DAR scores are unduly affected by the liking and nature of the program. For example, DAR scores of commercials in new programs average 25 and more percent below commercials in other shows. Third, of eight relevant studies seven found practically no association between recall and measures of persuasion. In contrast, there is substantial evidence linking persuasion measures with sales. Thus, copy test interest has turned toward persuasion.

PERSUASION

Forced Exposure Brand Preference Change

Theater testing, pioneered by Horace Schwerin and Paul Lazarsfeld in the 1950s and briefly described in Chapter 9, is now done by McCollum/Spielman, ASI, and ARS.[6]

The McCollum/Spielman test uses a 450 person sample spread over four geographically dispersed locations.[7] The respondents are recruited by telephone to come to a central location in order to preview television programming. Seated in groups of 25 in front of television monitors, they respond to a set of demographic and brand/product usage questions that appear on the screen. The respondents view a half-hour variety program featuring four professional performers. At the midpoint in the program seven commercials including four test commercials are shown.

Performer A	Performer B	T 1	C	T 2	C	T 3	C	T 4	Performer C	Performer D

C = constant commercials   T = test commercial

[4]Hubert A. Zielske, "Does Day-After-Recall Penalize 'Feeling' ads?" *Journal of Advertising Research 22* (Feb/March 1982) 19–22.

[5]Lawrence D. Gibson, "Not Recall" *Journal of Advertising Research 23* (February/March 1983) 39–46.

[6]Lipstein *op. cit.*

[7]AC-T Advertising Control for Television, Undated publication of McCullum/Speilman Research.

After audience reactions to the program are obtained, an unaided brand name recall question is asked that forms the basis of the Clutter/Awareness Score (the percent who recalled that the brand was advertised). The Clutter/Awareness score (C/A) for 30 second commercials averages 56 percent for established brands, 40 percent for new brands.[8] The four test commercials are then exposed a second time surrounded by program material:

Program Intro.	T 1	Program	T 2	Program	T 3	Program	T 4	Program

T = test commercial

An attitude shift (AS) measure is obtained. For frequently purchased package goods, such as toiletries, the preexposure designation of brand purchased most often is compared with the postexposure brand selection in a market basket award situation. The respondents are asked to select brands they would like included if they were winners of a $25 basket of products. In product fields with multiple brand usage, such as soft drinks, a constant sum measure (i.e., ten points to be allocated to brands proportional to how they are preferred) is employed before and after exposure. For durables and services, the pre- and post-preference is measured by determining:

The favorite brand

The next preferred alternative

Those brands which would not be considered

Those brands which are neither preferred nor rejected.

An important element of the McCollum/Spielman test is the use of two exposures. McCollum/Spielman and many advertisers argue that less than two exposures represents an artificial and invalid test of most advertising.

Finally, diagnostic questions are asked. Some of the areas that are frequently explored include:

- Comprehension of message/slogan
- Communication of secondary copy ideas
- Evaluation of demonstrations, spokesman, message
- Perception of brand uniqueness/brand differentiation
- Irritating/confusing elements
- Viewer involvement

[8]*Ibid.*

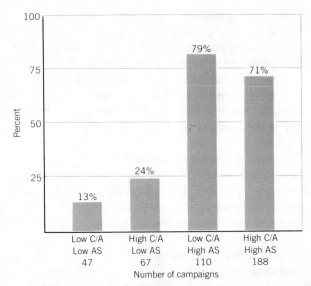

FIGURE 21–2 The percentage of campaigns exceeding marketing objectives by their performance in the McCollum/Spielman Test

Source: Adapted from Peter R. Klein and Melvin Tainter, "Copy Research Validation: The Advertiser's Perspective," *Journal of Advertising Research, 23* (October/November 1983) pp. 9–18.

In a rare copy-test validity check, McCollum/Spielman asked advertisers of 412 campaigns (some campaigns consisted of several commercials) that were tested over a three year period whether the brand has exceeded marketing objectives during the time that the campaign was being aired.[9] These advertising campaigns were then divided into four groups.

High AS (Attitude Shift) & High A/C (Awareness/Communication)

High AS and Low A/C

Low AS and High A/C

Low AS and Low A/C

The results are shown in Figure 21–2. Clearly, the AS persuasion measure was a good predictor of campaign success. The A/C recall measure, on the other hand, may have diagnostic value, but it had little relationship to campaign success.

The ARS approach is similar, except that their proven recall measure is the percent of respondents that claim to have seen the advertisement and can give some playback of it 72 hours later.[10] ARS obtained a correlation of .78 with their proven recall measure

[9]Peter R. Klein and Melvin Tainter, "Copy Research Validation: The Advertiser's Perspective" *Journal of Advertising Research 23* (October/November 1983) 9–18.

[10]"Advertising Quality Deserves More Weight!" Research Systems Corporation (August 1983).

and the unaided brand awareness level achieved by 24 new brands in test markets. Their pre/post persuasion measure had a correlation of .85 with the trial rate of 26 new brands in test markets. Further, on four occasions the ARS persuasion score correctly predicted which of two commercials achieved higher split-cable test market sales.

ASI, which uses a central Los Angeles location, relies upon a pre/post measure of brand selection in a prize/drawing context. Reliability studies across 100 commercials in 15 product categories yielded test-retest reliability correlations from .81 to .88. Fifteen hundred commercials per year are tested by ASI so well developed and current norms are available.[11]

The Buy Test design of the Sherman Group does not involve a central location, because the respondents are often recruited and exposed to advertising in shopping malls.[12] A series of unaided questions on advertisement and copy recall identify those in the "Recall/Understand" group. The advertising "Involvement" group are those who had a favorable emotional response, believed that the brand positioning fit the execution, and felt that the advertisement was worth looking at (or reading). The Buying Urgency group is identified in part by intentions to buy, improved product opinion, and the motivation to tell someone something about it. A basic measure, the BUY score, is the percent of those exposed who become part of all three groups.

On-Air Tests—Brand Preference Change

In a Mapes & Ross test, commercials are aired in a preselected prime-time position on a UHF station in each of three major markets. Prior to the test, a sample of 200 viewers (150 if it is an all male target audience) are contacted by phone and asked to participate in a survey and cash award drawing that requires viewing the test program. During the telephone interview, respondents provide unaided brand name awareness and are questioned about their brand preferences for a number of different product categories. The day following the commercial exposure, the respondents again answer brand preference as well as DAR questions. The key Mapes & Ross measure is pre- and post-brand preference change.

A Mapes & Ross study involved 142 commercials from 55 product categories and 2241 respondents who were recontacted two weeks after participating in a test. Among those who bought the product category, purchases of the test brand were 3.3 times higher among those who changed their preference than among those who did not change.[13]

The ASI Apex system differs from the Mapes & Ross approach in several important ways.[14] First, before exposure, brand preference is measured by determining the brand bought most often and the brand most likely to buy next. Thus, people who both use the brand and plan to buy it next are distinguished from those who answer only one or none

[11]ASI Laboratory Methodology, ASI Market Research, Inc., New York, Undated.

[12]Milton Sherman, "The BUY Test", Presented to the The Market Research Society, Manchester, England, May 20, 1982.

[13]Descriptive material from Mapes & Ross.

[14]APEX, ASI Market Research, Inc., New York, March, 1984, 46.

of those questions positively. The impact of sample composition with respect to brand usage is thus potentially controlled (although the test samples of size 200 are limiting in this respect). Second, the after exposure brand preference measure, based upon the brand to be selected if the respondent won a drawing and the brands they would consider if their preferred brand was unavailable, differs from the before measure. The use of different before/after measures reduces the likelihood that the before measure will influence the after measure. Third, the results are compared to a control group of 600 who goes through the complete procedure but does not see the test advertisements. Thus, the impact of the procedure itself on brand preference for a given product class can be determined.

Customized Measures of Communication/Attitude

Standardized copy test measures are useful because they come with norms sometimes based upon thousands of past tests. Thus, the interpretation of the test becomes more meaningful. Some objectives, particularly communication objectives, are necessarily unique to a brand, and may require questions tailored to that brand.

For example, Chevron ran a series of 12 print ads in 1980, such as the one shown in Figure 21–3, mostly telling people that Chevron made a lot less profit than people thought.[15] A posttest sample of 380 respondents in seven major markets were interviewed. The percent of those who were aware of at least one of the print ads that agreed with the statement "Chevron makes too much profit" fell from 81 to 72 percent.

Interestingly, however, data from the same study showed that people seeing these print ads and the very positive "Energy Frontier" television campaign actually had less attitude change toward Chevron than those seeing only the television ads. Thus, the print ads (20 percent of the budget) actually reduced the effect upon the attitude toward the firm. Creating a positive attitude obviously had a positive impact on all belief dimensions. Calling attention to a source of irritation, namely oil company profits, tended to counteract the positive attitude change. The Chevron experience graphically illustrates the risk of measuring a part of a campaign in isolation.

PURCHASE BEHAVIOR

Coupon Stimulated Purchasing

In the Tele-Research approach, 600 shoppers are intercepted in a shopping center location usually in Los Angeles and randomly assigned to test or control groups. The test group is exposed to five television or radio commercials or six print ads. Around 250 subjects in the test group completes a questionnaire on the commercial. Both groups are given a customer code number and a packet of coupons, including one for the test brand, which can be redeemed in a nearby cooperating drugstore or supermarket. Selling effectiveness

[15]Winters, *op. cit.*, 28.

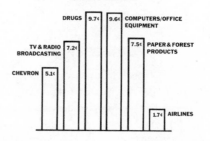

FIGURE 21–3 A Chevron "Profit" print ad.

576

score is the ratio of purchases by viewer shoppers divided by the rate of purchases by control shoppers. Purchases are tracked by scanner data. While the exposure context is highly artificial, the purchase choice is relatively realistic in that real money is spent in a real store.

Split-Cable Tests

Information Resources Inc's (IRI) BehaviorScan is one of several split cable testing operations (Burke and Nielsen being two others). BehaviorScan was in part described in Chapter 4. A consumer panel of 3000 people in each of eight cities (like Pittsfield, Massachusetts; Marion, Indiana; Midland, Texas; and Eau Claire, Wisconsin) each carry ID cards that they present to supermarkets (and some drugstores) when buying something. Their purchases are all monitored by IRI. In addition, in-store information such as special prices, features, and displays are also monitored.

An additional capability of split-cable testing makes it extremely important in advertising research. The panelists have a device connected to their TV set that not only allows the channel selection to be monitored, but also allows the advertiser to substitute one advertisement for another in what are called "cut-ins." Thus, a host of tests can be conducted such as the impact of specific commercials, sets of commercials, advertising budget levels, bunching the ad exposures, the time of day or program in which the ad appears, the commercial length, or the interaction with promotion programs.

Split cable testing is the ultimate in testing validity. However, it can cost from 5 to 20 times that of a forced exposure test ($100,000 to $200,000) and can take six months to a year or more before the results are known. By that time new brands or changing consumer preferences could make the results somewhat obsolete. For these reasons most firms use split cable testing far less than alternatives.

COPY TEST VALIDITY

The copy test validity refers to its ability to predict advertising response. Figure 21–4 provides an overview of some of the important ways in which copy tests can differ. Each dimension involves validity issues and trade-offs with cost. There follows a discussion of several important considerations involved in evaluating validity.

The Stimuli

One issue is whether a rough mock-up of an ad is used or a finished ad. Several copy test firms have reported high correlations with mock-up measures and finished copy measures. The seriousness of the problem will depend upon the difference between the mock-up and the finished commercial and the impact of this difference upon audience response. For example, it is very difficult to test humor in rough form.

The Advertisement Used

Mock-Up
Finished Advertisement

Frequency of Exposure

Single exposure test
Multiple exposure test

How it's Shown

Isolated
In a clutter
In a program or magazine

Where the Exposure Occurs

In a shopping center facility
At home on TV
At home through the mail
In a theater

How Respondents are Obtained

Prerecruited forced exposure
Not prerecruited/natural exposure

Geographic Scope

One city
Several cities
Nationwide

Alternative Measures of Persuasion

Pre/post measures of attitudes or behavioral
    that is, pre/post attitude shifts
Multiple measures
    that is, recall/involvement/buying commitment
After only questions to measure persuasion
    that is, constant sum brand preference
Test market sales measures
    that is, using scanner panels

Bases of Comparison and Evaluation

Comparing test results to norms
Using a control group

FIGURE 21–4   Alternative Methods of Copy Testing.

Another issue is the frequency of response. To what extent can a copy test predict the response to a campaign that will involve dozens or even hundreds of exposures? Can a single exposure provide meaningful results or should a minimum of two or three be used?

Still another issue is the context in which the test advertisement is embedded. The use of a clutter of advertisements embedded in a program or magazine is the most realistic but adds complexity and is possibly confounding.

The Exposure

The approaches such as the theater tests or mall intercept exposure contexts are termed forced exposure tests because the setting is artificial and the respondent is required to watch. Respondents thus tend to pay more attention to the advertisement than under normal conditions where they are much more likely to ignore it completely. The others, such as the BehaviorScan split cable testing are termed "on-air" tests because the exposure is a natural home setting in the context of watching a show. Approaches such as the ASI Apex method are on-air but the respondents realize they are in a test and are not watching a show they would watch at a time they would normally watch it. Thus, there is still concern that the exposure context may affect the results.

The Sample

The sample should be representative of the target population. In all copy test approaches the biggest concern is with the bias introduced by nonresponse. The danger is that those who refuse to participate may respond differently than those who do agree to respond. In addition, mall intercept methods obviously access only mall shoppers, and cable based tests miss those not connected to a cable. There is also the question whether one or even three or four cities can provide a representative sample.

Measuring Response

There is a concern with the reactive effect of the study; the respondent's reaction may be affected by knowing that actions and opinions are being recorded. There is evidence that this problem is minor in a system like BehaviorScan when the panel member becomes acclimated to the system. However, it is of greatest concern in systems which demand that the respondent give an attitude response. Is the respondent willing and able to respond accurately?

Appropriateness of the Response Measure

Obviously, copy test validity will depend upon the advertising response that is desired. A campaign that is designed to gain awareness may not be best measured by a test that focuses upon immediate behavioral response. A campaign that attempts to create an image or an association with a feeling such as warmth might require many repetitions and a subtle measurement method—perhaps asking some questions directed at the use experience. A single exposure test with a coupon redemption measure may not be appropriate at all. Thus, the usefulness of the various criteria used in testing need to be evaluated in the context of the advertising objectives involved.

Natural versus Artificial

Running through the validity considerations is a spectrum from artificial to natural. At one extreme there would be a forced exposure to a commercial mock-up with a paper and pencil response using a convenience mall intercept sample. At the other would be the BehaviorScan system where the audience member realizes he or she is in a panel but everything else is completely natural including multiple exposures over time.

TRACKING STUDIES

When a campaign is running its impact is often monitored via a tracking study. Periodic sampling of the target audience provides a time trend of measures of interest. The purpose is to evaluate and reassess the advertising campaign, and perhaps also to understand why it is or is not working. Among the measures that are often tracked are advertisement awareness, awareness of elements of the advertisement, brand awareness, beliefs about brand attributes, brand image, occasions of use, and brand preference. Of particular interest, is knowing how the campaign is affecting the brand as opposed to how the advertisement is communicating.

Figure 21–5 shows the tracking of an advertising campaign directed at children for a beverage product.[16] Personal interviews were held with children from 6 to 12 years old. They were shown visual stimuli such as pictures of brand packaging or line drawings of advertising characters. The mostly open-ended questions were consistently coded over five years. The interest was in the ''main character,'' who was the personification of the brand and playback of the ''story'' of the advertising, the main creative element.

The successful campaign of year one was expanded with additional executions, which apparently did not have comparable impact. The disappointing results of year two led to a fresh round of copy development aimed at making it more modern and relevant for kids. However, the decline continued in year three. An analysis of verbatim playback suggested that the main character's actions were too predictable. As a result, new ads were developed, which placed the character in a more heroic role—rescuing children in adventurous situations. In year four the main character measure turned up. For the next season the campaign used situations from a child's real life in an attempt to make the advertising more relevant. The result in year five was a dramatic increase in recall of the central creative element and an important increase in two other measures. The tracking program provided in this case actionable information over time allowing the advertising to be adjusted around the same theme to become more effective.

[16]Douglas F. Haley, ''Advertising Tracking Studies: Packaged-Goods Case Histories'', *Journal of Advertising Research* 25, (February/March 1985) 45–50.

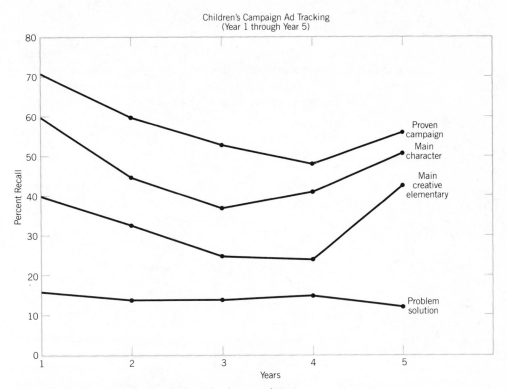

FIGURE 21–5 Tracking a childrens' ad campaign

Source: Douglas F. Haley, "Advertising Tracking Studies: Packaged-Goods Case Histories," *Journal of Advertising Research, 25* (February/March 1985) 49.

The TEC Audit

The Eric Marder firm provides one approach to obtaining tracking data without doing customized studies.[17] They maintain a panel of 3000 women from 1000 areas. Each woman keeps a record of all television commercials she sees in the course of one randomly assigned day each month. Before watching television on her assigned day, she records her buying-intention for each product category. On the assigned day she watches television normally, except that she records the time, the channel, and the brand advertised from every ad she sees, and her buying-intention immediately after exposure. The received-messages (RM) are defined as the total number of commercials recorded per 100 women. The persuasion rate (PR) is defined as the net percent of the RM that produce a shift in buying-intention from some other brand to the advertised brand. Subscribers obtain quarterly reports of the RM and PR from all competitor brands in the product class.

[17]The TEC Audit, TEC Measures, Inc. New York, N.Y.

DIAGNOSTIC TESTING

A whole category of advertising research methods are primarily designed not to test the impact of a total ad but rather to help creative people understand how the parts of the ad contribute to its impact. Which are weak and how do they interact? Most of these approaches can be applied to mock-ups of proposed ads as well as finished ads.

Qualitative Research

Focus groups research is widely used at the front end of the development of an advertising campaign. In one study of the techniques used by 112 (out of 150 surveyed) of the top advertisers and agencies, focus groups were used 96 percent of the time to generate ideas for advertisements, and 69 percent of the time to test reactions to rough executions.[18] In such groups, people will discuss their opinions about the product and the brand, their use experiences, and their reaction to potential advertisement concepts and actual advertisements.

Audience Impressions of the Ad

Many copy test approaches append a set of open-ended questions designed to tap the audience's impressions of what the ad was about, what ideas were presented, interest in the ideas, and so on. One goal is to detect potential misperceptions. Another is to uncover unintended associations that may have been created. If too many negative comments are elicited, there may be cause for concern. A Volkswagen commercial showing a Detroit auto worker driving a VW Rabbit because of its superior performance, was killed because a substantial part of the audience disliked the company disloyalty portrayed.[19]

Adjective Check Lists

The BRC mail questionnaire, shown in Figure 20–1, includes an adjective checklist that allows the advertiser to determine how warm, amusing, irritating, or informative the respondent thinks that it is. Similar checklists are used by ASI, TeleResearch, and other firms and agencies. The agencies Leo Burnett and Y & R use a similar phrase check list extensively. Several of their phrases tap an empathy dimension. "I can see myself doing that," "I can relate to that," and so on. Some believe that unless advertisements can achieve a degree of empathy they will not perform well.

[18]Benjamin Lipstein and James P. Neelankavil, "Television Advertising Copy Research: A Critical Review of the State of the Art" *Journal of Advertising Research 24* (April/May 1984) 19–25.

[19]"WV had some clinkers among classics" *Advertising Age,* Sept. 9, 1985, 48.

Eye Movement

Eye movement devices, such as those used by Perception Research and Burke, record the point on a print ad or package where the eye focuses 60 times each second. An analysis can determine what the reader saw, what he or she "returned to" for reexamination, what point was "fixed upon." In package research the package can be "placed" on a shelf with competing packages, and the respondent can be asked to "find" the test brand.

Physiological Measurement

Of particular interest in advertisements that are intended to precipitate emotional responses is the use of measures that reflect physiological arousal that is normally uncontrollable by the respondent. Among the measures used are GSR, skin resistance, heart beat, facial expressions, muscle movement, and voice pitch analysis. The difficulty is in the interpretation, because a variety of reactions can stimulate arousal. The key is to operate in a context such that the response is clearly interpreted. For example, GSR is correlated with other measures of warmth for warm commercials, but is not so correlated for humorous or irritating commercials.[20]

Monitoring Commercial Response

In the ASI theater test, 200 seats are equipped with dial interest recorders that allow the respondents to continuously dial their interest in the material. The output allows advertisers to determine which parts of a commercial are interesting. The output provides diagnostic information as to the points in the commercial that stimulate responses and those that do not. Aaker, Stayman, and Hagerty have used a computer joy stick driven monitor to allow respondents to record their feeling of warmth. It can also be used to monitor other feelings such as irritation, humor, or liking.[21]

Market Facts has developed a system in which a respondent presses a button when something in the commercial strikes her or him as especially interesting or irritating. The respondent is then shown the commercial again and asked why the button was punched at each point. The result is a second by second understanding of the audience reaction.

THE BUDGET DECISION

Providing analytical, research based judgments as to the optimal advertising budget is surprisingly difficult. However, there are research inputs that can be helpful. Tracking studies that show if the advertising is either surpassing or failing to reach communication

---

[20]David A. Aaker, Douglas M. Stayman and Michael R. Hagerty, "Warmth in Advertising: Measurement, Impact and Sequence Effects" *Journal of Consumer Research*, March, 1986.

[21]*Ibid.*

objectives can suggest that the budget should either be reduced or increased. Forced exposure testing of multiple exposures can suggest the optimal number of exposures per month for an audience member. Such a number can help guide the establishment of an advertising budget. More direct approaches include regression analysis of internal sales and advertising data, field experimentation, and split-cable experimentation.

Regression Analysis

A direct approach is to use internal data of advertising and sales over time, or perhaps over geographically defined sales regions, or perhaps both. The challenge is to explain sales movements using advertising as an independent variable. The regression coefficient would then be the change in sales obtained from a change in advertising.

Although such an analysis is relatively inexpensive and can be useful there are many serious difficulties with it.[22] First, there is often little variation in advertising (except that due to seasonable factors). With little variation, it is impossible to detect the impact of changing advertising. Second, it is difficult to control for other marketing variables, competitor actions, and other factors affecting sales, because data describing them is unavailable. Third, if a business spends a certain percentage of sales on advertising, a change in sales could cause a change in advertising, instead of the reverse. Fourth, and most important, it is most difficult to detect the delayed or carry-over impact of advertising on sales.

Field Experimentation

The lack of variation in advertising can be remedied by a field experiment in which advertising is deliberately increased or decreased in certain areas. The subsequent sales are then monitored. The Budweiser experiments, in the mid-1960s, discussed in Chapter 9, led to dramatic reductions in the Budweiser advertising budget.

Field experiments have problems of their own. First, it is virtually impossible to control for the other factors, particularly competitor factors that can affect sales. In fact, competitors, in order to protect their share or distort a test, may engage in extraordinary actions. Second, field experiments are costly to run, partly because of the costs of deliberately over- or under-advertising in some areas. Third, reliable results are still not guaranteed because of the variability between markets. Fourth, because of the elapsed time of the test the results could be rendered obsolete before they can influence decisions. Finally, field experiments are conducted in view of competitors who are free to observe and monitor them.

[22]David A. Aaker and James M. Carman, "Are You Overadvertising?" *Journal of Advertising Research 22* (August/September 1982) 57–70.

Split-Cable Testing

The scanner-based split cable tests solve many of the problems of field experimentation, and provide an excellent option for those products using television ads and distributed through markets that are monitored by the scanner systems. The advertising budget tests can be tightly controlled in that matched households received different levels of advertising. It is also hidden from the view of competitors. Although it can cost from $150,000 and up, and can require six months to a year or more to read because of potential carry-over effects, it can provide a valid estimate of the impact of different levels of advertising.

Hundreds of budget tests have been run on split-cable systems during the past decade, but few tested have reduced advertising levels. Aaker and Carman suggest that the relevant decision makers might be biased against such "down-weight" tests.[23] Agencies basically get paid a commission on advertising and thus have a conflict of interest. Further, it is psychologically and logically inconsistent to be excited and positive about a new campaign and propose a budget reduction. Finally, the product manager who controls the advertising and is measured in part on short-run sales, views advertising as a way to protect short-term market position and react to competitor activities.

MEDIA RESEARCH

In evaluating a particular media alternative such as *Time* magazine or "Dynasty", it is necessary to know how many advertising exposures it will deliver and what will be the characteristics of the audience. A first cut of the vehicle's value is the cost per thousand, the size of the audience divided by the advertisement insertion cost.

Measuring Print Vehicle Audiences

Print vehicle circulation data is easily obtained, but neglects pass-along readers both inside and outside the home. Thus, to measure a vehicle's audience, it is necessary to apply approaches such as recent-reading, reading-habit, and through-the-book to a randomly selected population sample.

In recent-reading, a respondent is asked whether he or she looked at a copy within the past week for a weekly publication, or during the last month for a monthly publication. One problem is that the survey is unlikely to represent an average week, so there is a seasonal factor to consider. Also, a reader could read several issues in one week and be incorrectly reported as not being a reader in another week. Another concern is the tendency to exaggerate readership of prestige magazines and minimize readership of those not matching people's self-image. Still another concern is the forgetting factor. One study

---

[23]*Ibid.*

found that 50 of 166 people who were observed reading magazines in a doctor's office said they had never read the magazine they had been observed reading.[24]

The reading-habit method, which asks respondents how many issues out of the last four did you personally read or look at, is also sensitive to memory difficulties. In particular, it is difficult to discriminate between reading the same issue several times from reading several issues. The through-the-book readership attempts to reduce the memory factor. Respondents readership is ascertained only after he or she is *shown* a specific issue of a magazine, and asked whether several articles were read and if they were interesting. The approach, which requires an expensive personal interview, is sensitive to the issue age. A too recent issue will miss later readers. A too old issue will risk forgetting.

The two major audience measuring services are Mediamark, which relies upon the recent-reading method and surveys 140 magazines, and Simmons.[25] Simmons, which interviews over 15,000 people each year, uses the through-the-book approach for 44 major magazines, and estimates another 81 using the reading-habit approach (downward adjusting the resulting reading-habit estimates).[26] Differences between the two have sparked sharp controversy through the years.

One comparison showed that Mediamark estimated the number of *Newsweek's* audit readers to be 92 percent of *Time's* 25.7 million, while Simmons estimated *Newsweek* to have 82 percent of *Time's* 20.035 million.[27] One explanation was that *Newsweek* does relatively better at out-of-home readership, which is detected easier by the recent-reading methodology. *Time,* in contrast, might get more serious, thorough readership, which is best measured by the through-the-book approach of Simmons.

Measuring Broadcast Vehicle Audiences

Television audience size is estimated by an audimeter and a diary. The audimeter is attached to a television set and monitors the set's activity 24 hours a day, recording any change or activity that lasts over 30 seconds. The familiar Nielsen national television ratings, the average number of households tuned to a given program as a percent of all television homes, are based upon 1750 Nielsen audimeter homes. Nielsen also provides estimates of nine cites.

The audimeter provides an objective measure of television viewer activity with no burdensome recordkeeping. To avoid self-consciousness, the meter is placed out of view, and a metered family is not used until several weeks of acclimatization have passed. The major problems with the audimeter is its cost and the fact that it cannot provide information

---

[24]William S. Blair, "Observed vs. Reported Behavior in Magazine Reading: An Investigation of the Editorial Interest Method," *Proceedings of the 12th Annual Conference of the Advertising Research Foundation,* 1967.

[25]"New Simmons Report May Stir Research War," *Advertising Age* (September 8, 1980) 20, 75.

[26]The total audience figures for the Simmons reading-habit approach is the total of the following percentages of those saying they have read the magazine in the last six months: 9% of those who claim to have read less than one out of four issues, 15% of those reading one out of four issues; 36% of the two of four group; 63% of the three of four issues group; and 73% of the all four issue group.

[27]Leah Rozen, "Reader Data Still Don't Jibe," *Advertising Age* (October 6, 1980) 118.

as to who is doing the viewing. A possible solution under consideration is to have each family member record entering and leaving the TV room by means of a wall switch assigned to him or her. Another is the diary.

Nielsen, in its national ratings estimates, supplements the audimeter with a matched sample, diary panel. A diary household notes the viewing activity, inlcuding who is doing the watching. A clocklike meter keeps track of how long the set is on so that Nielsen can make sure that the diary is complete. Using the diary information, Nielsen can break down the audience estimates by age, sex, and geographic area.

The diary is the basic data-gathering instrument for local television and radio ratings. Nielsen and Arbitron both monitor over 200 local markets. The sample size of the Nielsen effort ranges from 2200 households in New York to several hundred in the smallest markets. Monthly reports are provided three to eight times a year, depending on the size of the market. Over the course of a year's time, over 800,000 households will be involved in a television diary panel for one of the two services.

The quality of diary data can vary. Some respondents do not fill out during the day, but try to recall the viewing activity. As a result, fringe programming generally does not fare as well from the diary as it does from the audimeter. Another problem is that the homemaker is often the one who fills it out, and is usually not conversant with kid shows and lesser known programs. The major problem is probably nonresponse bias. It has been suggested that the diary panel tends to understate the younger audience. The cooperation rate among the 18 to 24 year old group is especially low.[28]

It is often useful to define a target audience in terms of purchasing patterns. Thus, the audience of heavy catsup buyers, or catsup buyers loyal to a competing brand, might be the target. Brand usage questionnaires in parallel with media usage information, can provide such information. However, a preferred approach is the combination of continuous monitoring of both purchases and media habits. BehaviorScan in fact does provide both sets of data for 6000 of their scanner panel members.

SUMMARY

Criteria used in copy testing can be usefully grouped into four types, recognition, recall, persuasion, and behavior. BRC uses mail questionnaires to measure television commercial recognition and brand name association: Communicus for television and Starch for print use personal interviews. Day-after-recall is widely used but controversial because of its inability to predict persuasion or behavior, especially for emotional appeals. Persuasion has been measured in forced exposure or on-air contexts, by change in brand preference, change in prize list brand preference, comparison of the effect on brand preference with a nonexposed control group, measures of advertisement involvement and brand commitment, and measures tailored to particular advertising objectives. Behavior measures include

[28]"ARB and NSI Defend Their TV Diaries," *Media Decisions* (October 1973) 72–74.

coupon stimulated buying after a forced exposure to an ad and scanner based monitoring of a panelist in a split cable testing operation.

Copy test validity concerns usually focus upon the naturalness of the exposure, the reactive (or guinea pig) effect of being in an experiment (especially when the exposure setting is not natural and when an attitude measure is required), the representativeness of the sample and the appropriateness and validity of the response measure.

A tracking study provides measures of advertising impact over time by taking periodic (monthly, quarterly or yearly) surveys of audience response. Awareness of the advertising or of specific claims or elements of the advertising is often included, but any measure relevant to the objectives can be included. Diagnostic testing, to evaluate the advertisement content at all stages of the process, includes qualitative research, audience ad impressions, adjective check lists, eye movement, physiological measures, and the monitoring audience response during the commercial.

Several research approaches are relevant to the budget decision. Regression analysis is limited by lack of variation in advertising data, the difficulty in controlling for other causes of sales variation, and in detecting the carry-over impact of advertising. Field experimentation is highly visible, relatively expensive in time and money, and subject to contamination by factors other than advertising such as competitor actions. A split-cable test solves most of the problems of the other approaches but is expensive and absorbs time.

Media research includes the measurement of vehicle audiences, which involves asking people about their reading habits, and by the use of audimeters connected to television sets.

QUESTIONS AND PROBLEMS

1 Why measure recognition anyway? Why would it ever be of value to have an audience member recognize an ad when he or she could not recall it without being prompted and could not recall its content? Why not just measure recall?

2 Compare the BRC recognition method with Cummunicus'. What are the relative strengths and weaknesses?

3 Is DAR widely used? Why? Would you use it if you were the product manager for Lowenbrau? For American Express? Under what circumstances would you use it?

4 Review the validity problems discussed in Chapter 4 inherent in the McCollum/ Spielman theater testing approach. Compare these to:

a The Mapes & Ross method.

b the Apex method.

c the TeleResearch approach

d the Sherman BUY test

e the BehaviorScan approach

5 Why conduct tracking studies? Why not just observe sales?

6 How will adjective check lists help a creative group? What about eye movement data?

7 A field experiment was conducted by DuPont for an improved version of Teflon several years after Teflon was first introduced. Four cities received 10 daytime commercial minutes per week during the fall months, five cities received five minutes per week, and four cities (the control group) received no advertising. Cities were randomly assigned to each of the three test conditions. The sales measure was purchase of Teflon cookware as reported by telephone interviews of 1000 housewives in each of the test cities. The total purchases turned out to be about 30 percent higher in the heavy advertising cities than in those cities with no or low advertising, but there was no real difference between the low and no advertising groups. Critique this test. What validity problems do you see? What changes would you make? Would you conduct the same test if the product change had been out for three years?

8 Mediamark estimated the total adult readers of *Family Circle Magazine* as 32.1 million, while Simmons estimated it as 18.3 million. Why the difference? Which is right?

9 In a survey of housewives, the readership of *Harper's* was exaggerated and the readership of *Modern Romance* seemed much less than circulation figures indicated. Why would respondents incorrectly report their readership in this manner? Can you think of ways to avoid this bias?

10 What are the weaknesses of the audimeter? What are some alternatives besides the diary? What are the weaknesses of the diary approach?

CASE 21–1
Levi Strauss & Co.

Sue Swenson, a member of the research group at Foote, Cone & Belding/Honig, a San Francisco advertising agency, was reviewing four copy-testing techniques, all of which cost about $10,000 per commercial (plus media costs where required):

1 Burke DAR (Spots are purchased in three markets for the test ads)

2 Mapes & Ross

3 McCollum/Spielman

4 TeleResearch

A meeting was scheduled with the Levi Strauss account group for the next day, to decide on which copy tests to employ on two new Levi's campaigns. The following week a similar meeting was scheduled involving a campaign for a new bar of soap for another client. In each case the task was to determine which testing approach would be used to help make the final selection of which commercials to use in the campaigns. Swenson knew that she would be expected to contribute to the discussion by pointing out the strengths and limitations of each test and to make her own recommendation.

Levi Strauss & Co. had grown from a firm serving the needs of miners in the Gold Rush era of the mid

LEVI'S® "ROUNDUP"

(Music) Yessir, this drive started over a hundred years ago, back in California.

Just a few head of Levi's Blue Jeans, and a lot of hard miles.

Across country that would've killed ordinary pants.

But Levi's? They thrived on it! If anything, the herd got stronger —and bigger.

First there was kid's Levi's. Ornery little critters...seems like nothing stops 'em.

Then there was gal's pants, and tops, and skirts. Purtiest things you ever set eyes on.

And just to prove they could make it in the big city, the herd bred a new strain called Levi's Sportswear.

Jackets, shirts, slacks... a bit fancy for this job, I reckon, but I do admire the way they're made.

Fact is, pride is why we put our name on everything in this herd.

Tells folks, "This here's ours!" If you like what you got, then c'mon back!

We'll be here. You see, fashions may change...

...but quality never goes out of style!

Levi Strauss & Co. Two Embarcadero Center, San Francisco, California 94106

FIGURE 21–6 A corporate commercial

ANNCR: If a man's suit jacket fits
    like a straight jacket . . .
WIFE: Hold on, Joe!
JOE: I can't raise my arms.

ANNCR: If his pants fit their worst
    around his waist,
WIFE: Sit down.
JOE: I can't — these pants are too
    tight.

ANNCR: Then he needs Levi's*
    Action Suit . . . perhaps
    the most comfortable suit
    a man can wear.

ANNCR: The waistband strrrr-
    retches to give more room
    when you need it.

JOE: Comfortable.
ANNCR: The jacket lets you
    move your arms without
    binding.

JOE: I can sit.
OLD LADY: Hmmmmmmph!

JOE: I can stand, too.

ANNCR: Levi's Action Suit from
    Levi's Sportswear.

Levi Strauss & Co. Two Embarcadero Center, San Francisco, California 94106

FIGURE 21–7 An Action Suit commercial

1800s to a large, sophisticated clothing company. In 1979 it had sales of over $2 billion, drawn from an international and domestic operation. The domestic company, Levi Strauss USA, included six divisions, Jeanswear, Sportswear, Womenswear, Youthwear, Activewear, and Accessories. In 1979, Levi Strauss was among the 100 largest advertisers, with expenditures of $38.5 million, primarily on television.

Concerning the Levi's campaigns, Swenson recognized that two very different campaigns were involved. The first was a corporate image campaign. The overall objective was to build and maintain Levi's brand image. The approach was to build around the concepts of "quality" and "heritage," the most meaningful, believable, and universal aspects of the Levi's corporate personality. Unlike competitors who claimed quality as a product feature, Levi's 128-year-heritage advertisements had an important additional dimension. More specifically, the advertising involved the following strategy:

1 Heritage-quality: communicate to male and female consumers, ages 12 to 49, that Levi's makes a wide variety of apparel products, all of which share in the company's 128-year commitment to quality.

2 Variety-quality: Communicate to male and female consumers, age 12 to 49, that Levi's makes a wide variety of quality apparel products for the entire family.

Figure 21–6 shows one of the commercials from the pool that was to be tested for the corporate campaign.

The second campaign was for Levi's action suits. In 1979, the Sportswear division responsible for action suits spent approximately $6 million on network television commercials and co-op newspaper ads to introduce Actionwear slacks, which topped the sales of both leading brands of men's slacks, Haggar and Farah, in that year. The primary segment was middle-aged males, who often suffer from middle-aged spread. Actionwear slacks, a blend of polyester and other fabrics with a stretchable waistline, were presented as a solution to the problem. The advertising objectives for the new campaign were guided by the following:

Focus: Levi's Action garments are comfortable dress clothes.

Benefits: Primary—comfortable; secondary—attractive, good looking, well made, long wearing

Reasons Why:

1 Levi's Action slacks are comfortable because they have a hidden stretch waistband and expandable shell fabric.

2 Levi's Action suit jacket is comfortable because it has hidden stretch panels that let you move freely without binding.

3 The Levi's name implies quality and well-made clothes.

Brand character: Levi's Action clothing is sensible, good-value menswear manufactured by Levi Strauss & Co., a company dedicated to quality.

Figure 21–7 shows a commercial from the pool for the Levi Action campaign.

Swenson also knew that previous Levi's commercials had proved exceptionally memorable and effective, owing to their distinctive creative approach. In part, their appeal lies in their ability to challenge the viewer's imagination. The advertising assumes that viewers are thoughtful and appreciate advertising that respects their judgments.

In preparing for the next day's meeting with the Levi account group, she decided to review carefully the four copy-testing services. The immediate problem was to decide which of the services to recommend for testing commercials from the two Levi's campaigns. She knew that similar issues would be raised in discussions with another of the agency's clients the following week concerning a national campaign for a bar-soap line extension. Positioning for the bar-soap essentially involved a dual cleanliness-fragrance theme. A demonstration commercial focused on these two copy points.

QUESTIONS FOR DISCUSSION

1 What copy-testing service or services should Sue Swenson recommend for testing the two Levi Strauss commercials?

2 What service or services should she recommend for testing the bar-soap commercial?

22

FORECASTING

Peter, an aggressive product manager for the widget product line for XYZ Electronics, was in a management meeting. The topic for discussion was his last quarterly sales forecast. It was only half of what sales actually had been, and as a result the manufacturing manager, Mary, needed to run the plant on overtime for six weeks after laying off people during the previous quarter. The controller, Charlie, was upset over the large fluctuations in the inventory level, and the general manager, George, recalled the order they bid below cost because of projected undercapacity. They were all discussing Peter's low forecast.

Mary: You are always low and wrong. Where do those numbers come from anyway, a random number table?

Peter: They come from the salesforce, who are on top of the market. You must realize that they don't like to put speculative orders into their forecast because they look bad if forecasted sales do not materialize. Because of that I actually increased their estimates somewhat.

Mary: We obviously need a better system and fast.

Charlie: I've been looking at the data over the last few years and the forecast is always low at this time of year. I think there is a seasonal effect brought about by the governmental purchases at the end of the fiscal year. Did you consider the seasonal effect?

Peter: No, it wasn't necessary because the salespeople already factor that into their estimates.

Charlie: You hope.

George: Didn't we hear that our competitor, Ajax, was at capacity and therefore probably would raise prices? Did the additional sales come from the region in which Ajax always has been strong?

Peter: That region was high but I've no information to suggest that it was due to a price change by Ajax.

George: Perhaps these forecasts signal a long-term change in the growth of the product line. Perhaps we should be adding plant capacity.

Peter: That's a possibility. I've always said that the widget line would take off with more sales and advertising support.

Charlie: In the meantime we need some short-term forecasts so that this debacle isn't repeated.

Mary: Amen.

Peter: You Monday-morning quarterbacks are really perceptive. I'd like to see you make forecasts instead of criticizing previous forecasts, for a change. Our best quarter ever and you complain about the forecast.

Forecasting, as the story illustrates, provides the basis for almost all planning and control. If the forecasts are unreliable, it is most difficult to make the right tactical or strategic decision. Try to think of decisions made by any organization that do not in some way rely upon a forecast of demand or sales. The story also indicates the varied considerations that can go into a forecast, considerations like seasonal effects, salespeople's biases, competitor's price, and long-term growth trends.

Peter was attempting to make short-term forecasts of the sales of an existing brand. There actually is a variety of types of forecasts. Figure 22–1 provides an overview of

---

BY TIME PERIOD
    Short term (3 to 6 months)
    Medium term (2 to 3 years)
    Long term

BY OBJECT
    Brand sales or usage
    Product class sales or usage
    Other consumer variables like attitude or intentions
    Macro variables like GNP, unemployment, or interest rates

BY SEGMENT
    Geographic area
    Customer type
    Product application

BY PRODUCT MATURITY
    New products
    Growth products
    Mature products
    Declining products

FIGURE 22–1   Types of forecasting tasks

some of the ways in which forecasting tasks can differ. Forecasts can be short-term (up to 3 to 6 months), medium-term (to 2 to 3 years), or long-term. The methods used and the forecast accuracy will be sensitive in part to the length of time to be forecast. It usually is much easier to forecast for short periods into the future because fewer factors will change in the short run.

There are countless objects that can be the focus of the forecast. Among these possible objects are brand sales (or usage) and product-class sales (or usage). Thus, a symphony manager might be interested in forecasting not only symphony attendance but the attendance at all cultural events, or product-class usage. Product-class sales can help refine the brand-sales forecast and also provide guidance to the marketing program. If attendance to all cultural events were expected to grow, that might have implications for the forecast for symphony attendance and also for ways to promote the symphony.

Often it is necessary to forecast by market segments or subgroups. A forecast by geographic area might be needed to plan warehouse-stocking decisions or to evaluate regional salesforce efforts. Long-range planning might need forecasts of customer types or of product applications.

In the next chapter the focus will be upon forecasting demand for new products. Approaches for new-product concept forecasting include obtaining the reaction of potential users to the new concepts. Test marketing will be discussed as a method for field evaluation of new products prior to full-scale introduction. In this chapter the focus will be on existing products and existing markets.

There is a variety of approaches that can be used for forecasting. Figure 22–2 summarizes those that will be discussed in this chapter. They are grouped into three categories. The first are qualitative in nature, such as the salesforce estimates Peter used. The second are time-series approaches where historical data are projected into the future. The third

---

QUALITATIVE METHODS
    Juries of executive opinion
    Salesforce estimates
    Surveys of customer intentions
    Delphi

TIME-SERIES EXTRAPOLATION
    Trend projection
    Moving average
    Exponential smoothing
    The seasonal and cyclical index

CAUSAL MODELS
    Leading indicators
    Regression models

FIGURE 22–2 Forecasting approaches

are causal approaches in which factors causally related to the forecast are identified. For example, the price charged by Ajax might be an important causal influence of widget sales and should be considered explicitly in the forecast.

QUALITATIVE METHODS

Time-series and causal-model approaches to forecasting both require an analysis of past data. In contrast, qualitative techniques are based upon the subjective judgments of individuals. Of course, the individuals may have access to quantitative information about the past, but the judgments themselves are subjective summaries or distillations of all the knowledge that is relevant to the forecast.

Jury of Executive Opinion

This approach involves combining the judgments of a group of managers about the forecast. The group normally would include a variety of concerned and informed managers representing such functional areas as marketing, sales, operations, manufacturing, purchasing, accounting, and finance. They each would bring to the forecast a different background, perspective, and set of biases. Often their judgments would be supported by background information that might include past data, economic and industry developments, competitive actions, and relevant news from customers or distributors. For example, the fact that a large retailer has decided to stock a competitor's product or is planning a large promotion might be relevant "news."

This technique has several advantages. First, it tends to be fast and efficient. Second, it tends to be timely in that the forecast is generated on the basis of the most current situation. Third, the knowledge upon which the forecast is based is extremely rich. It includes at least potentially all the collective knowledge and experience of the involved managers. Fourth, it has no formal requirements in terms of historical data.

The disadvantages are due to the subjectivity involved, because the information upon which the individual forecasts are based could differ from period to period. In one period the marketing manager might have just returned from a trade show or from a sales meeting and have better information than usual. Even the composition of the group might differ. Because the content and background can differ from period to period, it is difficult to make adjustments when forecasts err, even when they err systematically.

Actually, this technique is one of the most widely used. The Conference Board conducted a survey of the use of five major forecasting methods of commercial firms. The results from 161 reporting companies are shown in Table 22–1. The jury of executive opinion is the technique most used in consumer products and service companies and the second-most-used technique in industrial products companies.

TABLE 22–1
Usage Levels of Major Sales Forecasting Techniques: Percentage of Firms Rating Techniques as First or Second Most Valued

Forecasting Method	All Firms	Industrial Product Firms	Consumer Product Firms	Service Firms
Jury of executive opinion	54%	50%	64%	72%
Salesforce composite	56%	62%	40%	42%
Survey of users' expectations	29%	35%	13%	7%
Time-series projections	30%	35%	46%	34%
Causal models	15%	14%	20%	36%
Sample size	161	93	39	29

SOURCE: Adapted from Stanley J. P. Kempner and Earl L. Bailey, *Sales Forecasting Practices: An Appraisal* (The Conference Board, 1970), p. 14.

Salesforce Estimates

The salesforce estimate involves obtaining the judgments from the salesforce. Usually, each salesperson will provide a forecast for each product or product type by customer. Since many of the decisions based upon the forecast—such as production quantities—are product-specific, the forecast usually is needed by product.

Uncertainty can be introduced in several ways. One way is to allow the salespeople to provide a sales estimate range in addition to the single number representing the expected sales level. Another is to have them estimate the probability of each potential sale. The sales forecast then will be the sum of all the potential sales, each weighted by its probability of occurring.

Although the technique is termed a salesforce estimate, it also can be employed in organizations that do not have salesforces. The principle is that those in the organization who are closest to the organization's customers or clients make the individual forecasts, which are then combined into an aggregate forecast. A welfare agency might use case-workers to forecast their own caseloads, for example. Or branch librarians each might be asked to forecast demand for various categories of books for their branches. The term salesperson, in this context, thus will mean any organizational position that has direct contact with the customers or clients whose behavior is to be forecasted.

Forecasts generated from the salesforce are based upon the salesperson's knowledge of the customer or client, which is often extremely complete, sensitive, and current. Like the jury of executive opinion approach, it allows the introduction of subjective judgments drawing upon rich experience. The approach can provide detailed information about product lines and customers, which can be used productively in diagnostically identifying problems in the marketing program. For example, if sales are forecasted to be below normal for a certain product line or geographic area, then an investigation might be prompted. Such an investigation based upon a forecast could be stimulated many valuable months before historical data provided the same signal.

This approach suffers from subjectivity, as does the jury of executive opinion approach. Furthermore, salespeople often lack relevant information about a company's plans and overall industry trends. In addition, there is a greater tendency for biases to occur. Individual salespeople can be naturally optimisitic or pessimistic, and such biases are often more serious when the forecast is linked to their performance measures. For example, compensation often is based in part upon quotas, and forecasts sometimes contribute to quota development. In such cases salespeople might have an incentive to forecast low. Salespeople sometimes are criticized for "lost sales," and they may thus fail to report prospects that are not sure things, in order to reduce their lost sales. To counter such tendencies, a salesperson could be given credit only for sales that were listed in the forecast, but, of course, that policy would encourage overly optimistic forecasts.

There are two ways to deal with biases. One is to identify and compensate for them. If one salesperson is, on average, 20 percent low over several reporting periods, his forecast could be increased by 20 percent. Another salesperson could be 30 percent high, and her forecast would be reduced by 30 percent. Another approach is to divorce the forecast from any performance appraisal and ask that it be made as objectively as possible. The problem then might be to motivate the salesperson to be conscientious about the forecast. If the value of the forecast, in terms of the planning of operations and production, is well communicated, the motivation can be generated, but it is nearly always difficult to maintain.

Table 22–1 shows that the salesforce estimate approach is one of the two most-used techniques, particularly in industrial firms. Industrial firms often have relatively few customers and rely heavily upon their salespeople to reach those customers. Thus, the salesforce is the logical group upon which to rely for forecasts. In contrast, in consumer and service firms advertising plays a much more important role in communicating with the customer and there are usually many more customers involved.

Surveys of Customer Intentions

The third judgmental method is a survey of customer intentions. Customers are asked to make their own forecast about their usage and buying intentions. Customer intentions will be based upon subjective judgments about future requirements.

All the considerations of developing a valid survey are involved. The product or demand to be forecasted, the forecast period, and the population all must be specified clearly, and the sampling plan needs to be developed. When production or service sales are being forecast, the sampling frame is usually the existing customer or client list, as the bulk of sales or demand usually comes from existing customers. The right person in the customer organization must be contacted, and questions must be addressed with care. As the last chapter indicates, various biases can emerge.

Obviously, the advantage of the approach is that the user-customer has the best information upon which to base a forecast. It works best when the customers, or at least the major customers, are few in number. With few people or organizations to contact, the survey sometimes can be conducted quickly by telephone. As Table 22–1 indicates, the greatest use of this technique is in industrial firms, which often are characterized as having a relatively small set of major customers.

Surveys can become expensive and time consuming, of course, and are thus inappropriate for some forecasting tasks. They also are difficult when a sensitive purchase decision is involved and those surveyed may be reluctant to provide information.

Delphi

In the jury of executive opinion a group of people gather and reach a consensus on a forecast. Such an effort is subject to group effects. In particular, judgments might be swayed by the persuasions of some group members who have strong personalities, special interests (a sales manager might be optimistic, to encourage production), or special authority. When long-term forecasts are involved, such effects are particularly likely to occur. On the other hand, the information of the group should lead to a better forecast than that of any one of the individuals.

A method to retain the wisdom of a group while reducing the effect of group pressure is the Delphi approach. In the Delphi approach, group members are asked to make individual judgments about a forecast. These judgments then are compiled and returned to the group members, so that they can compare their own previous judgments with those of the others. They then are given an opportunity to revise their judgments, especially if they differ from the others. They also usually can state why they believe that their judgment is accurate, even if it differs from that of the other group members. After three or four iterations, group members usually reach their conclusions. There still remains group pressure, of course, but it is less overt since the individual is rating anonymously. The technique has been used with thousands of respondents, but more often it involves only from 10 to 40 respondents.

TIME-SERIES EXTRAPOLATION

A reasonable approach to forecasting is simply to extrapolate historical data forward. This approach, termed time-series forecasting, can be very effective, especially for short-term forecasting. A time series is simply data collected over time, such as weekly sales data for three years.

Three factors must be present for time-series forecasting to be appropriate. First, time-series data must exist. Without reliable past data there is nothing to extrapolate.

Second, the future must be like the past, at least with respect to forces influencing the time series. Since past data are being extrapolated forward, any environmental change influencing the time series can make the extrapolation err. In particular, a time-series forecast has little ability to forecast "turning points," where the rate of growth or decline of the time series will change significantly. Thus, time-series forecasting is best suited in rather stable situations and for short-term forecasting when the assumption that the future will be like the past is acceptable. Third, it must be possible to detect patterns or trends in the past data. If there is a large random element in the data, it might be difficult to detect any useful trends or other patterns.

Time-series forecasting involves several questions. First, what is the nature of the trend? Is it linear, for example? Second, how much historical data should be used? Third, how should seasonal and other cyclical fluctuations be handled?

Trend Projection

An advantage of time-series forecasting is that it is easy to understand conceptually. Historical data simply are plotted and extrapolated forward. The process can be done completely visually, or it can be done by using a regression program. In either case, a plot of historical data usually provides a useful feel for the data that a computer output sometimes lacks.

The simplest trend is the straight line, shown in Figure 22–3(i). The equation is simply:

$$y = a + bt$$

where t is time.

Figure 22–4 shows the domestic demand for oil products, a key item in energy-consumption forecasting. Suppose that the problem was to forecast the consumption for 1972 and 1973 using data from 1957 to 1970. A straight-line (least-squares) fit to this data would be:

$$8.1 + .43t$$

and is shown in Figure 22–4. Notice that the line is above the actual consumption during the 1961 to 1967 period and that its forecast for 1972 and 1973 is extremely low. A better straight-line forecast is obtained if the line is based only on the period from 1963 to 1971. The straight-line (least-squares) fit to the 1963 to 1971 data is:

$$9.7 + .61t$$

and also is shown in Figure 22–4. Notice the fit is quite good and that the forecast, although still low, improves.

In a linear or straight-line model, the growth is assumed to be a constant amount per year (0.61 millions of barrels per day for the 1963 to 1971 data). If the market instead grows at a constant percentage rate (such as 5 percent each year), then the appropriate

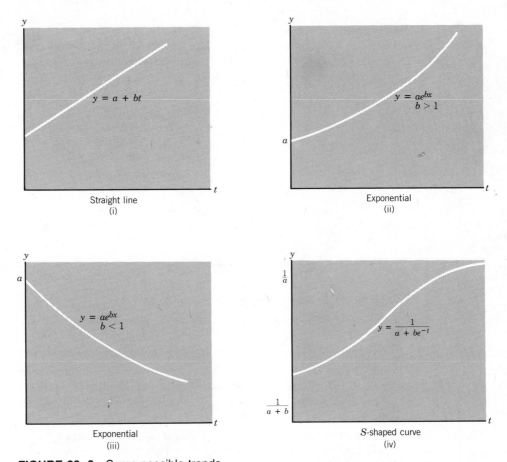

FIGURE 22–3 Some possible trends

model is the exponential model shown in Figure 22–3(ii).[1] The Figure 22–4 data actually follow the exponential curve very closely through 1973, so closely that a plot would tend to confuse the figure. However, if an exponential curve is fitted to the data from 1957 to 1973 the consumption forecast for 1974 would be 18.5, far above the 16.7 that actually occurred in 1974. The reason, of course, is that the consumption growth pattern was broken in 1974 by the Arab oil embargo. The example illustrates the inability of a time series to predict when there will be a dramatic shift in the underlying environment of the

[1]The exponential function can be converted into a linear equation so that it can be estimated by a regression program by taking natural logarithms of both sides of the equation. Thus,

$$y = ae^{bt}$$

can be transformed to

$$\log (y) = \log (a) + bt$$

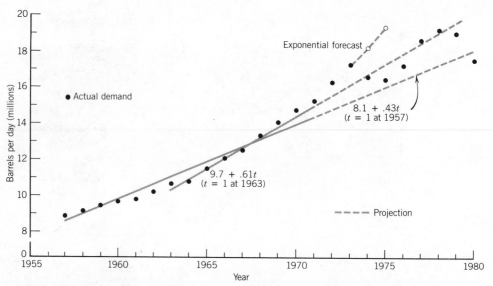

FIGURE 22–4 Domestic demands for oil products

Source: Standard and Poor's Industrial Survey. June 16, 1977; October 29, 1981.

forecast. The exponential model, which could provide very accurate predictions for any year prior to 1974, became inappropriate because of the oil embargo. However, because the oil embargo was so unexpected, there was probably no forecasting device that would have predicted it.

An important forecasting task is to forecast the growth, maturity, and decline of new products. Such a pattern is illustrated nicely by Figure 22–5, which shows the sales pattern for black-and-white and color television sets. The decline phase of a product life cycle often follows a downward-sloping exponential curve, as shown in Figure 22–3(iii). In Figure 22–5, an exponential curve is fitted to the black-and-white television set sales using only the data from 1966 to 1973.

Still another useful curve, an S-shaped curve, is shown in Figure 22–3(iv). It is appropriate when there is an introduction stage, a rapid growth stage, and finally a maturity stage. In Figure 22–5 the black-and-white data from 1946 to 1966 seem to follow this type of curve, as do the color television sales from 1960 to 1973.

Sometimes it is useful to separate initial purchases and replacement purchase demand and forecast each separately. An initial purchase is the first purchase such as the first purchase of a television set. A replacement purchase is made when the first set breaks down or becomes obsolete. Initial purchases tend to follow a growth-and-decline cycle, as the number of potential customers eventually declines. Replacement or repeat purchases, however, usually grow to a very stable plateau.

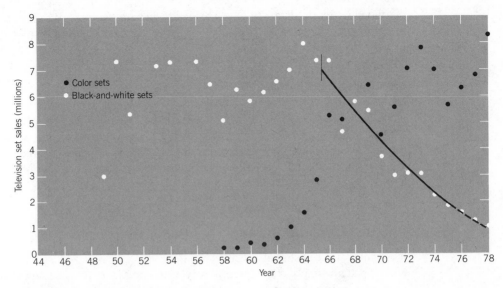

FIGURE 22–5 Sales of television sets

Sources: U.S. Industrial Outlook, 1968, 1970, and 1980 (Washington D.C.: U.S. Department of Commerce); *Statistical Abstracts of the United States,* 1959 (Washington D.C.: U.S. Bureau of the Census); and *Historical Statistics of the United States, Colonial to 1957* (Washington D.C.: U.S. Bureau of the Census).

Weighting the Data

How much historical data should be used? At first glance, it would seem all available data should be used. However, data that are too old will represent conditions that have changed and therefore actually could tend to detract from the forecast. Recall the superior prediction performance of the Figure 22–4 line based only on the 1963 to 1971 data. At one extreme, only the last data point should be used, since the conditions surrounding it will be the closest to those of the future. There are three intermediate positions that deserve mention: moving average, exponential smoothing, and past turning points.

Moving Average.   An alternative to using the last data point is to use the average of the last *n* data points. For example, if the task were to forecast the shipments of the monthly volume of mail delivered to a particular mail route, we might use the average of the last 12 months, and each forecast then would be based upon that figure.

Exponential Smoothing.   In this approach, instead of weighting the last *n* data points equally, we use exponentially decreasing sets of weights so that the more recent data are weighted more heavily than less recent data. This technique allows all the data to be used, but the more recent data will have more influence on the forecast. There are other, even more general weighting schemes; however, the added conceptual complexity and cost are usually not justified.[2]

Identifying Past Turning Points.   If a past turning point, a point in time where there was substantial change in the growth rate caused by an environmental change, can be identified, then a forecast might be based upon data since that point in time. The year 1966 represents such a turning point for black-and-white television sales, because, as Figure 22–5 indicates, it was in that year that color television sales became very substantial. Thus, the use of data from 1966 on to form the basis for a forecast of black-and-white television sales is reasonable.

The Seasonal and Cyclical Index

It is important to distinguish between a trend and a seasonal or cyclical fluctuation. A growth pattern simply may represent a cyclical upturn or even a seasonal fluctuation. Of course, if a 12-month moving average is used, the seasonal effect will be removed. However, it is useful to consider other ways to remove seasonal and cyclical effects that do not restrict one to using 12-month moving averages. Further, in short-term forecasting, the time period involved will be weeks, months, or quarters, and it becomes necessary to forecast the seasonal and cyclical effects as well as the trend. The solution is to develop indexes that will represent the seasonal and cyclical effect.

The Seasonal Index.   The seasonal index represents the effect of seasonal fluctuations. It can be created in a variety of ways.[3] A commonly used index, developed by the Bureau of the Census, is based upon the ratio of a given month's sales to the average monthly sales over a 12-month period. The 12 months used are centered at the month in question. If the month were September, for instance, the year would include 5.5 months before September and 5.5 months after. The seasonal index for September might then be the average of this ratio over a period of years.[4]

---

[2]One of these is termed the Box-Jenkins technique. Two researchers compared Box-Jenkins with exponential smoothing in the forecasting of tourists in Hawaii and found that both techniques performed equally well. See Michael D. Geurts and I. B. Ibrahim, "Comparing the Box-Jenkins Approach with the Exponentially Smoothed Forecasting Model: Application to Hawaii Tourists," *Journal of Marketing Research, 12* (May 1975), 182–188.

[3]One approach is simply to use an additive term reflecting the amount, on the average, that a given month differs from the average monthly level. It could be estimated by introducing a dummy variable for a season in a regression. The coefficient would reflect the average difference between demand in that month over demand in other months. If, however, there is a growth trend, it might be more appropriate to say that October is 15 percent more than the average month than to say it is 34,000 units more than average. In that case, an index based upon a ratio should be used.

[4]For a more complete discussion, including a historical perspective, see Lawrence Salzman, "Time Series Analysis," in Robert Ferber, ed., *Handbook of Marketing Research* (New York: McGraw-Hill, 1974), pp. 2–326 to 2–366. An excellent program, termed Census Program X-11, is available, which has provisions for seasonality, trend, and averages. See Julius Shiskin, *The X-11 Variant of the Census Method 11 Seasonal Adjustment Program* (Washington, D.C., U.S. Bureau of the Census, 1965).

TABLE 22–2
Seasonally Adjusted Museum Attendance (in thousands)

Quarter	Seasonally Adjusted Attendance	Seasonal Index	Actual Attendance
1	150	.80	120
2	140	1.05	147
3	135	1.20	162
4	130	.95	126
Total	555		555

Table 22–2 provides an illustration using the quarterly attendance at a museum. The right column shows the actual attendance. The middle column contains the seasonal indexes. If there were no seasonal effects, the first quarter would be expected to have 25 percent of a given year's demand. However, because of seasonal factors, the first quarter, on the average, gets only 80 percent of this amount (or 20 percent of a given year's demand), whereas the third quarter gets 120 percent (or 30 percent of a given year's demand). The seasonally adjusted attendance is in the left column. If the seasonally adjusted attendance for the first quarter, 150, is multiplied by the seasonal index, .80, the actual attendance is:

$$150 \times .80 = 120$$

Trends can be estimated and forecasts made using seasonally adjusted data. Then the seasonal index can be used to convert the forecast to actual numbers. For example, the seasonally adjusted data in Table 22–2 indicate a decline in attendance. Projecting this decline, the forecasted seasonally adjusted attendance for the first quarter of the next year might be 125. Applying the seasonal index of .80 would mean an actual forecast of 100.

The seasonal index also can be used to interpret past data. For example, actual attendance in the third quarter appeared good and reflected a nice growth trend; but, in fact, after applying the seasonal index, the attendance in the third quarter was disappointing, indicating a decline.

Cyclical Fluctuations.   Cyclical indexes can be developed in the same manner; however, most cycles, like business cycles, do not behave as regularly as seasonal factors, and it can be most difficult even to determine the length of the cycle.[5]

[5]For a discussion of market cycles that applies cycles of lengths of 40 months, nine years, 18 years, and 54 years, see Henry O. Pruden, "The Kondratieff Wave," *Journal of Marketing, 42* (April 1978), 63–70.

CAUSAL MODELS

Time-series approaches are limited by their simplistic assumption that the future will be the same as the past. Time-series approaches use only historical data on the variable to be forecasted. Causal models refer to the introduction into the analysis of factors that are hypothesized to cause or influence, either directly or indirectly, the object of the forecast. Thus, if forecasting transit usage is the goal, such causal factors as population growth, the price of gasoline, and frequency of service might be introduced as factors that might cause or influence transit usage.

There are at least three reasons for moving to a causal analysis. First, time-series analyses usually cannot predict turning points and thus are incapable of forecasting accurately at times when an accurate forecast is most needed. If causal factors can be identified and linked to the forecast, then they can be used to help predict turning points. Actually, some of the qualitative techniques used, like the jury of executive opinion, consider causal factors but not in a specific formal way. Second, sometimes there is too much variation in a time series to enable the detection of a trend. If a factor can be identified that is causally linked to some of that variation, the potential exists to remove it from the time series, just as seasonal components were removed. Third, an understanding of causal relationships can be interesting and useful. For example, if the effect of schedules upon transit usage could be predicted, policy concerning schedules might be affected.

Leading Indicators

Perhaps the simplest form of causal analysis is to attempt to identify leading indicators of the object to be forecasted. These indicators then could be monitored. In particular, we would hope that sharp changes in the growth rate of the indicators would predict turning points. Examples of leading indicators include the following:

1 The sales of color television are a leading indicator of the demand for components of color television sets. The sales of a product class are always a leading indicator of the sales of a supplier.

2 An analysis of demographic data frequently can provide useful indicators. The number of births is a leading indicator of the demand for education, and the number of people reaching 65 is a leading indicator of the demand for retirement facilities.

3 In technological forecasting, a leading indicator of the speed of commercial aircraft is the speed of military aircraft.

4 Economic data, such as disposable income, often are used as leading indicators of demand for such durables as automobiles, compactors, and the like.

Regression Models

A more formal causal model would be in the regression context. The dependent variable would be the object of the forecast. The independent variables would be the causal factors that are thought to cause or influence the forecast. The task, then, is to identify the causal factors and to obtain data representing them.

It is possible to include time as an independent variable, just as in time-series analyses. The causal factors then will be additional independent variables. The sales of the Simmons Company, makers of Beautyrest Mattresses, were hypothesized to have a linear trend and, in addition, to be caused by marriages during the year, housing starts, and annual disposable personal income.[6] The resulting model was:

$$S = 49.85 - 0.07M + 0.04H + 1.22D - 19.54T \qquad r^2 = .92$$
$$\qquad\quad (1.2) \qquad (3.1) \qquad (2.0) \qquad (8.4) \qquad (7.3)$$

where

$$S = \text{annual sales}$$
$$M = \text{annual number of marriages}$$
$$H = \text{annual housing starts}$$
$$D = \text{disposable income}$$
$$T = \text{time in years (the first year is 1, the second 2, etc.)}$$

The numbers in parentheses, which are the t-values, indicate that the trend is highly significant, as is the disposable-income variable.

In an effort to improve the model's validity and performance, three changes were explored. Since marriages were thought to be related positively to sales, a negative coefficient was unexpected and cast doubt upon the use of this variable, and the variable was therefore deleted. Also, the housing-start variable was thought to cause sales activity after about a year. To represent this lag between cause and effect, the number of housing starts in the previous year, H_{t-1}, was used instead of the number of current housing starts. Finally, last year's sales, S_{t-1}, is introduced to reflect current sales momentum. If last year's sales were exceptionally good, perhaps conditions that contributed to their success still will hold. Thus, the inclusion of last year's sales might provide a better model. The new model has the following form:

$$S = -33.51 + 0.37S_{t-1} + 0.03H_{t-1} + 0.67D - 11.03T \qquad r^2 = 0.95$$
$$\qquad\quad (2.1) \qquad\quad (2.8) \qquad\quad (2.4) \qquad (5.7) \qquad (5.1)$$

The revised model has an improved fit to the data, as reflected by the r^2. Of course, the fit to the data is only an indication of the model's ability to forecast, in the future. In evaluating a causal model, an important consideration is how reasonable and defensible

[6]George G. C. Parker and Ediberto L. Segura, "How to Get a Better Forecast," *Harvard Business Review* (March-April 1971), 99–109. The firm is identified in Robert A. Levy, "A Clearer Crystal Ball," *Dun's Review*, 98 (July 1971), 50.

the causal variables and their coefficients are. In this case, the revised model was thought to represent more closely the realities of the modeling problem.

Forecasts also can be made by cross-sectional data, data that involve a fixed point in time. For example, one firm wanted to forecast the soft-drink consumption per capita by state.[7] The hypothesis was that consumption was influenced by the mean temperature and by per-capita income. The resulting model was

$$C = -145.5 + 6.46X - 2.37Y \qquad r^2 = 0.66$$

where

$$C = \text{soft drink consumption per capita}$$
$$X = \text{mean annual temperature}$$
$$Y = \text{per capita income}$$

Thus, the consumption rate of a particular state can be predicted by knowing the values of the two causal variables. Such a prediction can be used to evaluate a special promotion in a particular state. The model can provide a basic prediction from which the results of the promotion can be compared.

SUMMARY[8]

There is a set of qualitative approaches to forecasting that includes the jury of executive opinion, the salesforce estimates, the survey of customer intentions, and the Delphi approach. These approaches are fast, inexpensive, flexible, and can integrate large quantities of information. They are extremely sensitive and can be used for difficult forecasting tasks such as long-range forecasting and forecasting turning points. They suffer from the biases, uncertainties, and inconsistencies inherent in the subjective judgments used.

Time-series forecasting, the projection of historical data, is well suited to short-term forecasts of data containing a clear trend or seasonal or cyclical patterns. It is not capable of forecasting turning points where the environment changes. One decision in time-series analysis is how much historical data to use and how much reliance to place on older data.

Causal models refer to the introduction of factors that directly or indirectly cause or influence the forecast. It can simply be the identification of leading indicators or the use of a formal regression model. Causal models allow for a deeper understanding of the process. The causal factors can be used to help predict turning points.

[7]Harper W. Boyd, Jr. and Ralph Westfall, *Marketing Research, 3rd ed.* (Homewood, Ill.: Richard D. Irwin, 1972), p. 577.

[8]The reader interested in learning more about forecasting is referred to a delightful, authoritative book by J. Scott Armstrong, *Long-Range Forecasting, From Crystal Ball to Computer* (New York: John Wiley, 1978).

QUESTIONS AND PROBLEMS

1   Assume you are the director of a large private hospital, which is one of four hospitals serving a medium-sized midwestern community. What types of forecasting tasks do you think the director will need? Answer this question for:

a   A university art museum

b   A small retail sporting goods store

c   A university

d   Delta Airlines

e   A maker of small computers sold primarily to educators in grades 1 through 8

2   Design a short-term (4 months) sales forecasting system for an electronics company that makes instruments that test such electronic components as transistors and integrated circuits. The instruments are sold to a variety of industries through a 20-person salesforce. Although there are thousands of customers, only about 300 provide about 85 percent of annual sales. The instrument normally has to be approved by people in manufacturing, purchasing, and quality control before it is purchased. Evaluate the various qualitative approaches in this context. Consider also the problem of forecasting sales potential five years out. The need is to make some basic decisions as to what product markets the company wants to be in.

3   Consider Figure 22–4. There are several alternatives to forecasting sales past 1974. Evaluate each of the following alternatives and describe what assumptions underlie each:

a   The straight-line fit $(9.7 + .61t)$ as shown, which predicts 17.6 for 1975

b   The exponential fit (to the data excluding 1974), which predicted 18.3 for 1974 and would predict approximately 19.4 for 1975

c   Use the exponential curve described in (b), except subtract 1.6 from it, since the actual 1974 value was 16.7 or 1.6 under the predicted value. The 1975 estimate then would be 17.8 $(19.4 - 1.6)$

d   Use only the 1974 data and assume 1975 would be the same (16.7)

What information would be needed to make an accurate forecast?

4   For Figure 22–4, generate a prediction for 1980 and compare your prediction with the actual demand. Predict the 1981 value.

5   Consider Figure 22–5. Take a piece of paper and cover the data from 1959 on, so that only the years 1946 to 1958 show. Forecast sales of black-and-white sets from the exposed data covering 1946 to 1958.

a   Why were you so far off? What additional information would you want to improve your forecast?

b Do the same, using only the 1946 to 1957 data. Repeat using the 1946 to 1956 data.

c What are your hypothesized reasons for the low sales in 1958?

d Do the same, using the data on black-and-white sets for 1946 to 1963. First, assume you do not know the future of color television. Just make some reasonable assumptions. Second, assume you know exactly what color set sales will be in the future.

e Project both color set and black-and-white set sales into the future.

f Would you advise a television set manufacturer to conduct an annual survey to determine the distribution of set purchases as to

    i Replacement of first purchase?

    ii Second or third set purchased versus first set purchased? Would such a survey improve the forecast?

g Use the data from 1946 to 1977 to predict 1978 sales of color sets. Evaluate your prediction.

6 What causal variables would you want to explore if you were forecasting

  a Furniture sales by region?

  b Student applications at Northwestern University over a 20-year period?

  c Attendance at the Chicago White Sox games by day for purposes of planning staff and food requirements?

  d Sales of a pizza sandwich at the Round Table pizza chain?

7 Using the seasonal index of Table 22–2, determine the seasonally adjusted attendance if the actual attendance for the four quarters (several years later) were 96, 134.4, 160.8, 136.8. What would be your forecast for the following year?

23

NEW PRODUCT RESEARCH

The development of new products is critical to the life of most organizations as they adapt to their changing environment. Since, by definition, new products contain aspects with which the organization will be unfamiliar, there will be uncertainty associated with them. Thus, it is not surprising that a large proportion of marketing research is directed toward reducing the uncertainty associated with new products.

In this section the role that marketing research plays in the new-product development process will be discussed. The purpose will be to position many of the marketing research techniques in their applied setting.

It should be fairly obvious that for some organizations their "product" is a service or a public policy program. It is less obvious—but nevertheless true—that the concept of a product often can be broadened to include the total marketing program. Thus, the material in this chapter often will apply to the development of any element of a marketing program. The problem of developing a new advertising campaign, a new package, or a new distribution channel is very similar to that of developing a new product.

The new-product research process can be divided into four stages, as shown in Figure 23–1. The first stage is the generation of new product concepts; the second is the evaluation and development of those concepts; the third is the evaluation and development of the actual products; and, finally, the product is tested in the context of the marketing program.

CONCEPT GENERATION

Many kinds of research can contribute to concept generation. Much of what is termed market analysis potentially can lead to concept ideas. It is useful to consider two types of concept generation research. The first might be termed **need research.** In need research, the emphasis is upon identifying unfilled needs that exist in the market—segments of the population that have a problem or are dissatisfied with existing product offerings for some reason. The second is termed concept identification. Here, an effort is made to determine

611

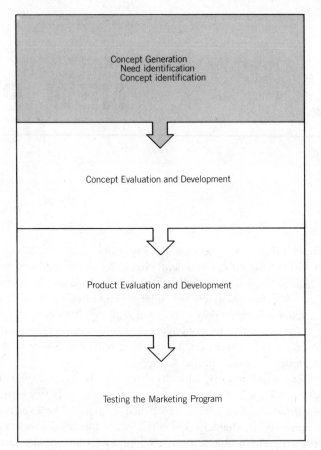

FIGURE 23–1 Phases in new product research

concepts that might fill the identified need. Sometimes the process bypasses the need-identification stage and is initiated by a concept.

Need Identification

There is a variety of ways by which marketing research can identify needs. Some are qualitative and others, like segmentation studies, can be quantitative. The following are some examples:

- Perceptual maps, where products are positioned along the dimensions by which users perceive and evaluate, can suggest gaps where new products might fit.
- Social and environmental trends can be analyzed. For instance, a trend toward natural foods might suggest fruit-filled cookies for a cookie manufacturer.

- An approach termed benefit structure analysis has product users identify the benefits desired and the extent to which the product delivers those benefits for specific use applications. The result is an identification of benefits sought which current products are not delivering.[1]

- Product users could be asked to keep a diary of a relevant portion of their activities. For example, a manufacturer of household cleaners might ask homemakers to recall in detail their cleaning experiences in the kitchen. For each incident, the product used, the surface involved (floor, counter, or sink), the time of day, the problems involved, the procedure used, and so on, would be noted. An analysis of such diaries can provide an understanding of unsolved problems associated with the cleaning task.

- In focus-group interviews product users could discuss problems associated with product-use situations. Thus, office managers might discuss various problems they had experienced with the postal service.

If several unsolved problems are identified, they need to be screened so that those with the greatest potential for attractive product concepts are identified. The advertising agency BBD&O, which relies heavily upon "problem detection" to generate new-product concepts and ideas for advertising campaigns, has developed a procedure for rating problems.[2] Each of 150 respondents, considered potential prospects, are asked to rank each problem as to whether:

1 The problem is important

2 The problem occurs frequently

3 A problem solution exists

A "problem score" is obtained by combining these ratings.

Using this technique, BBD&O found that the problem with hamburger outlets was that hamburgers were prefabricated. The result was a Burger King campaign based on allowing the customer to "Have It Your Way." In other words, the customer could order a "custom-made" hamburger. Western Airlines responded to a leg-room problem in their coach sections by altering their planes to provide first-class leg room in coach. A dog-food study revealed that buyers felt that dog food

- Smelled bad

- Cost too much

- Did not come in different sizes for different dogs

Subsequently, products responsive to these criticisms emerged.

---

[1] James H. Myers, "Benefit Structure Analysis: A New Tool for Product Planning," *Journal of Marketing, 40* (October 1976), 23–32.

[2] E. E. Norris, "Your Surefire Clue to Ad Success: Seek Out the Consumer's Problem," *Advertising Age* (March 17, 1975), 43–44.

Concept Identification

There is also a variety of approaches to the identification of concepts. Some are neither user-based nor follow from an identification of unfilled needs. For example, there may be a technological breakthrough that can suggest concepts, as when the freeze-dry process suggests freeze-dried fruit in cereal. Or competitors may introduce a new product that represents either a threat to or an opportunity for our organization. One role of marketing research is to monitor the environment in a systematic way to learn of technological or competitive developments that may suggest new concept ideas.

Other approaches are based upon the identified needs. Brainstorming groups could be formed to try to think of concepts that would be responsive to the identified need. These groups could consist of "experts" in a relevant area or simply end users who have experienced the need.

Users often can provide concept ideas directly. Most organizations receive many "why don'tcha" letters each year. Another role of marketing research is to organize and analyze the many user suggestions and complaints that flow into the organization.

CONCEPT EVALUATION AND DEVELOPMENT

During the new-product development process there is usually a point where a concept is formed but there is no tangible usable product that can be tested. The concept should be defined well enough so that it is communicable. There may be simply a verbal description, or it might include a rough idea of a name, package, and advertising approach. But the concept will not be developed fully into a product and marketing program. The role of marketing research at this stage is to determine if the concept warrants further development and to provide guidance as to how the concept might be improved and refined. Thus, research questions might include:

Are there any major flaws in the concept?

What segments might be attracted to it?

Is there enough interest to warrant developing it further?

How might it be altered or developed further?

There are approaches to concept testing that do not involve obtaining reactions from relevant people. One is to attempt to identify a set of similar products and to learn what the market response to them has been. Thus, a new crossword puzzle aid might be partly evaluated by determining the sales of similar products such as crossword puzzle dictionaries or of such complementary products as crossword puzzle magazines. If a variety of such products can be identified and their market performance determined, some insight into the potential success of the new product can be obtained.

Most concept testing, however, involves exposing people to the concept and getting their reactions. In exposing people to the concept, the market researcher needs to address a series of questions:

How are the concepts exposed?

To whom are the concepts exposed?

To what are they compared?

What questions are asked?

How Are the Concepts Exposed?

The researcher should be aware that the nature of the concept presentation can have a substantial influence on the respondent's reaction to the concept. The addition of a brand name or the inclusion of a visual demonstration to a verbal description can affect the results dramatically. In one experiment, eight different copywriters each prepared a copy statement for several different appeals.[3] The results showed significant variation in results across copywriters (more than across appeals) and illustrates rather graphically the sensitivity of the results to the presentation.

There always will be a trade-off between the timing of the concept test and the development of the marketing program. The whole point of concept testing is to determine if development of a marketing program is worthwhile. So it is not realistic to hold off concept testing until a marketing program exists. Still, there is always the danger that the reaction to a faulty concept presentation might be misleading. Greenhalgh suggests that

> The most practical approach would seem to be to build into the concept testing stage those elements (of the marketing program) which are necessary to convey the proposed new product idea adequately (bearing in mind its possible novelty and uniqueness) and seem likely to interact significantly. And to leave out those which, on judgment, are unlikely to interact to any significant extent. This would suggest that the concept test should often include:
>
> (a) the emotional aura surrounding the product, as well as its functional claims;
>
> (b) the creative execution up to a fairly advanced stage;
>
> (c) its expression in the chosen main medium;
>
> (d) and very possibly its proposed name, price, etc.[4]

Sid Heckler, a Young and Rubicam advertising executive, points out that a more complete presentation involving at least rough executions of advertisements will be needed

---

[3]Russell I. Haley and Roland Gatty, "The Trouble with Concept Testing," *Journal of Advertising Research* (June 1968), 23–35.

[4]Colin Greenhalgh, "Research for New Product Development," in Robert M. Worchester, ed., *Consumer Market Research Handbook* (London: McGraw-Hill, 1972), p. 388.

when an emotional appeal is involved.[5] (An example is an ice cream that makes any occasion fun.) In contrast, a simple verbal concept statement may be adequate for a rational appeal. (An example is a light, tasty ice cream that won't fill you up.)

Normally, the concept is exposed through personal contact, either in the respondent's home, office, or plant or in some central location like a shopping center. However, there have been efforts to avoid a personal interview. Market Facts, a research firm, did a study in which four products were exposed to controlled mail panel members (a group of people who have agreed to cooperate with the firm by regularly filling out mail questionnaires).[6] Colored prints of the products were used to communicate the concept. The reactions were somewhat more positive than in personal face-to-face data collected on the same products, but the relative rankings were very comparable. Another approach involves the exposure of the concept over cable television followed by telephone interviews. The approach will be dictated largely by the ability of the respondents to grasp the concept. If the concept is simple enough, such as a proposed new bus route, it might be possible to explain it verbally over the telephone.

To Whom Are the Concepts Exposed?

The respondents normally should include those who would be among the target segments. Since the goal of concept testing is to determine if a viable market exists, care should be taken to avoid omitting a potential segment from the study. It also is desirable to get opinions from those who will influence the purchase decision in addition to the user— particularly in industrial contexts.

When the concept is unique and quite different from those familiar to potential users, the respondents should be "experts" in a relevant area instead of potential users. For example, to evaluate the proposed crossword puzzle aid the opinions of editors of cross-word puzzle magazines or managers of game departments in department or specialty stores might be obtained. Retail store managers contacted in such a concept test indicated that the item would be most likely to be bought as a gift for crossword puzzle addicts by friends or relatives. This opinion altered substantially the concept (i.e., from a $1 item to a $5 gift item, and from direct-mail to specialty-shop distribution).

To What Are They Compared?

Usually several versions of a concept or several product concepts responsive to a user need will be explored in the same concept test. For example, in the mid 1960s Whirlpool engineers, in response to an identified need for a household garbage disposal system, tested four concepts: a disposable garbage can, a garbage compactor that would hold two

---

[5]Sid Hecker, "A Brain-Hemisphere Orientation toward Concept Testing," *Journal of Advertising Research, 21* (August 1981), 11, 55–60.
[6]Jack Abrams, "Reducing the Risk of New Product Marketing Strategies Testing," *Journal of Marketing Research, 6* (May 1969), 216–220.

weeks' worth of garbage, a built-in kitchen compactor, and a portable kitchen compactor.[7] The concept test showed the last two alternatives to be definitely superior.

Merging several concept alternatives into one test is not only efficient, but it tends to generate richer and more useful information. People can generate more perceptive comments when comparing alternatives than when only one is presented for evaluation. Further, the relative evaluations tend to be much more reliable than absolute evaluations. If possible, it is useful to include a ''concept'' reflecting an existing product (which could be marketed in another area), so that a real-world reference is involved. If a concept test has been applied many times with similar products, then norms can be developed that can serve the same functions. Without some point of comparison, however, it can be very risky to use the results to make absolute judgments.

What Questions Are Asked?

For the evaluative aspects of concept testing, it is necessary to include some overall indication of attitudes, interest, and likelihood of purchase. The purchase likelihood, for example, could be scales as:

Definitely Would Buy	Probably Would Buy	Might or Might Not Buy	Probably Would Not Buy	Definitely Would Not Buy

Again, caution is needed in interpreting the results absolutely, particularly when they are encouraging, since the exposure, even if presented in a relatively neutral way, will sensitize the respondent to the product. The result usually is an exaggerated tendency to indicate that a purchase would be likely. Further, it is often important to know not only if prospects are likely to buy the product but from which segments they are drawn. Some segments may be undesirable because they are already customers or because for some reason they are expensive to reach.

In addition to a general evaluation, there is generally a need for diagnostic information. Questions can be posed which determine

- The respondents comprehension of the product
- The perceived attributes
- The perceived advantages and disadvantages
- The situations in which it would be used
- The frequency of use
- Which products it might replace

One of the primary functions of a concept test is to help refine the product, determine how it should be positioned, and suggest aspects of the marketing program. It is rare that

[7]E. Patrick McGuire, *Evaluating New-Product Proposals* (New York: The Conference Board, 1973), p. 47.

the only (or even the dominant) purpose of the concept test is a go/no-go decision based upon intention-to-buy responses.

Greenhalgh discusses a technique that is designed to get some in-depth diagnostic information.[8] Termed ''word-of-mouth chains,'' it involves having successive informants communicate and discuss the concepts in their own words. The result can be new insights into the most promising appeals associated with the new concept.

The necessity of asking the right questions is illustrated by an experience of Kraft Foods.[9] They developed a flavored rice that was to compete with Rice-A-Roni varieties. The Kraft product did not require sautéeing and thus far outscored the competition on an ease-of-preparation scale in consumer tests and was equal on other relevant scales. Just before going into the test market, they decided to ask a few more questions of prospects regarding their frequency of product usage and their satisfaction with current brands. They found that almost half the flavored rice users prepared the dish less than once a month and that only about 11 percent felt that their existing brands were too difficult or too time consuming to prepare. As a result the product was not pursued.

Concept Testing: An Overview

It is unrealistic to expect a concept test to prove that the concept is sound or faulty or to demonstrate definitively how it should be altered. However, it should identify obvious failures, and, in the other cases, it should provide information to help make a judgment as to whether to proceed and should suggest some directions in the subsequent developmental phase. The goal of concept testing should be, in part, to avoid prematurely killing off promising ideas while at the same time avoiding bringing along ideas with little potential.

Concept testing is particularly important for durable goods and many industrial products because they rarely employ use testing or test markets[10] (the techniques of product evaluation). Neither the Sony Betamax videotape recorder nor the RCA SelectaVision video disc player were in test markets, although both used a regional roll-out that allowed some adjustment to the marketing program. The problem is that it is really not practical to develop or produce such equipment on a pilot basis. A major commitment is required and it would not be realistic economically to withdraw the product after a test market.

PRODUCT EVALUATION AND DEVELOPMENT

The process of product evaluation and development or product testing is very similar to that of concept testing, in terms of both the objectives and the techniques. The aim is still to predict market response to determine whether or not the product should be carried forward. There is still a need for diagnostic information to suggest modifications and

[8]Colin Greenhalgh, *op. cit.,* p. 391.
[9]''Kraft's Clark Urges Testing to Avoid Mistakes, 'Bombs','' *Advertising Age* (November 18, 1974), 22.
[10]Dylan Landis, ''Durable Goods Good for a Test?'' *Advertising Age* (February 9, 1981), 5–18.

specifics for the elements of the marketing program. Further, the same methodological questions have to be addressed in the product test context: How is the product to be exposed, to whom, to what is it to be compared, and on what questions will the test be based?

There are, however, at least two important differences. First, because the product and at least part of the marketing program have been developed, a more realistic product exposure plan can be undertaken. Thus, the results are potentially more valid and reliable than in the concept-testing situation, and the organization can therefore justify a more complete and elaborate test. Second, since the product is available, it is possible for respondents to try it to see if they like it and determine whether they would purchase it subsequently. Many products and programs are concerned not only with initial interest and trial usage but also with acceptance and repeat usage. A concept test is suited best to measuring initial interest. Some kind of usage test is needed to determine how the product will be accepted after it is tried. Some approaches to use testing will be described first. Then some methods for predicting trial purchase will be reviewed. Finally, the laboratory product test approach will be discussed.

Use Testing

The simplest form of use testing furnishes the product to the users and, after a reasonable amount of time, asks them their reactions to it, including their intentions to buy it. The respondents can be contacted in shopping centers, by personal visit to their homes or offices, or—initially—by telephone. Burlington Industries, producer of fabrics, calls randomly selected telephone numbers to locate adult females who make many of their own clothes and who would be willing to evaluate a new dress fabric.[11] The fabric then is sent by mail and a second telephone interview two months later solicits her description of her experience with it. Corning Glass Works, in order to control sample composition (particularly non-response problems) maintains a 1500-homemaker panel that helps in evaluating the company's new cooking utensils.[12] A subset of 200 homemakers usually participates in any particular evaluation. Many firms, particularly food and drug companies, use employee panels to evaluate the products. They have the advantage of being convenient, inexpensive, and capable of maintaining a high level of confidentiality.

For frequently purchased products or frequently used public policy programs it is often possible to go beyond asking respondents for their reaction and buying intentions and actually to give them the opportunity to buy the product. This process can be repeated so that the respondents have an opportunity to "repurchase the product" perhaps four or five times. The number of sales waves needed depends upon the length of time necessary to detect a stabilization of usage and purchase behavior and the emergence of boredom (especially with a product that has a fad characteristic and might not be able to maintain interest over time).

There are several problems associated with use tests. First, because of unclear in-

[11]McGuire, *op. cit.*, p. 58.
[12]*Ibid.*, p. 44.

structions, a misunderstanding, or lack of cooperation, respondents may not use the product correctly and may therefore report a negative opinion. Or they may not use it at all and simply fabricate an opinion. Second, the fact that they were given a free sample and are participating in a test may distort their impressions. Third, even when repurchase opportunities are made available, such decisions may be quite different than when they are made in a more realistic store situation with special displays presenting the new brand and those of its competitors. Fourth, there is the issue of the product's acceptance over a long time period. This problem is especially acute when repurchase data cannot be or are not obtained. Finally, there is the inflation of the intentions-to-buy question. In one study, consumers were given a product sample and asked 10 days later if they would buy the product.[13] Of the 48 people who said they probably would or definitely would buy and who were exposed to it in the store, only 35 percent actually bought.[14] If relative acceptance based upon paired comparison questions is involved, the reactions are often fairly reliable.

A particular type of use test is the **blind use test,** which is most appropriate just after the product emerges from the research-and-development laboratory. Even though a product may be proved superior in the laboratory, the consumer may not perceive it to be superior. For example, one consumer product company developed a window cleaner that was a definite improvement over existing products. The new product, however, was clear in color, whereas the existing products had a bluish tint. A blind use test, however, showed that consumers preferred the existing products. One hypothesis was that the blue color of the existing products was the reason consumers preferred them over the new, clear product. To test this hypothesis, a blind use test pitted the new product against blue-colored water. Over 30 percent of the respondents preferred the water. Thus, the color of the new window cleaner was identified as the problem in the blind use tests and was addressed in subsequent product development.

Predicting Trial Purchase

Hopefully, the product use test will provide an estimate of the repeat purchase rate of those who try the product. The analyst still needs an estimate of how many will try the new product or program to provide an estimate of ultimate sales or usage when the product is eventually launched.

Several models have been developed to predict trial levels of new, frequently purchased, consumer products.[15] The model termed ESP (Estimating Sales Potential) is typical.[16] Data from 45 new-product introductions were obtained and used to estimate the

[13]James W. Taylor, John J. Houlahan, and Alan C. Gabriel, ''The Purchase Intention Question in New Product Development: A Field Test,'' *Journal of Marketing, 40* (January 1975), 90–92.

[14]It should be noted that, although the question was biased, it still was predictive in that none of the 42 people who failed to indicate they would buy it actually bought it, even though they were exposed to it.

[15]Henry J. Claycamp and Lucien E. Liddy, ''Prediction of New Product Performance: An Analytical Approach,'' *Journal of Marketing Research, 6* (November 1969), 414–420; Gert Assmus, ''NEW-PROD: The Design and Implementation of a New Product Model,'' *Journal of Marketing, 39* (January 1975), 16–23.

[16]Gerald J. Eskin and John Malec, ''A Model for Estimating Sales Potential Prior to the Test Market,'' *1976 Educators Proceedings* (Chicago: American Marketing Association, 1976), pp. 230–233.

model. Trial levels (the percentage of a sample of consumers who had purchased the product at least once within 12 months after launch) were predicted on the basis of three variables:

Product class penetration (PCP)—the percentage of households purchasing at least one item in the product class within one year[17]

Promotional expenditures—total consumer-directed promotional expenditures on the product

Distribution of the product—percentage of stores stocking the product (weighted by the store's total sales volume)

Knowledge of these three variables enabled ESP to predict trial levels of the 45 new products extremely accurately (the regression model explained 95 percent of the variance with the three variables). Once the model is estimated it can be applied to other new products. The manager simply estimates the percentage of households using the product class, the total promotional expenditures planned for the new product, and the distribution level that is expected. The model will then estimate the trial level that will be obtained.

Trial also can be estimated directly using controlled shopping experience. A respondent is exposed to the new production promotion and allowed to shop in a simulated store or in an actual store in which the product is placed. The respondents then will have an opportunity to make a "trial" or first purchase of the product. An example of such an approach will be described in the context of a laboratory test market.

Laboratory Test Markets

An important tool for companies involved with frequently purchased consumer products is the laboratory test market. It is a mechanism that can be used to simulate an actual test market and can provide estimates of initial purchase and of ultimate repeat purchase rates. One such laboratory test market, termed ASSESSOR, will be described[18]

Table 23–1 shows an overview of the design.[19] The first step (O_1) is to intercept shoppers (normally about 300) in a shopping center and qualify them as members of the target segment of interest. The selected shoppers are then taken to a nearby laboratory facility location where they are asked to complete a questionnaire.

In the questionnaire (O_2), the respondents identify, by an unaided recall question, those brands in the product class of interest with which they are familiar. Brands that are considered both acceptable and unacceptable to them are included. They are then asked for their preference among the brands in their "response set." A constant-sum paired-

---

[17]In situations where no definition of the product class exists, a product appeal measure obtained from a concept test is used to estimate the size of the relevant product class for that particular product.

[18]Alvin J. Silk and Glen L. Urban, "Pre-Test-Market Evaluation of New Packaged Goods: A Model and Measurement Methodology," *Journal of Marketing Research, 15* (May 1978), 171–191.

[19]As discussed in Chapter 9, the symbols O_1, O_2, etc., refer to a measure or observation and X_1, X_2, etc., refer to experimental treatments.

TABLE 23–1

The ASSESSOR Laboratory Test Market Research Design and Measurement[a]

Design	Procedure	Measurement
O_1	Respondent screening and recruitment (personal interview).	Criteria for target group identification (e.g., product class usage).
O_2	Premeasurement for established brands (self-administered questionnaire).	Composition of "relevant set" of established brands, attribute weights and ratings, and preferences.
X_1	Exposure to advertising for established brands *and* new brand.	
$[O_3]$	Measurement of reactions to the advertising materials (self-administered questionnaire).	Optional, e.g., likability and believability ratings of advertising materials.
X_2	Simulated shopping trip and exposure to display of new and established brands.	
O_4 • • •	Purchase opportunity (choice recorded by research personnel).	Brand(s) purchased.
X_3 • •	Home use/consumption of new brand.	
O_5	Post-usage measurement (telephone interview).	New brand usage rate, satisfaction ratings, and repeat purchase propensity. Attribute ratings and preferences for "relevant set" of established brands plus the new brand.

SOURCE: Adapted from Alvin J. Silk and Glen L. Urban, "Pre-Test-Market Evaluation of New Packaged Goods: A Model and Measurement Methodology," *Journal of Marketing Research*, 15 (May 1978), 178.
*Note: O = measurement; X = advertising or product exposure.

comparison question is used to elicit preference. An example of such a question would be to ask a respondent to distribute 10 points among two brands in such a way as to reflect the respondent's relative preference between them. They also are asked to assign importance ratings to a set of attributes and their beliefs as to the extent to which each brand offers each attribute.

The third step (X_1) is to expose the respondents to a set of advertising materials for the new brand plus the leading established brands. Perhaps 5 or 6 commercials are included in the presentation.

The fourth step is a measure of reactions to the advertising (O_3). This step is optional and is included only if diagnostic information is desired. Obviously, the inclusion of this step, while potentially providing helpful information, will tend to increase their sensitivity to the advertising and therefore could distort somewhat the exposure to the product.

The fifth step is a visit to a simulated retail store where the new product is displayed along with a full set of competing brands. The respondents are given $2.00, which they can use to buy one of the products. In two studies involving antacids and deodorants, the proportions of respondents making a purchase were 64 and 74 percent, respectively. Respondents who do not purchase the new brand are given a quantity of the new brand free. Such a gift is intended to simulate a free sample.

The next observation, O_4, is a record of whether a brand was purchased and, if so, which brand. The final "experimental treatment," X_3, is the use of the product in the home.

The post-usage survey (O_5) is conducted by telephone. The respondents again are asked their brand preferences and their attribute beliefs and importance ratings, but this time the new brand is added to the brands in their "response set." Respondents are offered the opportunity to repurchase the new brand, which would be delivered by mail. If they choose not to repurchase the new brand, they are asked to indicate on a five-point scale what their buying intentions would be if the product were available in a store at a later date.

Two approaches are used to predict market share for the new brand. The first is based upon the preference judgments. The preference data are used to predict the proportion of purchases that a respondent will make of the new brand, given that the new brand is in her or his response set. These estimates for the respondents in the study are coupled with an estimate of the proportion of all people who will have the new brand in their response set to provide an estimate of market share. A useful byproduct of this approach is an analysis of the concomitant market share losses of the other brands. If the firm has other brands in the market, such information can be critical.

The second approach involves estimating trial and repeat purchase levels based upon the respondent's purchase decisions and intentions-to-buy judgments. The trial estimate is based upon the percentage of respondents who purchase the product in the laboratory plus an estimate of the product's distribution, advertising (which will create product awareness), and the number of free samples to be given away. The repeat purchase rate is based upon the proportion of respondents who make a mail-order repurchase of the new brand and the buying-intentions judgments of those who elected not to make a mail-order repurchase. The product of the trial estimate and the repeat purchase estimate becomes a second estimate of market share.

The method has a host of limiting assumptions and limitations, most of which are obvious. Perhaps the most critical assumption is that the preference data and purchase and repurchase decisions are valid predictors of what actually would happen in the marketplace. The artificiality of the product exposure and such surrogates for purchase decisions in the marketplace is a problem common to all laboratory approaches. In particular, the repurchase judgment made after the use experience does not reflect any in-store promotion. In one application of the model, the repeat purchase rate was grossly underestimated and the in-store promotion factor was cited as the probable reason.[20] Another problem is related to the convenience sampling approach and the fact that there will be attrition from the original sample (in one study, 16 percent of the respondents did not use the brand and another 16 percent could not be reached for the telephone interview).[21] The laboratory technique probably will work best when the product class is rather well established and defined and consumers can comprehend and make judgments about new products relatively easily.

Despite these limitations, laboratory test markets have been called "one of the biggest success stories in marketing research" by Edward Tauber, the editor of *Journal of Advertising Research* and a seasoned marketing research professional.[22] They have several attractive characteristics.

First, in comparison to test markets, they are fast, relatively cheap, confidential, and flexible. A basic ASSESSOR test can be conducted in three months with a cost that starts around $60,000 (most tests will compare alternative tactics and cost more), much less that test markets. The time and lack of confidentiality of test markets can be damaging. One firm developed a deodorant containing baking soda. A competitor spotted the product in test, rolled out its own version nationally before the first firm completed its test, and later successfully sued the product originator for copyright infringement.[23] Further, for a relatively modest incremental cost, a laboratory test market can evaluate alternative executions of elements in the marketing program such as packaging, price, advertising, product features, and location within the store. One such experiment found that a gravy base did 42 percent better when placed in the bouillon section instead of with the gravies.[24]

Second, the accuracy experience is impressive. Test market performance data were obtained for 44 products that had ASSESSOR estimates and the following results were obtained:[25]

1 The correlation between ASSESSOR and test market predictions was .95.

2 The average difference between ASSESSOR market share predictions and actual market share was .61 share points, indicating a small upward bias.

3 The average absolute difference between ASSESSOR share predictions and actual share achieved was 1.54 market share points, which is just over 20 percent of the

[20]Silk and Urban, *op. cit.*, 45.

[21]*Ibid.*, 12.

[22]Keven Higgens, "Simulated Test Marketing Winning Acceptance", *Marketing News* (March 1, 1985) 15.

[23]*Ibid.*

[24]Joel Robinson, "Simulated Test Marketing Reduced Risks," *Marketing News* (September 18, 1981) 3–4.

[25]Glen L. Urban and Gerald M. Katz, "Pre-Test-Market Models: Validation and Managerial Implications" *Journal of Marketing Research 20* (August, 1983) 221–34.

average test market share of 7.16. It was slightly lower for 13 health and beauty aid products and slightly higher for 20 food products.

4 The marketing plan and market conditions can change between the ASSESSOR reading and the test market or during the test market. If the ASSESSOR forecast was adjusted with respect to awareness achieved, distribution, and sampling to reflect such changes, the average absolute difference was reduced to .88 of a share point and the average difference was reduced to zero.

5 About 65 percent of the 27 cases in the sample that ASSESSOR deemed successful were considered a success. In contrast, all six products for which ASSESSOR forecasted failure were judged to be big failures in the test market.

Another laboratory test market (COMP) reported average differences, estimated from actual, of only .125 (or 1.5 percent of market share) for eight brands.[26]

The number of new product introductions is large and growing. New products introduced into food and drugstores, for example, has grown from 1268 in 1980 to 1510 in 1982 to 1988 in 1984.[27] It is understandable why the laboratory test market has been successful.

TEST MARKETING

In terms of providing a realistic evaluation of a marketing program, there is no substitute for conducting an experiment in which the marketing program (or perhaps several versions of it) are implemented in a limited but carefully selected part of the market. The impact of the total marketing program, with all its interdependencies, is determined then in the market context as opposed to the artificial context associated with the concept and product tests that have been discussed.

There are two primary functions of test marketing. The first is to gain information and experience with the marketing program before making a total commitment to it. The second is to predict the program's outcome when it is applied to the total market.

The test market fulfills the first function by being a pilot operation for the marketing program, just as a pilot production facility might serve to debug a manufacturing process. There are all sorts of possible and unanticipated problems associated with a marketing program. The physical problems of transportation, handling, stocking, and shelf life, for example, can generate difficulties. One prominent manufacturer tested a small compact box of facial tissues and found that, in the South, the tissues absorbed dampness and caused some boxes to explode after being on the shelf for a month. Clearly, without such

---

[26]*Ibid.*, p. 221.
[27]Laurie Freeman, "Battle for Shelf Space" *Advertising Age* (February 28, 1985) 16.

"I can't remember the brand name, but it has a commercial with a lot of people running in all directions."

© Ned Hilton/Consumer Reports.

a test the manufacturer might have gone national immediately, with disastrous consequences. It was only by actually having the product on the shelf for a month that the problem was uncovered. When the goal of the test market is to try out the marketing program and when prediction is not required, it is not so necessary to develop elaborate experimental designs, although there should be some concern that the test is general enough to expose problems. Thus, if the tissue manufacturer had not bothered to test the program in the South, the problem with the dampness would not have been uncovered.

The second function of a test market is to predict the outcome of the market program when it is applied to the total market. Although the test market does provide a realistic test of the impact of a marketing program, it also has a variety of methodological problems associated with it that make prediction difficult, as we shall see. As a result, the ability of test markets to predict is much less than one would expect.

There are really two types of test markets, the sell-in test market and the controlled-distribution scanner markets. The sell-in test markets are cities in which the product is sold in just as it would be in a national launch. In particular, the product has to gain distribution space. The controlled-distribution scanner markets are cities for which distribution is prearranged and the purchases of a panel of customers are monitored using scanner data. First we will discuss the design of sell-in market tests.

Designing the Sell-In Market Test[28]

The market test design involves several elements. First, the test cities need to be selected. Second, the market programs need to be implemented and controlled in each city. Third, the length of the test market must be established. Finally, a set of measures must be devised to evaluate the program.

Selecting the Test Cities.   City characteristics that are usually relevant in the selection of cities to use in the test market include:

1   **Representativeness.** Ideally the city should be fairly representative of the country in terms of characteristics that will affect the test outcome, such as product usage, attitudes, and demographics. Of course, the results can be adjusted to compensate for differences that are well known, if their impact upon sales can be estimated. For example, southerners use more biscuits, teenagers drink more soda, older people have more use for pharmaceutical products, and some towns have harder water (which could affect a bath soap test).

2   **Data availability.** It often is helpful to use store audit information to evaluate the test, as it provides sales data adjusted for inventory changes and gives other useful information such as shelf facings and in-store promotions. If so, it would be important to use cities containing retailers who will cooperate with store audits.

3   **Media isolation and costs.** Its desirable to avoid media spill over. Media that "spill out" into nearby cities is wasteful and increases costs. Conversely, "spill in" media from nearby cities can contaminate a test. Media cost is another consideration. Some media begin to charge exorbitant rates when they know they are in popular test markets.

4   **Product flow.** It may be desirable to use cities that don't have much "product spillage" outside the area.

Table 23–2 lists cities that are on the recommended list of Dancer Fitzgerald Sample, Inc. (DFS). DFS revises the list periodically, dropping and adding cities, reflecting changes in unemployment rates, media costs, overusage as a test market, and other factors.

Another issue is the number of test cities to use. A survey of 28 major consumer grocery and drug product companies found that the "norm" was to run a test market in three areas for one year.[29] However, Achenbaum recommends that, for a consumer product test market that is to be projected nationally, a large number of randomly dispersed markets covering over 20 percent of the entire United States is needed to achieve meaningfully

---

[28]This section draws upon the excellent overview of market testing by Alvin A. Achenbaum entitled, "Market Testing: Using the Marketplace as a Laboratory," in Robert Ferber, ed., *Handbook of Marketing Research* (New York: McGraw-Hill 1974), pp. 4–31 to 4–54.

[29]Jack J. Honomichl, "Test Marketing Practices Are Documented in Private Survey," *Advertising Age, 43* (April 10, 1972), 10.

TABLE 23–2
Recommended Test Markets

Boise	Green Bay	Phoenix
Buffalo	Indianapolis	Pittsburgh
Charlotte	Kansas City	Portland
Chattanooga	Knoxville	Roanoke-Lynchburg
Cincinnati	Lexington	Rochester
Cleveland	Little Rock	St. Louis
Columbus	Louisville	Salt Lake City
Des Moines	Minneapolis	Seattle-Tacoma
Erie	Milwaukee	South Bend-Elkhart
Evansville	Nashville	Spokane
Fargo	Oklahoma City	Syracuse
Fort Wayne	Omaha	Tulsa

SOURCE: Taken from a list of 49 markets recommended for new product testing by Dancer Fitzgerald Sample Inc. as reported in Keven Higgens, "Simulated Test Marketing Winning Acceptance", *Marketing News,* (March 1, 1985) 15.

precise predictions.[30] His judgment is extreme, but it reflects the reality that the market share and sales for most products vary enormously from city to city. Thus, there will be uncertainty in extrapolating from a test of one or even a few test cities. In fact, the ability of test markets to project national results is not nearly as strong as one would like. In a study by the A. C. Nielsen Company, the first-year national market share positions of 50 new brands were compared with their test market performance; the study concluded that the odds are about 50–50 that the national performance will match test results within a plus-or-minus 10 percent.[31]

Implementing and Controlling the Test. A second consideration is to control the test by insuring that the marketing program is implemented in the test area so as to reflect the national program. This step is not as easy as it may sound. A national program may not be defined precisely enough or it may not decompose easily to the local level. A national advertising budget, for example, may not be easy to allocate to a local level or it may not be well defined in terms of exactly how the television coverage is to be scheduled.

The test itself may tend to encourage those involved to enhance the effectiveness of the marketing program. Salespeople may be more aggressive in obtaining distribution. Retailers may be more cooperative than usual because they are told it is an "interesting and important test market." Those implementing a test public policy program may be more motivated and involved than could be expected when the program goes "national."

[30]Achenbaum, *op. cit.,* p. 4–46.
[31]Nielsen Marketing Service, "To Test or Not to Test," *The Nielsen Researcher, 30*:4 (1972), 3–8.

Considerable discipline must be applied to insure that the marketing program is applied as intended.

There is also the reaction of competitors. At one extreme they can destroy the test by deliberately flooding the test areas with free samples or in-store promotions. More likely, however, they will experiment with retaliatory actions and monitor the results themselves. The question is: What impact will their actions have on the results? Even if they do nothing, there is a concern with how the results will change when the program goes national and they *do* react. Each test market should be monitored carefully so that competitive reactions and other relevant market parameters are tracked over time and their impact on the market response detected.

Timing. A third consideration is timing. If possible, a test market normally should be in existence for one year. Even after a year has passed, if the program goes national, the test market should continue to be monitored to detect the impact of changes in the environment. An extended time period is needed for several reasons. First, there are often important seasonal factors that can be observed only if the test is continued for the whole year. Second, initial interest is often a poor predictor of a program's staying power. There is usually a fatigue factor that sometimes can take a long time to materialize. Cereal with dried fruit is one product that did very well during a short test but fizzled later because customers tired of it. Third, it is useful to allow the competition and other market factors to adjust to see what impact they will have on the results. An analysis of 141 test markets by the A. C. Nielsen Company indicated that, after the first six months of testing, the chance of adequately predicting market share at the end of 12 to 18 months is only one in two, but this rises to about two in three after eight months.[32]

Measurement. A crucial element of the test market is the measure used to evaluate it. A basic measure is sales based upon shipments or warehouse withdrawals. One problem with such information is that inventory fluctuations can distort this measurement, and it is not a very sensitive measure of consumer response.

Store audit data provide actual sales figures and are not sensitive to inventory fluctuations. They also provide variables such as distribution, shelf facings, and in-store promotional activity. Knowledge of such variables can be important in evaluating the marketing program and in interpreting the sales data.

Measures such as brand awareness, attitude, trial purchase, and repeat purchase are obtained directly from the consumer, either from surveys or consumer panels. Such variables as brand awareness and attitude also serve as criteria for evaluating the marketing program and can help interpret sales data. The most useful information obtained from consumers, however, is whether they bought the product at least once, whether they were satisfied with it, and have either repurchased it or plan to.

There is also the potential to project the levels of awareness, trial rates, and repeat

[32]John Davis, "Market Testing and Experimentation," in Robert M. Worchester, ed., *Consumer Market Research Handbook* (London: McGraw-Hill, 1972), p. 494.

purchase rates that will be achieved by a new product in a test market using survey data from the first three or so months of the test. A series of surveys would be conducted starting just prior to the test market launch. BBDO has developed a set of models termed the NEWS/Market system to do just that.[33]

In the NEWS/Market system, the surveys monitor new product awareness (aided and unaided recall), receipt and use of samples or coupons, trial purchases, and repeat purchases. Advertising and promotion expenditures are also monitored. Some relationships such as the drop in awareness among those not reexposed to the advertising, are estimated from prior research on other products. Of 34 NEWS/Market projections for which an ultimate test market share or sales were available, the average predictive error was 17.5 percent of the actual market share achieved. In 90 percent of the cases the prediction was within one share point, and in 70 percent of the time it was within 1.5 share points.

Predicting share from panel data will be discussed under controlled distribution scanner test markets because panel data is readily available in that context. The early prediction of test market results is important because it provides the potential to reduce the cost and time associated with test markets.

Cost of a Test Market

In making cost-benefit judgments about test markets, it is important to determine the costs accurately. Many of the costs associated with test marketing naturally are related to the number of areas used and their dispersion. A major cost is the development and implementation of the marketing program. Since a test market is an application of the marketing program, the marketing effort—including packaging, displays, promotion, and so on—must be completed. Further, the costs of implementing the program may not be covered by profits associated with it, since the product often will be produced and distributed in an inefficient manner. Another significant cost is the cost of providing the measures needed to evaluate the program. Information gained from direct consumer panels or surveys is the costliest approach. Still another cost is associated with pulling out of tests that prove unsuccessful.

There are also several costs that often are not associated with the number of test areas. One is the cost of planning and administering the test and analyzing the results. The key element to this cost is the management time that otherwise might be spent on other areas of operation. Another is the loss of confidentiality. A test market runs the real risk that a competitor will monitor the results and, if they seem positive, will be able to come to market first—perhaps even improving on the marketing program.

A test market can cost from \$1 to \$4 million or more, depending on the number of areas used and the other associated costs. Further, a study conducted by the A. C. Nielsen Company reported that only about one-half of 300 new brands that went into test markets

---

[33]Lewis G. Pringle, R. Dale Wilson, and Edward I. Brody, "NEWS: A Decision Oriented Model for New Product Analysis and Forecasting", *Marketing Science 1* (Winter, 1982) 1–30.

(103 test markets in 1961 and 204 in 1971 were studied) ultimately were launched nationally.[34]

There are several ways to react to the high cost of a test market. One is to fully use alternatives such as laboratory test markets and controlled-distribution scanner markets before committing to a test market. Another is to bypass a test market. Some companies like Philip Morris bypass test markets as a matter of policy. Their low-tar Merit cigarettes were introduced successfully in 1976 with a $40 million promotional effort but no market test.[35] Two years earlier they reached the market with the 120mm Saratoga on the same day as their competitor's More by skipping the test market. However, not all decisions to bypass a market test have been as successful. The Brown-Forman Distillers spent nearly $500,000 conducting concept and product tests launching their Frost 8/80, a "dry white whisky," without a test market.[36] The product flopped, costing the company about $2 million dollars. The public apparently was confused by the product and did not know how to use it; in the product-test situation, this confusion did not seem to surface.

Controlled-Distribution Scanner Markets

The characteristics of controlled-distribution scanner markets (CDSM) such as IRI's BehaviorScan, Nielsen's Testsight and Burke's ScanAmerica, have already been described in Chapter 4 and in Chapter 21 (where they were termed split-cable testing). Basically they tap into the retail distribution system collecting data on all the grocery store purchases and a growing amount of drug and other retail store types. They are here termed controlled distribution because they have agreements with the retailers to allow new products under test to have access to shelf space. An important feature is that a consumer panel is maintained of around 3000 people whose purchase activity is monitored.

CDSMs have four major advantages over test markets. First, they are less expensive. Although it is difficult to generalize, they are probably from one-sixth to one-third of the cost of a full test market. Second, there is the potential to do more experimenting with marketing variables in a CDSM. The advertising seen by panel members is controllable. Further, the in-store activities such as promotions and pricing is under more control than it would be in a sell-in test market. Third, the scanner based data is probably more accurate, timely and complete than that generally available in a sell-in test market. Fourth, there is the potential to provide accurate early estimates of the test market results using the consumer panel information.

The most obvious disadvantages of a CDSM is that it provides no test of the products ability to gain shelf space, special displays, in-store promotions, and so on. Since gaining distribution can be a crucial issue for some products, leaving it unaddressed can be

[34]Nielsen Marketing Service, "New Brand or Superbrand?" *The Nielsen Researcher*, 29:5 (1971), 4–10.

[35]"Philip Morris: The Hot Hands in Cigarettes," *Business Week* (December 6, 1976), 60–64.

[36]"An Untimely End: How a New Product Was Brought to Market Only to Flop Miserably," *The Wall Street Journal* (January 5, 1973), 1.

troublesome. Of course, many distribution problems may not surface in a few sell-in test markets.

Another major CDSM disadvantage is the limited choice of test cities. Several questions arise. Are the available test cities (i.e., IRI has four pairs of cities including Midland, Texas and Eau Claire, Wisconsin; and Nielsen has two cities including Sioux Falls, South Dakota) have adequate projectability for a particular product? Typically one or two cities are used. Is that adequate? Do the residents of these cities particularly the panel members become so exposed to new products that their reaction begins to differ from those in cities not associated with a CDSM system?

Projecting Trial, Repeat and Usage Rate Using Panel Data. The most accurate way to project trial and repeat purchase in a test market is by using panel data where the purchase and repurchase decisions of individual consumers can be monitored.

To estimate the ultimate trial level the percent of product class buyers who will try the new brand at least once is monitored over time. Figure 23–2 provides a graph of the trial rate for a new toilet soap (Brand T) by four week periods starting from the launch data. The projection could be made by observation but is normally based on some function such as those described in Chapter 22.

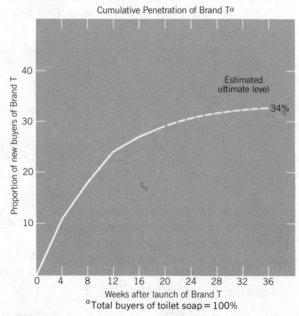

FIGURE 23–2

Source: Adapted from J. H. Parfitt and B. J. Collins, "Use of Consumer Panels for Brand Shave Predictions," *Journal of Marketing Research* 5 (May, 1968) 132.

Each person who tries the new product is then monitored and the time between the first (trial) purchase and second purchase is noted. The percent of new product triers who rebuy the product (the repeat rate), is plotted against the time between the first and second purchase and projected. Figure 23–3 illustrates.

The market share estimate is thus the product of the two projections. In the example illustrated by the figures it would be .34 times .25 (which equals .085) or a market share projection of 8.5 percent.

There are a number of refinements that can be made to this basic approach:

1 Sales will depend upon usage levels as well as market shares. If the initial buyers on average are heavy product users the estimate could be adjusted.

2 For some product classes (snack foods or cereals, for example) new brands may gain one or even two repeat purchases only to have customers lose interest in them. In those cases, it is important to not only estimate first repeat, but to also estimate second repeat (the percent of those buying the new brand twice that buy it a third time) and even third and fourth repeat.

3 Accuracy can often be enhanced, if repeat is estimated separately for those who try the brand early in the test from those that try it later. Early triers are generally more enthusiastic about a new brand and tend to have higher repeat rates.

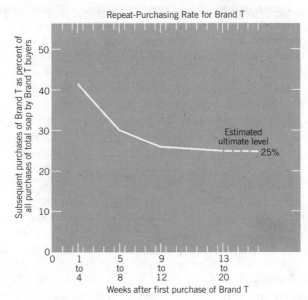

FIGURE 23–3

Source: Adapted from J. H. Parfitt and B. J. Collins, "Use of Consumer Panels for Brand Shave Predictions," *Journal of Marketing Research 5* (May, 1968) 133.

4 If there is no well defined product class, trial rates are defined as the total number of triers instead of the percent of product class users who try the new brand. An analysis similar to that illustrated in Figure 23–2 is still used.

Market share and sales projections made using this modeling logic can be very accurate as the experience of Parfitt and Collins illustrate.[37] They predicted the market shares of 24 successful, new, frequently purchased consumer products. In all 24 cases, their predicted market share, made 24 weeks after launch, was within the highest and lowest actual monthly market share encountered between months 12 and 18 after launch. Projections of trial and repeat have obvious diagnostic value. Weakness in achieving trial is usually due to a problem with the introduction effort, whereas low repeat usually signals a basic product problem.

SUMMARY

The first stage in new-product research is concept generation, which involves research first to identify needs and second to identify concepts that will be responsive to those needs.

The second stage is concept evaluation and development, getting relevant people's reactions to concepts. The purpose is usually to help make a judgment as to whether to proceed and to suggest some directions in the subsequent development phase. The exposure is based upon a concept description, which should include the elements of the marketing program (such as price) that are critical to concept acceptance.

The third stage is product evaluation and development, where a more realistic product exposure is possible because the product and much of the marketing program have been developed. In particular, the product will be available for use tests, where potential customers try it and provide reactions. Such use tests are used to predict product acceptance and repeat purchase. To predict trial, the laboratory test market, where respondents are exposed to the product and then given the opportunity to make a trial purchase in a simulated supermarket, can be used.

The fourth stage is the test market, where the product and the marketing program actually are implemented in the field. In a sell-in test market the product is sold just as it would be in a national launch. In designing a sell-in test market, the number and identity of test cities, the length of the test, and the criterion measures all need to be specified. In a controlled-distribution scanner market (CDSM) test, distribution is prearranged and purchases are monitored using scanner data. Using CDSM markets is cheaper, allows more experimentation, and provides scanner data for a panel of consumers that allows accurate projections of trial and repeat rates. It does not provide realistic tests of the ability

[37]J. H. Parfitt and B. J. K. Collins, "Use of Consumer Panels for Brand Share Prediction", *Journal of Marketing Research 5* (May, 1968) 131–45.

of the new brand to gain distribution and retailer support of the introduction, and is restricted to the established CDSM test cities.

QUESTIONS AND PROBLEMS

1 Develop a research design to provide a demand estimate for the following new products:

     a A plastic disposable toothbrush that comes in a cylinder 5/8 in. in diameter and 3 in. in length. Its unique, patented quality is that the toothpaste already has been applied.

     b A lemon condiment. Lemon enhances the flavor of many foods, including corn-on-the-cob, fish, and melons. The lemon condiment would be in a crystallized form that would capture the essence of lemon and be served in a "lemon shaker" that would complement the salt and pepper shakers.

     c A clear plastic umbrella attachment for bicycles, which folds away behind the handlebars when not in use.

     d A vibrator secretarial chair which contains a gentle vibrator device designed to provide relaxation and blood circulation for people who must sit for long periods of time.

     e A battery-powered, two-passenger automobile with a top speed of 40 mph and a range of 120 miles.

2 In benefit structure analysis 500 or so respondents are asked to react to a large number (75–100) of specific product benefits and to many product characteristics. The reactions are in terms of both the desire for and perceived deficiencies (of current brands) with respect to each benefit and characteristic. The focus is upon a specific use occasion. For example, if a household cleaner were involved the respondent would focus upon a single cleaning occasion. The brand used also would be asked. How would you generate the list of benefits and product characteristics? Develop a sampling plan. What data analysis would you conduct?

3 In evaluating a new product idea, what criteria should be used? What role should marketing research play in evaluating the idea against each of the criteria?

4 How would you find a name for a new brand of soda that is a new "natural drink" made out of carbonated apple juice with some ginger and lemon added? For a new bank verification card?

5 Identify five new products. Consider a concept test for each. Which could be exposed via a mail questionnaire? Via a phone interview? Via cable television? Which, if any, of these products would you take directly to market, bypassing a test market? Why?

6 How can the bias of a purchase-intention question in a concept test be measured?

7 What are the key assumptions of the laboratory test market? What improvements could you make in the laboratory test market to improve its validity?

8 The laboratory test market has been extremely important in testing new packaged goods products. Design a comparable system for services like financial or health care services and for durables such as cars or video tape players.

9 Compare and contrast the controlled-distribution scanner markets with sell-in test markets. What are the advantages and disadvantages of each? When would you want to use a sell-in test market?

CASE 23–1
Brown Microwave

Brown Microwave was one of the leaders in the area of microwave ovens for the home, with about 15 percent of the market in 1977. Although microwave cooking had been around for many years, its use in homes was in a major growth stage.

Brown was considering two new cabinet designs for their 1979 line of countertop microwave cookers. Both represented a sharp departure from the modern chrome designs that had been available from Brown and its competitors. One was an "early American" design and the other was made out of heavy dark wood and was more of a Mediterranean design. The concept was to add charm, warmth, and style to a product that had a "chrome-computer" image. The new design would add about 15 to 20 percent to the price of the unit.

The new designs would have to provide a net increase of Brown's sales of 15 to 20 percent to be considered worthwhile. There would be a substantial investment required to produce them, and their introduction would require a large percentage of the marketing budget and sales effort.

Before committing the company to one or both of these designs, a product test was proposed. The concept was to modify a large van so that half of it would simulate three kitchen segments. The segments would differ in the type of paneling and cabinets used. One

was dark, Mediterranean in appearance, another was light-oak "early American," and the third had a contemporary look. In this setting five countertop microwave ovens were displayed: Two were competitive models, one was the existing Brown design, and the remaining two were the proposed Brown designs. Each had very comparable features and specifications. The major difference was the cabinet.

The plan was to bring the van into five cities throughout the Eastern United States and in each city to recruit 100 women. The women would be recruited from shopping areas near or connected to office buildings. The hope was to obtain a reasonable number (like 25 percent of the sample) of working women who would be on a lunch break or would be shopping after work. The women would be asked to help evaluate some new kitchen appliances. A gift was promised for participants. The cities would be selected from cities frequently used as test markets.

Each woman would be shown each of the five models. The common performance capabilities would be explained, but it would be emphasized that the major difference was appearance and price. The price of each would be noted on an attached sign. After the women saw the five models, they would be asked to indicate their first, second, and third choices, assuming they were buying such an appliance now. The following information also would be obtained regarding the respondents' status prior to exposure to the new models:

1 Did the respondents own a microwave oven?

2 If so, what type and make?

3 If not, were they familiar with microwaves and did they plan to purchase one during the next year?

After exposure to the new models:

1 What were their intentions of buying a microwave oven during the next year?

2 What were their age, education, income, and family size?

3 Size of home or apartment? Rent or own?

4 Occupation?

5 What type of outlet would they go to if they were considering buying a microwave oven?

Assignment

Evaluate the research design. Would you make any changes? Plan a data analysis strategy.

CASE 23-2
National Chemical Corporation (B)

The Tiger-Tread spray product designed to free cars stuck in ice or snow had been delayed due to problems with packaging. In the summer of 1980, the problems were solved and the product was ready to go. There were, however, a host of basic decisions that needed to be made, and Charley Omsrud was considering the value of delaying a national introduction of the product and running a test market.

One issue involved the amount of production capacity to plan both for the 5-ounce can (good for two or three use occasions) and the 10-ounce can (good for four to six use occasions). Although the 200 people from the Toledo lab that tried product samples did not seem to have problems using it, there was always the lingering concern that unanticipated product problems could materialize in a broader test.

An issue that had recently emerged is whether the market should be restricted to fleets of cars. A colleague

of Charley Omsrud, the marketing manager, had observed that for every fleet car there was well over ten other potential customers. If a consumer effort were mounted the nature of the marketing program needed to be decided. In the test market used in 1970, extensive advertising and distribution was obtained. Charley felt that a middle course might make sense. His idea was to distribute the product through service stations and support it with point-of-purchase display stands and brochures. After all, the consumer did rely upon the service station to provide antifreeze and other winterization services.

Charley was evaluating a proposal from a local marketing research firm to conduct a test market through the coming winter in a snow-belt city of around two million. The plan was to reach fleet owners with their existing sales force and to reach individual car owners through service stations supported by point-of-purchase advertising. The cost would be $50,000 for running the test and evaluating the results. Among the outputs would be:

The percentage of households that:

were aware of the product

purchased the product

made a repeat purchase.

The number and size of fleets that:

were aware of the product

were aware but did not order the product

ordered the product

ordered the product and made repeat purchases.

The type and incidence of any product problem.

QUESTIONS FOR DISCUSSION

1 What will be learned from the test?

2 What would you add or change about the test?

3 What else would you like to know before making a decision about the test?

CASE 23-3

U.S. Department of Energy (B)

The U.S. Department of Energy wanted to determine public attitudes toward six different windmill designs, including the familiar old Dutch windmill design and more futuristic designs such as the Darrieus (eggbeater) design. One proposal was to expose 300 adult respondents to slides of the six designs. Each design was to be shown in three different scenes, a flat-land setting, a setting of hills, and a shore setting. The respondents were to be recruited from six locations, one of which was near a large working windmill.

QUESTIONS FOR DISCUSSION

1 Evaluate the research design. How would you select the cities and recruit the respondents?

2 How would you have them evaluate the six designs (actually the 18 different slides).

3 Would you use an evaluative scale or a paired or triad comparison?

GLOSSARY

Accuracy a criterion used to judge whether a market research study is logical and presents correct information.

Additive Causal Relationship a causal relationship in which the causal effects of two variables upon a third variable are added.

Affective/Feeling/Liking Component that part of attitude representing the person's overall feelings of liking or disliking for the object, person, or event.

Aided Recall a questioning approach that attempts to stimulate a respondent's memory with clues about an object of interest.

Analysis of Dependence a multivariate analysis where one or more variables are predicted or explained by other variables.

Analysis of Interdependence a multivariate analysis where the interrelationships within a set of variables are examined and no variable is seen to be a dependent variable.

Analysis of Value an estimate of the benefits gained by undertaking a market research study.

Analysis of Variance (ANOVA) a method of testing a hypothesis regarding the difference between several means.

Associative Scaling a scale in which the respondent is asked to associate alternatives with each question.

Attitudes mental states used by individuals to structure the way they perceive their environment and to guide the way in which they respond. A psychological construct comprised of cognitive, affective, and intention components.

Attribute a characteristic or property of an object or person

Attribute Judgment the judgment an individual makes about the numerous characteristics or attributes that are possessed by an object.

Automatic Interaction Detection (AID) a technique for finding interactions in a sample by using nominally scaled independent variables to find subgroups that differ with respect to a dependent variable.

Bar Graph a graph of bars whose length indicates relative amounts of the variable.

Before Measure Effect the alerting of respondents to the fact that they are being studied, due to the presentation of a before measure, causing unnatural responses.

Behavior the past and present overt reponses of subjects.

Behavior Recording Device a mechanical observation method, such as a traffic counter, that continuously monitors behavior, usually unobtrusively.

Benefit Segmentation a type of market segmentation based on the benefits that people seek from products.

Bipolar Scale a scale bounded at each end by polar adjectives that are antonyms.

Blind Use Test a use test where consumers are asked to evaluate product alternatives without being aware of brand names.

Bottom-Up Measurement a method of determining market potential that has as its starting point the identification of product use situations or applications.

Case Study a comprehensive description and analysis of a single situation.

Causal Relationship a precondition influencing a variable of interest, or, more strictly, a change in one variable that produces a change in another variable.

Causal Research research having very specific hypotheses that is usually designed to provide the ultimate level of understanding—a knowledge that one construct under certain conditions causes another construct to occur or to change.

Census Tract a group of city blocks having a total population of more than 4000 and generally used to approximate neighborhoods.

Chi-Square Statistic a measure of association between two nominally scaled variables.

City Block the smallest identifiable unit in the U.S. Census, being bounded by four streets or some other physical boundary.

Classification Variables variables used to classify respondents, such as demographic and socio-economic measures.

Close-Response/Structured Question a question accompanied by the presentation of responses to be considered by the respondent.

Cluster Analysis a set of techniques for grouping objects or persons in terms of similarity.

Cluster Sampling a sampling method where a random sample of subgroups is selected and all members of the subgroups become part of the sample.

Clutter/Awareness the percent who recalled a brand was advertised when exposed in a "clutter" of 7 ads in a McCollum/Speilman test.

Coding the categorization and numbering of responses.

Cognitive/Knowledge/Awareness Component that part of attitude representing a person's information about an object, person, or event.

Communality the proportion of a variable's variance explained by all of the factors in a factor analysis solution.

Compensatory Model any multiattribute model in which one attribute compensates for another in the overall preference for an object.

Completion Test a projective technique in which the respondent is asked to complete a series of sentences.

Compositional Approach an attitude measurement approach in which the overall preference judgment for each object is obtained by summing the evaluative rating of each attribute times the importance of that attribute.

Computer-Retrievable Data Bases secondary records accessible by a computer system.

Concept Test a test of a product concept where the concept is evaluated by a sample of the target segment.

Concurrent Validity criterion validity that is established by correlating the measurement score with the criterion variable, both measured at the same time.

Conjoint/Trade-Off Analysis a method of obtaining the relative worth or value of each level of several attributes from rank-ordered preferences of attribute combinations.

Consideration/Evoked Set all the alternatives that potential buyers would consider in their next purchase of the product or service.

Constant Sum Scale a scale in which the respondent must allocate a fixed number of points among several objects to reflect the relative preference for each object.

Construct a concept, usually psychological such as attitudes and values, that is not directly observable.

Construct Validity the ability of a measurement instrument to measure a concept or "construct"; generally, construct validity is demonstrated by showing both convergent and discriminant validity.

Controlled Distribution Scanner Markets (CDSM) distribution for new product test is prearranged and results are monitored with scanner data.

Contingency Coefficient a chi-square statistic corrected for sample size.

Continuous Purchase Panel a fixed sample of respondents who are measured on several occasions over a period of time.

Contrived Observation an observation method in which people are placed in a contrived situation so that their responses will reveal some aspects of their underlying beliefs, attitudes, and motives; examples are tests of variation in shelf-space, product flavors, and display locations.

Convenience Sampling   a sampling method in which convenient sampling units are contacted, such as church activity groups or student classes.

Convergent Validity   the ability of a measurement instrument to correlate or "converge" with other supposed measures of the same variable or construct; the opposite of discriminant validity.

Correlation   a number between $+1$ and -1 that reflects the degree to which two variables have a linear relationship.

Criterion/Empirical Validity   the validity of a measurement instrument as determined by empirical evidence that correlates the measurement instrument with other "criterion" variables.

Cross-Tabulation/Contingency Table Analysis   the determination of a frequency distribution for subgroups.

Data   unassimilated facts about the market.

DAR (day-after-recall)   the percent of the audience who can recall something specific about the commercial the next day.

Decompositional Approach   attitude measurement approach in which the utilities of each attribute are obtained from the overall preference judgment for each object.

Delphi   a group judgment method where each member makes an individual judgment and then each member is given an opportunity to revise his/her judgment after seeing the others' initial judgments, until, after several iterations, the group members reach their conclusion.

Descriptive Research   research that usually is designed to provide a summary of some aspects of the environment when the hypotheses are tentative and speculative in nature.

Direct Observation   an observation method in which the researcher directly observes the person or behavior in question.

Discriminant Analysis   a statistical method for developing a set of independent variables to classify people or objects into one or more groups.

Discriminant Function   the linear combination of variables developed by discriminant analysis for the purpose of classifying people or objects into one or more groups.

Discriminant Validity   the ability of a measurement instrument to not correlate with supposed measures of other variables or constructs; the opposite of convergent validity.

Drop-Off Approach   the hand delivery of a questionnaire to sampling points.

Dummy Variable   a variable taking on the values of either 0 or 1, which is used to denote characteristics that are not quantifiable.

Efficiency   a criterion used to judge whether a market research study produces the maximum amount and quality of information for the minimum expenditure of time and money.

Expected Value   the value obtained by multiplying each consequence by the probability of that consequence occurring and summing the products.

Experimental Control   the control of extraneous variables through experimental procedures such as randomization or block designs.

Experiments   studies that require the intervention by the observer beyond that required for measurement.

Exploratory Research   research that usually is designed to generate ideas when the hypotheses are vague or ill-defined.

Exponential Smoothing   in time-series extrapolations, the weighting of historical data so that the more recent data are weighted more heavily than are less recent data, by exponentially decreasing sets of weights.

External Source   a marketing data source found outside of the organization.

External Validity   the applicability of experimental results to situations external to the actual experimental context.

F-Statistics   the statistic used in the analysis of variance to test for differences in groups.

Face/Consensus Validity   the validity of a measurement instrument as determined entirely by subjective argument or judgment.

Factor   an underlying construct defined by a linear combination of variables.

Factor Analysis a set of techniques for the study of interrelationships among variables, usually for the purposes of data reduction and the discovery of underlying constructs or latent dimensions.

Factor Loading the correlation (or sometimes the regression weight) of a variable with a factor.

Factor Rotation the generation of several factor analysis solutions (factor loadings and scores) from the same data set.

Factor Scores a respondent's score or value on a factor.

Factorial Design an experimental design in which two or more experimental variables are considered simultaneously by applying each combination of the experimental treatment levels to randomly selected groups.

Field Experiments experiments in which the experimental treatment is introduced in a completely natural setting.

Focus-Group Discussion a group discussion focused on a series of topics introduced by a discussion leader; the group members are encouraged to express their own views on each topic and to elaborate or react to the views of each other.

Forced Exposure respondents are exposed to an ad in a facility as opposed to an "on-air" test in the home.

Frequency Distribution a report of the number of responses that a question has received.

Full-Profile Approach a method of collecting data for trade-off analysis in which respondents are given cards that describe complete product or service configurations.

Goodman and Kruskall's Tau a measure of association for nominally scaled variables based on a proportional reduction in error.

Hierarchical Clustering a method of cluster analysis that starts with all objects in one cluster and divides and subdivides them until all objects form their own single-object clusters.

History Effect any influence on subjects, external to an experiment, that may affect the results of the experiment.

Hold-Out Sample a sample used to test a model developed from another sample.

Home Audit a method of collecting continuous purchase panel data in which the panel members agree to permit an auditor to check their household stocks of certain product categories at regular intervals.

Hypothesis a possible answer to the research question.

Ideal Object the object the respondent would prefer over all others, including objects that can be conceptualized but do not actually exist; it is a combination of all of the respondent's preferred attribute levels.

Independence in statistics, the property that the knowledge of one variable or event offers no information as to the identity of another variable or event.

Individual Depth Interview a qualitative research method designed to explore the hidden (deep) feelings, values, and motives of the respondent through a face-to-face interview with the researcher.

Information data that have been transformed into answers for specific questions of the decision makers.

Information System a system containing marketing data and marketing intelligence.

Instrumentation Effect the effect of changes in the measuring instrument on the experimental results.

Intention/Action/Conative Component the part of an attitude that represents the person's expectations of future behavior toward the object, person, or event.

Interactive Effect the case where the effect of one variable on another variable depends on the level of a third variable.

Internal Records a marketing data source found within the organization.

Internal Validity the ability of an experiment to show relationships unambiguously.

Interval Estimation the estimation of the interval in which an unknown population characteristic is judged to lie, for a given level of confidence.

Interval Scale a scale with the property that units have the same value throughout the scale (i.e., thermometer).

Intervening Variable any variable positioned between two other variables in a causal path.

Interviewer Error   a source of error in personal interviews due to the impression the respondent has of the interviewer and the way the interviewer asks questions, follows up partial answers, and records the responses.

Itemized Category Scale   a scale in which the respondent chooses among one of several response options or categories.

Judgmental Sampling   a nonprobability sampling method in which an ''expert'' uses judgment to identify representative samples.

Laboratory Experiment   an experiment in which the experimental treatment is introduced in an artificial or laboratory setting.

Laboratory Test Market   a procedure whereby shoppers are exposed to an ad for a new product and then taken on a simulated shopping trip in a laboratory facility.

Latin Square Design   an experimental design that reduces the number of groups involved when interactions between the treatment levels and the control variables can be considered relatively unimportant.

Leading Indicators   a variable that tends to predict the future direction of an object to be forecast.

Likert/Summated Scale   a scale developed by the Likert method in which the subject must indicate his/her degree of agreement or disagreement with a variety of statements related to the attitude object and which then are summed over all statements to provide a total score.

Lockbox Approach   the delivery by mail of a small, locked metal box containing a questionnaire and other interviewing exhibits.

Mail Diary Method   a method of collecting continuous purchase panel data in which panel members record the details of each purchase in certain categories and return a completed mail diary at regular intervals.

Mail Panel   a representative national sample of people who have agreed to participate in a limited number of mail surveys each year.

Mail Survey   the mailing of questionnaires and their return by mail by the designated respondents.

Market Potential   the sales for the product or service that would result if the market were fully developed.

Market Segmentation   the development and pursuit of marketing programs directed at subgroups or segments of the population that the organization could possibly serve.

Marketing Planning and Information System   a system of strategic and tactical plans and marketing data and intelligence that provides overall direction and coordination to the organization.

Marketing Research   the specification, gathering, analyzing, and interpretation of information that links the organization with its market environment.

Maturation   during a research study, changes within respondents that are a consequence of time.

Mean   the number obtained by summing all elements in a set and dividing by the number of elements.

Measurement   the assignment of numbers by rules to objects in order to reflect quantities of properties.

Monopolar Scale   a scale bounded at each end by polar adjectives or phrases, one of which is the negation of the other.

Mortality Effect   the effect on the experimental results of respondents dropping out of an experiment.

Multiattribute Model   any model linking attribute judgments with overall liking or affect.

Multidimensional Scaling   a set of techniques for developing perceptual maps.

Multistage Designs   a sampling procedure that consists of several sampling methods used sequentially.

Multivariate Analysis   the simultaneous study of two or more measures on a sample of objects.

Need   a want, an urge, a wish, or any motivational force directing behavior toward a goal.

Need Research/Identification   a type of concept-generation research with the emphasis placed on the identification of unfulfilled needs that exist in the market.

New-Product Research Process   a sequential four-state process consisting of concept generation, concept evaluation and development, product evaluation and development, and product testing.

Nominal Scale   a measurement that assigns only an identification or label to an object or set of objects.

Nondirective Interview   a type of individual depth interview in which the respondent is given maximum freedom to respond, within the bounds of topics of interest to the interviewer.

Nonprobability Sampling   any sampling method where the probability of any population element's inclusion is unknown, such as judgmental or convenience sampling.

Nonresponse Error   an error due to the inability to elicit information from some respondents in a sample, often due to refusals.

Observation   a data collection method where the relevant behaviors are recorded; examples are direct observation, contrived observation, physical trace measures, and behavior recording devices.

Omnibus Survey   a regularly scheduled personal interview survey comprised of questions from several separate firms.

On-Line Telephone Interview   an interview where the interviewer (1) reads the questions from an on-line cathode-ray-tube (CRT) terminal that is linked directly to a computer and (2) records the answers on a keyboard for entry to the computer.

Open-Response/Unstructured Question   a question with either no classification of responses or precoded classification of responses.

Order Bias   the bias of question responses due to the order of question presentation.

Ordinal Scale   a measurement that assigns only a rank order (i.e., "less than or greater than") to a set of objects.

On-Air Test   a test ad is shown on a channel viewed at home.

Paired Comparison   a scale in which the objects to be ranked are presented two at a time so that the respondent has to choose between them according to some criterion.

Parameter   a number constant in each model considered, but varying in different models.

Perceptual Map/Reduced Space   a spatial representation of the perceived relationships among objects in a set, where the objects could be brands, products, or services.

Personal Interview   a face-to-face interview between the respondent and the interviewer.

Phi-Squared   a chi-square statistic corrected for sample size.

Physical Trace Measure   an observation method, such as a home audit, in which the natural "residue" or physical trace of the behavior is recorded.

Picture Interpretation   a projective technique based on the Thematic Apperception Test (TAT), in which the respondent is asked to tell a story on the presentation of a series of pictures.

Potential Rating Index Zip Markets (PRIZM)   the classification and grouping of residents of ZIP code areas based on demographic data derived from the census.

Predictive Validity   criterion validity that is established by correlating the measurement score with a future criterion variable.

Pretest   the presentation of a questionnaire in a pilot study to a representative sample of the respondent population in order to discover any problems with the questionnaire prior to full-scale use.

Primary Data   data collected to address a specific research objective (as opposed to secondary data).

Principal Components/Principal Factor Analysis   a type of factor analysis that seeks to explain the greatest amount of variance in a data set, thus providing data reduction.

Probability Sampling   any sampling method where the probability of any population element's inclusion is known and is greater than zero.

Problem or Opportunity Definition   a process of understanding the causes and predicting the consequences of problems or a process of exploring the size and nature of opportunities; the second phase of marketing program development.

Profile Analysis   the comparison of evaluations of the alternatives in a consideration set, on the important and determinant attributes.

Projective Techniques   a set of presentation methods of ambiguous, unstructured objects, activities, or persons for which a respondent is asked to give interpretation and find meaning; the more ambiguous the stimulus, the more the respondent has to project himself into the task, thereby revealing hidden feelings, values, and needs; examples are word association, role playing, completion tests, and picture interpretation.

Qualitative Research   research designed primarily for exploratory purposes, such as getting oriented to the range and complexity of consumer activity, clarifying the problem, and identifying likely methodological problems; examples are individual and group interviews, projective techniques, and case studies.

Quick Clustering   one method of cluster analysis.

Quota Sampling   a judgmental sampling method that is constrained to include a minimum from each specified subgroup in the population.

Random Error   measurement error due to changing aspects of the respondent or measurement situation.

Randomized Block Design   an experimental design in which the test units first are grouped into homogeneous groups along some prespecified criterion and then are assigned randomly to different treatments within each block.

Rank-Order Scale   a scale in which the respondent is required to order a set of objects with regard to a common criterion.

Ratio Scale   a measurement that has a true or meaningful zero point, allowing for the specification of absolute magnitudes of objects.

Reading Habit   measuring print media exposure by asking how many issues of the last four you have read.

Refusal Rate   a measure of any data collection method's ability to induce contacted respondents to participate in the study.

Refusals   a source of nonsampling error caused by a respondent's refusing to participate in the study.

Regression Analysis   a statistical technique that develops an equation that relates a dependent variable to one or more independent (predictor, explanatory) variables.

Relative Market Potential   the market potential of one segment relative to other segments.

Relevance   a criterion used to judge whether a market research study acts to support strategic and tactical planning activities.

Reliability   the random error component of a measurement instrument.

Research Approach   one of the following six sources of data—the information system, secondary and standardized data sources, qualitative research, surveys, observations, and experiments.

Research Boundary   a delineation of the scope of the research study in terms of such items as population characteristics, locations, and product markets.

Research Objectives   a precise statement of what information is needed, consisting of the research question, the hypotheses, and the scope or boundaries of the research.

Research Process   the series of stages or steps underlying the design and implementation of a marketing research project, including the establishment of the research purpose and objectives, information value estimation, research design, and implementation.

Research Proposal   a plan for conducting and controlling a research project.

Research Purpose   the shared understanding between the manager and the researcher regarding the decision alternatives, the problems and opportunities to be studied, and who the users of the results shall be.

Research Question   the statement(s) of what specific information is required for progress toward the achievement of the research purpose.

Research Tactics   the development of the specific details of the research, including the research approach, sampling plan, and choice of research supplier.

Response Bias   the tendency of respondents to distort their answers systematically for a variety of reasons, such as social desirability and prestige seeking.

Response Style   the systematic tendency of respondents to select particular categories of responses regardless of the content of the questions.

Retail Store Audits   audit data collected by research firms whose employees visit a sample of stores at fixed intervals for the purpose of counting stock and recording deliveries to estimate retail sales.

Role Playing a projective technique in which the respondent assumes the role or behavior of another person so that the respondent may reveal attitudes by projecting him or herself fully into the role.

Sample a subset of elements from a population.

Sampling Frame a listing or an accessing of population members that is used to create a random sample.

Sampling Unit any type of element that makes up a sample, such as people, stores, and products.

Scanner Data the scanner is a device that reads the universal product code off a package as it is processed at a retailer's check-out stand. Scanner data includes data on all transactions including size, price and flavor. It also normally includes in-store information like special displays.

Scatter Diagram a two-dimensional plot of two variables.

Screening Sample a representative sample of the population being studied that is used to develop or pretest measurement instruments.

Seasonal Index a representation of the effects of seasonal fluctuations in making a forecast.

Secondary Data data collected for some purpose other than the present research purpose.

Selection Bias differences among subjects, prior to an experiment, that affect the experimental results.

Sell-in test market the new product being tested must be sold to the retailer. Shelf space is not pre-arranged.

Semantic Differential Scale a scale in which the respondent is asked to rate each attitude object in turn on a five- or seven-point rating scale bounded at each end by polar adjectives or phrases.

Sensitive/Focused Individual Interview a type of individual depth interview in which the interviewer attempts to cover a specific list of topics or subareas.

Sensitivity the ability of a measurement instrument to discriminate among meaningful differences in the variable being measured.

Sequential Sampling a sampling method in which an initial modest sample is taken and analyzed, following which, based on the results, a decision is made regarding the necessity of further sampling and analysis; this continues until enough data are collected.

Significance Level the probability of obtaining the evidence if the null hypothesis were true.

Similarity/Judgment the judgment an individual makes about whether two objects are similar or different without specifying specific attributes.

Simple Random Sampling a sampling method in which each population member has an equal chance of being selected.

Snowball Design a judgmental sampling method in which each respondent is asked to identify one or more other sample members.

Social Indicators statistical series that describe trends in social rather than economic variables.

Split-Ballot Technique the inclusion of more than one version of a question in a questionnaire.

Split-Cable Testing exposing two or more groups of a cable system to different ads and monitoring their purchases.

Spurious Association an inappropriate causal interpretation of association due to an unmeasured variable influencing both variables.

Standard Deviation the square root of the variance.

Standard Error of Estimate in regression analysis, the amount of variation in the dependent variable left unexplained by the regression equation.

Standard Industrial Classification (SIC) System a uniform numbering system developed by the U.S. Government for classifying industrial establishments according to their economic activities.

Standard Metropolitan Statistical Area (SMSA) census tracts that are combined in counties containing a central city with a population of at least 50,000.

Standardized Marketing Data Sources external sources of marketing data collected by outside organizations for several information users who have common information needs.

Statistics any of several characteristics of a sample.

Statistical Control the control of extraneous variables through statistical methods.

Strategic Plans plans that focus on strategic decisions of resource allocation with long-run performance implications, usually having time horizons of more than one year.

Stratified Sampling a sampling method that uses natural subgroups or strata which are more homogeneous than the total population.

Survey Method a method of data collection, such as a telephone or personal interview, a mail survey, or any combination thereof.

Systematic Error measurement error due to constant aspects of the person or measurement situation.

Systematic Sampling a sampling method that involves systematically spreading the sample through the entire list of population members.

Tactical Plans plans that specify in detail the decisions that need to be made to develop and to implement current marketing programs, usually having a time horizon of one year or less.

Target Population a population defined by the research objectives of a research study.

Telephone Prenotification Approach a telephone call that asks permission to mail a questionnaire to a potential respondent.

Telescoping Time a source of response inaccuracy due to the tendency among respondents to remember events as occurring more recently than they actually did.

Test Marketing a test of a new product by introducing it into a part of a market such as two or three test cities.

Test-Retest Reliability test reliability that is measured by repeating the measurement with the same instrument and the same respondents at two points in time and correlating the results.

Testing Effect the respondent's awareness of a test situation, causing him or her to be sensitized and not to respond naturally.

Third-Person Technique a projective technique in which the interviewer asks the respondent how his friends,

neighbors, or the average person would think or react in a situation.

Thurstone/Equal-Appearing Interval Scale a scale developed by first having a group of judges categorize a set of items and then selecting those items that were similarly categorized; the scale is administered by having respondents choose those statements to which they agree.

Top-Down/Chain-Ratio Approach a method of determining market potential that has as its starting point the identification of the total and available markets.

Tracking Studies monitoring the performance of advertising by regular surveys of the audience.

Trade-Off Approach a method of collecting data for trade-off analysis in which the respondent is asked to rank each combination of levels of two attributes from most preferred to least preferred.

Through-the-book measurement of exposure to print media by asking respondents if they recognized articles in an issue

Unaided Recall a questioning approach in which the respondent is asked to remember an object of interest without the assistance of clues from the researcher.

Use Test a type of product evaluation where the product is given to consumers; after a reasonable period of time, the consumers are asked for their reactions to it.

Utility in trade-off analysis, the worth or value of each level of each attribute relative to the other levels.

Validity the ability of a measurement instrument to measure what it is supposed to measure.

Variance a measure of dispersion based on the degree to which elements of a sample or population differ from the average element.

Varimax Rotation a rotation method that searches for simple structure, a pattern of factor loadings where some loadings are close to one, and some loadings are close to zero.

Word Association a projective technique in which the respondent is asked to give the first word that comes to mind on the presentation of another word.

APPENDIX: TABLES

1 Standard Normal Probabilities

2 X^2 Critical Points

3 F Critical Points

TABLE A–1

Standard Normal, Cumulative Probability in Right-Hand Tail For Negative Values of z;
Areas Are Formed by Symmetry

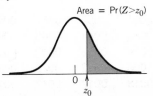

Area $= Pr(Z > z_0)$

					Second Decimal Place of Z_0					
Z_0	.00	.01	.02	.03	.04	.05	.06	.07	.08	.09
0.0	.5000	.4960	.4920	.4880	.4840	.4801	.4761	.4721	.4681	.4641
0.1	.4602	.4562	.4522	.4483	.4443	.4404	.4364	.4325	.4286	.4247
0.2	.4207	.4168	.4129	.4090	.4052	.4013	.3974	.3936	.3897	.3859
0.3	.3821	.3783	.3745	.3707	.3669	.3632	.3594	.3557	.3520	.3483
0.4	.3446	.3409	.3372	.3336	.3300	.3264	.3228	.3192	.3156	.3121
0.5	.3085	.3050	.3015	.2981	.2946	.2912	.2877	.2843	.2810	.2776
0.6	.2743	.2709	.2676	.2643	.2611	.2578	.2546	.2514	.2483	.2451
0.7	.2420	.2389	.2358	.2327	.2296	.2266	.2236	.2206	.2177	.2148
0.8	.2119	.2090	.2061	.2033	.2005	.1977	.1949	.1922	.1894	.1867
0.9	.1841	.1814	.1788	.1762	.1736	.1711	.1685	.1660	.1635	.1611

TABLE A–1 (*continued*)

Z_0				Second Decimal Place of Z_0					
	.00	.01	.02	.03	.04	.05	.06	.07	.08	.09
1.0	.1587	.1562	.1539	.1515	.1492	.1469	.1446	.1423	.1401	.1379
1.1	.1357	.1335	.1314	.1292	.1271	.1251	.1230	.1210	.1190	.1170
1.2	.1151	.1131	.1112	.1093	.1075	.1056	.1038	.1020	.1003	.0985
1.3	.0968	.0951	.0934	.0918	.0901	.0885	.0869	.0853	.0838	.0823
1.4	.0808	.0793	.0778	.0764	.0749	.0735	.0722	.0708	.0694	.0681
1.5	.0668	.0655	.0643	.0630	.0618	.0606	.0594	.0582	.0571	.0559
1.6	.0548	.0537	.0526	.0516	.0505	.0495	.0485	.0475	.0465	.0455
1.7	.0446	.0436	.0427	.0418	.0409	.0401	.0392	.0384	.0375	.0367
1.8	.0359	.0352	.0344	.0336	.0329	.0322	.0314	.0307	.0301	.0294
1.9	.0287	.0281	.0274	.0268	.0262	.0256	.0250	.0244	.0239	.0233
2.0	.0228	.0222	.0217	.0212	.0207	.0202	.0197	.0192	.0188	.0183
2.1	.0179	.0174	.0170	.0166	.0162	.0158	.0154	.0150	.0146	.0143
2.2	.0139	.0136	.0132	.0129	.0125	.0122	.0119	.0116	.0113	.0110
2.3	.0107	.0104	.0102	.0099	.0096	.0094	.0091	.0089	.0087	.0084
2.4	.0082	.0080	.0078	.0075	.0073	.0071	.0069	.0068	.0066	.0064
2.5	.0062	.0060	.0059	.0057	.0055	.0054	.0052	.0051	.0049	.0048
2.6	.0047	.0045	.0044	.0043	.0041	.0040	.0039	.0038	.0037	.0036
2.7	.0035	.0034	.0033	.0032	.0031	.0030	.0029	.0028	.0027	.0026
2.8	.0026	.0025	.0023	.0023	.0023	.0022	.0021	.0021	.0020	.0019
2.9	.0019	.0018	.0017	.0017	.0016	.0016	.0015	.0015	.0014	.0014
3.0	.00135									
3.5	.000 233									
4.0	.000 031 7									
4.5	.000 003 40									
5.0	.000 000 287									

TABLE A–2

χ^2 Critical Points

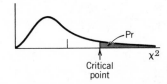

Pr d.f.	.250	.100	.050	.025	.010	.005	.001
1	1.32	2.71	3.84	5.02	6.63	7.88	10.8
2	2.77	4.61	5.99	7.38	9.21	10.6	13.8
3	4.11	6.25	7.81	9.35	11.3	12.8	16.3
4	5.39	7.78	9.49	11.1	13.3	14.9	18.5
5	6.63	9.24	11.1	12.8	15.1	16.7	20.5
6	7.84	10.6	12.6	14.4	16.8	18.5	22.5
7	9.04	12.0	14.1	16.0	18.5	20.3	24.3
8	10.2	13.4	15.5	17.5	20.1	22.0	26.1
9	11.4	14.7	16.9	19.0	21.7	23.6	27.9
10	12.5	16.0	18.8	20.5	23.2	25.2	29.6
11	13.7	17.3	19.7	21.9	24.7	26.8	31.3
12	14.8	18.5	21.0	23.3	26.2	28.3	32.9
13	16.0	19.8	22.4	24.7	27.7	29.8	34.5
14	17.1	21.1	23.7	26.1	29.1	31.3	36.1
15	18.2	22.3	25.0	27.5	30.6	32.8	37.7
16	19.4	23.5	26.3	28.8	32.0	34.3	39.3
17	20.5	24.8	27.6	30.2	33.4	35.7	40.8
18	21.6	26.0	28.9	31.5	34.8	37.2	42.3
19	22.7	27.2	30.1	32.9	36.2	38.6	42.8
20	23.8	28.4	31.4	34.2	37.6	40.0	45.3
21	24.9	29.6	32.7	35.5	38.9	41.4	46.8
22	26.0	30.8	33.9	36.8	40.3	42.8	48.3
23	27.1	32.0	35.2	38.1	41.6	44.2	49.7
24	28.2	33.2	36.4	39.4	42.0	45.6	51.2

TABLE A–2 (*continued*)

d.f. \ Pr	.250	.100	.050	.025	.010	.005	.001
25	29.3	34.4	37.7	40.6	44.3	46.9	52.6
26	30.4	35.6	38.9	41.9	45.6	48.3	54.1
27	31.5	36.7	40.1	43.2	47.0	49.6	55.5
28	32.6	37.9	41.3	44.5	48.3	51.0	56.9
29	33.7	39.1	42.6	45.7	49.6	52.3	58.3
30	34.8	40.3	43.8	47.0	50.9	53.7	59.7
40	45.6	51.8	55.8	59.3	63.7	66.8	73.4
50	56.3	63.2	67.5	71.4	76.2	79.5	86.7
60	67.0	74.4	79.1	83.3	88.4	92.0	99.6
70	77.6	85.5	90.5	95.0	100	104	112
80	88.1	96.6	102	107	112	116	125
90	98.6	108	113	118	124	128	137
100	109	118	124	130	136	140	149

TABLE A–3

F Critical Points

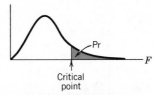

Pr

Critical
point

	Pr	Degrees of Freedom for Numerator										
		1	2	3	4	5	6	8	10	20	40	∞
1	.25	5.83	7.50	8.20	8.58	8.82	8.98	9.19	9.32	9.58	9.71	9.85
	.10	39.9	49.5	53.6	55.8	57.2	58.2	59.4	60.2	61.7	62.5	63.3
	.05	161	200	216	225	230	234	239	242	248	251	254
2	.25	2.57	3.00	3.15	3.23	3.28	3.31	3.35	3.38	3.43	3.45	3.48
	.10	8.53	9.00	9.16	9.24	9.29	9.33	9.37	9.39	9.44	9.47	9.49
	.05	18.5	19.0	19.2	19.2	19.3	19.3	19.4	19.4	19.4	19.5	19.5
	.01	98.5	99.0	99.2	99.2	99.3	99.3	99.4	99.4	99.4	99.5	99.5
	.001	998	999	999	999	999	999	999	999	999	999	999
3	.25	2.02	2.28	2.36	2.39	2.41	2.42	2.44	2.44	2.46	2.47	2.47
	.10	5.54	5.46	5.39	5.34	5.31	5.28	5.25	5.23	5.18	5.16	5.13
	.05	10.1	9.55	9.28	9.12	9.10	8.94	8.85	8.79	8.66	8.59	8.53
	.01	34.1	30.8	29.5	28.7	28.2	27.9	27.5	27.2	26.7	26.4	26.1
	.001	167	149	141	137	135	133	131	129	126	125	124
4	.25	1.81	2.00	2.05	2.06	2.07	2.08	2.08	2.08	2.08	2.08	2.08
	.10	4.54	4.32	4.19	4.11	4.05	4.01	3.95	3.92	3.84	3.80	3.76
	.05	7.71	6.94	6.59	6.39	6.26	6.16	6.04	5.96	5.80	5.72	5.63
	.01	21.2	18.0	16.7	16.0	15.5	15.2	14.8	14.5	14.0	13.7	13.5
	.001	74.1	61.3	56.2	53.4	51.7	50.5	49.0	48.1	46.1	45.1	44.1
5	.25	1.69	1.85	1.88	1.89	1.89	1.89	1.89	1.89	1.88	1.88	1.87
	.10	4.06	3.78	3.62	3.52	3.45	3.40	3.34	3.30	3.21	3.16	3.10
	.05	6.61	5.79	5.41	5.19	5.05	4.95	4.82	4.74	4.56	4.46	4.36
	.01	16.3	13.3	12.1	11.4	11.0	10.7	10.3	10.1	9.55	9.29	9.02
	.001	47.2	37.1	33.2	31.1	29.8	28.8	27.6	26.9	25.4	24.6	23.8
6	.25	1.62	1.76	1.78	1.79	1.79	1.78	1.77	1.77	1.76	1.75	1.74
	.10	3.78	3.46	3.29	3.18	3.11	3.05	2.98	2.94	2.84	2.78	2.72
	.05	5.99	5.14	4.76	4.53	4.39	4.28	4.15	4.06	3.87	3.77	3.67
	.01	13.7	10.9	9.78	9.15	8.75	8.47	8.10	7.87	7.40	7.14	6.88
	.001	35.5	27.0	23.7	21.9	20.8	20.0	19.0	18.4	17.1	16.4	15.8
7	.25	1.57	1.70	1.72	1.72	1.71	1.71	1.70	1.69	1.67	1.66	1.65
	.10	3.59	3.26	3.07	2.96	2.88	2.83	2.75	2.70	2.59	2.54	2.47
	.05	5.59	4.74	4.35	4.12	3.97	3.87	3.73	3.64	3.44	3.34	3.23
	.01	12.2	9.55	8.45	7.85	7.46	7.19	6.84	6.62	6.16	5.91	5.65
	.001	29.3	21.7	18.8	17.2	16.2	15.5	14.6	14.1	12.9	12.3	11.7

Degrees of Freedom for Denominator

TABLE A–3 (*continued*)

	Pr	\multicolumn{10}{c}{Degrees of Freedom for Numerator}
		1	2	3	4	5	6	8	10	20	40	∞
8	.25	1.54	1.66	1.67	1.66	1.66	1.65	1.64	1.63	1.61	1.59	1.58
	.10	3.46	3.11	2.92	2.81	2.73	2.67	2.59	2.54	2.42	2.36	2.29
	.05	5.32	4.46	4.07	3.84	3.69	3.58	3.44	3.35	3.15	3.04	2.93
	.01	11.3	8.65	7.59	7.01	6.63	6.37	6.03	5.81	5.36	5.12	4.86
	.001	25.4	18.5	15.8	14.4	13.5	12.9	12.0	11.5	10.5	9.92	9.33
9	.25	1.51	1.62	1.63	1.63	1.62	1.61	1.60	1.59	1.56	1.55	1.53
	.10	3.36	3.01	2.81	2.69	2.61	2.55	2.47	2.42	2.30	2.23	2.16
	.05	5.12	4.26	3.86	3.63	3.48	3.37	3.23	3.14	2.94	2.83	2.71
	.01	10.6	8.02	6.99	6.42	6.06	5.80	5.47	5.26	4.81	4.57	4.31
	.001	22.9	16.4	13.9	12.6	11.7	11.1	10.4	9.89	8.90	8.37	7.81
10	.25	1.49	1.60	1.60	1.59	1.59	1.58	1.56	1.55	1.52	1.51	1.48
	.10	3.28	2.92	2.73	2.61	2.52	2.46	2.38	2.32	2.20	2.13	2.06
	.05	4.96	4.10	3.71	3.48	3.33	3.22	3.07	2.98	2.77	2.66	2.54
	.01	10.0	7.56	6.55	5.99	5.64	5.39	5.06	4.85	4.41	4.17	3.91
	.001	21.0	14.9	12.6	11.3	10.5	9.92	9.20	8.75	7.80	7.30	6.76
12	.25	1.56	1.56	1.56	1.55	1.54	1.53	1.51	1.50	1.47	1.45	1.42
	.10	3.18	2.81	2.61	2.48	2.39	2.33	2.24	2.19	2.06	1.99	1.90
	.05	4.75	3.89	3.49	3.26	3.11	3.00	2.85	2.75	2.54	2.43	2.30
	.01	9.33	6.93	5.95	5.41	5.06	4.82	4.50	4.30	3.86	3.62	3.36
	.001	18.6	13.0	10.8	9.63	8.89	8.38	7.71	7.29	6.40	5.93	5.42
14	.25	1.44	1.53	1.53	1.52	1.51	1.50	1.48	1.46	1.43	1.41	1.38
	.10	3.10	2.73	2.52	2.39	2.31	2.24	2.15	2.10	1.96	1.89	1.80
	.05	4.60	3.74	3.34	3.11	2.96	2.85	2.70	2.60	2.39	2.27	2.13
	.01	8.86	5.51	5.56	5.04	4.69	4.46	4.14	3.94	3.51	3.27	3.00
	.001	17.1	11.8	9.73	8.62	7.92	7.43	6.80	6.40	5.56	5.10	4.60
16	.25	1.42	1.51	1.51	1.50	1.48	1.48	1.46	1.45	1.40	1.37	1.34
	.10	3.05	2.67	2.46	2.33	2.24	2.18	2.09	2.03	1.89	1.81	1.72
	.05	4.49	3.63	3.24	3.01	2.85	2.74	2.59	2.49	2.28	2.15	2.01
	.01	8.53	6.23	5.29	4.77	4.44	4.20	3.89	3.69	3.26	3.02	2.75
	.001	16.1	11.0	9.00	7.94	7.27	6.81	6.19	5.81	4.99	4.54	4.06
18	.25	1.41	1.50	1.49	1.48	1.46	1.45	1.43	1.42	1.38	1.35	1.32
	.10	3.01	2.62	2.42	2.29	2.20	2.13	2.04	1.98	1.84	1.75	1.66
	.05	4.41	3.55	3.16	2.93	2.77	2.66	2.51	2.41	2.19	2.06	1.92
	.01	8.29	6.01	5.09	4.58	4.25	4.01	3.71	3.51	3.08	2.84	2.57
	.001	15.4	10.4	8.49	7.46	6.81	6.35	5.76	5.39	4.59	4.15	3.67
20	.25	1.40	1.49	1.48	1.46	1.45	1.44	1.42	1.40	1.36	1.33	1.29
	.10	2.97	2.59	2.38	2.25	2.16	2.09	2.00	1.94	1.79	1.71	1.61
	.05	4.35	3.49	3.10	2.87	2.71	2.60	2.45	2.35	2.12	1.99	1.84
	.01	8.10	5.85	4.94	4.43	4.10	3.87	3.56	3.37	2.94	2.69	2.42
	.001	14.8	9.95	8.10	7.10	6.46	6.02	5.44	5.08	4.29	3.86	3.38

Degrees of Freedom for Denominator (left vertical axis label)

TABLE A–3 (*continued*)

	Pr	\multicolumn{11}{c}{Degrees of Freedom for Numerator}
		1	2	3	4	5	6	8	10	20	40	∞
30	.25	1.38	1.45	1.44	1.42	1.41	1.39	1.37	1.35	1.30	1.27	1.23
	.10	2.88	2.49	2.28	2.14	2.05	1.98	1.88	1.82	1.67	1.57	1.46
	.05	4.17	3.32	2.92	2.69	2.53	2.42	2.27	2.16	1.93	1.79	1.62
	.01	7.56	5.39	4.51	4.02	3.70	3.47	3.17	2.98	2.55	2.30	2.01
	.001	13.3	8.77	7.05	6.12	5.53	5.12	4.58	4.24	3.49	3.07	2.59
40	.25	1.36	1.44	1.42	1.40	1.39	1.37	1.35	1.33	1.28	1.24	1.19
	.10	2.84	2.44	2.23	2.09	2.00	1.93	1.83	1.76	1.61	1.51	1.38
	.05	4.08	3.23	2.84	2.61	2.45	2.34	2.18	2.08	1.84	1.69	1.51
	.01	7.31	5.18	4.31	3.83	3.51	3.29	2.99	2.80	2.37	2.11	1.80
	.001	12.6	8.25	6.60	5.70	5.13	4.73	4.21	3.87	3.15	2.73	2.23
60	.25	1.35	1.42	1.41	1.38	1.37	1.35	1.32	1.30	1.25	1.21	1.15
	.10	2.79	2.39	2.18	2.04	1.95	1.87	1.77	1.71	1.54	1.44	1.29
	.05	4.00	3.15	2.76	2.53	2.37	2.25	2.10	1.99	1.75	1.59	1.39
	.01	7.08	4.98	4.13	3.65	3.34	3.12	2.82	2.63	2.20	1.94	1.60
	.001	12.0	7.76	6.17	5.31	4.76	4.37	3.87	3.54	2.83	2.41	1.89
120	.25	1.34	1.40	1.39	1.37	1.35	1.33	1.30	1.28	1.22	1.18	1.10
	.10	2.75	2.35	2.13	1.99	1.90	1.82	1.72	1.65	1.48	1.37	1.19
	.05	3.92	3.07	2.68	2.45	2.29	2.17	2.02	1.91	1.66	1.50	1.25
	.01	6.85	4.79	3.95	3.48	3.17	2.96	2.66	2.47	2.03	1.76	1.38
	.001	11.4	7.32	5.79	4.95	4.42	4.04	3.55	3.24	2.53	2.11	1.54
∞	.25	1.32	1.39	1.37	1.35	1.33	1.31	1.28	1.25	1.19	1.14	1.00
	.10	2.71	2.30	2.08	1.94	1.85	1.77	1.67	1.60	1.42	1.30	1.00
	.05	3.84	3.00	2.60	2.37	2.21	2.10	1.94	1.83	1.57	1.39	1.00
	.01	6.63	4.61	3.78	3.32	3.02	2.80	2.51	2.32	1.88	1.59	1.00
	.001	10.8	6.91	5.42	4.62	4.10	3.74	3.27	2.96	2.27	1.84	1.00

Degrees of Freedom for Denominator (vertical label at left)

INDEX

INDEX

659